Amateur Gardening

COMPLETE GARDENING ANSWERS

D1329065

Amateur Gardening

COMPLETE GARDENING ANSWERS

Chris Day and Rob Keenan

Robinson
LONDON

Robinson Publishing Ltd
7 Kensington Church Court
London W8 4SP

First published by Robinson Publishing Ltd 1999

Copyright © IPC Magazines Ltd, 1999
Illustrations copyright © Peter Rigby, 1999

A copy of the British Library Cataloguing in Publication data
is available from the British Library

ISBN 1 84119 037 3

Printed and bound in the EC

10 9 8 7 6 5 4 3 2 1

Amateur Gardening is published weekly by IPC Magazines Ltd, Kings Reach Tower, Stamford Street,
London SE1 9LS. For subscription enquiries and orders call 01444 445555 (fax no: 01444 445599). For
credit card orders call the subscription credit card hotline (UK orders only) on 01622 778778.

Contents

Introduction

Amateur Gardening magazine has been around for 115 years, and in that time the world of horticulture, and more importantly that of the domestic gardener, has changed beyond recognition.

Who, a 100 years ago, would have thought that windows in the greenhouse could open and close by timed computer control? Likewise, who would have known that solar-powered lawnmowers would eventually be used to cut grass without the help of man? And who would have anticipated that tomatoes could be bred for growing in hanging baskets?

When it comes to micropropagation, plant breeding and genetic engineering, we're only just beginning to discover what potential there is.

And throughout all this time, *Amateur Gardening* has been there. Through two world wars, the depression of the 1920s and 30s, and throughout the modern technological revolution *AG*, as it has become known to its readers and admirers, has been dispensing weekly gardening advice more or less non-stop.

The philosophy of *AG* is to make gardening – *good* gardening – accessible and enjoyable for all. Part of the strategy to achieve this has been to talk about plants and practices simply and in layman's terms. We certainly don't advocate the gratuitous use of Latin names when they're not necessary. Nor do we go into great detail about the old layering or budding practices used by professional gardeners of yesteryear.

But we do know that our readers are not raw, novice gardeners. They know how to sow more than the odd seed and take more than the odd cutting. What they want is clear advice on gardening's more challenging aspects. They want to know the latest techniques, and they certainly want information on the latest plants and products.

In what has become a vast media "jungle" – with television and radio gardening programmes, coverage in local newspapers, and gardening columns in general interest magazines – this is the strength of our magazine.

There are gardening books, of course: there have been specialist tomes devoted to all manner of gardening subjects and themes, from alliums (or ornamental onions) to zucchini, with a fair sprinkling of bonsai, cacti, topiary and meat-eating plants in between. And bookshops are not short of general gardening books either. But there is still a distinct lack of publications that answer the common questions asked by ordinary gardeners. And this is where *Amateur Gardening Complete Answers* comes into play. Nearly 2,000 questions, culled from ten years' worth of *Amateur Gardening*, edited and updated, form the basis of this brand-new book.

We reckon that, since the first issue of the magazine came out in 1884, over 100,000 questions have been posed to us by our readers. But of course many of these will be on the theme of: "What can I plant in celebration of the life of our great Queen Victoria?", or "How do I help the war effort through my gardening?"

We have also had impossible questions to answer. I remember the famous occasion when one of our secretaries gingerly opened a matchbox sent in by a reader. It contained a dead goldfish in an advanced stage of decay, with a screwed-up note asking if we could say what it had died of! We were tempted to write back saying "lack of water in box", but thought better of it!

But back to the present. In this book of questions and answers, there are such valuable and essential posers as: "How soon can I sow cabbage to get an early crop?" "When is the best time to sow a new lawn?" "Which variety of cooking apples keeps the best?" "How do I overwinter pond plants?" "Which rose is recommended for a Golden Wedding Anniversary present?" "When is the best time to take pelargonium cuttings?" "How do you get rid of whitefly?"

All these questions and hundreds of others are asked of us by our readers practically every day. Our staff and experts, who between them have hundreds of years of horticultural experience, are not often foxed by a difficult question, and those mentioned above are, of course, relatively simple to answer. But some of the more taxing questions take a bit more research, such as: "Is the rose Dorothy Perkins and the person after whom the shop was named, one and the same?" Or, "Is it true that there are more plant species still to be discovered than have already been?" Or even, "Does the Dutch hoe come from Holland?" (The answers in case you want to know are: yes, probably and no!).

But it's the ordinary, everyday questions that are the driving-force of this book. Compartmentalized into useful sections for easy location, here are the answers to all the problems faced by the average UK-based domestic home gardener of the late 20th century.

This book contains just honest, good, down-to-earth, yet up-to-date gardening advice from the experts who work on the magazine, and who really do know what's what!

Chris Day and Rob Keenan are the key people in all of this. As "staffers" for a number of years, they have seen thousands of questions come and go, and much information and advice has rubbed off onto them. They have selected the best, and most frequently asked questions, and updated them, and both the publishers of this book, and humble little me, owe a great debt to the both of them.

GRAHAM CLARKE
Editor-at-Large,
Amateur Gardening

Alpines

Rock garden conifers

"I would like to have one or two small-growing conifers to add interest to my rock garden. I have seen them growing in rock gardens I have visited, but have not been able to discover their names. Can you help me?"

Yes, there are several conifers that make compact growth and do not grow too large. *Juniperus communis* "Sentinel" makes narrow, columnar growth and has grey-green foliage. It will grow in most well-drained soils and will tolerate some lime in the ground.

Another good conifer for a rock garden is *Juniperus communis* "Compressa". It has silvery grey foliage and takes about ten years to grow 2ft (0.6 cm) in height.

Others to consider include: *Chamaecyparis lawsoniana* "Minima Glauca", dwarf, conical habit; *Picea mariana* "Nana", dwarf, rounded shape; and *Thuja occidentalis* "Tiny Tim", slow-growing, forming rounded bushes.

Cyclamen seed

"Last August I bought some small rockery cyclamen which flowered through the winter. The plants grew tentacles and what appeared to be new corms. What do I do with them?"

Your cyclamen is probably *C. neapolitanum*. The corm-like objects on the coiled stems are the seed capsules. Left as they are they should soon produce small seedlings.

If you prefer, collect the seed and sow it in small pots of good seed compost. When seedlings appear, put them individually in small pots. When large enough, plant them in their permanent positions.

Propagating aubrieta

"I have grown some aubrieta plants from seed. They flowered very well last spring. One plant has very dark blue flowers and I would like to increase it. Do I have to split up the plant or can I take cuttings from it?"

If you do not want to disturb your aubrieta plant, cuttings can be taken from it. Do this in the spring after flowering by making cuttings from new, young growths. You could also take cuttings of firmer shoots in late summer. Root them in small pots of gritty soil covered with a plastic dome or polythene bag. Once rooted pot the young plants individually. Plant out once good growth has been made.

Trim to size ❧

"I have several large aubrieta plants in a dry, stone wall that have flowered very well this spring. As they have become rather straggly, will they stand trimming or must I start again with new plants?"

Your aubrieta plants will benefit from trimming and it is not necessary to scrap them. Trimming must be done only after flowering.
Use sharp secateurs and cut the old stems back hard.
New growth will develop in the summer which will flower next spring.

Pasque flower ❧

"I have bought two pasque flower plants in pots. Can you tell me what sort of soil and position they like?"

The pasque flower, *Pulsatilla vulgaris*, is a delightful plant for a rock garden, producing its silky flowers in spring and early summer. It likes a sunny position and fertile, gritty and well drained soil. It will not mind a chalky soil. Plants do not like being disturbed and should stay in the same place for a number of years.

Dainty Dresden China ❧

"I have a plant of the daisy called 'Dresden China'. How can I propagate it? Can I grow it from seeds?"

"Dresden China" is a variety of *Bellis perennis*. It is a pretty, double daisy but it is sterile and does not set seed. The best way of propagating the plant is to lift clumps after flowering and divide them into several pieces. Some strains of *Bellis perennis* can be raised from seed. This should be sown outside in June. The seedlings should be transplanted into nursery rows until the autumn when they should be planted out in their flowering positions. There are many fine strains which are used extensively in spring bedding schemes.

Snow in summer ❦

"I have a dry, sunny bank in which little grows. Would snow-in-summer be any good in this position and can it be raised from seed?"

Yes, snow-in-summer (*Cerastium tomentosum*) would be ideal for your dry, sunny bank. Plants are easily raised from seed. It can be sown outdoors in finely raked soil in the spring, where the plants are to grow. Keep the soil well watered to ensure good germination.

Alternatively, sow it in a pot, pricking out seedlings into boxes as they appear and planting them out in the open when they are large enough.

Use boulders (larger the better) in scale with your plants

Rock plants ❦

"I am building a small rock garden and would like to know the names of plants that are easy to grow. If I obtained plants in pots, can I plant them in the summer?"

Suitable plants for your rock garden are *Veronica austriaca teucrium*, *Campanula carpatica* varieties, aubrietas, *Dianthus gratianopolitanus*, dwarf bearded irises, *Gypsophila* "Rosenschleier", *Phlox subulata*, *Saponaria ocymoides*, *Aurinia saxatilis*, *Artemisia* "Silver Queen", and *Sedum spurium*.

Provided pot-grown plants are purchased, they can be planted throughout the summer. After planting do not neglect to water them in dry weather.

Sinking feeling ❧

"I have an old sink in which I plan to grow small alpine plants. Can you recommend suitable kinds?"

Aim to grow alpines of moderate size in your sink and avoid vigorous types such as aubrieta and arabis. Suitable plants are: *Aethionema* "Warley Rose"; *Anchusa caespitosa*; *Armeria juniperifolia*; saxifragas; soldanella; *Mentha requienii*; small dianthus; *Douglasia dentata*; *Gentiana verna*; *Raoulia australis*; sempervivums and *Campanula arvatica*. A dwarf conifer to grow is *Juniperus communis* "Compressa".

Dwarf shrubs include: *Betula nana* "Glengarry"; *Cytisus demissus*; *Genista delphinensis* and *Salix boydii*.

Slopes offer a great challenge when it comes to planting alpines.

Recipe for disguise ❧

"Could you please let me know how to make a sand and cement mixture for coating an old glazed sink? I want to make an alpine garden in it."

The hypertufa mix you need for covering a glazed sink consists of two parts peat, one part sand and one and a half parts cement.

Add a little water and trowel on an inch-thick layer. It sticks better if you first paint the glazing with Polybond adhesive.

Annuals and biennials

Golden moss

"Can you tell me the name of a plant with golden foliage that I have seen used as an edging for flower beds in a public park? I was told it was golden moss. Can it be grown from seed?"

The plant that you have seen edging beds of summer flowers is the golden-leaved feverfew, *Tanacetum parthenium* "Aureum".

It has attractive mossy, yellow foliage. Plants are easily raised from seed, sown in the spring under glass and grown on in small pots, ready for planting outside in late May and early June.

Wilting asters

"I normally have an excellent display of asters but this year they all shrivelled up and died a month or so after planting. Is it something in the soil I can treat?"

This is the result of aster wilt, a soil-borne fungal disease. There is no effective treatment to clear the soil of the infection, but all is not lost.

Seed catalogues do list some wilt-resistant varieties of aster, and although the range is a little restricted, they would enable you to continue to grow asters. Look for "Milady" mixed in D.T. Brown's seed catalogue, and "Starlight Rose" from Unwins.

Spotted honesty

"I grew honesty this year to use the dried seed pods for decoration, but most of them developed raised white spots which spoiled them. What would have caused this, and how could it be prevented another year?"

White blister fungus was responsible for the damage caused to your honesty seed pods. This is a fungus that can attack all plants in the cabbage family, although it is more commonly found on sprout and cabbage leaves than on honesty. Destroy all infected plants.

If there are overwintering seedlings or young plants of honesty that show no signs of the trouble now, spray them with a copper fungicide as a precaution.

Next spring, as new growth starts, again apply a copper fungicide.

Dried annuals ❦

"I want to grow some annual flowers this year specially for drying for winter arrangements. I do not have a greenhouse and the seeds will have to be sown direct in the garden. Can you tell me the best types to grow?"

Annual flowers that can be dried for flower arrangements include calendula, clarkia, larkspur, nicandra (shoo fly plant), amaranthus (love-lies-bleeding), candytuft, cornflower and nigella (love-in-a-mist).

All these can be sown outside in early April. Choose a sunny and sheltered position. The flowers must be picked at the right stage; pick calendulas, clarkia, amaranthus and nigella when the flowers are fully open.

Others, such as larkspur, should be picked before the lower flowers begin to fall.

Dried flowers ❦

"I was told that the flowers of the globe thistle are good for drying. I have these plants in my garden, but I have never been able to dry them satisfactorily. Do they need any special treatment?"

You have probably picked globe thistle (*Echinops ritro*) flowers too late. To dry them successfully, cut the stems just before the flowers are open. If the flowers are cut when fully open, they will not dry properly and will almost certainly fall to bits.

The leaves are also decorative and well worth drying.

Preserving cowslips ❦

"Cowslips are beginning to appear naturally at the end of my lawn. How do I look after them so that they will spread?"

To preserve the cowslips and encourage them to seed you must not cut the grass where they are growing until seeds have formed. This is likely to be in July.

Why not reserve an area for the cowslips so that you can cut the rest of the lawn? If any cowslip seedlings appear outside their area, transplant them into it.

Free seeding love-in-a-mist

"I grew some love-in-a-mist plants from seed last year. Now the area is carpeted with new seedlings that have come up like mustard and cress."

In a spot to their liking, love-in-a-mist (nigella), will seed itself freely as yours have done. The seedlings are worth keeping as they will flower earlier than seed sown in the spring. If they are overcrowded, thin them out carefully.

Surfina petunia

"I bought a plant labelled 'Surfina' but I cannot find it in any reference book. Has it got another name?"

"Surfina" is the varietal name of a petunia that trails well and blooms for most of the summer. You can increase it from non-flowering cuttings taken in August and September. There are several different forms with purple, blue, pink, red or white flowers.

Damping off

"My husband sowed the first of his bedding plant seed a week or two ago in a heated propagating frame. There are patches of dead seedlings in some of the boxes now. What action should he take, please?"

The problem is due to damping off diseases. These are encouraged by excess humidity, so are more of a trouble when the seeds are sown rather thickly, when the compost is over-wet, or where old, infected compost has been used.

   The best action would be to cut out the dead patches plus some of the surrounding seedlings and then to water with a copper fungicide such as Cheshunt Compound or Murphy Traditional Copper Fungicide. Watering should then only be done when the compost is on the dry side, and as much ventilation as possible should be given.

   Each time watering is required, add the appropriate fungicide. As more seeds are sown, spread them as thinly as possible to give the seedlings plenty of air, and prick them out just as soon as they are large enough.

Prairie gentian

"I have bought flowers of lisianthus many times as a cut flower. Where can I get seeds and any growing tips?"

A particularly fine strain of *Lisianthus* (*Eustoma*) "Double Eagle Mixed" is stocked by Thompson & Morgan, Poplar Lane, Ipswich, Suffolk IP8 3BU.

In its native America – its common name is prairie gentian – it is a perennial shrub but in Britain it is best grown as a half-hardy annual greenhouse pot plant.

Set seeds in a temperature of 21–4°C (70–5°F) in February. Grow the plants on in good light in a temperature of 10–15°C (50–60°F), nipping out the shoot tips to encourage branching and more flowers.

Persistent annuals ❧

"I was under the impression that antirrhinums were annuals and had to be grown from seed each year. Why is it that they are often found growing year after year in old walls and derelict sites?"

The best results are obtained by treating antirrhinums as annuals and raising new plants from seed each year. Strictly speaking, they are short-lived perennials and will last for a number of years in positions to their liking. Plants also scatter their seed freely and seedlings often appear on waste ground.

Marvel of Peru ❧

"I have been given some seeds of a plant called marvel of Peru which, I am told, flowers only around four o'clock in the afternoon. Can you tell me anything more about the plant?"

The marvel of Peru is called *Mirabilis jalapa*. It is frost tender and, as you say, flowers around four p.m. each day. It grows from 2–4 ft (60–120 cm) tall and reaches 2–2$\frac{1}{2}$ ft (60–75 cm) across.

Sow the seed in a heated propagator and pot the seedlings singly in 3 in. (7–8 cm) pots. Plant them outside in early June. They will do well in containers.

Lift the plants in early autumn and keep them in pots in a frost-free place for winter. Plant them outside again in early summer.

Sowing honesty ❧

"Can you tell me whether honesty is an annual or biennial? When should the seed be sown?"

Honesty (*Lunaria annua*) is a biennial. Sow the seed outside in a nursery bed in June or sow it in modules.

Plant out the seedlings in rows and transfer them to their flowering positions in the autumn. The plants should flower next spring.

Potted sweet peas ❧

"I would love to grow sweet peas but my soil is very heavy clay. Could I grow them in pots and what kind of soil should I use?"

There is no reason why you should not grow your sweet peas in large 10 in. or 12 in. (25 cm or 30 cm) pots. Make sure that there is drainage material in the base then fill with good John Innes Compost No 3.

After planting the sweet peas, train the stems up trellis or through a tripod of canes. It is essential that the soil does not dry out in the summer and also remember to feed the plants each week with a good liquid fertilizer.

Scatter hardy annual seeds over a border.

Hardy annuals ❧

"I have been told that some annual flowers can be sown in September to flower outside in early June. Is this a good idea in my district and if so could you give me the names of suitable annuals to grow?"

Many hardy annuals can be sown outside in September to stand the winter outside for flowering in May and June of the following year. Annuals such as love-in-a-mist (nigella) will do this naturally.

Others that you could grow include calendula, godetia, candytuft, annual alyssum, clarkia, annual coreopsis, cornflower, larkspur, Shirley poppies and annual scabious.

Annual or perennial? ❧

"I want to grow some Iceland poppies. Can you tell me whether they are annuals or perennials?"

Iceland poppies, *Papaver nudicaule*, are, strictly speaking, perennial but are best treated as biennials. Sow the seed in pots in June. When large enough, transfer the seedlings to small pots which can be stood outside for the summer.

Transfer the plants to their flowering positions in the autumn or early spring, choosing a position where the soil is well drained and fertile.

Companions for wallflowers ❧

"I have a round bed in my front garden in which I intend to plant wallflowers. I would like to edge the bed with another low-growing plant. Would double daisies be suitable?"

Indeed they would, or another option could be white arabis for edging your bed of wallflowers.

Sowing wallflowers ❧

"Wallflower plants that I have bought in the past have not been very satisfactory and the variety is never given. I have decided to grow my own from seed. When should it be sown?"

If you want particular colours or mixtures it is much the best thing to raise your own wallflowers. Sow the seed outside in May or June, in shallow drills. When the seedlings are large enough to handle, lift them and plant them out in nursery rows 6 in. (15 cm) apart. Transfer the plants to their flowering positions in October.

Bonsai

Bonsai care

"Can you tell me how to care for a conifer bonsai plant which I was given last Christmas. Is it best kept in a heated room or does it prefer cool conditions?"

Your bonsai plant will not do well if it is kept in a heated room indoors. The conifer is perfectly hardy and for most of the year it should be stood outside in a sheltered position. The pot or container in which the plant is growing may be vulnerable to frost and it should be insulated against the cold. It is best not to stand the plant on the ground as worms can get among the roots.

Regular trimming will keep your tree in shape

If possible stand it on staging raised above ground level. The plant can, of course, be brought indoors from time to time for short periods but it will suffer if kept indoors for long periods.

Blighted bonsai ❧

"I have grown some pine seedlings with a view to training them as bonsai trees in a few years' time. Now I find that they are all covered with a sort of woolly pest or mould."

The damage is due to the attack by a pest known as the Scots pine adelges, *Pineus pini*. It is a fairly close relative of the greenfly, and produces wax wool in the same way as the woolly aphid does on apple trees. There can be three or more generations of the pests each year, so prompt control will help to prevent further build up. A drenching spray with Rapid would be a good choice as this product is virtually specific to aphids so wouldn't damage any natural predators which may be attracted to the adelges.

When selecting plants from the garden centre, make sure you read the label!

Bonsai bother ⚜

"My 14-year-old bonsai acer is looking very poorly, with round objects on the stems and wilting leaves. Help please."

The round objects are hemispherical scale insects which feed on the plant sap. Eggs laid under the protection of the scales hatch out and the young wander off to find new feeding sites.

Pick off the scales as you find them and then spray with Tumblebug or Sybol to clear up any tiny new ones. Repeat the spray two weeks later.

Bulbs, corms and tubers

Dwarf bulbs for pots ❧
"I want to plant some dwarf bulbs in window boxes and containers this autumn. What kinds would you recommend?"

There are a great many dwarf bulbs that are suitable for growing in window boxes.

A few suggestions are: *Crocus chrysanthus*; *Narcissus* "Tête-à-Tête" and "Peeping Tom"; double early tulips; muscari; *Tulipa kaufmanniana*; *Anemone blanda*; hyacinths; *Iris danfordiae*; *Iris reticulata*; snowdrops; chionodoxas and *Scilla siberica*.

Plant the bulbs as soon as they can be obtained and use a good potting compost for the containers.

Pecking disorder ❧
"How do I stop hens from pulling out my bulbs?"

The only way to stop hens pulling out bulbs is to protect them with netting or temporary fencing until they have made enough root growth to withstand this attack.

Bulbs for Christmas ❧
"I want to grow some bulbs for flowering at Christmas. When should they be planted?"

For flowering at Christmas choose bulbs that have been specially treated for early flowering and plant them now. Narcissi such as "Grand Soleil d'Or" and "Paper White" are both well worth growing for a Christmas display.

Light bulbs ❧
"I have some pots of bulbs which have been kept cool and in the dark since they were planted. When can I bring them into the light?"

Bulbs should be kept in the dark for 10–12 weeks. This cool period allows the bulbs to make a good root system. After this period put into a light place in a cool room – do not put them in a warm room until growth is well developed.

Starting achimenes ⚜

"I have been given some achimenes tubers to grow in my greenhouse. When do I start them into growth?"

Achimenes are attractive plants for a cool greenhouse, grown in pots or hanging baskets. Plant several tubers together in a 5 or 6 in. (12–15 cm) pot filled with a good potting compost.

March is a good time to start the tubers into growth in a temperature of about 10°C (50°F). The thin stems usually need supporting with twiggy sticks.

When the plants are in full growth keep them well watered and fed each week with a liquid fertilizer.

Winter aconites ⚜

"I never have much success with winter aconites. Can you give me some tips please?"

You need to buy fresh corms, and not dried-up stock, and the best advice we can give is to try to buy growing plants in March or April.

There are two main species, *Eranthis cilicica*, and the better known *E. hyemalis*. Both have golden-yellow flowers in February–March, and *E. hyemalis* will seed freely.

Tender agapanthus ⚜

"I have plants of the very tall, white agapanthus which I keep in an unheated greenhouse during the winter. They are in large plastic containers and I find it difficult to move them. Can I plant them out in a flower border?"

Your plants are probably the half-hardy *Agapanthus orientalis*. They are liable to be damaged in temperatures lower than 0°C. If you decide to plant them out, cover them with a deep layer of bracken, straw or similar material.

It would be worth splitting the clumps into several pieces, potting some in smaller containers. These could be protected under glass in the winter so that even if the outside plants were killed off you would still have some safe and sound under cover.

Jersey lily ❧

"I have some Jersey lily bulbs in my garden but they never flower. Can you tell me why?"

The probable reason why your bulbs of the Jersey lily, *Amaryllis bella-donna*, do not flower is because they are not in a suitable position. They must have a warm, sheltered spot in full sun and well-drained soil. If they do not get enough sun they will not flower and you may have to move your bulbs to a more suitable position. Bulbs are already starting to make new leaves and this would be a good time to move them.

Choose a spot at the foot of a south-facing wall. Take out a deep hole for them and fill it with good potting soil containing plenty of coarse sand. Replant the bulbs with their tips at soil level. Feed the bulbs in the spring and early summer with a liquid fertilizer.

If you do not have a suitable position you could grow the bulbs in large pots kept in a frost-free greenhouse.

Lily confusion ❧

"Are the Jersey and Guernsey lily one and the same plant?"

The Jersey and Guernsey lilies are entirely different bulbs. The Guernsey lily is *Nerine sarniensis*. It is not fully hardy in this country and has to be grown under glass.

The Jersey Lily, *Amaryllis belladonna*, can be grown outside in this country and likes a border at the foot of a south-facing wall. Its pink, trumpet-shaped flowers appear in late summer.

Planting amaryllis ❧

"I have bought a bulb of Amaryllis belladonna. Can you tell me when is the best time to plant it and what sort of situation does it like? How deep should the bulb be planted?"

Bulbs of the Belladonna Lily, *Amaryllis belladonna*, like to be planted in a warm and sunny situation. Ideally, plant your bulb at the foot of a south- or west-facing wall. The soil must be well drained. Place the bulb with the tip at soil level.

The leaves appear in the autumn and grow through the winter until the following summer when they disappear. The flowers appear in early autumn before the leaves develop. If you prefer, you could grow your bulb in a pot kept in a cool greenhouse.

*Bulbs can brighten up the garden provided you
don't get them mixed up with the lighting kind.*

Leaves but no flowers ❧

*"I have had some bulbs of Amaryllis belladonna in my garden for several years.
Although they produce lots of leaves they do not flower. Can you tell me why?"*

It is possible that the situation in which you have planted the amaryllis
bulbs is unsuitable. To flower well they need a hot and sunny situation.
Ideally, the bulbs are best planted at the foot of a south-facing wall where
they can be thoroughly ripened. If yours are not in a sunny spot, we
suggest that you lift them after the leaves die down in the summer and
replant them in a more suitable position.

Normally, the bulbs resent disturbance and you may find that flowers
will not appear until the bulbs are well settled in their new home.

Channel potting ❧

*"I received a Jersey lily bulb and potted it in a 4 in. pot. After producing
three pairs of leaves it has stopped growing. Do I plant it in another pot or put
it in the garden?"*

The Jersey Lily, *Amaryllis belladonna*, produces pink, trumpet-shaped flowers in late summer before the leaves appear.

The bulbs lose their leaves in the summer and your bulb is probably resting. Bulbs may not flower in the first season after planting as they take a little time to settle down.

We suggest that you plant your bulb outside against a warm south- or west-facing wall. Do this as soon as possible, covering the tip of the bulb with about 6 in. (15 cm) of soil. Sunshine, shelter and warmth are essential for this South African bulb. The young leaves, which appear in late autumn, must be protected from damaging frosts.

Related anemones ❧

"Can you tell me the difference between Anemone blanda *and* A. appenina?"

Anemone appenina and *A. blanda* are very closely related and, basically, the difference between them, from a gardener's point of view, is hardly worth bothering about. However, from a botanist's point of view, the main distinguishing features are that the leaves of *A. blanda* are glabrous beneath whilst those of *A. appenina* tend to be less smooth-skinned and slightly hairy.

A. blanda flowers often have more petals than *A. appenina*.

Bulking up arum lilies ❧

"On lifting one of my arum lilies I discovered little bulbs forming around the main plant. What is the best way of growing them? Should I plant them in seed compost?"

The small bulbs or offsets may be removed from your arum lily, *Zantedeschia aethiopica* and put into small thumb pots. This is best carried out once the plant has finished flowering. We suggest that you use a multipurpose potting compost mixture. Once the plants increase in size move them on into large pots. They will be happy outside during the summer but are best kept under cover for the winter.

Arum scarum ❧

"My husband started his arum lily plants into growth as usual earlier this year, but now the leaves are infested with yellow and black aphids. We haven't seen this type before and would welcome identification and advice please."

The pest species you describe is the mottled arum aphid. Typically the older specimens have a yellow body with a black, U-shaped mark on the back. This species can attack a very wide range of greenhouse plants but will be well controlled by Rapid insecticide, which won't adversely affect any beneficial insects present.

Right way up ❧

"I have bought some dry begonia tubers. According to the instructions I should start the tubers in a tray of peaty soil and, when growth appears, put them in separate pots filled with potting compost. However, I am not told which way the tubers should be planted. Does it matter?"

There is a right and wrong way of planting begonia tubers.

On one side you will see that there is a hollow. This is the top side and it should be planted uppermost.

Planting Indian shot ❧

"I bought a root of the Indian shot plant (canna) earlier this year and started it off in a room indoors. It is growing well in a small pot and I have moved it to my greenhouse. What should I do now? When can I plant it outside?"

Cannas are not completely hardy and cannot be planted in the open until late May or early June when all danger from frost has passed. As your plant is in a small pot we suggest that you move it into a slightly larger one of good potting compost, so that you have a really good plant to put out in a few weeks' time.

Choose a sunny, sheltered position for the plant and good, fertile soil well enriched with decayed organic matter.

Lift the plant in early autumn and store it in a frost-free place for the winter.

Rest period ❧

"I have grown some cannas in pots this summer and they flowered well on my patio. How should I treat them in the winter?"

Cannas must be kept in a frost-free, dry place for the winter. After cutting back the foliage, stand your pots in a frost-free greenhouse or in an unheated room indoors.

Keep the soil in the pots almost dry in the winter and only water when it is very dry. Repot the roots in March using fresh potting compost and start the plants into growth in a greenhouse or in a light, cool room indoors. Move the plants outside in late May or early June.

Autumn crocus ❧

"Can you tell me when is the best time to plant bulbs of the autumn crocus? Can it be done in spring? I am told these flowers are not real crocuses. Is this true?"

The best time to plant bulbs of autumn crocus is in the dormant period. Normally, bulbs are on sale in July and August and they usually flower straight away. After flowering, leaves are produced which continue growing until late spring; the bulbs are dormant until early autumn.

The botanical name for autumn crocuses is colchicum. Although the flowers look similar to crocuses, close examination will show that each has six stamens, and it is a member of the lily family. True crocuses, on the other hand, have only three stamens and they belong to the iris family.

Congested corms ❧

"Some years ago I planted a patch of crocosmia and have not lifted the corms until now. They have grown on top of each other and whilst the oldest are clearly rotten, the ones near the top are not. Will the lower 'fully fleshed' corms grow again on separation or should I throw them away?"

Congested clumps of crocosmia corms can be lifted and divided every three to four years after flowering or before growth starts in the spring. Any corms that are firm are likely to grow and can be replanted. Squashy or damaged corms should be discarded.

Prepare the site by adding well-rotted manure or compost to the soil. Plant corms 4–6 in. (10–15 cm) apart and 2–3 in. (5–7.5 cm) deep. Mark the planting site with a label or small cane.

Gappy crocus ❧

"I planted 200 crocus bulbs in grass a couple of years ago. Last year they came up but this spring only a couple came up to flower."

We suspect that the bulbs have been damaged by mice or squirrels, as both creatures are liable to dig them up and eat them.

Apart from applying animal repellents such as Stay Off or Scent Off, which have to be renewed periodically, there is no other way to stop the animals stealing your bulbs.

It is also important to allow the foliage of the crocus corms to die down naturally after flowering. It must not be cut off whilst it is still green otherwise it will affect flowering in the following spring.

Hardy cyclamen   ⅜

"I have two Cyclamen hederifolium *in a small alpine bed planted close together about six years ago. From the size of the plants I thought they should be lifted and sorted out. I was amazed to find some corms 4 in. (10 cm) across. I have also found a number of small corms. I have replanted one large one and put the other in a pot. What should I do with it? Could I let it die back and start it again next summer and would it make a house plant?"*

Cyclamen hederifolium is a hardy plant not suited to indoor cultivation. The tubers (commonly but incorrectly known as corms) cannot be divided but as the flowers set seed freely you can leave the tubers undisturbed and allow the self-sown seedlings to develop naturally. Place your potted tubers in a cold frame or unheated greenhouse to prevent them freezing and replant them in the open in spring. Water as required but do not let the soil dry out.

Cyclamen puzzle   ⅜

"I had a lovely show of outdoor cyclamen but on one of the plants I have found some strange curled objects. Are these natural, or something I should be worried about?"

Lucky you. The objects you have found are seed pods, attached to the curled-up flower stems. After successful pollination, the stems curl up to bring the seed pods close to the soil.

The pods can be left to mature to sow the seeds themselves, or the ripe seeds can be gathered and sown in the open ground or in pots of compost.

Miniature cyclamen difference   ⅜

"Can you tell me the difference between Cyclamen coum *and* Cyclamen hederifolium?"

The main difference between Cyclamen coum and *Cyclamen hederifolium* is that *C. coum* flowers in late winter and *C. hederifolium* flowers in autumn. The leaves of *C. coum* are more rounded than *C. hederifolium* which has ivy-like leaves.

Blind daffodils ❧

"Last spring, many of my daffodils produced flowerbuds that failed to open. Some of this year's early ones now seem to be doing the same. Can you explain why?"

This condition, where the buds appear to be normal but then turn papery and fail to open is known as blindness. It can be the result of various factors.

Following exceptionally wet conditions, the most likely reason is root waterlogging of the plants. Other reasons include dryness of the soil, pest damage, nutrient shortage and high temperatures during the storage of the bulbs.

Except in the case of pest damage there is little that can be done other than trying to avoid the factors given above.

Box of delights ❧

"Would you be good enough to advise me on suitable plants for a north-facing windowbox during the winter? I had considered planting 'Tête-à-Tête' daffodils, but you may possibly have some more suitable suggestions."

"Tête-à-Tête" daffodils would be ideal for a winter windowbox. Other bulbs that you could also grow are crocuses, snowdrops, hyacinths and kaufmanniana tulips.

Plants that would be suitable are winter-flowering pansies, trailing, small-leaved ivies in various leaf colours, ajugas, dwarf wallflowers, polyanthus and carex.

Miniature conifers could also be used as a foil for the colourful bulb flowers.

Leave daffodil leaves well alone ❧

"Now that my daffodils have finished flowering do I remove the green seed pods and can I tie the leaves in bundles to tidy them up?"

It is a good idea to remove the green seed pods on daffodils so that all the energy goes into bulb production, but do not tie the foliage in bundles. This is likely to damage the leaves and prevent them from producing nourishment for the bulbs.

The foliage must be allowed to grow naturally for at least six weeks after flowering before it is cleared away.

Daffodil problem ❧

"A few of the older daffodils in my garden are coming up distorted this year. The leaves are twisted and there are small yellow spots down the leaf edges. From my reference book this sounds like eelworm, but no treatment is given. Can anything be done?"

The symptoms you describe do fit stem and bulb eelworm damage all too well. As a further check you could cut across one of the bulbs to look for the brown rings in the bulb scales. Unfortunately there is no easy control and the best action would be to dig up and burn the bulbs to reduce further spread. Remove all the bulbs in each cluster where even just one is showing signs of damage.

No Angel's tears ❧

"Can you tell me how to make my Angel's tears narcissi flower? They have only ever produced the odd flower and lately they have made leaves without any flowers. What should I do to make them flower?"

There are various reasons why daffodil bulbs do not flower. If the leaves are removed soon after flowering this will prevent flowers appearing in the following spring. The foliage should remain for at least six weeks after the flowers fade, preferably until the leaves die down naturally. Tying the leaves together in a knot is detrimental as it prevents them functioning properly. Dryness at the roots, particularly after flowering, is another reason why flowers do not form, although a waterlogged soil can make the bulbs rot.

To help your bulbs flower next spring feed them several times after flowering with a liquid fertilizer. Keep up the feeding until the foliage naturally withers.

Daffodils in grass ❧

"I want to plant some daffodil bulbs in an area of rough grass. What is the best way of planting them?"

If you intend planting a lot of daffodil bulbs, get hold of a bulb-planting tool which takes out a core of soil and turf for each bulb.

Another method is to carefully remove patches of turf with a spade. Fork over the soil and plant the bulbs, returning the turf afterwards. To create a natural effect, do not plant the bulbs in straight lines but in informal groups. After flowering allow the bulb foliage to develop and do not remove it for at least six weeks. It also pays to remove the green seed heads. At the same time feed the bulbs with a liquid fertilizer or a general garden fertilizer. This will help to build up the bulbs so that they flower well the following spring.

Feeding daffodils ❧

"We have 'Tête-à-Tête' and 'February Gold' daffodils in troughs. How should we look after them so that they flower again next year?"

Help your "Tête-à-Tête" and "February Gold" daffodils to flower next year by feeding them now with 2 oz. per sq. yd (56g/m²) of fish, blood and bonemeal. Sprinkle it over the surface of the soil. Or use a liquid fertilizer.

If the soil is dry, keep it well watered. Allow the foliage to die down naturally and do not remove it for at least six weeks after flowering. Feed the daffodils each spring to keep them flourishing with good size blooms.

Miniature narcissi ❧

"Last spring I saw lots of very small narcissi or daffodils and would like to grow some in my garden. Can you recommend some good varieties and when should the bulbs be planted?"

There are a great many small narcissi or daffodils. The following are some of the most reliable *cyclamineus* hybrids having swept-back petals: "February Gold", "February Silver", "Jenny", cream; "Peeping Tom", yellow; "Tête-à-Tête", lemon-yellow. Other small narcissi are: *Narcissus bulbocodium*, yellow; "Minnow", lemon-yellow; "Rip Van Winkle", yellow, double; and *N. pseudonarcissus obvallaris*, yellow, the Tenby daffodil.

Obtain the bulbs as soon as possible from a specialist bulb merchant or garden centre and plant them on arrival – the sooner that they are in the ground the better.

Pebbles and paper ❧

"I have bought some bulbs of 'Paper White' narcissi. I want to grow them in a bowl of moist pebbles. Do I have to keep them cold before bringing them into my greenhouse?"

"Paper White" narcissi do not need a cool period after potting in the same way as most other bulbs. If you pot them in pebbles now, they should be flowering in about six weeks' time. If you want them flowering for Christmas, delay potting until early November.

Keep them cool and dry in the meantime.

Naturalising bulbs can be great fun.

Giving daffodils a lift ❧

"I have some daffodil bulbs growing in a border. I want to move them to a new position. When can I lift them?"

Daffodil bulbs can be lifted once the foliage withers and turns brown. Don't lift the bulbs until at least six weeks after flowering otherwise they are not likely to flower very well next year.

Planting dahlias ❧

"I bought some dry dahlia tubers this spring and planted them in large pots. They are growing well in my conservatory. When can they be planted outside in this cold district?"

Dahlias are tender plants and you should not put your plants in their flowering positions until all danger of frost has passed. In your district it should be safe to plant out in the first week of June. Unless they are bedding dahlias, put stakes in the ground where the plants are to grow. This should be done before the dahlias are planted so that one plant can be supported by each stake.

Early flowers 🕯

"I want to grow some freesias in my greenhouse. Can you tell me when to pot the corms so that I can have flowers early next spring?"

Start freesia corms into growth in August. Pot about five corms in a 5 in. (12 cm) pot of good John Innes compost.

Stand the pots in a cold frame to allow a good root system to develop. Green shoots will soon appear and in late September take the pots into a frost-free greenhouse.

Stand the plants in a light position. As the foliage develops, support it with twiggy sticks placed around the edge of each pot. The fragrant flowers should appear in late winter.

Native delight 🕯

"I want to plant some bulbs of the snakeshead lily. When is the best time to plant? Will they grow in ordinary garden soil?"

Plant bulbs of the snakeshead lily, *Fritillaria meleagris*, in the autumn. This is a native flower that still grows wild in one or two places in the country. The plant seems to grow best in moist soil although it must not be waterlogged. It can also be grown in moist soil in rock gardens. Plant the bulbs about 3–4 in. (7.5–10 cm) deep and 6 in. (15 cm) apart.

Crowning glory 🕯

"A few weeks ago I collected some bulbils growing on the stems of a crown imperial, Fritillaria imperialis. *Hoping to grow them on, I planted 15 in a seed tray. I am pleased to see that they have rooted. What do I do with them now?"*

The bulbils of the crown imperial should be treated in the same way as seedlings. This spring, prick out the largest into an outdoor nursery bed or a cold frame. Grow them on until they are large enough to flower – usually two to three years. At this stage plant the bulbs out into their flowering positions.

Crown imperials 🕯

"I planted some crown imperial bulbs last autumn but they did not grow well and what growth appeared was weak. Are these bulbs difficult to grow?"

Crown imperial bulbs (*Fritillaria imperialis*) are not easy to get established.

They must have good, deep, fertile soil – they are not happy in poor, light soils.

To avoid water collecting in the centre of the bulbs, plant them on their sides in holes 4–5 in. (10–12 cm) deep.

After flowering it is a good idea to feed the bulbs with a good liquid fertilizer to build them up for the following year.

Ginger lily ❧

"I bought a ginger lily bulb three years ago. It produces leaves but has never flowered. Can you please tell me where I have gone wrong?"

We assume that your ginger bulb is hedychium, a member of the ginger family and a perennial with rhizomatous roots.

The plant needs a rich compost and a container not exceeding 12 in. (30 cm) across.

It also needs warm conditions if it is to flower well. Keep the plant fairly dry in the winter, but from March onwards give more water as new growth develops. Also give regular feeds of a high potash liquid fertilizer, such as a tomato feed, every 10–14 days in spring and summer. Grow the plant in a sunny part of the greenhouse and maintain a minimum temperature in the winter of 7°C (45°F). If the plant is very root bound, repot it in fresh compost.

Spotty gladioli ❧

"My son grew gladioli for the first time this year. Most were good, but the later varieties produced flowers that were spotted with white marks, whilst their leaves were streaked with silvery marks. Can this be prevented?"

The damage was due to feeding by thrips. Also known as thunderflies because they are most troublesome in overcast, warm conditions, thrips feed on leaves and petals of a wide range of plants.

After lifting and drying the corms at the end of the season, your son should dust them with malathion dust to control the thrips seeking to overwinter under the scales. Next summer, at the first sign of damage, or when thundery weather is forecast, spraying with a general insecticide would greatly reduce damage to leaves and flowers.

Early glads ❧

"I would like to grow some of the small, early-flowering gladioli. Is it best to grow them in a greenhouse?"

The early, small-flowered gladioli can be grown outside in warm districts but in your area it is probably best to grow them in pots in a greenhouse. Pot the bulbs as soon as you can get them and keep them outside until late September when they can be brought into a frost-free greenhouse.

Good varieties to grow include: "The Bride", white; "Comet", red and "Amanda Mahy", pink.

Cornish purple gladiolus

"Could you tell me the name of a plant that grows like a weed in Cornwall? The plants grow 10–12 in. (25–30 cm) tall and look like a gladioli, but these flowers are smaller than ordinary gladioli and are purple in colour."

We believe that the gladiolus-like plant that you have seen in Cornwall is *Gladiolus communis byzantinus*. It is commonly found growing wild in mild areas such as in Cornwall and the Scilly Isles. Corms can be purchased from most bulb specialists including Avon Bulbs, Burnt House Farm, Mid-Lambrook, South Petherton, Somerset TA13 5HE.

It's sow time for those glads!

"Last year I grew 70 gladioli corms and in October lifted the plants to dry off. I have now cleaned the corms and find I have 425 cormlets. How should these now be grown?"

If you kept your gladiolus corms cool, in a temperature of about 10°C (50°F) during the winter, they should have kept fine and be ready now for sowing in trays of seed compost. Start them into growth in gentle heat. In May, when they are several inches high, transplant them 4 in. (10 cm) apart in a nursery bed outdoors.

Alternatively, you could sow them *in situ* outdoors in mid-May.

Lift them in autumn and store in a dry, cool place. Plant them out in their flowering positions the following spring. Some may flower that year; the majority will flower the year after.

Potting gloriosa

"I have bought a root of Gloriosa rothschildiana. *I now discover that it needs high temperatures and I am wondering whether I can grow it in my greenhouse which is heated to exclude frost."*

You should be able to grow the gloriosa in your cool greenhouse. It is true that the plant revels in hot, moist conditions and, once the spring arrives, the temperature in your greenhouse will rise from sun heat.

We suggest that you start the tubers into growth in March. Plant one root in a 6 in. (15 cm) pot or several in a larger pot using good John Innes compost or a soilless mixture. Place the tubers vertically in the pot and cover them with about 2 in. (5 cm) of soil.

Starting gloxinias from scratch ❧

"I have bought some gloxinia tubers. What size pot should they be put in?"

The size of pot to use depends on how big the tubers are. We suggest that you first press the tubers into a shallow tray of peat so that their tops are exposed. Kept warm and moist, new shoots should soon appear. Once this happens, the tubers can be potted individually. Small tubers can be put in $3\frac{1}{2}$ in. (9 cm) pots and larger ones can go in a $4\frac{1}{2}$ in. (11 cm) pot. When established, the plants can be moved on into slightly larger pots. Once the final pots are full of roots, feed the plants each week with a liquid fertilizer.

Glory of the snow ❧

"Several years ago I planted some bulbs of Chionodoxa luciliae. They have spread considerably and form a carpet of pale blue flowers in early March. As they seem very crowded can I lift the bulbs and split them up for replanting?"

As your chionodoxa bulbs have increased so well it would be a good idea to split them up for replanting. Do this after flowering and before the leaves wither. Replant the bulbs straight away as they will be happier in the soil than being kept dry for the summer. Choose a sunny position for the bulbs and soil that is well drained.

Blood lily ❧

"I have been given a bulb called Haemanthus multiflorus. It is growing in a pot. Can I grow it indoors or does it need a greenhouse? When should it be repotted?"

You should be able to grow your haemanthus in a room indoors provided it is placed in a light window. Keep it cool when the bulb is resting when the soil in the pot should be kept almost dry. Repotting is necessary only every four or five years. The bulb resents disturbance and may not flower the year after repotting.

Worth the wait ✿

"About two years ago I was given some amaryllis seed which I sowed in pots in my cool greenhouse. After a considerable time they germinated and I now have plants with inch-wide leaves. Can you advise me how to grow them on?"

The bulbs with large, trumpet-shaped flowers, often wrongly called amaryllis, are in fact hippeastrums and we assume that this is the plant that you have. Keep your seedlings in a warm part of your greenhouse. Only water them through the autumn and winter when the compost in the pots shows signs of dryness. If the pots are full of roots in the spring, move the seedlings on into slightly larger pots, keeping the top half of the bulb above soil level. During the spring and summer feed the bulbs each week with a feed. The bulbs will slowly increase in size but it may take up to five years before flowers can be expected.

Pot that hippeastrum! ✿

"I have been given a hippeastrum bulb. Do I pot it now or in the spring, and how deep should the bulb be planted?"

Pot your hippeastrum bulb without delay. Place the bulb in the centre of a 5 in. (12 cm) pot and leave most of the bulb above the surface of the compost. Firm fresh potting compost around the roots but leave space at the top for watering.

Keep the bulb in a light place and not in a high temperature otherwise growth will be long and spindly. Water sparingly until growth becomes active.

Dealing with leggy growth ✿

"Last Christmas I was given a hippeastrum bulb in a box with a bag of compost. It has produced a stem so fast that it is becoming long and leggy and needs support. Is there anything wrong with the bulb?"

No, we do not think that there is anything wrong with your hippeastrum bulb. We suspect that the cause of the trouble is a lack of light and you are keeping it too warm. Can you move your plant to a light window in a cooler room? This may help it to produce more sturdy growth.

Feeding hippeastrum bulbs ✿

"My amaryllis bulb flowered around February and had four blooms. Later another spike appeared with five more blooms. How should I look after it?"

We were delighted to know that your hippeastrum (amaryllis) bulb flowered so well. Encourage it to perform strongly again next year by feeding it regularly with a liquid fertilizer and water it whenever the soil seems dry. Keep it well nourished until September when watering and feeding should cease.

Allow the foliage to die down and rest the bulb in an unheated room from autumn to late winter. In February or March start watering and feeding again to encourage the bulb to make new leaves.

Home-sown hippeastrum seedlings ?❧

"I collected some seed from my hippeastrum plant which I sowed in the spring. The seedlings have grown like grass. Please tell me how to care for them to produce flowering size bulbs and how long will they take before they flower?"

We suggest that you leave the hippeastrum seedlings as they are for the winter, preferably in a warm greenhouse. Keep the soil moist but not too wet.

Next February put the seedlings separately in small pots of potting compost. Grow them on in a warm greenhouse and feed them in the summer with a liquid fertilizer. Move them on to slightly larger pots a year later.

When the bulbs flower depends on how well they are grown but you cannot expect flowers until the plants are at least four years old. The colour of the flowers will probably be variable and you may have some interesting results. They will all be new varieties and, if you have one with very good flowers, it would be worth giving it a name.

Hyacinths for Christmas ?❧

"If I want to grow hyacinths to flower at Christmas, when do I pot the bulbs?"

Specially treated hyacinth bulbs should now be available at garden centres in August or you should order them without delay from a bulb nursery. Pot the bulbs as soon as you can. After a good watering stand the bulbs in a cold, dark place for at least 10 weeks to allow them to make a good root system before being brought out into the light.

Cool it ?❧

"I have planted some hyacinth bulbs in bowls of bulb fibre. At the moment they are kept in the dark in our garage. How soon can I bring them into a room indoors?"

Hyacinth bulbs must be kept cool and in the dark for at least 10 weeks before they are taken into a living room indoors. This cool period is essential so that the bulbs can make a really good root system before they are taken into warmer conditions.

If the bulbs have insufficient roots, they will not grow properly and the flowers will be distorted.

Drainage problem solved ❧

"Last winter I grew some hyacinths and winter-flowering pansies in an ornamental container, stood on a flat base. There were small holes in the base of the container for drainage but the soil seemed to become very wet and the bulbs and pansies rotted. What can I do to prevent this happening again?"

We suspect that your plants rotted off last winter because of poor drainage. The holes in the base of the container must be large enough to ensure that all surplus water drains away. It is a good idea to raise the container a little with special pot feet which can be obtained at garden centres. Also, make sure that you use a potting compost containing coarse sand or grit. Ordinary garden soil is not suitable.

Bulb flower mystery ❧

"Two years ago I acquired a bulb of the Peruvian daffodil, but for the second year running it has not flowered. It produces leaves and nothing else. I have planted the bulb in early spring in a semi-sunny position and average soil. What am I doing wrong?"

Although the Peruvian daffodil, *Hymenocallis narcissiflora*, can be grown outside in mild districts, it is not fully hardy and we think your bulb might do better if it was grown in a pot of sandy soil and kept in a greenhouse.

It needs well-drained soil and a hot, sunny situation. Give it very little water in winter but water it freely in spring and summer.

Winter iris eaten ❧

"Our winter-flowering iris, Iris unguicularis, has been badly damaged by some pest or other, with nearly all the flowers being spoiled. Can you suggest what is responsible and what we should use to stop it?"

The damage is being caused by slugs, feeding mainly at night. The best control would be to water plants and the soil around with Slugit Liquid.

This will kill the slugs as they move over the treated soil or feed on the leaves or flowers.

Doing the Kaffir splits ❦

"I have some Kaffir lilies which have made a sizeable clump. Should this be split up and when?"

To start, there is some confusion over the name Kaffir lily. The hardy outdoor kind is schizostylis, and the tender indoor kind is clivia – they're both distantly related, in the lily family, but require completely different cultural conditions. Once Kaffir lilies (schizostylis) have made large clumps it is best to split them up as left alone the flowers are not so good in the autumn. You should still be able to divide your clump now and replant the young pieces in a new position where the soil is fertile.

This Kaffir lily is all white ❦

"I have a white-flowered indoor Kaffir lily. The plant has been passed down in my family for 30 years and in all that time it has flowered in just its 26th year and again in its 30th year. I do not know anything about this plant and I hope you can tell me why it does not flower on a regular basis?"

To ensure your Kaffir lily flowers regularly, allow it to rest in the winter in an unheated room with a temperature of 4°C (40°F). Give water only sparingly and do not feed it until the spring. It is best kept in good light but not in direct sunlight. When the pot becomes very full of roots repot the plant in the spring after it has finished flowering.

Your white-flowered Kaffir lily, *Clivia miniata*, is quite unusual as the flowers are normally orange-red.

Kaffir lily choice for outdoors ❦

"I want to grow some Kaffir lilies. Can you tell me the best variety to grow and what sort of soil and situation suits the plant best?"

The Kaffir lilies or schizostylis are delightful plants for an autumn display. They are not fussy about soil, provided it is well drained. Choose a sheltered, sunny position for the plants.

There are several good varieties. *S. coccinea*, red flowers and "Mrs Hegarty", pale pink flowers, are reliable kinds. Several new varieties have appeared recently including the white "Snow Maiden" and "Sunrise" salmon-pink.

After-flower care

"My Clivia miniata, has finished flowering and I am not sure what to do with it now. Do I leave the flower stalk to die down or should I cut it off? I want to look after the plant well so that it flowers again next year."

Once the flowers have faded on your clivia, cut off the stalk as close to the base as possible. Keep the plant in a light place in a cool room but away from strong sunshine.

From June to early September stand it outside in a lightly shaded spot. Feed it each week until August with liquid fertilizer and keep it well watered.

In September return the plant indoors. Allow it to rest from October onwards by keeping the plant in a cool room and giving very little water. Only water when the soil becomes very dry.

A flower spike should begin to appear in February – wait until it has grown about 6 in. (15 cm) tall before resuming normal watering. Sponge the leaves from time to time to remove dust.

Scarborough lilies

"I have grown some Scarborough lilies (vallota), four per 3 in. pot, which have formed small bulbs. Could you tell me at what stage I should pot them singly? How long will the bulbs take to flower and will they have flowers true to the parent plant?"

The Scarborough lily (vallota) has beautiful flowers in September.

It is a slow process raising plants from seed and you may have to wait five years before you see flowers. However, the wait is worthwhile.

We suggest that you put your seedlings in separate 3 in. (7.5 cm) pots in March or April. Grow them in a warm and sunny place. From May to August feed the bulbs each week with a liquid fertilizer.

The bulbs resent disturbance and they should not need complete repotting for two to three years as long as feeding is not neglected in the summer.

The seedlings should have flowers similar to those of the parent bulb.

Madonna lily

"When should bulbs of the Madonna lily be planted and will they grow well in chalky soils?"

Late July or early August is the best time to plant bulbs of the Madonna Lily, *Lilium candidum*. Set them in the ground shallowly so that the tops of the scales are just below soil level.

The bulbs will grow well in chalky soil if it has been enriched with well decayed manure or compost. They often succeed best planted at the foot of a warm, south-facing wall.

Lily beetles on the rampage ❧

"Every year my lilies and a few other plants are devastated by shiny red beetles and some slimy-looking grubs. Having attacked in spring, they usually come again later on in the year as well. What are these pests and how can I stop the next attack?"

The red beetles are lily beetles, and the slimy grubs are their larvae. The larvae cover themselves with their black droppings, presumably as a form of protection. This species of beetle attacks fritillaries and Solomon's seal as well as lilies.

As soon as the summer generation of adult beetles is seen, spray thoroughly with BugGun, Tumblebug or Safer's Garden Insecticide, and repeat after a couple of weeks as necessary. This should greatly reduce the numbers of adults and the eggs and larvae they produce.

Lilies in pots ❧

"I obtained some lily bulbs recently, but because the ground outside was very wet, I planted the bulbs in pots. I am not sure what to do now. Should I plant the bulbs outside in the spring or can I keep them in their pots?"

Your lily bulbs could be planted outside in the spring in some well-prepared soil, or you can leave them in their pots if they are large enough. Lilies look very attractive in containers for decorating a patio.

If you have a greenhouse and you want early flowers, the pots could be taken inside, when the shoots are about 3 in. long. Do not try to force the lilies in high temperatures.

Once they are growing well, feed lilies in pots regularly with a liquid fertilizer.

Planting lilies ❧

"I have bought some bulbs of Lilium speciosum rubrum. *As the soil in the garden is too wet for planting can I grow the bulbs in large pots?"*

Yes, lily bulbs can be grown successfully in large pots or tubs. Make sure that there are drainage holes in the base of the container and cover them with a layer of rubble to ensure good drainage. Use a good potting compost and cover the bulbs with about 3 in. (7.5 cm) of compost. Do not fill the container to the rim but leave sufficient space for watering.

Stand the containers outside in a cool, sheltered position.

Lily bulbils

"I have some tiger lilies. They have small, round and black pods on the stems. Are these bulbils and will they grow if I take them off?"

Yes, the black, shiny bulbils on the stems of your tiger lilies can be used to raise more plants. Take them off directly after flowering and sow them like seeds in small pots of gritty soil. When new shoots appear pot each plantlet in a small container of well-drained, good-quality potting compost.

Nerine bulbs to light up autumn

"I have bought some bulbs of Nerine bowdenii. How deep should they be planted?"

Plant these bulbs as soon as possible. To grow well nerines should be planted in a warm and sunny position, preferably at the foot of a south-facing wall. Plant them in well-drained soil with the tip of each bulb just below soil level.

Leave nerine bulbs undisturbed for many years but remember to cover them with straw or bracken to afford them some protection in winter.

Hot flowerer

"I planted some bulbs of Nerine bowdenii several years ago but they have never flowered. They make masses of new leaves each year. Can you tell me why they don't flower?"

We cannot be sure why your nerines are not flowering from the information you have given, but we suspect that they are not growing in a suitable position.

They must be planted in a hot and sunny spot, preferably at the base of a south-facing wall. The soil must be well drained and the bulbs prefer a sandy soil. If you have them in an unsuitable site we suggest that you lift the bulbs now, as they start to make leaves, and replant them in a more suitable spot. Replant them with the tips of the bulbs slightly below soil level.

Storing ranunculus ❧

"I have grown some Turban ranunculus from tubers this year. Now that the flowers have finished, what should I do with them?"

Once the foliage of your ranunculus withers, lift the tubers carefully and dry them off. Store them in a dry, frost-free place for the winter and replant them again in early spring.

Dividing snowdrops ❧

"I have several large clumps of snowdrops. Can I split them up and when should it be done?"

It is a good idea to lift and divide large clumps of snowdrops as they are likely to flower better afterwards. The best time to do this is after flowering but whilst the foliage is still green.

Snowdrops in the green ❧

"I have several large clumps of snowdrops. I would like to lift and divide them so that I can replant a larger area with them. When would be the best time to do this?"

Snowdrops will transplant much better whilst still in growth, so now is the best time to lift clumps for replanting, whilst the foliage is still green.

Tiger flowers ❧

"I have grown some tigridias this year. One has four petals instead of the usual three. Is this unusual? If so, how do I propagate it?"

Tigridias normally have three large, outer petals and an inner ring of three. We assume your plant has four outer petals. This is unusual and you really should try to preserve it.

All you can do is to mark it, so that when you lift the corms, after the foliage withers, you can keep the corm separate from the rest.

Replant it next spring in the hope that it will continue to produce similar flowers.

South African bulb ❧

"Last summer I came across a charming plant called Tulbaghia violacea. *It looked something like a small agapanthus. Can you tell me whether it can be grown outside in my district [Westbury]?"*

Tulbaghia violacea is a choice bulb with thin, graceful stems of lilac flowers in July. It will tolerate a light frost but, in your area, to be on the safe side, grow it in a large pot kept under cover for the winter. Bring it out to a sunny patio for the summer. "Silver Lace" is a very choice form with cream-striped leaves. Growing bulbs "in the green" are available directly from Hopleys Plants, Much Hadham, Herts, SG10 6BU.

Their catalogue is available by sending five first-class stamps.

Delayed planting ❧

"I bought some tulip bulbs in September but, because of building work, I cannot plant them until the end of December. Will it be too late then?"

Although December is late for planting tulip bulbs, they should still flower. But why not plant them in large pots or tubs filled with good potting compost? Keep them outside and when your ground is ready, sink the pots into the soil.

Multi-flowered tulips ❧

"I have some red tulips in my garden with several flowers on a single stem. Is this a new type? Other tulips have only one flower per stem."

There are several tulip varieties that have multi-flowered stems. The best known is *Tulipa praestans* "Fusilier" which has bright red flowers. *T. praestans* has been used for hybridizing and there are now numerous varieties carrying several flower heads on a single stem. "Georgette", yellow with a red edge and "Happy Family", pink, are two good varieties.

Cacti and succulents

Prickly wool   ❧

"Our conservatory cacti are developing what looks like a woolly coating around the bases of the spines. I presume this is some pest, perhaps mealy bug. Could you suggest a control method please?"

The pests would be mealy bugs, as you suggest. The best control is to give a thorough spray with a systemic insecticide such as Tumblebug or Long-Last. The active ingredient gets into the sap of the plant and will then kill the mealy bugs wherever they are feeding.

Stunning bloomer   ❧

"My epiphyllum cactus flowered for the first time this year, although I have had it for a number of years. How should I look after it now?"

When your epiphyllum has finished flowering, water it when the compost shows signs of dryness.

From November onwards rest the plant by giving it very little water and no feeding. Keep it in a temperature of about 10°C (50°F) until late February. After that time, keep the plant cool and only water when the compost begins to dry out. Once flower buds form increase the temperature to 15°C (60°F).

Cactus cuttings   ❧

"I have an epiphyllum cactus plant which has grown rather large. Can I take cuttings from it so that I can start again with a young plant? What part should I take as a cutting?"

Epiphyllum cuttings are easy to root. All you have to do is to cut off a mature leaf blade and cut it horizontally into sections, about 2 in. (5 cm) wide.

Insert these vertically to about half their depth in a tray filled with seed compost, to which has been added extra coarse grit or sand.

Kept in warm, humid conditions, the cuttings should begin to root in the spring or summer. Once good roots have been made, pot each plant up into separate pots.

*Wrap corrugated cardboard around your 5ft cactus plant
at tricky repotting time as it can be awkward!*

Tight fit ❧

"My cleistocactus and cereus cacti are still in their original 6 in. (15 cm) pots. The cereus is 37 in. tall and the cleistocactus is 35 in. tall. Could you please tell me how and when to repot them?"

We suggest that you move your cacti into slightly larger pots as soon as possible. To avoid painful injury from the spines on the plants, hold them with a band of stout paper wrapped around the main stem.

Remove the present pot and tease out some of the old, spent soil from among the roots. Transfer each plant to a pot 2–3 in. (5–7.5 cm) larger than the original one.

Use a gritty potting mixture of three parts (by volume) John Innes No. 3 and one part coarse grit. Also add a sprinkling of bonemeal. Water carefully and only when the compost shows signs of drying out.

Seasonal blooms ❧

"I have a healthy Christmas cactus indoors. How should I look after it so that it flowers again next winter?"

Keep your Christmas cactus in a light place, in an unheated room until late May or early June. Water it thoroughly whenever the soil seems dry but do not stand it in a saucer of water.

From June to September stand the plant outside in a partially shaded spot. Keep it well watered and feed it each week with a liquid fertilizer. Return the plant indoors in late September to an unheated room.

Repotting cacti ❧

"I have a small cactus plant called Notocactus crassigibbus. *It has completely filled its pot and I am wondering whether it should be repotted?"*

As your notocactus has filled its pot it would benefit from repotting. The spring is a good time for repotting as new growth begins. Move the plant into a pot a little larger than the present one. Ready-made cacti composts can be purchased or you can use a mixture of a normal potting compost and Perlite in equal proportions. Make sure that there are some broken crocks in the base of the pot to ensure good drainage. To avoid the sharp spines of the cacti, hold the plant in a collar of folded paper when repotting it.

Easter cactus cuttings ❧

"I have an old Easter cactus plant which is rather straggly. Can I take cuttings from it to raise some young plants? When is the best time to do it?"

Cuttings of the Easter cactus are not difficult to root. Use pieces of stem with one or two segments for each cutting. Cut them off with a sharp knife. Insert them upright in small pots of peat and gritty sand.

The best time to take the cuttings is in the spring and summer. Once new roots form, pot each rooted cutting in a 3½ in. pot of good potting soil.

Orchid cacti in winter ❧

"I have an epiphyllum plant called 'London Glory', it was given to me in a pot in early spring and it produced some lovely flowers in the summer. How do I keep it through the winter? It is stood in a window in my living room as I do not have a greenhouse."

"London Glory" is a very fine epiphyllum variety and is not difficult to grow. During the winter keep it cool in a temperature of about 5°C. Your living room will probably be too warm and we suggest you stand it in an unheated room until March when it can be given warmer conditions.

During the winter water very sparingly. When the soil seems dry, give a little water to prevent the soil drying out completely. If you keep it too warm in the winter, more water will be needed and the plant will make weak spindly shoots which are of little use.

Succulent cigars ⅔

"I keep my epiphyllum plants under the greenhouse staging during summer and they flowered profusely in June. I hadn't watered them much so decided to repot them to buck them up. In each pot were numbers of quarter-inch diameter tubes, around an inch long and green or brown, apparently made of leaf sections. When opened up I found a white grub inside each section. What is this creature and how serious is it? I have repotted the plants and removed all the 'cigars'."

The cigar-like objects are cells made by the leaf-cutter bee. The adult bee cuts semi-circular pieces from the edges of rose and certain other leaves and then constructs the cells which are provisioned with nectar and pollen before an egg is laid in each one.

The cells are positioned in plant compost, sandy soil, or sometimes in rotting wood. Pots of cacti and succulents are favourite places as the compost is normally kept fairly dry. Left undisturbed, the grubs would pupate and then emerge as new adults in spring. The cells do no harm and the adults are useful pollinators, so no controls are needed.

Cape cowslips ⅔

"I have been given some lachenalia or Cape cowslip bulbs. When should they be planted?"

Pot your Cape cowslip, lachenalia, bulbs without delay. Partly fill a 5 or 6 in. (12–15 cm) pot or pan with good potting compost and plant the bulbs close together. Cover them with about an inch of potting compost and give them a good watering. Stand the pots in a cool place under cover until green shoots appear. Then move the bulbs into a light place in a frost-free greenhouse. They can also be stood in a light place in an unheated room in the winter.

The bulbs grow through the winter and will flower in February and March.

Flowerless ❧

"I recently took some cuttings from my Kalanchoe blossfeldiana. I now have 15 beautiful, healthy plants about 8 in. high, but none of them have flowered. Can you tell me where I have gone wrong? I feed them each week with Phostrogen."

We suspect that your *Kalanchoe blossfeldiana* plants have not flowered because they are, as yet, immature. They will bloom, almost certainly, next year. Encourage them to do so by siting them in full sun. You are doing the right thing to feed them weekly, from spring to late summer, with a high potash liquid fertilizer.

It is best to keep the plants in small pots, so that the roots are relatively pot bound.

Fragrant bloomer ❧

"I bought an indoor plant called Epiphyllum cooperi at a plant sale. It looks quite healthy but has never flowered. Can you tell how to make it produce flowers?"

Your epiphyllum is a very old variety and it is sometimes difficult to flower well. Normally, flowers appear in June and have a wonderful fragrance which is particularly noticeable in the evening. To get your plant to flower, stand it outside for the summer in a partially shaded spot and keep it well watered. Return it to a frost-free greenhouse or unheated room for the winter. Give it very little water in the winter. Once it is thoroughly pot bound it should flower. It's one plant that seems to thrive on neglect!

Lack of flowers ❧

"I have had a plant of Epiphyllum cooperi for some years but it does not flower very often. How can I make it flower each year?"

Epiphyllum cooperi is an old hybrid having wonderfully scented flowers. Unfortunately, it does not flower freely, only when it has grown into a large plant.

To help your plant make good growth feed it in the spring and early summer with a liquid fertilizer such as Phostrogen. Standing the plant in the open during the summer will help to ripen the growths and induce flowering.

Do not stand it in full sunshine as this could scorch the stems but keep it in a partially shaded position. Return the plant to an unheated room in September.

Keep dry   ❧

"I have a notocactus cactus plant which has been kept indoors on a sunny windowsill all through the summer. How do I look after it in the winter?"

Keep your cactus plant cool and dry throughout the winter months.

Ideally it should be kept in a frost-free greenhouse and given very little water, as this is its resting period. If you do not have a greenhouse, keep the plant in a light window in an unheated room. If it is kept too warm and moist the plant will start making spindly growths which are useless.

Once the days become longer in March, more water can be given as it starts up into growth once more.

Cactus flowers   ❧

"I have several Christmas cactus plants raised from cuttings. They have all developed well, having been kept outside all summer and fed regularly. However, in spite of looking healthy and lush, they have only produced two to four blooms each. Where have I gone wrong?"

Christmas cacti should be kept outside for the summer. To help them to flower, keep them in a cool spot in July and August, giving less food and water during this period. This will help to ripen the stems which formed earlier in the summer.

Increase watering gradually during the autumn. Flower buds are less likely to form on lush growth; we suggest you use a high potash fertilizer at half strength. Stop feeding from August onwards until the following spring.

Cactus is not beyond the pale   ❧

"I have two very big Christmas cacti, both believed to be more than 40 years old, which I inherited 20 years ago. They spend June to September outdoors.

One is fine but the other is rather shrivelled and pale. Should I repot it and feed it, or is there some other problem?"

Rejuvenate your ailing Christmas cactus by tapping it from its pot and teasing out old soil from the roots. If any roots are black and dead, cut them back to live tissue.

Then trim back any long shoots on the plant to make it more compact.

Repot in John Innes No. 1, adding a quarter part grit or sharp sand to improve drainage. Water in and keep it in a warm, light place for it to recover.

Climbers

Trumpet vine ✷

"We have a Campsis radicans growing on a south-facing wall. We have had it for about seven years. It grows every year but does not flower. We prune it severely each February. Have you any idea why it does not flower? We give it some growmore in the spring. Should we feed it more?"

Yours is a common problem. To flower well, the growths of *Campsis radicans* need to be well ripened and plants must be grown in a hot, sunny situation. Instead of using growmore we suggest that you apply sulphate of potash fertilizer each February to the soil around the plant. This should encourage firm and sturdy growth to be made.

You may be pruning too severely, which is encouraging growth at the expense of the flowers. Prune the climber each February by shortening all the side shoots close to the main stems. The new shoots should flower in late summer if they are well ripened.

Pruning a Russian vine ✷

"I have a Russian vine which has never been pruned. When is the best time to do it?"

The Russian vine, *Polygonum baldschuanicum*, is a rampant climber. It is most effective when allowed to ramble without pruning. However, when this becomes necessary, do it in late winter, cutting back the growth hard.

Chilean bellflower ✷

"Can you give me any information about a beautiful climber I saw last year trained up a wall in a Cornish garden? It is called the Chilean bellflower. Will it grow outside in my district [Crawley] or does it need a greenhouse?"

As you say, the Chilean bellflower, *Lapageria rosea*, is a very beautiful climber, producing pendulous, waxy, rose-pink flowers. It can only be grown successfully in the open in very mild districts and in your area it would be best in a greenhouse. It likes a moist, shaded position and good fertile soil that is free from lime. It is best planted in a border of well-prepared soil rather than in a large pot or tub.

Hop, skip and replace ❧

"Having planted a golden hop two years ago, we are disappointed that we have had no flowers as yet. The plant itself is flourishing. Any advice please? Our plan was to dry the flowers."

You have chosen the wrong hop! The golden-leaved form does not flower very well and it is grown for its attractive foliage. As you want the flowers for drying you should plant the common hop with plain green leaves, *Humulus lupulus*.

Golden hop ❧

"I have a two-year-old golden hop, Humulus lupulus *'Aureus', and wish to move it to another site in the garden. When is the best time to do it? Also, is it possible to propagate the plant from cuttings?"*

Lift your golden hop carefully with a good ball of soil attached to the roots. Transplant it in its new home in autumn or in early spring.

Leaf bud cuttings can be taken in the summer from young growths. These consist of a leaf and short piece of stem with a bud in the joint of the leaf. Dip the base of the cuttings in hormone rooting powder and insert them in pots filled with gritty soil or Perlite.

Put the cuttings in a heated propagating case until rooted.

Clematis cuttings ❧

"When is the best time to take cuttings of Clematis *'The President'?"*

Increase this clematis from double leaf-bud cuttings in late June or July. Choose a stem and make a cut just above a pair of leaves and another one 3 in. below them. Insert the cuttings in a pot of seed and cutting compost and root them in a lightly shaded heated propagator. Spray the cuttings with fungicide at 10-day intervals.

Pruning clematis ❧

"I have a plant of Clematis montana *which has gone mad and made growths all over the place. Can I cut it back now?"*

The correct time to prune *Clematis montana* is after flowering in the spring. If you cut it back severely now you will lose most of the flowers for next spring. We suggest that you simply trim back growths that are in the way now and prune more severely after flowering. This way you should have a reasonable display of flowers next spring.

Planting clematis ❧

"I want to plant a clematis against the wall of my house and train the stems up trellis. Can you tell me how deep to plant?"

As the soil against the wall of your house could be poor and dry, it would be wise to excavate a special hole for the plant. Make it about 2 ft (60 cm) square and 2 ft deep. Break up the bottom with a fork and fill the hole with good potting soil. Plant the clematis at least 1 in. (2.5 cm) lower than when it was in its pot. This helps to overcome possible trouble from clematis wilt disease, allowing new growth to develop from the base of the stem. Disentangle the roots and firm the soil well. Because the soil close to a wall gets very dry, plant about 1 ft out from the wall and train the clematis stems towards the trellis.

Seeds or shoots? ❧

"A neighbour has a wonderful plant of Clematis tangutica *which is covered each autumn in white, fluffy seed heads. If I collected some of them are they likely to produce similar plants?"*

It would be worthwhile collecting some seed from your neighbour's clematis. Sow it in the spring and within a few weeks it will have germinated.

Plants usually grow very fast and may flower later in the same year. However, results may be variable and some plants may be inferior and have small flowers.

To be sure that you raise plants the same as in your neighbour's garden, take cuttings from young shoots in June and July. Each cutting should consist of a joint or node with leaves and a piece of stem 1½–2 in. (4– 5 cm) below it.

Insert the cuttings upright in small pots of gritty soil. Enclose them in a polythene bag until roots begin to appear. Afterwards, pot each plant separately.

Avoid clematis wilt by careful planting ?‹

"I planted a clematis last autumn. It started to grow this spring and then withered. Is this clematis wilt disease and what can I do about it?"

It would seem that your clematis is affected by wilt disease. We suggest that you leave it alone for the time being as new growths may appear from below soil level.

As a precaution against the disease, always take out a large hole when planting to a depth of 2 ft (0.6 m) and 18 in. (45 cm) wide. Fill it with good, fertile soil to which has been added well-decayed compost or manure. Soak the roots of the clematis in water for half an hour before planting and place the stems 6 in. (15 cm) deep before returning the soil and firming it. This deep planting is recommended as growth will sometimes develop from below ground level when the top part has died. Mulch the ground around the base of the plant with compost to conserve soil moisture.

Monster mildew ?‹

"This year, our clematis shoots were white, with what we assumed to be some sort of mildew. What should we do now, and what can we do next year?"

The white deposits would be due to powdery mildew, and this disease can affect the growth considerably. It reduces leaf size as well as curling the leaves, even preventing flowering.

The best action now would be to cut out all the mildewed shoots. Depending on the variety of clematis, this could prevent or reduce next year's flowering, but is necessary to remove the existing infection. Next spring and summer, spray with Nimrod-T or Tumbleblite at the first sign of any mildew.

Tattered clematis ?‹

"Several of my clematis flowers have been badly eaten this year, but I've not been able to find any pest on them. Could you let me know the likely culprit and any available control measures?"

Clematis flowers appear to be irresistible to earwigs, but snails are also frequently found eating the leaves and petals.

Earwigs are best kept away by trapping them in pots filled with straw or crumpled newspaper and placed on the tops of canes close to the plants. The traps should be shaken out every morning.

Snails are less easily controlled as they can hide amongst the foliage or climb up at night and down again before the morning. A watering around the plants and over the foliage with Slugit Liquid should prove effective.

Clematis upset ❧

"I have a clematis 'The President' which started to wilt as it came into full bloom. At first I thought it must be clematis wilt, but a closer examination showed that the leaves and flowers were absolutely covered with greenfly. Could this really have caused so much damage, or do you think there could be a wilt attack?"

A severe attack of greenfly can certainly bring flowering of many plants to an abrupt end, cause plants to wilt, and in some cases virus diseases are also introduced which compound the damage. Fortunately there are no virus complications in this instance.

If the plant is now making better growth – especially if growth is coming from the tips of damaged shoots, then the greenfly would have been the cause of the problem.

On the other hand, if no new shoots are developing, and the wilted shoots continue to die down – then wilt would be likely. I would expect the cause in your case to be greenfly, in view of the heavy infestation you refer to.

Cutting survival ❧

"I have taken some cuttings of a white clematis which makes prolific growth up the wall of my house. The cuttings are doing well. How do I ensure that they survive through the winter?"

We assume your clematis cuttings have been rooted in a pot. Once they have made a good root system, pot them individually into a 4 in. pot of a multi-purpose compost.

Keep them well watered in the summer and stand the plants outside. A good root system should have formed by the autumn, allowing you to move them to their permanent home.

Prepare a new site for the plants, digging a large hole for each clematis and filling it with good soil or potting compost. Ideally plant the clematis in late September or early October, allowing it to quickly establish before winter. When planting the clematis it is important to ensure that the top of the rootball is 3–4 in. (7.5–10 cm) below soil level.

Evergreen clematis

"I have a plant of Clematis armandii. It is evergreen but the leaves tend to turn brown for part of their length. Is this unusual and can I take cuttings from the plant?"

Clematis armandii takes a long time to replace one set of leaves with another, so older leaves are often half green and brown. A good ploy is to prune after flowering, cutting back older, flowered stems to encourage strong new shoots to replace them.

Propagate the clematis from internodal cuttings in late spring. Make a cut just above and an inch or so below a pair of leaves. Shorten the leaves by about half their length and insert the cuttings in pots of gritty sand. After watering, enclose the cuttings in a plastic bag. Keep them warm in a light, shaded position until roots form six to eight weeks later.

Layering clematis

"If I peg a shoot of clematis in the soil will it form roots and make a new plant?"

Clematis stems allowed to trail on the ground will often form roots on their own. This is a simple and natural way to propagate these plants.

Once roots have developed, sever the young plants from the parent and plant them in well-prepared soil in their permanent positions.

Layering can be carried out between autumn and spring if you use mature stems or in spring and summer if you use stems made in the current season.

Green but mean

"Can you tell me why my clematis, planted three years ago, has never flowered? It grows in a tub and the foliage is healthy and green."

The reason for your clematis not flowering, while still looking exceedingly healthy, is probably overfeeding with a nitrogen-rich fertilizer. It would pay to balance it with a high potash feed such as Phostrogen which could be given each week in the spring and summer.

Lack of flowers

"Can you tell me why my wisteria produces only one or two flowers each year? It grows well and appears healthy."

If you bought an unnamed seedling wisteria you may have a poor flowering form and it may never give a good display. Named varieties are more expensive to purchase but they give the best results.

Pruning may help. In July cut back the new long side-growths by about half their length and in the following February shorten them further to within an inch of their base. New growths required to extend the framework of the wisteria should not be pruned but tied into position.

Feed the plant with sulphate of potash fertilizer in February. This should encourage sturdier growth to be made which should flower better. If this treatment does not improve flowering it would be best to dig out your plant and start again with a named variety.

A cut above ❧

"I have a large wisteria trained on the front wall of our house to which we have moved recently. Can you tell me when and how it should be pruned?"

Wisterias need to be pruned each year, otherwise they become a tangled mass of shoots.

Prune all the new side shoots arising from the main framework of branches in July.

Shorten them to about six buds from the junction. In the following February, shorten the side shoots further back, to two or three buds.

Saving glory flower seed ❧

"My plant of the glory flower, Eccremocarpus scaber, has produced lots of seed pods. If I collect some of them when can I sow the seed?"

Extract the seed and store it in envelopes in a cool, dry place. It should be sown in February in small pots in a greenhouse in a minimum temperature of 7°C (45°F). Sown early, plants should flower in late summer.

Handsome ivies ❧

"There is a dark corner in my garden with a high wall facing north. To brighten the position I thought of planting ivies with colourful leaves. Do you think they would succeed and what varieties would you recommend?"

Ivies would be excellent climbers for your dark, shaded situation. They tolerate poor soil but to ensure that they make good growth improve the ground with liberal dressings of decayed compost and bonemeal. There are a great many varieties from which to choose but the large-leaved

"Sulphur Heart", also known as "Paddy's Pride", is hard to beat. It has brightly coloured green and yellow leaves.

Hedera colchica "Dentata Variegata" is another large-leaved variety with dark and light green leaves bordered with bright yellow. "Goldheart" is an excellent small-leaved variety, having dark green leaves coloured bright yellow in the centres.

Mildew on ivy ❧

"Every summer, the leaves of the large-leaved ivy on my courtyard wall get covered with a white powder, presumably some form of mildew. Can this be prevented?"

The powdery coating will be powdery mildew, as you suggest. It is a fungal disease, and spores are carried on the wind so it is difficult to prevent completely. Mildew is often more severe under dry soil conditions, so regular and adequate watering of the soil will help to delay attack.

To arrest the current infection, spray two or three times at fortnightly intervals with Tumbleblite or Nimrod-T. For attacks later this year, or in subsequent years, spray at the first sign of attack and again give a few repeat applications.

Clinging ivy ❧

"I cut the roots of some ivy growing against the house wall eight months ago. The ivy is now dead but the stems still cling to the wall. What is the best way of removing them?"

Ivy can take a year or more to release its grip, but the adventitious roots will eventually weaken to allow you to prise them off the wall. There are no chemicals that will hasten the process.

Fruits to relish ❧

"Instead of roses we have a passion flower. It is now producing fruit which looks like olive-green 'Victoria' plums. Is the fruit edible? How should we care for the plant?"

Your passion flower is most probably *Passiflora caerulea*, the most commonly grown species. Helped by a long hot summer, many plants often produce egg-like fruits. These turn yellow when mature. The fruit is edible but not as sweet and tasty as the commercial species such as *Passiflora edulis*. The top growth of the plants is usually killed off by hard frosts in the winter but new shoots appear from the base in the spring. In late winter, cut off dead growth and thin out weak, congested growths. If the plant is a tangled mass, you could cut back all the side shoots close to their base.

Red passion turning yellow ❧

"I have a plant of Passiflora antioquiensis *which I grew from seed. This is its first year and the plant is in an 8 in. (20 cm) pot. The lower leaves have started to turn yellow. Is there something wrong with the plant?"*

It is natural for the lower leaves to turn yellow and wither as they age. *Passiflora antioquiensis*, the banana passion fruit, is a very beautiful species with attractive red flowers. It is not hardy, so needs the protection of a frost-free greenhouse or a cool room during the winter. Give water sparingly in winter but keep the plant well watered in spring and summer with regular feeds of a liquid fertilizer.

Passion flower cutting upset ❧

"In September 1992 I was given a cutting of a passion flower. It has now grown to 4 ft. tall. It has had no flowers, probably because I have kept the plant indoors. It is now looking rather sickly with just a few green leaves. I wish to put the plant outside. When is the best time to do it?"

If your plant is the usual kind, *Passiflora caerulea*, plant it outside now against a warm and sunny wall. Prepare the soil by forking in old manure or garden compost mixed with blood, fish and bone meal. Train shoots up trellis or a grid of wires. Every spring, cut back all the previous year's shoots to within 2 in. of the woody main stems. The plant should do much better outside.

Passion story ❧

"I am anxious to know the story of the crucifixion that is connected to passion flowers. Can you help?"

Different parts of the passion flower (passiflora) symbolize Christ and the Crucifixion. The outer ring of ten petals represents the ten apostles who witnessed the crucifixion. A ring of ten filaments within the petals is said to be the crown of thorns. The five stamens represent the wounds of Christ and the three stigmas the nails.

Passion flower rampage ❧

"I have a blue passion flower which has made tremendous growth during the summer. Will I harm the plant if I cut it back to reasonable proportions?"

Once frost has scorched your climber you can trim it back a little if you wish. Cold weather in the winter will kill off more of the growths. Next spring cut back all the side-growths close to the main stems. This treatment may seem drastic but you will find that healthy new growths will soon appear once the weather becomes warmer next spring.

Sowing sweet peas ❧

"When is the best time to sow sweet pea seeds?"

Sweet peas can be sown at different times. For early blooms sow seed in October or November in a cold greenhouse or frame. Overwinter the plants in small pots ready for planting outside in April.

Seed may also be sown in a warm greenhouse in February or outside in April.

Pinching out sweet peas ❧

"I am told that sweet pea plants should have their growths pinched. Can you explain what to do?"

Sweet peas to be grown on the cordon system, which gives the best quality flowers, do need to have the growths pinched. The young seedlings should have their tips pinched out to encourage several shoots to form.

After planting out, select the strongest stem to form the cordon and pinch out the weaker ones. As the main stem grows pinch out the tips of the side shoots as well as the tendrils.

Everlasting pea ❧

"Is it true that there are sweet peas which last from year to year and would they be suitable for screening a shed? Are there different colours?"

The most commonly grown perennial sweet pea is *Lathyrus latifolius*, which is often found growing wild on railway embankments. It is an excellent plant for screening a shed or covering a fence. Plants can grow up to 12 ft tall or they may be allowed to sprawl down a bank.

The flowers are usually magenta in colour, but seed can be obtained in mixtures of pink, white and red. Separate colour varieties are also available, including "White Pearl" and "Pink Pearl".

Sow seed in modules under glass in early spring, or sow where the plants are to grow outside in April. At the end of the season, cut back the old stems close to the ground.

Climbing companion ❦

"I have a forsythia bush. What climber could I grow through it?"

A clematis would look very attractive growing through a forsythia, or try the perennial pea, *Lathyrus latifolius.*

The soil at the base of the bush is likely to be poor so make the planting hole about 2 ft (60 cm) from the forsythia. Fill it with really good soil and decayed compost.

Train the climber along twiggy sticks and into the bush.

Odd growth on vine ❦

"We have a young outdoor vine, trained up a pergola along one side of the lawn. The leaves have suddenly become much more rounded, the younger stems have started to twist and the stems are sprouting what look like roots. Please help!"

The symptoms are very typical of contamination by lawn weedkiller. It may be that it was carried by the wind during a recent lawn treatment or that the vines were watered using a can previously used to apply weedkiller.

Sadly there is no reliably effective treatment. The affected shoots will be worthless so should be pruned out, cutting below any damage.

Whether the vine will recover and grow normally next year remains to be seen, but this is, I am afraid, rather unlikely.

Choice climber – but is it hardy? ❦

"Last September I admired a climber called Tropaeolum tuberosum *in a Dorset garden. It looked like a nasturtium and I would like to grow a plant. Will it thrive in my district?"*

The climber that you saw belongs to the nasturtium family. As its name suggests it has tuberous roots. Flowers do not appear until late in the season. It is a choice climber but is rather tender.

Apart from in very mild gardens, it is wise to lift the tubers in the autumn and store them like dahlias in a frost-free place.

There is a form called "Ken Aslet" which flowers much earlier and is the best one to grow. Plant the climber against a warm, south-facing wall.

Climbers can quickly get out of hand if you are not careful!

Canary creeper from seed ❧

"I have grown some canary creeper plants from seed, covering a fence with a mass of yellow flowers. Will they last for another year or do I have to grow new plants from seed each year?"

The canary creeper, *Tropaeolum peregrinum*, is a perennial but is best treated as an annual. It is easy to grow and is valuable for covering a fence or screen quickly. Start the plants of each year from fresh seed in March sown in pots in a greenhouse. Or sow the seed outside in April or May.

Honey monster ❧

"My honeysuckle is ruined every year by large greyish greenfly. They spoil the leaves and even prevent proper flowering. Please help."

The pest is the honeysuckle aphid which feeds in spring and summer, moves off to other hosts in late summer and then returns to honeysuckle in autumn prior to laying winter eggs.

It is necessary to use a systemic insecticide such as Tumblebug or Long-Last to obtain full control. Spray at the first sign of attack in spring and repeat if necessary.

Alternatively, the whole plant can be cut down in spring and burned. This will remove the damaged growths from previous years as well as any pests present. Drastic action, but well worth it for consistently severe attacks.

Honeysuckle leaf miner ❧

"Each year, our honeysuckle leaves get badly marked by a leaf-mining pest. Can you tell us what pest is involved and the best method of control?"

Mines in honeysuckle leaves are caused by the larvae of a small fly known as *Phytomyza*.

Typically, the damage starts as a number of radiating mines but then changes to a more winding type. It occurs widely on wild honeysuckle plants.

Best control is by simply squashing the larvae in the mines, or by removing the damaged leaves as soon as they are seen.

Tender lobster ❧

"I admired a lobster claw plant in a garden centre the other day but I could not find out anything about it. Will it grow outside or does it need a greenhouse?"

The lobster claw, *Clianthus puniceus*, always attracts attention because of its striking red flowers.

It is not fully hardy, and in most parts of the country must be grown in a frost-free greenhouse.

However, in mild districts, which do not normally get hard frosts, it can be grown in the open, trained against a warm, south-facing wall.

It is a shrubby plant with a lax habit, and the stems need supporting with wires. In your district, it would be best to grow the plant in a pot and keep it in a greenhouse through the winter. However, it could be stood outside for the summer.

Or plant it in a soil border and train the stems against a wall inside the greenhouse.

Climbers for problem location ❧

"One of our boundaries is a 6 ft-high fence, facing north. In front of it we have made a border which is planted with shrubs. On the other side of the fence are two large oak trees. Until the shrubs double their size the fence is very bare in winter. Can you suggest climbers, preferably evergreen, to cover it?"

The following are climbers that you could consider for your fence: *Akebia quinata*, beautiful, semi-evergreen, quick-growing climber with five-foliate leaves and fragrant, chocolate-purple flowers borne in racemes during April and May; *Holboellia latifolia* is a quick-growing climber with luxuriant, dark green, shiny foliage, producing white and purple, fragrant flowers in April and May; *Pileostegia viburnoides* is a self-clinging climber with dark-green leaves and white, hydrangea-like flowers; *Hydrangea petiolaris*, the climbing hydrangea has white flowers in June and colourful leaves in autumn but is not evergreen; *Lonicera japonica* "Halliana", the evergreen Japanese honeysuckle, has shiny leaves and fragrant, white and yellow flowers. It is very vigorous.

Trailing plant ideas ❧

"I have two pillars with shallow tubs on top of them in which I would like to plant something that would trail down to the ground (about 4 ft). Can you make some suggestions?"

There are a number of plants suitable for growing in tubs in the way you suggest. Black-eyed Susan (*Thunbergia alata*) would look attractive. Clematis are normally allowed to climb but they can also be allowed to trail. Other suggestions are: everlasting pea (*Lathyrus grandiflorus*), honeysuckle (*Lonicera periclymenum*), *Tropaeolum peregrinum* and *T. speciosum*.

Plants for a north wall ❧

"One of the walls in my garden faces north. What climbing plant could I grow against it to make it look more attractive?"

One of the best shrubs for growing against a north-facing wall is pyracantha. It is evergreen and has masses of white flowers in the spring followed by red, yellow or orange berries, depending on the variety you grow, in the autumn. Winter-flowering jasmine, *Jasminum nudiflorum,* also grows well trained to a north wall. It has numerous, attractive yellow flowers in the winter.

The climbing hydrangea, *Hydrangea petiolaris*, once given initial support, is self-clinging. It has white flowers in June and the leaves turn yellow in the autumn. Many of the variegated-leaved ivies will also brighten up a north wall.

Best shady characters ❧

"I have a courtyard garden which is partially shaded for most of the day. What climbers would you suggest for growing against the walls?"

We suggest that you try some of the ivies with colourful, variegated leaves. One of the best is "Gold Heart" which is neat in habit and has dark green leaves splashed with bright yellow. Pyracanthas (firethorns) could be trained against the walls. These shrubs are evergreen and are covered with white flowers in spring followed by red, yellow or orange berries in the autumn.

Other suggestions are: winter-flowering jasmine, *Jasminum nudiflorum*, which has bright yellow flowers in winter; *Hydrangea petiolaris*, the climbing hydrangea, having white flowers and rich yellow leaves in autumn. There are also several varieties of *Euonymus fortunei radicans* with silver or golden variegated leaves.

Wall shrubs go west ❧

"Can you give me the names of some plants to grow against a west-facing wall, 5 ft tall? The soil is alkaline."

Plants suitable for growing against a wall where the soil is alkaline are as follows: *Caryopteris x clandonensis*, deciduous, blue flowers, August to September; *Chaenomeles speciosa*, Japanese quince, white, pink or red blossoms in spring; *Chimonanthus praecox*, winter sweet, yellow, scented flowers in winter; *Clematis alpina*, violet-blue flowers April to May; *Garrya elliptica*, Californian catkin bush, evergreen, silvery grey catkins in winter and early spring; *Jasminum nudiflorum*, yellow flowers, November to April; *Lonicera fragrantissima*, semi-evergreen, creamy white, fragrant flowers, December to March; *Parthenocissus tricuspidata* "Veitchii", vigorous, deciduous climber, flame-tinted leaves in autumn; *Polygonum baldschuanicum*, Russian vine, very vigorous, deciduous climber, white flowers in late summer; *Pyracantha angustifolia*, firethorn, evergreen, white flowers in spring, orange berries in autumn.

House trained ❧

"I have a pyracantha shrub trained against my house wall. How and when should I trim the bush to keep it compact?"

Pyracanthas trained against walls need trimming twice a year. Carry out the first pruning after flowering, taking care not to remove the immature berries.

Prune again in August or early September and shorten the new growths to expose the clusters of ripening berries.

Mile-a-minute vines can quickly take over the house.

Pruning jasmine ❧

"A large plant of the common white jasmine covers the south wall of our house. The growths are very congested and some pruning is needed. When should this be done? I would still like to have some flowers this summer."

When growths get very congested, prune your white jasmine, *Jasminum officinale* in early spring.

You can prune it severely, thinning out most of the older stems. Flowers should still appear on the new growths in the summer.

Congested jasmine ❧

"I have a winter jasmine trained against trellis which is a mass of congested growths. Can I prune it without harming the plant?"

Prune your winter jasmine, *jasminum nudiflorum*, after the flowers have faded. Cut back all the stems that have flowered close to their base, leaving a framework of older branches. New growth will soon form which will flower next winter.

Overgrown jasmine ❧

"I have a very overgrown Jasminum beesianum which did not flower very well last year and obviously needs pruning. When should I do this?"

The best time to prune plants of *Jasminum beesianum* is after flowering.

As flowers are produced on the shoots made in the previous season, if you prune in the winter you are likely to cut out shoots that will flower in the coming season, but as your plant is overcrowded you could cut out some of the older stems now to get it back into shape.

Gooseberry fooled ❧

"I came across a climbing plant with most unusual pink leaves with a green tinge. Could you give me its name?"

The climbing plant that you saw is *Actinidia kolomikta*. It is related to the Chinese Gooseberry or Kiwi fruit. However, this species is grown for its ornamental, creamy white and pink variegated leaves. It's best to grow plants against a warm, south-facing, sunny wall. Once established they can quickly reach 15 ft in height.

Pruning Japonica ❧

"I have found a Japonica shrub trained against a wall of my new home. Will it need pruning?"

Japonica or chaenomeles trained on walls do need annual pruning to keep them within bounds. Just shorten the side growths after flowering to within two to three buds of their base and this will encourage woody spurs or short flowering growths to form.

Pruning garrya ❧

"I have a shrub of Garrya elliptica *growing against a wall. Some of the stems are straggly and need trimming back. When is the best time to prune the shrub?"*

Garrya elliptica is a fine evergreen shrub which normally needs very little pruning. The best time to cut back straggly growths is directly after flowering in early spring. Any dead or withered stems can also be removed at the same time.

The long attractive catkins are produced at the tips of the shoots made on the previous year's growth.

Easy annual vine

"I grew two cobaea plants from seed last year but they did not produce any flowers. Where did I go wrong?"

You may have sowed the cobaea (cup and saucer vine) seeds too late for the plants to flower in the same season. Sow some seeds now in a heated propagator and grow the young plants on in pots in a warm greenhouse. Plant them outside in a sunny spot in early June.

Cobaeas are perennial but must be kept under glass in the winter, so you could try growing a plant under glass through the summer.

Conifers

Composted conifers ❧

"Please tell me whether shredded conifer clippings can be used for composting. A friend tells me that they poison the ground."

As far as we are aware, there is no good reason why conifer clippings should not be composted. Shredding them beforehand speeds rotting. Sandwich them in the compost heap between layers of other waste material. The cuttings should then rot down without trouble. The resin and other substances will break down into beneficial humus.

You can bank on it! ❧

"I came across a low-growing conifer the other day but I cannot find out its name. Could you identify it from the piece I am sending?"

Your conifer is the savin or *Juniperus sabina tamariscifolia*. It has blue-green foliage and makes a low mound of foliage arranged in horizontal layers.

It is a most attractive conifer and very useful for covering a bank as ground cover. It is also useful for planting near a manhole cover to disguise it, but at the same time, allowing access to the drain if this is ever needed.

Plants grow 3–4 ft tall and spread to 6–10 ft.

A reason for the resin ❧

"I have a Christmas tree in my garden which has grown to 35 ft (10.5 m) tall. At the base of the trunk and at about 25 ft (7.5 m) resin is leaking out. At the higher level there is a distinct ring around the trunk. Will this make the tree unstable?"

Pine trees commonly ooze resin from the trunk or branches, particularly if damaged by birds or pests. It is not possible to say what has caused the ring and whether the tree is unstable. Contact a reputable tree surgeon who will examine it for you.

Rocky subjects ❧

"I have made a small rock garden and would like to plant some dwarf conifers in it. What types would you recommend please?"

Dwarf conifers that would be suitable for your rock garden include *Juniperus communis* "Compressa", *J. communis.* "Hornibrookii", *Chamaecyparis* "Minima Glauca", *C.* "Compacta", *Cedrus libani* "Comte de Dijon", *Pinus mugo* "Gnome" and "Mops".

Browned off conifer ❧

"One side of a dwarf conifer in my garden seems to be dying off. It is turning brown and looks very unhappy. Is there any cure?"

It seems probable that a disease known as phytophthora foot rot is responsible for the damage. Typically, attacks start at ground level from soil-borne infection, and then spread through the tissue up one side of the plant. Conifers and heathers are particularly susceptible to attack.

Sadly there is no satisfactory control for this disease, but we would suggest trying severe pruning out of the brown shoots first.

Should the damage be due to other factors then the plant could recover. Should no recovery occur, then dig out and burn the conifer and leave the spot unplanted.

A more refined conifer ❧

"What is the difference between Cryptomeria japonica *and* C. j. 'Elegans'*?"*

Cryptomeria japonica is the Japanese cedar and it makes a large tree. The form "Elegans" is more refined and retains its young feathery juvenile foliage throughout its life. The foliage also turns a wonderful bronze colour in autumn and winter.

Larch adelges ❧

"Can you please tell me what has attacked my bonsai larch tree? The shoots are covered in white pests, very much like woolly aphid of apple trees, but I think it must be a different insect."

The insects are larch adelges, a species quite similar, although distinct from, true aphids. They can also live on spruce (picea) species where their feeding causes galls to develop.

For best control spray with a systemic insecticide such as Tumblebug or Rapid.

Conifers on the move ❧

"I have a conifer bush which is now about 4 ft (1.2 m) tall. I can see it is getting too big for its position. When is the best time to move it?"

The autumn is the best time to move your conifer, whilst the soil is still reasonably warm. Make sure you lift the plant with a good ball of roots and give it a good watering beforehand if the soil seems dry.

Replant the conifer as soon as possible in its prepared position. Pour some good soil around the roots and tread it firm. Mulch the soil around the plant with decayed compost or manure. Make sure that the soil is kept thoroughly moist next spring and summer.

Check that dwarf conifers are just that!

Pine puzzler 🍂

"Some of the new shoots on our pine tree (Pinus radiata) *are hanging down and appear to have a caterpillar inside them. Help please?"*

It sounds as if the pine resin gall moth has been at work. Eggs are usually laid on the new shoots and the caterpillar bores into the base of a needle, this can also damage the shoot surface. The shoots tend to hang down as you mention and resin is often visible. In time, a small gall develops and this persists into the following year and grows up to 1 in. across.

The following spring the caterpillar pupates and then a new generation moth emerges.

To interrupt the cycle and prevent further shoot loss, prune out the infested shoot tips now or during the winter. On the other hand you may prefer to let them be and observe the full cycle.

Trimming leylandii 🍂

"I have a young hedge of Leyland cypress. How often should it be trimmed and when do I take out the tops?"

To keep hedges of Leyland cypress, *Cupressocyparis leylandii*, neat they need trimming two or three times during the spring and summer.

When the main stems of the plants reach the desired height take out the tips of the main stems and keep the top of the hedge trimmed in the same way as the sides.

Cupressus casualty 🍂

*"I have a normally lovely silver weeping conifer (*Cupressus lusitanica *'Pendula') in my garden, but this year and last lots of the young growths turned brown and died, starting in spring and continuing through the summer. Is this a disease and, if so, can it be treated?"*

The damage would have been caused by severe winter frost or freezing winds. This particular species is a native of Mexico, and although it can survive normal winters here, it can be severely damaged by the low temperatures experienced in East Anglia during the last two winters.

It is possible to cut out all the dead and discoloured shoots and the tree will send out new growths, but the damage will occur again if the coming winter includes very severe frosts.

Blue cedar   ⽊

"I want to grow a blue-leaved conifer in my front garden. In a garden centre I have seen one called Cedrus libani atlantica *'Glauca' but no-one could tell me how big it will grow. Do you think this cedar would be suitable for my garden?"*

Cedrus libani atlantica "Glauca" is a magnificent tree but it is not suitable for a small garden as it not only grows fast but can grow very large eventually.

A better choice would be *Abies lasiocarpa* "Compacta". It has silver-blue leaves and forms an attractive pyramid growth. It is also much slower growing.

Another that you could consider is *Juniperus chinensis* "Pyramidalis" which has soft blue foliage and compact upright growth.

Rooting thuja cuttings   ⽊

"I want to root some cuttings of Thuja plicata *to make a conifer hedge. When is the best time to take them and can they be rooted outside?"*

The best time to take thuja cuttings is in September to early October. Select young shoots a few inches long with a "heel" of older wood left attached. Remove the lower leaves. Ideally your cuttings should be 2–4 in. (5–10 cm) long. Use a seed compost to which has been added extra coarse sand or Perlite to root the cuttings in. Dip the base of each cutting in hormone rooting powder, and tap off excess. Insert the cuttings around the edge of a $3\frac{1}{2}$ in. (9 cm) pot and firm them in well.

After a good watering, stand the cuttings in a cold frame or under a polythene tent inside a greenhouse. Roots may form in a few weeks but keep the cuttings in the frame over winter.

The cuttings will not root satisfactorily in the open garden.

Variegated conifer   ⽊

"I found a variegated chamaecyparis among several plain green ones in a friend's garden. Is this unusual?"

It is not unusual to find a variegated shoot among chamaecyparis with plain green leaves. The genus is relatively unstable and new varieties are constantly being developed. As variegated shoots lack chlorophyll they seldom grow vigorously and it is difficult to propagate them.

We suggest that you show it to a local tree and shrub nurseryman who may feel that it is worth multiplying by grafting on to a robust stock plant.

Conservatories

Pruning bougainvillea ✿

"I bought a bougainvillea plant in a pot last summer and have kept it cool and dry in the winter. Should I keep it in its pot or would it be better to plant it in the greenhouse border? Does it need pruning?"

Bougainvilleas can be planted in a greenhouse border but they tend to grow rampantly and we feel it would be better to keep your plant in a large pot. With the roots confined, you should find it also flowers better.

Repot the plant in the next few weeks using a good potting compost. Before potting, prune all the sideshoots on the main stems by cutting them back to within one or two buds of their base.

Stephanotis seed ✿

"I have a stephanotis climber indoors and it seems to be doing very well. I noticed that two green fruits have appeared on one stem. Are these seed pods and can I grow them?"

Yes, the green fruits on your stephanotis plant are seed pods and you can sow the seed when it is ripe. It may take a year before the pods turn yellow and split open to reveal the flat, brown seeds. Sow it in the spring or summer in a small pot of good seed compost kept in a temperature of 21°C (70°F). The seedlings do not always perform well and you tend to get variable results. Some may not even flower. However, we hope you have good luck.

Munching maggots ✿

"There are lots of small black gnats or midges around the compost surface of our conservatory plants. Do they do any harm apart from being a nuisance every time we water?"

The insects are sciarid flies. The flies are harmless, but the maggots feed on the plant roots. Seedlings can be killed, and plants generally made less healthy by the loss of new feeding roots.

The best control for the adults is a spray with a house plant insecticide over the compost surface, and the maggots can be killed by a "friendly" nematode that hunts for them. One type of nematode can be bought by mail order from Defenders Ltd.

Under control ❧

"Is there an effective control for red spider mite under glass? My cucumber leaves are showing typical signs of pale yellow stippling. Last year my crops were cut off in their prime by a similar attack."

I had excellent results with Polysect insecticide from Monsanto a couple of years ago, when my cucumbers were found to be badly infested. One thorough spray under and over the leaves cleared up the attack.

No interval has to be left between spraying and picking the edible crops which are listed on the label.

Mealy bug cure ❧

"Is there any really effective cure for mealy bugs? Many of our conservatory plants are attacked and we seem unable to get on top of the problem. Many of the plants are too big to move outside to spray."

Probably the best spray would be one based on fatty acids. These are the modern equivalent of the old soft soap sprays, and a good application should wet the mealy covering of the pests and give control. Look out for Phostrogen Safer's Insecticide in ready-to-use form and Savona which is diluted in water.

There is also a beneficial insect which can be purchased for biological control, a ladybird relative called *Cryptolaemus*.

Fern failure ❧

"This year ferns growing in my conservatory were devastated by largish green caterpillars. Could you tell me what sort they would have been and how I can prevent or control any further attacks?"

The caterpillars were probably those of the angle-shades moth. The velvety green (or brown) caterpillars attack a wide range of outdoor herbaceous plants as well as those in a greenhouse or conservatory, and can cause a lot of damage, as you have found.

When fully fed the caterpillars pupate in the soil and the adult moths emerge in May to June, with a few more at intervals through to September.

Light digging of the compost in any large pots now could be worthwhile to discover the brown cocoons. Otherwise look out for the pale yellow eggs under the leaves during summer and autumn next year.

If caterpillar damage should start, remove any caterpillars you can find and then spray with a fatty acids, pyrethrins or permethrin insecticide.

Lemon tree pest ❧

"My lemon tree, started off many years ago from a pip, has very sticky leaves, and a growing infestation of greenfly. How would you advise me to clean up this cherished plant?"

The stickiness is due to the sugary honeydew which the greenfly produce as they feed. Often it will turn black as sooty moulds colonize the deposits. Spraying with a house plant insecticide should take care of the pests, and a careful wipe over with lukewarm water will remove the honeydew. It would be worth inserting a Phostrogen Plant Pin into the compost to prevent any further infestations.

Greenfly make a sticky mess ❧

"The leaves on my lemon tree, growing in a heated conservatory, were becoming sticky and then I noticed a massive invasion of greenfly on one of the shoots. Help is needed here please."

When greenfly feed they produce masses of sugary honeydew which falls onto the leaves below, making them sticky to the touch. Soon, the honeydew becomes colonized by sooty mould fungi and this results in the leaves turning black.

Spray the plant with a fatty acids ready-to-use insecticide which will quickly solve the pest problem, and then gently sponge the leaves with tepid water to remove all traces of the honeydew.

The natural way ❧

"Some of our conservatory plants have mealy bug colonies. I have used insecticides before, but the smell penetrated into the house. Is there an alternative method?"

When you can maintain a minimum temperature of 20°C (70°F) you would be able to control the mealy bugs with the biological agent known as *Cryptolaemus*.

This is a form of ladybird which wipes out the pests as they are its natural food. It originally came from Australia and is supplied by post by Defenders Ltd, PO Box 131, Wye, Ashford, Kent TN25 5TQ. Phone 01233 813121 for details.

Greenhouse gloxinias

"I bought some gloxinia tubers on a market stall but I am not sure how to grow them. Can you tell me when to plant them? I have a heated greenhouse."

Gloxinias are not difficult to grow if you have a warm greenhouse for them.

Start the tubers into growth now by pressing them into a tray of moist peat and coarse sand.

When growth begins, pot the tubers singly in 3 in. (7.5 cm) pots using a good potting compost. Shade the plants from strong sunshine. Once good growth has been made move the young plants on into 5–6 in. (12–15 cm) pots.

Give liquid feeds in the summer at weekly intervals. In early autumn gradually withhold water from the pots and keep the tubers dry and in a frost-free place for the winter. Start them into growth again the following spring.

Suffering stephanotis

"I have a stephanotis plant in my conservatory which was a picture of health until this year. Now, the stems are covered with numbers of pale objects – I am not sure if they are mealy bugs or scale insects. Can you please identify them and suggest an appropriate control measure?"

The objects on your stephanotis are scale insects, although they are particularly pale in colour. This scale species should be controlled by a biological agent known as *Metaphycus*, available by mail order from Defenders Ltd.

Bird of paradise flower

"Having seen bird of paradise flowers growing in Madeira, I want to grow a plant in my heated greenhouse. If I raise plants from seed, how long will they take to flower and how should I treat them?"

Bird of paradise, *Strelitzia reginae*, plants can be raised from seed. However, it will be four or five years before you are likely to see flowers.

Sow the seed in a small pot of a good seed compost. Keep the seed container in a warm, moist propagator with a temperature of 18–21°C (64–

70°F). As the plants grow, move them on each spring into slightly larger pots. Eventually, your plant can be grown in a large pot or tub or be planted in a greenhouse border.

Lack of flowers 🍂

"I have had a Coelogyne cristata *orchid for three years but it hardly has any flowers. The plant seems healthy and is kept in my greenhouse which is heated. Can you tell me why it does not flower properly?"*

Coelogyne cristata is usually regarded as a good orchid for beginners. It can, however, be difficult to flower. The trick is to withhold water from it at the end of the summer when growth for the season has finished. The green pseudo-bulbs may shrivel during this resting period, but this does not matter and they will soon fill out again once watering resumes in the spring.

Orange aid 🍂

"I have been given an orange citrus plant. It is in a small pot which I keep in my conservatory. Does it need repotting?"

If the present pot is full of roots, repot in spring. Keep it in a minimum temperature of 5°C (41°F) in winter.

Oranges and lemons 🍂

"I would like to grow some orange and lemon trees. Where can I obtain the seeds?"

Orange and lemon trees are not fully hardy in this country and must be kept under glass in winter in frost-free conditions. They can be stood outside in summer in a sunny spot.

   Plants raised from seed do not give very good results and it is much better to purchase named varieties. One of the most popular lemons is "Meyer's Lemon" and "St Michaels" is a good orange. Details of these and many others can be obtained from Reads Nursery, Hales Hall, Loddon, Norfolk NR14 6QW.

Winter care of bougainvillea 🍂

"I bought some bougainvilleas this year and they are in full bloom. How do I look after them through the winter?"

Overwinter bougainvilleas carefully, watering just enough to keep the compost damp but never soggy. If the compost dries, some leaves may be lost but this is not damaging. Ensure that the plants receive as much light as possible.

In late winter scrape a little compost from the top of the pot and replace it with fresh, loam-based potting compost. When roots push through the drainage holes, move the plants to new pots using John Innes Potting Compost No. 2.

Hoovering up the hovers ᴥ

"My hoya plants all flowered beautifully this summer and the nectar attracted literally hundreds of hover flies into the conservatory. Sadly, the floor had to be continually swept to remove dead hover flies. Is the nectar poisonous, or is there some other explanation?"

The nectar is not poisonous (unlike that of certain lime and rhododendron species, for example), the hover flies were simply unable to find their way out of the conservatory after feeding. They would tend to fly to the roof of the conservatory and in the very high summer temperatures the heat in the apex would have been sufficient to kill them.

Hover fly larvae feed on aphids so are very useful in the garden, so perhaps next summer you could net the conservatory doorway or hang plastic strip curtaining up during the hoya flowering period, to prevent the same fate befalling these allies.

Soft and hard ᴥ

"Some of my conservatory plants are badly infested with scale insects. Is there any easy solution?"

Scale insects are divided into hard scales and soft scales. Soft scales can be controlled biologically by a small wasp known as *Metaphycus helvolus*.

Hard scales can only be controlled by systemic insecticides but the two systems must not be used at the same time as the chemicals would kill the wasps.

Most of the conservatory plant infestations I have seen are of soft scale so it would be worth trying this method first.

The wasps are obtainable by mail order from biological control suppliers.

If not successful, you may have hard scales. In that case, spray thoroughly with Long-Last, Tumblebug or Sybol and repeat, if necessary, 14 days later.

Sowing morning glory ❧

"I sowed some seeds of morning glory in my greenhouse in early March but only one or two germinated. I would like to sow more seed. Is there anything I can do to ensure better results?"

Morning glory seeds germinate best in a temperature of 21–4°C (70–2°F). We suspect that your seeds did not germinate better because the temperature was too low. Once natural temperature get higher you should have better results, particularly if you sow the seed in pots stood in a warm, moist propagator. Sow the seed in a good seed sowing compost. To save pricking out the seedlings, sow the seed individually in modules or small pots.

Avocado pear plants ❧

"I have grown an avocado pear plant from a stone. It is getting very tall and I am not sure what to do with it. Can it be planted outside?"

Although your avocado pear plant can be stood outside for the summer, it is not hardy and will be killed by the frost in the winter. Once it becomes too large for your room, we fear that you will have to dispose of it and start again with another stone.

Care for lemon ❧

"I have seen lemon plants for sale in garden centres and I would like to try one. However, the smallest plant costs £15 and I do not want to spend this amount if the plants are difficult to manage. I have a small greenhouse which is heated in winter to exclude frost. Can you tell me how easy they are to grow?"

As you have a greenhouse from which frost can be excluded you should be able to grow a lemon in a large pot or tub. "Meyer's Lemon" is the most popular variety although there are several others. The flowers, which appear in the spring, have a delicious scent and the fruits follow later in the season. In the summer stand the plant outside in a sheltered and sunny situation but return it to the greenhouse in September.

During the spring and summer feed the plant each week with a liquid fertilizer. This should cease in August to avoid sappy growth being made late in the season.

Scale insects are a problem on all kinds of citrus fruits. The scales exude a sugary substance which forms a black, sooty mould. Spray the plant two or three times during the season with malathion to keep it clear of the pest. Do not allow the soil to dry out in the summer as this can cause the leaves to drop.

Dwarf gerbera ❧

"Can you tell me how to look after a pot gerbera I have been given. It has very colourful flowers and I would like to keep it as long as possible. Would it be best to keep it in my conservatory?"

Gerberas have long-lasting flowers and are best kept in a frost-free greenhouse or conservatory in the winter. The plants can be taken into a living room for short periods when in flower but for most of the year they are best in a greenhouse.

They do not like cold, wet conditions, so grow them in a freely draining potting compost containing plenty of coarse sand. Water very sparingly in winter and ventilate the greenhouse whenever possible to avoid damp and stuffy conditions. During the summer, until August, feed the plant with a liquid fertilizer each week. In hot weather give it plenty of water.

Curbing mimosa ❧

"I have a plant of Acacia dealbata *which is getting too big for my conservatory. Can I cut it back?"*

Acacia dealbata or mimosa does make a large tree and under glass needs regular pruning in the spring after flowering. Stand the plant outside for the summer.

Meyer's lemon ❧

"I have been given a Meyer's lemon in a pot. Should it be kept in a greenhouse?"

Meyer's lemon, like most citrus species, needs a greenhouse with a minimum temperature of 12°C (55°F) in winter. However, during the summer stand the plant outside in a warm, sheltered position, but return it to the greenhouse in September.

Give it plenty of water in the summer and feed each week with a liquid fertilizer between April and August. Water very sparingly in winter. Prune back straggly shoots in March.

Ginger lily

"Last summer I saw a beautiful scented flower which I was told was a ginger lily. It had a tall spike covered at the top with lots of yellow flowers. Can you tell me anything about the plant as I would like to grow one?"

The plant that you saw last summer was most probably *Hedychium gardnerianum*. This is one of the ginger lilies and produces its beautiful spikes of scented yellow flowers in July. It is not fully hardy and must be kept in a frost-free greenhouse for the winter.

Start the roots into growth in a large pot in March, preferably in a frost-free greenhouse. Stand the plant outside for the summer. The pot can be sunk in a flower border as the foliage is very ornamental. Cut back the stems in October and return the pot to a greenhouse for the winter.

Banana aphids

"I have found some very dark aphids on my indoor palm fronds. Is this the ordinary blackfly, or have I got some unusual new species?"

These black pests are banana aphids. They feed on palms and bananas and a few other plants under warm growing conditions. Whenever banana aphids are feeding they seem to attract ants, so presumably are producing plenty of sugary honeydew. This tends to be colonized by sooty moulds so leaves soon turn black.

To remove the aphids pull the palm fronds through a moist sponge or soft cloth, but should the attack persist, spray with an insecticide based on fatty acids.

South African proteas

"I have successfully germinated two protea seedlings from seed brought home from South Africa. How do I look after the plants from now on, considering the cold British climate?"

Proteas are not hardy plants and cannot be grown outside all the year round in this country, apart from mild areas such as the Scilly Isles, where they grow in the open on the island of Tresco.

Keep your seedlings in a frost-free greenhouse for the winter. If they have filled their present pots with roots, move them on to slightly larger pots. Otherwise do not repot the plants until early spring.

Use an ericaceous, lime-free potting compost. Water the plants sparingly in winter but never allow the soil to dry out in the summer. Feed the plants with Epsom salts (magnesium sulphate) in the spring and summer. Stand the plants outside in a sunny, sheltered position for the summer but return them to a greenhouse in September.

Frangipani seedling ⅍

"I have been given a frangipani seedling. It is 5 in. tall and has a very dark green stem. How should I look after it, how tall will it get and when will it flower?"

Ideally, you should keep your frangipani plant in a warm greenhouse as it is a tropical plant. If you do not have a greenhouse, stand it in a sunny window. Plants can grow 20 ft (6 m) tall but this applies to plants grown in a border of soil. They are not likely to grow so tall in a pot.

During the winter keep the plant in a cool room and give it very little water so that the soil remains dry. From spring to autumn water the plant whenever the soil is dry. Give liquid feeds whilst it is in growth in the summer.

The beautiful clusters of scented flowers appear at the tips of the stems. You are not likely to see any flowers for at least a year. Once the plant fills its present pot with roots, move it on to a larger pot using a good potting soil mixture.

Aspidistra treatment ⅍

"I have a variegated aspidistra with lots of pale stippling on the leaves. Can you tell me what this is and what to do about it?"

The pale markings are where red spider mites have been feeding. Wait until late spring, late April–May, and then use the predatory mite biological control agent Phytoseiulus.

The predatory mite is supplied in an inert carrier and the product needs to be sprinkled evenly over the infested leaves.

Blue plumbago ⅍

"Last year I planted a Plumbago capensis *in a border in my greenhouse. By the end of the summer it was covered in beautiful blue flowers. As it has made so much growth I feel it needs pruning but I am not sure when to do it. Can you help?"*

The plumbago flowers on the tips of the new shoots and so it is safe to prune it after flowering in the autumn by cutting back all the side shoots close to a main branch. If you are training your plant against a wall, select several stems to form a framework of branches and cut out surplus shoots as well as those growing outwards. At the same time cut back the side shoots close to their base. The new shoots that develop next spring will flower in the summer.

Repotting ❧

"I have had a plant of Crassula ovata 'Argentea' *for a number of years and it has never been repotted. As the pot is full of roots do you think it is time to do it now?"*

As your crassula has filled its pot with roots, you could move it on to a slightly larger pot. Do it in spring or early summer so that the plant has settled down before temperatures fall in the autumn.

The fresh potting compost should contain extra grit or coarse sand to provide a well-drained mixture. Give the plant plenty of water in the summer but water sparingly in the winter when it should be kept in a light place in an unheated but frost-free room.

Datura protection ❧

"Last April we bought three daturas (brugmansia). Two were put in large pots and the third was planted in the open ground. They have grown and flowered well. How do I protect them in winter? Can the one planted outside remain there?"

Daturas are not hardy and will be killed by frost. Lift the plant in the open and plant it in a large pot. Keep all of them under cover in a frost-free place. If you keep them indoors put them in an unheated room. Give them very little water until new growth begins again in the spring.

Pruning datura ❧

"I have a datura growing in a pot which has been stood outside for the summer. It has made so much growth that I cannot get it back into my greenhouse. Can I cut back the stems now to make the plant a more manageable size?"

One way of dealing with your datura plant is to cut back the stems by about half their length. This will not harm the plant and it will soon produce new shoots. Another way is to take some cuttings of the tips of young shoots. Root them in a heated propagating case. Once roots form pot the plants individually. These can then take the place of the older plant which can be discarded.

Handle the plant carefully as the sap is very poisonous.

Geranium cuttings   ❧

"I have several geraniums in pots in my conservatory. The plants are healthy but have grown nearly 18 in. (45 cm) tall and are now top-heavy. When can I cut them back? Can I use some of the prunings as cuttings?"

As your geranium plants have grown rather tall you can cut the stems back in March.

Use a sharp knife and cut just above a leaf joint. As new growth appears repot the plants in fresh potting compost. The prunings can certainly be used as cuttings if you want more plants. Use the tips of the shoots, making the cuttings about 4 in. (10 cm) long. Remove the lower leaves and trim each cutting with a sharp knife just below a leaf joint. Insert the cuttings in pots of gritty soil or use a mixture of peat and perlite. Water the cuttings very sparingly until they have rooted. Kept too cold and wet, the cuttings will suffer from black leg rot.

Winter cherry mystery   ❧

"Last year I raised some winter cherry or solanum plants from seed. They grew well but there were no berries. I kept the plants and they are in flower again. How do I ensure that they set berries?"

Solanum capsicastrum flowers are sometimes difficult to set. Keep your plants in the open and each morning, when they are in flower, spray them overhead with water. Another way is to hand-pollinate the flowers. All you have to do is to touch each flower lightly with a piece of cotton wool on the end of a stick to transfer the pollen from flower to flower. Ideally, do this in the morning on a warm day when the pollen is fairly dry.

Winter jasmine   ❧

"I would like to know if I could tidy up my winter jasmine. It is growing strongly and hanging like spaghetti!"

Winter jasmine flowers best on year-old shoots that are allowed to waterfall from the main branches, so please do not cut back too many of these or you will jeopardize the display.

Sensitive subject ❧

"A neighbour was given a sensitive plant last spring but it now seems to be dying. How are these plants propagated?"

Sensitive plants (*Mimosa pudica*) do tend to die off towards the end of the season. However, these plants are easily raised from seed which should be sown in the spring, in a warm propagator in a greenhouse.

Give it a rest ❧

"I have been given a passion flower in a 14 in. (35 cm) pot. I have put it in my greenhouse for the winter. Could you now give me some advice on feeding and pruning and should I repot it?"

Allow passion flowers to rest in the greenhouse through the winter. Water very sparingly and only when the soil seems dry. The leaves will fall.

Next spring cut out any dead stems and shorten side shoots close to their base.

Instead of repotting the plant, remove the surface compost in March and replace it with fresh John Innes No. 3.

Feed the plant each week during the summer with a liquid fertilizer.

Angel's trumpet ❧

"I have a datura plant in a container. It grew and flowered well last summer and has one stem about 3½ ft tall. Should it be cut back in the spring?"

Keep your datura (angel's trumpet) in a frost-free greenhouse in the winter and give water sparingly.

Cut back the main stem by about half its length in the spring. This will induce side branches to develop.

The plant will need repotting at the same time. Either move it into a larger container or shake out some of the old soil from among the roots and repot it with fresh potting compost. Feed the plant each week in the summer with a liquid fertilizer high in potash.

Sharon fruit ❧

"We have raised some plants from Sharon fruit seeds. How do I look after them?"

The Sharon fruit, *Diospyros kaki*, is frost-tender and best grown in a greenhouse or conservatory. Grow your seedlings in small pots of good potting compost and move them on to larger pots as they develop. Feed them weekly in summer with a tomato fertilizer. Water freely in summer but less in winter.

In time they will produce pale yellow flowers ½ in. (13 mm) across. They may even fruit if warm enough.

Tropical shrub ❧

"Last summer in the Algarve we admired some orange-red flowering shrubs called lantana. They had flowers like a verbena. Can they be grown in this country?"

Lantanas are commonly seen in the Mediterranean region and also in the Algarve. They are not hardy in this country but are excellent plants for a frost-free conservatory. They can also be treated as tender bedding plants to provide a colourful display in the summer. Cuttings root very easily and, if taken in late summer, can be overwintered under glass as small plants. Plant out in the open in late May or early June. The kind with orange-red flowers is most commonly seen but there are also several named varieties with flowers in various colours including red, pink and white.

That's a Jaffa, I'm sure of that, and the other's a Jiffy, it says so on the fruit!

Unhappy orange ❧

"I have an orange bush growing in a large pot in my greenhouse. Last summer, when I was away on holiday, it lost most of its leaves. Could you tell me what would have caused this?

Fortunately, the plant has now recovered but I do not want it to happen again. Could I plant it into a border in my greenhouse?"

The most probable reason for the orange bush losing its leaves is because the compost in the pot was allowed to dry out when you were away on holiday. Citrus are very prone to drying out and it can harm them badly.

To prevent it happening again in the future it would be a good idea to water the plant with automatic trickle irrigation.

If there is space in your greenhouse you could plant the orange in a border. Grown in this way, the soil is not likely to dry out so rapidly in hot weather.

Azalea advice – keep them moist ❧

"I have been given an Indian azalea in a pot. It is in full flower. How do I look after it?"

Hot and dry conditions will cause the leaves to turn brown and fall, so stand your azalea in a light window in an unheated room. The soil in the pot can dry out very quickly. When water is needed stand the pot in a bowl of rainwater for an hour or so until the compost is well moistened. Then, stand the pot on a tray filled with pebbles which should be kept damp to create humidity around the plant. Light overhead sprays with water will also be beneficial.

Twin peaks ❧

"I have a yucca in my conservatory which has two trunks and has grown 9 ft tall. It is now hitting the roof. What is the best way to prune it?"

Your yucca is obviously receiving tender loving care. Although it may appear to be cruel and drastic, the plant should not suffer if the stems are neatly sawn through, as low as about 9–12 in. (23–30.5 cm) above the rim of the pot.

After a couple of months, new shoots should sprout from the remaining stems and they will slowly develop into new branches.

The best time to carry out this operation is in the spring; pruning late in the year may result in the stems remaining inactive until the arrival of warmer weather in the spring.

If you wish, cut the severed stems into cane cuttings 4–6 in. (10–15 cm) long and try rooting them in a warm, moist environment.

Tropical trailer ❧

"I have been given a small plant of Columnea hirta. *Can I grow it indoors or does it need a greenhouse to succeed?"*

Columnea hirta is a tropical plant from Central America. It likes a position with dappled light and a moist atmosphere.

Indoors this may be difficult to provide as the air in a room is usually too dry. Unless you can provide a humid atmosphere for the plant, it would be best to keep it in a lightly shaded greenhouse. A minimum temperature in winter of 12°C (55°F) is desirable.

Sun scorch ❧

"We have a foliage house plant which has always had nice shiny green leaves. It is growing in our conservatory and one day recently we found nearly all the leaves had turned pale and brittle, particularly around the edges. Is this simply sun scorch or something more sinister? There is no shading in the conservatory, but the plant has been there for several years without any previous damage."

The markings are typical of damage caused by hot, direct sun falling on the leaves. The weather was particularly bright and sunny during March and April and it may be that whilst the plant has been able to cope with summer sunshine gradually building up through spring, the sudden early spring sunshine this year came before it had acclimatized.

Most of the affected leaves will drop so it would be better to cut the shoots back now and encourage replacement growth with repotting and regular feeding.

Taking care of crotons ❧

"I have a croton plant indoors. How should I look after it?"

Crotons, or codiaeums, are grown for their handsome leaves. They keep their colour best if the plant is kept in good light. It likes warm conditions in a temperature of 13°C (55°F). Kept too cool and in a draughty position the leaves will drop off.

Water the plant sparingly in winter but freely in the summer. Feed it each week from April to July with a house plant liquid feed.

To create humidity around the plant, stand it on a tray of pebbles which should be dampened regularly.

Pruning leadwort 🌴

"I have a blue plumbago in my greenhouse which flowered well last summer. It has also made a lot of growth which has become very congested. How and when can I prune the plant?"

Your plumbago (*P. auriculata*) is also known as leadwort. It can be pruned hard in winter and we suggest that you train out several main stems as a framework and prune all the sideshoots close to their base. All the main stems can also be reduced in height. Strong new growth should result next spring which will produce an abundance of flowers in late summer.

Growing bananas 🌴

"My sister recently brought home a banana plant from Madeira. I have put it in a 12 in. (30 cm) pot. Where do I keep the plant in the winter?"

The winter hardiness of your banana depends on the species that you have. The toughest is *Musa bajoo*. The probability is that you have a *Musa cavendishii*.

If at all feasible, move your plant to a heated greenhouse or conservatory in October. If not, enclose the stem in large bore plastic piping, tucking wood wool between the stem and pipe to insulate the plant from damaging frost. Cover the top as well.

Remove the wrappings in the spring.

Amazing aspidistra 🌴

"My variegated aspidistra produced some strange growths on the surface of the compost. Were these flowers, or something more sinister?"

The odd objects are the flowers of the aspidistra. They do not flower at regular or frequent intervals so you have done well to see them.

Scale away 🌴

"My wife has found what we assume to be scale insects on a new variegated agave plant in our conservatory. The objects are hemispherical, quite hard, but can be picked off. The leaves are quite sticky around the insects, but

luckily there are not many of them as yet. What treatment would you recommend?"

Yes, the objects you describe would be scale insects, and would probably be the species known as the hemispherical scale. The stickiness is due to honeydew, which is produced by the insects and can soon turn black, as it becomes colonized by sooty mould fungi.

As there are only a few at present, pick them off and then sponge the leaves with tepid water to remove the honeydew.

Should more scale insects appear, spray the plant with Tumblebug.

Fruit

Apple pollination ❧

"I have a ten-year-old 'Cox's Orange Pippin' apple tree. It has a good aspect and has been regularly fed and professionally pruned.

For the past three or four years it has blossomed extremely well but has produced only a handful of fruits. Close by is a large 'Bramley's Seedling', a 'James Grieve', a 'Worcester Pearmain' and a russet – all cropping well. Is there anything that can be done to improve the cropping of the 'Cox'?"

It is puzzling why your "Cox's Orange Pippin" apple tree is not fruiting better, particularly as the other trees are cropping well. As the tree produces plenty of blossom, poor pollination could be the cause, although both "James Grieve" and the "Worcester" are good pollinators for "Cox".

When the trees come into flower, we suggest you hang some flower sprays of "James Grieve" in the "Cox" tree to assist cross pollination.

It would also be a good idea to hand-pollinate some of the "Cox" flowers by lightly touching the open blossoms on a sunny morning with a piece of cotton wool on the end of a stick.

Also, try feeding the tree as soon as possible with a general fertilizer.

New fruit trees ❧

"We planted three 'column' fruit trees a couple of years ago. We did not expect fruit in the first season but not one of the trees had fruit buds this spring. The trees are growing well and other fruit trees on dwarfing stocks all flowered well."

The behaviour of your new fruit trees is not unusual. They need time to recover from the shock of transplanting. Initially, leaves, stems and roots are produced rather than flowers and fruit buds.

Provided you continue caring for the trees – feeding, watering and pruning to establish a sound framework – they will eventually become fine fruiting trees.

Over-vigorous Bramley ❧

"About five years ago I inherited a large 'Bramley's Seedling' apple with a span of about 35 ft. As it was too big for the garden, I pollarded it. The amount of new growth that resulted was fantastic. I have now got a decent shaped tree but it does not flower. In a recent issue you suggested bark ringing. Would this solve the problem?"

It is well known that hard winter pruning of apples will result in very vigorous growth at the expense of fruiting. It would have been better to have thinned the tree over several winters rather than all at one time. If you prune the tree very lightly in the winter for a year or so, it will probably settle down and start flowering and fruiting without further attention.

Grassing down the ground beneath the tree will also help to curb its vigour. Bark ringing could also be tried, particularly if there are no flowers this spring. It must be done very carefully otherwise you could harm the tree. It should be done at blossom time. The ring must be no more than $\frac{1}{2}$ in. (125 mm) wide. Using a really sharp pruning knife make two parallel cuts around the main trunk of the tree, down to the hardwood. Remove the strip of bark and tissue between the cuts and cover the wound with tape. This should curb the growth and induce flower buds to form.

Cooking apple choice for long-keeping ❧

"I want to grow a good cooking apple that will keep as long as possible after picking. Which should I have, do you think, 'Bramley's Seedling' or 'Blenheim Orange'?"

Both are good cooking varieties. "Bramley's Seedling" will keep in good condition until March, however "Blenheim Orange" does not usually keep much beyond January.

Both are triploid apples which means they must have a suitable pollinator such as "Lane's Prince Albert", "Sunset" or "James Grieve".

They are also both vigorous in growth and in small gardens they should be grown on a dwarfing rootstock.

Apples from seed ❧

"I have raised a few apple seedlings from an eating apple and they are quite sturdy. Will they eventually fruit?"

Your seed-raised apples are unlikely to bear fruits identical in quality and size to the parent as they are, in fact, new varieties. You may also have to wait many years – up to a dozen or more – for flowers and fruit to form. But not knowing what to expect adds to the fun of raising your own trees.

Pick of the crop ❧

"In the garden of our new home is a 'Sunset' apple tree. It has lots of fruitlets but I know nothing about the apple. Can you tell me when it is ripe and the best time to pick the fruit?"

"Sunset" is a very good dessert apple, similar to "Cox's Orange Pippin", and a useful alternative to it where it is difficult to grow Cox. Pick the fruit in late September. It should keep in a cool store until December. It tends to produce heavy crops of small fruits. Should your tree set a lot of fruit, it would be a good idea to thin the fruitlets a little, so that you have some apples of reasonable size.

Dying apple branch ❧

"A large limb on our mature apple tree has started to die, with virtually all the leaves turning brown. Looking under and around the tree we found little piles of sawdust on the ground. Can this be some form of woodworm attack?"

Clearly a wood-boring insect has been at work. As a large branch is dying, it would seem that a large insect is responsible, and the caterpillar of the leopard moth would be number one suspect.

Cut back the branch from the youngest growth back to the trunk and you may find the hollow area and the large yellowish-white caterpillar with black spots and brown head. The pest is fortunately not too common, but very damaging when present.

Sometimes it is possible to find an obvious entry hole in the shoot (look for the sawdust on the bark) and to hook out or kill the caterpillar with a piece of wire.

Golden Delicious ❧

"I understand that the 'Golden Delicious' apples we buy are mainly imported from France. Can you tell me why the variety is not grown more widely in this country?"

A good question. The reason is mainly because the climate in this country is not suitable for the variety. It can be grown in this country but it only does well in hot summers. To succeed it needs high temperatures and better light than we normally have.

We can grow "Cox's Orange Pippin" well in many parts of this country and this is a far superior variety for flavour than "Golden Delicious".

Fruit cages are your first line of defence
in the war against unwanted visitors, including birds!

Fruit drop ❧

"I have a row of cordon apple trees in a fruit cage. All are well fed, sprayed and mulched. Trees of 'Sunset' drop their fruit every year in late July. The fruit is first class in size when they fall. Can you tell me why this happens?"

The apples could be dropping because of dryness at the roots at a critical stage of development. If your soil is inclined to dry out, it would pay to water it thoroughly when the fruit is swelling. Faulty nutrition could also be responsible.

The fruit is large so they may be having too much nitrogen. Feed them in February with sulphate of potash to balance the nitrogen.

June drop ❧

"My young apple trees have set some fruit this year, but I have been warned to look out for June drop. What is this, and is it not possible to prevent it happening?"

June drop occurs when young apples which have not been fully pollinated fall off. Also, when a tree sets too many apples for it to carry to maturity it will shed a number, sometimes in June, although more often in July. This is a normal occurrence, so is nothing to worry about.

Apple sucker ❧

"Some of my apple buds are falling as they start to develop, and others are turning brown. Examination with a hand lens has revealed green insects feeding on the buds. What are they and what should I do?"

The pests will be apple suckers which can be quite damaging, particularly where a winter wash has not been applied for a few years.

Spray now with a systemic insecticide such as Murphy Tumblebug, Long-Last or Sybol to gain control. Consider using Mortegg or Clean-Up next winter.

More feed ❧

"Each year the leaves on my young 'Cox' apple tree develop rounded, orange-brown marks. No fungicides seem to help, can you?"

The spots are due to a condition known as cox spot, although it also occurs on some other varieties. It is not due to disease but to a physiological disorder or growth problem.

The exact cause is not fully understood, although it is related in some way to a lack of certain elements in the leaves.

It can sometimes be reduced by spraying the leaves a few times during the summer, using a complete foliar feed such as Liquinure, Fillip or Phostrogen. Keep the tree well watered in any dry spells and mulch over the soil to help conserve moisture.

If planning to plant any further apples, bear in mind that "Greensleeves" and "Discovery" are little affected by cox spot, but that trees growing on the rootstocks M9 and M26 appear to be more susceptible to attack.

What a "Discovery"! ❧

"Last September I bought some 'Discovery' apples in a greengrocer. They were delicious; can you tell me whether they can be grown in this country?"

Malus "Discovery" is an English dessert apple and can certainly be grown successfully in this country. It is an early apple, in season between the middle of August and mid-September and is a comparatively new variety, having been introduced by Matthews Fruit Trees Ltd, Bury St Edmunds, in 1963. The blossom tolerates frosts well and it has resistance against scab disease. It has been given an Award of Garden Merit by the RHS.

September apples ❧

"I want to grow an apple for eating that is ripe in August and September. Can you suggest varieties that I could grow?"

One of the best early apples is "Discovery". This can be eaten in late August and early September. Pick the fruits in mid-August. The red apples are attractive to look at and also have good flavour. Another good early variety is "Lady Sudeley". It crops well and the flavour is good. "Beauty of Bath" is an even earlier apple which is ripe at the beginning of August.

Ballerina apples ❧

"I have two Ballerina apple trees, purchased four years ago. Last year there was no fruit and only one small flower on them. How do I treat the trees?"

Ballerina apple trees are grown as cordons but the leading shoot – the end of the main stem – is not pruned. It should be allowed to grow freely. These trees do eventually grow very tall. The side shoots are naturally spur-bearing but can be summer pruned in July by shortening each back to five leaves. These shoots are further pruned back to a visible fruit bud in winter.

The pollination of the flowers is dependent on pollinating bees and other wild insects which need shelter and warm weather to work freely. A lack of fruit could be due to cold and wet weather last spring – perhaps this spring will be different.

Old fruit 🐝

"When I was a schoolboy during the war and evacuated to South Devon, there was a lovely pale yellow, juicy apple called "Keswick" in the orchard. Is it possible to obtain this tree today and where from?"

We believe the apple is "Keswick Codling". This is a very old apple which was introduced in 1790. It is ripe in October and is ready for picking in late August. Trees of this variety are still available from a few specialist nurseries including R. V. Roger Ltd, The Nurseries, Whitby Rd, Pickering, North Yorkshire Yo18 7HG. Phone 01751 472226.

Fruit gap 🐝

"I planted two apple trees in my garden last winter. They are growing well and fruitlets have now formed. I am now told that I should have nipped out the blossom to prevent the trees fruiting in their first year. Is this true?"

Yes, newly planted apple trees should not be allowed to bear fruit in their first season and you should nip out the fruitlets that have formed. The trees must be allowed to make a good root system before they take on the strain of bearing fruit.

Next year only allow a light crop to form. The aim should be to allow the trees to make good growth before allowing them to carry fruit.

Granny Smith apple 🐝

"Can you tell me anything about an apple called 'Granny Smith'? Is it a cooker or an eating apple?"

"Granny Smith" originated in Australia and was introduced to this country in 1935. It is grown extensively in Australia, New Zealand and South Africa as a dessert apple. It needs hot summers to develop its full flavour and, unless we have a hot summer, the flavour is poor when the apple is grown in this country. Many growers, in fact, list it as a cooking apple. Trees normally crop well and the fruit keeps until April.

Spraying by the book 🐝

"I have been advised to spray my apple trees at different bud stages. Can you explain what these are?"

At one time fruit growers sprayed their apples in the winter with a tar oil wash when the buds were dormant. Spraying was also carried out with other pesticides and fungicides at bud burst; when the flowers were in green clusters; when they were showing pink buds and at petal fall.

It is now felt that for ordinary gardeners so much spraying is not necessary provided a small amount of damage from pests and diseases is acceptable.

A simpler system is to spray in winter with tar oil wash once in three years to clear moss and kill off insect eggs. Further spraying can depend on the particular insect involved. As soon as there are signs of attack, spraying should be carried out. This is a better approach rather than following a rigid spray programme.

Apple growths ❧

"In our newly acquired garden, the old apple trees have considerable growths of what we believe to be mosses and lichen. Are these any threat to the general health of the trees?"

It is quite common for apple trees to become a host for mosses and lichen in the more westerly areas and in wet districts. The growths are no real problem to the trees unless they get out of hand, when the extra humidity created could assist apple scab or canker to establish.

A winter wash could be applied every few years just to keep things in check. However, should aphids become a persistent pest, an annual winter wash would help by killing the overwintering pest eggs. Complete any winter washing whilst the trees are still dormant – normally by the end of February, but possibly earlier in Cornwall.

Pruning times ❧

"We have an old 'Worcester Pearmain' apple tree in our garden, which is 34 years old and a tip bearer. How should we prune it in winter and summer?"

As your tree is well established and a good age, the main pruning should be done in winter. Remove dead and diseased wood and any over-crowded branches so that the crown of the tree is receiving good light when covered in leaves. All laterals with fruit buds at their tips should be left unpruned. Summer pruning is not necessary on a mature tree other than to remove any dead or diseased shoots or fresh growths that cross mature branches.

Apple choice ⚘

"Russet apples do not seem to be grown very much. I recently tasted 'Merton Russet' which was delicious. Are there any others?"

Most people prefer colourful apples and are not impressed with the appearance of russet apples. However, as you say, they usually have excellent flavour and are well worth growing.

"Merton Russet" is a very good apple and the flavour is good. "Rosemary Russet" is another well-flavoured variety keeping until March. "Egremont Russet" is also a reliable apple of good flavour. It will keep until December and seems to resist most pests and diseases.

Apples will be ready to pick in good time – you don't need to help them!

Out of date ⚘

"I had a good crop of 'Sunset' apples last year and kept the fruit in a cool garage. By December the remaining apples all rotted off. Is there any reason for this?"

"Sunset" is a very good dessert apple but it will not keep after early December. In other words, your apples were past their sell-by date. This year get them used up by November.

Picking Worcesters 🐾

"There is a 'Worcester Pearmain' apple tree in my new garden. When will the fruit be ready for picking and how long will it keep?"

"Worcester Pearmain" apples are ready for picking in the first two weeks of September, ripening in September and October. They do not keep for long.

Poor relations 🐾

"I have had a 'Bramley's Seedling' apple tree for five years which has not borne any fruit. I also have a 'Charles Ross' and 'Newton Wonder'. Is it possible to tell me why the apple tree is reluctant to fruit?"

"Bramley's Seedling" apple is a triploid variety which means that two other varieties of the same flowering period must be grown together to ensure successful pollination and fertilization. "Bramley's Seedling" and "Charles Ross" have the same flowering period (group 3) but "Newton Wonder" (group 5) flowers later. If you have room, plant another tree of either "Cox's Orange Pippin", "Discovery", "Fiesta", "Granny Smith", "James Grieve" or "Worcester Pearmain". We assume that the tree is flowering well in the spring. If it is not, it may be making growth at the expense of flowers. In this case, prune lightly in winter to slow up the growth and to induce flowering spurs.

Storing fruit 🐾

"I have a 'Lane's Prince Albert' apple tree which has a good crop of fruit this year. When should I pick it? And how should I store the apples?"

"Lane's Prince Albert" is a late keeping cooking apple. It should be picked in early October. To store, select only sound fruits without any blemishes. Apples must be stored in a cool, dark, frost-proof place where there is an even temperature. A shed or garage in shade may be used but avoid lofts and attics as they become too hot and dry.

Potting an apple tree ❧

"As I have a small patio garden, is it possible to grow a small apple tree in a large pot or tub?"

Yes, apple and pear trees can be grown in large pots or tubs. Most apple varieties can be grown in tubs but it is best to avoid tip-bearing varieties such as "Ellison's Orange", "Laxton's Superb" and "Worcester Pearmain".

Pot the tree in good potting compost such as John Innes No. 3. Make sure that there is a drainage hole in the base of the container. Before planting the tree, cover the base of the container with broken crocks or rubble to ensure good drainage. Firm the potting compost well around the root ball of the tree and leave space at the top of the container for watering. Keep the swollen, graft union near the base of the main stem a few inches above soil level.

During the spring and summer never allow the compost to dry out. Give a liquid fertilizer each week during the summer months but cease feeding in early August.

Wait for new apples ❧

"I planted some cordon apple trees last winter. They are growing well and have flower buds. Will they fruit this year?"

As your apple trees were planted only last winter we would not advise you to allow any fruit to form this year. The trees must be allowed to make a good root system before they take on the strain of bearing fruit, so nip out any flowers that appear.

Step-over apples over the edge ❧

"I have seen apple trees trained to form an edging to a path. Can you tell me anything about them?"

The apple trees that you have seen are called step-over trees and they can form an attractive edging to a border. They are, in fact, single-tier espalier trees usually grafted on M27 rootstock and can be obtained from specialist fruit growers.

The single arms are supported on a low horizontal wire. They are normally planted 5 ft (1.5 m) apart. To keep them compact they need summer pruning in the same way as for espalier and cordon trees.

Fruit trees can be trained into cordons,
espaliers and unusual shapes but there are limits!

Cordon apples need training ❧

"I am planning to grow some cordon-trained apples on wire supports. Should
they be planted at an angle or can I plant them vertically? If they are sloped
should they face the south?"

It is best to grow cordon-trained apples at an angle of 45°, preferably in a
row running north and south with the trees pointing to the north. This will
ensure that the trees get equal amounts of light on each side to provide
balanced growth.

Cordons planted vertically are difficult to manage, as the sap tends to
rush to the top of the stem, resulting in stronger growth at the top than at
the bottom.

Apples in trouble ❧

"A month or so ago, we noticed that several of the tips of apple shoots were
snapped over as though someone had just broken them. We were puzzled and

so looked more closely and found that in each withering tip was a little grub. Can you please tell me what the insect is?"

The damage is the work of the apple twig cutter, a species of weevil. An egg is laid in each shoot tip and then the weevil makes a series of punctures around the stem on the tree side of the egg. The tips then wither, and in some cases fall, and the weevils complete their development inside the tip. When fully fed they eat their way out and pupate in the soil. There seems to be an increase of this insect recently, probably because fewer sprays are being applied.

The damage is not too critical as new laterals will develop from lower down, although on young trees where establishment of a correct framework is needed it may be necessary to apply a contact insecticide such as Tumblebug just before flowering at pink bud stage.

Control apple sawfly now 🥂

"My young Cox apple tree always suffers from some maggot that attacks the very small apples, often boring through a few before it has finished. How can I prevent attacks this year?"

There is just time to take action to stop apple sawfly, the pest responsible for the damage you describe. At the end of flowering, just as the last petals are falling, and after pollinating insects have ceased working the blossoms, spray with Tumblebug or Picket. One good spray will catch the maggots as they move over the surface of the fruit and before they bore into the flesh. The maggots drop to the ground when fully fed where they pupate, so if the tree is in soil (not under grass) winter soil cultivations may also help in the control.

Miner losses 🥂

"My three-year-old 'Jupiter' apple tree has been losing leaves for some months. They turn brown and fall off. This has happened for the last three years. Can you tell me why?"

Apple leaf-miner is the pest responsible. The mines often double back on themselves, killing out patches of tissue. Infested leaves do often turn brown and fall early. There are three generations per year with adults present just before flowering in April, and then in June, August and finally the ones that overwinter being around in October.

Best control would be by spraying next spring at green bud and pink bud stages using a spray such as Tumblebug. Pick off any infested leaves when seen next year, and repeat the spray control each time adult moths are expected.

Mined apples

"My apples were ruined by severe damage in the flesh which I have never seen before. All eight of my trees were affected. What burrowed through them and how can I prevent it this year?"

The damage has been caused by caterpillars of the apple fruit moth, *Argyresthia conjugella*. Eggs are laid on the young fruitlets in June and the larvae burrow through the flesh until fully fed by early October. They then drop to the ground to overwinter just beneath the soil in a silken cocoon.

The pest was first recorded in Devon in 1898, but is now more plentiful in Scotland than England.

Soil cultivation around the trees in winter will help in the control of this pest, as will spraying with Picket or Tumblebug in mid-June, as for codling moth control.

Loopy caterpillar

"I was sitting under my Bramley apple tree the other day when a large (about 2 in. long) pinkish grey and brown caterpillar dropped onto me. It was very stiff and stick-like, with legs at each end only. Any ideas?"

The caterpillar would be one of the "looper" group, so called because, with no legs in the middle of their bodies, they move in a series of loops. The group scientific name is Geometridae and many of the caterpillars resemble twigs when at rest.

From your description, I believe the caterpillar was probably the larva of the brindled beauty moth, *Lycia hirtaria*. This is a fairly widespread, but not abundant species, feeding on fruit trees and also on elm, lime and willow. No great damage is done as numbers never appear to be great.

The caterpillars pupate in the soil from around July and the next generation of adult moths emerges in the following March to April.

Woolly chaos

"My old apple tree produced several strong new shoots from the trunk this year but they became covered with a cotton wool-like substance. I believe this is some form of blight; can you recommend a suitable treatment please?"

The cause of the cotton wool-like material is the pest woolly aphid, which was widely known to gardeners at one time as American Blight. Gardeners have long memories – the pest was first reported to have reached England from America in 1787! The vigorous new shoots would be best pruned out unless a few are needed for a new branch framework.

This would also remove the pest, but for any remaining, a spray made with Safer's Garden Insecticide Concentrate, or an application of Sybol should prove effective.

Wasps again!

"My early apples, 'Discovery' variety, are regularly attacked by wasps, just as they are getting close to ripening and picking. What would you advise me to do to stop these attacks?"

You could hang a proprietary wasp trap in the tree, or a home-made one containing jam diluted with water. Hopefully these will attract the wasps away from the apples. "Discovery" does seem to be particularly prone to wasp attack immediately before ripening, so if the tree is still small enough to reach easily, it may be worth encasing the fruits in old tights or similar protection.

Apple suckers

"The blossom and leaf trusses on my apple tree are being severely damaged. The flower petals turn brown as the buds start to open, leaves are distorted and there is a sticky substance present."

Apple sucker feeding is the cause of the damage. These overwinter as eggs on the trees and hatch in April to start the new season. The young nymphs feed very actively at this time of year and, as you are finding, damage can be very severe.

A spray with Tumblebug, Sybol or malathion, drenched well into the trusses, will control these pests. An alternative way to prevent damage would be to apply a Mortegg winter wash between early December and late February to kill the overwintering eggs.

Touch of the vapours

"I am finding a number of objects on my apple trees that look like cocoons, but they are covered with masses of eggs. Can you tell me what they are and if they are likely to be damaging?"

The eggs are of the vapourer moth, and the caterpillars feed on a wide range of tree foliage. The eggs are laid in autumn, close to the cocoon by the newly emerged and mated female moth, and hatch at intervals in spring.

To prevent damage it would be wise to collect and destroy any further egg masses that you find.

Not very rosy ❧

"Earlier this year I had a very bad attack of blue-coloured greenfly on my apple tree. The leaves were all twisted up by the attack and many of the fruitlets were deformed."

The pest is the rosy apple aphid, also known as blue bug because of its colouring. The leaves stay green, which distinguishes this species from the rosy leaf-curling aphid (which is also blue in colour; but which causes the leaves to turn red).

Some of the rosy apple aphids stay on the tree through to autumn; others migrate to plantains for the summer and return to apple trees for egg laying.

If the pests can still be seen, spray thoroughly with Phostrogen Organic Insecticide or Tumblebug. Should the pest attack again next spring then it would be worth spraying the apple tree in the following winter with Mortegg to clear up the overwintering eggs.

Sawfly scars ❧

"Several of my apples have winding scars on the skins. What do you think caused them?"

The scars were made by larvae of the apple sawfly. After feeding inside a fruitlet the larva eats its way out and then may feed around the surface of another fruit.

It then sometimes bores into the flesh, in which case the damaged apple would fall well before harvest time, but in other instances the larva will feed on the outside of a few apples before boring in, and it is this surface feeding that results in the scarring you have found.

Apple trap ❧

"I have an apple tree which normally has masses of fruit each year. This year I decided to use a codling moth trap but there is not a single apple. I cannot

believe that this is coincidence. A nearby tree with no trap has some fruit, but fewer apples. Can you tell me whether the moth trap could be responsible?"

Codling moth traps have been used for well over 15 years by commercial growers as a means of monitoring moth populations. It also gives them information on when to spray for best effect. No adverse effects on fruit have been reported during that time.

We think that the lack of fruit is probably more related to frost or to a period of low temperature or rain during the blossoming period. Frost could have killed the flowers, whilst low temperatures and rain would both keep pollinator activity at a low level.

We feel that the lack of fruit is simply a coincidence and was in no way affected by the moth trap.

Banish biologically ❧

"Is there a really effective non-chemical way to stop caterpillar damage, short of netting over everything to stop egg laying or having to squash the caterpillars by hand?"

The most effective non-chemical control for caterpillars, apart from hand removal or netting would be to spray with the bacterium *Bacillus thuringiensis*. After eating the bacterium, the caterpillars stop feeding and die within a few days, although it is harmless against humans and animals. The treatment would need to be repeated after rain or after seven days, when new caterpillars are hatching.

Deadly scent ❧

"I believe it is possible to stop damage by codling moth to apples even on large trees by using a form of trap. Could you please let me have details?"

Yes, it is possible to stop codling moth damage by attracting and killing male codling moths before they can mate. Hang a Trappit or a Pagoda trap in the tree as soon as possible now for maximum benefit.

If not stocked locally, write for details of Trappit to Agralan Ltd, The Old Brickyard, Ashton Keynes, Swindon, Wilts SN6 6QR, and for the Pagoda trap to Oecos Ltd, 11 High Street, Kimpton, Herts SG4 8RA. The traps contain a substance called pheromone that attracts males, like the substance emitted by the female codling moth.

Rabbit damage ❧

"Last winter I discovered that rabbits had eaten the bark of some of my young apple trees. What is the best way of preventing further damage this winter?"

Rabbits can cause considerable damage to the stems of fruit trees as well as ornamental trees and shrubs, particularly in a hard winter when the rabbits are short of food.

The best way to protect the stems of young trees is to fix special guards to them. These are available at most garden centres. Or instead, nylon mesh can be fixed to stakes around the tree. Special glues are also available that can be applied to the lower trunks of trees to deter the rabbits.

Brown rot strikes again ❧

"Some of the apples on my Cox tree are already showing signs of a brown rotting, even whilst still on the tree. It seems to happen most years."

There is a brown rot fungus which would be responsible for the rotting you are finding. It is principally a wound parasite, so it is likely that the apples have been damaged first by wasps, by bird pecking or by codling moth or other caterpillar.

Pick off all the rotting apples you can find now, and when picking later for storing, reject any apples that show signs of external damage. During winter, remove any mummified fruit remaining on the tree and next year take what measures you can by means of netting, trapping and spraying to prevent the fruits being damaged.

A systemic fungicide as used for scab or mildew may also have a useful effect against the brown rot fungus.

Apple tree in trouble ❧

"Our rather elderly apple tree, variety unknown but quite a good eater, is suffering from what I thought was canker, but now the damaged areas seem to be sprouting cotton wool. Help!"

There will be apple canker present which is eating away the tissue of the branch, but such sites are often used as feeding sites by woolly aphids. The "wool" will be from these pests.

Best treatment would be to wirebrush the cankers, if they are in branches which cannot be cut out, and then to paint over with Arbrex. This should stop both problems. On younger wood the woolly aphid often attacks first, and the canker then invades the damaged tissues.

Apple scab control ❧

"When should I start a scab control programme on my apple trees? I thought scab was a wet weather disease, but I had a lot of damage in 1997 despite a fairly warm and dry year."

Scab is normally more troublesome in wet seasons, but the spores will germinate as long as the leaves remain wet for a certain period. The length of this period depends on temperature and the higher the temperature the less time the leaves need to remain wet. Scab was quite troublesome in several areas of the country last year.

Early spring is the ideal time to apply the first spray in a scab control programme. It is round about this time that the overwintering scab fungus starts to release its spores to infect the new leaves. Use a carbendazim-based systemic fungicide such as Supercarb or Murphy Systemic Action Fungicide and apply three or four sprays at two- to three-week intervals. This should prevent the infection getting an early hold.

Wilting shoots ❧

"Every spring a number of young shoots on my apple tree wilt, turn brown and die. The tree is about 20 years old, crops well, but always looks unhappy with the brown patches of dead shoots."

The cause of the damage is the blossom wilt fungus which gets into the spurs and then lies in wait until the following year when it invades and kills the new growths. The only control is to prune out all the wilted shoots, cutting the growths back $\frac{3}{4}$–1 in. (2–3 cm) further than the wilted portion. The disease spores are spread on the wind so vigilance is needed each year to keep on top of any potential problem.

Bitter bramleys ❧

"Our bramley apples have developed brown spots just under their skins. There is no sign of pests and the skin doesn't appear to be broken. Please help."

Bitter pit is responsible. This is not caused by pest or disease, but by a lack of calcium uptake into the fruit. Hot, dry summers, large fruits from small trees, and excess nitrogen applications are all predisposing factors. "Bramley's Seedling" is one of the more sensitive varieties. The damage shouldn't get any more severe in storage.

Next year, spray the tree with Chempak calcium nitrate every three weeks from June to September. Use a rate of $1\frac{1}{2}$ oz. per gallon of water, adding a wetting agent.

Apple canker control ❧

"We have some old cordon-trained apple trees that seem to be increasingly attacked by canker. Is there any effective cure for this trouble?"

If major trunks and branches are badly eaten into by canker then it may be very difficult to eradicate the attack, and a clean start could be the best way to go. If attacks are not as bad as that, then treatment can be given. Take a wire brush and thoroughly clean up the cankers and surrounding bark.

In severely cankered areas, cut out the damaged parts with a sharp knife, collecting up all the parings, and paint over the cuts with a proprietary wound paint such as Arbrex or Medo to protect from further infection.

As an extra safeguard, spray the trees each autumn, at the start of leaf fall and again half way through leaf fall, using a copper fungicide. This will protect the leaf scars – the main source of new attacks by the apple canker fungus.

Mildew menace ❧

"Several of the developing flower buds on my little Cox's apple tree are coated with what I believe to be mildew. I know from last year that these buds will die out without setting any crop; what action should I take now please?"

You are correct in assuming the disease to be apple mildew. The disease spends the winter on the shoots and in the buds and in spring the primary infection sites produce spores which spread the fungus further.

Pick off and burn all the infected blossom and vegetative buds you can find. This may be sufficient action to take now, but should any further mildew attacks be noticed again remove the infection but then follow with a couple of sprays with Supercarb fungicide.

Soft in store ❧

"Some of our stored apples are beginning to develop a greenish blue mould and are then going soft. What is this, and how can we prevent it please?"

The growths are of a fungus known as blue mould, which is a species of penicillium. Attacks occur through wounds in the fruit skin, caused by insect feeding, damage during picking or sometimes by hailstones in late summer. The way to prevent attack is by avoiding as many forms of skin damage as possible, by good pest control and careful handling during picking and storing.

Fruit tree lichen ❧

"Our apple trees are covered with dense growths of lichens. Do these harm the growth or can they be left alone?"

Lichens do no real harm to fruit trees so can be left alone. They can act as homes for various pests, but beneficial insects will also hide there so that probably evens things up. Tar oil winter-washing removes lichens very effectively if you should ever wish to clean up the trees.

Apple attack ❧

"We didn't get many apples this year due to a late frost, and some of the ones that did set stayed small, about half size, and were all bumpy and coloured up early. The leaves were also curled and the stems twisted, looking almost like weedkiller damage, but no weedkillers were used."

The symptoms you describe are an accurate account of rosy apple aphid damage. Feeding in spring results in the different types of damage you have described. Winter-wash the tree with Mortegg between December and the end of February to kill the overwintering eggs and stop damage next spring.

June drop ❧

"I have a tree of the apple 'Sunset' which usually sets plenty of fruit. However, most is small. Should I thin out some of the fruitlets in the hope of getting larger apples?"

It would certainly pay you to reduce your apple crop by thinning out the fruitlets. Wait until the June drop has taken place. This is when many of the fruitlets will fall off naturally and it normally takes place in late June. If the fruitlets are still very crowded, thin them out with sharp scissors to leave the remainder about 4 in. (10 cm) apart. Remove any that are deformed or damaged.

Apart from thinning, water the soil thoroughly in dry weather to help produce apples of good size. One or two liquid feeds with a balanced fertilizer before the end of July will also be helpful.

Grease bands ❧

"*Why are grease bands put on fruit trees?*"

Grease bands are put around the main trunks of fruit trees to trap insects crawling up them. They are particularly good at catching the wingless, female winter moths, preventing them laying eggs. These would normally hatch in the spring and the caterpillars can do considerable damage to young foliage.

"To wash, or not to wash . . ." ❧

"*I am a long-standing and happy reader of AG. Each winter you publish articles on the virtues of winter washing fruit trees. I have a small orchard in Suffolk, and have complied with your instructions. My trees appear to be healthy. They are also fruitful. Recently, however, I've noticed that advice has changed to recommending that fruit trees should be winter washed only once every two or three years. As I had not sprayed my trees for a couple of years, I did so last January. Then, to my horror, I read that this practice is likely to do more harm than good. Your comments, please?*"

Although winter washing with tar oil rids apples and other fruit trees of overwintering pests – aphids, suckers and scale insects among them – and cleanses bark of suffocating moss, algae and lichen, it also kills red spider mite predators and other beneficial insects. On balance, therefore, unless the tree is heavily infested with, say, scale insect, it's better not to winter wash, but to control pests by using insecticides. On the other side of the coin the choice the gardener should be making is whether he or she is going to apply any form of spray. One either sprays or one doesn't. If one does, then a winter wash would be a biologically sound start, and should reduce the number of pests needing to be controlled in the active growing season.

Unfruitful apricot ❧

"*I have a container-grown 'Moorpark' apricot approximately six years old. The container is about 2 ft in diameter and one foot deep. In the tree's third year, after bark ringing, it was covered in blossom and I picked 45 good apricots. The tree is about 8 ft high, trained to an upturned goblet shape container, and housed in a south-facing conservatory. Each year, as much soil as possible is renewed and the tree is generally fed with Phostrogen interspersed with sulphate of potash. Last year and this year, although the*" *tree looks healthy, it has produced only one flower and no fruit. Any suggestions, please?"*

Apricots can be grown in the open in southern England but are well known for being fickle about fruiting. We assume that the tree is making plenty of new side shoots each year and we wonder whether these are getting well ripened in the summer because it is in the conservatory.

We suggest that you stand the plant in the open in a sunny, sheltered place. The tree can stay outside until next January when it can be brought under cover. This will protect the flowers from inclement weather. You have not said anything about how you prune the tree and we hope you are not cutting off potentially fruitful shoots! It is best to apply sulphate of potash fertilizer in January.

Beyond the pale ❧

"I have raised an avocado pear plant from the seed of a fruit. It has grown rather spindly and the leaves are yellowish in colour. What can I do to improve its growth?"

Avocado pear plants do tend to grow spindly, particularly if they are not getting enough light. We suggest that you stand your plant in a light window.

It will be happy outside in a sunny position during the summer from June to September. To help improve the colour of the leaves, feed the plant with a liquid fertilizer, such as Phostrogen or Miracle-Gro, from spring until early September.

If your plant has filled its present pot with roots, repot it into a larger pot using a good potting mixture.

Blackberry choice ❧

"I want to plant a blackberry in my garden but I am not sure which variety to choose. I would prefer a thornless variety. Which one would you recommend?"

There are a number of thornless blackberry varieties. One of the most popular is "Oregon Thornless" which has attractive cut leaves. "Loch Ness" is a new variety bred at the Scottish Crop Research Institute. The stems have an upright habit and are thornless. "Black Satin" is another thornless variety originating from the USA.

Fruit under siege   🍃

"Earlier this year, all the new leaves on our blackberries were opening out full of rounded holes. I think the damage has now stopped, but we would be interested to know what caused the damage and how to stop it another time."

The damage has been caused by caterpillars of a sawfly, most probably the small raspberry sawfly which can attack most cane fruits.

Adults are on the wing in May, no males are known, and lay eggs under the leaves. Feeding on opening leaves by the caterpillars causes the holes which often appear almost symmetrical when the damage is done whilst the leaves are still partially folded. The fully fed larvae pupate on the leaves and there is a second generation in August. Should more damage be seen shortly, or next year, spray with derris or a permethrin insecticide.

Blotched berries   🍃

"A number of my blackberries have failed to ripen fully, resulting in part of the fruit being black and part red. Is this anything to worry about?"

The two-tone effect is known as red-berry disease and follows feeding by the blackberry mite. Toxic saliva is injected into the berries by the mite as it feeds, and this results in the failure of the attacked part of the berry to ripen.

Control is quite difficult, but prune out the shoots that carried damaged berries as soon as possible now, and in the next year that the symptoms occur, directly after picking is finished.

In winter, tie in the new canes fairly low, and then in the spring and summer, tie in the new canes above the older ones. Train the new canes above the older ones.

Prune to resume   🍃

"I planted a 'Himalayan Giant' blackberry last winter against a wire support. It has made lots of growth. How should I prune it?"

Prune blackberries in the autumn or winter by cutting out the canes that have carried fruit and retaining the new canes for fruiting in the following year. Your blackberry will need little pruning this winter but the canes should be trained and tied into place. There are various systems of training aimed at keeping the old canes separate from the new ones. You could train all your new canes to one side and tie them to the wires. Next year train all the new canes to the opposite side. Instead, train the canes out as a fan to left and right, leaving the space between them clear. Next season train the new canes vertically up this space. At the end of the season cut out the old fruiting canes and tie in the new canes in their place.

Galled blackberry

"On a recent walk I saw several odd swollen growths on a clump of blackberries. Some were rather like pods along the stems, others curled the stems in a complete circle. What would have caused this and can it affect garden blackberries?"

The cause of the swellings is an attack by a gall wasp. Eggs are laid in the young stems in spring and as many as 200 larvae can be found in individual cells within the gall. New adults emerge in March to April in the following year.

Eggs are mainly laid in low-growing bramble stems, specially when partly concealed by grasses, so attacks on garden blackberries, although possible, are not often experienced.

Blackberry blues

"Checking on my blackberries as they were starting to ripen, I found many of the leaves to have a pale yellow stippled effect, with small, pale leaping insects under the leaves. Can you please explain what the problem was?"

The problem was an attack by leaf-hoppers. The wingless nymphs feed under the leaves on the sap, resulting in the bleached spots. As they mature, wings gradually develop until they are fully adult insects. When disturbed they make the characteristic short leaping flights that you mention.

The damage they cause can be prevented by spraying under the leaves with a permethrin or a fatty acids insecticide.

Currant affairs

"I want to plant some blackcurrant bushes in my garden this winter. Can you recommend some good varieties? How far apart should the bushes be planted?"

Good blackcurrant varieties are "Boskoop Giant", which is early, "Ben Nevis", a mid-season variety, "Ben Sarek" mid to late season and "Black Reward" which is late.

Most varieties should be planted 5–6 ft (1.5–1.8 m) apart, but "Ben

Sarek" can be planted closer at 4 ft (1.2 m) apart and is useful in small gardens. After planting, cut back all the stems to within a few inches of ground level. This is done to encourage strong new growth which will fruit next year. Expect no fruit this year.

Pruning blackcurrants ❧

"I am not sure when to prune my blackcurrant bushes. Some people tell me to prune after picking the fruit and others say wait until the autumn. Who is right?"

Blackcurrants are usually pruned in the autumn after the leaves have fallen. However, some gardeners like to thin out a few of the lower stems after picking the fruit to allow light and air into the bush. The main pruning should be done in autumn, though.

Aim to remove about a third of the older stems. This hard pruning encourages good strong growth the following season, provided the bushes are well fed in the spring.

Planting a blackcurrant bush ❧

"I plan to plant some blackcurrant bushes this winter. How far apart should the bushes be spaced and how deep should they be planted?"

Blackcurrant bushes can be planted until March provided the ground is not too wet or frozen. Space the bushes 5–6 ft (1.5–1.8 m) apart in each direction. Plant at the same depth, or a little deeper, as the old soil mark at the base of the stems.

After planting prune the stems by cutting them back close to ground level. This will help stimulate new growth in the spring and summer which will produce fruit the year after.

Currant capsid concern ❧

"The leaves on my blackcurrant bushes are showing some nasty yellow spots and quite a bit of distortion. Is this a virus attack, and is there any cure?"

The spotting and distortion are the result of feeding by capsid bugs so fortunately control measures are available. Where the pests insert their feeding tubes the leaf tissue is killed and shows up later as a yellow, then brown, spotting; attack on young leaves also results in the distortion you have seen.

Spray thoroughly under the leaves, and on the soil around the bushes, with Safers Organic Insecticide Concentrate or you could use either Sybol or Tumblebug.

Currant green fly ❦

"Each spring, our currant bushes seem to be infested by masses of greenfly and the new shoots are damaged before we can gain control. Is there any way we can prevent attacks?"

If you spray your currants any time from November to February with a tar oil winter wash, Mortegg or Clean-Up, the overwintering eggs of the greenfly will be killed, and this will mean a clean start in the following spring.

Hollow currant stems ❦

"I am finding a number of wilted blackcurrant shoots in my bushes. When I cut them off the stems seem to be hollow."

The stems have been hollowed out by the caterpillar of the currant clearwing moth and this causes the shoots to wilt and die. You may find the brownheaded, creamy white grubs inside some of the shoots.

Continue to cut out affected shoots for burning, pruning them back to their bases. Any weak-looking stems can be gently bent over; bored ones will snap. There is no special control, but permethrin sprays in early and late June should cover the egg-laying period next year.

Blistered currants ❦

"Every spring, our blackcurrant leaves are covered with blisters. They start off green but then change to purple. Is there any action we can take now to prevent this happening again?"

The blisters are caused by the currant blister aphid, and this pest can be treated in winter. Using a tar oil winter wash (Mortegg or Clean-Up), spray the bushes before the end of February and this will kill the overwintering eggs.

Woolly currant shoots ❦

"Some of the shoots on my blackcurrant bushes have patches of woolly growths, and they seem to start under hard, shell-like objects. Help please?"

The curious outgrowths on your currants are the work of the woolly currant scale insect. The "wool" consists of masses of waxy threads and contains the eggs of the scale insect. The wool is dispersed by wind during the summer months. Red and white currants are subject to attack, along with blackcurrants as well as flowering currants and gooseberries.

Spray with Long-Last and during the winter months apply Mortegg or Clean-Up winter wash.

Currant casualty ❧

"A few of my blackcurrant shoots wilted and died back. When I pruned them out the inside of each shoot was brown and hollow and seemed to have had the pith eaten out. Can you throw any light on this please?"

The insides of the shoots had indeed been eaten out, the culprits being larvae of the currant clearwing moth. The adult moths, black with yellow stripes, and with transparent wings, are active in June and July and lay eggs, one at a time, close to the buds. The larvae bore into the stems and feed through the summer and autumn, and pupate in the following spring.

Infested shoots die, as you have found, but often the damage is not noticed until winter time when the shoots may snap.

Control by pruning out any suspect shoots, cutting back enough to remove the pupating insects.

Any control for currant big bud mite? ❧

"Many years ago I used to use lime sulphur to control blackcurrant big bud mite. Since this disappeared from the market I haven't found anything that is recommended against this pest. Any ideas please?"

There is no effective chemical control for use by gardeners against big bud mite. Control is by removing the swollen buds whenever they are seen.

If any are present now, remove them immediately, as the mites will be starting to disperse. Some dispersion is on wind currents, but the tiny mites also attach themselves to the legs of greenfly and other insects.

If you cover the blackcurrant plants with fine netting, such as Enviromesh, it may not exclude the actual mites, but it would keep out the mite-carrying insects.

Currant problem ❧

"Many of my blackcurrant shoots were all crumpled as they started growing in spring. I pruned out these shoots, but as they sent out further ones, these too

were crumpled and soon turned black. There was also some leaf twisting. Is this some virus problem, and is there any cure?"

The damage has been caused by the blackcurrant leaf midge. There are three or more generations each year, and your new growths were clearly infested by a later generation. The adult midges lay eggs in the new growths and many larvae feed together, resulting in the damage you describe. The insects then pupate in the soil to emerge as adults a couple of weeks later to repeat the cycle.

To control now, again cut out the affected shoots and try a spray with Tumblebug or a fatty acid-based insecticide to reduce reinfestation. Next year, apply a spray when the flower buds become visible.

Cut backs, but when? ❧

"Can you tell me when my blackcurrants should be pruned? I prune the bushes in winter but I have been told that it should be carried out after picking the fruit."

The main pruning of blackcurrants should be done after leaf-fall in the autumn. However, some pruning may be done after picking the fruit. Cut out a few overcrowded, old, dark branches in the base of the bush to allow air to circulate and help ripen the wood.

After leaf-fall, aim to remove about a third of the older branches, cutting them out at the base of the bush. The older stems are darker in colour. This hard pruning is necessary to encourage strong basal growths to appear in the following season. Retain the strong new growths made in the current season.

Soil for blueberries ❧

"I would like to grow some blueberry bushes in my garden and I am told that they must have a soil free from lime. Mine is neutral. Will it be suitable?"

Blueberries must have an acid soil with a pH of about 4.5, so your neutral soil (pH 7) is not suitable. However, you could grow a bush in a large pot or tub filled with an acid, ericaceous compost.

Alternatively, you could prepare a special planting position for a bush. Take out a hole about $2\frac{1}{2}$ ft by $2\frac{1}{2}$ ft (76 × 76 cm) and 18 in. (45 cm) deep. Line it with black polythene and fill it with an acid potting compost. Make a few holes in the plastic at the bottom of the hole to allow surplus water to drain away. The plastic lining prevents alkaline water seeping into the hole.

Starting with blueberries ❦

"Where can I get seed of blueberries? We developed a taste for them whilst on holiday in America. I am sure that I have read somewhere that they can be grown in this country but I cannot find anyone selling the seeds."

Seed of blueberries is not generally available and, in any case, it is better to purchase a bush of a named variety which is known to fruit well. Good varieties are "Berkeley", "Bluecrop" and "Spartan".

Blueberries must be grown in an acid, lime-free soil. If your soil is naturally alkaline, it would be best to grow the bushes in large pots or tubs containing an acid, ericaceous compost.

Good plants can be obtained from James Trehane & Sons Ltd, Stapehill Road, Hampreston, Wimborne, Dorset BH21 7NE.

Blueberries in pots ❦

"I would like to grow a blueberry bush which I understand needs an acid soil. As my soil is chalky, can I grow a bush in a large tub filled with a lime-free potting compost?"

Blueberry bushes may be grown successfully in large tubs or pots filled with an acid compost as used for rhododendrons and heathers.

Stand the containers in a sunny position and water with rainwater whenever possible as hard tap water contains lime. Feed the plants each spring with an acid fertilizer such as Miracid. The fruit begins to ripen in July and August when the bushes should be netted to keep birds away from the ripening fruit. Apart from the delicious fruit, the foliage is highly ornamental in the autumn when it turns bright red.

"Bluetta" and "Bluecrop" are two good varieties.

Cape-able berries ❦

"Can you tell me whether Cape gooseberries can be grown outside in this country?"

Cape gooseberries, *Physalis peruviana*, are usually treated as half-hardy annuals. Plants can be grown outside in southern England during the summer, provided they are given a warm, sheltered position. Better results are obtained by growing them under glass. They can be treated in a similar manner to tomatoes.

Raise plants from seed under glass in spring and plant in the open in late May or early June. Alternatively, plant them in a greenhouse border.

The berries, contained in a fibrous pod, are green at first and turn golden yellow when ripe. The berries may be eaten raw or stewed for desserts.

Bird damage   🌿

"Can you tell me what I can do about birds pecking out the buds on my gooseberry bushes?"

Yours is a common problem. The most effective way of preventing birds pecking out the buds on your gooseberry bushes is to grow them in a fruit cage. Proprietary models are available or they can be made with stout galvanized metal or wooden supports to a height of about 6 ft (1.8 m). Cover the framework with nylon netting of $\frac{3}{4}$ in. (2 cm) mesh.

Chemical deterrents are also available but, as they are easily washed off by rain, repeated sprayings are necessary.

It is also best to delay winter pruning until February so that shoots can be pruned to living buds.

Cape gooseberries   🌿

"Can Cape gooseberries be grown outside in this country? I like the sharp flavour of the fruit and want to grow some next year."

Cape gooseberries can be grown outside during the summer in this country. They need similar treatment to tomatoes. In a good summer the fruit will ripen outside but normally the fruit has to be picked and ripened indoors on a sunny windowsill. Better results are obtained by growing the plants in large pots under glass.

Sow the seed in a warm greenhouse in March. Prick out the seedlings into small pots and later move them on to larger pots. Plant outside in mid-May under cloches. Remove the covering in June and tie the plants as they grow to stout stakes. Remove the tip of each plant when it is about 1 ft tall to induce a bushy habit. Feeding the plants with sulphate of potash will help fruits to form.

Marked cherry leaves   🌿

"Most of the leaves of my flowering cherry are absolutely full of holes. They seem to get brown spots and then fall out. Is there anything I can do?"

There are two possible causes of the shot-like holes in your cherry leaves. Bacterial canker has a shot-hole stage in summer (and a canker stage in winter), and there is also the fungal disease *Stigmina*. The fungus is encouraged by waterlogging of the soil. Bacterial canker is the likely choice. Spray the tree quickly with Bordeaux mixture or a copper fungicide and repeat in two weeks' time and again in mid-October. These sprays encourage early leaf-fall and then protect the leaf scars from infection.

Falling cherries ❧

"I have a four-year-old 'Morello' cherry which is fan-trained against a south-east facing wall. This year it was a mass of flowers and, as it was cool and not many pollinating insects around, I hand-pollinated every bloom. Nearly all the flowers set fruit, but over the following weeks, most fell off. What caused this to happen?"

Although you hand-pollinated all the flowers on your cherry tree, we do not think that the flowers were fertilized satisfactorily. This was probably due to poor weather conditions. The best time to pollinate the flowers is in the middle of a warm and sunny day when the pollen is dry. The flowers must be touched gently with the aid of a soft camel-hair brush or with a piece of cotton wool on the end of a cane. Despite doing this, poor weather conditions can prevent successful fertilization of the flowers. Dryness at the roots can also cause the fruit to drop.

Single cherries ❧

"I want to grow a cherry in my garden but I am told that I need two trees to pollinate each other. Are there any self-fertile varieties as I have space for only one tree?"

Yes, there are self-fertile sweet cherries, and only one tree need be grown. These are fairly new introductions, and until recently, it was necessary to have two varieties together for pollination.

"Stella" is a reliable variety producing dark red fruits which ripen at the end of July. Others are "Cherokee", dark red cherries ripe in mid-August, and "Sunburst" which has black fruit in late July.

The sour cherry "Morello" is also self-fertile and only one tree need be grown.

"Morellos" for a north wall ❧

"I have a north-facing wall in my garden on which I would like to train a fruit tree. Would an apple grow in this situation? If not, what would you recommend?"

We do not think an apple would do very well on a north-facing wall. Apples, generally, do best planted in the open and they can suffer badly from red spider mites if trained on walls. The best fruit to grow on a north-facing wall is the "Morello" cherry. This is an acid cherry of excellent flavour and good for making jams and preserves.

Plant a fan-trained tree supported to horizontal wires fixed to the wall. Other fruits that can be grown as cordons on a north-facing wall are gooseberries and redcurrants. They fruit later than bushes grown in the open.

Sweet cherry ❧

"I would like to grow a dessert cherry but I am told that I need two varieties for pollination. I do not have space for more than one tree. Are there any self-fertile varieties?"

At one time all sweet cherries needed another variety as a pollinator, but in recent years a number of new self-fertile varieties have appeared. "Stella" is a reliable variety with dark red fruit. "Lapins" is said to yield even better and "Sunburst" is another good black variety in season at the end of July. Make sure that the tree is grown on a dwarfing rootstock such as "Inmil" or "Damil".

Cherries v. birds ❧

"Can you give me any advice on protecting my cherry trees from birds? I have two trees which bear plenty of fruit but I never get any ripe cherries as the birds beat me to the fruit."

The only satisfactory way of protecting fruit trees from birds is to cover them with nets. Chemical bird repellents are available but these are quickly washed off the trees and repeated spraying is necessary. We realize that if your trees are large it could be difficult to net them but if they are compact we suggest that you build a cage over them. The sides of the cage can be covered with nylon or galvanized wire netting. Use nylon netting for the roof of the cage as galvanized wire netting can result in harmful zinc deposits on the trees. It is easier to protect wall-trained trees of cherries and peaches from birds. Hang netting from the top of the wall down to the ground to enclose the tree.

If you can visit the Royal Horticultural Society's garden at Wisley, Surrey, you will be able to see their model fruit gardens where most of the fruit trees and bushes are enclosed in cages $6\frac{1}{2}$ ft (1.8 m) high.

Blossom wilt ❧

"Some of my cherry blossom and new shoots failed to develop and then died back. Is this something I should be concerned about?"

The sample showed blossom wilt to be responsible for the damage. The best treatment now is to prune out all the affected shoots to remove the disease. If left, the infection can pass further down into the shoots and be even more troublesome next year. There is some evidence that a tar oil winter wash, as applied for pest control in December, will reduce blossom wilt attacks.

Cherry bacterial canker ❧

"A few weeks ago I noticed that my cherry tree leaves had a large number of orange-brown spots on them. Now the spots are falling out, leaving lots of rounded holes. I cannot find any pests on them."

The damage has been caused by bacterial canker infection. One form of this disease attacks the branches in the crotch of the tree, girdling and killing branches. The other type, seen on your tree, is known as the shot hole form. Now is the ideal time to tackle the infection to reduce damage for next year. Spray thoroughly with Bordeaux Mixture or Murphy Traditional Copper Fungicide in mid-August and repeat in mid-September and mid-October. These sprays condition the leaves for early leaf-fall and then protect the leaf scars from infection.

Cherry under attack ❧

"During July we noticed a browning of our cherry tree leaves and then they were suddenly covered with masses of yellow and black, slightly hairy, caterpillars. Much of the foliage was destroyed. Help please."

The caterpillars you describe are those of the buff-tip moth. They feed on the under surface of the leaves first, resulting in the brown appearance and then devour the entire leaf. They always live in large colonies. When fully fed in autumn they pupate in the soil.

Look out for attack from next June onwards, and remove the pests by hand when seen. For severe attacks, spray with Phostrogen Safer's Insecticide or Long-Last.

Cherry fly ❧

"Each year we get a mass of blackfly on our cherry tree. The leaves become curled and growth is severely affected. Will winter spraying prevent this problem?"

A winter spray with Mortegg will kill the overwintering eggs of cherry blackfly and prevent the early damage.

There may be some later damage from aphids flying into your garden from nearby unsprayed cherry trees, but these could be cleared up with a spray of malathion or Tumblebug.

Cherry trouble ❧

"My cherry tree leaves were reduced to just a network of veins by some pest last summer. How can I avoid the problem this year?"

The pest that caused the damage would be the pear and cherry slug-worm. The larvae are slug-like, black and shiny and feed on the leaf surface, to cause the skeletonized leaves you describe. There are up to three generations per year and the pests overwinter in cocoons in the soil.

Winter cultivations around the trees may help a little, but main control would be with a contact insecticide such as permethrin or pyrethrum, in summer or autumn as necessary.

Figs outdoors ❧

"I am very fond of figs and would like to grow a tree. I do not have a greenhouse and am wondering whether I could grow a fig outside in my district. If so, what is a good variety that you would recommend?"

Figs can be grown outside in southern England and if you have a warm, south-facing wall you should be able to grow a tree successfully. A good variety to grow is "Brown Turkey".

The fig could be planted in a pot or in an outside border against the wall. However, the roots need confining in an enclosed bed measuring approximately 2 × 2 ft (0.6 × 0.6 m) and 2 ft (0.6 m) deep. If the roots are not confined in an enclosed bed the fig will grow too rampantly at the expense of the fruit.

Planted against a wall, the shoots should be trained to horizontal wires fixed in the wall. The tips of the shoots, which carry the embryo figs, can be damaged in hard winters and it is wise to enclose the whole tree in bracken or straw for the winter to protect the shoots. Keep the covering on between November and April.

Caring for a fig ❧

"I would like advice on growing a 'Brown Turkey' fig. It was bought in August in a 14 in. (32 cm) pot. I put it in a sunny spot outside my shed but when the leaves started to turn black I moved it inside."

The leaves on your fig turned black late in the season as they normally fall at that time of year.

It was a good idea to move the plant into the shed for the winter – wrap a blanket around the pot if temperatures fall severely. When new buds break in spring and hard frosts are over, move it back outdoors. Nip out side shoots when four or five leaves have formed, to encourage twiggy growth and good crops.

Culling figs ❧

"I have heard that you should take off this season's figs in November as they will never swell properly and will fall off rather than ripen next summer. Is this true?"

What you say is true. Fig fruits that have not ripened by November are likely to fall off and can be removed. The figs for next year can be seen at the tips of the shoots as rounded, fat buds. These need to be protected from frost with bracken or insulating material otherwise they will not develop next year.

Regular figs ❧

"I planted a 'Brown Turkey' fig in 1985 in an enclosed bed against a south-facing wall. It normally produces a single fig in August but none last year. In the autumn it had a lot of second crop figs about the size of walnuts which I ripened in an airing cupboard. Can I do anything to persuade the tree to produce figs at the proper time?"

Fig trees will crop three times a year in warm Mediterranean climates and will often produce two crops in a warm greenhouse in this country. Unfortunately, outdoor figs usually fail to ripen properly because our summers are so short. Any unripe figs on your tree in the autumn will shrivel and fall off during the winter.

However, the tiny embryo figs situated near the tips of shoots often survive. In spring, these tiny protuberances, if protected from frost, will grow into figs and be fully ripe by August.

Successful fig culture depends on encouraging the fig to produce short growths from midsummer onwards. These will produce small embryo figs near their tips. You should pinch out the tips of the side shoots at five leaves, no later than the end of June. This will encourage the production of more shoots that should carry the embryo figs later on.

Pinch back about half the shoots (every other side shoot along the branches) one year and the other half the following year. This is necessary to accomplish regular cropping, otherwise you will have a crop of figs every other year. Protect the fig stems from frost with bracken or evergreen branches.

Disease-free gooseberries ❧

"We are about to plant up a new fruit cage and would welcome your suggestions on disease-free gooseberry varieties. In our previous garden our old bushes suffered a lot from leaf spot: is there a resistant type available?"

The gooseberry "Greenfinch" is resistant to both leaf spot and mildew so would be a good choice. Other varieties to consider include "Invicta" and "Rokula", both resistant to mildew, and "Pax" which is mildew resistant as well as being prickle-free.

Cordon gooseberries ❧

"I would like to grow some gooseberries as cordons with a single main stem. I have some rooted cuttings ready for planting out. How far apart should they be planted and how do I prune them?"

Plant your gooseberries about 1 ft (30 cm) apart. If you have more than one row, allow 5 ft (1.5 m) between them. After planting, cut back all the side growths on the lower 4 in. (10 cm) of the main stem so that it is left clear of shoots.

Cut back the leading shoot by about half its length and all the side shoots to within three buds of their base. Support the main stem to a vertical cane.

In subsequent years shorten the new growth on the leading shoot by about a quarter in the winter and cut back the side shoots to 3 in. Also, summer prune the side shoots in late June, shortening the new growths to five leaves. These are cut back further in winter.

Control gooseberry sawfly   ❧

"Around this time last year my two-year-old gooseberry bushes were deva-stated by caterpillars which stripped off every single leaf. What would the caterpillars have been and how do I prevent such damage this year?"

Gooseberry sawfly caterpillars would have been responsible. The adults are on the wing in April and May and insert eggs into the leaf tissue using their saw-like ovipositors – hence the name sawfly. They choose the lower leaves and ones in the centre of the bushes so often the damage goes unseen at first.

Examine the lower and central leaves for small holes as soon as flowering is over and, at the first sign of damage, spray forcibly with Phostrogen Safers Organic Insecticide, Tumblebug or Picket. Repeat if necessary should damage continue.

Two- and three-year-old bushes are most commonly attacked, so after this year your gooseberries should be at less risk of serious damage.

Under the weather   ❧

"Many of my gooseberry leaves fell early this year. I assumed it was the dry weather, but looking at some at the weekend there does seem to be some spotting as well. Is this the cause of the problem?"

The leaves sent in show quite a bad attack of leaf spot fungus. This can result in early leaf-fall and no doubt the hot, dry weather and the disease combined to bring the leaves off early. It may be worth giving the bushes a drenching application with a copper fungicide now to help clear up any infection, but try also to rake up and burn the fallen leaves. Spray again with copper or with Dithane 945 fungicide in spring when new growth starts. If you are planning any further plantings of gooseberries, I would suggest the variety "Greenfinch" which is resistant to both leaf spot as well as mildew.

Summer trim   ❧

"I planted some gooseberry bushes last winter. I understand that they need pruning in summer. Do I cut back the new growths?"

Gooseberry bushes need pruning both in winter and summer. From the middle of June onwards shorten all the new season's side shoots to five leaves.

In late winter cut these back further to one bud. This encourages a system of spur growths to develop. As they get older they will need thinning out in winter.

Increasing gooseberries ❧

"Is it possible to grow gooseberries from cuttings? When is the best time to take them and how long do they take to form roots?"

Gooseberries can certainly be grown from cuttings. These are best taken in late September or early October. Select firm growths made in the current season and make the cuttings 12–15 in. (30–38 cm) long. Trim the top of the cutting just above a bud and below a bud at the base. Dip the base of the cuttings into hormone rooting powder. Insert the cuttings by about half their depth in slits made in the ground with a spade. Pour some coarse sand in the base of the slits to assist rooting. It has been found that better rooting occurs if the cuttings are inserted through black polythene laid on the surface of the soil. It helps to conserve soil moisture and prevents weeds developing among the cuttings.

Rooting should have taken place 12 months later when the cuttings can be lifted after leaf fall and planted in their permanent positions.

Mildew control ❧

"Is there a really good way to control mildew on gooseberry plants? Each year our bushes are badly attacked and the fruit is ruined."

Mildew on gooseberries can be controlled, but several sprays will be needed. A sulphur fungicide can be used, such as Phostrogen Safer's Garden Fungicide, although some varieties of gooseberry are sulphur shy, so may suffer leaf damage. Unfortunately, this concerns the commonly grown varieties "Leveller" and "Careless". For best control, a systemic fungicide such as Supercarb or Murphy Systemic Action Fungicide should be used, with sprays just before the flowers open. Repeat applications at fruit set and 14 days later.

If you are planning to replace your gooseberry bushes shortly, it would be wise to choose "Greenfinch" which is resistant to mildew.

Spotty gooseberries ❧

"Our gooseberry plants didn't produce much of a crop this year and the leaves were spoiled by masses of dark spots. What would your advice be?"

Gooseberry leaf spot fungus would have been responsible for the spotting of the leaves, and the early leaf-fall that this induces can result in poor cropping in the following year.

If your bushes are getting on a bit we would suggest replacing them with new bushes of the variety "Greenfinch" which is resistant to leaf spot attack. Use a new site for the replanting.

Curious gooseberries

"Our gooseberry leaves have developed strange, orange, wart-like swellings. Can you help us to clear up whatever it is?"

The swellings are known as cluster cups and are the result of attacks by a species of rust fungus. As is the case with many rust fungi, this one alternates between different hosts during its life cycle, and cluster cup rust spends one stage on sedges (carex species).

Implementing good weed control, including the removal of any sedges in wet areas would help, as would cutting out infected shoots and pulling off any damaged leaves. Following this, spray with a copper fungicide now, and next year take preventative action by applying a copper fungicide just before flowering.

Seedling grapes

"I have grown some grape seedlings from white grape pips. They are in a container outside and are 4–7 in. (10–18 cm) high. How do I look after them?"

If the grape seeds were from imported white grapes, we do not think that they will fruit very well in this country. Being seedlings, they are an unknown quantity and will give varying results.

However, you may like to grow them for fun and see how they behave. After the leaves have fallen, pot the seedlings separately in 5 in. (13 cm) pots of good potting compost. Cut the stems back to within 1–2 in. (2.5–5 cm) of soil level. This is done to encourage strong new growth next spring. If you have a greenhouse, put the seedlings inside in March. Once the pots are full of roots, move the plants to larger pots.

Vine to Menorca

"I have a small house and garden in Menorca. If I took a 'Black Hamburg' vine out there would it flourish?"

There's no reason why a "Black Hamburg" grape vine should not flourish outside in Menorca. The vine itself is hardy in this country and it is one of the easiest grapes to grow, but it needs glass protection in this country to assist pollination of the flowers and to protect the developing grapes.

Vine cuttings ❧

"A friend has a 'Black Hamburg' grape vine and has offered me a cutting from it. When is the best time of year to take it?"

The easiest way to propagate a vine is to take hardwood cuttings. Wait until your friend has pruned the vine in late November or early December and use the prunings. Select pieces of firm stem made in the previous season. Cut them into lengths of 9 in. (23 cm) with sharp secateurs. Cut above a bud at the top and below a bud at the base and insert the cuttings outside in well-drained soil by about half their length. Put coarse sand in the base of the planting holes to encourage rooting. The cuttings will have rooted by the following autumn when they can be transplanted to their permanent positions.

If you have a heated greenhouse with a propagator, single bud cuttings root without difficulty. Select firm, plump buds. Cut the stems into pieces about 2 in. long with a bud in the centre. Press the cuttings horizontally into small pots of gritty soil with the buds uppermost. Stood in a warm and moist propagating case, the "vine eyes" will root in a few weeks. Once roots are made, pot the young plants in a good potting compost.

Vine mess ❧

"Our outdoor vine is growing well but appears to have a lot of fluffy white growths around the buds. What would this be and what action is needed please?"

Scale insects are responsible for the growths you are finding. The white substance surrounds the new nymphs as they crawl out from under the old parent scales. Scrape down the vine stems now and then spray with Mortegg tar oil to kill any remaining eggs.

If the wall behind the vine is pale-coloured, don't use the tar oil which could be staining, but spray with malathion in spring and summer.

Planting a grape vine ❧

"I have bought a young vine in a pot for planting in a border outside my greenhouse. Do I plant with the root ball intact or should the roots be spread out?"

So that the vine gets off to a good start, shake the soil from the roots in the pot and spread them out in the planting hole before covering them with soil. Mulch the surface of the soil with decayed compost in the spring to help keep it moist during the summer.

Mouldy grapes 🍂

"My greenhouse grapes are covered in mould and several are now shrivelled and brown. How can I prevent this next year?"

Powdery mildew has attacked your grapes. This fungal disease is encouraged by lack of water at the roots, but the spores are carried on air currents, so most grapes can be attacked. Grape powdery mildew normally starts on the leaves and then spreads to flowers and fruit.

Next year, therefore, take action at the first sign of the tell-tale white, powdery patches on the leaves. Action consists of spraying or dusting with sulphur or spraying with a systemic fungicide, giving three or four fortnightly applications.

Vine care 🍂

"My husband bought a vine over two years ago and although it is growing vigorously, it has not produced any fruit."

Your grape vine will not fruit until it is mature – about three years old – and has been pruned correctly.

Whether you are growing the vine in a greenhouse or outdoors to cover a wall, tie the laterals or side shoots – those growing from the main leading stem or rod – to horizontal wires 15 in. (38 cm) apart. In spring, rub out all but one bud at each joint (spur) and shorten laterals that spring from them to one leaf beyond the flower bunch. Reduce non-flowering shoots to six leaves. In November cut back all fruited and non-fruited shoots to within one or two buds of their base to encourage spurs (a cluster of several buds) to form.

Why not consult *The Fruit Expert* by David Hessayon for full details on pruning.

The great escape 🍂

"When we gathered the hazel nuts from some bushes in our garden, several of the shells were empty and had a circular holed drilled into them. What sort of creature could have made these holes?"

Hazel nut weevil (*Curculio nucum*) is the culprit. The weevil lays eggs in June by boring a hole in the shell whilst it is still soft and the larvae feed on the developing kernel. When fully fed the grubs squeeze out through the same hole, which will have increased in size as the hazel nut matures, and transfer to the soil where they pupate until the following May, emerging as adult weevils to start the cycle again.

If you wish to stop the damage, cultivating around the hazel bushes in winter will disturb and perhaps kill the pupae, whilst a late May spray with permethrin or pyrethrin will kill the egg-laying adult weevils.

Nut galls

"Do hazel buds suffer from blackcurrant big bud mite? Quite a lot of our hazel buds are swollen and don't open normally in spring. Is there any treatment, as I'm sure we must be missing some crop of nuts from the trouble."

Hazels don't get attacked by the blackcurrant gall mite, but they do have a gall mite of their very own! The damage is not normally too severe in terms of crop loss as generally there are plenty of other, healthy buds. There is no special control or treatment, just regular removal of buds or whole stems, as appropriate.

Just what are Jostaberries?

"Can you give me any information on Jostaberries?"

The Jostaberry is a hybrid between a blackcurrant and a gooseberry. They look like large blackcurrants and are well flavoured.

Kiwis will fruit, but only if conditions are right

"Can Kiwi fruits be grown to produce fruit in this country?"

Kiwi fruits, also known as Chinese gooseberries (*Actinidia chinensis*) can be grown successfully in southern England but fruiting can be uncertain as the young shoots and flowers are prone to damage from spring frosts. Male and female flowers are borne on separate plants and it is necessary to grow both to ensure the development of any fruit.

One of the best varieties to grow is "Hayward" which is late flowering and usually misses those damaging spring frosts.

Kiwi fruit plants are vigorous climbers and need plenty of space. Grow them against a warm south-facing wall and enjoy the creamy white flowers.

Waiting for loganberries ❧

"I planted a loganberry the year before last. Growth was good but no fruit formed last year. What can I do to ensure it fruits for me this year?"

The reason why you did not have any fruit from your loganberry in the first year after planting is that berries form on one-year-old canes. Those produced last year, therefore, should fruit this year.

All the new canes on your plant should be tied carefully to the supports. Once the fruit has been picked this year, cut out the old canes at ground level, retaining the new canes for fruiting in the following year.

Pruning loganberries ❧

"Can you tell me how and when to prune a loganberry?"

Prune loganberries in the autumn after picking the fruit. Cut out all the stems that have fruited, at ground level, and retain the strongest new canes made during the current season. Train these to the left and right as a fan, leaving space in the centre for the new canes that will be produced the following season. Tie the canes to horizontal wires with soft string.

Loganberry tips ❧

"When is the best time to take loganberry cuttings?"

Loganberries are not normally propagated from cuttings. The easiest way is to layer the tips of the shoots. Just peg the tip of a stem in the soil beside the main plant and it will root in a few weeks. You may find plants will often root on their own without assistance. Once rooted, cut off the new plant and replant it in its permanent position.

Non-fruiting loganberry ❧

"I planted a loganberry four years ago. Every summer it has good foliage and a mass of flowers which do not set fruit. Can you tell me why?"

Loganberries normally set fruit fairly easily because they are self-fertile, so it is surprising that your plant has never fruited. To get the best from it, give it plenty of moisture this summer and feed it with a balanced liquid plant food, such as Miracle-Gro, to encourage fruit and healthy growth. Water the roots and drench the foliage with the liquid feed.

Loquat fruit 🙌

"I have raised a loquat plant from seed. Can it be grown outside in this country and will it fruit?"

The loquat, *Eriobotrya japonica*, is cultivated mainly in warm climates. Although it can be grown outside in this country it is unlikely to produce fruits. This is mainly because it flowers in the winter and the blooms will be killed off by hard frosts. However, it is well worth growing for its handsome leaves.

Outdoors, plant it against a warm, south-facing wall, or grow it in a large pot or tub which could be kept under glass in the winter but stood outside for the summer. The white, hawthorn-like flowers are sweetly scented – a real late winter treat.

Exotic fruit 🙌

"Is it possible to grow a mango from a kernel and can ginger be grown from a root?"

As mangoes are normally picked underripe and left to mature in transit, the stone will probably not be fertile. However, it may be worth putting it to the test.

Half bury the seed horizontally in a pot of seed and cutting compost and water it in. Keep it moist in an airing cupboard. When the stone splits and a shoot emerges, move the plant to a warm, sunny windowsill.

Ginger, on the other hand, is normally easy to propagate from a section of root. Plant it shallowly in a tray or pot of gritty cutting compost and keep it warm and moist. Roots soon form and new shoots will appear.

Ripe medlars 🙌

"On a recent gardening television programme, medlar fruits were discussed. Is it an ornamental tree or is it simply grown for its fruit, and are they good to eat?"

Medlars are small, wide-spreading trees which make good subjects for a large lawn. The large white flowers, which appear in May and June, are followed in the autumn by unusual brown fruits. Leave them on the tree until October, after the first frosts, and store them in a cool place so that they can "blet" or become fully ripe. The full flavour of the fruits does not develop until they are overripe.

They are not to everyone's taste eaten raw but they can be made into a delicious jelly. "Nottingham" and "Large Russian" are by far the best varieties to grow.

Melons under glass ❧

"I have an unheated greenhouse and would like to grow some melons this year. What is a good variety and when should the seed be sown?"

As your greenhouse is not heated sow the melon seed in mid to late April, ideally in a heated propagator set at a minimum temperature of 18°C (65°F). Failing this, sow the seed indoors in a warm room. Sow two seeds together in a small pot and when the seedlings appear, select the strongest and pull out the weaker one.

Plant the young melons in a greenhouse border or in growing bags or large pots of good potting soil. Train the stems to canes or wires up to the greenhouse roof.

A good early variety to grow is "Sweetheart". "Ogen" is another good early melon.

Netting melons ❧

"I am growing some melon plants in my greenhouse. A number of fruits have set; how many should be left on each plant? And what is the best way of supporting the fruit as it swells?"

Now that your melons are swelling, select four of similar size on each plant and remove the remainder. If they are of unequal size, they will swell unevenly. Only allow one fruit per lateral shoot.

The individual fruits need supporting as they swell. Ideally, use nets to hold the melons, tied at the top to wires under the greenhouse roof.

Melon failure ❧

"Last summer I grew some melon plants in my greenhouse which did not do very well. I planted them in a growing bag at the end of June under the greenhouse staging. At first only male flowers appeared and when female flowers showed, they did not set properly. I want to try again this year. Can you tell me where I went wrong?"

We suspect that your melons did not get enough light under the greenhouse staging. This year we suggest that you put the growing bags on top of the staging. Sow the seed in early April in a temperature of at least 18°C (65°f).

Plant in the growing bags when the plants have made four leaves. Maintain a high and humid atmosphere. Train the stem of each plant up the greenhouse roof and tie it to wire supports. When it reaches the top, nip out the tip. Side shoots will form. Pinch out the tips of each one at three leaves.

The flowers are produced on the side shoots. Pollinate the female flowers with the male flowers. When four of equal size have set, pinch out the remainder. Only allow four fruits to form on each plant.

Good varieties to grow are "Galia" and "Sweetheart".

Eaten alive ❧

"Our young melon plants, standing on the floor in our heated greenhouse, are being eaten. We cannot find any pests on the leaves. Please help."

The damage could be due to slugs or snails, or to woodlice. If slime trails are present, they would indicate the former.

Check under the pots for pests as they tend to feed mainly at night and hide by day. If you scatter Slug Guard pellets lightly around the pots and over the greenhouse floor, the damage to your melons should cease.

Mad about mulberries ❧

"I want to plant a mulberry tree in my garden. What sort of soil and situation is best for the tree? How long will I have to wait before I can expect fruit? Are there any special varieties?"

One of the best mulberries is the variety "Chelsea". This is available from Reads Nursery, Hales Hall, Loddon, Norfolk. Plant it in good, well-drained soil and choose a warm, sunny situation. Young trees begin fruiting usually about three years after planting. Mulberries can also be grown in large containers.

Sunshine fruits ❧

"I have a nectarine tree in my garden which is now about seven years old. It produces healthy leaves but does not fruit. Could you give me some advice?"

The nectarine, like the peach and apricot, needs great summer heat to ripen the wood. For this reason it does best grown under glass or on a south-facing wall. It should be grown fan-trained against the wall with the main branches spread out evenly.

The fruits are borne on good lateral shoots of the previous season's growth. They should be tied flat to the wall between the main branches. The fruit buds on these shoots will blossom and carry fruits, provided the flowers are successfully pollinated. You will need to protect the open flowers from cold winds and carry out pollination on sunny days, using a rabbit's tail or camel-hair brush. To protect the blossom, drape a covering of horticultural fleece over the branches during the blossoming period.

By the end of the season, each fruit-bearing shoot, having done its work, is cut out and a replacement shoot is tied in its place.

Full details on growing all kinds of fruit can be found in *The Fruit Garden Displayed* by Harry Baker, published by the Royal Horticultural Society.

Lemon aid ❧

"I have grown two lemon plants from pips indoors. They are 24 in. (0.6 m) high and are in 5 in. pots. Should I transfer them to larger pots? What feed is suitable?"

Lemon seedlings often take several years before they start flowering and fruiting. To help ripen the shoots, stand the plants outside for the summer in a sheltered and sunny spot.

From September to late May keep your plants in a light place in an unheated room indoors. They are unlikely to survive the winter outside in Yorkshire. Water the plants sparingly in winter but freely in summer.

Special feeds for citrus plants are available from Global Orange Groves UK, PO Box 644, Poole, Dorset BH17 9YB.

Chewed citrus ❧

"The leaves of my pot-grown calamondin orange tree are being eaten away, particularly the youngest leaves. What is doing this and how should I treat it?"

Wingless weevils, most probably the vine weevil, are responsible. The adult weevils feed at night and by day hide in the compost so are rarely seen. If the roots are also being eaten away the weevil grubs will be present as well.

These are best controlled by a "friendly" eelworm, now being sold through selected garden centres and by mail order. To control adults only, dust the compost with Sybol dust.

Yellowing lemons

"I am having trouble with my lemon tree. It is growing in a large pot and at the moment it is kept in a conservatory which is heated to exclude frost. During the summer it is stood outside. A number of the leaves have turned yellow and fallen off. How do I prevent more leaves falling?"

We suspect that the leaves on your lemon tree are turning yellow and falling because of incorrect feeding. It is now felt that feeding should be carried out both in summer and winter. A high nitrogen feed is recommended for the summer and a more balanced feed for the winter. Don't forget: trace elements are also important.

Citrus trees do not like an alkaline soil which can result in yellowing of the leaves. It should be slightly acid. An alkaline soil can be made more acid with flowers of sulphur; apply two teaspoonfuls evenly to the soil for each plant and repeat in one month's time.

Red spider mites

"I have an orange tree which is about seven years old. Since I put it outside for the summer it has developed a cobwebby substance on its leaves. I cannot see any insects. Can you tell me what is causing this?"

Your orange tree is probably being attacked by red spider mites. These are very small and can only just be seen with the naked eye. If you look through a hand lens you will see the tiny mites moving around among the cobwebby threads. They thrive in hot and dry conditions and spraying the plant each day with water will help to discourage them. However, you will probably have to spray with malathion insecticide to get rid of them.

Fruit can be a real headache

"I suffer from bad migraine, and citric acid is one of the worst triggers, giving me a severe eight-hour attack. But I can't find a list of fruit and vegetables that contain citric acid other than the obvious lemons, oranges, grapefruit and limes. Can you help me?"

Apart from the citrus fruits you have listed, a wide range of soft fruits such as gooseberries, raspberries, etc. contain citric acid, although not in the same quantities. We suggest that you give all soft fruits a wide berth and even treat rhubarb and spinach with caution. It may help to discuss your problem with a homoeopathic practitioner, who might be able to suggest a remedy to you.

Passion fruit   ❧

"I am very fond of the passion fruits that can be purchased at supermarkets. Can they be grown in this country? I have a passion flower climber in my garden but it produces yellow fruits which are not very pleasant to eat."

There are several different passion flower species that are grown for their fruits in the tropics. The one most commonly seen is the purple passion fruit or granadilla, *Passiflora edulis*. This can be grown in a frost-free greenhouse or conservatory. A single plant grown in a 12 in. (30cm) pot is capable of producing up to 50 fruits.

Another kind, *P. quadrangularis* or giant granadilla, has spectacular flowers and can be grown in a small greenhouse if it is kept in a large pot. The flowers need hand-pollinating to set fruit. Seed of several species is available from Chiltern Seeds, Bortree Stile, Ulverston, Cumbria LA12 7PB. Plants are also available from Reads Nursery, Hales Hall, Loddon, Norfolk NR14 6QW.

Peach seedlings   ❧

"I have managed to raise three peach trees from seed. When should I plant them in the open and what type of soil do they need? At what height should I begin shaping them?"

We assume that your peach seedlings are in small pots. Once roots fill the pots, repot the seedlings into 6 in. pots using a good potting compost. Later move the plants on into 9 in. (13 cm) pots. Stand the plants outside in a warm sunny spot. When they are well established in their pots, feed them each week during the summer with a liquid fertilizer.

Plant the trees in the open at the end of the second season after the leaves have fallen. To grow well, peaches need fertile, well-drained soil. They will not thrive in shallow, chalky soils.

Prune the tree in early spring. Cut back the leading stem to where there are several lateral shoots about 2 ft (0.6 m) above ground level. Shorten the lateral shoots by about half their length to outward facing buds. Remove surplus lateral shoots. The trees are likely to be four to five years old before they start to fruit. As they are seedlings the quality of the fruit will be variable.

New peach tree   ❧

"Earlier this year I purchased a 'Peregrine' peach tree and planted it against the west-facing wall of my potting shed. It is about 3ft high. To train it

laterally, I pruned the fore and aft branches, leaving five laterals to the right and six to the left. These were carefully tied to wires. I now find that the nearest half of each branch to the trunk is in leaf but the outer halves have only tiny buds and look as if they are dying. In between the branches, new green shoots are sprouting but no blossom. Your advice please?"

It is not unusual for some of the stems on a new peach tree to wither at the tips in the first spring after planting. We suggest that these are shortened to where a new young shoot is appearing. This should be tied into place to serve as a replacement stem. It is not a good idea to allow a new tree to flower and fruit the first season, as it must be allowed to become well established before taking on the strain of bearing fruit. As your wall is only 3 ft (1 m) high you may find it difficult to train the shoots evenly. It is best to train the stems in a fan. Remember that the peach flowers and fruits on stems made in the previous season. After picking the fruit, the old stems that have carried fruit should be cut out and the new young shoots tied into their place.

Peach cuttings ❧

"We have a 5 in. (12 cm) rooted cutting of a peach tree. Every book says that peaches should be grafted. Why?"

Good question. Peaches are not usually easy to propagate from cuttings. It is more economical to bud named varieties on a suitable plum rootstock which controls the ultimate size of the tree.

The "Brompton" rootstock produces vigorous trees and "St Julien" is not so vigorous. Good results have also been had by raising peaches from the stones taken from imported fruit. However, seedlings are variable and many can be inferior.

It is better to purchase a named variety, such as "Peregrine" or "Rochester", which is known to produce good quality fruit.

Plum rootstocks sometimes produce sucker growths with roots from the base. If your cutting was one of these it will, of course, not produce peaches.

Potted peach ❧

"My garden is not large but I have a sunny patio. Could I grow a peach tree in a large pot or container? If so, what variety would you recommend?"

Peaches can be grown successfully in a large container and your sunny patio should be ideal for it. Good varieties to grow are

"Peregrine", ripening in late August, and "Rochester", ripening in early August.

A large 10–12 in. (25–30 cm) pot is needed. Make sure that a layer of broken pots or rubble is placed in the bottom for drainage. For potting, use John Innes No. 3. The compost in the pot is likely to dry out rapidly in the summer and special attention must be given to watering. Also feed the tree each week in the summer with liquid fertilizer.

Alternatively, add a slow-release fertilizer to the potting compost each year. One application will last for six months.

Peach nightmare ❧

"A lot of my peaches this year were split down the middle, often the stone was also split in half. There were lots of earwigs in the fruits, but I don't think they were the main cause. Any ideas?"

Your peaches were affected by a growth disorder known simply as "split stone". It is not caused by pest or disease but by a combination of several factors including a lack of calcium, fluctuating water supplies and lack of complete pollination. Earwigs feed and shelter in the damaged areas but they are not the major cause.

Apply a light dressing of garden lime over the soil in winter, then as the flowers open, hand-pollinate with a fine brush or rabbit tail. Incorporate a rose fertilizer to the soil and ensure adequate water is available at the roots.

Fan train or not?

"I have a peach tree which is about 10 years old and planted close to a south-facing wall. Rather belatedly I would like to fan-train it. How should this be done?"

A fan-trained peach tree should have a short main stem with two low side branches carrying the remaining shoots. It will be difficult to turn your wall-trained tree into a fan shape and severe pruning may cause dieback which may ultimately mean replacing the tree.

If you still want to have a go, carry out the reshaping over two or three years, thinning out over-vigorous shoots each year. As peaches are susceptible to silver leaf and canker diseases, prune in June and July to discourage infection.

If the tree's initial response to pruning is good, follow the pruning instructions in a good fruit tree book such as the *RHS Manual of Pruning and Training* by C. D. Brickell and published by Dorling Kindersley.

Peach poser ❧

"Visiting a stately home recently (I had better not say which one!) I saw quite a lot of leaf damage in the peach house, due I believe, to red spider feeding. The stippling on the leaves was severe, but also on the leaves were what looked like granules of vermiculite. Could you suggest what this would have been?"

The granules would indeed have been of vermiculite. At least one brand of red spider biological control, the predator *Phytoseiulus*, is supplied in small tubes of vermiculite and the tube contents are then lightly scattered over the infested leaves.

The predatory mites do a very good control job, but of course the leaf damage will remain until leaf-fall.

Mouldy peaches ❧

"My young peach tree has cropped for the first time this year, but a few of the fruits developed a blue-coloured mould shortly after picking. Is this something I could have prevented?"

This is blue mould, a species of penicillium, chiefly a wound parasite, infecting tissue injured in some way, such as wasp damage, bruising during picking, or by bird pecking.

If storing any fruit, select ones that are completely free from skin damage, and keep them slightly apart. There is no practical way to prevent this occurring, but you were quite unlucky to have an attack.

Peach of a problem ❧

"Some of our peaches started to rot on the tree, even before they were fully ripe. The fruits developed rings of buff-coloured growths. What can we do next year to prevent such losses?"

The rotting would be due to the brown rot fungus. This mainly attacks damaged tissue, so would infect any areas attacked by wasps, birds or damaged by hailstones. Prevention is rather difficult, but catching wasps in a trap and using netting to deter birds may help a little.

Planting fruit trees ❧

"I want to plant some apple, plum and pear trees. I have read not to bury the union, at the point of grafting, on a pear tree. Does this apply to other fruit trees?"

What you have read is correct. The union at the point of grafting on all fruit trees must be kept several inches above soil level when a tree is planted. If the union is buried it is likely that the top part of the tree will form roots and the beneficial effects of the rootstock will be lost.

Assuming that the union is buried on a tree of "Bramley's Seedling" grafted on a dwarfing stock, it is likely that the tree will begin to grow very vigorously and the dwarfing effects of the rootstock will be lost.

Pear pair failure

"I have two pear trees, the newer one 'Conference', planted to help the first one set a better crop. This year, however, both lots of fruit were odd, swelling early but then turning black and shrivelling. Can you provide a reason and a cure please?"

Attack by pear midge would have been responsible for the damage you describe. Up to 30 eggs are laid in the flower buds as they start to show white petals and the grubs feed inside the fruitlets. The young pears swell encouragingly but then turn black and shrivel as you mention.

Control next year by spraying with Tumblebug or Sybol as the first white petals appear and then by removing and burning any fruitlets that do appear infested. Treat in the following year also, but that should hopefully put an end to the local infestation.

Williams pear

"I planted a small tree of 'Williams' Bon Chrétien' pear last winter. It has settled down well and has a number of small fruits on it. When should the fruit be picked?"

As your pear tree was planted only last winter you should not allow it to fruit this year. The fruitlets that have formed will in all probability fall off as the tree is not yet strong enough to carry fruit. It must be allowed to make a good root system before taking on the strain of bearing fruit. After two to three years you can let some fruit mature. They should be ready for picking at the end of August but will not keep much beyond the middle of September.

Pear for Bristol

"Can you tell me anything about a pear called 'Bristol Cross'? As I live near Bristol it is a variety that appeals to me."

"Bristol Cross" is an excellent pear having been raised in the 1930s at Long Ashton Research Station. Its parents are "Williams' Bon Chrétien" and "Conference", to which it is very similar.

The fruit is ready for picking in the middle of September and is ripe in early October – they are juicy and delicious to eat. It has resistance to scab disease but its pollen is poor and it is not good as a pollinator.

Pear to please ❧

"I want to grow a well-flavoured pear. Can you recommend a good variety to grow? Do I need more than one variety for pollination?"

A pear with excellent flavour is *Pyrus* "Beurre Superfin". It is ready for eating in October and should be picked in late September.

Pear trees should be grown near other suitable varieties to ensure a good set of fruit. "Conference", "Beurre Hardy" and "Williams' Bon Chrétien" are all good pollinators.

Dimpled pears ❧

"I had my pear tree professionally pruned this year but the crop was very poor. The pears were full of dimples and the flesh under these areas was hard and gritty."

The misshapen appearance and sunken spots are the result of attack by the stony pit virus. Sadly there is no way to eradicate the virus and the only satisfactory action would be to remove the tree, replacing it with a virus-free pear in another part of the garden.

Rotting pears ❧

"We had a poor set of pears this last year and most of those that did set became rounded. They then turned black and rotted, whilst only thumbnail size. Is there any winter action we can take?"

Pear midge was responsible for the damage to the pears, the poor set probably being due to adverse weather at flowering time. This reduces pollinator activity. If the pear tree is growing in bare soil, and not in grass, cultivating lightly around the tree may expose the overwintering larvae.

Best control is by spraying the tree at late green bud/early white bud stage with a permethrin insecticide such as Long-Last or Tumblebug.

Browned off ❧

"Our pear tree crops very well every year, but quite a lot of fruits are spoiled by turning brown and rotting, both before picking and in store. What causes this, and how can we prevent it?"

Brown rot fungus is the main culprit but this is primarily a wound parasite, infecting damaged areas on the fruit which is caused by pear scab, codling moth and often by wasps.

Control pear scab with Supercarb or Murphy Systemic Action Fungicide, which will both also reduce brown rot attack. Codling needs to be prevented in early summer, the best way being by hanging a Trappit codling moth trap in the tree when flowering has just finished. Wasp traps are available which may divert these insects from the pears, but if any wasp nests can be found, destruction will be helpful.

At leaf-fall, remove any mummified pears remaining on the tree as these would act as a source of infection for the following year.

Pear drop ❧

"For the last few years my pear trees have been disappointing. The pears swell up quickly after petal fall but then turn black and fall off. Inside the tiny pears are numerous white maggots. Is it possible to prevent attacks this year?"

The pest responsible is pear midge and it should be possible to prevent any serious attack this year. The adult midge lays her eggs in the flowers just before or just after they open and they soon hatch into the yellow-white larvae which feed inside the developing pear fruitlets. As many as 100 larvae have been found in a single fruitlet.

As you mention, the infested pears swell rapidly at first, usually into a rounded shape, but then blacken after a few weeks. The larvae enter the ground when fully fed and pupate there until the next year.

The damage can be prevented by a spray of permethrin, such as Picket, Tumblebug or Long-Last at early white bud stage. If the trees are in bare earth, the larvae may also be disturbed and killed in winter by soil cultivations.

Blistery pears ❧

"Every year our pear leaves have lots of spotty pimples on them, starting out green but turning red, then blackish. What are they, and can we stop them this year?"

The damage is due to attack by the pear leaf blister mite. There is no satisfactory cure, as none of the available sprays has any worthwhile effect.

If your pear trees are still quite small, then pick off all the infested leaves you can see. Although the fruits can also be spotted in severe cases, the attack is generally more unsightly than damaging. The mites overwinter under the bud scales, so severe pruning will reduce their numbers.

Summer pruning pears

"There are some cordon-trained pears in the garden that I have taken over. They have made lots of growth this year. I am told that I should prune them in the summer. Is this correct and when should it be done?"

Yes, your cordon pears do require to be pruned in summer. This should be done when the bases of the new growths have hardened and turned dark brown in July and August. Cut back all shoots longer than 9 in. (23 cm), arising from the main stem, to three leaves of the basal cluster of leaves.

Side shoots appearing on old spur growths should be cut back to one leaf above the basal cluster of leaves. The shoots that are shorter than 9 in. can be left unpruned. Summer pruning should be carried out only when the base of each shoot has hardened. If it is done too early, new unwanted growth may develop.

Asian imports

"I have purchased and eaten Asian pears obtained from a supermarket. Can they be grown in this country?"

Asian pears, many of Japanese origin, can be grown in this country but they do not often produce worthwhile fruits, which often tend to remain small with little flavour, particularly in a poor summer. It is better to grow the well-known European pears of which there are many excellent varieties.

Pear canker

"Can apple canker also attack pears? I thought I had cut out all the disease from my old apple tree but now I'm finding some dying shoots on my new pear tree. The damage looks identical to apple canker."

Both apples and pears (and also poplar and willow) are attacked by the same canker species, *Nectria galligena*. Cutting out affected shoots is the best treatment for a young pear tree to ensure the disease is removed completely.

It would be worth spraying the pear tree, and the apple as well, with a copper fungicide at the start of leaf-fall and again half way through leaf-fall. These sprays protect the leaf scars from canker infection, one of the main points of entry of the disease.

Gritty pears

"My 'Conference' pears this last year produced fruits that were full of dimples. When eaten, they were very gritty around the dimpled areas. Is this something that we can prevent happening to this year's crop?"

The dimpling and gritty particles were due to attack by a virus disease, giving a condition known as stony pit. Sadly there is no recommended cure and the usual advice would be to grub out and burn the tree.

In some countries, fruit growers cut back infected trees quite severely and then graft with "Williams' Bon Chrétien" shoots. Williams' pears do not show the symptoms of stony pit, and you may be able to find a nurseryman, or skilled local amateur fruit grower, who could carry out this top working for you.

Wilting fruit

"Several of our fruit trees this spring produced flower buds but they shrivelled up and didn't open. This affects both apples and plums, so we don't think frost was responsible. Can you help please?"

The problem appears to be blossom wilt which is a form of the brown rot fungus and it can attack apples, pears, plums and cherries, both the fruiting and the ornamental types. The infection can pass from the flowers and leaf clusters down into the stems which become cankered and then die.

The best treatment is to prune out as many of the affected shoot tips as possible, removing the dead blossom remains or dead leaves. This is a fiddly job, but well worth the effort. Then, in winter, give a good drenching spray with Mortegg or Clean-Up which should kill any fruiting pustules of the fungus, and so prevent attacks next year.

Asian pears

"Can you tell me anything about Asian pears. How do they compare with our usual pears and can they be grown successfully in this country?"

Asian pears are natives of China and Japan where they have been grown for centuries. They are also now being grown successfully in California and Australia. Imported fruits are also sold in supermarkets. The white flesh is sweet and juicy.

Trees can be grown in this country but the quality of the fruit produced is not usually good. In poor summers the fruit is small and of poor flavour. We feel you will have much better results with the well-tried varieties such as "Conference" and "Doyenne du Comice".

Scabby spray

"Last year our pears were covered with rough, dark coloured marks which spoiled their appearance. I think the problem is pear scab. Could you confirm, and give some advice on prevention this year?"

Yes, the problem you describe would have been pear scab. The best control would be obtained by spraying in April with Nimrod-T, Supercarb or Murphy Systemic Action Fungicide.

Repeat this spray two or three times (perhaps more if the spring is wet) to protect the leaves and young fruits from the damaging early scab infection.

Winter moths

"Are grease bands still a valuable method of pest control on fruit trees?"

Putting grease bands around the trunks of apple and some other fruit trees, or applying special grease such as Trappit to the trunk itself is aimed mainly at stopping winter moths. With winter moth, and the related March moth and mottled umber moth, the female has no functional wings so must climb up the trunk to lay her eggs. The grease prevents this. Most of the egg-laying will be done in November or December, so you have probably missed the chance this year. To control the caterpillars hatching from any eggs already laid, spray with a contact insecticide such as pyrethrum or permethrin next spring. Use the grease band method next October.

Pear problem

"We have lost a lot of our crop from our young pear tree this year. The fruit turns brown and gets covered in cream-coloured spots, and wasps eat out the flesh. Can you tell us if the wasps or the rot come first, and how we can stop the problem?"

The wasps normally start the damage by eating into the top shoulder of the pear. This damaged area is then susceptible to attack by the brown rot fungus. This is the cause of both the rot and the cream-coloured spots, which are the spore-bearing pustules of the fungus.

There is no real way to prevent wasps, other than seeking out and killing any nests found, generally in the soil under hedges, or in roof spaces.

Brown rot can be prevented from attacking by spraying a few times with Supercarb or Murphy's Systemic Action Fungicide. Next year, you may think it would be worth enclosing a number of the fruits in plastic bags, or sleeves cut from nylons, and tied to the shoot above the pear and also below the pear. This would keep wasps out and if the tree is not too large it would be possible to protect all the pears in this way.

Plum pollinator

"I have a 'Cambridge Gage' plum which has blossomed but does not set fruit. A tree of 'Early Transparent Gage' is planted nearby as a pollinator but it does not seem to have much effect. What is a good pollinator to plant for 'Cambridge Gage'?"

We are sorry to learn that your "Cambridge Gage", despite having "Early Transparent" nearby, failed to set fruit after flowering. We suggest that you consider "Victoria". Alternatively, there is "Marjorie's Seedling", "Giant Prune" and "Kirke's Blue" which should be good pollinators.

Plum rust

"My plum tree leaves are covered in yellow spots on the top surface and orange, rusty spots underneath. I believe this is called rust. Does it harm the tree and, if so, are there any control measures to take? The tree is quite big."

The disease you describe is the plum rust fungus, *Tranzschelia discolor*. The attack can result in early leaf-fall but this doesn't seem to have any noticeable effect on the tree's cropping ability. There are no practical control measures which you could take apart from checking on any anemones in your garden. The plum rust fungus alternates between plum and anemone, so destroying any infected anemone plants would help the plum tree a little.

Plum-less

"We have a four-year-old, 14 ft-tall cherry plum. It is regularly covered in blossom in early spring. In order to encourage the fruit to set, we have been

advised to apply a tourniquet of wire around the trunk. How and when should this be done?"

As your myrobalan cherry plum (*Prunus cerasifera*) flowers well, we suspect that it is not setting fruit because the blossoms are being damaged by spring frosts or cold winds. This plum flowers very early and is prone to frost damage. If the tree was shorter, you might have been able to erect a frost barrier to protect the flowers.

We do not think it would be a good idea to put a wire tourniquet around the trunk. This would do more harm than good.

Winter in March ❧

"The leaves on my plum tree are being eaten away by green caterpillars. I have picked them off the lower shoots, but although the tree is not too tall I cannot, at age 81, get to all the branches. Ready-to-use sprays are too small for my needs, so what alternative could you suggest?"

The caterpillars would be those of the winter moth, which can feed through until the end of May. You could spray the tree now with Picket or Tumblebug which would give a good control before the flowers open. If you are in an early area and the blossoms are already beginning to open out, delay spraying until after the spring flowering period.

Plum aphid ❧

"My plum tree leaves became covered on the undersides with a grey form of greenfly shortly after flowering last summer. Please help me to avoid a similar problem this time."

Mealy plum aphid would have been the pest you found, and attacks normally occur from late May to late June. For an existing attack a systemic insecticide would be best. There is little that can be done to prevent the aphid, but attacks are not always severe. In winter, a spray of Mortegg or Clean-Up would kill the overwintering eggs of this pest.

Plum crazy ❧

"My son's plum leaves have developed lots of little swellings, mainly underneath the leaf. Is this something that he should be taking action against?"

The swellings are the work of a tiny gall mite, and it is more commonly associated with blackthorn leaves. No great damage is being done, so no action is needed.

Sticky plums ❧

"I have had excellent results from my dwarf 'Victoria' plum but sticky globules appear at the base of the plums as they ripen."

Gumming of plum fruits is a common problem. It is not a result of disease but is a natural process as the plum tries to heal a small split in the skin. This can be a result of insect injury or the skin can crack if the soil dried out at some time.

Keep the soil watered in dry weather, particularly when the fruit is swelling.

Thinning is all that's needed ❧

"I have a large plum tree which seems healthy. When do I prune it?"

Plum trees do not need much pruning. Any thinning out of old growths should be done in June.

Plums must not be pruned during the winter months as silver leaf fungus disease spores are active at this time and can infect a tree through the pruning wounds.

Sick plum just needs a prune ❧

"Some of my developing plums are a very strange shape, being flattened and hollow on one side. There doesn't appear to be any stone in the affected plums and they look most odd. Is this something that will spread to the rest of the crop and is there any control?"

The condition you describe is known as pocket plum. It is the result of infection by a fungal disease related to peach leaf curl and crops up from time to time without any apparent rhyme or reason. Diseased plums develop a white coating of spores which can spread the disease although often the problem does not occur in successive years. This is just as well as there is no recognized control other than pruning out the twigs bearing affected plums.

Take care when pruning your fruit trees!

Victoria plum in trouble ❧

"I have a three-year-old Victoria plum tree which has been very unhealthy this year. For several months the leaves have been covered in brown spots; the spots then fall out leaving a lacy-looking leaf. What is wrong and what can I do about it please?"

The spotting and subsequent holing are the result of attack by bacterial canker.

Sometimes the leaf damage is the only symptom, in other cases the canker can girdle the shoots, often in the crotch area, killing whole branches.

The infection gains entry mainly through the leaf scars left as the leaves fall, and this can be reduced by spraying with a copper fungicide such as Bordeaux Mixture. Ideally, spray in mid-August, mid-September and mid-October to induce early leaf-fall and then to protect the leaf scars.

Quince leaf blight ❧

"The leaves on my edible quince tree are developing reddish spots on both sides of the leaf which gradually darken and become black. This also happened last year when the spots spread to the fruit as well. Is there any control at this time of year?"

The spotting is due to attack by a fungus known as quince leaf blight, which is commonest in wet seasons. It can result in early leaf-fall and loss of vigour, as well as the fruit damage you report.

Look for any cankers on the stems immediately (and again in winter) and cut these out. A spray now with a copper fungicide (which could cause some leaf damage of its own) or a systemic fungicide should cut down any later attacks.

Pears are also susceptible to leaf blight, particularly when in close proximity to diseased quince trees.

New raspberries ❧

"Can you tell me when is the best time to plant new raspberry canes and how far apart should the canes be spaced? Is it best to have the rows running east to west or north to south?"

Plant raspberry canes anytime in the winter but no later than the end of March. Avoid planting when the ground is very wet or frozen. Space the canes 15 in. (38 cm) apart in the row. If you should plant more than one row allow 6 ft (1.8 m) between them. It is preferable to have the rows running north to south so that either side receives roughly the same amount of light for even growth. After planting cut all the canes to within 9 in. of ground level.

Raspberry mix-up ❧

"I planted a row of 'Glen Clova' raspberries last spring and cut the canes down to ground level. Strong, new canes formed and were trained to a wire fence. I was surprised to find that four of the 12 plants started fruiting in October and continued producing fruit until mid-November. Is this unusual?"

It seems that four of your summer-fruiting "Glen Clova" raspberry canes are, in fact, an autumn-fruiting variety. Your best option is to assume that you have some autumn fruiters and leave the cropped canes until February when they should be cut back to 2 in. (5 cm) from the ground.

The remaining canes should be pruned after fruiting in late summer when they should be reduced to 2 in. (5 cm) from their base.

Raspberry canes ❧

"A neighbour has promised to give me some raspberry canes for my garden. How far apart should they be planted and do the canes need pruning?"

If your neighbour has had the raspberry canes for a number of years they could be affected with virus and not worth transplanting in your garden.

Viruses gradually weaken raspberries and they are spread largely by greenfly. Some experts would recommend that it would be better for you to purchase new canes that you can rely on being from certified virus-free stock.

Plant the canes in well-manured ground. Spread out the roots and cover them with about 2 in. (5 cm) of soil. Space the canes 15 in. (38 cm) apart and if you have more than one row allow 6 ft between them. After planting cut back each cane, just above a bud, about 9 in. (23 cm) above ground level.

Autumn raspberries ❧

"Which raspberries fruit in the autumn?"

There are several good autumn-fruiting raspberries. "Autumn Bliss" is a heavy cropper and has received an Award of Garden Merit from the Royal Horticultural Society. "Ruby" is another good variety.

Cut the canes down to ground level each winter.

Picking raspberries ❧

"My raspberry canes are fruiting for the first time and the berries will soon be ready for picking. Should they be picked with the plugs still on or removed and what is the average weight of fruit that I can expect to pick?"

It is usual to pick raspberries without the plugs unless the fruit is needed for showing, when it is best to leave the plugs and stalks on the fruits. Raspberries for showing must be handled very carefully to avoid bruising. Pick the berries with scissors. Yields vary according to variety and season but $4\frac{1}{2}$ lb per yard of row is a good average.

Pruning raspberries ❧

"Can you tell me how and when to prune raspberries?"

Prune summer-fruiting raspberries as soon as the fruit has been picked. Cut out all the old canes that have carried fruit down to ground level. Select eight of the strongest new canes made this season and tie them into place on the supporting wires. Any thin, weak canes should be cut out at ground level. The canes that are retained will fruit next summer.

Raspberry suckers ❧

"My neighbour has a bed of raspberries and the suckers are coming up in my flower bed. Is there any way I can get rid of them without damaging the raspberry canes?"

As the raspberry suckers are appearing among your flowers it will not be possible to use weed killers without harming them. The best thing to do is to hoe them out as soon as they appear.

It is natural for raspberries to send out suckers. When raspberries are grown in rows against wires the suckers that appear between the rows have to be hoed out whenever they are seen otherwise they would become a tangled mess.

Pale raspberry leaves ❧

"Many of our raspberry leaves are showing patches of yellow and we would like to take appropriate action to correct the problem. Help please."

If the yellowing is fairly even and between the veins, with the veins themselves remaining green, then nutrient deficiency would be the problem. Should the yellowing have started at the base of the canes a shortage of magnesium is indicated and if at the tops then iron deficiency is indicated. Supply magnesium with a light dressing of Epsom salts to the soil and a spray using 2 oz. per 1 gal. (57 g per 4.5 l) of water. For iron deficiency, water leaves and soil with Miracid or Sequestrene. More serious would be an irregular yellow spotting with some leaf distortion. This indicates raspberry mosaic virus, for which there is no control. If many canes are affected it would be best to dig them all up after cropping this year.

Start off new canes in a different position, selecting a newer variety such as "Glen Moy", "GLen Ample", "Malling Leo" or "Malling Delight", all of which are resistant to attacks by aphids. Mosaic virus is normally spread by sapsucking aphids.

Rotten raspberries ❧

"A lot of our raspberries were spoiled this year by raspberry beetle grubs being found inside at picking time. Is there anything we can do in the winter time to reduce damage next year?"

The raspberry beetle spends the winter months as a pupa in an earthen cell in the soil, constructed by the larva after it has left the fruit. The larvae move down to between 2–8 in. (5–20 cm) into the soil to make the cells. If you cultivate carefully around the canes you may be able to find and remove, or to damage, the cells to prevent or reduce attacks next year. Having said that, one spray with permethrin when the first pink fruit appear next year would give virtually complete control of the pest.

Raspberry sawfly attack ❧

"What would have eaten these elongated holes out of my raspberry leaves? Fruiting didn't seem to be affected, but could it have been if the damage had been more widespread?"

The damage you have found has been caused by the raspberry sawfly, *Empria tridens*. Although the damage looks quite severe, attacks are usually reasonably light and general growth and cropping are very rarely adversely affected.

Raspberry mildew ❧

"The backs of my raspberry leaves were absolutely white with what I presume was some disease infection. Can you suggest what it was and how I could prevent it next year?"

The disease would have been powdery mildew, which in some years can be very severe. It is generally encouraged by dryness at the roots and by overcrowding of the canes. Thin out the canes now to allow adequate space between them and keep watered in dry spells in spring and summer next year. Should the disease still attack, apply a sulphur or systemic fungicide.

Spotty raspberries ❧

"Some of my raspberry canes have oval spots on them and I also noticed last year a similar marking on some of the leaves. Is this something I should be treating?"

Damage is the result of raspberry cane spot fungus, and all infected canes should be cut out and burned. If untreated, the disease will spread, and can have a serious effect on the new, flower-bearing shoots. In May and June, the disease spreads to the foliage, causing the leaf spotting.

Having cut out the spotted canes, spray with Supercarb, and repeat the sprays every two to three weeks until the end of flowering.

If you intend to plant any new raspberry canes, choose "Leo" or "Malling Admiral" which have some resistance to this disease.

Colour change can be altered ❦

"I moved some redcurrant bushes three years ago. They are now well established. Four of the bushes appear to have reverted back to white fruit. Is this possible?"

The whitecurrant is a sport derived from the redcurrant, so they are closely related. However, it is not usual for redcurrants to change to whitecurrants, at least not the whole bush; a single branch may become white-fruited. It is likely that your redcurrants suffered a shock when they were transplanted and this year's crop will probably be red.

Give your bushes a feed of 2 oz. (56 g) sulphate of potash, 2 oz. (56 g) superphosphate and 1 oz. (28 g) sulphate of ammonia per sq.yd (m²) as soon as possible, and water the plants in summer.

Starfruit seedlings ❦

"Last year I potted a few seeds from a starfruit which I was using for a fresh fruit salad. To my total amazement one of them sprouted and I now have a very attractive house plant which is 12 in. high. I have been unable to find any details on how to care for the plant. Can you oblige?"

Well done! The starfruit, *Averrhoa carambola*, is a handsome native of warmer parts of India and China.

Encourage your seedling to grow by gradually moving it on into larger pots until it is in a 10 in. size pot. Use a good potting compost.

The plant needs a warm and humid environment so mist it daily with a fine spray of water and maintain a temperature of 18–21°C.

The flowers, when they appear, will be red and borne in short racemes.

Early berries under glass ❦

"I have a cold greenhouse and would like to grow early strawberries in growing bags on the staging. I can keep the temperature to a minimum of 5° C. When is the best time to plant?"

We suggest that you plant "Emily", "Pegasus" or "Tamella" bought in pots or Jiffy 7's, from a strawberry specialist such as Ken Muir, Honeypot Farm, Weeley Heath, Clacton-on-Sea, Essex CO 16 9BJ.

Ideally, this should be done in July and August. Set the plants in 5 or 6 in. (12–15 cm) pots of John Innes No. 2 potting compost. Plunge the pots to their rims in well-drained soil outdoors. Move them into the greenhouse in January or early February. Hand-pollinate the flowers when they appear and ventilate the greenhouse when the temperature rises above 18°C (64°F). With luck you should have fruits in late April or May.

First season care 🐾

"I have grown strawberries for the first time this year. I understand that commercial growers burn off their strawberry fields. This seems too drastic for me in a small garden. What is the best option in this case? Also, when should I make new plants from the runners?"

We suggest that you simply cut back and burn old leaves, which may be diseased, on your strawberry plants. Cut back the leaves to within 4 in. (10 cm) of the crowns. Healthy new leaves will soon appear.

Remove weeds and rubbish from the strawberry bed and work ½ oz. (14 g) of sulphate of potash per sq.yd (m²) into the soil around the plants to toughen up the growth for winter. Strawberry runners are best pegged down in June and detached, nicely rooted, in August.

Putting plants to bed 🐾

"I have had a strawberry bed for the past four years and during this time I have had some wonderful crops. This year the berries were smaller and the pickings poor. Does this mean that the plants are worn out? Do you think that I should scrap the plants and start again with fresh stock?"

The life of a strawberry bed is about four years as the plants gradually degenerate with virus diseases. We feel that it would be a good idea to scrap your plants now and replant with fresh, virus-free stock as soon as you can get the plants. Choose a new position for them and plant in ground that is fertile and has been well manured.

The ideal time for planting a new bed of strawberries is in early August so that good plants develop for fruiting next year. If planting is delayed until the autumn or late winter, it is best not to allow the plants to fruit in their first season by removing the flower buds as they appear. This allows the plants to make good strong growth for fruiting in the following year.

Strawberries forever? ❧

"I understand that August is the best time to plant new strawberry plants. Can you recommend a couple of varieties that may be less prone to disease attack than previous ones?"

The varieties "Pegasus" and "Pandora" are both resistant to verticillium wilt and are claimed to be less suspectible to mildew and grey mould. Strawberries planted now should establish well to crop next year. Marshalls of Wisbech are selling module-grown plants of "Pegasus", which get off to a even better start than traditional runner-grown plants.

Strawberries from seed ❧

"Could you give me advice on germinating seed of alpine strawberries?"

Sow alpine strawberry seed thinly in 4 in. (10 cm) pots of seed or multi-purpose compost. Immerse the pot in 4 in. (10 cm) of water, removing it when the surface is shiny-wet.

Germinate the seeds in bright light in a temperature of 13°C (55°F) and prick the seedlings out 2 in. (5 cm) apart in seed trays. Set them outdoors in their fruiting positions when large enough.

You can sow the seeds outdoors in shallow drills ½ in. (13 mm) deep. Rake the seed bed to a fine tilth. When the seedlings are 1 in. (2.5 cm) high, plant them 3 in. (7.5 cm) apart in a nursery bed for transplanting later.

Greenfly control on strawberries ❧

"I am bringing along some strawberries in pots in a slightly heated greenhouse, hoping for some early fruits. Now I am finding lots of greenfly on the leaves. What can I spray these with without affecting the subsequent crop?"

You could apply a drenching spray of a fatty acids insecticide such as Safer's Insecticide for Fruit and Vegetables or a natural pyrethrins-based one like BugGun or Nature's Answer to Insect Pests. On the other hand, if considerable leaf curling has occurred, you may prefer to use a systemic insecticide such as Tumblebug. None of these sprays would affect the later crops of strawberries.

Strawberries in bags ❧

"I want to grow some strawberries in growing bags for an early crop next year. When should they be planted and what are the best varieties to grow?"

For an early crop next year plant your strawberries in growing bags as soon as possible. Good varieties to grow are: "Elvira", "Honeoye" and "Tamella".

Wilting strawberries ❦

"Some of our strawberry plants are wilting and dying, but most are growing strongly. They have been there a few years, and were previously all healthy. What could be amiss?"

It sounds as if strawberry wilt is responsible. Dig up one of the plants and examine the roots. If there is no discoloration, and no white grubs feeding, then wilt is most probable.

There is no easy control, so dig out all the affected plants, plus some of the surrounding soil, and dispose of them carefully. Do not put on the compost heap. Try watering the other plants with a fungicide such as Benlate or Supercarb at fortnightly intervals as a preventative measure.

The root of all weevil? ❦

"A number of my strawberry plants looked rather sick and a few have shrivelled and died. When I removed them I found the enclosed specimen feeding on the roots, along with several similar grubs."

The leg-less grub is one of the many species of weevil that attacks strawberry roots. Eggs are laid on the leaf stalks and, depending on the species, they feed there for a short or long time before moving into the soil and attacking the vulnerable roots. Dig out all the plants showing signs of distress and remove all grubs found.

Any plants that are clear of pests, and look to be still alive, could be replanted, but it would be better to wait until next spring or summer and then establish a new strawberry bed on a fresh site. Regular hoeing and an overall application of Sybol Dust should help control the soil pest.

Fruity mites ❦

"My strawberry plants are looking rather pale with a lot of yellow stippling on the leaves. What would you suggest to cure the problem?"

The damage will be due to feeding by red spider mite. Spray thoroughly, covering both sides of the leaves, using a pyrethrum or fatty acid insecticide and repeat again a week later. If your plants are already in flower, delay treatment until after flowering is finished.

Should the damage persist into the summer you could try using the beneficial, predatory mite, *Phytoseiulus persimilis*, as sold for control of red spider under glass. The outside temperature should be high enough in the summer for the predator to give good control.

Strawberry runners

"My strawberries are producing runners with plantlets. I would like to have a few more plants. What is the best way of rooting them? Do I cut off the surplus?"

Provided your strawberries are young and vigorous you can root some of the runners. It is not worth doing it if the plants are old and weak which suggests that they are affected with virus diseases.

Peg the runners into the soil with a bent piece of wire or weight them down with a stone. A better system is to sink small pots filled with good soil into the ground near the plants and peg the runners into them. The advantage of this method is that when the plantlets are severed from the parents and planted out, the roots are not disturbed unduly and the young plants settle down more quickly in their new home.

Strawberry virus

"Some of my strawberry plants grew normally this year but others are very small and yellow and look rather sick. What would be the cause and should I dig them out?"

Almost certainly one of the many viruses that can attack strawberries is responsible for the symptoms you describe. Sadly there is no control, and the affected plants should be removed and burned as soon as possible. Keep a careful watch on the remaining plants, and remove any that show signs of going the same way.

Frosted strawberries

"Last spring many of my strawberry flowers developed black 'eyes' because of frost. I think my garden is in a frost pocket. How can I protect my plants from frost?"

One of the easiest ways of protecting strawberry flowers from frost is to cover the plants with polypropylene fleece (Environmesh). Do this as soon as flowers form. It should give good protection from frost and allows light to reach the plants. Alternatively, cover the plants with cloches.

To obtain early crops many gardeners plant young strawberries in August and cover them with cloches in late February.

Strawberry grey mould ❧

"Some of my later strawberries turned grey and rotten after a rainy spell. Was this just the rain or is some disease involved which can be prevented?"

Strawberry grey mould disease, caused by the botrytis fungus, was responsible for the rotting, but it is encouraged by wet conditions. Often the infection sets in on the petals as they are trapped between the green calyx and the swelling fruit, and then spreads to the actual strawberry.

Best control is with a systemic fungicide applied a few times at four-day intervals, with the first spray just before the flowers open. The fungicide will protect both the petals and the fruit from the disease. Slug control is also important, as berries damaged by slugs soon become infected with grey mould.

Cockchafer pest ❧

"Whilst digging around my strawberry plants I found several had been eaten off close to ground level, and I also found some large and nasty-looking creatures in the soil. Did these do the damage?"

The creatures are cockchafer larvae and they feed on a wide range of plant roots, including strawberries. Remove as many as you can find, and then dust with Sybol Dust to take care of any that might have been missed.

Strawberries and caterpillars ❧

"The leaves on many of my strawberry plants are coming out in holes. I have not seen this before in many years of gardening and wonder what is causing the damage and why. I cannot see any sign of slugs or their slimy trails."

The damage is due to feeding by caterpillars of the strawberry tortrix moth. Eggs are laid under the leaves in autumn and feeding by the young caterpillars starts in late April to early May in an average season. Later, the caterpillars web leaves together and feed under the protection that creates. They may also feed on petals which they web together. They pupate in June and another generation of adults emerges by July.

There is a naturally occurring parasitic wasp which may have kept your local strawberry tortrix caterpillars in check in previous years, but which failed last year, hence the appearance of damage this spring. Seek out and hand-pick the small green caterpillars which can be quite difficult to spot until you "get your eye in". Spraying may prove necessary with a severe attack.

Strawing strawberries ❧

"I have some strawberry plants that are coming into flower. When should I put straw around them to protect the fruit?"

Do not put straw around strawberries too early, wait until the fruit begins to form. At this stage tuck the straw under the plants so that the fruit can rest on it.

Instead of straw, special strawberry mats can be used or black polythene can be laid along the ground. This will help to conserve soil moisture and keep down weeds.

Greenhouses

Splitting grapes

"I have a five-year-old 'Black Siegerrebe' grape vine. Each year the berries split. I water the vine each week and keep the ground mulched. How can I stop the berries splitting?"

Splitting of grape berries is usually associated with irregular growth as a result of the soil drying out followed by heavy watering. Mulching the ground is a good thing but as soon as the soil shows signs of dryness, give it a good watering. Do not water again until the soil seems dry once more. In very hot weather it may be necessary to water each day.

Scaly vine

"What would you advise me to treat my greenhouse vine with; it is covered with scale insects."

Scrape down the vine rods now to remove scaly and loose bark. This should also remove quite a lot of the scale bodies.

Provided there are no signs of buds breaking on the rods, they could be sprayed with Mortegg to complete the control. If the buds are already moving, spray with malathion and repeat when the buds have produced a few leaves.

Ripening grapes

"I have a 'Black Hamburg' vine in a greenhouse and the grapes are ripening. Should I keep the greenhouse well ventilated or close it at night?"

Unless there is plenty of air circulation moulds are likely to develop, so leave the ventilators open at night unless the weather becomes very cold.

Propagating a vine

"I thought I'd be a bit adventurous and take cuttings from my vine to give to friends, but I think I need a bit of advice before I make a start."

Grape vines are very easily increased from "eyes" which are prepared in early winter after the vine leaves have fallen and the vine is dormant.

Kept warm over winter, in February the bud on each "eye" should start to swell and soon make a new shoot. Roots will also form and when the pot becomes full of roots move the young vine on into a larger pot. Stand the vines outside for the summer.

Castor oil plant ❧

"Can you help me about the castor oil plant? I thought it was an indoor plant with thick leathery leaves. However, last summer in a public park I saw some plants with large purple leaves which were labelled castor oil plants! Can you tell me the correct name for the plant?"

Common names can be confusing but the true castor oil plant is *Ricinus communis*. This is the plant you saw in the public park. There are several different forms of it. The one with purple leaves is most commonly seen in large bedding displays.

The other plant you mention is incorrectly called the castor oil plant. Its correct name is *Fatsia japonica*. It can be grown outside in southern England. Its large, shiny, green leaves are very handsome. It is also sometimes grown as a house plant. Plants of *Ricinus communis* are highly poisonous and should be handled very carefully.

Sowing time ❧

"When is the best time to sow seed of Primula obconica?*"*

Seed of *Primula obconica* can be sown anytime between June and September depending on when you want the plants in flower. The early sowings will flower by the end of the year and the later ones in spring of the following year.

Sow the seed in a soilless seed compost in a temperature of 16°C (60°F). Grow the young plants on in small pots and stand them in a cold frame for the summer with light shade from strong sunshine. Return the plants to a frost-free greenhouse by the end of September.

A sensitive issue ❧

"I grew some sensitive plants, Mimosa pudica *last year. They did well but died off in the autumn. I will grow some more from seed this year in my greenhouse, but how can I stop the plants dying off?"*

Plants of *Mimosa pudica* do not usually last very long and they resent the cooler conditions and short days of autumn and winter.

There is not a lot that can be done about it. The best policy is to raise new plants from seed each spring. For better germination, soak the seeds first in water before sowing.

Rusty geraniums ❧

"I have 56 geraniums that have spent the winter in an unheated greenhouse, protected from frost with a covering of fleece. The leaves are now showing brown spots and holes. I am afraid I may lose them."

Grey mould and rust diseases are both involved and both can be encouraged by the humidity under the fleece. Ventilate as much as conditions allow and water in the mornings to allow the excess moisture to evaporate before putting the fleece back over.

To control the diseases, pick off all the affected leaves and spray with Tumbleblite II or Nimrod-T, allowing the spray to dry before covering again.

Rust may attack again, so continue to pick off leaves showing concentric brown rusty rings.

Carnivorous plants ❧

"I have a 12 ft by 8 ft (3.6 m × 2.4 m) heated greenhouse with a built-in bench along one side. I am thinking of using this to grow carnivorous plants. Any advice would be appreciated."

Making a table display of carnivorous plants is very easy and relatively inexpensive. Obtain enough polythene to lay on the bench as a base. Then add moss peat (avoid sedge peat as it is too limy). Shape the display using some old stumps of wood and stone to make a minimum depth of 3 in. (7.5 cm) and a maximum of 6 in. (15 cm).

Temperature levels need to be a minimum 0°C (32°F), maximum 30°C (86°F) and the plants will need full light.

Suitable plants include Venus fly trap (dionaea); various sundews (drosera); American pitcher plants (sarracenias); bladderworts and Mexican butterworts. All these are perennial and are dormant over winter from November to February. Just cut back any dead foliage during this period and reduce watering, but flood the bog in spring when new growth starts. Keep it wet in the summer.

Geranium "black leg"   ❧

"Last September I took some geranium cuttings but several of them went black and rotted. I have taken more cuttings this spring but the same thing is happening. What is causing the trouble?"

The trouble you have had with your geranium cuttings is commonly known as "black leg". It is always worse if the cuttings are kept too wet and cold. Cuttings made from soft, sappy stems are also more prone to the rot. Some gardeners leave their cuttings on an open bench for a couple of days before potting them. This is done to harden them and make them less prone to rotting. Always insert the cuttings in an open, free-draining compost containing plenty of coarse grit or perlite. Water very sparingly until roots have developed.

Resting begonias   ❧

"I have grown some begonias from tubers and they flowered well last summer. After the foliage died down I kept the soil in the pots dry. When do you suggest I start the tubers into growth again? They are kept in a frost-free greenhouse."

Remove the soil from the begonia tubers and keep them in dry peat or perlite. Press the tubers, hollow side up, into a tray of moist peat. Kept in the warmest part of your greenhouse new sprouts will soon appear. At this stage pot the tubers individually in good potting compost.

Shrimp plants from seed   ❧

"I have some shrimp plant seeds and would appreciate knowing when and how I should plant them."

Sow shrimp plant (beloperone, now known as justicia) seeds in spring. Fill a clean 3 in. (7–8 cm) pot with seed or multi-purpose compost and firm it gently. Stand it in a container of water until the compost is damp.

Sow the seeds very thinly and just cover them with a thin layer of vermiculite or fine grade perlite. Cover the pot with plastic film wrap and place it in a propagator heated to around 16°C (60°F) or put it on a radiator in good light. Seedlings can take several weeks to appear.

Geranium cuttings   ❧

"Can you tell me when is the best time to take geranium cuttings? I usually take them in the autumn but a number turn black at soil level and rot."

Geranium cuttings can be taken any time during the summer and early autumn. They root more readily in the summer when temperatures are high and can, in fact, be rooted in the open garden if the soil is well drained. After preparing the cuttings, stand them on the greenhouse staging to allow the cut surfaces to dry before potting them. Only water the cuttings when the compost in the pot is very dry. Black rot occurs if the cuttings are kept too wet in cold conditions. Once roots form, pot the cuttings individually.

Whitefly attacking fuchsia ❧

"Why is it that every time I try to grow fuchsias in my conservatory they become plastered with whitefly in a matter of weeks? Is there any really effective cure?"

Fuchsias are indeed very attractive to whitefly. We suspect that there is a resident low-level population of the pests on other plants in your conservatory. Once the fuchsias are introduced the whitefly adults would migrate to their favoured host plant and rapidly build up to plague proportions.

Probably the best control now available is the biological one known as *Delphastus.* The whitefly are reduced first by spraying with a fatty acids insecticide such as Safer's Garden Insecticide, and then the *Delphastus* are introduced under a cover to confine them to the plants and prevent them escaping through doors or open windows.

Defenders, who are at Occupation Road, Wye, Ashford, Kent, TN25 5EN supply the predator.

Storing cannas ❧

"I have grown some canna plants this year. What is the best way of keeping them during the winter?"

You must lift your canna plants before frosts can damage them. Cut off the top growth and pack the roots close together in boxes. Firm potting compost around the roots and store them in a cool, frost-free place. Give the plants very little water and keep them almost dry. If they are in a damp place moulds are likely to develop.

Next March or early April shake the soil from the roots and pot them in fresh potting compost. Kept in a warm greenhouse, new growth will soon begin. Plant outside in late May or early June.

Pot it up ❧

"I have an arum lily in a large pot which I keep under glass in the winter. It has been stood outside for the summer and is now very crowded in its pot. When is the best time to repot it?"

August is a good time to repot arum lilies, particularly if they are over-crowded in their pots.

Tap your plant out of its pot and split the clump into several pieces.

Repot two or three of the strongest in a 10–12 in. (25–30 cm) pot of John Innes No. 3. If you need more plants, pot the smaller pieces in 6 in. pots.

Keep the plants outside for the rest of the summer but take them into your greenhouse by the end of September. The larger plants should flower again from late winter into early spring.

Once established in their pots, feed with a liquid fertilizer regularly from March to September.

Fuchsia care ❧

"I have bought a small plant of a fuchsia called 'Hampshire Prince' which is growing in my conservatory. Can you tell me how long it should stay in its present pot? The plant is about 6 in. high."

You will need to move your plant into a larger pot if it is to make a plant of decent size. The time to do this is when the plant is beginning to fill its pot with roots. As it is 6 in. (15 cm) tall the plant is most probably ready for a move now. If it is in a 3½ in. (9 cm) pot, it could be moved on into a 6 in.(15 cm) pot. Use a good potting mixture such as John Innes Potting Compost No. 2. If the plant has only one stem, pinch out the tip to induce bushy growth. The side shoots that appear should also have their tips removed so that you have a well-proportioned bushy plant. Once the plant is established in its final pot, feed it each week in the summer with a liquid fertilizer.

Care for clivia ❧

"I was given a plant of Clivia miniata *for my 70th birthday. As the blooms are now falling off, can you tell me how to care for the plant from now on?"*

Grow your clivia in a light place in a cool room or frost-free conservatory. Whenever the soil in the pot seems dry give it a good watering and allow it to drain. Do not let the plant stand in water. During the spring and summer feed it each week with a liquid fertilizer such as Phostrogen.

In the winter keep the plant much drier and only water it when the soil is very dry. At the same time keep the plant in a cool room so that the plant can rest. This resting period is important in encouraging the plant to produce flower spikes. Repotting is only necessary when the pot is very overcrowded and is best carried out in the spring.

This ailing yucca needs a new lease of life

"I have had an indoor yucca for ten years. It stands in a south-facing living room and is put outside for the summer. It has not been repotted for years and is now not looking very healthy. Can you tell me how to improve it?"

Give your yucca a new lease of life by repotting it now. Water it the night before repotting, then gently tap its congested root system from the pot. Carefully tease away old, spent compost and reset the plant in Levington House Plant Compost. Water it in and when strong new leaves appear, cut back any old ones that have shrivelled.

Six weeks after repotting start feeding each week with a liquid house plant fertilizer until early autumn.

Failed fuchsia cuttings

"In the past I have found that fuchsia cuttings are easy to root. Some I took in March have failed. I covered the cuttings in the pot with a plastic bag to conserve moisture. When I removed it, the cuttings had dropped their leaves and looked dead. If the plastic touched the cuttings would this be the cause or was the temperature too low?"

We suspect that the demise of your fuchsia cuttings was because of low temperatures. They do not mind having the plastic against them provided the temperature is around 12–16°C (52–61°F). Below this, rooting is difficult and the cold soil could trigger the development of fungus diseases. Next time root the cuttings in a heated propagator. In the summer, when natural temperatures are high, cuttings will root outside or in a frame if they are kept misted with water. Dipping the base of the cuttings in hormone rooting powder will help to encourage roots to form.

Greenhouse red spider mite

"Can you tell me please what is wrong with my greenhouse cucumbers? The leaves are very pale and there seems to be a fine webbing over the youngest shoots. Growth and cropping has almost stopped."

Your cucumbers have been attacked by red spider mite. These pests are often more green than red, are just visible to the naked eye and feed mainly under the leaves and on the younger growths.

There would still be time to control the infestation by introducing the predatory mite known as *Phytoseiulus*. Control will be slow at first, but as the predators build up the pests will gradually be brought under control, although it may be necessary to make more than one introduction.

Datura cuttings ❧

"I have a datura plant in a large pot which I keep in my greenhouse in the winter and stand it outside in the summer. It has now got very big and too large for my greenhouse. Can I take cuttings from it so that I can start again with a new plant?"

Yes, cuttings can be taken from datura plants during the summer. They are not difficult to root at this time. Choose young shoots and make the cuttings about 4 in. (10 cm) long. Remove the lower leaves and trim each cutting just below a leaf joint. Insert the cuttings around the edge of a small pot filled with seed compost to which has been added extra coarse sand or perlite. Cover the pot with a polythene bag to conserve moisture. Once rooted, pot the cuttings separately in small pots of good potting compost.

Greenhouse insulation ❧

"I have an 8 ft × 6 ft (2.4 m × 1.8 m) aluminium greenhouse which I line with bubble plastic from apex to floor, leaving no gaps. I also use a paraffin heater to keep the temperature above 2° C (35° F). Is it wise to cover the whole area or leave gaps for the air to circulate from the louvre ventilator?"

Whenever you use gas or paraffin heating, considerable amounts of water vapour are released into the atmosphere and this makes the greenhouse very wet. It is important to leave a little ventilation on in the greenhouse and ventilate freely whenever possible during mild spells in the winter.

Also, water your plants with great care and keep the greenhouse as dry as possible. It is advisable to leave a gap in the bubble insulation around the ventilator so that you can ventilate the greenhouse effectively in mild weather.

Reading a thermometer ?℮

"I am heating my greenhouse by electricity. I am only keeping cuttings growing as well as some tender plants. What temperature do I need? Could you please tell me how to read a maximum/minimum thermometer?"

Your plants will require a minimum winter night temperature of 10°C (50°F). An occasional fall of a few degrees below the desired minimum during severe weather will seldom do much harm if plants and the atmosphere are on the dry side.

A maximum/minimum thermometer consists of a U-shaped glass tube containing a column of mercury. It records the minimum temperature in the greenhouse at night and the maximum temperature that occurred during the previous day. Each morning, read the lowest temperature in one column and the highest temperature in the other column, reading to the bottom of the internal indicators. On modern instruments a push button is used to reset the indicators at the start of each day.

Damping down adds valuable moisture to the atmosphere.

Summer shade ❧

"My small greenhouse gets very hot when the sun is shining. Apart from opening the ventilators, how can I keep the air cooler?"

Temperatures rise very rapidly in small greenhouses when the sun is shining and doors and ventilators must be kept fully open. Some form of shading is also desirable to prevent sun scorch. This can done with roller blinds or a special paint which is applied to the outside of the greenhouse. This should last for the summer and be washed off in the early autumn.

Not all plants need shading. Cucumbers must have shade but melons do not need it. Light shade only is necessary for tomatoes. To prevent the air becoming too dry in the greenhouse, damp the floors and staging with water in hot weather. This will also help to lower the temperature.

Leaf cuttings ❧

"I have a plant of Begonia rex *in my sitting room. I am told that new plants can be grown from the leaves. Is this true?"*

Yes, the leaves of *Begonia rex* can be used to raise new plants. It is best done in spring and summer when temperatures are naturally higher than in the winter.

Cut off a mature leaf with a short stalk and make several cuts in the veins on the underside of the leaf. Lay the leaf on a mixture of moist peat and coarse sand, keeping the slit veins in contact with the mixture by putting some stones on the surface to hold it down. Enclose the leaf in a warm propagator or in a polythene bag.

Roots should form where the veins were cut. Put the young plants in small pots of good compost such as multi-purpose compost and grow in good light. Water carefully until established.

Sowing cinerarias for Christmas! ❧

"I have seen cinerarias growing in the open in Madeira. Can they be grown outside in this country? If so, when is the best time to sow seeds?"

Although cinerarias flourish in the open in Madeira, they need greenhouse conditions in this country. To have plants flowering for Christmas sow the seed in early May or delay sowing until June if you want spring-flowering plants.

They may be grown in cold frames during the summer and need light shade from strong sunshine. Watering must be done very carefully. If the compost is kept too wet the plants may collapse.

Saintpaulia plantlets

"I inserted some saintpaulia leaves in a jar of water covered with cling film. I now have many small plantlets at the base of the leaf stalk. What do I do next?"

A good question. You must carefully separate the small plantlets from the base of the old leaf stalk and pot them individually. Treat them as if they were young seedlings. Fill some small pots or modules with a soilless compost and, with the aid of a dibber, put a single plantlet in each pot. When they have filled the small pots they can be moved on to slightly larger pots. If you pot the whole cluster of plantlets they will make lots of leaves but no flowers. Once you have removed the plantlets, the old leaf can be put back in the jar of water and more plantlets will form at the base once again.

Greenhouse sterilization

"Most of my old gardening books say it is necessary to sterilize my greenhouse soil each year, using formaldehyde. I cannot find this chemical now; what is the latest thinking?"

Soil sterilizing was designed to prevent soil diseases such as fusarium and pests such as root knot eelworm building up in the soil. The easier way now is to select tomato varieties that are resistant to such problems, or to use growing bags rather than the greenhouse soil. "Counter", "Cyclon", "Piranto" and "Primato" are all suitable varieties. Where eelworms are known to be a problem you can graft your chosen variety on to the KNVF rootstock.

Lantana seed

"Can you please tell me how to increase our stock of lantana? After our plant flowered it produced small green 'pips' which turned black. Each one contained a hard seed. When should we sow it and can we take cuttings from the plant?"

Collect the hard seeds of your lantana and keep them cool and dry. Sow them in small pots of good seed compost in warmth in February or March. When the seedlings appear, move them to small pots of good potting compost. When well established move them on to slightly larger pots. The plants should flower in the summer and they can be planted out in the open from June until September.

The flowers of seedlings will vary in colour. Any with particularly good colours can be perpetuated by taking cuttings. Firm, young shoots, a few inches in length, will root easily in the summer. Put the cuttings in small pots of gritty soil. Keep the plants in a frost-free greenhouse or unheated room for the winter.

Blackened tomatoes ❧

"My husband's tomatoes, especially at the start of the season, had black marks at the end away from the stalk. Can he prevent the same thing happening next year?"

The blackening is a condition known as blossom end rot. No disease is involved, and the damage is basically due to lack of calcium in the fruits. The deficiency is worse where inadequate or uneven watering is given or where excess ventilation results in leaves losing too much water. Prevent by careful watering and ventilation and by adding calcium nitrate, available from Chempak, to the water once a week.

Pepper poser ❧

"I grow sweet peppers every year in my greenhouse and this year had the healthiest-looking plants ever. Sadly, the fruits are now turning dark-coloured at the ends and I am anxious to prevent any further losses. Help please."

The darkening and sunken look of the ends of your peppers away from the stem is known as blossom end rot. This problem is quite commonly found on tomatoes but less commonly on peppers. The cause is a lack of calcium in the fruits which can result from an actual lack in the soil or compost, or from inadequate or irregular watering interfering with calcium uptake.

To correct the problem, keep the plants adequately and regularly watered and feed with a tomato or other fertilizer which includes calcium in the list of ingredients. If growing in growing bags, Miracle-Gro fertilizer would be ideal. Phostrogen Tomato Food would be a suitable alternative.

Fuchsias for baskets ❧

"Can you recommend some fuchsia varieties that are suitable for growing in hanging baskets?"

Fuchsias with a pendulous habit that are suitable for growing in hanging baskets are: "Dusky Rose", double, deep pink; "Anne of Longleat", semi-double, coral and lavender; "Cascade", single, white and carmine; "Golden Marinka", single, yellow foliage, red flowers; "Lena", semi-double, pink and magenta; "Trailing Queen", single, red; "Snow White", double, white, pink streaks; "Swingtime", double, red and white.

A fan of the blue fan

"I have some plants of Scaevola *'Blue Fan'. Is it possible to take cuttings from them as I do not have space for the large plants in my greenhouse over the winter?"*

Take cuttings of young shoots from your scaevola plants without delay. Make them about 3 in. (7.5 cm) long and remove the lower leaves before inserting them in small pots filled with a seed compost to which has been added extra coarse grit or perlite. This will encourage new roots to form. Stand the cuttings in a heated propagator until they have rooted.

Frost-free

"What measures are necessary to maintain a frost-free greenhouse?"

The temperature in the greenhouse should not be allowed to fall below 2°C (35°F). This is most easily done by using an electric heater with a thermostat, which can be set to switch on automatically when the temperature falls below a pre-set level. Gas or paraffin heaters could also be used.

If your heater is not thermostatically controlled, use a maximum/minimum thermometer to check that the correct temperatures are being maintained, particularly overnight. A frost alarm can be a useful additional safeguard. This can be set to sound an alarm (usually somewhere in your house) if the temperature unexpectedly falls to near freezing, for example if the heater breaks down or if there is a power failure.

Watering tomatoes

"I have planted some tomatoes in growing bags in my small greenhouse. The plants are growing well but I am not sure about watering. How often do I need to water the bags?"

How often you should water your tomatoes depends on temperatures and how long the plants have been in the bags.

After planting, not a great deal of water will be needed but as the plants get larger they will require more water.

Once the bags are full of roots and in hot weather it may be necessary to water two or three times a day. Keep a close watch on the compost in the bags. If it is really moist, watering is not necessary but once it shows signs of dryness give it a thorough watering.

On dull days much less water will be required but plants in bags do dry out very rapidly and a close watch must be kept on them in summer.

If the soil does dry out badly, the tomatoes could be affected with blossom end rot. The base of the fruits are sunken and show black blotches. This is entirely due to a shortage of water at some stage.

Don't overfill your greenhouse or you won't get the best from it!

Trimming geraniums ⁊

"I have kept several geraniums in pots in my greenhouse through the winter. All have grown rather tall and leggy. Can I cut them back now and hope that they will produce new shoots?"

It would be a good idea to cut back the stems of your geraniums now to induce fresh growth. After trimming we suggest that you repot the plants in fresh potting compost. Grow them in a light and sunny position and plant them outside in late May or early June.

The tops of the stems may be used as cuttings should you want more plants.

Ailing cyclamen ❧

"I was bought a cyclamen for Christmas but the leaves keep turning brown and falling off. Could you tell me how I should look after the plant?"

The main requirements of cyclamen are a steady temperature – but not too warm – good light and even watering. Any deviation from these will result in leaves turning brown or going limp and rotting.

Watering is best done by letting the compost become fairly dry, and then soaking the pot in a bowl of water. After half an hour or so, remove the pot from the water and allow any excess water to drain away.

Keep the plant on a well-lit windowsill. A cool room is preferable to an overheated one.

Leggy Busy Lizzies ❧

"I had eight pots of busy Lizzies in full flower in my porch. One night the temperature in the porch fell to 5° C (42° F) so I brought the plants into a cool bedroom. Now, all the plants have grown outwards and the stems seem very weak."

Your impatiens are growing outwards in search of light. Find them a brighter spot, and they will be more stocky, neater plants. If they become too large, cut them back by half. New shoots will soon appear.

Chrysanthemum leaf-miner ❧

"I had some lovely chrysanthemum cuttings and young plants coming along but now the leaves are being attacked by leaf-miners. Apart from regularly removing infested leaves, is there any other action I can take? Isn't it a bit early for such pests?"

The chrysanthemum leaf-miner breeds continuously throughout the year given suitable temperatures, so often attacks young chrysanthemums. Continue to remove infested leaves, or simply squash the grubs within the mines. Also try spraying with malathion. There are some biological control agents used by commercial growers to check leaf-miners, and these could well be made available to gardeners in the future.

The pests can breed in summer on a range of weeds, so keep these well controlled to remove at least one source of reinfestation.

Damping off disaster ❧

"I started my bedding plants off from seed in the usual way, but this year I am finding patches of seedlings are dying off. Is it too late to resow to make up numbers?"

Your seedlings (*Impatiens)* have been attacked by damping off, a fungal infection that can arise from too much water, disease-infected water as from an old tank, or from too low a temperature. Prevent further damage by watering more sparingly, using clean water, and adding a copper fungicide each time you do water.

There should be time to start most bedding plants off from seed again, but any shortages could be made up from plug-grown plants which are now supplied through the post by most seed companies, or are obtainable from garden centres.

Controlling condensation ❧

"During winter my greenhouse drips with condensation. Is there any way of lessening it?"

Condensation is a problem in most greenhouses during the winter. The only way of curbing it is to ventilate the greenhouse whenever the weather is favourable. Try to open a ridge ventilator each day, even if it is only for a few hours. The use of an extractor fan in mild weather also helps and can be used throughout the year.

Winter care ❧

"This year I grew some Lotus berthelotii *and planted them in a container. They did very well. Can I keep them in the container over winter?"*

Your lotus plants will need protection over the winter. They cannot stand temperatures below 5°C. Ideally, keep the plants in a greenhouse or in a spare room, in a light place and put them back in the garden in early June. Water sparingly and only when the compost is becoming dry.

Falling leaves ❧

"I have a datura (brugmansia) growing in a 10 in. (23 cm) terracotta pot on my south-facing patio. Although it keeps its shape perfectly, leaves are continually turning yellow and falling off."

It is natural for datura leaves to turn yellow and fall from the base upwards. However, red spider mites are very fond of datura leaves and because of their activities the leaves will wither and fall.

The mites are very tiny and can only just be seen with the naked eye. They cause a white mottling on the leaves and in a bad attack fine webs are formed. If you find any signs of the pest spray the plant with malathion regularly.

Fern spores ❧

"How do you grow ferns from spores?"

Fill a 4 in. (10 cm) pan with a mixture of equal parts peat and sharp sand, then pour boiling water over it to sterilize it. Cover the pot with a pane of glass while the compost is cooling.

When the mixture is cold, sprinkle fern spores over it and replace the glass. Germinate them in a warm and lightly shaded spot – beneath a greenhouse bench is ideal. Within a few weeks, you will notice a green film of germinating spores. Prick out the small plants singly in an ericaceous compost when they are $\frac{1}{2}$ in (1.25 cm) high.

Blotchy tomatoes ❧

"During the height of summer, as many of our greenhouse tomatoes ripened, the colour was a mixture of yellow and red, and under the yellow areas the flesh was rather hard. Can you explain?"

The condition you describe is known as blotchy ripening, and it is generally more severe in hot, sunny weather. High temperatures, high light intensity and also high nitrogen and low potash all seem to encourage the problem.

Reduce damage in another year by shading the greenhouse glass in the late spring and by ventilating as fully as conditions allow. Once cropping is under way, feed with a high potash tomato fertilizer.

Shady cucumbers ❧

"I have two cucumber plants in my greenhouse. In hot weather they go limp but recover when the sun goes off them. Do they need shading?"

Cucumber plants must be given shade in the summer otherwise the foliage will become scorched. Apply a special shading paint on the outside of the greenhouse or use blinds. Cucumbers like hot and humid conditions so give the plants plenty of water in the summer. Also regularly damp down the inside of the greenhouse.

Seed from Australia

"I have been sent some seed of Boronia heterophylla *from Australia. Can you tell me anything about the plant? Can it be grown outside?"*

Boronia heterophylla is an evergreen shrub which grows 4–5 ft (about 1.5 m) tall. It is not hardy in this country and is best grown in a frost-free greenhouse. Cultivated in pots, plants can be stood outside for the summer. The clusters of rosy pink flowers appear in the spring and are pleasantly fragrant.

Sow the seed in a small pot in a warm greenhouse or by a light window indoors in April. Plants need to be grown in a lime-free potting compost. Prune the plants after flowering by shortening the stems that have flowered.

Bougainvillea care

"I have a bougainvillea which is about 3 ft (90 cm) tall in a frost-free greenhouse. Can you tell me how to look after it in winter and how to propagate from it?"

We assume your bougainvillea is in a large pot or tub? As the weather becomes colder give it very little water and keep the plant almost dry in January and February. Prune the plant in February by cutting back all last year's side shoots to within an inch of their base. Retain a framework of old branches. Water the plant freely during the spring and summer and give liquid feeds frequently.

Cuttings can be taken during the spring of young shoots with a heel of older wood attached. Dip the base of the cuttings in hormone rooting powder and put them in small pots of gritty soil. Stand the cuttings in a warm and moist propagator.

Elephant trouble

"My fuchsias are being stripped of foliage by some menacing creatures. Can you identify them and suggest a control?"

It sounds like the caterpillar of the elephant hawk moth. In gardens they feed on fuchsia and Busy Lizzie, and in the wild on willowherb.

The large spots on the side of the body are false eyes. When threatened, the caterpillar retracts the front part of the body and rears up, appearing much larger and menacing than it really is. When danger is over the front of the body extends again, looking a little like an elephant's trunk. The caterpillar pupates just under the soil and pink and pale brown adults appear in June the next year.

Control measures are not really justified for such an interesting creature, but in cases of severe damage you could remove the caterpillars by hand and put them onto wild willowherb plants away from your garden.

Aubergine rot ❧

"Some of my aubergines developed a furry fungal growth on their sides just before they were ready to pick; very disappointing. What would be the best way to avoid it happening again?"

The damage would be due to grey mould. This is mainly a wound parasite so there was probably some prior damage to the aubergines. Likely contenders would have been caterpillar feeding or sun scorch.

Grey mould is encouraged by over-moist air, so avoiding damage and ventilating the greenhouse fully should prevent injury to your next crop.

Splitting tomatoes ❧

"Towards the end of cropping, my outdoor cherry tomatoes all suffered from a splitting of the skins, leaving unpleasant scars around the sides. Is this due to some pest feeding, or another cause?"

The splitting would have been due to heavy rainfall or watering occurring after a period of drought or underwatering.

Under dry conditions tomato skins become hardened and are then unable to cope with any rapid expansion of the fruits after sudden uptake of water.

Prevent this in another year by regular, steady watering during any dry periods.

Red spider attack ❧

"I believe it is now possible to control red spider with some form of beneficial insect. If this is so, could you please tell me where I can obtain them?"

The controlling agent is a predatory mite, *Phytoseiulus persimili.* They can be obtained by mail order from Defenders Ltd, PO Box 131, Wye, Ashford, Kent TN25 5TQ, or Green Gardener, 41 Strumpshaw Road, Brundall, Norfolk NR13 5PG.

Sowing cinerarias ❧

"I bought a packet of cineraria seed but I am not sure when to sow them. Can they be sown now in my greenhouse which is kept frostfree in the winter?"

Cineraria seed can be sown any time between April and August. Sow the seed in a small pot or make use of an old butter/margarine container, making sure that there are holes in the bottom to allow surplus water to drain away.

Aubergine attack ❧

"We grow aubergines in our greenhouse every year and every year we seem to get an attack of greenfly on them. They are clear at present, so is there any way to protect them from attack?"

If your greenhouse has been free of plants during winter it is unlikely that the greenfly would overwinter there. Keep them out now by covering the door with a fine netting curtain. Enviromesh would be ideal, hung so you can push it aside as you enter.

If plants have been present over winter, spray them all now using a pyrethrin-based spray, such as Bug Gun or Nature's Answer to Insect Pests, or use a systemic insecticide such as Tumblebug or Rapid. Later in the season, when the temperatures rise, and full ventilation is needed, introduce an aphid parasite for biological control.

Arum lilies ❧

"I thought that arum lilies were greenhouse flowers but last summer I saw several large clumps growing outside around the edge of a stream on the Isle of Wight."

Arum lilies, *Zantedeschia aethiopica*, are usually grown in large pots under glass for their early white flower spathes. However, in mild areas they can be grown outside if they are given winter protection. They survive well, as you have seen on the Isle of Wight, if they are planted deeply in the margins of a stream or pond. "Crowborough" is a variety that is reputed to be hardy in southern gardens.

Begonia bulbils   ❧

"I have a plant of Begonia sutherlandii. *I notice what seem to be bulbils on the leaves. Can these be used as a method of propagation? How should I treat the parent plant in the winter?"*

The bulbils that you have found on the leaves of your *Begonia sutherlandii* can be removed and grown on as seedlings. They will soon attain flowering size. This begonia has attractive orange flowers and is very easy to grow. It makes an attractive plant for a hanging basket and is one of the tuberous types which should be rested in winter.

When the foliage begins to wither, gradually withhold water until the compost is dry. Store the tuber in a cool, frost-free place until starting it into growth next spring.

Canna care   ❧

"Two or three months ago I was given a canna lily. One leaf went black and I was told this was because of sun scorch. It is in flower now but all the leaves are black. Can you help?"

We do not think you are treating your canna correctly. It should remain dormant in winter and be kept dry. In early spring, repot the tuber in fresh potting compost and recommence watering to start the plant into growth. At the end of May plant the canna in the open and it will flower in the summer. Lift the plant in the autumn and store it in a dry, frost-free place for the winter.

Shooting fuchsias   ❧

"I have some fuchsia plants in pots in my greenhouse and they are now producing shoots. Can these shoots be used as cuttings to raise new plants?"

These young fuchsia shoots can be used as cuttings. Insert them in small pots filled with gritty seed compost or perlite and stand them in a heated propagator until roots form when the plants should be put in individual small pots.

Fuchsia attack can be avoided   ❧

"Several of the fuchsia plants which we have kept growing over winter have what looks like tufts of cotton wool sprouting from the leaf joints. The leaves also are quite sticky. Can you please explain what is at fault?"

The cotton wool-like growths are waxy threads produced by mealy bugs and the stickiness is honeydew. Honeydew is excreted by the insects as they feed and it drops down onto the leaves below.

To control these pests (which are fairly unusual on fuchsias), it would be best to take the plants outside on a mild day and to spray them thoroughly with malathion, Sybol or Murphy Tumblebug. Return the plants inside when the spray has dried but repeat the treatment if necessary a couple of weeks later.

Seedlings in trouble   ❧

"My trays of young bedding plants are starting to die off in patches and the areas get larger by the day. How can I stop this and prevent it for later sowings?"

Your seedlings are being attacked by damping off fungi. Keep the compost as dry as possible, and when watering is required add some Cheshunt Compound to the water in the can.

For new sowings, use new, reliable brand compost, sow as thinly as you can, and then add the Cheshunt Compound to all waterings.

Plants for sale   ❧

"I want to sell plants that I can grow in my heated greenhouse. Would you tell me what plants I could start from seed?"

There are several plants that you can grow from seed to provide pot plants for sale at most times of the year. We suggest you select small, compact varieties. Some suggestions are: schizanthus, portulacas (ideal in small, indoor hanging baskets), pansies, thunbergia (trained up a cane, or a tripod of canes), *Begonia semperflorens*, impatiens, solanum, cyclamen, primulas, fuchsias, cinerarias, exacum, browallia, calceolaria and rechsteineria.

Bug bother   ❧

"Could you please give me some details of any biological control for mealy bugs? There is a nasty infestation on my conservatory plants."

There are three different biological controls available against mealy bug, but they are only active in the warmer summer months.

For the present, reduce numbers with sprays of fatty acids using Phostrogen Safer's Rose & Flower Insecticide, or permethrin, using Long-Last or Tumblebug.

Next summer, if mealy bugs are still a problem, introduce the ladybird-type beetle known as *Cryptolaemus* or the mixture of parasitic wasps Leptomastix, Leptomastidae and Anagyrus.

Where different species of mealy bug are present, use both the beetle and the wasps for the best results.

Fragrant freesias   ❧

"I have a greenhouse and intend to grow freesias. Should I buy corms or seeds? When should I plant them?"

If you want to have freesias for next spring you should plant corms in pots in late summer: in August and September several may be grown in a 5 or 6 in. (12–15 cm) pot of John Innes potting compost. After potting, keep the corms in a cold but frost-free place, but once young shoots appear, keep the pots in a light position in a cool greenhouse. Support the stems as they grow with twiggy sticks.

Corms started into growth in September usually flower in February and March – yours are likely to be later. Do not try to hurry them with extra heat, as this will cause the leaves to grow thin and spindly and the flowers may be deformed.

Freesias can also be grown from seed which should be sown in the spring to flower in the following winter.

Side splitting   ❧

"We have had some really good tomatoes this year in our greenhouse, but since we have returned after a week's holiday we have found that many of the skins are starting to crack around the tops, as seen in the specimens I am enclosing. What causes this and how can we stop it please?"

The cracking is due to irregular watering. The tomatoes probably went short of water during your holiday. Once short of water this causes the skins to become hard. When there is a sudden uptake of water into the fruits the skins split. Correct by watering regularly now, and I would suggest applying more water each time than usual so that there is always a plentiful supply. This problem is common and can affect a wide range of plants.

Scented bedding   ❧

"I bought some heliotrope plants this spring, and although they flowered well, there was no scent. Did I buy the wrong kind?"

Your cherry pie (heliotrope) plants were probably grown from seed as most seed strains have little scent. To have scented bedding plants, grow a named variety noted for its scent such as "Chatsworth" or "W.H. Lowther".

Once you have a plant, it can be perpetuated by taking cuttings from it in late summer. Heliotropes are not hardy and plants must be kept in a frost-free greenhouse for the winter.

Storing begonias ❧

"Can you advise me how to save my begonia tubers, as I usually make a mess of it and have to buy new ones each year. Also, what is the best method of propagating begonias?"

Lift your begonia plants just before the first frosts arrive. Remove as much soil as possible from them and reset them in pots or boxes filled with gritty compost.

Transfer them to a greenhouse that is gently heated through the winter. When the leaves turn dry and wither, detach the old flower stems. Keep the tubers dry until February or early March, then plant them in trays of a peaty compost to sprout. Water carefully and raise the temperature to 16°C. (61°F).

Propagate tuberous rooted begonias by rooting 2 in. (5 cm) basal stem cuttings in a propagator in spring. Make a cut below a joint and dip the base in rooting hormone powder.

Pot up ❧

"I have rooted a number of geranium cuttings. At the moment there are several together in 3 in. (7.5 cm) pots. Can they stay like this for the winter or is it necessary to pot them individually?"

Now that your geraniums have rooted, it would be better if they were given individual 3 in. (7.5 cm) pots. Left in their present pots, they are likely to become starved. But potted separately, they will make nice sturdy plants by next spring.

Pot the rooted cuttings using a gritty potting compost. During the winter, particularly when it is damp and cold, water the plants sparingly. Kept too wet, the stems are likely to rot.

Morning glory ❧

"Last spring I raised some plants of Ipomoea *'Heavenly Blue' from seed. The young plants made poor progress and the leaves went yellow. What did I do wrong? Please help me as I want to grow some more next year."*

The leaves of *Ipomoea* "Heavenly Blue" become yellow and sickly when temperatures are too low for the plants. We suggest that you wait until the middle of April before sowing the seed.

Germinate it in a warm propagator and grow the seedlings on in a greenhouse. Do not plant out until June and choose a warm and sunny spot. Plants always do better in a good, hot summer.

Regular pinching out promotes bushy growth.

ℒily-pot ❧

"I want to grow some lilies in pots for flowering in my conservatory. What kinds should I grow and when should I plant the bulbs?"

Lilies that grow well in containers and pots for flowering in a conservatory include *L. regale*, *L. speciosum*, *L. longiflorum*, *L. auratum*, "Enchantment" and "Destiny". Purchase top-quality bulbs from a bulb specialist and plant them as soon as they can be obtained.

Use a good potting compost and ensure that there is adequate drainage material in the base of the pot. Cover the bulbs with at least 3 in. (7.5 cm) of compost.

Stand the pots outside under a thick layer of sand or leaves, or in a dark cellar so that the bulbs can make a good root system. When the stems are about 3 in. (7.5 cm) tall, take the pots into a cool greenhouse to flower, but do not allow the temperature to rise too high until the flower buds are well formed. Keep the lilies in a light position. Greenfly can be a problem and spraying may be necessary with a suitable insecticide if the insects appear.

Outdoor bananas ❧

"Last week I saw banana plants grown outside among the summer flowers in a public garden. They looked wonderful. Can you tell me whether they are a special hardy sort and can stay outside in the winter?"

Banana plants have large, handsome foliage and they are often used as specimen plants in summer floral displays. However, they are not hardy in this country and have to be kept in a frost-free greenhouse for the winter. Plants are easily grown from seed.

Musa uranoscopus grows to about 4 ft (2 m) and *Musa ensete*, the Abyssinian banana, grows much taller. Sow the seed in a warm place in February/March. Best results are obtained by starting the plants off in a warm greenhouse.

Potting cyclamen ❧

"I raised some cyclamen plants from seed last September. The plants have grown well and are now in 3½ in. (9 cm) pots. When should I move them into their final pots and should they be put in 5 or 6 in. (12–15 cm) pots? Do I keep the plants in the greenhouse during the summer?"

Move your young cyclamen plants into their final pots when roots begin to fill the small pots. For final potting, use either 5 or 6 in. containers depending on how much space you have and the size of plants you want. Really good specimens can be grown in 6 in. (15 cm) pots.

When repotting, make sure that you keep the tuber just above soil level. Once the plants are well established in their final pots, feed them each week until the autumn with a liquid fertilizer.

Cyclamen like cool, moist conditions in summer with light shade from strong sunshine. From June to September keep the plants in a cold frame.

Friendly mouse plant ❧

"I would be grateful if you would name the plant from the specimen I am sending. There is a profusion of leaves and the strange-looking flowers are totally hidden under the leaves. I have looked in various gardening books but I cannot trace it."

Your plant is *Arisarum proboscideum*, commonly called the mouse plant, because of the curious appendages at the tips of the flower spathes. It is a delightful, choice plant that is well worth preserving.

It grows best in soil that is well enriched with decayed organic matter and prefers a shaded position. The flowers are hidden by the leaves, so try to grow it at the edge of a path where it is less likely to be overlooked. Some gardeners grow it in shallow pots stood in an unheated greenhouse or frame so that the flowers can be better appreciated when they appear.

Resistant solution ❧

"I find it simpler to grow my greenhouse tomatoes in the border soil rather than in growing bags. I have been told it will be necessary to change the soil every few years to stop disease build-up. Is this really so?"

If you grow tomato varieties that have an inbred resistance to the main soil-borne diseases, you should be able to continue growing in the soil for some years without changing it.

"Cyclon" from Unwins Seeds is resistant to fusarium and verticillium wilts (as well as to virus and leaf mould) and "Piranto" from Marshalls is resistant to brown root rot as well as to most other tomato diseases. For prevention of damage by root knot eelworm and other soil-borne troubles, the variety of your choice could be grafted onto a resistant rootstock known as KNFV.

This imparts resistance against root knot eelworm as well as corky root, stem rot, and fusarium and verticillium wilts, but there is no resistant variety against cyst eelworms.

Flush the soil through at the end of each year to remove excess salts and use plenty of manure or compost to keep the plants growing well.

Myrtle berries ❧

"We recently bought a plant of Myrtus communis *but I cannot find out whether the fruit is edible. I purchased the plant, thinking that it was the same myrtle which I have seen as a tree in the South of France which produced delicious berries. In the same region is a plant that grows as extensively as gorse in this country. It is almost identical but the flowers are scented. Can it be grown in this country?"*

The myrtle that you have seen in the South of France is most probably not the same as *Myrtus communis,* which can be grown outside in mild areas of this country. It is possibly *M. luma,* which has edible berries, or *M. ugni,* now correctly called *Ugni molinae,* the Chilean Guava. The latter produces delicious, blue-black berries but can only be grown outside in Cornwall.

There are several different types of gorse and we cannot be sure which one you have seen in France. The common gorse that grows in this country is *Ulex europaeus.* The flowers are scented, producing a coconut fragrance.

Fuchsia cuttings ❧

"I have a fuchsia pot plant in my greenhouse which has lots of new shoots on it. Can I cut some of them off as cuttings? When is the best time to do it and how long should each cutting be?"

Some of the young shoots on your fuchsia could be taken as cuttings. Now that the days are becoming longer and warmer the cuttings should soon form roots. Some gardeners make the cuttings about 2 in. (5 cm) in length but even tiny cuttings, about $\frac{1}{4}$ in. long, root without difficulty.

Insert the cuttings in modules or small pots filled with a good seed compost to which some perlite has been added.Once the cuttings have been taken, keep them moist at all times until roots have formed.

Mealy bug ❧

"I have a young myrtle plant, grown from my daughter's wedding bouquet, and it is doing well apart from some cotton wool-like growths in the shoots and leaf axils. I would hate to lose the myrtle, can you advise please?"

How nice to learn you are carrying on the tradition of growing a myrtle plant from a wedding bouquet. The pest you describe will be mealy bug and it is reasonably easy to control.

The pest feeds on the sap, weakening the plant, but also deposits sticky honeydew over the leaves and that soon turns black and unsightly. If the myrtle is in the house or conservatory, put it outside on a mild, calm day and spray thoroughly with malathion. This is a good systemic insecticide so will kill the mealy bugs wherever they are feeding, and also kills on contact. Wash the leaves after a few weeks to remove any sticky honeydew.

Rusty carnations ❧

"My greenhouse-grown carnations are looking rather poorly with dusty, brown to orange spots on the leaves. I suppose this is some form of rust, but is there any control?"

Yes, the spots are due to attack by carnation rust and yes, it can be controlled. Remove the worst of the infected leaves and then spray thoroughly with Tumbleblite or with a copper fungicide.

Using a cold frame ❧

"I have bought a cold frame but do not know what to use it for. Can you help me?"

A cold frame is a valuable piece of garden equipment and a wide variety of plants can be grown in it. During the winter you could grow winter lettuce in it. Sow a variety such as "Novita" from September to mid-February. Early radish and carrots could also be grown in the frame. If you are more interested in ornamentals, grow small bulbs, such as dwarf irises, crocuses and daffodils in pots. Plant the bulbs in the autumn for early spring flowers.

Seeds of half-hardy annual flowers can be sown in pots in the spring. Grow the seedlings on in boxes in the frame for planting out at the end of May. During the summer months melons or cucumbers could be grown in the frame.

Sticky traps ❧

"I hang up sticky yellow traps in my greenhouse to try to keep whitefly numbers down. In a commercial nursery I saw both yellow and blue traps hanging up; are the blue ones more effective or do they catch different pests?"

The different wavelengths of the yellow and blue traps do attract different pests to some extent. Yellow will attract whitefly, greenfly and thrips plus some other pests. The blue is more specific to thrips, and where this is a major pest then the blue traps are worth using. They can be obtained from Oecos, 130 High Street, Kimpton, Herts SG4 8QP. Phone 01438 832481.

Greenhouse lining ❧

"I lined my 10 ft by 6 ft greenhouse with bubble plastic last autumn. This has insulated the greenhouse successfully and kept the frost out. As it is now the start of the seed-sowing season, I am wondering whether the lining will allow sufficient daylight through to keep the seedlings sturdy. Can I take part of the plastic down?"

Seedlings sown under glass in late winter or early spring need very good light to keep them sturdy. Rather than taking down the complete lining, while the weather is still cold, remove a section from the side of the greenhouse that receives most sun. After germination, place the seedlings on the staging or, preferably, on a shelf fitted near the roof and close to the unlined area.

Do make sure that seedlings are not harmed by very strong sunshine and keep away from cold draughts.

Cheshunt Compound on edible crops ❧

"I use Cheshunt Compound regularly against damping off with my flower seedlings, but wonder if it is safe to use it on edible crops? Would it affect them later on after growing and when they are ready for eating? Earlier in the season I lost some tomato seedlings to damping off and would like to know, for future reference, if I could have treated them."

Cheshunt Compound is based on copper and is purely a contact fungicide, so is not absorbed into the plant system. It can therefore be used on edible plant seedlings and young plants without any later complications.

By law, under the Control of Pesticides Regulations, any restrictions regarding treatment of edible crops must appear on the product label. Where no warnings or restrictions appear, the product would be approved for application to edible crops.

Too rich ❧

"I have geraniums growing in my conservatory that make lots of leaves and no flowers. They are in John Innes Potting Compost No. 2 and are

fed every fortnight with half-strength tomato fertilizer. How can I make them flower?"

Almost certainly you are over-feeding them. Cease regular feeding with the tomato fertilizer and instead, give them sulphate of potash – a tiny pinch per pot.

Next year pot the plants in John Innes No. 1 (No. 2 is too rich) and do not feed them.

Indoor control   ❧

*"I have a pony tail plant (*Beaucarnea recurvata*) that is badly infested with mealy bugs. The mealy areas can be found on virtually all the leaves but as it is in our conservatory I am reluctant to spray. Can you tell me about biological control – I read a little while ago in* AG *about a beetle that can be used."*

The biological control agent to use is known as *Cryptolaemus*. This is a ladybird relative which will feed on the mealy bugs and also lay eggs to be followed by larvae which also feed on the pests.

Obtain supplies by ordering by post from Defenders Ltd, PO Box 131, Wye, Ashford, Kent TN25 5TQ.

Glory lily   ❧

"I have been given some tubers of the glory lily, Gloriosa superba *'Rothschildiana', to grow in my greenhouse. When should the tubers be planted and how tall do the plants grow?"*

Gloriosa "Rothschildiana" is a superb plant for a warm greenhouse. It is a climber and clings by means of tendrils, growing up to 6 ft. (1.8 m) tall.

Plant the tubers in early spring in large pots or containers filled with a good potting compost. Train the stems under the roof in your greenhouse or provide twiggy sticks in the pot to support the stems. Once the plants are in full growth, water them freely in the summer and feed them each week with liquid fertilizer.

In the autumn, when the leaves begin to fade, gradually give less water and keep the tubers dry in the winter.

New arrival   ❧

"Can you tell me anything about the plant called Scaevola aemula *as I cannot find anything about it in any of my gardening books. All I know is*

that it is suitable for hanging baskets and patio containers. Is it an annual or perennial?"

Scaevola aemula is a half-hardy perennial. This means it can be grown outside in the summer but it must have the protection of a frost-free greenhouse for the winter.

The best way to keep the plant is to take some cuttings in late summer and root them in a pot of gritty soil. Pot them up when new roots have been made and keep the young plants in a frost-free greenhouse through the winter. This is simpler than trying to keep the old plant which will have grown fairly large by the end of the summer.

Bright, not breezy ᘓ

"Two years ago, I was given an ixora plant. It is now almost 2 ft (60 cm) high and has clusters of small red flowers. At present it is in a 4 in. (10 cm) pot and is kept in my greenhouse at 10–15° C. Please tell me how to treat it."

The ixora is a tropical plant that appreciates a bright position throughout the year. During the winter keep it in a minimum temperature of 15–18°C, but slightly warmer at the roots. A windowsill that has a radiator underneath would be suitable, provided the plant is not subjected to draughts or very dry air.

During the winter, only water the compost when it shows signs of drying out, and use rainwater if possible.

When new growth starts in the spring, gradually increase the water supply and stand the pot on a tray of gravel which should be kept damp.

Feed the plant regularly with liquid fertilizer in the spring and summer; it could be transplanted into a 7 in. (17 cm) pot in April.

Too tender for our winters ᘓ

"On holiday in the Algarve I admired colourful lantana bushes. I obtained some cuttings which I have rooted at home. Will these plants survive winter outside in this country?"

Lantana bushes are not hardy in this country so we would advise you to keep your plants in a frost-free greenhouse for the winter. They can be planted outside again next summer if you wish.

Take cuttings again in the summer and these will provide you with plants for the following year.

Green shoots

"I have some fuchsias in pots which have been kept dry in my greenhouse during the winter. When can I start them into growth and should I prune the old stems?"

Your fuchsias may be started into growth in February and March. Do it as soon as you see new green leaves appearing on the stems. Cut back the old stems to where a strong new shoot is appearing and cut out all thin and weak ones. Shake out some of the old soil from amongst the roots before you repot the plants in fresh potting compost.

Which way up?

"I have bought some begonia tubers but I do not know which way up to plant them."

Take a look at the tubers and you will see a hollow on one side. This should be planted facing upwards.

To start tubers into growth press them into the surface of the compost in a shallow tray so that the top of the tuber is just above the level of the compost.

Keep them warm and moist and once new growth begins pot them individually using a good potting compost.

Shrubby calceolaria

"I thought that calceolarias were tender plants for a greenhouse but last summer I saw some plants covered in small, yellow flowers. It looked as if they were planted outside permanently. Is this a special hardy form?"

The calceolaria that you saw last summer was probably the shrubby *C. integrifolia*. This is not hardy but in mild, frost-free gardens it will often last for several years outdoors. It likes a hot, sunny spot, preferably at the foot of a south-facing wall and soil that is well drained.

As a precaution, take a few cuttings in the summer and keep them under glass for the winter.

Sowing calceolarias

"I would like to grow some calceolarias in my greenhouse which is heated in winter to exclude frost. When is the best time to sow the seed?"

Greenhouse calceolarias can be sown between May and July to flower early in the following year. They do not like hot conditions so delay sowing if the weather is very hot.

Once germinated, grow the plants in cool conditions and provide light shade from strong sunshine. You can expect blooms about 18 weeks after sowing.

Succeeding with cinerarias ❧

"Can you tell me whether cinerarias can be grown outside in this country? They seem to flourish in places like Madeira but is our climate too cold for them? And when is the best time to sow the seed?"

Cinerarias are not hardy in this country, although it is possible they might succeed in mild gardens in Cornwall or the Isles of Scilly. They are normally grown as pot plants under glass for flowering in the winter and spring. Seed can be sown throughout the summer to give flowering plants in about six months' time.

Sow the seed in small pots in a cool greenhouse. When large enough, prick out the seedlings into small pots and move them on individually later into 5 or 6 in. (12–15 cm) pots.

The dwarf strains make attractive small plants and may be flowered in $3\frac{1}{2}$ in. (9 cm) pots.

Scented cherry pie ❧

"I have been given a cherry pie plant. The flowers have a lovely scent and I would like to grow more plants. Can it be propagated from cuttings and, if so, when is the best time to take them?"

Cherry pie, heliotropium, is a fine plant for growing outside in summer beds or as a pot plant in a greenhouse or conservatory. Grow named varieties which are known to have good scent.

Plants are easily propagated from cuttings, made from sturdy, firm young shoots, taken in the summer. Make each one about 2 in. (5 cm) long and trim off the lower leaves. Insert the cuttings in small pots of gritty soil and stand them in a heated propagator until roots form.

New greenhouse cropping ❧

"We have just put up a new greenhouse, with a central path and beds on each side. Is it all right to plant up tomatoes and cucumbers in the soil, or would we be better off growing them in bags or pots?"

If you prepare the soil well with organic matter and fertilizer you should obtain very good crops by growing directly in the border soil. Plants there would also be under less stress in hot weather if watering was delayed for any reason.

After a few years there could be a build-up of soil-borne diseases such as wilt or brown root rot, so should crops fail in any year, switch to growing in bags from then on.

Before the advent of growing bags, keen gardeners used to change the greenhouse soil every two or three years, and you could take this alternative if you wished.

Top dressing for ficus ❧

"I have an indoor Ficus benjamina *plant growing in a large pot which is full of roots. I cannot move it into a larger pot, so what should I do?"*

As it is not possible to repot the ficus, scrape away a large amount of the surface compost and replace it with fresh potting compost. In the spring start feeding with a liquid fertilizer or use a slow-release fertilizer which provides enough nutrients for the plant for a whole season.

Fuchsia cut-backs ❧

"I have a hardy fuchsia with lots of dead stems. Some have young shoots on them. Do I cut them all back or leave those with young shoots?"

You can cut all the stems on your hardy fuchsia back to the ground. New growth will soon appear which will flower in late summer and autumn. However, if several of the stems have strong, young growths appearing on them, you may cut the withered tips of the stems back to where the growths are appearing and you will probably finish up with a taller bush.

Angel's trumpets ❧

"Are angel's trumpets the same as datura and are they dangerous to animals?"

Angel's trumpets is the common name, in this instance for datura, now *Brugmansia sanguinea*. It is a very handsome plant but poisonous. But provided the sap is not taken into the body and the leaves are not eaten, daturas should cause no serious problems.

Sensitive plant ❧

"I have four plants of Mimosa pudica *which I have grown from seed. All are doing well. But every now and then, I find the leaves shrivel and die. How and when is it safe to repot them?"*

Mimosa pudica originates from Brazil and is a short-lived sub shrub which, in this country, is usually grown as an annual and discarded at the end of the season. You could try to keep your plants over the winter if they can be kept in a warm greenhouse. The possible cause of the shrivelling of the leaves may be because the plants have been kept too dry at some stage.

Damping of blooms ❧

"My greenhouse chrysanthemums were disappointing this year, with several of the flowers turning brown and rotting just before they were fully open."

The flowers have been attacked by a fungal disease known as damping of blooms. It is a form of the ever-present grey mould fungus botrytis and is encouraged by lack of ventilation and associated damp air.

Enclose damaged flowers in plastic bags and then cut them off for disposal; this prevents spores spreading to other flowers during the removal process.

Give as much ventilation as the outside weather conditions allow, and heat a little in dull and cold conditions.

Sowing those indoor primulas ❧

"I have been given some seed of Primula 'Kewensis'. When should it be sown?"

Like other indoor primulas, such as *Primula malacoides* and *P. obconica*, seed of *P.* "Kewensis" should be sown in late spring or early summer in a propagator.

Grow the plants on in a greenhouse, giving light shade from strong sunshine in the summer. Maintain a minimum temperature in winter of 7°C (45°F). Water sparingly in winter and never allow the compost to become too wet.

The plants should flower in the spring after sowing.

Barberton daisy ❧

"I have been given a gerbera pot plant. It has bright red and yellow flowers. I have it in a light window, but would it be better moved into the greenhouse after flowering?"

The dwarf gerbera hybrids (Barberton daisies) are attractive pot plants but they are unlikely to grow well if kept permanently in a living room, so after flowering do as you suggest and put the plant in your greenhouse.

Give it light shade from strong sunshine in the summer and in the winter maintain a minimum temperature of 7°C (45°F). Water the plant freely in the summer and feed with a liquid fertilizer, but water only sparingly in winter when temperatures are low.

Repot the plant in early spring in John Innes potting compost No. 1 to which can be added extra coarse grit or sand to ensure good drainage.

Heathers

Ailing heathers

"Seven years ago we made a large rockery of heathers and a couple of small conifers. The site is very windy and last winter and spring we lost a lot of plants. Please can you explain what may be wrong."

We are sorry to learn of your unhappy heathers. We are wondering whether you are growing summer-flowering heathers and the soil is too alkaline for them. Check the soil by testing it with Rapitest kit to see how acid or alkaline it is. Ideally, the result should be a pH6 or less. If it is higher, add plenty of pulverized bark and grow only the winter-flowering, *Erica carnea* varieties which do not mind a slightly chalky soil. If you wish to reduce the pH even more, work flowers of sulphur into the soil.

Heathers for lime

"I want to plant a border with heathers and dwarf conifers but I have discovered that the soil is slightly alkaline. I know that heathers need an acid soil but are there any that will put up with a little lime in the soil?"

Yes, there are a few heathers which will tolerate some lime in the soil. Choose the winter-flowering *Erica carnea* and its many varieties, as well as *E.* x *darleyensis*. Before planting, work plenty of acid peat into the soil plus decayed leaves and woodland soil which will help to make the soil more acid.

Heathers in tubs

"I am very keen on heathers but I cannot grow them as my soil is chalky. Can I grow a few plants in tubs? What sort of soil should I use?"

Yes, heathers can be grown in tubs. Use an acid, ericaceous potting compost which you can obtain ready mixed at garden centres. Make sure that there are drainage holes in the base of the tubs and cover the bottom with broken crocks or rubble before adding the compost.

Although your soil is chalky you can still grow the varieties of *Erica carnea*, the winter-flowering heather, which tolerate an alkaline soil. Mix plenty of peat and leafmould in the soil before planting.

Heathers and lime   ?❧

"I thought that heathers could only be grown on lime-free soil. Passing a garden in a chalky area the other day I saw a wonderful display of pink and white heathers. Why were they doing so well?"

The heathers you saw were probably varieties of *Erica carnea*, the winter-flowering heather. These will tolerate lime in the soil unlike most of the summer-flowering heathers. *E.* x *darleyensis* will also tolerate lime in the soil.

Healthy trim   ?❧

"Last autumn I planted a number of young calluna plants in my garden. Can you tell me whether they should trimmed and when it should be done?"

Trim your young callunas during the next few weeks with sharp secateurs, cutting off the old flower heads. This will induce bushy new shoots to form which should flower in late summer.

Cut back   ?❧

"I have a bed of winter-flowering heathers which are doing very well. I have been told that they should be trimmed each year; when should this be done?"

Heathers respond well to an annual trim. This keeps the plants compact and they flower better. Trim your winter-flowering heathers with shears or secateurs after flowering. Summer-flowering kinds should be trimmed in late March or early April.

Trimming heathers   ?❧

"I have some winter-flowering heathers which are very colourful at the moment. However, they are spreading a bit. Can I cut them back and if so, when?"

Heathers benefit from an annual trim to keep them compact. Do this after flowering in early spring, using a sharp pair of shears.

Hedges

Seaside blockade ❧

"I have an evergreen cotoneaster hedge 7–8 ft tall. My neighbours have cut some of the foliage away so that the plants are spindly. What evergreens could I plant in containers to screen the gap? I live close to the sea and the garden is constantly subjected to strong, salty winds."

There are several evergreen shrubs suitable for planting in tubs in an exposed situation on the coast that is liable to salt winds. Suggestions include: *Aucuba japonica, Cistus laurifolius, Elaeagnus pungens* "Maculata", *Escallonia* "Crimson Spire", *Euonymus japonicus, Hebe salicifolia, Ilex aquifolium, Lonicera pileata, Olearia* x *haastii* and *Arundinaria japonica*.

Flowering hedge ❧

"I would like to have a flowering hedge to cover an ugly chainlink fence. It is in a sunny situation. I have been told that rosemary makes a good hedge. Can you recommend any other flowering hedges and is rosemary easy to plant and maintain?"

Rosemary makes an attractive flowering hedge. Choose "Miss Jessop's Upright" form. As the name suggests the growth is upright and well suited for hedging. A light trim can be given after flowering.

Other flowering hedges that you can grow are: *Berberis stenophylla*, yellow flowers, evergreen; escallonia, evergreen, red or pink flowers; forsythia; ribes (flowering currant); *Spiraea* x *arguta*, white flowers in spring and *Rosa rugosa*, red flowers and colourful hips in autumn.

Hedges on chalk ❧

"My soil is very chalky. What are the best shrubs to grow for a hedge on this type of soil?"

Suitable shrubs for making a hedge on a chalky soil are: *Cotoneaster simonsii*, escallonias, *Lonicera nitida, Viburnum tinus, Fagus sylvatica* (beech), *Berberis stenophylla* and *Ligustrum ovalifolium* (privet). If you need a low, evergreen hedge about 2–3 ft (up to 1 m) tall, *Cotoneaster microphyllus* has neat, compact foliage. The best time to establish the hedge is during the autumn.

Cold comfort

"We always get snow here at some time during the winter. What can we do to help the wildlife during these snowy spells?"

Snow is not the real problem; it is prolonged freezing temperatures that cause the most hardship. When the ground is frozen on the surface it is impossible to dig or scrape for insects or plant roots, and water is very difficult to come by. Animals hibernating under a blanket of snow find their nests those important few degrees warmer and snow can be eaten to provide water.

The best way to help animals survive cold spells is to provide suitable food in the autumn and winter so that they can fatten themselves up; supply suitable nesting or hibernation sites and put out fresh water regularly in freezing conditions.

Brown leyland

"Both this year and last, areas of my lovely green leyland hedge turned yellow or brown and dead-looking. I cut out the dead areas but couldn't find any bugs. There was a black powder on the shoots though; is this some disease?"

The damage to your leyland hedge is due to attack by the cypress aphid. Most aphid species simply feed on the sap and excrete honeydew, although this does then turn black due to sooty mould growth. Some species also spread virus diseases. The cypress aphid is even more damaging as where the pests feed the whole shoot beyond that point dies out.

The aphids are quite large and are pale grey in colour with two black lines on the back. They live mainly on young shoots, excreting honey as they feed. "Castlewellan" and other golden forms of leyland seem more at risk. Control next year with drenching sprays of a systemic insecticide such as Long-Last or Sybol, with the first application in mid-June.

Leylandii headache

"I have recently moved to a house with an overgrown boundary hedge of Cupressocyparis leylandii. I believe that the top can be cut back drastically without killing the hedge but I am not sure how hard I can prune the sides which spread some 5 ft (1.5 m) out from the trunk."

Cupressocyparis leylandii does not respond well to renovation when it is drastically pruned so there is a strong possibility that when you cut back the side branches, the whole will look bare and bleak. The top will not be so bad as it will tend to develop new growth in this area.

We planted these leylandii conifers to get on the telly!

Leylands in trouble ❧

"There are brown areas of foliage scattered along our otherwise lovely Castlewellan 'leyland hedge' and where the worst browning occurs there is also a black deposit. No pests are visible."

The browning and death of the shoots is the result of feeding by the cupressus aphid, *Cinara cupressi*. Where the pest feeds the shoots die back, and become coated with sugary honeydew excreted by the pests. This becomes colonized by black sooty mould fungi. New attacks are likely to start from April to May.

Cut out affected shoots now, remembering, however, that old, leafless wood may not sprout new growth. Keep a lookout for the large, yellowish brown aphids and, if found, apply the aphid-specific Rapid insecticide as a forceful drench.

Bindweed in a hedge ❧

"I have an 8 ft (2.4 m) high leylandii hedge which has become partly covered with bindweed. Is there a selective weedkiller I can use to get rid of the bindwind without harming the conifer?"

Unfortunately, there is no selective weedkiller available that can be used without harming the hedge.

What we suggest you do is disentangle the bindweed and lay it away from the hedge. Once clear of the hedge it can be treated with a glyphosate weedkiller. Do this in the spring as the new growth emerges, but in the meantime, try to fork out as much of the weed as possible.

Trimming beech ❧

"How often should a beech hedge be trimmed?"

Beech hedges need to be trimmed only once a year, in July or August.

Messy pest ❧

"My beech hedge is being attacked by a pest that looks like apple woolly aphid. The leaves are sticky, the leaf edges are turning brown, and it all looks very messy. Help please."

The pest responsible in this instance is the beech aphid which is very similar in appearance to woolly aphid.

The pests produce sugary honeydew which is soon colonized by sooty mould fungi, turning the leaf surface black.

For best control, apply a systemic insecticide such as Tumblebug or Long-Last to kill the pests deep inside the hedge as well as those nearer the outside. As the pest is so damaging, repeat the spray after a couple of weeks to ensure total control.

Spread out ❧

"I have a beech hedge growing between two concrete paths 8 in. (20 cm) apart. The concrete is beginning to crack because of the expanding roots. The trunks are now about 6 in. (15 cm) in diameter. Can I restrict further expansion by bark ringing?"

Bark ringing is done mainly on apple trees to curb the vigour of the top growth. We do not think it will curb root development on your beech hedge. In fact, it could seriously harm the hedge. The only way to deal with the problem is to move the paths further away from the hedge or take the hedge out.

Planting a hedge ❧

"I am thinking of planting a beech hedge. Is it better to arrange the plants in a single or a double row, and how far apart should the plants be spaced?"

Beech plants can be grown in a single or double row, although a double row will make a more robust and sturdy hedge. If planting a double row, set the plants 18 in. (45 cm) apart, in two staggered rows. In a single row space the plants 10 in. (25 cm) apart.

Planting may be carried out throughout the winter although November is an ideal time.

Holey laurel ❧

"Our laurel hedge leaves are being eaten around the edges by something, but we can never find any insect on them. I also thought laurel leaves were poisonous, so would be unaffected by pests."

Vine weevils are responsible for the damage. They feed mainly at night so are rarely seen at work. Insects dropped into a screw-top jar containing crushed laurel leaves will be killed, and yet the vine weevil is able to survive on a diet of laurel leaves. Control is therefore by using a contact insecticide such as Tumblebug; spray the ground as well as the leaves to catch the weevils in their daytime resting places.

Mildewed hedge ❧

"Is there a really effective control for mildew on roses? My rose hedge, Rosa x damascena versicolor *gets a very bad attack each summer which spoils it for the rest of the year."*

Rose mildew can be controlled, but it does take perseverance. Start now by mulching the soil below the rose hedge with compost or bark after applying a rose fertilizer. Give the soil a good watering if it is dry. This will help to conserve moisture – dryness at the roots can be a contributory factor in rose mildew attack. If there is any sign of mildew now, spray thoroughly with Nimrod-T or Systhane and repeat a fortnight later.

Keep the soil moist in dry weather, pruning out any mildew attacks, and spray with one of the above fungicides, or with Safer's Natural Garden Fungicide a few times during the summer and autumn. This will prevent mildew spoiling your hedge.

Scale of the problem

"Several of the shoots in our evergreen euonymus hedge are coated with a fine white encrustation which spoils its appearance. From the samples enclosed, would you please let us know what is responsible and if there is any cure?"

The white deposits are the remains of an attack by the euonymus scale insect, and the brown objects also visible are the living adults. Prune out the shoots that can be spared without spoiling the hedge and then spray with Tumblebug in June. This is when the next generation of scales will be on the move.

As there is such a dense infestation, it would be worth giving two sprays a couple of weeks apart and repeating the two-spray treatment in September.

Box clever

"The growing points of lots of shoots in our box hedge are curling into rounded growths and there are several greyish insects inside. Can you identify the problem and suggest a control measure please?"

The pest responsible for the curling is the box sucker. These mealy pests feed on the sap and exude sticky honeydew which in time turns the leaves black. The curled, infested shoot tips are known as artichoke galls.

Hedge trimming should remove many of the pests, along with the young growth, but burn or otherwise safely dispose of the prunings. Any that remain can be controlled by a systemic insecticide such as Sybol.

To feed or not to feed?

"We always keep our bird table well stocked, and have plenty of visitors through the winter, but when spring comes the birds hardly ever visit. Where are we going wrong?"

Most birds prefer to be self-sufficient: it's often only when bad weather drives them to it that they will feed from bird tables. In spring, when they are raising young, there should be plenty of natural food about. In any case, the food we often provide, such as peanuts and coconut, is fine for adult birds, but could actually be harmful to nestlings.

Hedging your bets ❧

"At the end of last year I purchased and planted some Rosa rugosa *bushes for a hedge. They have all taken and started to produce suckers. Should I leave these to produce a dense thicket or remove them to let the original bush have all the goodness?"*

Allow your bushes of *Rosa rugosa* to continue making suckers so that you have a good thick hedge. Apart from the large, attractive flowers, this rose also produces handsome hips in the autumn.

Quick hedge – but not conifers ❧

"I want to plant a hedge at the bottom of my garden to separate the ornamental part from the vegetable garden. I want a fairly quick-growing plant but do not want conifers."

If you don't want conifers for your hedge, the choice of other shrubs is rather limited. Suggested evergreens for your hedge include: *Cotoneaster lacteus*, escallonias and pyracantha and planting distances between the shrubs should be about 18 in. (45 cm). Improve the soil before planting with rotted manure or compost. Container-grown plants can be put out at most times of the year but in the summer careful attention must be paid to watering.

Pimple problems ❧

"A maple tree in my hedge has sprouted little yellow pimples on the leaves. They look quite attractive but I would rather be without them. Any suggestions please?"

Maples and sycamores can be attacked by at least seven different gall mites. On maple, some cause little red pimples and others, like those on your plant, cause yellow ones. Yours would most probably be a species of *eriophyes* and is specific to species of acer.

There is no satisfactory control, but picking off and disposing of infected leaves would help.

Silver Y moth ❧

"There were literally hundreds of moths on my lavender hedge at flowering time. I am worried that they may breed and that their caterpillars could be damaging. Comments please."

This would be the adult silver Y moth, so called because of the characteristic Y mark on each forewing (the scientific name is *Autographa gamma*, indicating that the mark also looks like the Greek letter gamma).

This moth is unable to survive our winters, except under glass, but it can be quite a serious pest in heated greenhouses, the caterpillars feeding on chrysanthemum, carnation, pelargonium and other flowers, leaves and buds.

The silver Y moth is a regular immigrant into this country from the Mediterranean areas of Europe. The damaging caterpillars are about 1½ in. (3 cm) long, pale to dark green with a pale yellow line along the body. Any seen on plants should be picked off by hand.

Lavenders for a hedge

"I want to plant a lavender hedge on either side of a path. What is the best dwarf kind?"

One of the best is "Hidcote". Another good dwarf form is "Nana Atropurpurea". Both have dark purple flowers and fragrance.

Keep in shape

"Over a year ago I planted lavender on either side of a path. The plants have grown very well and are nice and bushy. I want to prevent them spreading and I feel they need a trim. When should this be done?"

Lavender hedges need trimming each year to keep them compact otherwise the growth will spread outwards, leaving the centres open.

Trim your hedges in the autumn, once the flowers have finished, with sharp shears or secateurs. If trimming has not been done in the autumn it can still be carried out in late winter.

Evergreen screening

"I have a mesh-type fence which I erected as a screen approximately 7 ft 6 in. (2.2 m) high by 12 ft (3.6 m) wide. It faces east but is sheltered on three sides and is in a semi-shaded situation. At the moment it is covered by a Russian vine but I would like to replace it with an evergreen covering. Can you offer any suggestions for a quick-growing climber?"

The choice of quick-growing, evergreen climbers for your situation is very limited. Ornamental ivies are worth considering, in particular *Hedera canariensis* "Variegata", *H. hibernica* and *H. colchica* "Dentata Variegata". Pyracantha varieties could also be considered, although these are shrubs and trimming would be required to keep them trained along your screen.

Berberis hedge ❧

"I am thinking of planting a hedge of Berberis darwinii. *Do you think that this is a good choice? Should the plants be put in a single or double row and how far apart should they be spaced?"*

Berberis darwinii is a first-rate evergreen shrub with masses of yellow flowers in the spring. It makes an excellent hedge and needs trimming only once a year after flowering. Plants may be grown in a single row spacing them 18 in. (45 cm) apart or they may be planted in a double, staggered row at 3 ft (90 cm) apart if a denser and wider hedge is required.

Hedge cuttings ❧

"I have a hedge of Lonicera nitida *and I want to extend it. Can I take cuttings from the existing plants?"*

Cuttings of *Lonicera nitida* root readily in April. Make the cuttings from firm, young growths to a length of 6–9 in. (15–22 cm). Insert them outside in a slit made in the ground with a spade. Put some coarse sand in the bottom of the holes to assist rooting.

Golden privet ❧

"I want to plant a hedge this winter and I am considering golden privet. Does it make a good hedge? Does it need any special kind of soil and how far apart should bushes be planted?"

Golden privet is a valuable ornamental shrub and it makes an excellent hedge. It is not fussy about soil, provided it is well drained. However, to ensure good growth, dig over the ground before planting and work liberal quantities of decayed compost or manure into the soil. Space the plants 1 ft (30 cm) apart. After planting, cut the bushes back by about half their length to induce bushy basal growth.

Mildew hits mixed hedge

"We have a long front hedge of mixed plants including elm, oak, beech and maple. Last summer the maple was white with mildew which quite spoiled the look of the whole garden. Will this mildew overwinter on the maple shoots to appear again next spring? If so, is there anything we can do?"

Some mildews that attack woody plants do spend the winter on the shoots or in the buds, but trimming the hedge in late autumn would remove most of any infection.

If the hedge was not trimmed, do this when new growth starts in spring and follow with a spray of fungicide as recommended for rose mildew.

Keep the plants well watered during dry spring and summer weather.

Make sure you keep your eye on the hedge when cutting your privet.

All trim and tidy ⅔

"I want to plant a formal hedge. Can you tell me how often different kinds need trimming?"

Most formal hedges such as yew, box and Lawson's Cypress need trimming twice a year in spring and late summer. Privet and *Lonicera nitida* need trimming three times in the season. Beech and holly need to be trimmed only once in late summer.

Caterpillar tents ⅔

"What is affecting my hedge? It is covered in a film of fine threads and inside are lots of hungry caterpillars. They even enclosed a dandelion seed head in the webbing."

A few different species of caterpillar can produce this type of webbing but the most likely would be those of the lackey moth. Adults are on the wing in late July to September and lay batches of up to 200 eggs in a tight band around the twigs, protecting them with a shiny, varnish-like coating. The eggs hatch in April to May and feed in vast numbers under the protection of the webbing which they spin, extending it as they move to new areas. The caterpillars are fully fed by July when they pupate, and emerge as new adults three weeks later to repeat the cycle.

Control by searching for, and pruning out, the egg bands, most clearly visible after leaf-fall.

Box sucker ❧

"My wife has established a nice little box hedge but the new shoots now have what looks a bit like woolly aphid on them. Small insects with white threads coming from them are making the hedge look unsightly and I'm sure are doing it no good."

The insects are box suckers. Overwintering eggs hatch in spring and feed on the sap in the growing points, often causing the young leaves to curl inwards like tiny cabbages. A spray now with a systemic insecticide such as Sybol or Tumblebug should be effective. Autumn trimming of the hedge is needed to remove the eggs, as they are not laid until late summer.

Screening shrubs ❧

"My daughter wants to divide her garden in two with an evergreen flowering hedge. What can you suggest please? We do not want shrubs with thorns or prickles."

There are a number of evergreen, flowering plants suitable for hedging that do not have prickles or thorns. A few suggestions include: *Cotoneaster lacteus* with white flowers in June followed by red berries in autumn; *Elaeagnus* x *ebbingei* "Gilt Edge", golden-edged leaves and fragrant white flowers in autumn; *Escallonia* "Donard Radiance", rose-red flowers in summer and early autumn; *Ligustrum delavayanum*, a small-leaved privet which bears white flowers with violet anthers in early summer, but not suitable for cold, exposed areas; *Osmanthus* x *burkwoodii* or *O. delavayi*, fragrant white flowers in spring; *Prunus laurocerasus* (cherry laurel), again white flowers, this time in early summer; *Prunus lusitanica* (Portugal laurel), fragrant white flowers in June; rhododendron hybrids, all spring-flowering and various flower colours – must have lime-free soil and *Viburnum tinus*, white flowers in winter.

Pruning yew

"I have a yew hedge which has been neglected and has spread out too much. Can the stems be cut back to keep the hedge to a reasonable width?"

Yes, you can certainly cut back your yew hedge as you suggest. Do the pruning in late winter. The hedge may look rather unsightly for a while, but new green shoots will soon break out from the bare brown wood. The hedge can be cut back into old brown wood and will soon recover.

After pruning, feed the soil around the hedge with bonemeal and mulch with manure or compost to help stimulate new growth.

Yew hedge

"I wish to plant a hedge in my garden to provide a dense screen about 6 ft (1.8m) high. I would like to plant yew but wonder whether this would take too long to mature. How far apart should the bushes be planted?"

Yew is an excellent choice for a hedge. It is not only dense, responds well to regular clipping but also grows fast once established. Give it a good start by taking out a trench 2–3 ft (just under 1 m) wide and 1 ft (30 cm) deep. Work old manure or compost into the soil and apply bonemeal over it. Set the bushes 1½ ft (45 cm) apart. Water copiously in dry weather and foliar feed each week in the summer with a high nitrogen fertilizer. This will help the hedge to get established. If your garden is windy, stretch twine from one end of the hedge to the other and tie the plants to it. Mulch the soil around the plants with a 2 in. (5 cm) layer of manure, compost or bark fibre.

Pruning yew

"I have a yew hedge which is cut regularly but is spreading out into a path. If I cut it back into older wood will I harm the hedge?"

Yew will stand being cut back severely if it is done at the right time. This hard pruning must be carried out only in early spring. Strong new growth should develop in the summer and the old bare stems will be quickly covered once again with green foliage.

Herbs

Herbal remedy

"I have often thought that it would be a good idea to grow a few herbs in a hanging basket but I have never seen one. Do you think they would grow well and are there likely to be any snags?"

Herbs can certainly be grown in a hanging basket. Grow them in the largest basket that you can obtain so that they can form good root systems.

Suitable kinds to grow include parsley, thymes (including the golden-leaved form), sage, rosemary and mints. The main problem likely to be encountered is watering in the summer.

The compost in the basket is likely to dry out rapidly in hot weather and it may be necessary to water the basket two or three times a day.

Give feeds of liquid manure in the summer once the plants are well established in the basket. It would be interesting to hear from other readers who have grown herbs successfully in a hanging basket.

Keen as mustard

"I want to grow some mustard and cress indoors for winter salads. Can you give me some tips on the best way to do it?"

Mustard and cress can be grown indoors in dishes lined with blotting or kitchen paper. Moisten the paper and sow the seed evenly over it. As mustard germinates more quickly than cress, sow the cress two days before.

After sowing, keep the trays in the dark but as soon as the seed germinates, bring the trays out into the light.

Cut the seedlings when they are about 2 in. (5 cm) tall. Sowing at intervals will provide a continuous supply.

Scented leaves

"I like to have plants in my garden with scented leaves. I am told that Agastache foeniculum *has fragrant foliage. What sort of soil and position does it need?"*

Agastache foeniculum is a sun-loving plant and needs good, well-drained soil. Plants grow about 3 ft. (90 cm) tall and produce attractive spikes of violet-pink flowers in late summer. The leaves are fragrant and are similar to bergamot.

Herbs at hand

"Is it possible to grow herbs satisfactorily in a windowbox or tubs? I would like to have some close to my kitchen door, so that they are handy when I need them for cooking."

Herbs can certainly be grown in a variety of containers and windowboxes – special clay herb pots are available from garden centres.

If possible, choose a sheltered and sunny spot for the herbs and fill the container with good potting compost. Make sure that there are drainage holes in the base of the container. A few herbs that you could grow in this way are thyme, sage, parsley, chives and a prostrate rosemary.

Planting a herb pot

"I was given an attractive herb pot for Christmas. What are the best kinds to grow in it and what type of soil should I use for planting?"

Choose compact and prostrate types of herb for the pot. Parsley is ideal as well as attractive plants such as sage, various thymes, chives and mint.

Make sure that the drainage hole in the bottom of the pot is covered with a piece of broken pot to allow surplus water to drain away. Fill the pot with good potting soil such as John Innes potting compost. As you fill the pot with the compost push a small plant into each opening in the side of the pot and firm the soil around the roots. Allow space at the top of the pot for watering.

The herbs will grow best if the pot is stood outside in a sheltered and light position. If it can be put close to the kitchen door the herbs will be handy for use as and when required.

Planting a herb pot for winter pickings

"Can I plant a herb pot in September as I would like to have one near my kitchen door where it would be handy to have herbs for picking in the winter?"

Herb pots can certainly be planted in the autumn. Suitable herbs for winter use include parsley, chives, mint and sage. Place a little rubble at the bottom of the container for drainage. Use John Innes Potting Compost No. 2 to fill the container.

Insert the herbs in the apertures in the side of the container and at the top. After planting, give the herbs a good watering to settle them in.

Sorrel sorrow ✺

"I had a lovely sorrel plant in my herb garden, but now the lower leaves are being shredded by some pest. I cannot find any slug trails or caterpillars present."

I have had exactly the same problem and found that sparrows were having a feast early each morning. Now the plant has had an old onion net placed over it and damage has ceased.

Sowing parsley ✺

"Can you tell me where I am going wrong with parsley? I made two sowings in March and April but hardly any seedlings appeared. Does the seed need to be treated in a special way?"

Your problem is not uncommon. Parsley can be difficult to germinate but given the right conditions you should not have much trouble. It will not germinate in cold, wet soil and you should wait until the soil warms up in the spring before sowing. The seed can be soaked in water overnight before sowing and some gardeners like to pour boiling water along the seed drill just before sowing. It is also important to use fresh seed as old seed will give disappointing results. You may have been sowing too deeply. A covering of $\frac{1}{8}$ in. is all that is needed.

Parsley pointers ✺

"I sowed some parsley seed in July and now have some nice sturdy plants. What is the best way of keeping the plants growing through the winter?"

One way of safely overwintering your parsley is to cover the plants with cloches in the autumn. Alternatively, lift some of the plants and put them in pots. Kept in a greenhouse or cool room indoors they will provide foliage for cutting through most of the winter.

Cover young parsley plants with cloches in the autumn to provide fresh leaves through the winter months.

Parsley puzzle   ❧

"One of my parsley plants started to change colour, and went from a dark green, through yellow and orange, to red. It also stopped growing and is now about half the size of the others. Any ideas?"

The damage you describe so well is typical of the effect that a couple of virus diseases have on parsley, and also on carrot, where the symptoms are known as motley dwarf disease. Carrot motley virus and carrot red leaf virus are both spread by the willow-carrot aphid, and the leaves of infected plants change colour exactly as you have described. Carrot fly attack can also have a similar effect on parsley, but the damage is not quite as marked.

There is no real control, as it only takes a small amount of feeding by the aphids to spread the infection. Destroy the plant to stop further infection being picked up by visiting aphids.

Parsley problem   ❧

"I have some French parsley in a pot on my kitchen windowsill which now has a developing population of greenfly. What can I spray with safely? Further, where did they come from?"

You could take the plant outside and spray with Tumblebug, which only needs one day between spraying and picking. However, I would try first to remove the pests with finger and thumb, or by picking off the worst leaves. There were probably one or two greenfly on the plant when you brought it into your kitchen, and they are now multiplying in the warm conditions.

Clipping bay   ❧

"I have a small bay tree in my garden. Can I clip it to keep it compact and when should it be done?"

April is a good time to trim bay trees and you will find that new growth will soon follow. Another trim can also be given, if necessary, in July.

Bay sucker   ❧

"Can you please tell me what is causing the thickening and yellowing of the leaf edges on my bay tree leaves and the best way to stop it?"

The puckering and yellowing is the work of the bay sucker. Adult insects spend the winter on the tree and start egg-laying in spring. Feeding and leaf damage continues through to October.

Control inside the curled leaves with a systemic insecticide, observing the necessary interval between spraying and using any leaves in the kitchen.

Blackened bay leaves 🎋

"My bay tree leaves are covered with a sooty black deposit. Although it washes easily off the leaves when brought into the kitchen for use, I would like to know what causes the blackening, and more helpful still, is there anything that can be done to stop it happening?"

The blackening is due to sooty moulds, but the underlying cause is an attack by scale insects. If you look along the main veins under the leaves you will see the actual flat scale insects. As they feed they exude a sugary honeydew, and it is on this that the sooty mould becomes established. Control the scale insects with a spray of Tumblebug, Bio Friendly Pest Pistol or Phostrogen Safer's Insecticide. Check the label in order to leave any necessary interval between spraying and use in the kitchen.

Standard bay 🎋

"I have just bought a standard bay tree in a pot. How do I look after it and when do I trim it?"

Make sure that the compost in the pot of your bay tree never dries out in the summer. Feed it each week with a liquid fertilizer to encourage new growth but cease feeding in early August.

Trim the foliage two or three times in the summer to keep the "head" neat and compact.

Bay watch 🎋

"I was given an established bay tree which is now growing in my conservatory, but there are scales under the leaves, plus a shiny substance which makes the leaves and floor sticky, and which also turns black. How can I treat it to cure the problem?"

The pests responsible are scale insects and you have described all their attendant problems very well. As they feed on the sap they exude sugary honeydew and this is soon colonized by black, sooty moulds.

Malathion is probably the most effective insecticide against scale insects, but it does have rather a pungent smell, which may be offensive in a conservatory. If the tree is small enough to take outside, once the weather warms up a little, then spray it outside and leave it to air before returning the tree to the conservatory. If too large, spray with Tumblebug or Sybol instead of malathion.

Planting garlic ❧

"I would like to grow my own garlic. How do I go about it?"

Garlic can be grown successfully in this country, but it needs a light, fertile soil and a sunny situation. As it likes a long season of growth, November and early December is the time to plant the cloves, the individual segments that make up a bulb.

Plant the cloves 4 in. (10 cm) apart in rows 12 in. (30 cm) apart, covering them with about an inch of soil. Keep the ground between the bulbs clear of weeds.

The bulbs should be ready for harvesting in July after the foliage has withered.

All tied up ❧

"What causes mint leaves to become tied up at the tops of the shoots? I think there is a caterpillar present, but it must wriggle out before I can get a good look at it."

There will be a caterpillar involved, namely a species of tortrix moth. Such caterpillars always wriggle rapidly backwards out of danger.

Picking off the affected shoot tips should give sufficient control, but dispose of the tips away from the mint plants to stop them crawling back!

Saucy ideas ❧

"Which mint makes the best sauce?"

Spearmint (*Mentha spicta*) is the one you want to grow to flavour your new potatoes, peas, beans and, of course, to mix with vinegar for your mint sauce!

There are several other mints worth growing, too. Woolly-leaved apple-mint (*M. suaveolens*) can be added to summer drinks, as can the dark-leaved peppermint (*M. piperita*). Gingermint (*M. gracilis*) has beautiful variegated golden and green leaves and will add a hint of ginger to salad leaves, while a bunch of leaves of the eau-de-cologne mint (*M. p.* "Citrata") can be held under the tap for a scented bath.

All these varieties will grow in almost any soil, but they prefer a rich, moist loam, and will tolerate shade better than most other herbs.

Mint going rusty 🌿

"Is it possible to cure mint rust or do I have to dig it all up and start again?"

The answers to your questions are "Yes" and "Yes"! The best way would be to dig all the mint out and burn it except for a few underground runners. Take tip cuttings from these and the plants that grow should be free from rust.

Mint can take over the entire garden and even the house if left to its own devices!

Scent for success 🌿

"I want to make a small area in a raised bed as a seat carpeted with fragrant chamomile. Is it best to buy plants or sow seed?"

The best chamomile to use for a lawn or seat is the double-flowered variety because of its compact habit. However, it does not come true from seed and you will have to buy in plants which can be expensive.

There is also a non-flowering form called "Treneague" which also does not come true from seed.

Depending on how many you need, you could buy a few as stock plants and propagate your own from them by detaching the offsets in the autumn or spring.

Alternatively, ordinary chamomile, *Chamaemelum nobile*, can be raised from seed. We suggest that you sow in seed boxes and prick out the seedlings before planting them out.

Plant at 6 in. (15 cm) apart in each direction. Any weeds that appear should be removed by hand as soon as they are seen.

Rosemary cutting ⅔

"I have a nice rosemary bush in my garden and would like to take some cuttings from it. Are they easy to root and when is the best time to take them?"

Rosemary cuttings root without difficulty. The best time to take them is in the summer. All you have to do is to pull off short side shoots with a "heel" of older wood attached. Strip off the lower leaves and plant them in sandy soil in the open. A better method is to remove side shoots about 4 in. (10 cm) long in July and August. If they have a "heel" of older wood attached, trim it with a sharp knife and remove the lower leaves. Insert several cuttings around the edge of a small pot filled with a mixture of peat and coarse sand or perlite. Once rooted, pot the cuttings individually. Plant out in the open when a good root system has been made.

Lavender cotton ⅔

"I have some bushes of cotton lavender or santolina. They have become rather leggy. Is it safe to cut them back without harming the bushes and can cuttings be taken from the plants?"

Santolina plants (cotton lavender) tend to become leggy and they should be cut back each year in March. Fresh, young grey foliage will develop soon afterwards.

Cuttings of young shoots removed with a "heel" of older wood attached may be taken in late summer. Insert the cuttings in small pots filled with a gritty compost.

Dividing chives ⅔

"I have a large clump of chives in my garden which has not been disturbed for some time. Can I split it up, and when is the best time to do it? How far apart should the pieces be replanted? Can I grow a plant under cover for winter supplies?"

It is a good idea to lift large clumps of chives and divide them into a number of pieces. It should certainly be done every three or four years. Spring and autumn are the best times to divide plants.

Plant the divisions 8–12 in. (20–30 cm) apart. They make an attractive edging to a border. One or two plants can be grown in pots and kept under glass for the winter to provide young foliage for cutting at inclement times of the year.

Chive talking ❧

"I bought some chive plants last spring and planted them in my garden. They have grown well but they are much taller than I expected, reaching 9 in. (23 cm) high. I was expecting small plants about 4 in. (10 cm) tall. Is there more than one type of chives? Should the plants be allowed to flower?"

Yes, there are two types of chives, the ordinary kind with fine leaves and a taller version. Yours is obviously the latter.

If you want to grow the plants for ornament, they can be allowed to flower and they make an attractive edging to a flower border. If you are mainly interested in producing foliage for flavouring dishes, remove the flower heads so that the plant's energy goes into leaf production.

Incidentally, the flowers may also be used in salads and for flavouring dishes.

Establishing chives ❧

"How do I go about getting a clump of chives established?"

You can raise chives (Allium) from seed or by dividing an old clump. A packet of seeds, available from all the major seed suppliers, will cost less than £1. Sow these in the spring, and when the seedlings are a few inches high, plant them out in clumps of about half a dozen seedlings, spacing the clumps 9 in. (23 cm) apart. They'll soon spread into larger clumps.

Mature clumps can be divided at any time from spring to autumn, and divisions will soon establish. Remember, though, chives need a humus-rich soil and plenty of moisture.

Rusty chives ❧

"Do chives suffer from leek rust disease? I had rust on my leeks once, but have never seen any on chives until this year. Is it the same species as the one that attacks leeks?"

Yes, the leek rust fungus can attack chives (and garlic) as well as leeks. On chives attack is often sufficient to kill off all the leaves and it is likely to be perennial within the plant. The only satisfactory treatment would be to dig out and burn the plants.

Dig the soil over well before carrying out any replanting in the same area.

Angelica seed ❧

"I was given some angelica seed and I sowed it in a shallow box in good seed compost. Not one seed germinated. Does it need any special treatment?"

We suspect that you got hold of some old angelica (*Angelica archangelica*) seed. It remains viable for only a short time after it is collected and it is important to sow it as soon as possible. This can be done in the autumn and certainly no later than the following spring. The seed also requires light for good germination and it should not be covered. A temperature of 12°C is ideal.

New herb to grow? ❧

"Can you tell me anything about a herb called Good King Henry. What is it used for?"

Although Good King Henry, *Chenopodium bonus-henricus*, has a grand name, the plant's appearance is not particularly striking. It is often found growing wild in waste spaces. It has arrow-shaped leaves and spikes of tiny green flowers. The leaves are used as a substitute for spinach and the young shoots can be cooked and eaten like asparagus. It is perennial in habit and can be easily raised from seed.

To assist germination, sow the seed in January in a box and leave it outside exposed to frosts. Then put the box in a warm greenhouse. Plant the seedlings in the open in June. A few leaves may be gathered in the autumn.

Established plants may be increased by lifting and dividing them in the autumn.

Drying sage ❧

"Can you tell me whether it is worth drying the leaves of golden variegated sage? I have a large plant of it which I grow as an ornamental plant. Does it have the same strong flavour of ordinary sage?"

The leaves of the golden variegated sage can be dried in the same way as ordinary sage but the flavour is milder. The purple or red-leaved variety can also be dried and has a stronger flavour than ordinary sage.

Variegated sage

"I have had a sage bush with green and grey variegated leaves for a number of years. Lately it has become rather straggly and I am wondering what to do with it? Can I cut back the stems?"

Your plant of variegated sage is probably past its best. Older plants tend to lose their colour. As young plants tend to produce the best foliage we suggest that you take some cuttings from your plant now. Choose sturdy side shoots, 2 in. (5 cm) long, for cuttings. Remove some of the lower leaves and put the cuttings in small pots of gritty soil. Once rooted pot them separately into 3½ in. (9 cm) pots. When a good root system has been made plant the young sage in the open garden. The old, worn-out plant is best thrown away.

Fragrant allspice

"I have been told that there is such a thing as an allspice bush. Can it be grown in this country?"

The allspices are American shrubs called calycanthus and they are easy to grow in this country. The flowers are reddish-brown in colour and both the flowers and leaves, when crushed, are pleasantly fragrant.

Lemon balm

"I want to grow some plants of lemon balm as I think the fragrance of the crushed leaves is delicious. Can you give me the botanical name for the plant and tell me, does it need a sunny or shaded position?"

The botanical name for lemon balm is *Melissa officinalis*. There is also a form called "Aurea" which has attractive, yellow-splashed leaves. Both are easy to grow. They succeed in most soils and prefer a sunny spot. Infusions made from the leaves have been used medicinally for centuries as an aid to relieving depression.

Curry aroma

"The curry plant in my garden attracts much attention, mainly for its pleasant curry aroma when visitors rub against it. I am often asked for cuttings from it, so when would be the best time to take them?"

The curry plant, *Helichrysum angustifolium*, is grown primarily for its attractive silver foliage and unusual curry aroma, which is strongest on a hot, sunny day. Plants are easily increased from cuttings taken in July and August.

Use young shoots that are not too soft and make them 2–3 in. (5–7.5 cm) long. Remove the lower leaves and insert the cuttings in small pots filled with seed compost to which has been added extra coarse sand or perlite.

Stand the cuttings in a cold frame or under a cloche and once rooted, pot the young plants individually.

Curry plant ❧

"Can you tell me whether the curry plant can be grown in this country? And is curry powder made from it?"

The curry plant is correctly called *Helichrysum italicum*. It has grey foliage and yellow flowers. In warm, sunny weather it gives off a distinctive curry aroma. Curry powder, which is a mixture of spices, is not made from it. However, sprigs from this plant can be used in cooking for its mild curry flavour.

It can certainly be grown in this country: it likes a warm, sunny position and well-drained soil.

Feverfew fever? ❧

"I have quite a lot of feverfew plants which I grow as an edging to flower beds. Now my plants have succumbed to a severe attack of mildew. What can I spray to cure the mildew and would I still be able to use the leaves in salads and sandwiches, which I find helpful against migraine?"

Miracle Spotless, Murphy Systemic Action Fungicide and Supercarb would all be effective against the powdery mildew on your feverfew. The fungicides can be used on a number of specified edible crops without any interval between spraying and picking. However, feverfew would not be one of the crops specified as edible on the label so it should not be sprayed and then eaten.

Instead, copious watering of any new plantings, and removal of leaves at the first sign of any renewed mildew attack would help to keep them free of infection.

Sowing feverfew

"I want to grow some feverfew plants as I am told that the leaves can be eaten to avoid migraine attacks. When should the seed be sown and are plants easy to grow?"

Feverfew (*Tanacetum parthenium*) is very easy to grow. Once you have plants in the garden, it is difficult to get rid of them as they seed themselves freely. Sow the seed in shallow drills in the open garden in early April and thin the seedings later to 12 in. (30 cm) apart.

The leaves have been used to relieve migraine but you should ask your doctor's advice as they can be harmful in excess or in pregnancy.

Oregano or marjoram?

"I'm confused. Are oregano and marjoram the same thing?"

Yes, they are. Oregano gets its name from the Latin name for marjoram, Origanum, although there are several different kinds.

The potted herb sold by many supermarkets as oregano is wild marjoram, *Origanum vulgare*, with its highly flavoured foliage. Pot marjoram, on the other hand, is *O. onites*, a compact plant ideal for growing, surprise, surprise, in a pot. Sweet marjoram, *O. majorana*, is the herb commonly sold as marjoram.

Here is one instance where the Latin name really does help, particularly when some seed catalogues simply list both marjoram, and oregano, with no explanation as to what is what!

The wrong colour

"I bought some plants last spring labelled Anthemis cupaniana. *I was expecting the plants to produce white flowers but, instead, they were a creamy-yellow. Can you tell me what they might have been?"*

We cannot be sure about your plants with yellow flowers without seeing them but we suspect the anthemis you bought was wrongly labelled.

Your plants are probably *Anthemis tinctoria*, commonly called golden marguerites. There are several different varieties including "Grallagh Gold", "E. C. Buxton", lemon-yellow and "Wargrave Variety", creamy-yellow. All are excellent border perennials.

Lovage lodgers ❧

"My lovage plants are being spoiled by brown blotches. I use lovage a lot in my cooking so I hope you can tell me how to correct the situation."

The damage is due to attack by a leaf-miner. Unlike some species of leaf-miner, this one causes the blotchy mines you are finding, rather than the more usual winding mines. There is no easy control, but picking off the worst leaves, and squashing the grubs inside the other ones, will reduce the damage to some extent.

Next year, at the first sign of damage, remove or squash the culprits and then spray a couple of times with a general insecticide, following the instructions regarding any necessary interval between application and picking for kitchen use.

Lifting horseradish ❧

"I planted some horseradish roots in March. Can the plants stay in the same position all year round or should I lift the roots in the autumn?"

Lift and store your horseradish roots in sand for the winter. Next spring cut off some of the thicker side roots and replant in the open in March. If the plants are left in the same position for several years they can become invasive, producing poor quality roots. Plant the roots with a dibber spacing them 12 in. (30 cm) apart.

Tansy uses ❧

"Can you tell me how the herb tansy is best used?"

Tansy is not used a great deal nowadays.

It is said that grown near fruit trees, it deters insects. Dried leaves placed under carpets are also said to repel ants. The attractive yellow flowers may be dried for winter flower arrangements.

Sowing clary ❧

"I want to grow clary among other herbs. Can you tell me whether it is an annual or perennial and when can the seed be sown?"

Clary, *Salvia sclarea turkestanica*, is a hardy biennial but usually grown as an annual. Sow the seed outside in the spring where the plants are to grow. Thin the seedlings out to 12 in. (30 cm) apart as the plants grow quite tall, up to 3 ft (90 cm) high.

Florence fennel ⁓

"I sowed some seed of Florence fennel last April but the plants bolted and were useless. Can you tell where I went wrong?"

Florence fennel can be tricky to grow and plants bolt easily if they are sown too early or if checked in growth by a lack of water. This year sow the seed outside in late May or early June. Thin the seedlings to leave them 12 in. (30 cm) apart. Remember to give them plenty of water and never allow the soil to dry out.

Choose a modern variety, such as "Cantino" which is not so inclined to bolt.

Bolting fennel ⁓

"I have never been successful in growing Florence fennel. Seed was sown in May but the plants bolted and did not form bulbs. How can I prevent this happening?"

Fennel seed sown too soon is inclined to bolt so try sowing later in June or early July. Sow the seed in small pots or modules and, when the plants are large enough, plant them outside. Checks to growth such as a lack of water or fluctuating temperature can cause bolting.

It would also be wise to use a bolt-resistant variety such as "Zefa Fino".

Italian cress ⁓

"Last autumn, when on holiday in Italy, we were served what we were told were rocket leaves in salads. They had a spicy taste and were very pleasant. Can it be grown in this country?"

Rocket, also known as Italian cress, is a hardy annual that can be grown successfully in this country. The leaves may be used in salads for their spicy flavour, or cooked.

As it is hardy, it is a useful substitute for lettuce in the winter. However, if sown in early autumn for winter use, cover the plants with cloches to have better quality foliage. Seed can be sown throughout the spring and summer, although plants tend to bolt and go to seed in hot weather.

Ginger root ⁓

"I bought some ginger roots in a supermarket. Would they grow if I put them in a pot of soil?"

Yes, the ginger roots you have will grow into attractive plants. The true ginger is *Zingiber officinale*. They are tropical plants and need a really warm greenhouse with moist, shady conditions. The unusual, club-like flowers appear at the base of the stiff stems of grass-like leaves, although it is unusual for plants to flower in this country. The best time to start a root into growth is in the spring.

Although not true gingers, the Ginger Lilies are more rewarding to grow. *Hedychium gardnerianum* produces spikes of highly fragrant, creamy yellow flowers in late summer. Pieces of root can be purchased from bulb suppliers. These should be potted in the spring and grown under glass, although they can be taken outside for the summer.

Grow your own ginger ❧

"Some months ago I put a piece of root ginger in a pot. It has produced a green shoot about 2 in. (5 cm) long. Does it require any special treatment?"

Root ginger, a form of hedychium, makes a fine foliage plant for a warm, moist situation. When mature it bears fragrant white flowers. Other forms, such as *Hedychium gardnerianum*, have handsome spikes of yellow flowers. For the moment, grow your plant in a pot of good potting compost and keep it in a light place. When the pot becomes full of roots move it on into a larger pot. Feed it regularly with a liquid fertilizer during the summer. The plant may not be large enough to flower this summer but next year it should flower in late summer. Keep the plant in a frost-free place for the winter.

Dandelions for salads ❧

"I have been told that dandelion leaves are good in a salad. Is this true? My impression is that the leaves are too bitter."

Although a common weed, dandelion leaves are often used in salads. They can be chopped or pulled apart into smaller pieces. On the continent special strains are cultivated for their leaves.

Choose the young leaves which have a milder flavour. Plants can also be blanched by putting an inverted pot over them. The drainage hole must be closed to exclude light. Blanched leaves are paler and have a sweeter flavour.

Herbs on the rocks ❧

"I have been told that herbs can be frozen in ice cubes. Do you think that this is a satisfactory way of preserving herbs?"

Freezing herbs in ice cubes is a very good way of preserving the leaves. Simply wash the herbs and then chop the leaves as finely as possible. Most cubes will hold a tablespoon of chopped herbs and a tablespoon of water. Use them as required and if the water is not required for cooking allow the cubes to thaw in a sieve.

House plants

Inside out

"Are there any of my house plants that can survive on their own in the ground outside?"

Most house plants are tender and will not survive the winter outside, but many can be put outside for the summer.

It is usual to sink the pots in the ground but, if necessary, they could be taken out of their pots and planted in the soil. However, they would have to be lifted and repotted in early autumn. Some of the more hardy house plants that could be treated in this way are *Solanum capsicastrum* (winter cherry), Indian azaleas, fuchsias, jacarandas, ivies, aspidistra and *Campanula isophylla*.

Home alone

"I cannot find anyone to water my indoor pot plants while I am on holiday. Can you tell me the best way to keep them moist while I am away?"

One of the easiest ways of keeping house plants moist during the holiday period is to stand them on capillary matting in a shallow tray. Water the plants thoroughly before you leave and also thoroughly moisten the matting. This should keep the plants moist for up to a week. If you are away longer, arrange a wick from a large jar of water, above the tray, down to the matting. Stand the plants out of direct sunshine.

House plant care

"I was given several house plants for Christmas but I am not sure how often to water them and when should they be repotted?"

Stand your house plants in a light place in a cool room avoiding hot and stuffy conditions. Only water when the soil seems dry.

Thoroughly soak the compost in the pot and allow it to drain. Do not water again until the soil is almost dry once more.

Repotting must not be done until early April and only then if the pot is very full of roots.

Give liquid feeds from April until August each week which should keep the plants growing healthily. It is a good idea to stand plants indoors on a tray filled with chippings which should be dampened each day. This will provide some humidity around the plants.

Jumping pests ❧

"When we water our house plants, little grey creatures appear on the surface of the compost and leap about. What are they, and are they harmful?"

The creatures you describe are springtails which have a special springing organ at the rear of their bodies. They feed on dead and living organic matter, and in pot plants can be quite damaging to the plant roots.

Control is not too easy, but watering the compost with a spray-strength solution of malathion is usually pretty effective.

Mouldy compost ❧

"The surface of the compost of some of our long-term house plants is grey in colour and looks as if a mould or something similar is at work. Is this likely to damage the plants?"

The greyness is unlikely to be harmful to your house plants. It may be due to oxidation of the peat at the compost surface or a form of mould, living on the dead organic matter of the compost.

A gentle stirring of the surface should reduce the visibility of the discolouration, whilst a watering with a copper-based fungicide used for damping off should check any fungal growth.

Browning leaves ❧

"The tips of many of my house plants are turning brown. Can I do anything about it?"

The browning of leaves of indoor plants is usually caused by dry air conditions. This can be overcome to a certain extent by standing the plants on a tray of pebbles that are kept damp. Light mistings of water each day with a hand spray will also be beneficial.

Most plants benefit from being stood outside in summer, in a partially shaded spot.

Leaf cuttings ❧

"Is it true that streptocarpus plants can be propagated from their leaves? I have a plant and would like to raise more from it to give to friends."

Yes, streptocarpus plants can be increased from cuttings made from the leaves. The best time to do this is in the spring and summer when there are higher temperatures to assist rooting.

Remove a mature leaf and cut it horizontally into sections each about 2 in.(5 cm) deep. Insert the sections upright in a small pot filled with a gritty cutting compost, burying them by about half their depth. Ideally, stand them in a warm, moist propagator or enclose them in a polythene bag in a warm position. The cuttings should form roots in a few weeks when they should be potted individually in good potting compost.

Mother-in-law's tongue ❧

"I have had a Sansevieria *'Laurentii', the one with yellow edges to the leaves, for at least 15 years. It is strong and healthy and I have given many cuttings from it to friends. During the last year the yellow edges on the leaves have disappeared. Can you explain why this has happened?"*

Your *Sansevieria trifasciata* "Laurentii" would seem to have reverted to the plain green form and nothing can be done to bring back the yellow banding. Incidentally, this plant, unlike other varieties, can only be propagated by division of the rootstock, not from cuttings, otherwise it loses its yellow margin.

Yellow leaves ❧

"My winter cherry pot plant has had lots of berries but the foliage has become yellow between the veins. Do you think that the plant needs feeding?"

We suspect that your winter cherry or *Solanum* is short of plant food and does need feeding. Cut back the side shoots close to their base. This will induce bushy, new growth in the summer. Without pruning plants tend to become very straggly.

After pruning, repot the plant in fresh potting compost. Shake off some of the old soil before adding fresh compost. The plant can stand outside for the summer. When it is in flower, spray it overhead each day with water to help the flowers set berries. During the summer feed the plant each week with a liquid fertilizer.

African hemp ❧

"I have been given a plant with the name Sparmannia africana *on its label. I cannot find the name in any of my books and so I do not know how best to treat it."*

Sparmannia africana, African hemp, is an appealing foliage plant with interesting flowers. A fascinating feature is its stamens. Tickle them gently and they respond by expanding slowly – like an opening umbrella.

Grow it in a light place in a cool room. Feed and water it regularly in spring and summer but give less water in winter.

If your plant grows too large for its position, prune it back in spring.

Annual care ❧

"I have been given a streptocarpus plant which is flowering well in my sitting room. When the flowers fade can I keep it for another year or should I throw it away?"

There is no reason why you shouldn't keep your streptocarpus for more than a year. During the summer keep it in a light place but away from strong sunshine. Stand the pot on a tray of pebbles that can be kept moist to create humidity around the plant. Feed it each week with a liquid fertilizer until the autumn.

During the winter keep the plant in a cool room to give the plant a rest. As the days become longer the plant should begin to flower again.

Leaf drop ❧

"Last year I was given an indoor plant called Heptapleurum variegata. *It is a most attractive plant with yellow variegated leaves. It has done well until the last few weeks when some of the leaves have fallen off. Is there any way I can stop this happening?"*

The probable reason for the dropping of its leaves is shock as a result of a change in conditions. This plant likes a warm, moist atmosphere in winter and if it has been subjected to a cold draught, this could cause the leaves to drop.

Grow it in a light place in a temperature of about 15°C (59°F). Stand the pot on a tray of pebbles that can be dampened to create humidity around the plant. Only water when the soil seems dry. Give it a good soaking and allow excess water to drain away. Do not water again until the soil seems dry. Wipe over the foliage from time to time to clear away dust.

Carrion flower

"I have been given a stapelia succulent plant in a small pot and have put it on a windowsill indoors. What treatment does it need?"

Like many other succulents, stapelias must be kept cool and dry in the winter. If they are kept too warm and wet, they will rot off. Your plant will be happy in a greenhouse with a minimum temperature of 8°C (48°F), provided the soil is kept dry. Plants like a really well-drained compost with plenty of coarse grit.

Often, they are grown in open lattice baskets suspended from the greenhouse roof. Without a greenhouse, keep your plant in an unheated room in winter. Once the weather becomes warmer in the spring, watering can be gradually increased. When plants become overcrowded they may be repotted in the spring.

Stapelias have curious star-shaped flowers which unfortunately give off a rather nasty rotten meat smell. This attracts flies which then carry out pollination.

Rare flowers

"I have a large sansevieria house plant. For the last three years it has produced large spikes of white flowers. Is this normal, as I have seen this plant exhibited at flower shows as a non-flowering house plant?"

Your sansevieria is obviously receiving the right care. Old, well-established plants that are pot bound are most likely to flower. If they are potted on and fed liberally they are inclined to make new growth and a few flowers.

Sansevierias are grown mainly for their attractive, sword-like foliage and not primarily for their flowers.

For this reason, it is permissible to exhibit them in a class for foliage plants. After all, *Begonia rex* is usually shown as a foliage plant and it is also capable of producing flowers.

Do the splits

"I have a sansevieria plant in my sitting room which is bursting out of its pot. I do not want to move it into a larger pot. Can I split it up into several smaller pieces and when is the best time to do it?"

Your overgrown sansevieria can be taken out of its pot and divided into several smaller portions.

Try to pull the plant apart in your hands or you may have to use a stout, sharp knife or secateurs to separate the rhizomes – they won't suffer.

Repot the separate pieces in a good potting compost, such as John Innes potting compost, firming it well around the roots. Until the plants start to make new growths, give water sparingly.

Peace Lily ❧

"I have a spathiphyllum or peace lily which has now completely filled its pot with growths. What is the best way to propagate the plant?"

Spathiphyllum wallisii is easily increased by dividing a large plant, and now is as good a time as any to divide your pot-bound specimen. Grow the divisions on in warm, moist conditions.

Powdery pest ❧

"I have a succulent plant called Tacitus bellus *that is not very 'bellus' just now. It is covered with some powdery pest, a little like a woolly aphid. Can you please identify it and supply a cure?"*

These pests are mealy bugs and produce a mass of waxy threads as a protection, in much the same way as fruit tree woolly aphids.

To control, take the plant outside on a mild day and spray thoroughly with malathion insecticide.

Mealy bugs will attack most kinds of indoor plants, and if there is a widespread infestation, consider using the biological control agent *Cryptolaemus* which is an effective predator.

Chusan palm ❧

"I have a clump of three Trachycarpus fortunei *palms in my garden which are about 30 years old and stand 6 ft high. One of the trees is now flowering for the first time with three large clusters of flowers. If I am lucky enough to get some seed, when should it be sown?"*

We were interested to know that you have three, thriving trachycarpus palms. Male and female flowers are often produced on separate plants but both sexes sometimes appear on the same plant.

If seed sets on your tree this year, collect it in the autumn and store it in a cool, dry place. Sow the seed in a pot or pan of seed compost in the spring.

Self-sown seedlings often appear around the base of the palms.

Tradescantia cuttings ❧

"I have a tradescantia plant with green and white leaves. It has now become straggly. If I cut off the tips of the stems as cuttings will they root?"

Yes, the tips of the shoots on your tradescantia plant can be used as cuttings. Cut them off with a sharp knife into lengths of about 4 in. (10 cm). Remove the lower leaves and insert the cuttings in a small pot filled with gritty potting soil or perlite. Cover the pot with a polythene bag to keep the cuttings moist. Inspect the cuttings from time to time and when signs of new growth appear it will indicate that new roots are being formed. Pot the rooted cuttings in new pots filled with a good house plant potting compost.

Glory bush ❧

"I have a plant of Tibouchina urvilleana *which I have in a large pot in my frost-free greenhouse. The plant has become rather straggly. Can I cut it back and when, and when is the best time to take cuttings?"*

It is natural for tibouchina plants, often called glory bush, to become straggly after a while. Prune your plant in early spring by cutting back long shoots by about half their length and cutting out thin, spindly growths. This should induce the plant to produce compact, bushy growth.

Cuttings are not difficult to root. Take them from firm, young shoots in the summer. Insert them in a small pot of gritty soil and stand it in a warm propagator.

Pick-a-back plant ❧

"I have a pot plant of the variegated Tolmiea menziesii. *I am told it is hardy and grows well in the open. Is this true?"*

Yes, *Tolmiea menziesii* is quite hardy and can be grown in the open. The variegated variety is particularly handsome. Young plants grow out from the older leaves, hence the name of pickaback plant.

This plant is good for ground cover and will soon form a carpet of foliage in cool, woodland conditions under shrubs.

Taff's golden outdoors ❧

"I have a pick-a-back plant with golden variegated leaves. I grow it in a pot indoors suspended so that the attractive foliage trails down. A friend tells me that it can be grown outside. Is this true?"

Your plant is *Tolmiea menziesii* and the golden-leaved form is called "Taff's Gold". It is an easy and attractive room plant but it can also be grown outside. *T.m. variegata* is another commonly grown form and the plantlets are easily propagated. Plant them in the front of a border in a lightly shaded position.

Fern help ❧

"My nephrolepis fern is not looking very healthy and some of the leaves are turning yellow. Should I repot the plant?"

It is not a very good idea to repot your nephrolepis fern in the middle of the winter as the plant is semi-dormant and making little growth. Wait until March before repotting, and use a good, lime-free potting compost. In the meantime, stand it in a light place in a room with a temperature of about 15°C. It does not like over-hot and dry conditions, so stand the plant on a tray of pebbles that can be kept damp to create some humidity around it. Also lightly spray the foliage with water whenever you can.

Yucca sucker propagation ❧

"I have a large yucca plant with lots of small shoots. Is it possible to cut these off to make new plants?"

Yuccas can be propagated from the sucker growths that appear around the base of the plant. In early spring carefully scrape the soil from around the suckers and if any have roots, detach them. Put the suckers in small pots of gritty soil so that a good root system can develop before the plants are put in the open.

Yuccas can also be propagated from root cuttings in the winter. Fork the soil from around the base of the plant to expose the root system. Cut off roots the thickness of a pencil and trim them into lengths of about 2 in. (5 cm). Plant them in a pot filled with gritty soil. Keep them under cover in the winter and new shoots should develop in the spring.

Unhappy venus fly trap ❧

"I bought a Venus fly trap plant in a pot but it does not seem to be doing very well in my sitting room. How can I make it grow better."

Your sitting room is probably too hot and dry for this plant, *Dionaea muscipula*. Fly traps grow naturally in swampy ground in Carolina, USA, and they must have a really moist atmosphere which is difficult to maintain in a living room.

Your plant would be better off in a cool greenhouse with the pot sunk in a bed of moist sphagnum moss. Plants enjoy regular light mistings with water as well as a light position.

Yuccas can grow too tall and action is required promptly.

Stag's horn fern ❧

"I have been given a plant of the stag's horn fern. How do I look after it?"

The stag's horn fern, *Platycerium bifurcatum,* is not difficult to grow and does well in a centrally heated room. It is best grown in a suspended hanging basket. Provide a reasonably light position: the plant prefers light shade to strong sunlight.

Water the plant by standing it in a bucket of rainwater for a short time each week. A little liquid fertilizer may be given to the plant in the spring and early summer.

Fly traps from seed

"I found the article about carnivorous plants very interesting. I was the owner of a Venus fly trap, but unfortunately I killed it by giving it some beef when flies were scarce. Where can I obtain seeds to start off another one?"

Seeds of this and other carnivorous plants are available from Marston Exotics, Brampton Lane, Madley, Hereford HR2 9LX. Tel: 01981 251140.

Water trap

"Some months ago I bought a Venus fly trap plant which I have kept indoors. It has not done very well and has now gone brown. How should I look after it?"

The venus fly trap plant, *Dionaea muscipula*, is very difficult to grow in a living room because the atmosphere is usually too hot and dry. In its natural habitat the plant grows in mossy, boggy conditions.

It is best to grow the plant in a frost-free greenhouse in a bed of sphagnum moss. Plants require a high moisture level and must be kept well watered in summer. Grow the plant in full sun with only light shade from very strong sunshine. Don't make the traps close artificially.

Arabian violets

"I bought an attractive pot plant the other day called Exacum *'Starlight Fragrance'. It has small mauve flowers that are nicely scented. Can you tell me whether I can keep the plant for next year or will it die after flowering? Can plants be grown from seed? I have a frost-free greenhouse."*

Exacums are usually treated as annuals and once the flowers have faded the plants are not worth keeping. They can be raised from seed sown in February/March in a warm propagator at a temperature of 18°C (64°F). The plants should be flowering six months later. Seed may also be sown in September to flower in the following spring.

Care for Indian azalea

"I have been given an azalea in a pot which has lots of flowers. I want to keep it so that it flowers again next year. How should I look after it?"

Keep your azalea in a cool room in a light window. Stand it on a tray or dish of pebbles that can be kept moist to create some humidity around the plant. Never allow the soil to become dry. Use rainwater for watering if at all possible as tap water is usually hard and contains lime which azaleas do not like.

During the summer stand the plant outside in a partially shaded spot. Keep it well watered in hot weather and feed it each week with a liquid fertilizer until August. Return the plant indoors in September and keep it in a light place in a cool room.

Brown tips ❧

"My aspidistra seems healthy but the tips of the leaves are turning brown. What is causing this to happen?"

Aspidistra leaves will become brown mainly because the plant is kept in a room where it is too warm and dry. Aspidistras are nearly hardy and are best kept in an unheated room in a light position during the winter. If you have to keep your plant in a heated room, stand it on a tray of moist pebbles which will create humidity around it. During the summer the plant may be kept outside in a partially shaded position.

Asparagus fern ❧

"Can you tell me how to grow asparagus fern? I have a small greenhouse with enough heat to exclude frost."

Asparagus fern, *Asparagus plumosus (A. setaceus)*, is not a true fern and, in fact, belongs to the lily family. The feathery foliage is highly decorative and it is well worth growing in a greenhouse. Sow the seeds in a small pot in the spring. Transfer the seedlings to individual pots and gradually move the young plants on to larger pots of good potting compost. The variety "Nanus" is compact in growth and is best for a small greenhouse.

Falling leaves ❧

"I have had a plant of Aphelandra squarrosa for several weeks but some of the lower leaves are falling off. Can you tell me what is wrong?"

Aphelandras are not the easiest indoor plants. It is common for them to lose their leaves if conditions are not to their liking. Cold draughts and hot, dry air can be responsible.

To create some humidity around the plant, stand it on a tray or dish of chippings which can be dampened and give the plant light overhead sprays of water. A steady temperature of 16°C (61°F) is desirable but if there are wide fluctuations between night and day temperatures this can cause the leaves to fall. Make sure that the compost in the pot does not dry out badly. When it seems dry give it a good soaking and allow surplus water to drain away. Do not water again until the compost seems dry once more. Never stand the plant in a dish of water.

Fern greenfly   ❧

"I have a bird's nest fern (Asplenium) *on my kitchen windowsill. It looks healthy, but I have now noticed an attack of greenfly on the fronds, and sticky deposits on the sill below. What would you advise?"*

If the attack is not too severe, hand-squashing of the pests may be enough, followed by a gentle washing of the fronds (and the windowsill) with mild soapy water to remove the sticky honeydew.

Should the attack persist, spray with a fatty acid insecticide, such as the Bio Friendly Pest Pistol or Phostrogen Safer's Insecticide.

Under the lonesome pine   ❧

"I have an indoor plant called Araucaria heterophylla. *Most if it looks healthy but the lower foliage is dropping off. How can I prevent this happening?"*

The Norfolk Island pine, *Araucaria heterophylla*, is an attractive conifer for growing indoors but it resents the hot, dry air in a centrally heated room which can cause the foliage to turn brown and drop. The plant is almost hardy and grows outside in the Isles of Scilly. Stand it outside for the summer but in early autumn take it into a frost-free greenhouse or an unheated room in a light position. The conifer will eventually grow too large for a room indoors. In Chile, its natural home, plants can grow up to 200ft (61 m) tall!

Aspidistra under attack   ❧

"My small, variegated aspidistra has very speckly leaves. I believe this is due to red spider attack, although I cannot see any actual pests on the foliage. As I only have one small plant, is there any alternative control to buying a bottle of insecticide or a whole container of biological control agents?"

The speckling will indeed be the result of mite feeding. The mites feed mainly on the undersurfaces of the leaves and being very small can only be seen clearly with the aid of a × 10 hand lens.

As only one plant is involved try a regular treatment of the leaves with a leaf shine product. Leaf shines work, whether in spray or wipe-on form, by coating the leaves with a fine oil. The same oil would tend to clog the breathing pores of the mites and could be expected to give a reasonable level of mite control.

Partridge-breasted aloe ❧

"I have a plant of Aloe variegata on a windowsill indoors. Would it better placed outside for the summer? There are several offsets around the base of the plant. Can these be removed?"

Aloes love the sun and your plant would be better outside in a sheltered position for the summer. The resulting plant will develop a good leaf colour and flowering will be encouraged. Return the plant indoors in September.

Keep it in a cool, unheated greenhouse throughout the winter months.

Aspidistra, a house plant ❧
with a cast iron constitution

"My aspidistra is not looking very happy and has brown edges to the leaves. Does it need feeding?"

Your aspidistra is probably suffering from the poor light conditions during the winter and you may have been keeping it in a room where the air is hot and dry. Aspidistras are nearly hardy and should be kept in a light place in a cool room.

From April to August feed the plant with a liquid fertilizer each week and during the summer stand it outside in a partially shaded position.

If the pot is full of roots, it would be a good idea to repot the plant with fresh potting compost in March or April.

Aechmea after flowering ❧

"Can you tell me what to do with my plant of Aechmea fasciata now that the flower has faded? The foliage still looks healthy."

Aechmea fasciata is one of the most popular bromeliads which have vase-shaped leaf rosettes. Once the flower dies, it means that the rosette will also wither away. Suckers will, however, appear around the base.

When these are large enough they can be carefully cut off the main plant with roots attached. Pot each one separately in small pots of good potting compost. Grow the plants in a warm, moist atmosphere and keep the vase of leaves topped up with water.

In hot water? ❧

"I have bought some achimenes tubers and have been told that they are also called hot water plants. Does this mean that they should be given hot water? When should the tubers be started into growth?"

Achimenes are called hot water plants because it was once thought that they needed hot water. We now know that this is not necessary.

Start the tubers into growth from March onwards in a greenhouse with a minimum temperature of 8°C. (48°F). Use a good potting compost and space the tubers about $\frac{1}{2}$ in. apart in a 5–6 in. (12–15 cm) pot.

Achimenes may also be grown in hanging baskets.

Spindly avocado ❧

"I have grown a plant from the seed of an avocado pear. It has healthy leaves but seems to be very spindly. Is this natural?"

Unless avocado pear plants are grown in good light they tend to become spindly. Keep your plant in a light window in a cool room for the winter. Too much warmth and poor light will result in more spindly growths.

In March repot the plant in a multi-purpose potting compost and cut the stems back by about half their length. Kept in a light place, new shoots should soon develop. The plant can be stood outside for the summer months.

An avocado tree, *Persea americana*, can be easily grown from seed. You need to germinate at a temperature of 18°C (64°F) for best results.

Lilac hibiscus ❧

"I have been given a plant called Alyogyne 'Santa Cruz' (lilac hibiscus). Can you tell me how to care for it? My plant came from the gardens at Abbotsbury in Dorset where it is growing in a border."

Alyogyne huegelii "Santa Cruz" is a native of Australia and can only be grown outside in frost-free gardens such as those at Abbotsbury and in the mild gardens in Cornwall.

Elsewhere it is best grown in a container which can be stood outside for the summer but returned to a frost-free greenhouse for the winter. Keep it well watered and fed regularly in the summer. Do any pruning required in spring.

Baby ferns

"I have been given an indoor fern called Asplenium bulbiferum. *It has dark green foliage on which appear to be small plantlets. Should these be left on the plant? What sort of position is best for this fern?"*

Asplenium bulbiferum is a handsome fern for a room provided it has a moist atmosphere. It should be kept shaded from strong light and a bathroom would be a good place for it.

As you have found, small plantlets form on the fronds. They do not have to be removed but one or two may be taken off when roots can be seen. Put the plantlets in small pots filled with a good potting compost.

Easy care

"I have been given a succulent indoor plant called Aeonium arboreum *'Zwartkop'. Does it need a warm or cool room and when is the best time to repot it?"*

Your aeonium would be best stood outside in a sunny spot for the summer. Keep it well watered. In late September return it indoors to a light place in an unheated room. Only water during the winter when the soil in the pot is really dry. Kept too warm and moist, unwanted, weak, spindly growth will be produced. Repot the plant in the spring but only if it is very pot-bound. Use a compost containing plenty of gritty, coarse sand.

Begonia care

"A friend gave me a magnificent present of a large plant of Begonia sutherlandii. *Could you tell me how to treat this unusual begonia?"*

The begonia that you have has become very popular in recent years. Its soft green foliage and orange flowers are certainly very attractive. Keep your plant in a light place indoors but with light shade from strong sunshine. Water the plant whenever the soil seems dry and allow it to drain. Do not water again until the soil is dry once more. Feed it each week in the summer with a liquid fertilizer to encourage good growth.

Towards the end of the summer mildew can be a problem, so keep it in a well-ventilated place. It is a tuberous begonia and from late September begin drying off the plant. Water it very sparingly until the soil is completely dry.

Remove the old foliage when it has withered. Keep the tuber dry through the winter in a cool place. As soon as new shoots can be seen in the spring, repot the tuber and start it into growth once again.

Shrimp plant ❧

"My Beloperone guttata has grown leggy. Could I take cuttings from it to start again with a new plant?"

Plants of *Beloperone guttata* are easily propagated from cuttings taken in the summer. Choose firm, young shoots a few inches long. Remove the lower leaves and trim each cutting just below a leaf joint. Dip the base of the cuttings in hormone rooting powder and insert them in small pots containing plenty of coarse sand. Stand the cuttings in a heated propagating case until roots form. At this stage pot the rooted cuttings individually.

If you want to keep the old plant, cut back the stems next spring and when new growth begins repot the plant in fresh potting compost.

Yellowing busy Lizzies ❧

"The leaves on my busy Lizzie plants turn a speckled yellow and then fall off. Many of the plants are now just bare stems. Help please."

Busy Lizzies are very susceptible to attack by red spider mites. The pests feed on the lower leaf surfaces and where they puncture the tissue to feed on the sap a pale patch develops. After a severe attack the leaves become lifeless and will fall off the plants.

A fine webbing can be seen over the leaves in serious infestations. To control, spray the plants, outside on a mild day, using a liquid derris insecticide or Long-Last. Repeat two weeks later. Indoors, mist the plants each day with water to reduce the attacks.

Bromeliad care ❧

"I have three bromeliads but I don't know the different types. What do I do with them once they finish flowering?"

Bromeliads enjoy a moist, warm atmosphere. Some kinds die after flowering. If yours do not, keep them in a warm, moist temperature and encourage robust growth by feeding them with dilute liquid fertilizer.

Pour this, like you would water, into the plant's vase. Remember to empty the vase if the temperature falls below 4°C.

Many kinds, such as *Aechmea fasciata*, produce suckers when the flowers fade. If yours does, detach the rooted suckers and pot them individually into peaty compost.

Spray plants daily with rain water.

Prize begonia ❧

"I have a ten-year-old Begonia rex *plant which has won several prizes at local shows. A judge told me to exhibit it at larger shows up country. Can you tell me how to go about it?"*

Two of the best regional flower shows where you could exhibit your *Begonia rex* are the Shrewsbury Flower Show (held in August) and the Southport Flower Show (held in August). For show schedules ring Shrewsbury 01743 364051 and Southport 01704 547147. The Royal Horticultural Society organize a great many shows and details can be obtained from their Shows Dept. Phone 0171 630 7422. The National Amateur Gardening Show (held in September) includes competitive classes for houseplants. For a show schedule, ring 01202 440840.

Hibernating house plant ❧

"I have a bougainvillea pot plant which has flowered for most of the summer. I want to keep it for next year. How do I look after it in the winter – at the moment it is in a greenhouse which is heated in winter."

Allow your bougainvillea to rest in the winter by gradually giving it less water. The soil in the pot can be allowed to become almost dry before more water is given. Keep the plant in a minimum temperature of 7°C. In early spring, shorten all the side shoots to within an inch or so of the main stems. Repot the plant in good potting compost.

Once new growth is underway, feed the plant each week with a liquid fertilizer.

Mealy bug menace ❧

"My indoor begonia plants and leaves have become covered with white fluffy growths. There seems to be some sort of creature inside the wool and a friend thinks this may be mealy bug. Advice please."

Your begonias are quite badly infested with the glasshouse mealy bug, a species that probably produces more of the waxy wool than other species.

The best plan would be to take the plants outside on a mild day and give a drenching spray with malathion or Phostrogen Safer's Insecticide, making sure to wet the "wool" thoroughly. Return the plants inside when the spray has dried.

If you have a large collection of plants, it would be worth using biological control, introducing the predatory beetle *Cryptolaemus* that feeds on mealy bugs.

Obtain supplies by post from Green Gardener, 41 Strumpshaw Road, Brundall, Norfolk NR13 5PG.

Christmas cactus botanically speaking ❧

"Can you give me the correct name for the Christmas cactus? And why do the small buds always seem to drop off?"

The botanical name of the Christmas cactus is *Schlumbegera* × *buckleyi* and there are many varieties. It is also often called *Zygocactus truncatus*.

It is common for the developing flower buds to drop. This can occur if the plant has been under any stress such as a sudden change in temperature or lack of moisture. Keep plants in a light position in a cool room. They also appreciate light overhead sprays of water each day.

Yellowing cyclamen leaves ❧

"Soon after I received a potted cyclamen, the leaves started to turn yellow and shrivel. Can you tell me how to stop this happening?"

The leaves of your cyclamen may be yellowing because the plant was in a draught and chilled before you received it. This can also occur if you have kept the plant where the air is too warm and dry. Overwatering and standing the plant in a dish of water can also result in the leaves turning yellow.

Keep the plant in a light window and in a cool room. Only water when the soil begins to dry out and never stand the plant in water as this will cause waterlogging. Give the soil a good soaking and allow surplus water to drain away. Do not water the plant again until the soil shows signs of dryness once more.

Frond point

"Can you give me any information on the holly fern, Cyrtomium falcatum. *What is the best position for it in the home?"*

Cyrtomium falcatum, in common with most other half-hardy ferns, thrives in a temperature of 13–18°C (56–64°F) and light shade. When the pot is full of roots, repot in the spring with J. Arthur Bower's ericaceous compost.

Remove fading fronds and position the plant on a tray of gravel kept moist at all times. Water and feed the plant freely from spring to late summer.

Clivia flowers

"I have a clivia plant indoors which looks healthy but last spring it produced only one flower spike which was dwarf and stunted. As I do not want this to happen again, can you tell me what went wrong?"

We suspect that your clivia produced a stunted flower spike because of incorrect watering. During the winter the plant should be kept almost dry in a cool room so that it can rest. Only water it if the soil seems very dry. When a flower spike appears, allow it to grow to a height of at least 6 in. (15 cm) before increasing the watering.

At this stage it can be put in a slightly warmer room but it will resent hot and stuffy conditions. The plant can be stood outside for the summer in a lightly shaded position.

Handsome leaves

"Can you tell me how to care for a caladium plant that I have been given. It has beautifully coloured leaves and I would like to keep it as a house plant for as long as possible."

Caladiums have highly decorative but rather fragile leaves. Unless you have a heated greenhouse we feel you will have difficulty in keeping the plant for very long indoors because they like a really warm and moist atmosphere.

To keep your plant for as long as possible, stand it on a tray of pebbles that can be kept moist to create humidity around the plant. A temperature of at least 16°C (61°F) is needed and the plant must be shaded from direct sunshine. If you have a heated greenhouse, grow the plant in the warmest part and maintain a humid atmosphere in hot weather. Keep it shaded from the sun. Allow the plant to rest in the winter by withholding water and keeping the soil dry. In early spring repot the tuber and commence normal watering.

Tip cuttings ❧

"I have had a lovely coleus plant for nearly a year, but recently many of the lower leaves have dropped off, leaving a few at the top of each stem. Can the plant be cut back so that the tips of the stems can be used as cuttings?"

We suggest that you wait until the spring, when the weather is warmer, before you cut back the stems of your coleus plant. Use the tips of the shoots as cuttings – they will root in a jar of water in a warm room.

If you wish to keep your old plant after cutting back the stems, repot it in the spring in fresh potting compost and keep the plant in a light place in a warm room.

Watery grave ❧

"I have grown some cinerarias from seed but several have rotted off in their pots. Can you tell me why this is happening as I do not want the trouble to affect the rest of the plants."

Cinerarias are likely to rot off if the compost in the pot is kept too wet. The trouble is usually worse in the autumn when the compost does not dry out very quickly, particularly when the nights become cooler. For the rest of the summer keep your plants in a cold frame with shade from strong sunshine. It's essential to only water the plants when the compost is showing signs of dryness and always use tepid water. Do not allow the pots to stand in water as this will keep the compost too wet and the plants are likely to rot off. Cinerarias can also collapse if poor drainage is a problem when you use a heavy loam-based compost.

Coleus cuttings ❧

"I was given a coleus plant in the spring and it has had lovely, colourful leaves all summer. The lower ones have fallen off and the stems are now rather spindly. Can I cut them back in the hope that new shoots will appear?"

You can cut back the stems of your coleus to induce more bushy growth, but the best time to do this is in early spring. The best way to deal with your plant is to take cuttings from it and start again.

Remove the tops of the stems and make the cuttings about 4 in long. Take off the lower leaves and cut each shoot just below a leaf joint. Insert the cuttings in small pots filled with perlite or coarse sand and put them in a propagator or in a polythene bag in a temperature of at least 18°C.

Once rooted, pot the young plants individually in 3 in. (7.5 cm) pots of good compost. They must be kept in a light place and in a temperature of about 16°C.

Money tree ❧

"A few years ago, a friend gave me a cutting of a succulent-type plant. It is now 16 in. tall and has dark, shiny, fleshy leaves. It also has a thick, woody stem at its base. I have been told it is called the 'money tree'. Can you give me its correct name? As my friend's tree is very large, can it be grown outdoors?"

Your succulent plant is *Crassula argentea*, also known as *C. ovata*. It is an attractive indoor plant for a light place in a cool room. It is sometimes also known as the jade plant. Plants can be stood outside for the summer but they cannot stand frost and must be kept indoors for the winter.

Plants can grow up to 10 ft. (3 m) tall. As your plant becomes older you will probably find that it will produce sprays of small, white flowers.

There are several varieties; "Basutoland", with white flowers, "Variegata", and "Hummel's Sunset" which has yellow striped and red-edged leaves.

Chrysanths in hot water ❧

"The leaves on some of my chrysanthemums last year developed brown, dead areas between the main veins and the flowers were rather 'thin'. I believe this was caused by eelworm attack. Is there any modern control; all my books refer to hot water treatment which sounds rather complicated."

There is no chemical treatment available to amateur gardeners. Hot water treatment can be used, but it is a bit of a bother. Wash all the soil off the dormant stools and then submerge them for 30 minutes in water held at 43°C (110°F). You must be careful with such hot water. The stools are then planted up in new compost and cuttings are taken in the normal way.

However, there are many suppliers of first quality chrysanthemums around, so unless your varieties are particularly valuable to you, and are no longer available, it would indeed be simpler to destroy your stocks and purchase new plants.

Cigar flower   ⅺ

"I have a cigar flower which I've planted out in the garden. It has made a large bush. What do I do with it as I do not want to lose it in the winter?"

The cigar flower, *Cuphea ignea*, is an attractive indoor plant and, although it is happy outside in the summer, it will be killed by the first frosts.

To keep your plant, take some cuttings of young shoots from it now. Make them a few inches long and insert them in gritty soil in a small pot. Cover with a polythene bag until the cuttings have rooted when they should be potted individually and kept in a frost-free greenhouse or cool room for the winter.

Long-term care   ⅺ

"I have been given a beautiful cyclamen as a Christmas present. I want to keep it for as long as possible. How do I look after it?"

To keep your cyclamen for as long as possible, stand it in a light place in a cool room. It will not like hot and stuffy conditions. It helps if the plant can be stood on a dish of pebbles. If they are kept moist they will produce humidity for the benefit of the plant.

Do not allow the plant to stand in water as this will keep the soil too wet. When the soil seems dry, give the plant a good watering and allow it to drain. Do not water again until the soil is dry once more.

Umbrella plant cuttings   ⅺ

"I have an umbrella plant, Cyperus alternifolius, *indoors and would like to propagate from it. Is it possible to take cuttings?"*

Cuttings of the umbrella plant are easy to root. All you have to do is to cut off a stalk with an umbrella of leaves at the top and place it upside down in water. It is best to prepare the cutting by shortening the foliage by about half its length and trimming the stem to leave 2–3 in. This makes it easier to stand the leaf in a tray of water with the stalk uppermost. When roots appear, pot the young plant in a small pot of potting compost.

Unhappy coleus   ⅺ

"I had a fine coleus plant last summer but in the autumn many of the leaves began to fall off. The plant is kept in my conservatory which is partially heated. Can you tell me why my coleus should lose its leaves?"

Coleus need a warm and moist atmosphere. If they suffer a shock from low temperatures and poor light conditions they are likely to lose their leaves. Keep your plant in the warmest part of your conservatory for the winter. In early spring cut back the stems.

As the days become longer and warmer the plant may recover. When new growth appears, repot it in fresh potting compost. During the summer feed it each week with a liquid fertilizer and never allow the soil to dry out.

Holly fern ❧

"I recently bought an indoor fern called Cyrtomium falcatum. *It has attractive, dark green leaves. Can you tell me how to look after it?"*

The fern you have is also known as the holly fern. It makes a good indoor plant, enjoying shade and a moist atmosphere. During the summer keep it well watered and feed it each week with liquid fertilizer. Wipe the leaves occasionally to clear any dust that may have collected on them. The plant rests in the winter and should be kept in a cool room with little heat. When temperatures are low give water sparingly. Do not feed the plant in the winter.

Leggy coleus ❧

"I have a coleus plant which has grown leggy. All the lower leaves have fallen except for a few at the top. What should I do with the plant? Is it worth keeping?"

We suggest that you use the tips of the stems of your coleus as cuttings to raise new plants. Make the cuttings 3–4 in. (7.5–10 cm) long and trim each one below a joint with a sharp knife. Remove the leaves, except for a few at the tip. Insert the cuttings in a small pot filled with potting soil to which perlite has been added which assists rooting. Place the pot of cuttings in a polythene bag tied at the top.

Once signs of new growth are apparent and roots have formed, pot the cuttings separately in small pots of good potting soil. Pinch out the tips of the shoots several times to induce a bushy habit.

Clivia suckers ❧

"I have a plant of Clivia miniata. *This year it had four flowers. There are two shoots coming from the base. Is it possible to take these to make new plants?"*

The best time to propagate a clivia is in early summer when the flowers have faded. Give the plant a good watering and remove its pot. Use a sharp knife to remove the two side shoots together with plenty of roots attached.

Set the new plants in small pots filled with Arthur Bowers' House Plant Compost, then keep in light shade for a few days to allow them to recover.

Cautionary tale ❧

"I bought a dieffenbachia house plant which has most attractive leaves. How should I look after it and is it true that it is a poisonous plant?"

The dieffenbachia is an attractive indoor plant but it is certainly poisonous and should be kept away from children and pets. If a child should eat a leaf, it is wise to seek hospital treatment without delay.

The plant likes a partially shaded position and plenty of atmospheric moisture. Stand it on a tray of pebbles that are kept damp but do not stand it in water. It likes a minimum temperature of 15°C (59°F) . Give plenty of water in the summer with feeds each week of a liquid fertilizer. In the winter water the plant more sparingly.

Dragon tree ❧

"When I was holidaying in the Canary Islands I saw several very old dragon trees. What is their botanical name and can they be grown in this country?"

The correct botanical name for the dragon tree is *Dracaena draco*. It is a native of the Canary Islands although it has become an endangered species in the wild because it has been exploited for its resin, known as Dragon's Blood.

It is not a hardy plant in this country and cannot be grown outside. It needs a frost-free greenhouse.

Plants in the Canary Islands live to a great age and the oldest one in Tenerife is reputed to go back to 1,000 years BC.

Indoor heather ❧

"Last January I was given a pretty pink and white heather, growing in a pot, called Erica hyemalis. *After a while it started to drop its leaves and I moved it to my conservatory which is cooler. Can you tell me how to look after the plant?"*

Your heather is one of the Cape heaths and it is not hardy. It is a popular pot plant for indoor decoration in the winter. Although needing frost-free conditions, it does not like hot and dry, stuffy air. This will cause the leaves to drop. The soil in the pot can also dry out rapidly and the best way of watering these plants is to stand the pot in a bucket of water until the compost is thoroughly wetted. Keep your plant in the conservatory for the time being. In early spring, trim the shoots back to keep the plant compact.

During the summer stand it outside. Heathers must have an acid soil and you should use rain water for watering. Hard tap water contains lime which heathers do not like.

Fig leaf drop ❧

"I have a plant of variegated Ficus benjamina *stood in a container in my hall. It did well in the summer, but the leaves have started to fall. How can I stop this happening?"*

We suspect that the leaves are dropping on your weeping fig plant, *Ficus benjamina*, because it has been exposed to cold draughts in the hallway. It should do better in a light place, in a warm room with a temperature of about 16°C (61°F) in winter. Avoid a room where temperatures fluctuate widely from day to night.

Light overhead sprays of water will also be helpful as the air in centrally heated rooms can become very dry. Only water the compost in the pot when it shows signs of dryness and do not allow it to stand in water. Feed the plant in the spring and summer with a good house-plant fertilizer.

Air layering ❧

"My rubber plant has grown very tall and lost a lot of its lower leaves. Can I cut the main stem back and hope that it will sprout new shoots?"

Yes, you can cut your rubber plant back as you suggest and it should send out new side shoots. A better way of dealing with the problem is to air layer the top of the plant.

About 9–12 in. (23–30 cm) from the tip of the plant make a 1½ in. (1.2 cm) slanting cut in the stem, starting under a leaf joint. Dust the cut surfaces with hormone rooting powder and keep the tongue open with a small wad of moss. Surround the cut with moist sphagnum moss and cover it with a piece of clear polythene. Seal the polythene covering by tying a piece of string firmly at the top and also at the bottom.

After a few weeks roots will begin to form and you should be able to see them through the polythene covering. When a good root system has been made, cut off the new plant from the parent just below the new roots with sharp secateurs.

Pot the new plant immediately in good potting soil. To help it recover quickly, put a plastic bag over the plant for a short time but remove it once it has settled down.

The old plant can be kept as new side shoots should soon form after the top is cut off.

Bridal wreath

"I am anxious to trace the name of a plant my mother had many years ago. It is called bridal wreath and has soft, slightly furry leaves and white flowers. It was trained around a cane in a semi-circle. Can you help?"

Bridal wreath was a favourite pot plant on cottage windowsills. Its botanical name is *Francoa ramosa*. Another species, *F. appendiculata* has pink flowers.

Fatsia facts

"I have a fatsia or castor oil plant growing indoors in a pot. It has handsome green, leathery leaves and has been stood outside for the summer. Can I plant it in an open border?"

Fatsia japonica is often wrongly called the castor oil plant, a name which applies to *Ricinus communis*, a poisonous plant grown for its ornamental foliage. Fatsia can be raised from seed sown in early spring for planting out in late May or early June. It can be planted in the open border, but in cold districts it will need shelter. Trusses of white flowers should appear in October.

Fuchsia flies

"Every year my pot-grown fuchsias are attacked by whitefly and are spoiled. How can I start off free from infestation?"

Try cutting the plants down to soil level in the pots. This will remove any whitefly adults, young or eggs and ensure a clean start. Should there be a renewed attack from other plants, spray with Monsanto Polysect, which gives by far the most effective control.

Not very busy Lizzie

"My previously healthy busy Lizzie is now very poorly. The leaves are pale and covered with minute speckles."

Your plant has obviously been attacked by red spider mites (two-spotted mites to give them their more correct name). Where they feed the tissue dies, leaving the speckles you describe.

The mite is difficult to control, but if not too severe, introduce the biological, predatory mite *Phytoseiulus*.

Hibiscus care

"I have a pot plant of Hibiscus rosa-sinensis *which I keep in a light window. Can you tell me how I should look after it, please?"*

Your hibiscus is a shrubby plant and is best stood outside for the summer in a sunny, sheltered position. Keep it well watered and fed each week with a liquid fertilizer.

Cease feeding from August until March and bring the plant indoors in September for the winter. Keep it in a cool room and a light place. Next spring, trim back the growths a little and repot the plant in fresh potting compost.

Living stones

"I have been given a pot of living stones. They are curious little plants but I do not know how to look after them. Can you give me a few words of wisdom?"

Lithops are succulent plants which need to be watered very carefully. Do not give them any water between October and the spring and keep the plants in a light place in an unheated room or in a frost-free greenhouse with a minimum temperature of 8°C.

In the spring and summer, water the plants when the soil in the pot becomes dry, but do not allow it to settle among the leaves or they may rot. The best way to water lithops is to stand the pot in water for an hour or so until the soil is well moistened. Afterwards, take it out of the water and do not water until the soil is dry again.

Sensitive plant

"This year I grew two sensitive plants from seed but they are now looking rather miserable. I keep them in my heated greenhouse. How can I get them to make new leaves?"

Sensitive plants, *Mimosa pudica*, tend to degenerate by the end of the season. There is not much you can do to improve your plants so it would be best to start again next spring with young plants which are easily raised from seed in a heated greenhouse.

Winter care of medinella ❧

"Can you tell me how to care for my medinella indoor plant?"

Keep your medinella in a temperature of 15–21°C (60–70°F) during the winter. Mist it with tepid water two or three times a week and stand the plant on a drip tray of gravel, kept moist at all times.

In spring, if the roots have filled the pot, tap the plant gently from its pot, tease out some of the old compost from the roots, which could be trimmed lightly, and repot in a good potting compost.

Plants for bottles ❧

"I have purchased an old glass carboy bottle in a junk shop and believe it can be used for growing indoor plants. Could you give me the names of suitable plants for it? I assume that they will have to be miniature kinds."

An old glass carboy planted with suitable plants can make an attractive feature for a room. The plants will not remain miniature and when the foliage overcrowds the bottle you will have to do some thinning.

Suitable plants to grow include *Ficus pumila*, peperomias, selaginella, *Saxifraga sarmentosa*, *Neanthe bella*, cryptanthus, ferns, maranta, small-leaved ivies and *Dracaena sanderiana*.

Garden centres often have special plant collections for bottle gardens, called 'tots', on sale in the indoor plant sections.

Cork stopper ❧

"I was given a bottle garden for Christmas without a stopper. The opening at the top is almost 4 in. across. Is it necessary to have a stopper?"

The fact your bottle garden came without a stopper suggests that the makers do not consider it important. Indeed, unless you are lucky, the moment you seal the neck, moisture from transpiration will mist the glass and obscure the plants. Despite this, some experts put stoppers in their bottles to dispense with regular watering. If you wish to use a stopper, make one from a piece of cork matting.

Egyptian star cluster ❧

"I have been given a plant called Egyptian star cluster. Can you please tell me how to care for it?"

The botanical name for your plant is *Pentas lanceolata* which comes from East Africa. It has attractive pinkish red flowers and can be grown successfully in a room or cool greenhouse. Avoid giving the plant too much water and in winter, particularly, water sparingly.

Indoors, grow the plant in a light position in a cool room. During the summer plants may be stood outside.

New plants are easily raised from the tips of young shoots which should be rooted in a heated propagating case in the spring. Pinch the tips of the shoots of young plants several times to produce a bushy plant.

Bottle gardening can go too far!

House plant cuttings ❧

"When is the best time to take cuttings from my indoor plant of Philodendron scandens? *The plant has grown large and seems very healthy. I would like to give some plants to friends."*

The summer is the best time to take philodendron cuttings whilst natural temperatures are high. Cut off shoots with a sharp knife and trim them just below a leaf joint so that they are 3–4 in. (7.5–10 cm) long. Remove the lower leaves and insert the cuttings in small pots filled with a mixture of equal parts peat and coarse sand or perlite. Cover the pots with a polythene bag to conserve moisture and keep the cuttings in a warm place until there are signs of rooting. At this stage pot each plant separately in a small pot filled with a good house plant potting compost.

Friendship plant ❧

"I've been given a cutting of a friendship plant and I wonder if you could tell me a bit more about it."

The "friendship plant" is *Pilea involucrata*. It needs a temperature that does not drop below 10°C (50°F) in winter and a position in good light or semi-shade. Shield it from hot sunlight. Water freely from spring to autumn but less in winter. Mist leaves with water regularly and feed weekly with liquid fertilizer in spring and summer.

In the dark ❧

"I have a poinsettia plant which looks healthy but the leaves stay green and do not turn red. How can I make them change colour?"

The poinsettia, *Euphorbia pulcherrima*, is a short day plant. This means that it will flower and produce its colourful bracts only when it has less than ten hours of light in a day.

For the rest of the time, it must be kept in total darkness. One way of ensuring this is to cover the plant with a black polythene bag, ensuring that no light reaches the plant. If you can do this you should have a colourful poinsettia soon.

Plants kept from year to year are likely to grow more leggy than newly purchased plants. This is because nurserymen treat their plants with chemicals to keep them compact.

Poinsettia pointers ❧

"I have been given a poinsettia plant in a pot. How should I look after it?"

Poinsettias should be kept in a light place in a cool room. They prefer a constant temperature of around 13–15°C (55–60°F). They do not like a room that is in shade with hot and dry air while cold draughts will cause the leaves to fall. Keep them away from radiators. Whenever the soil seems dry give it a good watering. Add a balanced liquid fertilizer monthly during the winter.

Nice & easy ❧

"I have a plant of Plumbago capensis *in my greenhouse which made masses of growth this year and was covered in beautiful blue flowers in July and August. It has grown so big that it needs pruning. When should this be done?"*

Plumbago capensis, Cape leadwort, is now correctly called *P. auriculata*. It is a very handsome, shrubby plant for a frost-free greenhouse or conservatory. Flowers are produced on the current season's growth. This means that you can cut back the stems on your plant fairly hard in the winter. The new growths made next spring will flower in the summer.

Parlour palm shake-up ❧

"I have a parlour palm which is 27 in. (68 cm) high and growing in a 7 in. (18 cm) pot. When should it be repotted?"

The time to repot is when the pot becomes full of roots and has used up all the goodness in the compost. Spring is an ideal time, but instead of moving the plant on to a larger pot, you could shake off some of the old soil from among the roots and replace it with fresh potting compost.

Once established in its new pot, feed the palm each week in the summer with a liquid fertilizer. Cease feeding by the end of August.

Pelargonium in winter ❧

"Could you tell me how to overwinter my large, old pelargoniums? They flower profusely all summer, and as I have no greenhouse I keep the plants on windowsills in the house. Being so large can I cut them down, and what about watering?"

As your pelargoniums are large cut back the stems to accommodate them on your windowsills. Use a really sharp knife and cut the stems back above a joint. They can be shortened by as much as two thirds of their length. Water very sparingly in the winter and keep the plants in a cool but frost-free room.

Next spring repot the plants in fresh potting compost as they start to make new growth. Some of the stems that you remove could be used for cuttings if you want more plants.

Instead of keeping your old plants through the winter, you could take cuttings from them in August. Once rooted, put the plants in small pots. They will not take up so much space in the winter as the older plants.

Corky spots look a mess ❧

"The undersides of the leaves on my ivy-leaved geraniums are producing raised, corky spots. What is the cause, and is this something I can cure or prevent?"

The leaves are affected by a condition known as oedema. Basically, there is more water reaching the leaves than can be evaporated away, so the cells are rupturing, resulting in the raised spots you are finding. Prevent further damage by reducing watering to a minimum until growing conditions improve and the geraniums are growing more rapidly. If the plants are in a humid atmosphere, move them to a drier one to encourage greater water loss from the foliage.

Preparing geranium cuttings ❧

"Is it better to keep whole geranium plants for the winter or take cuttings from them?"

It is probably more convenient to take cuttings from geranium (pelargonium) plants and overwinter the young plants in small pots in a frost-free greenhouse as they take up less space than mature plants. Cuttings can be taken through August and September. Make cuttings about 4 in. (10 cm) long and trim each one just below a joint. Use a seed compost to which has been added extra coarse sand to root them in. Single cuttings can be put in a 3 in. (7 cm) pot or several may be rooted together in a larger pot. To avoid "black leg" rotting, do not water the cuttings for a week after potting. Thereafter, water very sparingly as cold, damp conditions encourage rotting.

Resting gloriosa ❧

"I have a gloriosa plant which I grew in a pot in my greenhouse this year for the first time. It had some nice flowers but now the foliage is turning yellow. Is this normal?"

It is normal for gloriosa plants to lose their leaves in the autumn as this is the beginning of their resting season. Allow the plant to dry off and give it no more water during the winter.

Keep it dry in a frost-free place until next March when the roots should be repotted in fresh compost. New growth should soon appear which will flower during the summer.

Gardenia care ❧

"I was given a gardenia house plant with lots of buds and flowers. I have sprayed the leaves daily and the plant looks very healthy. Now it has finished flowering, do I need to continue spraying?"

It is not necessary to continue spraying your gardenia when it is not flowering. The reason for spraying is to stop the flower buds falling, which they will do if the plant is growing in dry air. Keep your plant warm – around 13–16°C (55–61°F) – and water it when the compost is drying out. Feed it with a high-potash liquid tomato fertilizer weekly from March to September, and monthly at other times.

Withered blooms ❧

"I recently purchased a gerbera plant in a pot and kept it on my kitchen table where it received plenty of light. The flowers soon dropped off. Can you explain why this should have happened?"

Probable reasons why the gerbera dropped its flowers are dry air, excessively bright, hot sunlight, draughts, or even stress which may have occurred at the garden centre before you bought the plant.

Provided its leaves are perky, new flowers can be encouraged by misting the foliage regularly and feeding with a high potash tomato fertilizer. Avoid placing the plant where it is exposed to draughts.

Gardenia from seed ❧
"Are gardenias difficult to grow from seed?"

It is not very easy to raise gardenias from seed. They are usually propagated from cuttings in a heated propagator. However, have a go. Sow the seed in a small pot of an acidic, soilless compost and stand it in a heated propagator at a temperature of at least 21°C (70°F). Grow the seedlings for a while in the propagator but when they are large enough, stand them on the greenhouse staging. A minimum winter temperature of 15°C (60°F) is needed.

The plants do not like lime so use rainwater if the tap water in your area is hard.

Lawns

Chamomile lawn ❧

"I would like to have a small chamomile lawn in my garden. If weeds appear in the lawn, how should they be dealt with?"

Weeds can easily appear in a chamomile lawn and the only satisfactory way of eradicating them is to pull them out by hand. Weedkillers cannot be used as they will also kill the chamomile.

Chamomile lawn ❧

"I would like to grow a chamomile lawn on a small strip in my garden. How do I prepare the ground?"

Unlike grasses, a chamomile lawn does not stand up well to heavy, continual wear so once you have laid your small area do not walk on it apart from when it needs clipping to keep it neat and tidy. Use the non-flowering strain called "Treneague" which is suitable for lawns.

Before planting, ensure that the area has been thoroughly cleared of perennial weeds and stones. After forking over the ground, rake the soil to an even level surface. Plant the chamomile 6 in. (15 cm) apart in each direction.

Seed or turf? ❧

"We have recently moved into a new house and I want to lay a lawn as soon as possible. Is it best to lay turfs or sow grass seed? When should the work be done?"

March and early April is a good time to lay a lawn, provided the ground is not frozen or too wet. Wait until the surface of the soil begins to dry out before working on the ground. The advantage of laying turfs for a lawn is that you get immediate results. However, turfs are a lot more expensive than seed. If you are prepared to wait a couple of months, seeding provides the most economical method of laying a lawn.

The seed usually takes about ten days to germinate. Two or three weeks later there is a good green cover. Light topping of the grass with a mower helps the grass to bush out and after a couple of months you will have a reasonable lawn. It will take a whole season to have a really thick sward. Watering must not, of course, be neglected in dry weather otherwise the young grass will suffer.

A book that you will find helpful is *The Lawn Expert* by Dr D. G. Hessayon, price £3.25. It is available at most garden centres and bookshops.

New lawn

"I sowed some grass seed for a new lawn in early September. The grass has come up well. When should I mow?"

Start mowing your grass when it is about 3 in. (7.5 cm) tall, but set the mower blades high so that only the top $\frac{1}{2}$ in. of the grass is cut off.

Laying turf

"I want to lay some grass turfs for a new lawn. Have I got to wait until the spring before I can do it?"

Grass turfs can be laid in the winter provided the ground is not too wet or frozen. If conditions are not right when the turfs arrive, lay them out flat temporarily as the grass will turn yellow if they are kept rolled up.

Too late to sow?

"I am about to make a lawn in my new garden. Can I sow seed now or must I wait until next spring?"

Early to mid-October is a good time to sow grass seed. The soil is still warm and it should be nicely moist. Before sowing make sure the ground is thoroughly cleared of any weeds and break the soil down to a fine tilth by raking and treading it evenly Make sure it is levelled by filling in hollows with soil.

Given good weather and moist soil, the seed should have germinated in nine to ten days.

Sowing rate

"I want to make a lawn from seed. What rate should I apply the seed?"

Sow grass seed at $1\frac{1}{2}$ oz. per sq. yd. (42 g/m^2). To ensure the seed is sown evenly, mark the lawn in yard (metre) squares with canes and sow the right amount of seed in each.

Buying turf off the roll couldn't be easier these days.

Dogged by lichen on the lawn ❧

"There are several patches of pale growths on my lawn. They are flat, brown on top, pale underneath and about three centimetres across, made up of overlapping plates. Can you please tell me what they are, and what is the best way to get rid of them?"

The growths are of the dog lichen *Peltigera canina*. Generally their presence indicates damp or over-compacted soil and spiking or hollow-tine forking would help to ease the problem.

The growths themselves should be killed by an application of a liquid lawn moss-killer such as MossGun or Tumbleweed Moss.

Lawn lichens ❧

"My daughter's lawn has many areas covered with strange growths. The growths are flat, lying close to the ground, and are brown on top and grey underneath. Advice please on identity and control."

The growths are lichens and are often most troublesome on poorly fed or compacted lawns. Feeding and spiking will help to reduce attacks, but where the lichens are very serious they can be killed by a dichlorophen moss-killer treatment.

Unwelcome lawn lichen ❧

"We are finding some odd-looking growths on our lawns. They are grey underneath, pale fawn on top and seem to consist of folds of tissue. They are flexible when damp, but become brittle in dry spells. What are they, and can we do anything apart from raking them off the lawn?"

The growths are of dog lichen, and they occur from time to time on lawns, more particularly when the soil is becoming depleted in nutrients and compacted. They are more common on shaded lawns.

Dog lichen is normally reasonably well controlled by lawn sand or a dichlorophen-based moss-killer, but the underlying soil conditions should also be addressed. Application of a good lawn feed now, plus aeration of the ground, will help to ensure that the lichens do not return.

Return of the sward ❧

"I was not able to water my lawn in the summer drought and it is now a sorry sight. How can I restore it back to good condition again?"

Now that we have had some heavy rain your lawn will soon look fresh and green again. However, the surface is likely to be compacted and it will need aerating.

Small machines can be hired to do this but it can also be done with a garden fork. Push the tines into the lawn to their full depth at intervals all over the lawn. Then, using a wire rake, remove dead grass and moss.

Follow this with a dressing of an autumn lawn fertilizer.

Spiking a lawn ❧

"During the heavy rains of last winter, I noticed that water collected on my lawn for short periods. Does this suggest that drainage is poor and what can I do about it?"

It is not surprising that water lay on your lawn last winter as there were spells of exceptional rainfall. As the water collected for only short periods we do not think that you have a serious problem. However, it would do your lawn no harm to aerate it.

Small mechanical tools can be hired or you could use a garden fork. This is more laborious.

Insert the tines of a garden fork to their full depth and work the fork backwards and forwards. Do this at intervals of 6 in. all over the lawn. This will help to improve drainage if the surface of the lawn has become compacted.

You can also brush gritty sand into the surface of the lawn to fill up the holes made with the fork.

Laying down the lawn 🍃

"The lawn in our new house is awful and I have dug it over hoping the frost will break up the soil. Can you give me information on what to do before laying turf?"

Prepare the site for laying the lawn in spring by forking out invasive perennial weeds. Follow by grading the site – using pegs and a spirit level – to ensure that it will be level for mowing. If the soil is heavy clay, sprinkle 3 oz. per sq.yd. (85 g/m²) of garden lime over the surface and rake it in to help pulverize it.

In early spring kill germinating weeds with Weedol. When these are dead, scarify the surface with a three-pronged cultivator and rake in 3 oz. per sq.yd. (85 g/m²) of fish, blood and bone meal. Tread the whole site firm and rake it level.

Ten days later, lay the turfs, working from a long, wide plank and starting at the longest side.

Rusty grass 🍃

"I have an area of grass where bulbs grow and which is not mowed too short. This autumn, patches of it turned orange-yellow, and close examination showed the discoloration to be due to the growth of what I presume to be rust on the leaf blades of the grass. Is this likely to kill the grass, and is there any treatment or feed I should apply?"

The disease you have found is yellow rust, and it can be very weakening on grass. We would recommend a late mowing, when conditions allow, and a good feed in spring. Should the disease reappear next year, then a couple of sprays with Tumbleblite or a copper fungicide should be an effective cure.

Rusty the dog? ❧

"My bearded collie started coming in with orange-coloured legs after her morning romp in the grass at the bottom of the garden. Investigation showed there to be an orange fungus or something similar on the grass blades. What is this, and is it serious?"

The cause of the orange spotting is attack by rust fungus. It is probably the same orange rust species that can be found on unsprayed cereal crops where it will reduce crop yields.

On your lawn, I suggest a late mowing, if soil and weather conditions allow, to remove most of the infection. Should the disease reappear in spring then Tumbleblite or a copper fungicide would probably be effective.

Tree stump ❧

"What is the best way to get rid of an old tree stump which I have growing in my lawn?"

Assuming the stump is still alive, treat it with a product sold as SBK Brushwood Killer, available from garden centres. Water the stump with a solution of sulphate of ammonia and then water every few weeks to accelerate the rotting process.

A shade too much ❧

"Part of my lawn is in the shade of a tree and the grass is not very good in the area. Is there anything I can do to improve matters?"

The reason why the grass does not grow well in the shade of the tree is mainly because the area does not get enough light to enable the grass to grow well. Also, the foliage of the tree prevents rain reaching the area and the soil dries out badly in the summer.

Seed companies can supply shade-tolerant grass-seed mixtures and we suggest you try sowing some in the affected area in spring. You must also keep the area well watered in the summer to prevent the soil drying out.

Low evergreens ❧

"I have recently covered my two front lawns, each 18 ft by 6 ft, with gravel over a black membrane. Rocks have been added at random over the area. Can you recommend suitable, low-growing, evergreen plants to give colour for as long as possible?"

Plants you could grow in your gravel garden are: *Berberis stenophylla* "Corallina Compacta"; *Cotoneaster* "Coral Beauty"; *Euonymus fortunei* "Emerald Gaiety"; *Hebe pinguifolia* "Pagei"; *Bergenia cordifolia*; *Pachysandra terminalis*; *Prunus laurocerasus* "Otto Luyken"; *Waldsteinia ternata*; and *Thymus serpyllum*.

Slimy lawn ❧

"Our lawn is full of slimy patches of dead grass. We have no idea what to do."

The black slime and patches of dead grass spoiling your lawn are due to bad drainage. Initially, kill the algae with Bio Moss Killer. Then improve the drainage. This could be done with a power-driven spiking machine which can be hired from a local dealer, like HSS Hire Shops.

If you find water tends to lie for periods on the lawn you may have to consider laying a herring-bone system of land drains leading down to a soakaway at the lower end of the site. You will have to lift the turfs for the drainage channels and fill the base with 6 in. (15 cm) of gravel before refilling with soil and replacing the turfs.

There is a very good section on draining a lawn in *The New Lawn Expert* by David (D. G.) Hessayon. It is available at most good bookshops and garden centres.

Killing moss ❧

"There is a lot of moss in my lawn. I don't want to use moss-killers, but is there any other way of getting rid of it?"

Rake out as much of the moss as possible with a wire rake, or an electric one. This may leave bare patches which can be scarified and resown with grass seed. Next spring feed the lawn from March onwards to encourage the grass to grow at the expense of the moss.

Clear off moss! ❧

"I have moss in my lawn. As there are bulbs in the grass I do not want to use chemicals to get rid of it. Is there any other way?"

Rake the moss out and sow any bare patches with grass seed. Encourage the grass by feeding the lawn several times in the spring.

Mechanical control ❧

"My front lawn is on the north side of the house and is full of moss. I don't want to use chemicals to get rid of it as crocus bulbs are planted in one area. Please tell me how to eradicate the moss without it harming the bulbs."

The simple non-chemical way of removing the moss from your lawn is to rake it out with a wire rake or with an electric lawn rake. You may, however, be left with bare patches which can be sown with fresh grass seed in autumn or spring. We would also suggest that you feed the grass in the spring with a high nitrogen lawn fertilizer. This will encourage the grass to grow at the expense of the moss.

Secrets of the mole catcher ❧

"I have a very large lawn which is being steadily ruined by the activities of moles. The lawn is too large for 'local' remedies such as buried bottles, windmills, or sonic deterrents. I have bought three mole traps, but have not had any success in using them. Can you help please?"

Mole trapping takes practice, but is usually fully effective, given time to learn the system. Start by flattening all existing molehills and then probe around the new ones with a cane. As the cane pushes through the soil into a tunnel there will be a sharp downwards movement of the cane. Take a small spade and dig out a triangular section of soil and then gently feel around the edges to locate the two runs where the tunnel enters and leaves the exposed area. Place the trap in the centre of the run and replace the soil and turf. Where children or pets have access to the lawn it is a good plan to cover the trap with an upturned bucket. This protects the trap and also excludes light.

Place three traps in the same manner and examine them each day. If no traps have been sprung within three or four days, repeat the process around different molehills, and persist until the moles have been caught; you will succeed in the end!

Scorched grass avoidance ❧

"Last year I scattered fertilizer on my lawn by hand. Unfortunately, I could not have applied it evenly as bare patches appeared and I realize I must have scorched the grass. What is the best way to apply lawn fertilizers?"

It is very easy to scorch grass by applying fertilizers unevenly. To avoid this, mark out the lawn with canes in square yards and apply the recommended amount of fertilizer as evenly as possible to that area. Better still, use a small fertilizer distributor. These are available at garden centres and can be set to apply fertilizers evenly at pre-set rates.

Fertilizers are best applied when the soil is moist. If rain does not fall for two days after applying the fertilizer, give the lawn a good watering.

Patchy lawn upset 🐾

"Brown patches appeared in my lawn in late summer. I hardly think they were due to the hot summer as the lawn was watered regularly. Your advice would be appreciated."

Refurbish your lawn by raking it gently to remove dead and clogging thatch and sprinkle the surface with a thin layer of sifted garden soil or spent potting compost.

Afterwards, sow a patch-pack of grass seed, stocked by garden centres, at $1\frac{1}{2}$ oz. per sq. yd (42 g/m^2). Lightly rake the seed into the surface soil. If the weather is mild the seeds will germinate within a fortnight.

Turfed aid 🐾

"My lawn is looking a sorry sight after the winter. What is the best treatment to give it to ensure a good, green sward this summer?"

Make a start on your lawn as soon as the ground begins to dry out – not a lot can be done whilst it is still sodden. Remove old dead grass by giving the lawn a good raking with a wire rake. If the ground is very compacted, use a garden fork, inserting the tines to their full length at intervals all over the area. Alternatively, you may be able to hire a hollow-tine aerating machine. Top dress the lawn with a mixture of sieved soil and gritty sand, working it into the surface with a besom broom. Lightly cut the grass as soon as it is reasonably dry. Afterwards, feed the grass with a lawn fertilizer and repeat the application several times in the spring and early summer. If there is much weed in the grass use a combined lawn fertilizer and weedkiller.

Fusarium patch 🐾

"Our once lovely lawn of fine grasses is producing pale yellow patches and they seem to be spreading and joining together. Please help."

The damage is the result of attack by fusarium patch disease which, sadly, does favour the finer grasses. The first step is to water the areas with

Benlate or Supercarb fungicide and repeat the treatment a month later. Longer term, keep the lawn fed in a balanced way, avoiding excess nitrogen and don't apply nitrogen after midsummer. Where possible, increase air movement, for example, by trimming back any overhanging trees. Attacks may develop under a covering of snow and activity starts up in spring, so repeat the treatment in March.

Odd growth

"I have just got back a picture taken last autumn of an area of rough grass in my garden showing a strange, creamy mass on the leaves. I have been unable to find any reference to this. Can you help?"

The creamy growths are due to a slime fungus known as *Mucilago crustacea*. It is not particularly common, and appears to do little harm to the grass. It can occur at any time of the year, although as with many fungi it is more prevalent in the autumn. If it occurs in abundance, an application of lawn sand or dichlorophen-based moss-killer should get rid of it.

Toadstools on turf

"At this time of year my lawn always starts to sprout a crop of toadstools. I haven't bothered before, but now I have a small daughter and am worried that the toadstools may be poisonous. What can be done?"

Most toadstools grow on dead organic matter in the soil. This could be the old "thatch" of grass mowings and roots, etc., or buried tree roots. There is no really effective control for toadstools although watering with Epsom Salts solution has been recommended in the past. All I could suggest is collecting up the toadstools each morning and disposing of them before your daughter goes out to play. Although not too many toadstools are really poisonous, it would be better not to take any risks and you could wear rubber gloves to be extra safe when collecting them up. I have no doubt that as soon as your daughter is old enough you will teach her not to eat anything in the garden without your approval.

Fairy rings

"My husband and I have seen rings of toadstools in the grass at a local park and we assume that these are fairy rings. Can you tell us something about them please?"

There is more than one type of fungus that can spread out in ring formation on grass, but the usual fairy-ring fungus is known as *Marasmius*. The fungus doesn't actually feed on the grass itself but on nutrients in the soil often liberated by dead grass tissue.

The main problem that arises with rings is that the underground feeding system of the fungus is very water-repellent, and this starves the grass roots of moisture. Typically there will be a ring of lush, green grass in which the toadstools appear, with a dead or brown ring of grass inside.

Professional groundsmen have access to specialist fungicides to control this fungus, but all the gardener can do is to spike the dead area of grass and squirt on washing-up liquid to enable the soil to become re-wetted. Continue to water the lawn on a regular basis thereafter.

Fairies in the garden?

"We have what we believe to be fairy rings on our lawn. Rings of toadstools appear and the grass grows strongly around them but turns brown inside the rings. They are gradually getting bigger and bigger. Please help."

Fairy rings behave exactly as you describe. Initially the fungus breaks down the organic matter in the turf and the nutrients released stimulate the grass as the fairy ring develops. A mass of waxy, water-repellent threads spread through the soil.

The grass roots then become deprived of water, resulting in the dead-looking areas inside the rings. The complete answer would be to dig out the infected soil in the ring and replace it with new soil, but this would involve moving a lot of soil as the area dug out should be at least a foot wide and deep.

An easier way is to help overcome the dryness of the soil by making a number of holes in the brown area, squirting in washing-up liquid and then hosing the area well. The detergent will allow the water to wet the soil and so enable the grass to grow normally.

Are there fairies at the bottom of my garden?

"We seem to have had more than our fair share of fairy rings on our lawn in autumn and there are several brown rings left by this fungus. Isn't it time someone discovered an effective cure?"

There is a fungicide which is effective against the fairy ring fungus but it is only available to professional groundsmen. You may be able to enlist the services of a suitably qualified professional gardener to treat your lawns.

The only other suggested treatment is to spike the area of the brown grass, squirt with washing-up liquid and then soak with water.

The dead areas are due to the soil being water-repellent after fungal activity, and the thorough wetting may help to overcome this effect. Repeat as necessary as the ring grows out.

Autumn mowing ❧

"The grass in my lawn has grown rather long. Will it do any harm if I mow it late in the season?"

There is no reason why you should not mow your lawn late. However, wait until there is a dry day and do it in the middle of the day, if this is possible, after dew on the grass has cleared. And don't cut the grass too closely.

First cut ❧

"My lawn seems to have made a lot of growth through the winter and the grass is very long. How soon can I cut it and should I feed the grass this spring?"

Your grass has made a lot of growth through the winter because of the mild and wet weather. Cut it as soon as the ground begins to dry out. Do not cut the grass too closely at first and keep the blades of the mower set fairly high. Heavy rains in winter will have washed nutrients out of the soil and you should begin feeding the grass with a good lawn fertilizer. Do this as soon as possible to encourage good growth.

Yellow grass ❧

"The grass on our lawns is very yellow and was the same at the end of last summer. We feed the grass in spring and autumn, and also aerate it. Can you tell me how to improve the colour?"

The yellow appearance of the grass is due to a lack of nitrogen. Replace it by applying sulphate of ammonia at 1 oz. per sq.yd (28 g/m²) in April. Repeat the application in mid-June. Alternatively, apply a balanced fertilizer, such as Toplawn, or fish, blood and bone meal. Water in granular fertilizers if rain does not fall within two days.

Applying lawn fertilizers ❧

"I do not seem to be able to apply lawn fertilizers very evenly by hand. As a result I get patchy growth of the grass. How do I apply it evenly?"

The best way to apply a lawn fertilizer as evenly as possible is to use a small fertilizer spreader which you can either buy or hire from a garden centre. The spreader can usually be set to apply the fertilizer at different rates. It is possible to cover the lawn evenly by hand if known areas are marked out on it with long canes. Measure the correct amount of fertilizer for each area and scatter it as evenly as possible.

Business is a real concern ❧

"Is there any way of getting rid of an invasive weed called mind-your-own-business? It has spread into the lawn and is taking over from the grass."

Unfortunately, mind-your-own-business, *Soleirolia soleirolii*, is one of the few weeds resistant to most broadleaf lawn weedkillers. There are also no chemicals available that can be sprayed over areas of cultivated plants without harming them. However, glyphosate (Tumbleweed or Roundup GC) is a total weedkiller that can be used as a spot treatment to kill this weed if it is used with care. You really only have the choice of using glyphosate on the affected areas of grass and reseeding or returning the lawn. The most effective period to apply the weedkiller is between early June and August when the weed is growing actively. Leave the area for at least three weeks for the weedkiller to take effect.

Lawn daisies ❧

"My lawn was full of daisies last summer. What is the best way of getting rid of them?"

Many people like the appearance of a few daisies in a lawn but if you don't use a selective weedkiller. Apply it as a combined lawn fertilizer and weed-killer at intervals in the spring and early summer. This will feed the lawn to encourage the grass to grow and, at the same time, kill off broad-leaved weeds.

Lawn weedkillers ❧

"My lawn is in fairly good condition but there are one or two dandelions and plantains here and there. I do not want to treat the whole of the lawn with weedkiller and wonder whether I can treat each weed individually or if it is best to dig them out."

If there are only a few isolated weeds in your lawn you could dig them out with an old kitchen knife or fork. However, it is probably easier to spot treat the weeds with a "weed gun", available at most garden centres. Treated in this way there will definitely be less disturbance to the lawn.

A wee problem ❧

"Our lawns suffer from the effects of our labrador bitch – where she 'performs' bleached areas develop. What can be done, please?"

The high concentrations of salts in the urine is responsible for the killing of the grass. The only feasible action is to follow your labrador round the garden with a watering can and to water the "performing spots" thoroughly. My dog-training friends tell me it is possible to train a dog to use a specific area in the garden. As labradors are very intelligent animals, this would be worth looking into.

Turn on the worm ❧

"My lawn seems to have more than its fair share of worms and the casts make mowing difficult. I don't really wish to kill them, but is there any alternative?"

Casting species of earthworms are a nuisance on fine lawns. The casts get flattened by mowers and feet, and then smother the finer grasses, providing sites for weeds to germinate. They also encourage moles to tunnel in the lawn. The deeper-living species do help by creating drainage pathways, but their good name is tarnished by the casting species.

Earthworms prefer alkaline conditions, so avoid liming or using alkaline fertilizers such as Nitrochalk, and use sulphate of ammonia instead. Daily dispersing of the worm casts with a besom will also help.

Orchids

Repotting cymbidium ❧

"I have a cymbidium orchid which seems healthy but the 'bulbs' seem very crowded in the pot. Does the plant need repotting? Can I stand the plant outside for the summer?"

When cymbidium pseudo-bulbs begin to fill the pot, it is time to repot the plant. The time to do this is after flowering in April or early May. We advise you to wait until next spring before repotting your plant. Plants can certainly be stood outside for the summer in a partially shaded position. Keep them well watered and spray them overhead with water in hot weather. In September return the orchid either back to the greenhouse or on to a light south- or west-facing windowsill indoors.

Orchid problem ❧

"My orchids (cattleyas) are developing a pale stippling on the leaves and generally look rather sick. Can you tell me what the trouble is and how to correct it?"

The stippling is the result of feeding by red spider mites. Under a hand lens the creatures themselves will be visible. Red spider mites are now pretty resistant to most chemicals, but it might be worth trying a few sprays with derris, pyrethrum or dimethoate. I would recommend burning all the badly affected leaves and then maintaining a buoyant atmosphere by daily misting with water.

If you have a valuable collection of plants, or where several other species are also infested, it would be worth introducing the biological control agent *Phytoseiulus*. This is a predatory mite that seeks out and eats red spider mites.

Hardy orchid ❧

"I would like to grow some plants of Orchis elata in my garden. Is it difficult to grow and what kind of soil does it like?"

Orchis elata is now correctly named *Dactylorhiza elata*. Despite the name, it is a superb plant. It likes a sunny spot but must have soil that is rich in humus and well laced with decayed leafmould. Heavy clay soils, as well as very light sandy soils, are unsuitable unless they can be improved considerably with organic matter.

Missing link ❧

"Last summer I admired some plants in a woodland garden and I would like to try some in my own garden. I believe they are orchids but I could only read part of the name on the label which was 'dact . . . elata'. Do you know the full name and is it easy to grow?"

The name of your orchid is most probably *Dactylorhiza elata*. It is a magnificent plant flowering in early summer and is not difficult to grow provided it is given good, fertile soil enriched with well-rotted leaves or compost. Choose a sunny position for planting, or one in partial shade will do. Plant the tubers about 3 in. (7.5 cm) deep.

Calanthe orchid ❧

"I have been given a calanthe orchid bulb to grow in my heated greenhouse. As I know little about this orchid can you tell me how to grow it?"

The calanthe is a very beautiful orchid with graceful arching flower stems. The pseudo-bulbs rest in a dry state during the winter. Start them into growth in early spring by partially inserting single bulbs in trays of peat and sand in a warm, moist propagator. When new shoots appear, pot the bulbs individually in a mixture of good fibrous loam, coarse sand and well decayed manure. Bury only the base of the pseudo-bulb in the potting mixture. Grow the plants in a warm, sunny part of the greenhouse and when in full growth water them freely and give regular feeds of liquid manure. The flower spikes appear in the autumn when the leaves wither. At this stage gradually withhold water and keep the compost dry through winter.

Care for cymbidium orchid ❧

"I have been given a miniature cymbidium orchid. The flowers were very beautiful and lasted for several weeks. How should I look after the plant from now on? I have a greenhouse with an electric heater."

Cymbidium orchids like cool, moist conditions during the summer. Stand your plant in a partially shaded position and on a base of shingle which can be kept moist. In hot weather spray over the foliage with water each day. Plants can be stood outside for the summer but they must be returned to the greenhouse in early September.

Feed the plant each week in the summer with a special orchid fertilizer or Phostrogen. Ideally, the temperature in winter should not fall much below 10°C. (50°F). Water the compost in the pot freely during the spring and summer when new growth is being made but more sparingly in winter when temperatures are low.

Wet or dry? ❧

"I have two cymbidium plants in my heated greenhouse. Should the compost be kept wet or dry in the winter?"

Keep the cymbidium compost just moist during the winter but never allow it to dry out completely. On the other hand do not keep it too wet, particularly when temperatures are low. The best advice is "if in doubt during the winter delay watering."

Madeira orchid ❧

"I have seen some orchids called Dactylorhiza maderensis *growing outside. I would like to grow some. What soil and position suits them?"*

Dactylorhiza maderensis is now correctly called *D. foliosa*. It is a very beautiful hardy orchid with tuberous roots. They are expensive to purchase, costing £7–8 each. For this reason, prepare the ground well for them, adding plenty of decayed compost or manure to the soil. Heavy clay and chalky soils are unsuitable. Grow the tubers in a sunny position and mulch the ground around them with decayed organic matter each spring.

Life lines ❧

"I have a number of orchids which flowered well last summer and which are still in the pots as supplied by the grower. What do I do with the aerial roots? Should they be cut off and can the leaves be cut back?"

Do not cut off the aerial roots from your orchids. They are the plants' lifeline and vital for their survival. Again, it would be unwise to remove any leaves from your cymbidiums. The leaves are their food factories and the plants would suffer if they were cut back.

Hardy orchid ❧

"Last summer I was greatly taken with a group of plants labelled Dacty-lorhiza elata *in a large garden that was open for charity. Can you tell me anything about the plant as I would like to grow it. What sort of soil does it like and is it difficult to manage? Can you tell me where I can buy plants?"*

The plant that you saw last summer is a hardy orchid and it is not difficult to grow if you give it the right sort of conditions. Plant the tubers in early autumn in good, deep soil, well enriched with decayed compost and leafmould. Choose a sunny, sheltered position with a little shade from strong sunshine – it is an ideal plant for a woodland garden where the soil is moist. It will not do well if the soil is poor and liable to dry out badly in the summer.

Two nurseries that should be able to supply the plant are: Paradise Centre, Twinstead Road, Lamarsh, Bures, Suffolk CO8 5EX and Roger Poulet, Nurse's Cottage, North Mundham, Chichester, Sussex PO20 6JY.

The roots of orchids can grow out of the top of the pot as well as the bottom!

Orchid roots ❧

"I have an orchid plant and the roots are growing out of the pot. Should they be cut off?"

No, the orchid roots should not be cut off. They are special roots which are covered in absorbent tissue designed specifically to absorb water. They are essential for the well-being of the plant.

Restless orchid ❧

"I have an orchid plant in my greenhouse called Coelogyne cristata. *I bought it, as I was told it was a good beginner's orchid. It grows well but it does not flower. Can you tell me where I am going wrong?"*

Coelogyne cristata is a delightful, small-growing orchid which should flower in the spring. But unless it is given a decided rest in the winter, it is not likely to flower very well, and this is probably why your plant has not flowered yet. At the end of the growing season, withhold water from the plant and keep it dry. The green pseudo-bulbs will shrivel, but do not worry, as they will soon recover when watering is resumed in the spring. Coelogynes also resent disturbance, and should be repotted only when they have outgrown their containers.

Patios

Blueberries in containers   ✺

"Last summer I tasted some blueberries. They were delicious. I would like to grow one or two bushes but my garden is very small. Can I grow them in large pots or tubs? What is the best variety to grow?"

Yes, blueberries can be grown successfully in tubs or containers standing on a patio. They must be planted in an acid, lime-free compost, so you should purchase a potting compost suitable for rhododendrons and azaleas.

Apart from their delicious fruit, sweet-smelling, white flowers appear in May and the leaves turn crimson in the autumn.

Make sure that there are drainage holes in the base of the container. During the summer do not use hard tap water which contains lime. Use rainwater instead.

Good varieties to grow are "Bluetta", "Berkeley" and "Spartan". These are available from James Trehane & Sons Ltd, Stapehill Rd, Hampreston, Wimborne, Dorset BH21 7NE. Phone 01202 873490.

Peach poser   ✺

"I have a dwarf peach growing in a large pot on my terrace. It has set some fruit and looked very healthy until this week, but now the leaves appear pale and with a very fine speckling. Help please."

The damage you describe is the work of the two-spotted spider mite, previously known more simply as red spider. Leaves become stippled with pale feeding marks, resulting in a dull, lifeless appearance followed by early leaf fall.

Plants that become short of water, or which are growing in a very dry spot, are typically more prone to attack. Try moving the pot to a more sheltered spot, keep it well watered, and spray the leaves daily with tepid water.

To control the existing attack, spray with an insecticide based on pyrethrins or on fatty acids.

Tub shrubs ❧

"*I would like to grow an ornamental shrub in a large tub to stand on the terrace in front of my house. Can you give me the names of shrubs that will grow happily in a tub?*"

Shrubs that you could grow in a large tub include *Acer palmatum dissectum*, *Laurus nobilis* (bay), *Fatsia japonica*, *Aucuba japonica* "Picturata", *Cotoneaster* "Hybridus Pendulus", forsythia, *Yucca filamentosa*, cordylines, rhododendrons and camellias (acid soil for these last two).

Fill the tub with good potting compost and make sure that there are drainage holes in the base of it. The soil is likely to dry out quickly in hot weather and watering must not be neglected in the summer.

Trees for pots ❧

"*Could you please tell me what sort of tree to plant in a large tub to make a screen to hide my neighbour's garden. I want one with a main stem and a rounded top.*"

Trees that you could grow in a large tub include *Caragana arborescens* "Pendula"; *Pyrus salicifolia*, grey-leaved weeping pear; *Cotoneaster* "Hybridus Pendulus" with red berries; *Salix caprea* "Kilmarnock", the weeping goat willow; and *Acer pseudoplatanus* "Brilliantissimum". Make sure that you purchase a standard-trained tree.

Lacklustre berries ❧

"*I have two skimmia shrubs but they never have any berries. Can you tell me why?*"

Some species of skimmia have male and female flowers on separate plants and to have berries bushes of both sexes must be grown adjacent to each other to ensure that the female flowers are pollinated. It would seem that you do not have the right combination. *Skimmia japonica reevesiana* is more reliable as its flowers carry both male and female organs. The white flowers appear in May, followed by deep red berries in the autumn. Unfortunately, this particular form does not like chalky soils.

Vegetables in containers ❧

"*As my garden is small I do not have space for a vegetable plot. However, I do like to have fresh vegetables straight from the garden. Could I grow some in containers on a sunny patio?*"

Most certainly. Many different kinds of vegetables can be grown success-fully in containers. Avoid brassicas, which need a long season of growth. Choose quick-growing kinds such as lettuce, spring onions, radish, beet-roots and carrots, as well as courgettes, tomatoes, French beans, auber-gines and peppers. A variety of herbs, such as sage, thyme and parsley, will grow well in containers.

Cropping bags or any kind of large tub or container can be used. Do not use ordinary garden soil but purchase good John Innes potting compost. Most vegetables need a lot of water as they develop and watering must be attended to very carefully, particularly when the weather is hot in the summer. Allow the soil to dry out and the vegetables will suffer.

Space-saving cropping ❧

"I do not have space for a vegetable plot as such, but I do have a sunny patio. What could I try in containers and growing bags?"

Choose quick-growing crops: beetroot, carrots, lettuce, spring onions and radishes, for example. Aubergines, courgettes, French beans, peppers and tomatoes can all also be grown in pots or growing bags, as well as a variety of herbs such as parsley, sage and thyme.

Select a large tub or container, make sure it has adequate drainage holes in the bottom and fill it with good John Innes potting compost: don't use ordinary garden soil.

Most vegetables require plenty of water as they develop, so pay close attention to this, as pots do dry out very quickly, particularly in hot weather. If the compost dries out, your crops will suffer.

Tub plants in a town garden ❧

"I have a courtyard town garden which is in shade for most of the day. I want to grow an evergreen shrub in a tub, preferably one with attractive leaves. What would you recommend?"

A shrub that should meet your needs is *Fatsia japonica*. This has large, attractively glossy leaves and does well in town gardens. It can also be grown in a large tub or container. In the autumn it produces trusses of white flowers. After a number of years the stems become leggy but they can be cut back in the winter as the plant makes new sucker growths from the base.

If you also plant variegated-leaved ivies in the tub, they will make an attractive combination with the fatsia.

Well contained ❧

"I need some evergreen plants for two containers standing on an exposed south-facing balcony. What would you recommend? A hydrangea and rhododendron have been there for a year but they are not happy and need replacing."

Evergreen shrubs that you could grow in your containers are: *Choisya ternata* (Mexican orange), evergreen, white scented flowers; *Skimmia foremanii*, evergreen, white flowers, red berries; santolina (cotton lavender), silvery leaves, evergreen; *Acer* "Flamingo", silvery, pink-flushed leaves; *Yucca* "Golden Sword", creamy-yellow banded leaves; *Camellia japonica*, scarlet, pink or white flowers, evergreen; berberis, several evergreen kinds; *Hebe* "Midsummer Beauty", lavender-purple, cone-like flowers. Don't forget to stand the containers on bricks to allow surplus water to escape. Fill the containers with John Innes Potting Compost No. 3. No plants will succeed if the soil dries out and particular attention must be paid to watering. It may be necessary to water twice a day in the summer.

Heathers in tubs ❧

"I would like to have some heathers in my garden but the soil is chalky. Could they be grown in window-boxes or tubs instead?"

Heathers can certainly be grown in windowboxes or tubs filled with an acid, ericaceous compost similar to that used for rhododendrons and camellias. Some heathers will tolerate lime in the soil, such as the winter-flowering varieties of *Erica carnea*.

Alpine gem ❧

"A friend of mine has sent me some seeds of Soldanella alpina *from Switzerland. This is a lovely small flower which blooms in the snow. Please tell me how to grow the seed."*

Sow your soldanella seeds now. Sprinkle them over the surface of a 3½ in. (9 cm) pot filled with a mixture of equal parts (by volume) shredded, sterilized loam, peat and coarse sand, or use a good proprietary seed sowing compost. Cover with a thin sprinkling of grit and moisten by standing the pot in a bowl of water until the surface is wet. Move to a cold frame to germinate. Shade from bright sunlight. When the seedlings appear, prick them out into a box of acid, peaty compost. When large enough, plant out the seedlings in a peat bed.

Raised alpine bed

"I would like to grow some alpine plants but the soil in my garden is rather heavy clay and I have not been very successful so far. How can I overcome the problem?"

Most alpine plants like a freely draining soil and to provide this we suggest that you build a raised bed for alpines. The retaining walls need not be very high and they can be made with bricks, stone or wood. Make sure that there are holes in the base of the walls to allow surplus water to drain away. For ease of management do not make the beds wider than 4 ft (1.2 m). The soil in the bottom of the bed must be forked over and a shallow layer of rubble put over the base before the bed is filled with good gritty soil. A suitable mixture consists of 1 part good soil, 1 part peat or decayed leafmould and 1 part stone chippings. This should be well firmed. After planting cover the bed with chippings to prevent moisture lodging around the base of the plants.

Coral gem

"Can you help me about the name of a plant I saw growing in a hanging basket in a botanical garden? The only name on the label was lotus. It had attractive pendulous stems with silvery leaves and coral-red flowers. Could you identify the plant for me and tell where I can get seed of it?"

From your description we believe the plant you have seen is *Lotus berthelotii*, also known as coral gem. It is an excellent plant for a hanging basket. As it comes from the Canary Islands it is not hardy in this country and needs to be grown in a frost-free greenhouse. It can be raised from seed but this is not generally available. However, several nurserymen offer plants for sale, including: Reads Nursery, Hales Hall, Loddon, Norfolk and Hopley's Plants Ltd, High Street, Much Hadham, Herts. SG10 6BU. The best variety to grow is known as "Kew Form".

Soft joints

"I am laying a limestone flag terrace and I want to fill the joints with a low, moss-type plant rather than a hard cement finish. Can you suggest what to grow, please?"

Rather than opt for moss to create "soft" joints between your limestone paving, you could plant New Zealand burr, *Acaena inermis*. This has ferny, bronzy-purple leaves and is far more durable than moss which could dry out in a prolonged hot spell.

Plants are available from most alpine specialists such as Potterton & Martin, The Cottage Nursery, Moortown Road, Nettleton, Caistor, Lincs LN7 6HX.

Power washing makes light work of keeping the slabs clean.

Pressure wash

"My brick-paved patio is covered with an unsightly and slippery green slime. How can I clear it off?"

The easiest and most efficient way is to use a pressure washer. The equipment is not expensive to hire and will do the job in minutes. This is far quicker than using proprietary chemicals which need applying periodically.

Potted spring glory

"My garden is very small and I grow a lot of plants in tubs and containers on a sunny patio. This summer I have planted them with begonias, geraniums and petunias. What can I grow in them for the spring?"

Universal pansies grow well in containers and will give you flowers through the winter and early spring. Ornamental cabbages and kales look particularly attractive if used in bold groups, or when combined with pansies. Polyanthus, dwarf wallflowers and forget-me-nots will also give a colourful display in the spring. In addition plant bulbs such as daffodils, tulips and hyacinths in the autumn.

Care for hanging basket ❧

"I have bought a hanging basket planted with a fuchsia. It seems healthy and I want to keep it in good condition all summer. How do I care for it and can I keep the fuchsia for another year?"

Once the fuchsia in your hanging basket is well established it will need feeding each week with a liquid fertilizer. Fuchsias need regular feeding to keep them flowering all summer. Watering is also very important. Plants in hanging baskets can dry out very rapidly, particularly in hot weather. Give the basket a good soaking each morning and, depending on the weather, water again during the day and in late afternoon.

You can keep the fuchsia for another year. If you have a greenhouse move the plant to a pot in September and keep it almost dry for the winter. Next spring, prune back all the side shoots close to their base and start the plant into growth by giving the plant a good watering. If you do not have a greenhouse, keep the plant in a fairly dry state in a frost-free shed or unheated room. Some gardeners bury their fuchsias in a trench in the garden covering them with about 9 in. (22 cm) of soil. In the spring they are lifted and started into growth once again.

Tub plant gift ideas ❧

"We are planning to give our relatives a planted container for a special wedding anniversary. Their garden is small, sheltered and sunny for most of the day. We would welcome suggestions for what would be suitable to plant in the container. The tub could be placed in an unheated greenhouse for protection in winter."

As the tub could be placed in a cold greenhouse during the winter, it would be a good idea to purchase a plant that would brighten up the days in the early part of the year. If you fill the container with an acid, lime-free potting compost you could plant a dwarf rhododendron or a camellia.

Rhododendron calostrotum is one of the azalea types having blue-green leaves. In spring it has purple or scarlet flowers. In the open it grows no more than 3–4 ft (1–1.2 m) tall and probably less in a container.

Most camellias can be grown in tubs. "Donation" is one of the best varieties, starting to flower in February in mild districts.

Winter windowboxes ❧

"I want to keep my windowboxes colourful through the winter months. What can I plant in them after the summer flowers fade?"

There is a vast range of plants that you could put in your windowboxes to provide colour through the winter including: winter-flowering pansies and heathers; ornamental cabbage and kale; dwarf conifers with colourful foliage; periwinkles and variegated-leaved ivies.

You could also plant dwarf bulbs, such as *Tulipa kaufmanniana* and its varieties, among the other plants for spring flowers. Other bulbs that you could plant include dwarf-growing cyclamineus daffodils, muscari and crocus.

Winter hanging basket ideas ❧

"My summer baskets are looking a little sorry for themselves now. Can I replant them for the winter?"

Give your baskets a good scrub, then replant for winter interest, using dwarf bulbs, winter flowering pansies, perhaps one or two young evergreen shrubs like *Aucuba japonica* or a dwarf hebe, and some trailing ivy to disguise the sides.

Hot spot contenders ❧

"My patio really bakes in summer. Are there any plants I could grow in containers on it?"

Potted plants for a hot spot include *Senecio cineraria*, *Helichyrsum petiolare*, petunias and spiraea.

Sink plants ❧

"Can you give me the names of plants suitable for growing in a sink or trough?"

Suitable plants for growing in a sink garden include: *Armeria caespitosa*, *Draba aizoides*, *Iberis saxatilis*, small Kabschia saxifragas, *Achillea chrysocoma*, *Gypsophila repens*, *Erodium reichardii roseum plenum*, *Sempervivella alba*, *Achillea chrysocoma* and *Sisyrinchium* "E. K. Balls".

Planting a sink garden   ❧

"I want to make a sink garden. Can you please let me know the type of soil to use and what plant varieties will thrive in a sink?"

A suitable soil mixture to use in a trough garden for alpine plants is John Innes Potting Compost No. 3 to which should be added an extra part of coarse sand or grit to ensure really good drainage. Cover the drainage hole in the trough with a zinc square or pieces of broken pot. Over this put a layer of rubble or broken pots followed by a layer of rotted leaves. Pour in the potting compost and firm it gently so that the final level is about an inch below the rim of the trough. This is to allow space for watering.

One or two rocks can be placed in the trough to give the appearance of an outcrop. A small conifer, such as *Juniperus communis compressa*, also adds interest to the trough garden.

Suitable alpine plants to grow are: *Saxifraga* "Cranbourne" and "Kath Dryden", varieties of *Thymus serpyllum*, *Sempervivella alba*, *Sisyrinchium* "E. K. Balls", *Achillea chrysocoma*, *Sedum cauticola*, *Dryas octopetala*, *Dianthus alpinus*, *Artemisia assoana* and *Helianthemum alpestre serpyllifolium*. Dwarf bulbous plants, such as dwarf irises, hardy cyclamen and miniature daffodils could also be grown in the trough garden. After planting, cover the surface of the soil around the plants with stone chippings.

Soil for a rockery garden   ❧

"Having discovered an old china sink long ago abandoned in the jungle of a garden I inherited when I moved, I can now fulfil an ambition to make an alpine sink garden. What soil do I use?"

Use John Innes Potting Compost No. 3, but add to it an extra part of coarse sand or grit to ensure really good drainage. Make sure your sink has adequate drainage holes before you start, then cover the base with a layer of broken crocks, followed, if possible, by a layer of rotted leaves. Pour in the compost and firm it so the final level is about an inch (2.5 cm) below the rim of the sink to allow for watering.

After you have planted it up with alpines, a small conifer perhaps, and some dwarf bulbs maybe, cover the surface of the soil around the plants with some stone chippings.

The right mix ❧

"I have an old glazed sink which I want to treat to give it a stone effect. What is the cement mixture I should use?"

The cement mixture used for giving a sink a stone appearance is called hypertufa. It is made from a mixture of 1 part cement, 1 part sharp sand and two parts of peat. Mix the ingredients with water to a smooth paste (do not add too much water). Score the sink to form a key for the hypertufa mixture and apply it with a trowel about $\frac{1}{2}$ in. (1 cm) thick. Use the finger tips to give the coating a textured finish.

That sinking feeling! ❧

"I have acquired an old stone sink and I want to grow alpine plants in it. What sort of compost should be used, and can you name a few suitable alpine plants for the trough?"

Fill your stone trough with a mixture of equal parts good top soil, peat, and coarse, gritty sand. Or you can use a prepared potting compost such as John Innes Compost No. 1. It is very important that there is a drainage hole in the base of the trough. Cover this with wire gauze and add a shallow layer of rubble or broken pots before pouring in the soil mixture to within an inch of the top of the trough.

Make sure it is well firmed – one or two pieces of rock can be set in the surface to give the appearance of a miniature rock garden. Suitable plants are: *Sempervivum arachnoideum*, *Genista villarsii*, *Saxifraga* "Cranbourne", *Dianthus* "Pike's Pink", *Achillea* x *lewisii*, *Thymus serpyllum coccineus*, *Penstemon hirsutus* "Pygmaeus", *Raoulia australis*, *Rhodohypoxis baurii*, *Fuchsia* "Tom Thumb", *Draba aizoides* and *Hypericum polyphyllum*. A miniature conifer such as *Juniperus communis* "Compressa" adds to the attractiveness of the trough garden.

All year interest ❧

"We have recently paved our small backyard and would like to plant a climber in a large tub to train round the window and door. Could you suggest a climber that looks good all the year round? I don't want a climber that looks dull in the winter. The wall gets plenty of sun."

There are very few climbers that are interesting all the year round. However, you could consider some of the large-leaved, variegated ivies such as *Hedera colchica* "Sulphur Heart" which has green and yellow leaves or *H. colchica* "Dentata Variegata" with green and grey leaves.

Pyracanthas, although not climbers, can be trained to walls. They are evergreen and have masses of white flowers in early summer followed by red, yellow or orange berries in autumn.

Another idea is to plant a climbing rose with winter-flowering jasmine. You will then have rose flowers in summer and the yellow flowers of the jasmine in winter. Use a good potting soil mixture in the tub and feed the plants through the spring and summer. Watering must not be neglected in the summer.

Tub clematis

"Can you tell me whether clematis can be grown in pots?"

Most clematis, apart from extra vigorous kinds such as *C. montana*, can be grown in containers. A large barrel is ideal. Drill holes in the base, cover with rubble for drainage and fill with John Innes Potting Compost No. 2. Grow plants up a pyramid of canes and keep the compost moist at all times.

Three varieties you might like to try are: deep purple "Beauty of Worcester", white "Gillian Blades" or mauve-blue "Etoile de Paris".

For further details on growing clematis in pots, check out *The Gardener's Guide to Growing Clematis* by Raymond Evison (David & Charles).

Shaded patio winners

"At the back of my house I have a concrete patio which faces north. It is shielded from the east but is exposed to west winds. Can you suggest any climbers, and berrying and flowering shrubs for this position? They would have to be grown in containers and large pots."

Climbers that should flourish in 15 in. (38 cm) pots or tubs of JI No. 3 on your shaded patio include *Akebia quinata, Hydrangea petiolaris, Clematis alpina* "Frances Rivis" and ivies, such as "Buttercup", "Goldheart", "Paddy's Pride" and "Angularis Aurea".

Shrubs include *Pyracantha* "Orange Glow", *Cotoneaster* "Skogholm" and "Coral Beauty", *Ilex* (holly) "Golden King" and "Golden Queen", *Euonymus* "Emerald 'n' Gold" and "Sunspot", *Aucuba* "Variegata".

Perennials

Moist perennial performers ❧

"There is an area in my garden where the soil is moist for most of the year. What border perennials would grow well in this position?"

Suitable plants for the area of damp soil in your garden include: astilbes, hostas, *Iris sibirica* and *I. kaempferi*, lysimachia, mimulus, primulas, rodgersias, veratrum, lythrum, monardas and trollius. If you have plenty of space you could also try *Gunnera manicata* which has giant, rhubarb-like leaves. The toothed leaves can grow up to 10 ft (3 m) across, so you have been warned!

A shade more ❧

"Several of the plants I have in a shaded border do not grow very well and I suspect that they need more light. Can you give me the names of perennials that do not mind a shaded situation?"

There are a good number of hardy perennial border plants that will grow happily in a shaded border. A few that you could try are *Dicentra spectabilis* (bleeding heart), bergenia, primulas, hellebores, convallaria (lily of the valley), campanulas, *Anemone nemorosa*, astilbes, polygonatum (Solomon's Seal), lamiums and *Gentiana asclepiadea*.

Splitting polyanthus ❧

"My polyanthus plants have finished flowering. Is it worth keeping them for another year?"

Polyanthus plants are well worth keeping for another year. After flowering, lift the plants and split them into several pieces. Plant these in a shaded position for the summer. In the autumn, lift the plants and replant them in their flowering beds and await next spring's display

Perennials from seed ❧

"To save money, I would like to grow my own border perennials from seed. Can you give me the names of some that are easy to grow from seed?"

Many border perennials can be raised from seed. Although it is cheaper than buying plants, it takes much longer to establish a border.

Plants that can be grown from seed are acanthus, *Achillea ptarmica* "The Pearl", *Aconitum napellus*, agapanthus, *Anchusa azurea*, delphiniums, lupins, scabious, *Dicentra spectabilis*, geums, heleniums, verbascums and *Rudbeckia* "Goldsturm".

Everlasting flowers ❧

"I want to grow some everlasting flowers from seed this year. Can you give me the names of some good kinds to grow?"

Some of the best everlasting flowers that can be raised from seed include: helichrysum, limonium (statice), xeranthemum, helipterum, globe amaranths, *Scabiosa stella* "Drumstick" and *Moluccella laevis* (bells of Ireland). There are many different colour strains for most of these flowers. Special mixtures of everlasting seeds are also available.

Raised colours ❧

"I have a raised bed in which I want to plant perennial, yellow flowers to last as long as possible. Can you suggest any that will fit the bill?"

The following herbaceous perennials and small shrubs have yellow blooms and foliage providing colour for most of the year. Perennials include *Aurinia saxatilis* "Compacta", *Primula vulgaris, Mimulus* "A. T. Johnson", *Sedum spathulifolium* "Cape Blanco", *Viola* "Jackanapes" and *Campanula garganica* "Dickson's Gold" (foliage).

Shrubs include *Helianthemum* "Wisley Primrose", *Genista lydia, Genista* "Vancouver Gold", *Epimedium perralderianum* and *Penstemon pinifolius* "Mersea Yellow".

Evergreen perennials ❧

"I grow a variety of herbaceous flowers in the front of a shrub border. When the foliage dies down in the autumn the area is very drab. I have planted some bergenias as they are evergreen. What other evergreen perennials could I plant to provide year-round interest?"

There are a great many evergreen perennial flowers which would add interest in winter to your border. Suggestions of what to grow include: hellebores, particularly *H. corsicus*, dianthus, euphorbias, *Anthemis cupaniana*, *Artemisia* "Powis Castle", *Campanula persicifolia*, *Doronicum* "Miss Mason", *Heuchera sanguinea*, pulmonarias, including *P.* "Redstart" and *P.* "Bowles' Blue", *Stachys olympica*, ferns, hardy geraniums and *Tellima grandiflora*.

Swift moth ❧

"Whilst dividing some herbaceous plants I found a number had been eaten into and semi-transparent caterpillars wriggled rapidly out of some of them. What is the pest, and how can it be controlled?"

The caterpillars would have been those of a swift moth. Both the garden swift and the ghost swift moth scatter eggs around herbaceous and other plants and the caterpillars feed underground on thick roots and fleshy storage organs for up to three years before becoming fully fed. Regular soil cultivation and good weeding will help control them, as would a scattering of Sybol Dust around the plants.

Seed coats ❧

"When growing hardy perennials from seed I have found that the seed coating sticks to the seed leaves and prevents them opening for some time. When I have tried to remove the seed coats, I have damaged the seedling."

It is not uncommon for perennial seedlings to emerge with seed coats firmly attached to the cotyledons or seed leaves. Don't pull them off as you may harm the seedlings. The husk will, in time, be shed naturally.

Mulching drought plants ❧

"To save watering the garden in the summer, I am growing mainly Mediterranean-type plants such as cistus, lavenders and grey-leaved plants like santolina. Will they mind having a mulch of coarse bark put around them?"

Although the Mediterranean plants you mention will tolerate dry conditions, they still need moisture at the roots. Mulching the surface of the soil with composted bark will help to conserve soil moisture and be of benefit to the plants.

Dividing border perennials ❧

"I have a large clump of day lilies (hemerocallis). It has been in the same position for many years. I want to split it up. When is the best time to do this?"

Overgrown clumps of border perennials, such as your clump of hemerocallis, may be lifted and divided in the autumn or spring. Lift the clump with a garden fork or spade then divide it into several portions.

Rabbit-proof ❧

"Could you recommend some perennials and spring bulbs that rabbits will not eat?"

Plants that are not usually damaged by rabbits include: agapanthus, alchemilla, aquilegia, artichoke, astilbe, bergenia, chionodoxa, colchicum, convallaria, primrose, tagetes, verbena, viola and zinnia.

Perennials from seed ❧

"To save money this year I would like to raise some border perennials from seed. What would be suitable kinds?"

There is a large number of perennials that can be raised from seed. Among the many you might like to consider are *Rudbeckia fulgida* "Goldsturm", *Scabiosa caucasia*, delphinium, verbascums, lupins, hollyhocks, hellebores, *Heliopsis scabra, Helenium autumnale, Gypsophila paniculata, Papaver orientale* and *Astrantia major*.

A firm that can supply seed of most of these plants by mail order is Chiltern Seeds, Bortree Stile, Ulverston, Cumbria LA12 7PB. Phone 01229 581137. Take a browse through their descriptive catalogue and discover even more perennials from seed.

Shady perennials ❧

"I have a border in my garden which is partly shaded and the soil generally moist. What border perennials would you suggest for this position?"

Perennials suitable for your border include: aconitums (monkshood, poisonous), ajuga (bugle), *Anemone hybrida* in variety, aquilegias, *Arum italicum* "Pictum", astilbes, *Dicentra spectabilis* (bleeding heart), doronicum, *Geranium sylvaticum*, hostas, lily-of-the-valley (convallaria) and *Meconopsis cambrica* (Welsh poppy).

What is AGM? ❦

"Some plants have the initials 'AGM' after them. What does this mean?"

The initials stand for Award of Garden Merit. This is an award given to a plant by the Royal Horticultural Society because they feel it has all-round excellence and can be recommended for general garden cultivation.

Michaelmas mildew ❦

"Every summer our Michaelmas daisies get coated with mildew, spoiling the look of the borders. Is there any treatment I can give to stop this happening again?"

Dryness at the roots is a contributory cause of mildew, but the spores are airborne so there is no real preventative action to take. However, you can replace the worst-affected varieties with less susceptible plants.

Look for varieties of *Aster amellus* and *Aster* x *frikartii*, neither of which suffers from mildew to any extent. The choice is not too wide, compared to the normal Michaelmas daisies (*Aster novi-belgii*) but specialist nurseries do provide a reasonable choice.

Jamaica primrose ❦

"I bought four plants called Jamaica primrose. They are a mass of yellow flowers at the moment. Can you tell me how to keep them from year to year?"

We believe your plant is *Argyranthemum* "Jamaica Primrose" once called *Chrysanthemum* "Jamaica Primrose". It is a first-rate plant but it will not survive the winter outside in your area. However, cuttings of side shoots root very easily and we suggest that you take some before the winter. Root them in small pots of gritty potting soil. Once roots form, pot the young plants individually and keep them in a frost-free place for the winter. A heated greenhouse would be ideal or you could try keeping them in a light position in an unheated room indoors. Put the plants in the garden again next May.

Aspect for astilbe ❦

"Having admired astilbes at last year's Chelsea Flower Show, I intend to plant some in the spring. What sort of soil and situation is best for them?"

Astilbes like to be grown in moist soil and thrive in boggy ground beside a stream or pool. Ideally, the soil should be acid and they do not like thin, chalky soils that dry out in the summer. Grow the plants in sun or partial shade. Plant in spring or autumn and lift and divide the clumps every three to four years.

Handle with care
"What is a monkshood?"

Monkshood is the common name for *Aconitum napellus*. It is a hardy perennial and there are several different species and varieties having hooded, deep blue or white flowers. Aconitums are relatives of the delphinium and thrive in light shade.

The roots are *very* poisonous and it is best not to grow it where there are young children. This plant should be handled with extreme care, wearing gloves.

Cascading seedlings
"I have found that there are seedling plants near my clumps of aubrieta. They are rather overcrowded. When can I move them to a better place? The old plants are rather straggly. Are they worth keeping?"

Wait until early autumn before transplanting your seedling aubrietas. Seedlings tend to produce pale colours and may not be the same as the parent plants. If you want to preserve plants with good, strong colours, you will have to take cuttings of young shoots from them during the summer.

Plant your seedlings in a sunny position where the soil is well drained. Old plants tend to become straggly. To retain their compact habit, trim hard back directly after flowering and topdress around the plants with some fresh soil or old potting compost.

Lady's mantle
"I want to grow some plants of Alchemilla mollis *so that I can use the flowers in floral arrangements. What sort of soil and position does it like?"*

Alchemilla mollis, lady's mantle, is a hardy perennial that is very easy to grow. The fluffy, yellow-green flowers are much sought after by flower arrangers. They may also be dried for winter displays. It is not fussy about soil, although it should not be too wet. Plants may be raised from seed sown in the spring but it is probably simpler to purchase small plants from a garden centre. Provided they are planted this spring, the plants should be flowering in the summer.

Arabis attacked

"I took a photo of an arabis at a garden centre recently and wondered if it was affected by something incurable or a new disease that I should have reported to the owner. At the time I couldn't find anyone available."

The spotting is due to a very severe attack by flea beetle, the same pest that attacks seedlings of turnip and other plants of the cabbage family. It could be controlled by dusting with derris or by spraying with permethrin. If you go to the same centre again, you could show the owner this reply!

Columbine decline

"The long-spurred aquilegias in my garden seem to be declining and the flowers are not as good as they once were. Is this normal?"

Aquilegias are not long-lived perennials and they tend to deteriorate after a year or so. Scrap your plants and start again with young plants which are easily raised from seed. This can be sown in February and March under glass or in June and July in a frame. Grow the seedlings in pots or modules of good potting compost before planting them in the open. They prefer light, well-drained soil and are not too happy in heavy, wet soils.

Mildewed bugle

"I have an area of my borders covered with creeping purple-leaved bugle (ajuga), which normally looks very attractive. This autumn the leaves were plastered with white deposits which I assume was some form of mildew. Should anything be done now, and what can be done next year?"

The deposits are of powdery mildew. It would be wise to cut out the mildewed shoots to remove the source of infection and then to spray with sulphur or a systemic fungicide. Next year, keep the area well watered in dry weather and at the first sign of any white spotting, spray again with sulphur or systemic fungicide. Two or three sprays, two weeks apart, should clear up the attack.

Prized lilies

"At a recent flower show I admired a display of alstroemeria hybrids. Can you tell me what kind of soil and situation they like. Are they fully hardy? When is the best time to plant them?"

There are some very lovely alstroemeria hybrids (Peruvian lilies) now on the market and they are certainly hardy in southern England, provided they are given some protection with bracken or bark fibre in the winter. The top growth will die down in the autumn and the fleshy roots must be protected. For this reason plant them 6 in. (15 cm) deep. Ideally, plant in May or June so that the plants are well established by the following autumn. Plant in good, well-drained soil and in a warm and sunny situation. Alstroemerias also make good tub plants, particularly in cold areas, as the containers can be taken under cover to a frost-free place in the winter.

Arum lilies outside ❧

"I understood that arum lilies were greenhouse plants but in several gardens I have seen them growing outside. Have they been put there for the summer or can they stay outside all the year round?"

It is true that arum lilies are grown under glass specially for their white spathes which are at their best at Easter. However, they can be grown outside in gardens in southern England. There is also a variety called "Crowborough" which is said to be hardier than ordinary forms. An effective way of growing arum lilies in the open is to plant them in the mud at the edge of pools and streams.

Tender loving care ❧

"How do I grow beautiful Amaranthus tricolor? *Mine were mainly all stunted and shrivelled."*

Your amaranthus could probably have done with some tender, loving care! Next year, start the seed off in a heated propagator in March, in small pots, using a good, proprietary compost. As soon as the seedlings can be handled, prick them out individually into modules or boxes. Grow them on in a light, sunny position.

Plant them outside in early June, choosing a site where the soil has been improved with decayed organic matter and where it is sunny and sheltered. Feed the plants at intervals with a liquid fertilizer such as Miracle-Gro or Phostrogen. Your plants may have suffered from drought this summer, so next year make sure the soil around them does not dry out.

Silver and gold mystery

"I have been given a plant called Ajania *'Silver and Gold' but I am unable to find out any information about it. Can you help?"*

Ajania pacifica is also known as *Chrysanthemum pacifica* and is a member of the daisy family. It is a mound-forming sub-shrub and is a native of exposed rocky hillsides in central and eastern Asia. It carries small yellow flowers in autumn.

High and dry

"I have some clumps of Achillea *'Gold Plate' and want to dry some of the flowers for winter arrangements. Can you tell me when to cut the flowers and how to dry them? Can I use my greenhouse for drying?"*

The flower heads of *Achillea* "Gold Plate" can be dried without difficulty. Cut the stems when the flowers are fully open and firm. Hang them up in bunches where it is dark, warm and dry. An airing cupboard is an ideal place. Success depends on drying the flowers quickly; a greenhouse is not suitable. The atmosphere is too moist; mildew would form and hot sunshine would bleach the flowers.

Lemon-scented verbena

"I have bought a plant of lemon-scented verbena as the leaves have such a delicious fragrance. What is the best position for it? Does it need sun or shade?"

Lemon-scented verbena, *Aloysia triphylla*, is a half-hardy shrub and we do not think it will survive outside in the winter in northern England. It could, however, be grown in a large pot or tub and taken under cover for the winter. It grows best in a warm and sunny spot.

Love-lies-bleeding

"I notice in a catalogue that love-lies-bleeding is a hardy perennial. What happens to the plants in the autumn? Are the stems cut down to ground level?"

Love-lies-bleeding is the accepted common name for *Amaranthus caudatus*, a half-hardy annual that dies at the end of the summer. The plant to which you refer is probably bleeding heart, *Dicentra spectabilis*. This is a hardy perennial which has arching flower stems from which hang several small, heart-shaped florets. Once the stems of this plant wither in the autumn cut them back to soil level. Do not disturb the plant often because the roots are brittle and easily damaged. It will send up fresh growth again next spring.

Perennial asters ❧

"I would like to plant some Aster *x* frikartii *(Michaelmas daisies). Can you tell me whether they are prone to mildew?"*

There are two good varieties of *Aster* x *frikartii* called "Monch" and "Wunder von Stafa". Both have received Awards of Garden Merit from the Royal Horticultural Society. Both are resistant to mildew. "Monch" has really good blue flowers and "Wunder von Stafa" tends towards purple.

Poppy anemones ❧

"I am very fond of the anemones that you can buy in florists' shops in the winter. When should they be planted?"

The anemones that florists sell in the winter are poppy anemones which are derived from *Anemone coronaria*. In Devon and Cornwall, and other mild districts, plant the tubers in October. In colder districts plant in February. If you have some barn cloches or a cold frame you could try planting in the autumn. The glass protection should provide you with early flowers. To do well the anemones need really fertile soil.

Wilting asters ❧

"For the last two years, my asters have died off just before flowering. Is this some form of soil sickness?"

The cause of the early death would be aster wilt. It persists in the soil so it could be called a form of soil sickness; it is actually a fungal disease. To overcome the problem, grow a wilt-resistant strain of aster, such as Marshall's "Starlight Mixed".

When to divide ❧

"A friend has a large clump of Achillea ptarmica *'The Pearl' and she has offered me some pieces from it. When is the best time to divide the clump? The double, white flowers are most attractive; can they be dried?"*

The best time to lift and divide the clump of *Achillea* "The Pearl" is in early spring. Choose young, vigorous pieces from the outside of the clump. Replant in well-drained soil and a sunny position.

Sunny spot for bugle ❧

"I am thinking of planting the purple-leaved bugle as a ground coverer. Will it grow well in a sunny situation?"

Yes, the purple-leaved bugle, *Ajuga reptans* "Atropurpurea", will grow in a sunny or partially shaded situation. The leaves will, in fact, colour best in a sunny situation. To grow really well the plant likes moisture-retentive soil that does not dry out badly.

Bear's breeches ❧

"Can you give me some information on a plant known as bear's breeches? Is it a perennial?"

Acanthus mollis, or bear's breeches, is a hardy perennial grown for its handsome foliage and interesting flower spikes which are a blend of purple and white. It grows 4–5 ft (1.2–1.5 m) tall and originates from southern Europe and north-west Africa.

Different windflowers ❧

"Can you tell me the difference between wood anemones, Anemone blanda *and 'De Caen' anemones?"*

All the anemones you mention are delightful garden plants and are popular florists' flowers. *Anemone nemorosa* is the wood anemone with small, white, daisy flowers in March and April. *A. blanda* flowers at the same time but has larger flowers which may be blue, mauve, pink or white. "De Caen" anemones (*A. coronaria*) have large single flowers in red and blue. The tubers can be planted at different times of the year. Those planted in April will flower in the summer. Others planted in September/October will flower in the winter if covered with cloches.

Ground colour ❧

"I have several different ajugas with coloured leaves which are planted for ground cover. I am told that some varieties have better flowers than others. Could you give me their names?"

There are a great many ajuga varieties with differently coloured leaves. Some of the best flowering kinds include "Pink Elf" and "Rosea", both with pink flowers, and "Alba" with white flowers and dark green leaves.

Agapanthus hardy and true ❧

"I have seen agapanthus plants grown in large tubs on a sunny terrace in Cornwall. Are they hardy enough to be grown outside further north?"

There are many different types of agapanthus. Some, such as *A. umbellatus*, are tender and can only be grown outside in the winter in very mild gardens. However, there are many hardier strains, such as the "Headbourne Hybrids", which could be grown successfully outside in the Midlands.

Off with their heads! ❧

"I have several clumps of lady's mantle. I am very fond of the feathery, greenish-yellow flowers but I find the mass of seedlings that appear around the plants is a nuisance. Is there any way of preventing the plant seeding?"

Alchemilla seedlings can be a nuisance although friends will be glad of them if you dig them out. However, the best way to overcome the problem is to cut off the flower heads before they set seed.

Plant advice ❧

"In July I bought a pretty plant called Anisodontea capensis. *I know nothing about it. Can you help?"*

Anisodontea capensis is a half-hardy shrubby perennial from South Africa. It flowers for months from summer to early autumn. Blooms are deep reddish-purple. It is frost-tender and will not survive temperatures lower than 5°C (23°F). Plant it in a large pot and plunge it outdoors for the summer. When nights turn chilly, move it into a heated greenhouse or somewhere indoors where it is light and warm.

Ornamental onions over ❧

"I have some allium bulbs growing in my garden. Now that they have finished flowering do I cut off the heads?"

Cut off the allium heads after flowering, but leave the green stems to die down naturally. The bulbs need to rest for the remainder of the summer, but in October apply bonemeal to the soil.

Some ornamental grasses grow taller than you think.

Onion heads

"I have grown some ornamental onions with large globular flower heads. Now that the flowers have faded should I cut off the flowering stems?"

If you want to use the heads in dried flower arrangements leave them until they are thoroughly dry before cutting them off. However, if you do not want to keep them, they can be cleared away as the bulbs are now dormant. They will probably have set and scattered a lot of seed and you may find that you have a crop of onion seedlings appearing next spring.

Pampas grass

"I would like to grow pampas grass in my garden but I do not want one that grows too big. Are there any compact types?"

Cortaderia "Pumila" is one of the most compact kinds, growing to about 4 ft (1.2 m) tall. "Sunningdale Silver" is another good variety, growing to about 5 ft (1.5 m), while "Gold Band" is an interesting variety as it has yellow-striped leaves and grows about 5 ft (1.5 m) tall.

Irishman's cuttings ❧

"Can you tell me what exactly is the difference between ordinary chrysanthemum cuttings and Irishman's cuttings? Is there any advantage of one over the other?"

Irishman's cuttings are partially rooted shoots that arise around the base of chrysanthemums and other plants. They are removed with a sharp knife when they are a few inches tall and with roots attached. It is a useful way of increasing a plant if only one or two cuttings are needed. Each one should be potted separately in small pots of good potting compost. Ordinary cuttings, made from basal shoots, are taken in the same way but without roots. Each cutting is trimmed just below a leaf joint before being put in pots of gritty soil.

Plant size ❧

"Can you tell me anything about a plant called Crambe cordifolia? *How tall does it grow? I understand it has white scented flowers."*

Crambe cordifolia is a magnificent border plant when it is covered in masses of white, scented flowers in June. It is not, however, suitable for a small garden as it grows up to 6 ft (2 m) tall and 4 ft (1.2 m) wide. It is very deep-rooted and needs well-drained soil and a sunny situation.

Ivy-leaved toadflax ❧

"I enclose two photos of ivy-leaved toadflax. One plant is growing in a wall and the other is in the ground with its roots in gravel at the base of the wall. Even though the photographs are at slightly different distances, you will see that the plant in the ground has much larger flowers. Does this mean that there are several species of ivy-leaved toadflax or does habitat make such a difference?"

There is only one species of ivy-leaved toadflax, *Cymbalaria muralis*. Although it is possible that some forms are better than others, we believe that habitat is responsible for the difference in the two plants. The one in the wall is starved of moisture and nutrients whereas the one in the ground has the benefit of abundant plant food and water. If the position is in shade, this may also have had an effect on the more lush growth.

Make sure you select plants of the right height to get the best from your border.

Chrysanthemum aphids

"I am just starting to take my chrysanthemum cuttings, but am finding various greenfly on the young shoots. What would be the best way to treat them at this stage?"

I would spray the stools and rooted cuttings with Rapid insecticide to clear up the current attack. In order to prevent any further infestation developing, I would then insert a Phostrogen Plant Pin into each pot of cuttings.

Trailing chrysanthemums

"A few weeks ago I saw some trailing chrysanthemums in France. I was unable to find out their name. Can you help me?"

The trailing chrysanthemums that you saw in France were probably cascade chrysanthemums. These are not often seen as they need careful training and a lot of attention. Plants can be raised from seed or from cuttings. They are naturally upright in habit. To induce them to cascade, the shoots must be made to grow downwards by training them to supports. In the summer plants are kept in the open on shelves, enabling the stems to be tied downwards on canes.

Mouldy chrysanths

"For the first time my early chrysanths were spoiled by some mould affecting the base of the blooms. What caused it?"

The damage you describe is known as bloom damping and is caused by the grey mould fungus botrytis. Botrytis is worse under thundery, humid conditions and often follows damage to the petals by thrips (thunder flies). Keep humidity under control next year and also fumigate with tecnazene smoke.

Charm chrysanthemums

"Last year I raised some charm chrysanthemums from seed. One or two plants have very good flower colours and I would like to keep them. Can I take cuttings from these plants instead of raising new plants from seed?"

Yes, you can take cuttings from your charm chrysanthemum plants. Do this within the next few weeks, using young basal shoots. Root them in small pots of gritty soil in a warm propagator.

Beware chrysanth rust

"A few of my chrysanthemum plants last year produced brown circular powdery patches which I was told was rust disease. I cut the plants down, but have taken cuttings from them and I am now wondering if that was wise."

The disease could still be in the plant tissue, so it would have been safer to have bought new plants from a reliable nursery. However, try a few sprays over the cuttings with Tumbleblite II which may well eradicate the infection. Should rust still appear, start again with new plants.

Comfrey food

"I have recently returned to holding an allotment and have inherited a row of comfrey. How do I use this plant as a feed for others?"

There are a number of options. Dig them directly into the soil, where they will be rapidly broken down by bacteria, or compost them with organic refuse. Alternatively, stuff the leaves into a large container – any size, from a four-gallon bucket to a water butt – that has seep holes at the base. Cover the container and allow the leaves to ferment. Within two weeks or so, a concentrated, black liquid will ooze from the base. Catch this liquid in a bowl and dilute it with 20 parts of water before feeding it to other plants.

Devon chocolate ❦

"Whilst on holiday in Devon we came across a plant called the chocolate flower. It really smelt of chocolate. Can you give me its correct name?"

The chocolate flower is *Cosmos atrosanguineus*. It produces attractive flowers with velvety, deep maroon petals and is unusual in having a chocolate fragrance. It's a tender perennial and will not survive the winter outside. Lift plants in the autumn and keep them in a frost-free greenhouse for the winter. Replant in early summer when cuttings can also be taken.

Chrysanth growths ❦

"Some of my young chrysanthemum plants, grown from cuttings, have developed nasty swellings at soil level. I have never seen this before and my gardening friends are unable to help. Can you please advise?"

The plants have been infected by crown gall, which is a bacterial disease. It is pretty unusual on chrysanthemums. This same disease can infect trees and shrubs, and your damaged plants should be burned along with any remaining soil or compost from that potting.

Use only sterilized soil, or reliable proprietary compost for further pottings. No chemical cure exists, but it may help a little to dust the compost of currently healthy plants with sulphur dust.

Charm chrysanthemums ❦

"Having read about charm chrysanthemums, I would like to grow some. Are they easy to grow, and who can supply cuttings?"

Charm chrysanthemums are normally raised from seed and several seed firms, such as Suttons Seeds of Torquay, Devon and Thompson and Morgan, Poplar Lane, Ipswich, Suffolk, have their own special strains.

Plants are not difficult to grow. If the seed is sown early in warmth, large specimens can be grown by the autumn when the mushroom-shaped plants become covered in masses of single, starry flowers in various colours.

Sow the seed as soon as possible in a heated propagator. When large enough, pot the seedlings individually in small pots. As they develop, move them on gradually to larger pots of good potting compost. Stand the plants outside for the summer and keep them well watered and fed regularly, once they are established in their final pots. Bring the plants into a cool greenhouse or conservatory in September.

Seedling care

"Last autumn I was given some eryngium heads which I put into a polythene bag and stored in a shed. Earlier this year I found a number were producing roots and I now have nearly 100 tiny seedlings."

To help your seedlings grow, put them singly in small pots of potting compost and grow them in a well-ventilated cold frame until they are large enough to move into the open garden.

Ornamental thistles

"Can you name the piece of plant that I am sending? It is growing in a friend's garden and I would like to know how to propagate it."

Your plant is *Eryngium tripartitum*. It has attractive, blue, thistle-like flowers which are good for drying for winter decorations. Grow the plant in a sunny position. It is not fussy about soil as long as it is well drained. Increase plants by sowing seed in the spring, or remove some of the roots in the autumn and use them as cuttings, making them 2–3 in. (5–7.5 cm) long and inserting them in pots of gritty soil.

Elephant's ears

"I want to plant some elephant ears in a shaded part of my garden. What varieties would you recommend?"

Bergenias or elephant ears are excellent ground-cover plants and there are some very good varities from which to choose, including "Sunningdale", pink flowers and coloured leaves in winter; "Profusion", pink; "Margery Fish", reddish-purple; and "Silberlicht" which has white flowers.

Tender daisies

"Can you name the yellow flower I am sending? I found it growing in a garden in Cornwall. The bush was covered in yellow, daisy flowers and looked most delightful."

The flower that you sent is *Euryops pectinatus*. It is a most attractive shrubby plant growing about 3 ft (1 m) high and 2 ft (0.6 m) across. The yellow daisy flowers appear for most of the summer. Unfortunately, the plant is not fully hardy and in cold areas it is likely to be killed off by hard frosts. It is well worth growing in the Midlands if you can give it a warm and sheltered position.

Spectacular echiums ❧

"While on holiday in the Scilly Isles I saw some plants with huge blue flower spikes up to 10 ft (3 m) tall. What are they are called?"

The plants you saw were most probably *Echium pininana*. They really are spectacular, but will only thrive in frost-free areas such as in Cornwall and the Isle of Wight. In these districts they seed themselves freely.

As they are biennial the plants die after flowering, but young plants can easily be raised from seed. There are several species which come mainly from the Canary Islands and Madeira.

Dividing bellis ❧

"I have a plant of Bellis *'Dresden China'. I was expecting it to die after flowering but it still seems healthy. Is it perennial?"*

Unlike most double daisies, *Bellis* "Dresden China" is sterile and does not set seed. It is perennial in habit and the only way to propagate the plant is to divide the clumps after flowering in the spring and replant the pieces about 6 in. (15 cm) apart.

Bloom damping ❧

"Several of my best chrysanthemum blooms have been ruined by some disease that has turned them brown from the outside. After a while the flowers then develop a greyish powder over them. Advice, please."

The problem is a disease known as bloom damping. It is caused by the grey mould fungus, botrytis, and is encouraged by too moist an atmosphere in the greenhouse. Remove any blooms still showing signs of the problem, first covering them with a plastic bag if they have got to the "mouldy" stage. Provide as much ventilation as possible, and apply a light dusting of sulphur from time to time.

Choice calceolaria ❧

"Can you tell me anything about an alpine calceolaria called 'Walter Shrimpton'?"

"Walter Shrimpton" is a choice hybrid between *Calceolaria darwinii* and *Calceolaria fothergillii*. It grows only a few inches tall and has curious flowers arising from a rosette of leaves. It needs to be grown in an alpine house in gritty, lime-free soil. Provide light shade from strong sunshine in the summer. Plants are very prone to attack from greenfly and a systemic insecticide should be used to keep them under control.

Leaf miners ❧

"A few years ago I gave up chrysanthemum growing as I didn't seem able to get on top of leaf-miner. I had another attempt to grow them this year but once again the crop has been badly attacked. Is there any wonder cure yet?"

Chrysanthemum leaf-miner has a very wide host range, including sow thistles and other weeds, so sadly, attacks are always going to be a possibility. No cure has emerged in the past few years, but try spraying regularly with malathion or Sybol.

Wax flower ❧

"On visiting a garden I was given a seed of Cerinthe major *'Purpurascens'. I do not know much about the plant other than it is from the Mediterranean. I put the seed in a 6 in. pot and six weeks later a seedling 1 in. tall had appeared. Can you tell me anything about the plant. Is it hardy and what should I do with it in the winter?*

Cerinthe major "Purpurascens" is listed in the latest catalogue of Thompson & Morgan (phone 01473 688821) as a new introduction. The leaves of the plant are fleshy and blue-green in colour. The small flowers are enclosed in striking blue bracts which are the main attraction. It is a native of the Mediterranean and described as an evergreen, hardy perennial. Plants grow 12–18 in. (30–45 cm) tall.

As your plant is still quite small we suggest you keep it in a greenhouse or frame for the winter and plant it outside in the spring; then it should flower in the summer.

Stately and edible cardoons ❧

"I have seen cardoon plants growing in a flower border. Can they also be used as a vegetable and what parts can be eaten?"

Cardoons (*Cynara cardunculus*) are stately plants growing about 6 ft (1.8 m) tall. They are often used as an ornamental plant but the blanched stems are also delicious to eat. They are, however, probably appreciated more on the continent than in this country.

Plants are raised from seed sown in April. To blanch the stems, draw them together and wrap the lower parts in black polythene, newspaper or brown paper, putting several ties around the wrapping. Do this in late August and in six to eight weeks the lower stems should be blanched and ready for eating.

Clump cuttings ❧

"I have a large delphinium clump with dark violet flowers. What is the best way of propagating the plant?"

The best way of propagating your delphinium is to take basal cuttings in February. Using a sharp knife, remove young shoots 2–3 in. (5–7 cm) long with a piece of the older hard stem attached at the base. Remove the lower leaves and dip the base of the cuttings in hormone rooting powder. Insert them in small pots filled with a gritty potting compost. Stand them in a cold frame or greenhouse.

Cuttings can also be rooted in jars of water. Once a good root system has been made, pot the young plants individually in small pots of good potting compost.

Increasing diascia ❧

"I bought a diascia plant this spring and it has been covered in pink flowers all summer. I would like to have more plants. Can I take cuttings from my plant?"

Diascias are first-rate border perennials. Most need a sunny position and a well-drained soil. Cuttings of young shoots, 2–3 in. (5–7 cm) long are easy to root, best taken in the late summer. Place them around the edge of a small pot of gritty compost covered with a polythene bag. It is a good policy to take a few cuttings before the autumn and to keep the young plants under glass for the winter as not all kinds of diascias are fully hardy. In very hard winters some diascias, being only half-hardy, may die off.

Pink pipings

"I have been told to propagate my 'Mrs Sinkins' pinks from pipings. How do I prepare the pipings and when should it be done?"

Pipings are the tips of the pink's shoots. They are simply removed by holding the top of the shoot between thumb and first finger and giving a sharp tug. The best time to take pipings is in late June/early July.

Insert the pipings, without any other preparation, in small pots filled with seed compost to which extra grit or perlite has been added. Stand the cuttings in a propagator until roots form, when the plants can be potted on separately.

You need to stake your delphiniums regularly to keep them straight.

Care for delphinium seedlings

"Could you tell me what to do with some delphinium seedlings. I shook some ripe seeds over garden soil in a seed tray last autumn and now have a thousand seedlings 2 in. high. Will they survive the winter? I could put them in an unheated conservatory."

Your delphinium seedlings will most certainly survive the winter because they are quite hardy. They will be safe in your unheated conservatory. Do not disturb them or try to prick them into seed trays – just leave them alone for the winter. Give them a sunny spot in the conservatory and water them very sparingly, but do not let them dry out completely.

In the spring prick out as many seedlings as you can manage in seed trays of good potting compost. When they are a little larger pot them singly in 3 in. (7.5 cm) pots and, finally, plant them outside at the end of May.

Sulphur so good

"Last summer some of my best delphiniums were spoiled by a dense growth of white mould on the flowering stems and leaves. What should I do this year to prevent a similar fate?"

The damage would have been due to attack by powdery mildew. Prevent damage this summer by keeping the plants well watered in any dry weather, and by spraying a few times, two or three weeks apart, using a sulphur fungicide such as Phostrogen Safer's Garden Fungicide or a systemic fungicide such as Bio Supercarb.

Conditions for hostas

"I have some hosta plants which seem healthy but they do not flower. They are growing in a moist and shaded position which I understand is the sort of situation the plants like. Should I move them to a new place and when is the best time to lift and divide large clumps?"

Hostas do like a moist and shaded position but if the shade is too dense they will not flower very well. Give some of your plants a sunnier situation and they should flower better. It does mean, however, that the soil is likely to dry out more often and you may have to water in dry spells. Also, make sure that you put plenty of well-rotted compost or manure in the soil to help keep it moist.

The best time to divide the plants is in the autumn or early spring. It is not necessary to disturb the whole of large clumps. Sections can be cut from them without disturbing the main plant.

Dividing doronicum ❧

"A friend has a large clump of doronicum or leopard's bane which is covered in bright yellow daisy flowers in April. It is such a good plant that she has offered me some pieces from it for my own garden. When is the best time to take them?"

Doronicums are valuable for their bright yellow flowers so early in the season. The best time to lift and divide your friend's clump is in the autumn. The plants prefer a moist soil and they will tolerate partial shade.

Dividing hosta ❧

"I have a large clump of Hosta glauca *which is in need of splitting up. When is the best time to do it?"*

Hosta clumps can be lifted and divided in early autumn or early spring. However, they do not need dividing very often. To avoid undue disturbance to a large plant, cut a wedge-shaped piece out of it. Replant without delay in good, moisture-retentive soil, well enriched with decayed compost or manure.

Splitting the roots of most perennials should be a simple process.

Hosta slugs ✿

"Is it ever possible to stop slugs ruining hosta leaves?"

With difficulty, yes! Water around the plants in early spring with Nobble or Fertosan slug killers and then surround the plants with sharp grit. As soon as new growth starts, water plants and soil with Slugit liquid, and repeat after heavy rain. There should then be no damage.

Baby's breath ✿

"I planted a root of baby's breath or perennial gypsophila last year but it did not grow. Do they require any special soil and position?"

Gypsophila paniculata or baby's breath is not usually difficult to grow and it is puzzling to know why your plant failed unless the soil was too wet. It grows best in well-drained limy soil and in a position in full sun. Plants do not like cold and wet soils. They do not like disturbance and should not be moved once planted.

Attractive leaves ✿

"I want to grow some plants of Heuchera *'Palace Purple' as the foliage is so attractive. Is it true that plants can be raised from seed?"*

Heuchera "Purple Palace" is a superb border perennial and it is true that it can be raised from seed. A few of the seedlings may have green leaves, but these are best discarded at an early stage. Grow the plants in semi-shade and where the soil is moist.

Pink pokers ✿

"I have grown some plants of pink pokers (Limonium suworowii) *from seed and I plan to dry the flower spikes later in the season. I shall put the plants outside at the end of May. In case we have a wet season, which might spoil the flowers, could I grow some plants in pots and keep them in the greenhouse all summer?"*

Limonium suworowii, commonly known as statice is an excellent tender annual and the pink flower spikes dry well. We think your idea of growing some plants in pots is an excellent one. They are most decorative and are often used in this way for interior decorations.

When the seedlings are large enough, put them in 5 or 6 in. (13–15 cm) pots, filled with a good potting compost. Grown in this way you should have superior flower spikes for drying later on. Cut the spikes when all the flowers are open.

Unsuitable soil ❧

"I have not been able to grow plants of Gypsophila paniculata *in my garden. I have tried several times, but the plants simply wither away. My soil is inclined to be wet and heavy. Is this the cause of the trouble?"*

Your cold, wet soil is probably the reason why you have not been able to grow *Gypsophila paniculata* successfully. It needs a well-drained, stony soil containing lime, and a sunny situation. If you want to try again, prepare a special position for the plant. Put coarse rubble in the base and add generous amounts of coarse sand and grit to the bed. It would be a good idea to remove the existing clay soil from the planting position and fill it with gritty potting compost. Planting is best carried out in early spring.

Not such a sweet pea ❧

"Could you give me some advice on growing the perennial sweet pea, Lathyrus latifolius? *I just cannot get this plant to establish itself. I am aware that I must sow the seed outside. Do I stop the growths like sweet peas?"*

The perennial sweet pea, *Lathyrus latifolius*, is not usually difficult to grow from seed and it is not necessary to remove the shoot tips as you would with annual sweet peas to encourage basal shoots. Try again by simply sowing the seeds shallowly in a sunny, well-drained patch and they should germinate like the proverbial mustard and cress.

Herbaceous problem ❧

"During the autumn and early winter our delphiniums and phlox plants started to die. During winter cultivations we unearthed quite a large number of these semi-transparent white grubs from around the plants. Are these the cause of the trouble, and how do we get rid of them?"

The white grubs are caterpillars of the swift moth. They feed on a wide range of herbaceous plant roots, with delphiniums and phlox amongst their favourites. Remove as many as you can find during digging and then apply a soil insecticide such as Bio Chlorophos to the soil. The caterpillars can feed for one or two years before pupating and emerging as adult moths.

Bleeding heart in pots

"In an old garden book it says that plants of dicentra or bleeding heart were once brought into flower early under glass. Can you tell me how it was done as I would like to try out the idea?"

It is not difficult to get plants of *Dicentra spectabilis* to flower under glass early. In the old private gardens of the past it was often done to produce early blooms for floral decorations.

Lift roots in October and put them in large pots of good potting compost. Stand the pots in a cold frame until February and then take them into a cool greenhouse. Once flowering is over replant the clumps in the open garden.

Diascia cuttings

"Last spring I put a small plant of Diascia rigescens *in a sunny spot in my garden. It has grown well, spreading into a large clump. The flowers have been lovely all summer. I am not sure how hardy it is. Do you think it will survive outside in the winter in Hampshire?"*

Diascia rigescens is one of the hardier species and it should survive the winter in your garden. It is a valuable perennial plant, flowering for most of the summer and well into the autumn. To make sure that you do not lose your plant, you could take cuttings of the young shoots in early autumn. They root very easily. Keep the young plants in a frost-free greenhouse for the winter and plant them outside in the spring.

Dividing dicentra

"I bought a plant of Dicentra spectabilis *last year and this spring it grew rapidly to 3 ft high and rather more across. I do not need to increase my stock but should I divide it this year anyway?"*

There is no need to divide your plant of *Dicentra spectabilis* this year if it is looking healthy and vigorous. When you wish to divide it, do it in late July/early August. Alternatively, wait until it is dormant and divide it in late March/early April. Either time is satisfactory.

Some gardeners divide their plants in late July/early August by cutting back the stems and lifting the clump. After pulling it apart into pieces they are replanted immediately. Give the freshly planted crowns plenty of water so that they make fresh roots before the winter.

Drooping dahlias ❧

"Some of my best dahlias are wilting. Watering didn't seem to help, so I dug one to check the roots. I found a lot of the roots had been eaten, and there were large tunnels in the tubers. In the tunnels were semi-transparent caterpillars, with brown heads. Identification and advice please."

Your excellent description makes it clear that the garden swift moth is the pest responsible. If not controlled, the caterpillars feed through the year and can take two years to complete their development. They can eat a lot of roots in that time!

Control is not easy once the attack has occurred, but it may help to dust around the wilting plants with Bio Chlorophos and gently work it into the soil. When the dahlias are lifted in autumn, check each tuber carefully and also dig the soil over well to expose any pests still present. When replanting in spring, dust with Bio Chlorophos after firming the soil around the dahlia plants.

Fancy foxglove ❧

"Last year I saw some unusual foxgloves with flowers that stood straight out from the stems, unlike ordinary foxgloves which have pendulous flowers. Are these a special kind and can they be grown from seed?"

The foxgloves that you saw last year were "Excelsior" hybrids. It is a very good strain with flowers in a mixture of colours ranging from cream to pink and purple. Plants can grow up to 5 ft (1.5 m) tall. They are easily raised from seed which can be sown between April and June in the open garden. Plants raised this year will not flower until next year. Grow the plants in partial shade. Seed is widely available.

Autumn hues ❧

"I have some bergenia plants in my garden which grow and flower well, although the leaves remain dark green. In other gardens the leaves turn a lovely dark red in the autumn. How can I get my plants to do the same?"

It is a matter of variety. The leaves of some bergenias do colour well in the autumn; others do not. One of the best varieties for coloured leaves is "Abendglut", also known as "Evening Glow". The semi-double flowers are magenta-crimson in colour and the undersides of the leaves become deep red. Plants grown in an open, exposed position have the best coloured leaves in winter.

Euphorbias

"Could you give me some information on two euphorbias I have been given
E. dulcis *and* E. x martinil? *Are they hardy and what soil and situation do
they like?"*

Both are hardy. E. dulcis has greenish-yellow flowers and colourful foliage
in the autumn. It is inclined to seed itself and seedlings can become a
nuisance. *E.* x *martinil* is a hybrid between *E. characias* and *E. amygda-
loides*, the wood spurge. Grow them both in full sun in a well-drained soil.

Ornamental cabbages

*"Last autumn I saw some plants called 'flower cabbage'. They looked really
beautiful. Are they a special type of cabbage and how are they grown?"*

Ornamental cabbage or kale is a special form that has become popular in
recent years for its highly colourful and frilly foliage. It is an excellent
bedding plant and is particularly useful for autumn and early winter
displays when the colours develop as the temperature falls in early
autumn. Plants are also suitable for growing in pots and containers.

Plants are grown from seed and new colour strains appear each year.
One of the latest is "Xmas Bouquet Series", an F_1 hybrid having magnificent white, frilly leaf rosettes. Most seedsmen offer colour mixtures
including shades of rose, pink and white.

Sow the seed in a greenhouse in April. It is preferable to sow in modules
to save pricking out the seedlings. When large enough, move the small
plants to $3\frac{1}{2}$ in. (9 cm) pots of good potting soil. Gradually acclimatize them
to outside conditions and plant outside in May. If you do not have a
greenhouse sow the seed in the open and when large enough to handle,
transplant the seedlings to their flowering positions.

Mealy aphids and cabbage white caterpillars can be a nuisance in the
summer and spraying may be necessary against the pests.

South African daisy

"I have admired plants of Euryops pectinatus. *Can you tell me whether the
plant can be grown in Wiltshire?"*

Euryops pectinatus is an attractive plant from South Africa, producing its
yellow daisies all summer. It is only likely to succeed outside in your
Wiltshire garden if you plant it against a warm, south-facing wall and
protect it in the winter with bracken or straw.

Take a few cuttings in late summer and root them in a greenhouse. Keep the young plants in a frost-free greenhouse for the winter and plant them outside in late May.

Holey bergenia ❧

"My elephants' ear plants (bergenia) all have their leaf edges notched. I thought at first that it was due to slugs or snails, but the border where the plants are is very dry and I have not seen any slime trails. Any ideas what has caused the problem and what can I spray with to stop the damage?"

The notching is the work of vine weevil adults. The weevils hide in the soil or under the plants by day and come out to feed at night. Probably the best short-term answer is to dust under the plants with Sybol Dust to reduce the numbers of adult weevils. In the longer term, water the area with Nemasys H obtainable by mail order from Defenders, Occupation Road, Wye, Ashford, Kent TN24 5EN (tel orders on 01233 813121). This product contains millions of "friendly" nematodes that seek out and destroy the vine weevil larvae in the soil.

Pruning euphorbia ❧

"I have a thriving clump of Euphorbia characias wulfenii. *The stems are very crowded, so can I prune out some of the older ones? And when can I take cuttings from it?"*

Plants of *Euphorbia characias wulfenii* flower on stems made in the previous season. Prune out the old stems after the flowers have faded. Cuttings of basal shoots can be taken in the summer. Make them about 4 in. (10 cm) long and insert them in small pots filled with 4 parts grit or coarse sand and 1 part seed compost. Stand the cuttings on open staging in a greenhouse.

Lady's mantle ❧

"I am a keen flower arranger and like to grow my own materials. I have bought some plants of Alchemilla mollis *as the greenish-yellow flower sprays are delightful in arrangements. Can you tell me whether the plant needs any special conditions and what soil is best for it?"*

The beauty of *Alchemilla mollis* or Lady's mantle is that it is very easy to grow and it will flourish in most situations. It will tolerate shade and any ordinary well-drained soil will do. In a position to its liking it can become a nuisance as seedlings can appear all over the place. Give it some good soil and a reasonably light position and it will reward you with an abundance of feathery flowers and foliage for your arrangements.

Ornamental onion

"At this year's Chelsea Flower Show I was very taken with an ornamental onion called Allium christophii. *The flower heads were huge. Is it a difficult plant to grow and when is the best time to plant bulbs?"*

Allium christophii is also known as *A. albopilosum* and it is very easy to grow. It does not mind poor soil provided it is well drained. It also likes a sunny situation. The large, purplish-blue flowers appear in early June and last a long time. The old flower heads are also useful dried for winter decorations. After flowering the leaves wither and the bulbs go into a resting stage. The best time for planting bulbs is in early autumn or as soon as they are available from bulb merchants.

Allium seedlings

"I have a bulb of Allium albopilosum *in my garden which flowers each year in May/June. I have discovered a lot of green shoots appearing around the plant. Could they be seedlings and are they worth keeping?"*

The green leaves around the base of your ornamental onion are in all probability seedlings from the mature plant. If they are left they will gradually increase in size and eventually flower. When the leaves die down you could lift the bulbs and plant them in a special nursery bed of good soil where they can grow to flowering size. When large enough, plant the bulbs in their flowering positions.

South African daisies

"Last summer I grew some plants of Venidioarctotis 'Wine'. *They flowered well and in the autumn I took some cuttings which all damped off. Can you tell me where I went wrong?"*

The venidioarctotis hybrids are very colourful daisy flowers which revel in hot and sunny situations. They are not fully hardy which means they will not survive the winter outside in most districts. The best way of preserving them is to take cuttings from the plants in the autumn and keep them in a frost-free greenhouse for the winter.

They are prone to damping off if conditions are too damp and cold, so another time, root the cuttings in small pots filled with a compost containing plenty of coarse sand. Stand the cuttings on the greenhouse bench and water very sparingly. Ventilate the greenhouse whenever weather conditions permit.

Planting wallflowers ❧

"I am thinking of planting a border in my garden with wallflowers for a spring display. When is the right time to plant them and how far apart should they be spaced? Can I plant bulbs with them?"

Plant your wallflowers as soon as possible. They like a sunny position and well-drained soil. Space the plants 9–12 in. (23–30.5 cm) apart. Purchase sturdy plants with dark green foliage and avoid over-large plants with lots of soft, sappy growth, which can suffer in the winter.

Bulbs can certainly be planted with wallflowers to enhance the display next spring. The yellow, lily-flowered tulip "West Point" looks particularly attractive with red wallflowers. The tulips can be planted between the wallflowers as late as November.

Wallflower seedlings ❧

"I have raised some wallflowers from seed. Do I need to move them before planting them in their flowering positions in the autumn?"

Your wallflowers will not make good plants if left in the seed rows. Lift them now and transplant them in a nursery bed, spacing the plants 6 in. (15 cm) apart. Plant them in their flowering positions in October, allowing 12 in. (30 cm) between the plants.

Mullein moth caterpillars ❧
– attractive but huge appetites

"I used to grow lovely mulleins, with large white, hairy leaves, but for the last few years the plants have been devoured by caterpillars. The caterpillars are very attractive with yellow, black and white bodies, but they eat leaves, flowers and then all but the hardest stems. Can you tell me a little of their life cycle so I know exactly when to look out for them?"

Adult mullein moths start their egg laying around the middle of April and continue through to late May in most years. The caterpillars are very attractive, as you mention, but growing as they do to about 2 in. (5 cm) long they do have large appetites.

When fully fed by June or July, the caterpillars leave the mullein plants and penetrate quite deeply into the soil where they pupate in silken cocoons. Surprisingly, the pupation period will last through four or even five winters, so in your garden you must have a number of overlapping generations of the insect for annual attacks to occur. Start to look out for the caterpillars from early to mid May.

Leggy wallflower ❧

"I am very fond of the old double wallflower called 'Harpur Crewe'. My plants have become very leggy. Is there any way of keeping them more compact?"

Erysimum "Harpur Crewe" is a fine, double-flowered wallflower. Its natural tendency is to grow leggy and it is difficult to do anything about it. We suggest that next summer you take a few side shoots as cuttings to raise new plants and start again with them. They are not difficult to root. Insert the cuttings in small pots of gritty soil. When rooted, pot them individually. When a good root system has been made, plant them out in the open garden.

Mallow malady ❧

"I have a mallow in the garden which has suddenly become home for lots of little beetles. They are quite pretty to look at, with metallic greeny-blue bodies and reddish-brown heads, but they are making a real mess of the leaves. I don't want to kill them, but would like to know what they are and if there is an alternative host plant I could transfer them to."

These attractive insects are a form of chrysomelid or leaf beetle. They occur in southern Britain, feeding on mallow and hollyhock. Perhaps you could find some wild mallow locally, or some out-of-the-way hollyhock where the beetles' feeding would not be too noticeable.

Tatty dahlias ❧

"What causes the tattered holes that have spoiled my dahlia leaves for much of the summer? I have not spotted any caterpillars or other insects on the leaves, but most of them have these irregular holes."

Capsid bug feeding was responsible. Capsids look rather like large, very active aphids but they drop off the plants at the first sign of danger so are not often seen at work.

If new foliage is still being attacked, try spraying the soil and the leaves with Tumblebug or BugGun. Very soon now, damage will cease as the capsids will be laying their winter eggs in tree and shrub bark, so look out next year for the first signs of attack and then spray before the damage is severe.

Shoo fly plant ❧

"I have been given some seeds of the shoo fly plant. I understand it gets rid of flies. Can you tell me how to grow it?"

The shoo fly plant, also known as apple of Peru, is called botanically *Nicandra physalodes*. It grows about 3 ft (90 cm) high and 1 ft (30 cm) across. It is fully hardy and needs a sunny, sheltered spot and a free-draining soil. In summer, light violet, white-throated flowers appear on the stems.

Sow the seeds in a heated propagator and prick out the seedlings 2 in. (5 cm) apart in a seed tray. Set the plants outside when they are large enough to handle.

Solomon's seal sawfly ❧

"In June of most years, our Solomon's seal leaves are suddenly eaten away, almost overnight it seems. We have occasionally found greyish grubs feeding in some numbers. Can we prevent attacks this year?"

Solomon's seal sawfly is responsible for the rapid disappearance of foliage. Eggs are laid in May and hatch in June. Once fed, larvae cocoons spend the winter in the soil, pupate and then emerge as adults in spring.

Soil cultivation now may help, by disturbing the pests, but it is difficult to prevent attacks as the adult sawflies can fly in from nearby gardens. The best plan is to keep a close watch under the leaves during June and spray with a contact insecticide as soon as any grubs are detected.

Some like it hot ❧

"When I was on holiday on the Isles of Scilly I bought a plant called Lampranthus roseus. *It has pink, daisy flowers. Will it survive growing outside all year round in my garden?"*

Lampranthus roseus is a tender, shrubby succulent plant. In the Isles of Scilly plants flourish in the mild climate and in spring and summer cover the ground with a blaze of colour.

The plant is not likely to survive a cold winter outdoors. However, you could take cuttings from the plant in September and root them in sandy soil in a greenhouse. Keep the young plants in frost-free conditions for the winter and plant them outside for the summer in late May.

Honesty problem

"Can honesty catch club root disease? Whilst clearing away some unwanted seedlings I came across several with the typical root swellings."

Yes. Being a member of the cabbage family, honesty, as well as stocks and other cabbage relatives, is susceptible to attack. Attacks are much less common, however, than on cabbages, sprouts and other vegetable members of the family. Burn infected plants, lime the soil in that area, and avoid growing flowers of the cabbage family.

Blistering honesty

"The leaves on my honesty plants have yellow and brown spots on them and underneath are raised, white patches. It is unsightly, but at present the plants are growing all right. What is causing this and is there any remedy to prevent it?"

The white growths under your honesty leaves, and the resulting discoloration seen above, are due to white blister fungus. This can attack a wide range of plants of the cabbage family and is frequently found on sprout leaves. In severe cases the whole of the underside of honesty leaves can be covered with the fungus and growth is then much impaired. There is no real control although attacks could perhaps be prevented or reduced by regular sprays with a copper fungicide. Complete removal of all infected leaves or plants could be sufficient to prevent attacks next year.

Giant rhubarb

"I would like to grow a gunnera (giant rhubarb). What sort of conditions does it like?"

Gunneras like to be grown in moist, boggy soils. They make huge plants and so are not suitable for small gardens as they need plenty of space. To protect the dormant crowns in the winter, cover them with the old leaves.

Cardinal flower ❧

"I want to grow some plants of Lobelia cardinalis *'Queen Victoria'. What kind of soil and situation will suit them best?"*

Lobelia cardinalis "Queen Victoria" is a first-rate border perennial, flowering in late summer. It must have moist soil in full sun or partial shade. It can be grown successfully in the moist soil beside a pool.

Prepare the ground ahead of planting by incorporating liberal quantities of decayed manure or compost into the soil. Spring is the best time to plant.

Chip and chit ❧

"I sowed some lupin seeds in a pot this spring and put them in a heated propagator. None of the seed germinated. Can you tell me why?"

Your problem is not unusual. According to the best lupin growers in the country, lupin seed should first be chipped. Use a sharp knife and remove a small piece from one end of the seed coating. Afterwards, chit the seed by placing it on damp kitchen paper inside a plastic box. Within 48 hours there will be signs of germination. At this stage place each seed in a small pot of good seed compost. A few days later, the first seed leaves will appear and the seedlings can be grown on in the usual manner.

Blackfly blitz ❧

"We had some very bad infestations of blackfly on our flowers this summer, probably the worst for many years. Some white campanulas were particularly badly attacked. What is the best way to control any repeat attacks in another year?"

If the attacks are not too widespread use a ready-to-use sprayer containing fatty acids, such as the Phostrogen Safer's Insecticide for Roses and Flowers, or pyrethrins such as Bug Gun or Nature's Answer to Insect Pests. Where the infestation is more widespread then I would mix up a sprayer-full of Tumblebug or Rapid.

Peruvian lilies ❧

"I planted a Peruvian lily in my garden last spring but it died. I would like to try again this year. What tips can you offer on growing this plant successfully?"

Peruvian lilies (alstroemeria) can be difficult to get established but once they have settled down, types such as *A. aurantiaca* can almost become a nuisance. They need a sunny situation with well-drained soil. Young pot-grown plants should be set out in spring. Plant them in a hollow so that they are 8–9 in. (20–23 cm) deep. The stems die down by early August and during the winter you should cover the dormant plants with a mulch of rotted compost.

Spit it out! 🌺

"Many of my herbaceous plants and my lavender are being spoilt by blobs of cuckoo spit. Can you tell me the name of the pest that causes this and how to control it?"

Cuckoo spit is the name given to the froth produced by insects known as froghoppers. Eggs are laid in autumn by the adult froghopper and these hatch the following summer into nymphs which suck the sap. They exude liquid and beat this into a protective froth.

No serious damage is done and the easiest control is to direct a strong jet of water from a hose at them. This will wash away the froth and dislodge the insects. They may re-establish themselves, requiring further hosings.

Shady intentions 🌺

"Having seen some plants of Trillium grandiflorum *at the Chelsea Flower Show, I would like to grow some in my garden. What sort of soil and situation do they require?"*

Trillium grandiflorum is a very beautiful, hardy perennial plant, which is commonly known as wake robin, originating in eastern North America. It is a woodland plant and likes cool conditions in a partially shaded position. The soil should be well enriched with decayed organic matter.

The white flowers are often spoilt by the weather and plants can be grown in pots in a cold greenhouse to protect the flowers. After flowering stand the plants outside in a shaded spot.

Let's split 🌺

"I have a clump of the red hot poker called rooperi *which flowers freely in the autumn. Is it possible to split the clump as I would like to have more of these plants?"*

The red hot poker, *Kniphofia rooperi*, is an excellent plant for the autumn garden. Old clumps may be lifted and split into several sections. This is best done in the spring. Keep the plants well watered through the summer to help them get established.

Handsome leaves ❧

"I acquired a plant of Tovara *'Painter's Palette' earlier this year. It has grown well in my mixed border. However, information about this plant is hard to come by and I only know that it is a hardy perennial. I would, therefore, welcome advice on general cultivation."*

Your tovara is also known as *Persicaria virginiana*. It is not difficult to grow but must have soil that does not dry out badly. It also needs a sheltered position to prevent the delicate leaves being damaged by sun and wind. Plants benefit from a mulch of decayed compost or leafmould in early spring to help keep the soil moist. Cut back the stems in the autumn once the leaves fade.

Variegated honesty ❧

"Can you tell me the name of the plant from the piece that I am sending? It looks like honesty but the leaves are variegated."

Your plant is the variegated-leaved honesty, *Lunaria annua variegata*. Plants are easily raised from seed which can be sown outside in early summer. Sow in autumn, and the plants should be flowering by next spring.

Not very sweet rocket ❧

"The tips of all my sweet rocket plants are being tied together and distorted by small green caterpillars. Can you tell me what sort they are and the appropriate action to take, please?"

The caterpillars belong to the large tortrix group. Typically, these caterpillars tie leaves together and feed under the protection. When disturbed they wriggle violently backwards and often drop from the plant on a silken thread. Hand removal of the tips of the shoots would give the best control as no insecticide treatment is likely to penetrate the tied shoots.

Save the seed ❧

"One of my forget-me-nots has produced pure white flowers this year, larger than the normal blue ones. Is this common?"

There are white-flowered strains of forget-me-not (myosotis) as well as colour mixtures, which produce white, blue and rose flowers.

Your plant is a result of a white-flowered seed becoming mixed with the true blue type. As you say it has large flowers, it would be worth saving seed from it.

Sow the seed in late June to provide plants for flowering next spring. There are likely to be blue and white-flowered plants. But if you continue saving seed each year from the best white-flowered plants, you will gradually build up your own unique strain of white forget-me-nots.

"Silver Sparkler" ❧

"This year I bought a plant called Osteospermum *'Silver Sparkler'. Can I leave it in the garden all the year round or do I have to put it in a greenhouse for the winter?"*

Your osteospermum is one of the modern hybrids of these attractive, South African daisies. It is hardy only in very mild gardens and we do not think it is likely to survive the winter outside in Essex.

Take some cuttings from it now. Choose firm side shoots and root them in small pots of gritty soil in a greenhouse. Once they have formed roots, pot them separately and keep them frost-free, ready for planting outside in the spring.

Welsh poppy ❧

"Can you tell me anything about a plant called the Welsh poppy? Is it easy to grow and can plants be propagated from seed?"

The Welsh poppy is *Meconopsis cambrica* and it is a native plant. It is an easy-going plant thriving in moist soil and a partially shaded position. The ordinary form has yellow flowers but others are orange and there is also a double-flowered form. In a position to its liking, plants will seed themselves freely about the garden.

Seed should be sown in pots or boxes in the spring or as soon as it is ripe if you can collect some from a plant. The plants grows about 18 in. tall.

Black leaves ❦

I came across a strange plant the other day which has black leaves. Can you name it?"

The plant is *Ophiopogon planiscapus* "Nigrescens". It always attracts attention as it is so unusual in having almost black, grass-like leaves. It is not difficult to grow and will succeed in ordinary soil and a sunny situation. It looks effective planted in groups at the front of a border.

Tender daisies ❦

"I have two varieties of osteospermum, 'Blue Streak' and 'Pink Whirls', and I am looking out for others. As I have not been able to find out anything about them in my gardening books, can you tell me how to care for them? Are they half-hardy perennials and do they like sun or shade?"

Most osteospermums are half-hardy perennials and need protection from frost in the winter. They flower all summer from May until the first frosts of autumn. They are sun-lovers and need well-drained soil. Do not give them rich soil as this is likely to make them produce foliage at the expense of the flowers.

Evening glory ❦

"An unusual plant 54 in. (135 cm) tall and 12 in. (30 cm) wide has appeared for the first time in my garden this year. Every evening its primrose-yellow flowers start to open but only last until the following day. Can you name it for me?"

This delightful intruder is a species of evening primrose, *Oenothera biennis*. It grows to around 6 ft (1.8 m) in height and is widely distributed.

As you say, it flowers late in the evening and has a pleasant scent. Being biennial, it flowers and dies in its second year. Happily it sets plenty of seed which normally produces an abundance of seedlings around the parent plant.

Wilting rudbeckia ❦

"In midsummer, a much-prized rudbeckia plant suddenly started to wilt and is now completely dead. What would have done this, and will it spread to my other herbaceous plants?"

It is difficult to be exact, but as the plant has now died it does seem probable that a root disease was involved. The most likely would be a fusarium, verticillium or phytophthora species. These can persist in the soil and could spread to nearby plants so dig out the dead plant together with a bucketful or two of adjacent soil and dispose of it all safely. Fill in with new soil and then replant. There is no really effective chemical control for these troubles.

Care for ranunculus

"I have some ranunculus plants which are still growing well with plenty of blooms. Can you tell me what to do with them when they finish flowering?"

Once your ranunculus plants have finished blooming, give them a feed with a granular fertilizer, such as growmore, or use fish, blood and bone fertilizer. This will build up their reserves for flowering next year.

Leave the plants in position – or move them and heel them in a spare piece of ground – until the leaves begin to turn yellow. At this point, lift the tubers and dry them in the sun. Afterwards, store them in a cool, frost-free place over the winter. Replant the tubers in the spring.

Sucker problem is only natural

"I have a plant of Romneya trichocalyx *which is flourishing and produces lovely, white poppy flowers for most of the summer. However, it sends out sucker growths all over the place. It has even sent them under a gravel path. How can I stop the plant producing these suckers? Is there a weedkiller that I could use on it?"*

It is natural for romneya plants to produce suckers and there is nothing that you can do about it apart from chopping them out whenever they appear. It is not possible to use weedkillers on the suckers as they would also harm the main plant as well.

Soil type

"Can you tell me what type of soil best suits Houttuynia cordata?"

Houttuynia cordata is an attractive plant grown mainly for its colourful foliage and ground-covering ability. Although it does best in moist soil, it will certainly tolerate dry soil. It is invasive because of its underground stems and may need controlling.

Golden grass ❧

"Can you tell me whether the grass called Bowles' golden grass will thrive in dry soil? I saw a plant of it last spring which was most colourful but I think it was growing in moist soil."

Bowles' golden grass (*Milium effusum* "Aureum") will tolerate dry soil conditions, preferring a partially shaded and sheltered spot. It is an excellent plant, producing bright golden foliage in March and April.

White poppies ❧

"I admired some romneya plants this summer. Their white, poppy-like flowers were most appealing. I understand that there are two kinds — Romneya coulteri and R. trichocalyx. What is the difference between them and are they difficult to grow?"

Romneyas, sometimes known as Californian tree poppies, thrive in a warm, sunny situation. They prefer good, well-drained soil. It is best to start off with a pot-grown plant as they are sometimes difficult to get established. Otherwise they are not difficult to grow.

Once settled they send out sucker growths in all directions. Well-rooted pieces can be cut off in the autumn and replanted in a new position. *R. coulteri* and *R. trichocalyx* are very similar. The former has scented blooms and the flower buds of the latter are bristly.

Lacking lilies ❧

"I have a clump of Kaffir lilies which normally flower well each year. This year I have had only a few flowers. Should I lift and divide them, as I have had the plants for several years?"

Clumps of Kaffir lilies (schizostylis) do need lifting and dividing every few years, otherwise flowering will gradually diminish. Do this in the spring and replant the young pieces, preferably in a new position.

Quick trim ❧

"I have a large clump of Euphorbia characias *in my garden. It has been covered in flowers since March. Some of the old flowering stems are becoming ragged. Can I cut them out without harming the plant?"*

Once the flowers fade on plants of *Euphorbia characias*, the old stems can be cut back to their base to allow the new, young growths to develop from the bottom of the plant. The cut surfaces will ooze white sap. This is harmful and can blister tender skin, so take care and wear gloves when carrying out pruning.

White blister on honesty

"Whilst clearing away my old honesty plants recently I noticed several with raised white patches on the leaves, and some on the seed pods as well. I assume this is some sort of mould – is it something that I should treat?"

The symptoms you describe are typical of the white blister fungus. It is more commonly a disease of sprouts and other brassicas, but will also attack flowering plants in the cabbage family, including honesty.

Keep new plants away from old, infected ones where possible, and dig up badly diseased plants when seen. Early in the year the infection may already be in the new seedlings, so spray them once or twice with a copper fungicide.

Dwarf lupins

"I am very fond of lupins but, as my garden is not very big, the normal varieties are likely to grow too big. Are there any dwarf strains, and can I grow them from seed?"

There are dwarf strains of lupins which can be raised from seed. "Dwarf Lulu Mixed" grows about 2 ft (60 cm) tall and "Dwarf Gallery Mixed" grows to between 9 in. (22 cm) and 20 in. (50 cm) tall.

Sow the seed early in spring, singly in modules of good seed compost, to avoid pricking out. When large enough, the young plants can be planted out in the garden. You may even have a few blooms this year but the plants will give their best display next year.

Top tips

"For the past three seasons I have had no success with sowings of Inula orientalis. *I would be grateful for your advice on how to germinate the seed successfully."*

Sow the seed thinly and shallowly outdoors on a prepared seed bed in late spring or early summer. Keep the soil moist, particularly in dry spells.

Latin for a Welsh poppy ❧

"Can you give me the botanical name of the Welsh poppy?"

The botanical name of the Welsh poppy is *Meconopsis cambrica*. Sow the seed in early spring in small pots in a cool greenhouse. Prick out the seedlings in boxes or modules and, when large enough, plant in a partially shaded spot.

Hollyhock rust ❧

"Are there any varieties of hollyhock that are resistant to rust disease? Our plants always seem to be attacked and the yellow spotting spoils the look of the leaves and the whole border where they are growing. If there are no resistant varieties, what is the best way to reduce attacks?"

As yet there are no reliably rust-resistant hollyhocks, although research and testing are being carried out all the time. The best plan is to treat hollyhocks as a biennial plant. Sow seeds in year one, ready to grow on for planting out for flowering in year two. In year two, sow seeds again and replace the first planting at the end of the year.

During the year, spray the seedlings every few weeks with Tumbleblite, Dithane, or a copper fungicide to protect them from attack. Any attacks which may occur during the flowering year will not be sufficient to spoil the display.

Straggly lavender ❧

"I cut off all the old flower stems on my lavender plants last summer. Some of the shoots are rather straggly. Can I trim these in spring?"

It is a good idea to trim straggly stems on lavender in spring to keep the plants compact. Use sharp secateurs or hand shears to do this.

Is Mavis a hardy geranium? ❧

"I bought a plant of Geranium *'Mavis Simpson' last spring. It spread and flowered all through the summer. I have now been told it is not fully hardy. Is this true?"*

Geranium riversleaianum "Mavis Pritchard" is an excellent hardy, pink-flowered geranium. It should come through the winter safely in Wiltshire provided it is growing in well-drained soil, as it does not like too much dampness around its base in winter. This variety is hardier than the other similar variety "Russell Pritchard", which has magenta flowers.

Hardy geraniums

"Can you tell me the difference between hardy geraniums and ordinary geraniums that are grown for summer displays? I am very confused!"

The so-called geraniums that we use for summer bedding displays are correctly called pelargoniums. Most of the true geraniums are hardy border plants that are easy to grow in sun or shade. They are plants that are in vogue at present and a great many kinds are listed by specialist nurserymen. A few good kinds are: *G. ibericum*, 18 in. (45 cm) tall, deep blue; *G.* "Johnson's Blue", 15 in. (32 cm) tall, violet; *G. macrorrhizum*, 18 in. (45 cm) tall, magenta, good for ground cover; *G. endressii*, 18 in. (45 cm) tall, pink; *G.* x *magnificum*, 24 in. (0.6 m), violet, good for ground cover; and *G. phaeum*, 24 in. (0.6 m) maroon, pendent flowers.

Sawfly attack

"I recently noticed thousands of purple caterpillars, about $\frac{1}{2}$ in. long munching the leaves of my Solomon's seal plants. What can I do to get rid of them and to prevent it happening again?"

Your Solomon's seal has been attacked by Solomon's seal sawfly, a pernicious pest whose caterpillars rapidly strip the leaves. Overcome it next year by spraying with Bug Gun for Flowers when the caterpillars are first seen.

Mouldy mysotis

"I was looking forward to a lovely display of forget-me-nots amongst spring bulbs, but all the plants are now turning white with some mildew or mould. Can this be cured?"

The powdery mildew fungus is responsible, and the white deposit contains thousands of disease spores.

With very severe attacks it is probably better to pull up and destroy the plants. The best fungicide treatment would be to apply Tumbleblite two or three times, two weeks apart.

Here's to a hardy fuchsia

"Can you give me the names of some hardy fuchsia varieties?"

Fuchsia megallanica is the hardiest of the genus and is commonly seen in Cornwall and in the hedgerows of Ireland and the Scottish islands.

Others to consider include: *F.* "Riccartonii", broad, dark crimson sepals; "Lady Thumb", semi-double with white petals showing pale veins and vivid pink sepals with a purplish hue; "Rufus", dark red sepals and dark red petals with a vivid pink hue; "Snowcap", semi-double flowers with red sepals and white petals with cherry-pink veins; and "Tennessee Waltz", double blooms, rose to reddish-orange sepals and mauve to rose petals.

Corky geraniums ❧

"The leaves of my ivy-leaved geraniums have raised corky patches underneath. The new leaves, made since planting in my tubs, appear normal. What could have caused this damage?"

The condition you describe so well is known as oedema. It is often found on ivy-leaved geraniums (pelargoniums) but does little harm. It develops as a result of more water being applied than can be transpired through the leaves in the usual way. The build-up of water ruptures the cells and causes the wart-like corky spots. Do not remove affected leaves, as this can do more harm than good. Next year, give less water and improve ventilation.

Spotty iris ❧

"My iris leaves looked very sorry for themselves this year. They have lots of long, orange/yellow spots along their lengths. Can this be treated or would it be better to start again with new plants?"

Iris leaf-spot fungus is the cause of the damage. Although not too serious for the health of the plants, it is very unsightly and well worth trying to eradicate. You should try cutting off the worst leaves now, or even cutting all the foliage off and burning it. This sounds a severe treatment, but iris have plenty of food reserves. Next spring, as new growth starts, a few fortnightly applications of Dithane 945 or Traditional Copper Fungicide should protect against new attack.

Dividing iris ❧

"I have some large clumps of flag irises which are not flowering as well as they used to do. Can I split them up and when is the best time to do it?"

Once clumps of flag irises become overcrowded they should be lifted and split up. Do this after flowering. Discard the old, worn-out rhizomes and select young pieces with leaves attached. Cut the pieces off with a sharp knife. Trim back the fan of leaves by about half their length. Replant the pieces in fresh ground, burying the roots but keeping the rhizome at soil level.

Attractive snowflakes

"Can you tell me when snowflakes flower? I thought they appeared in the spring but I have seen some flowering late in summer."

Leucojum vernum is the spring snowflake which flowers in April. *L. aestivum* is taller and also flowers in spring. *L. autumnale* is less often seen and has dainty flowers on wiry stems in August and September.

Giant greenfly attack lupins

"My lupins are being attacked by the biggest greenflies I have ever seen. I measured one and it was 5 mm long. Is this a new species and how should I control it?"

The species is the lupin aphid which came to southern England from North America in 1981 and has since spread quite widely. It is a very large species, and can cause considerable damage to the lupins.

   The pest spends the winter in the crown of the plants so it is at hand as soon as new growths start each year. Best control will be obtained by spraying with a systemic insecticide such as Tumblebug or Sybol whenever attacks are seen. Spray again when growth starts up next year.

Tea plant

"I have been given a plant commonly called a tea plant. It has leaves similar to rosemary and pink flowers, but I cannot find any reference to it."

The botanical name of your tea plant is *Lycium barbarum*. It is a member of the nightshade family (Solanaceae) and is a native of North Africa. It is not commonly seen but thrives in most soils and situations. Increase it from cuttings or by pegging low shoots into the soil.

Tree lupin

"Whilst on holiday on the Scilly Isles we saw some lupins growing on the sand dunes. They had yellow flowers and were more shrubby than the lupins I grow in my garden. Can you tell me what sort they are as I would like to grow some?"

The plants you saw were tree lupins, *Lupinus arboreus*, which grow well on sandy shores. They are excellent plants for growing near the sea but soon exhaust themselves because they produce seed so freely.

The easiest way to start is to raise plants from seed sown in a pot in the spring. When large enough they can be planted out in their permanent positions. After flowering cut off the old flower heads to prevent seeds forming which exhausts the plants.

Slimy creatures ❧

"I have a few phygelius plants in my borders. Some slimy creatures attacked the leaves last summer. Later, they were followed, or changed into, hard, round objects but then disappeared."

These are the larvae of the figwort weevil. The grubs eat away the tissue from one surface of the leaf. Figwort weevil feeds on phygelius, mullein and buddleja as well as on figwort. The hard objects you found were the pupal cases and the new adults would have emerged from them. The adults would have then laid eggs to repeat the cycle and the final generation of adult weevils will now be hibernating in the soil.

Look out for the little black and white weevils and the slimy larvae again this spring and if control is necessary spray with an insecticide based on pyrethins, permethrin or fatty acids.

Hopping mad ❧

"Many of my primroses were spoiled this spring by a form of leaf spotting. Can you suggest a cause and a cure?"

The spotting is the result of feeding by leafhoppers, most probably an outdoor attack by the glasshouse leafhopper. This species can attack quite a range of greenhouse and garden plants and primulas are among the favourites. Various weeds, specially chickweed, are also attacked, so good weed control is important.

Spray the undersides of the leaves with Safer's Garden Insecticide, Long-Last or Tumblebug. A couple of thorough applications in spring, with a repeat in early summer, should help to clear up the problem.

Perfumed peony ❧

"I have a white, perfumed peony in my garden. I know these plants do not like being moved but can I increase the plant?"

Multiply your peony in October. Scrape away some of the soil from the side of the clump without lifting the whole plant, and very carefully slice off a rooted and budded portion. Dust the cut surface with flowers of sulphur to protect the tissues from disease and replant the division in a sunny spot in well-prepared soil enriched with decayed compost.

Un-pampered pampas 🌿

"I have a large, untidy and not very attractive clump of pampas grass. Even when showing its plumes it is not particularly attractive; clearly a poor seedling originally. I'd really like to kill it off."

Cut back the pampas using a hedge trimmer and then wait for the regrowth. As soon as that is a foot or so high, spray it lightly with a glyphosate weedkiller such as Murphy Tumbleweed or Miracle Tough Weed Killer. Take care to confine the spray to the pampas. Normally one such application will kill even a large old plant completely.

Choice polyanthus 🌿

"Can you tell me anything about a polyanthus which is called 'Garryarde'?"

Usually known as *Primula* x *garryarde* "Guinevere", this is a most attractive polyanthus-type primula. It has bronze, crinkled leaves complementing the soft pink flowers. It grows about 8 in. (20 cm) tall and flowers in the spring. Grow it in moist soil in a partially shaded position. Plants can be increased by splitting them up after flowering.

Penstemon problem 🌿

"We have some lovely penstemon plants that survived the last hard winter, only to start dying this summer. Whole shoots turned brown, wilted and died off. Can you suggest any reasons and offer any control measures?"

The plants have most probably been affected by one of the wilt diseases. These tend to be soil-borne infections, gaining entry through the roots. There are no really effective control measures apart from removing the plants together with a bucketful of surrounding soil. But first, it may be worth just cutting out the affected shoots and drenching with a systemic fungicide.

Pasque flower was a failure

"I planted a Pasque flower last spring but it gradually faded away. It is such a lovely flower that I would like to try again. What situation and soil does it like?"

Your plant may have failed because the soil it was growing in was too heavy and inclined to dampness in the winter. The Pasque flower, *Pulsatilla vulgaris*, flourishes in the wild on chalk downlands. In our gardens it needs a sunny position in well-drained soil. Obtain pot-grown plants and improve the soil with well-decayed compost.

Poorly peonies

"I have had a large clump of the peony 'Sarah Bernhardt' in my garden for many years but lately it has not flowered very well. Should I lift and divide the clump?"

Your peony is not flowering very well because of a lack of plant food. To encourage it to flower better, scatter bonemeal on the soil around the plant now, followed by a thick mulch of rotted compost or manure.

Peonies do not like being disturbed, but if feeding does not improve the situation you may have to lift the clump carefully and divide it into several pieces. This is best done in October. Replant the divisions in well-manured soil. Make sure that the tops of the crowns are not planted deeply but at about the same depth as they were before. The plants will probably not flower in the first season after transplanting, but if you feed them well they should recover quickly.

Ripe for sowing

"Seed pods are forming on some cowslip plants in my garden. When is the best time to collect and sow the seed?"

Leave the seed capsules on your cowslip plants until they are fully ripe in late summer. The seed will germinate quickly if it is sown straight away, rather than saving it until the following spring.

Sow it in pots or pans of a good seed compost and cover each container with a piece of glass. When the seedlings are large enough, prick them out into boxes, small pots or modules and grow them in a cold frame or greenhouse. Plant in their permanent positions when they have reached a manageable size.

More, please ❧

"I have a plant of Penstemon *'Alice Hindley' which has been flowering since June. It is a very attractive variety and I would like to have more of it. Can I take cuttings from it and when is the best time to do it?"*

Penstemon cuttings root readily at this time of year. Collect firm young shoots and make the cuttings about 3 in. (7 cm) long. Trim each one with a sharp knife just below a leaf joint and carefully remove the lower leaves.

Insert the cuttings in a small pot filled with seed compost to which is added extra coarse sand or perlite. Stand the pot in a propagator or enclose it in a polythene bag. Once rooted, pot the young plants individually and keep them under glass for the winter. Plant them in the open in early spring in good, fertile, well-drained soil.

Lift and divide ❧

"I have a large clump of oriental poppies which I would like to propagate. When can I lift and divide it?"

Your clump of oriental poppies can be lifted and divided in early autumn or in spring. Do this with a garden fork and try not to damage the roots too much. If any pieces are left in the ground they will soon develop into new plants. The roots can also be used as cuttings. In the autumn, cut pieces of root into 1–2 in. (2.5–5 cm) lengths. Make a horizontal cut at the top and a sloping cut at the base to ensure that the cutting is inserted the right way up. Insert them upright in boxes of gritty soil. Once growth begins in the spring, put the young plants in individual pots and plant them out in early autumn.

Penstemons from seed ❧

"Penstemons seem to do well in my dry soil. I have been told that they can be raised from seed. When is the best time to sow?"

Penstemons can certainly be raised from seed but named varieties have to be propagated from cuttings. There are several good seed strains, including "Skyline", which produce a variety of colours.

A sowing can be made in early August to produce good plants for flowering the following year. Grow the young plants on in small pots and keep them under glass for the winter, planting outside in the spring. Sowings can also be made under glass in February and the plants should flower later in the summer. To perpetuate particularly good colours, take a few cuttings from the plants during August–September.

Plant particulars ❧

"Can you tell me anything about a plant I bought last spring for my herbaceous border? It is called Polemonium pulcherrimum. *It has done really well but I cannot find any reference to it in any of my books."*

Your plant is a hardy perennial and, as it grows about 18 in. (45 cm) tall, it is often planted in rock gardens. The tubular blue flowers appear for most of the summer. Grow it in a sunny position in well-drained soil.

Pampas grass ❧

"Can you tell me how old pampas grass plants have to be before they flower? Is it possible to transplant a clump to a new site?"

Given good conditions, pampas grass should begin to flower in the second year after planting. They must have an open, sunny position and well-drained soil. They will not flower in a shaded spot. Transplanting can be tricky. Do it in early spring and make sure that the roots do not dry out.

Wilting peonies ❧

"We always lose a proportion of our peony flowers with what we believe is called peony wilt. The flower buds develop so far but then fail to reach maturity and don't open. Is any treatment possible?"

There is a form of the grey mould fungus *Botrytis* that attacks peony buds and causes them to stay closed. They soon become covered with the typical grey mould spores. Peony buds can also fail to reach full flowering stage because of drought, frost damage, too deep planting or root disturbance. Take care when weeding or digging around the plants, keep them well watered in any spring droughts and, if possible, cover with plastic or netting if frost threatens.

Seedling failure ❧

"I have been trying to grow Salvia farinacea *'Victoria' from seed this year but have been totally unsuccessful. The seedlings emerge but quickly damp off, even though I water them thoroughly with Cheshunt Compound. What I am doing wrong?"*

It is not usually so difficult to raise plants of *Salvia farinacea* "Victoria" from seed. The seed is best sown as thinly as possible on the surface of a good seed compost in a small pot. It is important to sow thinly as overcrowded seedlings are prone to damping off.

Stand the seedlings in a light, airy place in a greenhouse but do not overwater them. Prick out the seedlings in trays or modules as soon as they can be handled. Hold each seedling by its seed leaves and not the stem. The trouble you have had could be because the seedlings were exposed to cold, damp conditions.

Figwort care ❧

"I recently purchased a plant of Phygelius aequalis, *the Cape figwort. Is it safe to leave it outside for the winter and what soil does it like?"*

Care for your Cape figwort by planting it in a sunny, sheltered border where the soil drains freely. If hard frost threatens, erect a small wigwam of conifer shoots, or some similar structure, over it to protect it from icy winds. It is not the hardiest of shrubs, so make sure the crown of the plant is well protected from low temperatures. Remove the covering when any danger of hard frosts has passed.

Oriental taste ❧

"I have a clump of the oriental poppy. It is lovely when it flowers in June but looks a mess afterwards. Can I cut back the stems and the foliage a little to tidy up the plant?"

Papaver orientale is a handsome plant in June but it becomes untidy afterwards. There is no harm in trimming back the foliage and stems a little. Despite this, the plant is dull for the rest of the season and it is a good idea to plant something close to the clump that will flower later and screen the poppy. That well-known gardener, Gertrude Jekyll, recommended planting *Gypsophila paniculata* behind oriental poppies to provide interest once the poppies faded. It is a tip well worth following.

Plant with own weevil ❧

"I have found a plant which I cannot identify and on the leaves are little weevils which again I have not come across before. Can you please identify the plant and the weevil for me?"

The plant is common figwort, *Scrophularia nodosum*, not over-common, but so called to distinguish it from other figwort species. Common figwort can usually be found growing in damp places.

The weevil is, appropriately enough, the figwort weevil, *Cionus globosa*. As well as feeding on figwort it also attacks *Buddleja globosa*, mullein and phygelius. Two generations occur each year, the second-generation adults hibernating until May in the following year. Damage on garden plants can occasionally be severe, but normally no controls are needed.

Penstemon cuttings

"I have a plant of Penstemon *'King George' which flowered all last summer. I would like to have more plants of it. Can it be increased from cuttings and when should they be taken?"*

You can take cuttings from your penstemon plant. They are not difficult to root if inserted in small pots of gritty soil. Take soft, young shoots in May and June, trimming each one below a leaf joint and removing the lower leaves. Put the cuttings in a propagator, or cover the pot with a polythene bag until they have rooted. Cuttings of firmer shoots can also be taken in July and August. Once rooted, pot the cuttings individually and plant them in the open later.

Wallflower cuttings

"I have a plant of the double-flowered wallflower 'Harpur Crewe'. It has become rather leggy and I am wondering what is the best thing to do with it?"

The old, double-flowered wallflower, *Cheiranthus* "Harpur Crewe", does have a tendency to grow long and lanky. When this happens it is best to take some cuttings from the plant and root them in small pots of gritty soil. You can then discard the old plant. Once roots have been made, pot the plants on individually and later plant them out in the border.

Spotty Christmas rose

"My Christmas rose never quite makes it to flowering stage by Christmas so this year I have tried to bring it on a bit with a plastic cover. Sadly, the leaves have become badly spotted and the damaged tissue then fell out."

Hellebore leaf spot is responsible for the damage and this may have been aggravated by the extra humidity under the plastic cover. Pick off the damaged leaves and then spray with Dithane 945 fungicide. Keep the cover over the plant, but lift it off during any warm, dry weather to remove any dampness.

Wall flowers ❧

"I have a long dry stone wall facing south on which I would like to grow aubrieta. I will need a large number of plants, so can you tell me whether I can raise what I need from seed? When is the best time time to sow?"

Aubrietas are easily raised from seed and plants will often seed themselves in the open garden if they are growing in a position to their liking. Seedsmen offer strains with blue, purple or red flowers, as well as mixtures. Sow the seed in the spring in a heated propagator under glass. When the seedlings are large enough to be handled, prick them out into trays or boxes. Later, move them to individual pots. Finally, plant them in their permanent positions outside in the autumn.

The great divide ❧

"I have a large clump of hellebores in my garden which I would like to split up for replanting. When is the best time to do this?"

The best time to lift and divide hellebores is in March. This must be done carefully as the roots are easily damaged. Replant the divisions as soon as possible in deep, fertile soil containing plenty of decayed compost or rotted manure. Plants resent being moved and they should be left undisturbed for a number of years.

Corsican hellebore ❧

"I bought a plant of Helleborus corsicus *last autumn. It has made lots of leaves but no flowers have appeared. Is there anything wrong with my plant and how can I get it to flower?"*

This hellebore usually makes leaves in its first year and you will probably find that flowers will appear on this year's stems next spring. It is one of the finest hellebores with large, pale green florets. The evergreen leaves are handsome all year round.

Spotty violets ❧

"I grow blue and white violets under my rose hedge and normally they are the picture of health. This year, for some unknown reason, the leaves are covered with bleached-out spots. What has caused this?"

Violet leaf-spot fungus would be responsible. Remove the affected leaves and then spray the plants with a copper or a mancozeb fungicide to protect the new growth. Repeat once or twice at two-week intervals.

Perennial for a sunny spot   ❧

"Can you tell me anything about a plant called Sisyrinchium striatum? What soil and position does it like?"

Sisyrinchium striatum is a herbaceous perennial producing fans of narrow, greyish-green leaves. In summer, 16 in. (40 cm) spikes of pale primrose blooms appear among them. The variety "Aunt May" has creamy, variegated leaves. They enjoy a sunny spot and deep loamy soil. They also romp in gaps in crazy paving where roots stay cool and moist in hot spells. They are, however, best grown in a sheltered spot, away from cold winds and hard frost which can blacken the leaves.

Blue Wonder   ❧

"Can you tell me how to overwinter my plant of Scaevola 'Blue Wonder'? Does it need cutting back and will it be safe in a frost-free greenhouse?"

Plants of *Scaevola* "Blue Wonder" should be safe in a frost-free greenhouse for the winter as it is a half-hardy shrub. Trim back the growths so that the plant is manageable and water only sparingly when temperatures are low.

Plants can be propagated from cuttings of young, firm side shoots taken in August. Root them in gritty soil and keep them warm, under glass, until they are rooted. Plants can also be raised from seed sown in a warm greenhouse in early spring.

Winter web   ❧

"I have been given a small houseleek plant called Sempervivum arachnoideum in a pot. How do I look after it? Can it stay outside all winter?"

The cobweb houseleek, *Sempervivum arachnoideum*, is perfectly hardy and can be planted in the open. It must have a sunny position and can be planted in a trough or in rock crevices. In a position to its liking, it will soon spread to form a large mat of attractive rosettes.

It must be grown in gritty soil that is well drained, as it seems to thrive in very dry conditions.

Removing dead flowers

"I have a plant of Scabiosa *'Butterfly Blue' which flowers well in the summer. I find the old flower heads unsightly. Is it a good thing to cut them off as the flowers fade? Does it need feeding?"*

The scabious that you have is a good garden plant and can flower all summer and winter provided all the fading flowers are cut off. This makes more flowers develop. As long as it's in good soil it needs no special feed, just a little bonemeal or Growmore in spring.

Slug lover

"I bought a plant for my border this year called Salvia *patens. It has wonderful blue flowers. Can you tell me whether it is hardy or does it need protection in the winter?"*

Salvia patens is not fully hardy; only in mild districts can it be left in the open during the winter. It has tuberous roots and should be lifted in late September and stored like dahlias, in a frost-free place. Incidentally, it is very prone to damage from slugs which can soon decimate a plant.

Beware late frosts

"I have some geraniums and salvias ready for planting outside. How soon can I do it?"

There is always a danger of a late frost until the end of May. If you wish, the plants could be stood outside under a warm wall and covered with bubble plastic at night if there is any danger of a late spring frost.

Mildewed phlox

"Almost every year our phlox plants become covered with white mildew just as they come into flower and should be looking their best. What is the answer?"

Phlox mildew is a fungal disease that is generally more troublesome on plants that are dry at the roots, so plenty of watering and mulching of the soil with organic matter will help. Once the disease appears, the choice of fungicides rests between the systemic Tumbleblite or the sulphur-based Safer's Garden Fungicide.

Sticky leaves ❧

"The leaves on our variegated vinca are turning black and sticky. There appears to be some black insects on the stems and leaves but I cannot see them well enough to be sure of what they are."

The cause of the damage you describe will be aphids, almost certainly the black bean aphid which has a wide host range. The pests exude sugary honeydew as they feed, and as this dries it turns sticky and is then colonized by sooty mould, causing the leaves to turn black.

As it would be difficult to get good spray coverage underneath the leaves, the best control would be obtained by spraying with a systemic insecticide such as Sybol, Tumblebug or Long-Last. One good application should clear up the problem.

Not for tidy gardeners ❧

"Should the dead stems of herbaceous plants be cut down in the autumn or left until the spring?"

The answer to this really depends on whether you are a tidy gardener. Some people like to tidy their borders in the autumn and get them manured before the spring rush. However, some gardeners find the dead stems covered in frost are attractive and brighten the winter garden. So the choice to tidy or not is yours!

Hot spot ❧

"There is a border in front of my house which faces south and gets very hot in the summer. What low-growing perennials would do well in this position?"

Plants that should succeed in your border include helianthemums, origanum, *Oenothera macrocarpa*, diascias, armeria, arabis, *Cerastium tomentosum*, dianthus, *Osteospermum jucundum*, *Lychnis viscaria*, iberis, *Genista lydia*, hebes and *Anthemis punctata cupaniana*.

Shady border ❧

"An old stone wall in my garden casts a shadow on what could be a sunny border. Plants such as delphinium and phlox grow very tall. With this obstacle in mind, could you suggest suitable small shrubs and perennials that would grow well in this position?"

There are several plants which should flourish in your shady border. They include aquilegia, astilbe, aucuba, bergenia, dicentra, euphorbia, fatshedera, fatsia, hedera, helleborus, hosta, *Hypericum calycinum*, lysimachia, mahonia, pulmonaria, saxifraga, skimmia, vinca and viburnum.

Vine weevil strikes again ❧

"I think my primulas have been attacked by vine weevil grubs. There are fat, legless grubs with orange heads feeding on the plants. How can I stop them spreading to other plants in my conservatory?"

The grubs were those of the vine weevil. Fortunately there is now a really effective cure in the form of a friendly nematode that seeks out and kills these grubs. Various suppliers exist; look out for BioSafe, Defender's Vine Weevil Control or Zeneca Nature's Friends for controlling vine weevil. The product is mixed with water to activate the nematodes (microscopic worm-like creatures) and then watered over the infested compost in the pots. It can also be used outdoors and will control a number of important soil pests as well as the vine weevil larvae.

Pests and diseases

Trouble in store ❧

"Living in the country, we always find quite a few mice coming into our garden store-room around this time of year. As we also have two dogs and a cat we are not able to lay mouse bait around and trapping doesn't always keep on top of the problem. Any other suggestions?"

The Miracle Garden Care "Mouser" was designed for exactly these conditions. This is a self-contained unit with the bait tucked safely away from all but small creatures. For a severe infestation, use two or three such units, although each one is able to kill as many as ten mice. Place them outside or inside the store, alongside a wall. The brodifacoum bait is effective against mice which may be resistant to other rodenticides.

Ant attack ❧

"I laid a new paved area last autumn but now I am finding that ants are excavating the sand from underneath the slabs. How would you recommend that I control this?"

Squirt Miracle Ant Gun! or Murphy Kill-Ant spray into the excavated holes and along the ant runs. Normally one treatment should be sufficient, but a follow-up may be needed if the runs under the paving are extensive.

Squirrel trouble ❧

"For several winters squirrels have dug up my bulbs and corms, especially crocus. Scoot deters them for a while but I am looking for a more permanent cure, such as humane trapping so I can release them in woodland."

It should be possible to purchase suitable traps from Rentokil or other companies offering a pest-control service. The problem is that further squirrels are likely to come into your garden from nearby as the resident squirrels are removed. Work by the Forestry Commission on squirrel control has shown little benefit from continued trapping. It may be possible to protect your bulbs, depending on the area involved, by placing some fine wire netting over the soil above the bulbs, and then removing it as the new shoots appear.

Fortunately, squirrels appear not to be too interested in the bulbs and corms once they are in active growth.

Woodlice ❧

"The garden of my new house has been neglected for some years and there are large numbers of woodlice. Will they do any damage and what can I do about them?"

In small numbers woodlice are not generally serious pests. Their main food is decaying plant material and they are often found on plants that have already been damaged by other pests and diseases.

However, they can sometimes reach nuisance proportions. Seedlings may be eaten off at ground level, and the stems, leaves and roots of older plants may be attacked.

Woodlice feed mostly at night and during the day will hide in moist, cool places where there is lots of debris to provide shelter. They can, therefore, become abundant in neglected gardens such as yours.

To reduce numbers, clear up accumulated plant debris and garden rubbish, and keep greenhouses and other areas clean and tidy. Dust or spray infested areas with HCH or carbaryl dust. You can also trap woodlice by putting down bait such as potato, turnip, orange, etc. and then dispose of them with chemicals or simply by pouring boiling water on them.

Sad but true ❧

"I have been told it is against the law to use soapy water to help to get rid of greenfly. Is this really true?"

Under the terms of the Control of Pesticides Regulations 1986 which are part of the Food and Environment Act of 1985, it is illegal to use ordinary soapy water for purposes of pest control, as it would not have been subjected to the necessary scrutiny.

Only substances that have been examined and have passed the necessary tests for safety to the user, the consumer of treated produce and the environment can receive the official approval for pest-control use.

Slugs are up and about ❧

"My winter-flowering iris (Iris unguicularis) *are being ruined by slugs. They are attacking by night and eating great pieces from the petals. Is there any way of stopping this damage?"*

To stop slugs in their tracks, water the plants and the surrounding soil with a solution of Slugit Liquid. This will kill the slugs as they move over the treated soil or as they feed on the flowers. Remember to repeat the treatment after rain.

Snakes in the grass ❧

"When digging over my compost heap last year I disturbed a grass snake. Why was it in such an unlikely place?"

Reptiles such as snakes and lizards are cold-blooded: they cannot produce their own body heat, but rely on outside sources of warmth to bring their body up to working temperature. Usually the sun supplies the warmth they need, which is why reptiles can often be seen basking – literally soaking up the sun. In spring and autumn they need to spend longer basking than in high summer, and when there is insufficient sun to provide the warmth they need they are forced to hibernate.

Fast mover, even faster eater ❧

"I was always taught that if a creature moved quickly in the soil it was likely to be a 'goody' whilst slow-moving creatures were 'baddies'. I have found some caterpillars, almost transparent to white, but although they move quickly, they do so backwards! Are they good or bad and if bad, what do they do and should they be controlled?"

It is nearly always correct that fast-moving creatures are hunters whilst the slow ones are plant feeders but the caterpillars you describe are those of the swift moths which are great eaters of herbaceous and other plant roots. As they can feed for two or even three years before pupating it is best to control them, and Sybol Dust would be a good choice.

Mole plant ❧

"As I have a mole problem in my garden, someone gave me a mole plant to deter them. It seems to have worked as last year we had no trouble."

Your plant is *Euphorbia lathyrus*, commonly known as caper spurge because the fruits are often mistaken for true capers. Fruits of the caper spurge must not be eaten as they are highly poisonous.

It is a biennial which means it will die after flowering. However, you will probably find that a crop of new seedlings will appear around your old plant. It can become a nuisance and most people regard this plant as a weed. It is often said that it will deter moles but it does not always work!

Smoking pot? ❧

"I recently emptied out some plant pots and found several cigar-like objects in the old compost. Can you tell me what they are and how they are made?"

The cylinders are composed of rolled-up leaf sections, most probably from rose leaves, and are the work of the leaf-cutter bee.

The adult bee bites semicircular pieces from the edges of rose leaves, or may use laburnum, lilac or a small number of other plants. These are rolled and inserted into sandy soil, pot-plant compost, rotting wood or soft brickwork, and each is filled with a mixture of pollen and nectar in which an egg is laid. A cap is then made from a further leaf portion and another cell constructed on top of the first one. The developing larvae feed on the provisions and emerge as new adults in the following June to repeat the life cycle.

Withdrawn from service ❧

"For years I have used Benlate for control of various garden diseases but now it seems to be unobtainable. Can you explain this and suggest an alternative?"

Under the terms of the Control of Pesticides Regulations, manufacturers of insecticides, fungicides and weed-killers are being asked for more detailed information relating to their products. Where this information would be more costly to provide than the profit being generated by the product, manufacturers have little option but to take the product off the market. This is the situation with benomyl, the active ingredient in Benlate, and you will find a number of long-established products disappearing for the same reason.

The alternatives to Benlate are Bio Supercarb and Murphy Systemic Action Fungicide. These are based on the active ingredient carbendazim which is broken down to benomyl within the plant.

Rodent rampage ❦

"Whilst lifting my last potatoes we found quite a number with strange marks. Have you any suggestions as to what caused them?"

The marks are made by rats gnawing at the potatoes. The damage was probably done a few months ago, during the dry August or early September weather when perhaps the rats were not finding their normal food or when water supplies were somewhat restricted. Look around sheds and outbuildings for holes or other signs of rat infestation and, if necessary, contact your local council for advice or control.

Suitable ready-to-use rodenticides are available from garden centres. Bio Racumin is best applied in any holes or where traces of rats have been found.

Overrun veg ❦

"My garden is invaded by rabbits which ruin my vegetable garden whilst this year the various cabbage caterpillars have eaten what was left!"

You could use either chemical or non-chemical methods, or a mixture of both. Rabbits could be excluded either by netting around your garden (or just your vegetable garden) with appropriately sized wire netting or by using Renardine around the boundary.

Caterpillars can be prevented from feeding on the leaves of brassicas by covering the crop with Enviromesh, or by regular sprays with a fatty-acids spray such as Phostrogen's Organic Insecticide or with a permethrin-based product such as Picket.

Mushroom menace ❦

"We had some super mushrooms in our lawn this year, but when we came to prepare them for cooking we found them to be full of holes, plus a few maggots. Is there any easy way to keep them free from such attacks?"

The maggots eating the holes in your mushrooms would have been the larvae of mushroom flies. The tiny adult flies lay their eggs on the developing mushrooms and the maggots quickly hatch out and get to work. It may be possible to reduce such damage by a light dusting with malathion dust, but probably the best way would be to pick the mushrooms as soon as they appear, rather than waiting for them to get to their full size.

Shield bug ❧

"I have an insect on my beans and believe it to be a shield bug. Can you let me have some information on its life history? Does it need to be controlled?"

Some shield bugs feed on plant sap but the damage is not significant and no control measures are called for. Other species feed on insects including pest species and so can be considered as friends in the garden. In orchards and soft fruit areas, one species, known as the "stink bug", produces a sticky secretion with an obnoxious odour, but it does also feed on caterpillars. Eggs are laid in large masses in spring and the young mature through a series of moults to become adult in late summer.

Organic control for cabbage caterpillars? ❧

"Is there a truly organic way to control caterpillars on cabbages? I know you can spray with pyrethrum or soft soap but if possible I would prefer to control them without any chemicals at all."

It is possible to control caterpillars on cabbages without the use of chemicals. If no attack has yet started, cover the crop with Enviromesh netting; the fine mesh will exclude the egg-laying butterflies. If there are already caterpillars on the crop, spray with the biological control agent *Bacillus thuringiensis*. This is a special bacterium species that attacks and kills caterpillars. It can be obtained from garden centres by completing the card inside Miracle Garden Care Nature's Friends for Caterpillar Control packs or by mail order direct from Defenders Ltd, PO Box 131, Wye, Ashford, Kent TN25 5BR.

Mole runs ❧

"In the lawn edge, alongside one of my flower borders, a mole has started to tunnel. There are no runs deep enough for a trap to be used but it is making a terrible mess of the grass. Some soil is being excavated, which leaves a hollow underneath, and in other places the grass over the runs is dying despite daily treading down. Is there any control you could suggest?"

The moles clearly cannot be trapped in the shallow runs, but they are likely to have deeper runs in your borders and it should be possible to find suitable places for traps there. Alternatively, or in addition, the moles can be deterred from passing from the border to lawn areas by using Renardine.

Organic panic

"My husband and I have just taken over a house with a garden and we are puzzled by the terms 'organic' and 'non-organic' when they are applied to pest sprays. If they are designed to kill insects does it really matter if they are naturally occurring substances or man-made ones? Also, is it possible to garden without using any sprays at all?"

There are virtually as many ways to garden as there are gardeners and the right way is, by and large, the one that you find works best for you. If you grow your plants well, pests or diseases may not become a major problem. There is always a risk of some losses, but if you plan to lose some and still have enough left over, all should be well. Check on varieties of plants that are resistant to various common problems and choose accordingly.

Natural explanation

"I have been reading about biological control and am unsure about the terms 'parasite' and 'predator'. Are the two words interchangeable or is there a difference?"

There is a distinct difference between a parasite and a predator, although sometimes the terms are used a little loosely. In biological control terms, a predator is an agent that seeks out and devours its prey from the outside, whilst a parasite attacks the prey from inside. It generally develops from an egg laid inside the host by the adult.

  Of the biological control agents commonly available, *Cryptolaemus*, which preys on mealy bugs, and *Phytoseiulus*, on red spider mites, are both predators, whilst *Encarsia*, which is used to control whitefly and *Aphidius* for greenfly both lay eggs in their hosts.

The love trap

"I recently read about pea moth. There is a pheromone pea-moth trap available which attracts and catches the male moths, thus preventing mating. I have used the similar trap against apple codling moth very successfully."

There certainly is a pheromone trap for pea moth which releases a man-made version of the female sex attractant, but it is not particularly effective as a control in the garden. Pea-moth females, unlike those of codling moth, fly considerable distances after mating, so the pheromone can be used as a guide for when to spray but not as a control measure in its own right.

Whitefly menace ❧

"We are suffering from the worst attack of whitefly on our tomatoes that we have ever seen. The fruit and leaves are becoming sticky and black and nothing seems to control the attack. Is there any hope, or should we dig the plants up?"

With an attack as severe as the one you describe, it would be very difficult to gain the upper hand. You could try spraying every two or three days with a fatty acid insecticide such as Phostrogen Safer's Organic Insecticide, but as the eggs and nymph stages are not well controlled, it could take several weeks before the infestation is brought down to acceptable levels.

Controlling whitefly with a handheld vacuum cleaner is great fun!

If you do decide to clear out the tomatoes, spray the plants and greenhouse well with insecticide before you start to reduce the chances of spreading the whitefly further. Wash the structure down with Jeyes Fluid during the winter.

On the right trap   ❦

"I have used yellow sticky-board traps in my greenhouse for a few years to catch whitefly. In a greenhouse recently I saw blue traps hanging up. Are these more effective?"

Blue traps are said to be more attractive to thrips, but yellow is still the best colour for whitefly. There is a relatively new greenhouse pest called western flower thrips; perhaps the owner of the greenhouse you saw was concerned about controlling that species.

Vine weevil strikes again   ❦

"Whilst getting my fuchsias and auriculas ready for winter I found an infestation of vine weevil grubs. I removed all I could find but am worried in case some remain. Is it the wrong time to use the nematode control and, if so, is there a chemical I could water in to kill them?"

The nematode vine-weevil control agents (Defender's Nemasys H and Miracle's Nature's Friends for Vine Weevil control) need a minimum of 12°C to be effective. If you are keeping your plants cool over winter, delay application until the compost temperature reaches this level in spring. If the plants are being kept in active growth and the temperature is correct, you can use the nematode product from January onwards. Keep a look out for a new compost from Levington to control a number of plant pests, including vine weevil.

Root them out   ❦

"I have lost a number of my greenhouse plants this year and have now identified the cause as vine-weevil grubs feeding on the roots. I think I have removed all the infested plants, but what would you advise as a treatment now?"

The most effective control for vine-weevil grubs, under glass as well as outside, is the biological method using nematodes. These seek out the vine-weevil larvae and a number of other soil compost pests and kill them (by contaminating them with a lethal bacterium). One such nematode is sold as BioSafe, a different species as Nature's Friends for Vine-weevil Control, and as Defender's Nemasys H.

Autumn is a good time to apply the nematodes in the greenhouse or conservatory (diluted in water and applied by a watering can) and late spring is generally best out of doors.

A flurry of fungus gnats ❧

"Some little black flies have invaded the compost of my newly potted house plants. Can you recommend a solution to my problem?"

The flies are fungus gnats, also known as sciarid flies, and in nature they live in organic matter such as leafmould or other decaying plant tissue. They find the damp peat present in most composts an ideal substitute but their larvae do also attack living plant roots. It is unlikely that the flies were in the freshly made compost, but the adult flies could have laid eggs in the bags during storage.

Repot your plants in a brand new type of compost sold as Levington Plant Protection Compost. This compost contains an insecticide which will control sciarid flies (and vine-weevil grubs) for a whole year, greenfly for three months, and will also give a useful control of whitefly.

Peppery aphids ❧

"The leaves of my greenhouse-grown peppers are becoming puckered and I see there are greenfly clustered around the foliage. What is the safest way to control this attack?"

If by safest you mean you wish to control the attack without any spraying, then you could introduce one of the biological control agents. Defenders supply the aphid parasite *Aphidius* which is a tiny midge that lays its eggs inside the aphid and the hatching larvae devour the host.

Alternatively, Miracle Garden Care supply *Aphidoletes* under the name of Nature's Friends for Aphid Control, via garden centres. This is another species of midge but one that eats the aphids from the outside.

For the squeamish, perhaps a spray with Rapid or Tumblebug would be a better choice.

Tomato blossom end rot ❧

"Nearly every year the first tomatoes produced in my greenhouse develop hard, dark areas on the base of the fruit. I have tried different varieties, changing the make of growing bag, different fertilizers, etc., but the trouble always occurs. As the season progresses, the problem goes away."

The problem you describe is known as blossom end rot, and is caused by a lack of calcium in the developing fruits. This may be due to low calcium in the compost, or to lack of uptake caused by too little or irregular watering.

Blossom end rot can be largely prevented by using a tomato fertilizer specially formulated to include adequate calcium. Miracle Garden Care have a product under the name of Miracle-Gro Tomato Booster. As well as calcium, it contains a whole range of trace elements so would be a suitable choice for use this year.

Scale away

"I have a problem with a 5 ft (1.3 m) high citrus tree and would appreciate your help. It stands outside in summer and in my warm greenhouse for winter. The leaves are getting a black deposit on them and this is getting worse all the time. Can you tell me what to spray it with, and also what I should feed the plant with?"

There are probably some scale insects underneath the leaves. The blackening of the citrus leaves is due to sooty moulds, and these are living on sugary honeydew secreted by the scale insects.

Carefully wash the leaves with tepid water to remove the sooty moulds and honeydew and then spray with a malathion insecticide. Feed the plant from now onwards with Miracid, possibly alternating this with Miracle-Gro or a tomato food.

Egg mixture

"Can you tell me what greenfly eggs look like on apple trees? A neighbour tells me I should be spraying my apple tree with Mortegg to kill the eggs, but I would like to know if there are any on the tree before I do any spraying."

Greenfly eggs are black, oval and shiny, about 2 mm in size and generally laid in thick clusters on young spurs and twigs. You can apply a Mortegg winter wash on apple trees up to the end of February and it will remove any mosses and lichens, as well as killing greenfly and other pest eggs.

Slug bug

"Last year, several of our asparagus stems were damaged by slugs underground. Is there any treatment that we could apply now to stop a repeat of the damage?"

As soon as the soil has warmed up to around 5°C (usually around mid March) apply the beneficial nematode known as *Phasmarhabditis hermaphrodita*. This seeks out the underground slugs and infects them with a lethal bacterium.

Obtain the nematode via a garden centre under the name of Zeneca Nature's Friends for Slug Control'.

Slugs controlled by torchlight using a bucket and a bag of salt!

Biological control of slugs ❧

"I have read about the use of nematodes for biological control of underground slugs and intend to try it this year. Can you tell me where I can obtain supplies and how soon can I start to use the product?"

There are two sources of supply, Defenders and Miracle Garden Care. For the Defenders product, sold as Nemaslug, write to PO Box 131, Wye, Ashford, Kent TN25 5TQ. For the Miracle product, sold as Nature's Friends for Slug Control, you purchase an empty product pack at a local garden centre, fill in the enclosed pre-paid card and send it to the suppliers.

The nematodes need a minimum soil temperature of 5°C, so in northern areas this would generally mean from April onwards, through to September. Further south, applications could be made from March to October.

Bar slugs with Mollbar

"What is likely to be eating my ligularia leaves? They are riddled with irregularly shaped holes. I have seen no signs of slugs, weevils or caterpillars, and other plants nearby do not seem to be affected."

The irregular shape of the holes indicates that slugs are responsible for the damage. They will be feeding by night and it is not uncommon for slugs to pick out their favourite food plants and leave others untouched.

Try protecting the ligularia with a new product sold as Mollbar. Composed of porous volcanic rock from Australia, slugs seem very reluctant to cross this material. It can be used as a barrier around susceptible plants or as a complete soil covering. Mollbar is sold by mail order by Defenders Ltd, Occupation Road, Wye, Ashford, Kent TN25 5EN.

Soil caterpillars

"I am finding greeny-grey caterpillars in my soil as I dig it over. I am quite concerned as they are up to 2 in. (5 cm) long and look as though they could do a lot of damage. What are they?"

The caterpillars are known as cutworms, and are the grubs of various moths, including the turnip moth and the yellow underwing. Cutworms do have large appetites and can eat down a long row of vegetable plants in a single night, biting them off at soil level.

Regular soil cultivation will expose numbers to the local birds, while in very wet conditions (of the kind experienced in January) cutworms tend to die off. A soil insecticide along the drills at sowing time could be a wise investment.

Big bud mite control

"My blackcurrant bushes are showing quite a few swollen buds which I believe is the work of the big bud mite. Is there any chemical control now available? My old books recommend lime sulphur but this disappeared from the market years ago."

There is no chemical control for blackcurrant big bud mite, or gall mite as it is more correctly known. If the infestation is severe then it is likely that the mites will have passed on the reversion virus to the bushes and cropping will be progressively poorer.

If the attack is not too bad, it may be sufficient to remove the infested shoots. For more serious attacks, consider cutting the bushes down to soil level. If the virus has not established a foothold the new shoots will grow out free from both the mites and the virus, although cropping will be lost for a year.

Cabbage aphid attack ❧

"I have just found an attack of purplish aphids on my sprouts; is this early?"

The cabbage aphid, *Brevicoryne brassicae*, lays eggs on stems of sprouts and cauliflowers in autumn and these hatch from February through to April. From mid-May to August, winged forms are produced which spread to the next lot of brassica crops. Winter egg-laying then continues from September and though into December.

Remove any old crop remains before May to prevent the migration to new host plants and then spray the crops at the first sign of damage in spring or summer. You can control by spraying with a fatty acids insecticide or, if you wish, use a systemic insecticide such as Tumblebug.

Blistering attack on currants ❧

"Every year about this time or a little later, the leaves of my currants start to develop blisters on the top. On the redcurrants the blisters are red, but they stay green on the blackcurrants. Is this due to some form of greenfly, and can you tell me what I should spray with?"

The pest involved is the redcurrant blister aphid. The eggs are laid in autumn, hatch in spring, and feeding by the aphids or greenfly underneath the leaves causes the blistering found on the upper surface.

Virtually all damage could be prevented in another year by a winter tar-oil spray to kill the overwintering eggs. For this year, spray forcibly under the leaves with a fatty acids insecticide such as Safer's Organic Insecticide Concentrate (suitably diluted), Bug Gun for Fruit and Vegetables based on pyrethrins, or spray with Tumblebug.

Starting apple mildew control now ❧

"Over the last few years my 'Bramley' tree has developed more and more mildew infection. What would you advise me to do to get on top of the problem?"

Examine your tree in April, looking for blossom and leaf trusses with any signs of the white powdery mildew coating, and carefully prune every one out. These are the primary infection sources that start off the early attacks. Then spray with a carbendazim fungicide.

Continue to prune out any trusses or shoots that show mildew infection during the year, and repeat the fungicide application a few times whenever the mildew seems to be increasing its attacks.

Buff-tip moth ❧

"Last summer my cherry tree was devastated by swarms of yellow and black caterpillars. They fed on the leaves in great numbers and stripped virtually all the foliage from parts of the tree in a short space of time. What were they and are they likely to attack again this year?"

The caterpillars would be the larvae of the buff-tip moth. They drop to the soil and pupate when fully fed so may well attack again this year. The buff-coloured adults are around from late May, so look out for the caterpillars from early June onwards.

Eggs are laid in batches of 50 or so, giving rise to heavy local infestations of caterpillars, so the easiest control is simply to prune out infested shoots, or to shake them vigorously to dislodge the caterpillars. Where the attack is too high for such action, fit an extension on a sprayer and give a good drench with Picket or Tumblebug.

How to beat carrot fly the belt and braces way ❧

"Over the many years that we have been growing vegetables, we have never fully controlled carrot-fly damage. We have tried all the various things recommended, such as adjusting sowing dates, using resistant varieties, dusting with insecticide and covering with mesh, but there has always been some damage. Can you suggest anything else we could try, please?"

Grow a carrot-fly resistant variety, such as Thompson & Morgan's "Fly-away", alongside a row of a non-resistant carrot variety. The carrot flies appear to select the non-resistant variety, leaving the resistant one alone. But also continue with the use of a fine mesh cover, well tucked into the soil to reduce the chances of the flies getting in under the edges.

This "belt and braces" approach should mean that if the mesh is completely successful you would get two rows of pest-free carrots, but if a few flies did gain entry, the non-resistant carrots should fulfil their sacrificial role to safeguard the resistant carrots.

Rootless cabbages ❧

"A lot of my cabbage seedlings are turning a purplish colour rather than a healthy green and when I dug a few up there were virtually no roots left on them. I have fed and watered them, so what has gone wrong?"

Purpling of the leaves of brassicas of all kinds is a sure sign of poor root action and a lack of roots would confirm that cabbage root-fly maggots have been at work on your plants. If there are no active maggots now present you may be able to save the cabbages by earthing-up the stems with soil and keeping it moist to encourage another set of roots to develop. Protect any new brassica plantings you may make from attack by placing a tight-fitting disc of roofing felt around the stems at soil level. This should prevent the root-fly adults from laying their eggs close to the plants.

Controlling cabbage whitefly with a gun should not be your first line of attack!

Cabbage whitefly patch ❧

"Whilst clearing the remains of my cauliflower plants I found odd-looking white patches under many of the leaves. Can you tell me what they are, or were?"

The patches are where brassica whitefly had been feeding and breeding during the winter. Keep a watch on your new brassica plantings for these pests. They don't do too much damage, compared with the greenhouse species of whitefly, but are quite unpleasant when on cabbages, broccoli or other brassicas when the leaves are served in the kitchen.

Rusty broad beans ❧

"Last spring and early summer, my autumn-sown broad beans suffered quite badly from what I was told was an attack of rust disease. I am sure the cropping was cut short by the severe leaf damage. My new crop is just coming up – is there any action I can take to keep these plants free from the rust fungus?"

Normally, bean rust occurs too late in the season to do much harm to cropping, but an unusually early attack certainly can stop growth very quickly. Plants suffering from low potassium levels may be more prone to attack, so apply sulphate of potash now and again in spring.

Copper fungicides used to be used against rust diseases on most crops, but it is doubtful if any now carry the necessary recommendations. Keep a close watch on the plants in spring and remove any that show signs of rust building up.

Blackcurrant midge blistering attack ❧

"What is causing the young leaves on my blackcurrant bushes to become puckered and fail to open properly? I have had this for three years now and would like to do something about it."

Blackcurrant leaf midge is the pest responsible. There are three, and sometimes four, generations of this insect each year, so the damage can be quite extensive. The white larvae feed inside the twisted leaves for a couple of weeks or less before dropping to the ground to pupate. The new adults emerge a fortnight later so the damage can be almost continuous.

Probably the best control is simply to cut off the affected shoot tips and burn them, each time the damage is seen, followed by a spray of the plants and soil with Picket or Tumblebug.

More than one cabbage white ❧

"My cabbages and other greens were badly attacked by cabbage butterflies until I managed to spray them and then erect a framework and cover. I found

that some of the butterfly eggs were laid singly but others in larger batches. Why is there a difference?"

A number of related species of cabbage butterflies will attack plants of the brassica family. Chief among these is the large white butterfly and this lays batches of orange eggs which hatch out into caterpillars that are bluish-green with yellow and black markings. The small white butterfly lays eggs singly, and the caterpillars are pale green in colour. A third species, the green-veined white, is mainly found on wild host plants.

Attack of the vapours ❧

"I found an interesting-looking creature eating the leaves of my raspberries. What is it and is it likely to cause a lot of damage?"

The creature is the caterpillar of the vapourer moth. Each caterpillar doesn't do too much harm, but the eggs are laid in batches of up to 300 so the overall effect of an attack can be quite devastating!

By now, a new generation of adult moths will have emerged to continue the life cycle. The females tend to stay by their cocoons until mated and will then lay their large batches of eggs, which hatch in the following spring. Control by inspecting trees and bushes in winter and removing the egg batches, which are frequently laid on and around the old cocoons.

Mealy aphid menace ❧

"Can you identify the problem affecting all my various brassicas (broccoli, sprouts, cabbage)?"

The pests present on the samples were mealy cabbage aphids. The winged forms of this pest can fly considerable distances on the wind, so it is not unusual to have attacks after an absence of several years.

Control the existing attack by spraying with Tumblebug. This will move through the sap to kill the aphids, even inside curled leaves, but then disappear from the plant leaving no residues. Edible crops can be harvested the day after treatment. This year, protect your brassicas by covering them over with Enviromesh netting.

Aubergine aphid attack ❧

"Help! My aubergine plants are plastered with greenfly. The attack occurred virtually overnight and now all my greenhouse-grown plants are suffering. How can I get rid of the pests without spoiling the fruit?"

Spray with Tumblebug. This kills greenfly by both contact and systemic action, but then evaporates out of the plant within 24 hours.

When insecticides are officially approved, the crops as well as the pests to be controlled are taken into account. This means that some products can only be used on a limited range of crops. However, Tumblebug can be used on all crops, as long as you leave 24 hours' delay between spraying and picking.

Hardy whitefly

"Am I right in thinking that the whitefly that attacks sprouts and other vegetables of the cabbage family is a different sort to the one found on greenhouse plants? It certainly seems to be able to withstand frosts. Is there any effective control?"

You are quite right. The glasshouse whitefly was originally a tropical and subtropical species and is unable to survive freezing conditions. The cabbage whitefly on the other hand is made of sterner stuff and the adults can survive even in hard winters. They are not too easy to control, because they are tucked away underneath the foliage, but thorough applications of Sybol, Tumblebug or Phostrogen Organic Garden Insecticide should prove effective.

Stinkhorn fungus menace

"We are being plagued by stinkhorn fungi and have to keep our doors and windows locked to protect us from the smell and from angry neighbours! We have so far dug out over 100 from a 20 square yard bed. No garden centre seems to have heard of them or is able to offer any help. Armillatox has not worked. Please help; we don't want to have to move house."

Sadly there is no specific cure for this problem. The stinkhorn fungus generally lives on buried, dead roots or other wood, so you may be able to dig around and unearth something.

Some gardeners used to swear by a strong dose of Epsom Salts for various toadstool attacks, using per square yard 4 oz. per gallon (113 g per 4.5l/m^2) although that is now probably illegal under EU rules. The only other suggestion would be to hoe through the soil frequently.

The early stage of the stinkhorn fungus is an egg-like growth just under the soil surface. If these could be hoed out or sufficiently damaged, the fungus could not complete its development. The "egg" stage is edible although not remarkable in terms of flavour, but I doubt if you would wish to eat your way through the problem!

Happy families? ⚬

*"I have a light attack of whitefly on my cabbages, and looking through a
× 20 hand lens there appears to be a ring of whitefly young feeding alongside
the adult. Do whitefly mothers look after their young in this way?"*

Whitefly females tend to lay their eggs in a circle, just moving their rear
ends as the eggs are deposited on the leaf. The adults also tend to stay put
and feed unless disturbed.

As the eggs hatch the early larval stages feed in the same positions as
the eggs before dispersing a little to new sites. So, although the picture
you saw suggested a mother and family all feeding happily together, there
were no maternal instincts in play.

Buff-tip moth menace ⚬

*"Last year we had a terrible caterpillar attack on our cherry trees. Masses of
yellow and black caterpillars attacked in late May and stripped the foliage in
very quick time. Is this likely to occur again this year, and if so is there any
way we can prevent it?"*

The caterpillars you describe would have been those of the buff-tip moth.
They feed on quite a number of different native trees and cultivated
varieties of them. The caterpillars enter the soil in autumn and pupate in
earthen chambers, with the new generation of moths emerging to lay eggs
during May.

It would be worth preparing to spray your cherry tree any time in May,
with Picket or Tumblebug being the best choices. Wait until the caterpillars
are first spotted before applying the spray, but don't waste any time after
that!

Humming-birds spotted in Coventry? ⚬

*"Can anyone identify the lovely creature that came into my garden in the
autumn? It was about 2 in. long and looked like a tiny humming-bird,
hovering over Busy Lizzie flowers, apparently feeding on the nectar by means
of a long proboscis. It was brown in colour with a black 'tail' which had white
bars. The almost round wings were transparent."*

The creature you saw was a humming-bird hawk moth, *Macroglossum
stellatarum*. (Macroglossum means long-tongued.) The insect comes over
from Europe every now and again, but is not able to survive the British
winter. As you observed, it feeds on flower nectar by means of its

proboscis, looking just like a real miniature humming-bird. The caterpillar
stage feeds on bedstraw and goosegrass.

Lettuce rot ❧

*"My wife grew a number of lettuces in her greenhouse over winter, but quite
a few rotted off at soil level before they were ready to pick. Is this something in
the soil, and if so, will it affect the tomatoes we grow there later in the year?"*

The rot was most probably due to the grey mould fungus botrytis. Attacks
often start on leaves in contact with the soil and then spread into the stem
bases, and losses are always more severe under wet conditions. The
fungus is always present, so your tomatoes would not be under any
greater risk. Next autumn, plant the lettuces on small domes of soil to keep
the basal leaves and stem bases slightly drier.

Whitened plums ❧

*"My plum leaves appeared to be white from the distance. When I got
close I found the leaves all covered with a white deposit and the
undersides absolutely plastered with greenfly. Where has the attack come
from and how can I control it? Will it come again next year or could I
prevent attacks?"*

The effect you describe is just typical of the mealy plum aphid. The pest
spends the winter in the egg stage on plums, damson and related host
plants and hatches out in spring. Numbers are generally low until late June
to July when they build up very rapidly, as you have found. Winged forms
then develop and fly off to reeds and waterside grasses, but they return to
plums in autumn for egg-laying.

Inspect your plum shoots in autumn and winter and, if large numbers of
the shiny black eggs are found, it would be worth applying a winter wash.
Otherwise, wait until May and assess the situation, being ready to apply a
systemic insecticide if necessary.

Horseradish under attack ❧

*"I have had a most horrendous attack of little, black, jumping beetles on my
horseradish leaves. As I pass by the plants the noise of them leaping off the
leaves is quite loud and they are making a terrible mess of the leaves, leaving
masses of small yellow spots where they have been. What are they and how can
I best control them?"*

The insects are flea beetles. Quite often such insects come off fields of oil-seed rape and then infest other plants in the cabbage family. If you spray the leaves with Bug Gun or Nature's Answer to Insect Pests (both sold in ready-to-use sprayers) the pests should be brought under control, although a few weekly sprays may prove necessary.

Wasp worry ❧

"How can I beat the wasps to my early-ripening 'Discovery' apples? I have had the tree now for six years and have barely had a decent apple."

As the tree will still be reasonably small, you could enclose each apple in a plastic bag, or in the feet of old nylon tights. This would keep the wasps and the apples apart. Traps are available which will attract and catch vast numbers of wasps, although not enough would be trapped to prevent all fruit damage.

Hazel mites ❧

"I have a row of old hazel-nut bushes in my garden and have noticed that many of the tip buds are swollen and flat rather than pointed. Is this something I should be concerned about?"

The bud damage is the result of attack by a tiny creature known as the filbert bud mite. Buds infested by the mite will fail to open properly in spring (rather like blackcurrant buds infested with big bud mite). There will be very little other adverse effect, perhaps just as well as there are no control measures, other than cutting out infected buds or shoots.

Bands of eggs ❧

"On some of our apple-tree twigs we are finding odd-looking objects which appear to be bands of eggs of some sort. Could you identify the creature responsible?"

The objects are indeed bands of eggs, and were laid by female lackey moths during early autumn. If left on the tree the eggs would hatch in April and May and the greyish-blue, white, black and red-stripped caterpillars will then feed actively on the leaves, living in communal tents. A lot of damage can be caused and whole trees can be stripped of foliage. Prune out all the egg bands you can find. Should any tents of caterpillars be found in spring, prune these out, too.

Club root resistance? ❧

"Are any varieties of brassicas resistant to club root? I discovered some of the characteristically gnarled roots when digging out my old cabbage plants."

Sadly, as yet the only club-root resistant vegetable is the swede "Marian". In time, either by selective breeding or by genetic manipulation, there will be a range of resistant cabbages, sprouts, etc. available.

Potato blight ❧

"I want to keep my potatoes free of blight attacks this year. When should I start to spray, and what is the best fungicide to use?"

Blight strikes from late June onwards. The disease needs a minimum of two mild and damp days; and the high relative humidity needed is often found as the haulm meets across the rows. Spray in advance of attack – so start in mid to late June – and continue, in suitable weather, every two to three weeks. Mancozeb and copper are the recommended fungicides.

When lifting potatoes, be sure to take out all the crop. It would also help to grow a less susceptible variety of potato, such as "Wilja", "Cara", "Record" or "Kondor".

Blistered currants ❧

"The leaves of my blackcurrants this year were all blistered with raised lumps, but I never found any insects on them. What caused the problem and how can I prevent it occurring next year?"

The cause was attack by the redcurrant blister aphid. This particular greenfly feeds under the leaves of red- and blackcurrants, resulting in the raised blisters you have seen. The blistering remains after the pests move off to their summer host plants. Winged adults return to currants in autumn when eggs are laid to overwinter.

The best way to prevent damage is to spray the bushes with Mortegg tar-oil winter wash in the dormant season (December to end of February) to kill the eggs.

Silver Y moth ❧

"Can you please identify this moth? I have found quite a few fluttering around my vegetable patch and wonder if they are up to no good."

This is a silver Y moth, so called because of the Y-like markings on its front wings. The Latin name, *Autographa gamma*, also reflects this marking, which resembles the Greek letter gamma.

Each moth can lay 500 eggs around vegetables and herbaceous plants, and in the greenhouse, and the night-feeding caterpillars, mainly green with a pale line down each side, feed on leaves, buds and flowers for a month or so before pupating. A further generation of adults emerges a few weeks later, but these can only survive our winter under glass. Control the caterpillars with a contact insecticide when damage is first seen.

Leek moth on the attack ❧

"The leaves of my husband's leeks are showing lots of holes and I found a pale caterpillar down in the centre of one plant. Can you help us to save our crop from further damage?"

Leek moth is the culprit and it can also attack onions, shallots and garlic. Damaged plants often rot, so the damage is even greater than holed foliage. There can be as many as three generations each year, so action needs to be taken as soon as possible.

Destroy the worst plants, as the caterpillars pupate within them, and try a couple of sprays with Tumblebug or Sybol, drenching well into the leek foliage. As the crop is harvested, remove and destroy all the old plant remains, in particular, any leeks not good enough to use in the kitchen.

Berry troubles ❧

"On a recent blackberrying outing we came across several leaves looking like lace curtains. The holes seemed too symmetrical to be caterpillars feeding; but what could have caused this to happen?"

The holes are the work of a sawfly caterpillar, but the feeding was carried out before the leaves fully unfolded. Rather like the patterns or strings of people you can cut out of folded paper, the caterpillar ate through several layers of leaf.

Sow to be clever ❧

"I had a lot of pea-moth damage this year. Is there anything I can do before next year to reduce attacks?"

Pea moths spend the winter as caterpillars in the soil and then pupate in spring. Digging over the soil during winter may disturb or expose the caterpillars for the birds to eat. If you choose varieties to sow next year for picking before early July, or sow after mid-June, the crops will normally escape attack.

Beat the fly

"We suffered damage from onion fly this year for the first time ever. Any advice would be most welcome."

Firstly, you could protect next year's sowings with a covering of Envir-omesh, which will exclude the egg-laying adult onion flies, or you could grow autumn-planted onion sets which normally escape attack. Unwins "First Early" or the new variety from Marshalls called "Radar" should give good results. Plant in September or October and the crop will be ready some weeks before the normal spring-planted or sown crop.

Wasp attack

"I know that in spring, wasps are supposed to be the gardner's friend, but in summer and autumn they make an awful mess of my fruit crops. They attacked my raspberries and plums earlier on this year and are now making holes in my apples."

It is true that in spring wasps feed caterpillars to their young, but as only the queen wasps will survive the winter I have no doubt about trying to control wasps at this time of year. New on the market is the Rescue! Trap for Wasps which is basically a high-tech version of the old jam-jar method. The special long-life attractant will lure the wasps away from your fruit and into the trap. There is also a Rescue! trap for fly control.

Stripped tease

"Could you please tell me when action should be taken against the spotty caterpillars that regularly strip the foliage from my gooseberry bushes? Attacks seem to start very rapidly and the whole bush is stripped of leaves within a short space of time."

Gooseberry sawfly eggs tend to be laid on leaves close to the ground and in the centres of the bushes, normally just after flowering. Attacks are nearly always severe, as you mention, as the larvae feed in colonies for about three weeks until fully grown.

Control by hand picking and spraying with derris, pyrethrin or perme-thrin. Young bushes seem to be singled out for the worst attacks, so your bushes may well escape any attack this year. Keep a close watch as soon as flowering is over, however, just to be sure.

Leaf blisters ❧

"I was determined to stop the pest that causes raised blisters to appear on my currant leaves, but rain in late winter prevented my tar-oil wash application. Can I do anything now?"

The pest you mention would be the currant blister aphid. On red and white currants the blisters are red to purple, but usually a pale green on blackcurrants. The aphids spend the winter on the plants, so could have been killed in the egg stage during the dormant period. The best control now would be a spray with Long-Last or Tumblebug at the first sign of the greenfly underneath the leaves, or at the very first sign of damage.

If you would prefer to use a spray based on fatty acids, such as Safer's Garden Insecticide, which is not systemic, a drenching application to both upper and lower surfaces of each leaf would be necessary.

Spot the difference ❧

"Several of the new stems on my thornless blackberry are showing a number of purple or brown spots and streaks. I think this may be cane spot or something similar. Would you please let me know what is wrong and what I should do about it?"

There would appear to be cane spot and spur blight diseases on your blackberry canes. The cane spot results in numerous purplish spots, which often join together, whilst the spur blight is mostly concentrated around the buds.

Although these diseases are more commonly found on raspberry, they can sometimes be quite damaging on other cane fruit. Prune out those canes showing the damage. However, if this involves removing too many of this year's fruiting canes, you could train the new canes above the old ones to protect them from infection, and then delay cane removal until directly after picking the crop.

Holey help ❧

"My swede seedlings have just come up but the leaves are being badly holed by something. I never find any slugs or insects on the leaves."

The small holes are typical of the damage done by flea beetles. They jump off the plants at the first sign of danger so are only rarely seen at work. Control by dusting along the rows using a derris dust. Repeat after rain or weekly for a few weeks until the older, less susceptible leaves have developed.

Caterpillar tracks

"Cabbage caterpillars seem to have been very troublesome this year and damage has continued for a long time. Do hot summers encourage them to live longer?"

There are several different species of cabbage caterpillars including cabbage moth, large white, small white and green-veined white. They all have slightly different life cycles so when they are all present the damage can go on for the whole of summer. Some pests can have an increased number of cycles per year, depending on the weather, but the various cabbage caterpillars do not respond in this way. Try netting over your plants next year to avoid damage.

Codling moth control

"This year my apples were bored into by a grub that I have been told was codling moth. My local 'guru', a retired head gardener, said I should spray in mid to late June, but he didn't know what was the latest and best insecticide to use. Can you advise me?"

The most modern approach is to use a pheromone trap rather than spraying. A pheromone is a substance produced by an animal (including insects) which has an effect on the behaviour of another animal, generally of the same species. In the case of codling moth, there is a man-made version of the female codling moth pheromone that is incorporated into a trap. Male codling moths are lured to a sticky death in the trap and so prevented from mating. The trap can be bought in garden centres under the name of the Trappit Codling Moth Trap.

Nutty problem

"My son gave me a peanut-growing kit and one seed germinated and grew into a good plant which was beginning to flower. Suddenly the leaves became pale and now there is a fine webbing over the plant and it all looks very unhealthy."

Your plant has succumbed to attack by two-spotted spider mite. This has been a major problem in many greenhouses and conservatories, due in part to high temperatures and dryness during the hot summer weather. Once webbing is produced the plants will be severely infested and satisfactory control is virtually impossible.

Try again, but maintain a buoyant atmosphere around the plant by standing it on a saucer of pebbles or proprietary clay granules that can be kept damp.

Parasitic damage ??

"We left a patch of ground at the bottom of the garden uncultivated, knowing there were a lot of nettles there. We hoped they would be fed on by the caterpillars of various butterflies. We were rewarded by the worst greenfly attack we have ever seen! After a little while, some of the greenfly became more orange, smooth and rounded, and appeared dead. These remained as the infestation faded away. We then noticed tiny holes in each of these orange greenfly bodies. Can you explain?"

The greenfly had been attacked by a parasitic wasp known as *Aphidius*. The wasp inserts an egg into the aphid body and the grub then feeds on the body contents before emerging as an adult through the tiny hole you spotted. These helpful wasps would have been encouraged by the higher-than-average temperatures of the summer.

Tortrix torture ??

"On my young apple tree I am finding that several of the leaves have been tied with a cobweb-like silk and on opening them up a little green caterpillar shoots out and drops down on a thread. Can you identify this for me and suggest a control?"

The caterpillar is a larva of one of the tortrix species. There are several different species that feed on the leaves, and also on the fruit, and typically they wriggle violently backwards when disturbed. The caterpillars on your trees are probably those of the summer fruit tortrix moth. Control by hand picking if there aren't that many, or by spraying with Picket or Tumblebug, or use Safer's Insecticide.

Caterpillar assault ??

"A hairy caterpillar attacked my rose blooms this summer. It is mainly red and black with white patches along the sides. It seemed capable of eating a whole rose flower in a day.'

The caterpillar seems to be that of the yellow-tail tussock moth. The adult is a pure white with a golden-yellow tail. It lays eggs on a very wide range of trees and shrubs – including fruit trees and roses – and covers them with protective hairs. The caterpillars hatch in August and feed until late September when they find a place to hibernate, under bark or moss, and cover themselves with a protective silk web. They emerge in spring, pupate in May and the new adults are flying and laying eggs from late June through July.

Jerusalem artichokes under attack from slugs

"My Jerusalem artichokes were spoiled by holes in the flesh. No pests were found in the crop but I assume underground slugs had been at work. I have read about the biological control of slugs; can you tell me how it works?"

Keeled slugs would almost certainly have caused the damage to your artichoke crop. Biological control is by nematodes, almost microscopic worms, which invade the slug bodies and infect them with a bacterium that kills the slug. The nematodes breed inside the slugs and then escape to continue their "seek and destroy" mission over the following six weeks or more. These nematodes are supplied by mail order and come in a form that is simply mixed with water and applied to the recommended area of soil.

Not berry nice

"I have found a lot of dried, white objects on the back of my strawberry leaves. The leaves themselves are somewhat crinkled and some plants appear stunted. Is this something I should be concerned about?"

The crinkling and stunting is the result of feeding by the shallot aphid, a particularly damaging species of greenfly. The dried objects are the cast skins of the pests. To prevent further spread and damage, spray as soon as possible with a suitable insecticide. Use Tumblebug as it is systemic so will kill pests under the leaves as well as those on top, but it evaporates within a day so there are no residual problems to worry about.

Open to infection

"Last year we lost several courgette plants, just as they were starting to crop, due to what was identified as mosaic virus. I believe this is spread by greenfly. How should we prevent attacks this year?"

The simplest way would be to grow the courgette variety "Tarmino", which has been bred to be resistant to mosaic virus. For varieties that are not resistant, it is virtually impossible to prevent infection, as even if greenfly are constantly controlled by spraying, the first feed they take could infect the plant. A fine Enviromesh net would be effective, but it would have to be lifted or pulled back every day to pick the crop.

Ghostly caterpillars ❧

"Whilst digging over the vegetable garden my husband came across some semi-transparent white caterpillars. They wriggled violently backwards when disturbed. He killed those he found. Was this correct and what other treatment may be needed?"

The caterpillars would have been those of either the ghost swift moth or the garden swift moth. The caterpillars feed on plant roots and other underground parts, preferring fleshy objects such as Jerusalem artichokes, celeriac, dahlias and other storage organs. Garden swift moth caterpillars feed for one or two years before pupating whilst the ghost swift moth caterpillars feed for two and sometimes three years.

Digging over the soil and hoeing regularly will help to control them by exposing the caterpillars. The soil is best treated with Sybol dust before sowing or planting most crops.

Watch the weather before you plan to spray!

Peach leaf curl control ❧

"I forgot to take my pot-grown peach under cover to prevent the rain spreading peach leaf curl. Is there an alternative method of control?"

It would still be worth protecting your peach from rain, even though some spread of the spores may have already occurred. However, before taking the tree under cover, spray it with a copper fungicide which should prevent any liberated spores from germinating.

Woolly aphid worry ❧

"Quite a number of my young apple shoots have been damaged. There was an attack of woolly aphid on them in the summer, but I don't know if they also caused the eruptions seen later."

Woolly aphid feeding often results in a distortion of the shoots and eruptions of tissue through the young outer bark. Apple canker can gain entry into the damaged tissue, making the attack rather more serious.

Prune out the worst of the damage during normal winter pruning operations and look out for any return of the woolly aphid next spring or summer. If an attack does occur, spray with a systemic insecticide or give a drenching application of a fatty acids insecticide.

Chafer trouble ❧

"Whilst digging over our vegetable plot I came across some evil-looking creatures that I am sure must be damaging my crops. Can you identify them and recommend any treatment?"

The creature you found is a chafer grub, the larval stage of the cockchafer, *Melolontha melolontha*. The larvae of other chafers such as the garden, summer and rose chafers are all basically the same. They feed on plant roots for up to three years before pupating to emerge the following year as adults (which are also known as June bugs).

Digging the soil to disturb the grubs or to expose them for hand removal is usually effective as a control. Treatment of the soil with an approved soil insecticide would also be appropriate.

White oaks ❧

"Why was 1997 such a bad year for mildew? Lots of my garden plants were attacked, even a new oak sapling. Could anything have been done to prevent these attacks of mildew?"

Much of the mildew problem was related to the very dry spell of weather earlier in the year. Plants under stress from lack of water do appear to be more susceptible to mildew attack and the dry conditions help in the airborne dispersion of the spores.

Where there were no restrictions on the use of hosepipes, then copious watering in the dry weather may have helped to reduce potential attacks. Alternatively, or in addition, a few sprays of sulphur or carbendazim fungicide would have stopped the disease building up on the leaves.

Grubbed out ❧

"While carrying out some quite severe pruning of my apple trees, I came across a branch that had been bored inside, and poking around, revealed a large yellowish caterpillar. What would this have been, and is it a common problem?"

The caterpillar could have been the larva of a leopard moth or a goat moth. The former tend to be found singly, while the goat moth tends to occur in groups and grows to 4 in. (10cm). Neither is particularly common, but they do crop up from time to time on various fruit and other trees. As you found only one, it is probable that it was a leopard moth larva. These feed for two to three years before pupating.

Spring sprays for fruit ❧

"I was unable to give my fruit trees and bushes their usual tar-oil winter wash. What would you expect to be the main pests that the plants would suffer from and how would you recommend I treat them?"

Various species of greenfly would be the main concern, and these could attack all your different fruit trees and bushes. A good choice of spray would be Rapid Insecticide as it is specific to greenfly.

Apple and pear suckers may also be present in the absence of a winter treatment and for these a systemic insecticide would be a better choice. Tumblebug or Sybol would take care of both types of sucker as well as greenfly and any tortrix or other caterpillars. Alternatively, drenching sprays of a fatty acids insecticide could be used.

Unhappy aspen ❧

"My aspen leaves have pale blisters on them. They are yellow when seen from above but from below the attacked area is hollow and seems rusty-coloured

*and hairy. The tree is far too tall to spray, but I would be interested to know
what the damage is caused by, and if there is any practical form of control."*

The raised spots are due to feeding by a tiny creature known as the poplar
erineum mite. As far as is known, this particular mite feeds only on aspen
and black poplar, and as there are not too many black poplars around
these days, the aspen is quite frequently attacked. The damage is
unsightly when present over many of the leaves, but little real harm is
done to the tree and no control measures are known.

Earwigs on the offensive ❧

*"I am a container gardener and have the usual odd problem with slugs and
caterpillars which I deal with using pellets and hands. However, something
else has been eating selected plants wholesale, whilst not touching others at all.
Leaves and flowers are eaten, particularly clematis, violas and romneya.
Tiarella and Solomon's seal are left untouched. No insects have ever been seen
at work. I have tried earwig traps (pots of straw on canes) without success."*

Earwigs are responsible for the damage you describe. Earwigs lay eggs in
December and January, with a further batch of eggs in May to June. There is
not likely to be much more feeding until spring, but a concerted effort then
should prevent any major trouble later on. A dusting around the plants and
over the compost with gamma-HCH dust in addition to the trapping will help.

Holey holly ❧

*"My holly tree leaves have been attacked again by a sort of blistering. There is
an unsightly brown area, usually in the middle of the leaf, and some of them
have a hole in the centre of the blotch."*

This damage is the work of the holly leaf-miner. The pest causes rounded
blotches, rather than the more usual winding mines of most other leaf-
miners. Eggs are laid in May and June and the larvae feed through to the
end of the year, pupating in the following spring to emerge as new adults
from late April onwards. The holes are where the adults emerged.

It may be worth spraying with Tumblebug or Picket a couple of times
over the next two or three weeks to catch the new generation as they lay
eggs or as the young miners hatch. Removing blistered leaves from winter
up to late April would prevent the new adults emerging, but as the adults
will fly in from elsewhere, control would not be complete without some
supplementary spraying.

Curing cutworm ❧

"I have found some fat, grey-green caterpillars feeding on my herbaceous plants, just below soil level. I have not come across these before and wonder what sort they are and what they mature into. I would also like to know how to get rid of them."

The creatures you have found will be cutworms which are the caterpillars of various moths. As you have found, cutworms feed on the stem bases of plants and quite frequently will eat their way along a row of vegetable or flower seedlings. Turnip moth is one of the most common of the adult forms of the cutworm; others include the yellow underwing and the heart and dart moth.

Good control will be obtained by watering the affected area with BioSafe. This is a biological control agent which seeks out and kills cutworms, vine weevil and some other soil pests.

Rusty rose ❧

"Is it possible to really control rust on my rose of Sharon? I was told that the rusty yellow patches under the leaves were due to rust disease, but I did a few sprays with a general fungicide last year without marked success. What would your advice be?"

All rust diseases are quite difficult to control. Cut the plants right down to ground level now, burning or disposing safely of the cuttings. As soon as there is any sign of regrowth, spray with Nimrod T or Tumbleblite II and repeat these sprays two or three times at two-week intervals. This should eradicate all the existing attack but should re-infection come in from elsewhere then spray again as necessary.

Box sucker at work ❧

"My box hedge has some pest or disease on it that causes the shoot tips to form little rounded cabbage-like growths and there is some white substance inside. Can you tell me what the problem is and how I can control it?"

The problem is due to attack by box sucker and severe infestations make box hedges look unsightly and may check growth. The insect spends the winter as an egg and the young nymphs hatch in spring and attack the developing new buds.

Normal trimming of the hedge will remove the suckers but if attacks are too severe, before you do any trimming, spray with Tumblebug or Sybol. If you spray again after autumn trimming, that should take care of any adult suckers before they can lay their winter eggs

Boring beetles living in logs ❧

"I have taken delivery of some logs for my wood-burning stove but am concerned that some of them show signs of boring. If there are any wood borers still present, do you think they could move from the logs to my furniture?"

The common furniture beetle woodworms do live on dead wood outside as well as in gardens, so if any larvae are present in the logs they could theoretically mature, pupate and then emerge as adults to lay eggs in your house. The logs would have to be in your house for a long enough period, though.

However, the borings may have been made by a species of bark beetle. These make their galleries just under the bark. If the logs are elm, the beetles would be the ones responsible for spreading Dutch elm disease.

Keeping hungry deer at bay ❧

"I have a problem with small deer coming into my garden and eating emerging shoots and buds on my roses. The deer come from woods backing on to my garden."

Apart from protecting your garden with a strong 6 ft (1.8 m) high wire-mesh fence, deer can be very difficult to control. Soak pieces of cloth in Renardine and tie them to canes inserted 1–2 ft (30–60 cm) apart around susceptible plants. Additionally, add 1 litre of Renardine to 25 kg of sand and sprinkle it evenly around gates and gaps, to deter the animals from entering your garden.

Nasturtiums on whose menu? ❧

"Which pest eats nasturtiums? I returned from an autumn holiday to find my lovely plants almost completely eaten away. There were some caterpillars, but they looked more like the ones that feed on cabbage plants."

The large white butterfly will lay eggs on nasturtiums just as readily as on cabbages. As the nasturtium plants are that much smaller, the damage is far more rapid and severe. Next year, a protective application of the biological control Dipel, or of a permethrin insecticide, would be a worthwhile insurance.

Aruncus attack ❧

"I have, or rather had, a lovely aruncus plant in my border. Suddenly, hordes of little caterpillars descended upon it and have stripped off nearly all the leaves. What are they and what can I do to save the plant?"

The caterpillars are those of the aruncus sawfly. It first came to Britain from northern Europe in 1924 and is now widely spread through the country. If the caterpillars are still feeding, spray thoroughly with Safer's Garden Insecticide, Tumblebug or Picket.

The fully fed caterpillars enter the soil to pupate and a second generation of adults will then emerge to lay eggs in late July to August, so be prepared to spray again in August and into September.

How many leaf-miners? ❧

"Are there lots of different sorts of leaf-miners, attacking specific crops or groups of plants, or just a few with very wide-ranging tastes? We seem to have had an awful lot of damage on all sort of plants."

There is a very wide range of different species of leaf-miner, some being the larvae of flies, others the larvae of moths. Some are very specific in what they will feed on, for example, the holly leaf-miner only feeds on holly and the lonicera leaf-miner only attacks honeysuckle and snowberry. On the other hand, the most common chrysanthemum leaf-miner species will also feed in the leaves of an extremely wide range of plants of the daisy family, including weeds and cultivated flowers. Once the miners are inside the foliage, little will control them other than a firm squash with finger and thumb.

Sick sycamore ❧

"Some of our local sycamore trees have leaves with pale yellow patches on them. Is this something that might spread to the Japanese maples in my garden?"

The patches are probably due to attack by one of the various eriophyid mites, which seem to have been quite troublesome. Such mites can move between different acer species, but most do seem to prefer the larger tree types. Keep a watch next spring and summer, however, and pick off any damaged leaves that may appear.

Blighted begonia ❧

"I grew a Begonia Rex from a cutting eight years ago. Last October, the stems had a white mould on them and now the new leaves develop with a dark spot, then dry up and fall off. Is there anything I can do to save the plant, or shall I have to get rid of it?"

The white mould on the stem and the dark leaf-spotting are the result of attack by powdery mildew. Begonias often just get dry, dead areas on the leaves, without the more usual powdery white coating of fungal growths. Take cuttings from the tips of the shoots, spraying them with Levington Nature's Answer Fungicide and Insect Killer as a precaution. It would be worth spraying the parent plant with the same product, but it's best done out of doors to avoid contamination in the house. If this treatment doesn't cure the diseased parent plant it is probably best scrapped, but you should get plenty of new ones growing on from the cuttings.

Going Dutch . . . again? ❧

"There are now lots of dead elms in our local hedgerows. Is there anything that can be done? I dread to think of the state of the hedgerows over the next few years."

The deaths are due to Dutch elm disease, a fungal problem first investigated around 1910 to 1920. However, in the 1960s one or more virulent strains of the fungus reached this country on imported elm timber and this killed vast numbers of the native elms over large areas of the country.

The disease spores are picked up by bark beetles as they feed and then spread to new elms when the beetles fly off to lay their eggs. Infection also passes from tree to tree by root junctions. Infected trees soon start to develop yellow leaves as the disease both produces a toxin and blocks the water-conducting vessels, and the whole tree will die within a few months. There was a lot of publicity about it in the early years but Dutch elm disease is not "news" any longer, particularly as there is no effective control.

Number one pest ❧

"Is there one particular pest that you would say is the number one enemy of garden plants? I find slugs one of my greatest problems but would be interested to know your opinion."

To be the number one enemy any pest would need to cause serious damage to a wide range of different plant types, so slugs and snails would be quite high on the list. Our choice, however, would be the vine weevil. The adults damage the leaves of rhododendrons and a range of other "hard-leaved" plants, while the larval stages feed on the roots of all kinds of plants, in the garden, greenhouse and home.

Examine the roots and compost of a wilting house plant and almost certainly you will find one or more legless, orange-headed weevil larvae present. Control is now possible using the nematode biological control agent, sold by mail order by Defenders and via garden centres by Miracle Garden Care as Nature's Friends for Vine Weevil Control. Both products can be used on soil or pot plant compost.

Bud attack ❧

"A number of my peony buds failed to develop properly this summer and stayed as tight buds. These buds are now brown and dead."

The peony may have been attacked by a disease known as peony blight, or it could be suffering from a growth condition known as pedicel necrosis. Remove all the darkened buds now and look for any sign of grey, furry growth on them which would indicate blight. If this is found, prevent it next year by spraying the new growths in spring with Bio Supercarb. Pedical necrosis is related to lack of water uptake due to drought or it can be related to lack of nutrients. Apply a rose feed in the spring and keep well watered during dry weather.

Pine-resin gall moth ❧

"Can you tell me why several of my pine shoots appear to be partially broken and are hanging down? As far as I know, no person or large animal could have caused the damage I have found."

It sounds as if the pine-resin gall moth has been at work. The moth lays eggs on the young shoots and the developing caterpillars feed at the base of the needles. The shoot tips tend to droop and resin is produced around the damaged areas. During the second year, a 1 in. (2–3 cm) gall develops at the site of the feeding and the caterpillars pupate in the following year. Further attacks may be reduced by pruning out all the damaged shoot tips you can find.

A major miner problem

"Is there any easy control for leaf-miner? I seem to have more than my share this year and even my perennial thalictrum has been badly damaged, which I don't remember happening before."

Once the leaf-miner adult has laid her eggs in the leaves, control is very difficult and the grubs can only be controlled by squashing them within the mines or by removing leaves. With a severe attack either course of action would be a very fiddly job. Incidentally, the leaf-miner involved, *Phytomyza miniscula*, only attacks thalictrum and aquilegia, although there are plenty of other species feeding on a wide range of plants. Next year, inspect the plants from late May onwards, especially the leaves that are more shaded where the bulk of the eggs will be laid. Squash the larvae within any mines and give a protective spray with Tumblebug or Bio Long-Last.

Mildew alert

"Our phlox plants have been very badly damaged by mildew. The leaves were attacked in late June, just as we went on holiday, and on our return most of our phlox were white with the disease."

Dryness at the roots can be a contributory factor in mildew attacks and a dry summer means that powdery mildew has been more of a problem than usual. Regular watering in the early months followed by soil mulching would help in another year. To help clear up the attack, after cutting down the stems after flowering (or before if preferred) spray with Tumbleblite. At the first sign of mildew next year, give two or three sprays a couple of weeks apart.

Lime mite

"These leaves came from a tree found in a hedgerow. Could you identify them and explain why they had red 'spikes' growing on them?"

The leaves are from a lime tree and the growths are due to feeding by the lime gall mite. The mites start to feed on the leaves in May and by June the odd-looking galls develop, sometimes pale yellow but also green, brown or red. Although unsightly, the galls do not interfere with normal growth.

Menacing spiders ❧

"Every year recently our house walls and window frames have been covered in summer by swarms of red spider mites. Spraying doesn't seem to clear them."

The mites are bryobia or clover mites, rather than the normal red spider mite. These mites feed on plants in the same way, but rarely cause severe damage. They seek winter quarters quite early in the summer, searching for a safe place to tuck themselves into. A gap of 18 in. (45 cm) round the house, in which no plants are allowed to grow, will often keep the mites off the structure but where this is not sufficient, frequent spraying with malathion is effective. Most chemicals are rapidly de-activated on masonry – hence the need for frequent applications.

Playing host ❧

"Our euonymus bush has suddenly become infested with masses of blackfly. It seems a little late in the year for such an attack. Why should this happen and any control?"

The black bean aphid spends the winter in the egg stage on spindle and also on *Viburnum opulus* and a few other hosts. The insects return in autumn to produce one more generation which in turn lays the overwintering eggs. In spring the pests build up before flying off to infest a wide range of secondary hosts. Control the infestation now, and you will thwart next year's attacks.

Willow fungus ❧

"Every year, as soon as our weeping willow comes into leaf, the steams and leaves develop nasty dark spots, the leaves twist and then they fall off. What causes this and is there anything that can be done?"

The trouble is due to a fungal disease known as anthracnose. If the tree is not too tall to reach, prune out all shoots showing the typical dark spotting and burn the prunings. As soon as the new leaves have unfolded, spray with a copper fungicide such as Bordeaux Mixture or Murphy Traditional Copper Fungicide. Should any spotting occur later in the season, prune out and spray as above.

Nipped in the bud ❧

"Would you please identify the pale green to yellow caterpillars that are eating the flower buds of my scabious plants? None of my gardening friends have ever seen this before."

The caterpillars are almost certainly the young of the angle-shades moth. The name comes from the wing pattern of the adult moth which is a clear V-shape in darker brown shades on a pale, pinkish wing. The caterpillars can be either a yellowish-green or a pale brown in colour and they will feed on a wide range of flower types, outside in the garden as well as under glass. Control these caterpillars by spraying the plants with Dipel, the biological control product based on a friendly bacterium, *Bacillus thuringiensis*.

Camellia scale ❧

"I have been given a lovely indoor camellia but have found masses of strange white objects under its leaves. There doesn't appear to be any sign of life in them, but I would like to know what they are, where they came from and how to get rid of them."

The white objects are egg-sacs of the cushion scale. The brown-coloured scale insects would have been feeding under the leaves where the females lay their eggs under the protection of the waxy egg-sacs that you have found. The females then die and drop off the leaves.

The egg-sacs could be carefully picked off the leaves but the main control would be by spraying with a malathion insecticide. Give one spray now and a further one in early summer when any new scale-insect nymphs are likely to be on the move.

Holey leaves ❧

"What causes the leaves of dahlias to become distorted and full of holes? Our plants suffer this damage every year."

Capsid bugs are probably responsible. The tissue dies out where they feed, so as the leaves grow the damaged areas become holed and distorted. The bugs overwinter as eggs laid in the shoots of woody plants and the pests move on to dahlias and herbaceous plants in June and July. Stop further damage by spraying with a general insecticide a few times, treating the soil around the plants, as well as the undersides of the plant leaves and the stems.

Blooming aphids ❧

"The arums which we are bringing along into flower have suddenly sprung a crop of aphids. What would be the best way to control them?"

If you are keeping them at a temperature of around 16°C, you could introduce a biological control. This will involve using either the predatory gall midge *Aphidoletes* or the parasitic *Aphidius*. Otherwise, spray with Polysect or Rapid.

Earwig-go ❧

"My clematis was spoiled by damage to the petals. I assumed this was due to slug or snail feeding, but the usual anti-slug methods have not improved matters. Please help."

The damage to the petals is the work of earwigs. Although it looks very similar to slug attack, and is done mainly at night, there are no characteristic slime trails and the holes tend to be more regular round the edges because they are chewed, not rasped away.

The traditional control for earwigs is to trap them in straw pushed into plant pots with the pots balanced on canes around the plants. The earwigs are shaken out and disposed of each morning. Alternatively, use crumpled newspaper instead of straw and dust it with Sybol Dust or some other insecticide in dust form, so the earwigs do not need to be shaken out and killed each day.

False alarm ❧

"Last autumn, as the leaves fell from our oak tree, we found many with raised 'discs' underneath. They appeared to be only loosely attached to the leaves. What would they have been, and if they are harmful how can we prevent them this year?"

The discs are known as spangle galls, and are due to feeding by a tiny wasp. The wasp spends the winter in the galls in the larval stage and adult females emerge in spring. These lay unfertilized eggs in the oak flowers, and feeding by the larvae which hatch from these eggs results in currant-like galls.

Male and female gall wasps arise from these larvae and, after mating, the females lay eggs on the leaves which give rise to the spangle galls. There is no real harm done by these interesting creatures, although on a small oak tree in a garden the galls could be considered unsightly. Gathering up the fallen leaves as soon as they fall would possibly reduce numbers in the following year where there are few other oak trees.

Achillea aphids

"I have grown some nice achillea plants from seed but notice now that there is a very dense attack of greenfly on the young shoots. What is the best way to control them?"

If only a few plants are involved a ready-to-use insecticide sprayer would be very convenient. Choose from Bug Gun!, Nature's Answer to Insect Pests and Safer's Rose and Flower Insecticide. Normally one treatment should be sufficient, but for any persistent attack repeat a week or two later to complete the control.

Mildew-free

"Most of the Michaelmas daisies in my garden suffer badly from mildew, despite spraying with fungicides. Are there any varieties that are resistant to the disease?"

The varieties of the novi-belgii asters or Michaelmas daisies suffer the most from mildew. Those in the novae-angliae group, such as "Barr's Pink" and "Lye End Beauty", are less affected. *A.* x *frikartii* "Monch" is a particularly fine variety and so is "Wunder von Stafa", both of which are resistant to mildew. These two have also received Awards of Garden Merit from the Royal Horticultural Society.

Burdock leaf problem

"I have some burdock plants in my wild garden area and they are being spoiled by leaf-miner damage. Is there any treatment you would recommend? I would prefer not to spray in this area, but the damage is too much to remove the damaged leaves."

The three alternatives would be 1, leave alone, 2, hand-pick the worst leaves and squash grubs in the others or 3, spray a few times with a general insecticide. As the plants are in your wild garden the first choice would be the most appropriate. Next year, perhaps a precautionary spray at the first sign of attack would be worthwhile.

Parsley in peril

"Is it usual to get greenfly on parsley? My plants are smothered and I would like to know how to get rid of them. They are in an unheated greenhouse."

Parsley under glass does appear to be much more susceptible to greenfly attack than when grown outside. You could spray with Rapid, which is virtually specific to greenfly, or you may like to use the biological control available from garden centres under the name of Nature's Friends for Aphids or the aphid parasite, *Aphidius*, available by mail order from Defenders Ltd.

Roses

Choosing a rose ❧

"I want to plant some roses but I cannot find the type I want. I do not like the big flowers of the hybrid teas and I am looking for a rose that produces large trusses of small, single flowers in soft pastel shades. Could you help me with the names of one or two roses of this type?"

You could not do better than plant "Ballerina". This is classified as a Hybrid Musk rose. It produces large sprays of single pink flowers, each with a white centre. It is a healthy, vigorous rose and it can be purchased grown as a standard. Another similar variety is "Mozart", but it differs in that the flowers are of a deeper pink surrounding the white centres. "Marjorie Fair" was bred from "Ballerina" and is very similar, except that the flowers are carmine-red in colour.

Replacing roses ❧

"I have had a rose bed in my garden for a number of years and now some of the bushes are beginning to fail. Can I replace them with the same varieties?"

If you replant in the same soil the new roses will not grow well because the soil will have become "rose sick". So before replacing the ailing roses you must dig out a hole where they were growing to a depth of 18 in. (45 cm) deep and 18 in. (45 cm) across. Remove the soil and replace it with new soil from a different part of the garden.

Blue Moon ❧

"Is there a rose called 'Blue Moon' and does it really have blue flowers?"

There is a rose called "Blue Moon", but despite its name the flowers are not true blue but more of a mauve-pink shade. It is a hybrid tea rose growing about 3 ft (90 cm) tall. It's available from all the leading rose growers.

Autumn roses

"Are there any bush roses that do well in the autumn?"

A few Hybrid Tea bush roses that give a good show in the autumn are: "Royal William", "Paul Shirville", "Fragrant Cloud", "Silver Jubilee", "Alec's Red" and "Just Joey".

Planting bare-root roses

"I want to plant some bush roses this winter. Is it better to buy bare-root bushes or container-grown plants?"

Bare-root bush roses are plants that are lifted in the nursery in the autumn and sold with no soil on their roots. They are available between November and March. Container-grown roses are available for most of the year.

If you intend to plant during the winter, choose bare-root roses. They are usually cheaper and, planted with care, will grow away well next spring and flower in the summer. Next February apply a good rose fertilizer and put a thick mulch of decayed compost or manure around the newly planted bushes.

Replanting roses

"In the autumn of 1983, I planted a number of roses in different varieties. 'Deep Secret' has proved to be too vigorous and 'Pascali' and 'Whisky Mac' have not put on much growth. I feel that they need replacing. I understand that this should not be done for ten years, or a hole 18 in. across and 24 in. deep has to be dug out and replaced with fresh soil for the new roses. Is this a practice you would recommend?"

If roses are planted in soil that has already grown roses, they will not do very well. The problem is usually described as "soil sickness". It applies to all kinds of plants and it is recommended that vegetables of similar types should be rotated, and not grown in the same piece of ground year after year. The best solution is that which you suggested. Take out a hole 18 in. (45 cm) across and down to the sub-soil. Replace it with fresh fertile soil that has not grown roses.

Rose hedges

"I have seen Rosa rugosa used for hedging. Are there any other roses that can be used for the purpose and what would be your recommendations?"

There are many roses that make effective hedges. A few suggestions are "Queen Elizabeth", "Iceberg", "Kassel", "Sarah van Fleet", "Sally Holmes", "Congratulations" and "Mountbatten".

Many of the musk roses, such as "Penelope" and "Felicia", make good screens, particularly if they are trained to a wire support. "Zephirine Drouhin", the thornless rose, can be treated in the same way. The deep pink flowers are pleasantly fragrant.

Ballerina rose ❧

"Can you tell me anything about a rose called 'Ballerina'? Can it be grown successfully in a large pot or tub? Does it get black-spot disease?"

The "Ballerina" rose is a delightful variety producing large sprays of pink and white flowers on bushes growing about 3½ ft (1 m) tall and spreading to about 4 ft (1.2 m). It is an excellent rose for bedding but can also be grown in a large pot for standing on a patio. It is also good grown as a weeping standard. Black spot can be a problem and to avoid damage it is wise to spray several times against the disease. Give the first spray as the new foliage emerges in the spring and repeat the spray at monthly intervals.

Rose poser ❧

"Can you tell me whether the 'Dortmund' rose is a climber or a shrub?"

Rosa "Dortmund" is usually regarded as a climbing rose as, trained against supports, the stems can grow 10 ft (3 m) tall and spread out to 6 ft (2 m). This is how it is best seen when the growths are covered with clusters of bright crimson flowers with white "eyes". They appear all summer and into early autumn. However, plants can be kept pruned and maintained as a shrub, if that is preferred.

Modern shrub rose ❧

"Last June I saw a beautiful rose cascading over a low wall. Its name was 'Raubritter'. As it seems to have a sprawling habit, would it be suitable for covering a bare bank that I have in my garden?"

The rose you saw would be ideal for covering a bank to eventually exclude weeds. Make sure that the ground is well cleared of weeds. Do this in the summer so that you can plant in the autumn. Afterwards, mulch the surface with plastic or bark fibre to stop weeds growing. "Raubritter" is a modern shrub rose with attractive, cup-shaped blooms. There is only one flush of bloom in June. The variety is also prone to attacks of mildew. The rose is wide, spreading to 7 ft (2.1 m), and attains 3 ft (1 m) in height.

Patio rose 🥀

"Can you tell me anything about a rose called 'Clarissa'? A relative of mine has the same name and I would like to give her some bushes. Naturally, I want to tell her something about the rose."

"Clarissa" is a delightful rose that was raised by Harkness, Hitchin, Herts. It is classed as a patio rose and grows to about 2½ ft (75 cm) tall. The flowers are described as coral and apricot. It has won many awards including a Trial Ground Certificate from the Royal National Rose Society after a trial in their gardens at St Albans. As a patio rose it can be grown in a large pot or tub or used for bedding. Growth is upright and it can make an attractive low hedge.

Fragrant roses 🥀

"Can you give me the names of some roses with really good fragrance?"

Roses having a good scent include: "Fragrant Cloud", "Golden Celebration", "Korresia", "Madame Butterfly", "Meilland Merril", "Papa Meilland", "Molineux" and "Velvet Fragrance".

For a fuller list you can consult the booklet *Find that Rose*, which lists 2850 varieties and where they can be obtained. Varieties with good scent are marked with a rosette. The booklet is available from the Editor, Find That Rose, Colchester, Essex CO4 5EA (cheques to be made payable to the British Rose Growers' Association).

Showy rose hips 🥀

"Last autumn I saw a rose bush covered in large, orange-red hips. I would like to grow a similar rose in my garden. Are there any special varieties that have handsome hips? What height do they reach?"

There are a number of shrub roses that produce handsome and colourful hips. The following are a few suggestions: *Rosa moyesii* "Geranium", 8 ft (2.4m); "Fru Dagmar Hastrup", 3 ft (1m); *Rosa rugosa* "Alba", 6 ft (2m); *R. rugosa rubra*, 5 ft (1.5m); *R. davidii*, 10 ft (3m); "Scabrosa", 5 ft (1.5m); and *R. virginiana*, 4 ft (1.2m).

Thorn-less issue

"Can you name the rose which comes from a bush that does not seem to have any thorns?"

This rose is "Zephirine Drouhin". It has thornless stems and clusters of double, well-scented flowers. It may be grown as a shrub or trained as a climber and, kept tied to a fence, makes an attractive screen or flowering hedge. It is an easy rose to grow although it is prone to mildew, particularly when trained against a wall.

Miniature roses

"I have bought two miniature roses in pots. They are in flower and look delicate. How should I look after them and do they need a warm or cool room?"

The miniature roses that you have bought have been given special treatment to make them flower early but they are, in fact, hardy plants that can be grown outside. They do not make good indoor plants as hot and stuffy rooms are not to their liking. For the time being enjoy your little plants indoors but stand them in an unheated room in a light window. Water them whenever the soil seems dry. Put the plants outside in early April. They look attractive in troughs and containers or in a rock garden. Give them good soil and several feeds through the summer and they will give you a good show of flowers.

Roses for northern exposure

"I have a 20 ft (6m) high north-facing garage wall and I would like to cover it with roses. What would you recommend?"

There are several climbing roses suitable for growing on a north-facing wall including: "Alberic Barbier", "Morning Jewel", "New Dawn", "Danse du Feu," "Gloire de Dijon", "Leverkusen", "Madame Alfred Carrière", "Nova Zembla" and "Paul's Lemon Pillar".

Potpourri concoction

"Can you tell me what is needed to make potpourri?"

Potpourri consists of a mixture of flower petals, aromatic leaves and spices. Rose petals and lavender are favourites, but others are wallflowers, orange blossom, freesias and honeysuckle. These can be mixed with more colourful flowers such as zinnias and small everlasting flowers.

Plants with aromatic leaves include bergamot, lemon balm, thymes and mints. All these are mixed together with a fixative powder, such as orris root, which holds the scents together. To make the mixture more intense, a small amount of essential oils can also be sprinkled over the ingredients. Seal the potpourri mixture in a container, kept in the dark in a warm place for six weeks, so that all the aromas are concentrated together. Afterwards, display the potpourri in an attractive bowl or similar container. The scent will lose its intensity after a few weeks, and you will need to add more oils.

Wait until the flowers are open before collecting the blooms for potpourri.

In the back row ❧

"I am planting a new double bed of roses against a 6 ft high wooden fence which is 30 ft long. I would like the back row to be of tall growing Hybrid Teas of different varieties and colours. I have already picked out 'Alexander', 'Queen Elizabeth' and 'L'Oreal Trophy'. Can you suggest other good varieties?"

In addition to the roses that you have selected, varieties that would serve your purpose are "Chinatown", yellow floribunda; "Congratulations", rose-pink Hybrid Tea (HT); "Elina", also known as "Peaudouce", cream HT; "Golden Showers", yellow climber; "High Sheriff", reddish-orange HT; "Mountbatten", yellow floribunda; "Royal William", dark red HT; "Silver Jubilee", salmon-pink HT; "Uncle Walter", dark red HT; "White Cockade", white climber. Although you have specified HT's, we have included two floribundas that produce large flowers, as you have included "Queen Elizabeth" in your selection. We have also included two HT-type climbers which are suitable for growing as big bushes – prune them fairly hard into the new wood each spring.

Instant coverage ❧

"Which ground-hugging roses would you recommend for Scotland and where can they be obtained?"

Some of the best ones observed in different locations, including Scotland are: "Avon", white; "Nozomi", blush white; "Wiltshire", deep rose-pink; "Flower Carpet", deep, bright pink; "Suma", light red; "Fairy Prince", crimson; and "Hertfordshire", carmine pink, light eye.

Most of these should be available from: Mattock Roses, Nuneham Courtenay, Oxford OX44 9PY, R. Harkness & Co Ltd, The Rose Gardens, Hitchin, Herts SG4 0JT or Fryer's Roses Ltd, Manchester Road, Knutsford, Cheshire WA16 0SX.

Rose for a wall ❧

"I want to grow a climbing rose on a south-facing wall. Would 'Albertine' be suitable? If not, could you make other suggestions?"

"Albertine" is a rambling rose which is prone to mildew if it is grown on a dry wall facing south. Better roses for you to grow on a south-facing wall are: "Etoile de Hollande", crimson; "Lady Hillingdon", yellow; and "Shot Silk", orange-pink.

Pergola roses ❧

"I want to plant some roses to cover a new pergola I have built in my garden. Could you suggest a few suitable varieties?"

There are a great many climbing and rambler roses suitable for covering a pergola. A few reliable kinds are pink "Albertine", white "Iceberg Climbing", red "Paul's Scarlet Climber", pink "New Dawn", red "American Pillar", pink "Madame Grégoire Staechelin", yellow "Maigold", and white "Felicité Perpétué".

Pillar roses ❧

"Can you recommend some red-flowered climbing roses for growing up pillars near a boundary fence? What I need is vigorous varieties with plenty of thorns."

You could not do better than plant some of the vigorous climbing roses raised by Kordes in Germany. "Dortmund" grows to 10 ft (3 m) and produces masses of single red flowers with white eyes. It has healthy, glossy foliage. Another is "Hamburger Phoenix" which has dark red, semi-double flowers and grows to about 9 ft (2.7 m). Growing even taller is "Parkdirektor Riggers". It has large clusters of deep red, semi-double flowers.

Wall for Madame ❧

"I want to grow a pink climbing rose up a sunny wall on my house. Would 'Madame Grégoire Staechelin' be suitable?"

Yes, very suitable for training against a sunny wall. It is vigorous in growth and carries masses of blowzy, pink flowers in early summer which are very pleasantly scented. Unfortunately, there is only one flowering, but this is so good that it easily makes up for the lack of later blooms. The large hips that follow the flowers are an added attraction in the autumn.

Pink climbers ❧

"I want to grow some pink-flowered climbing roses. Could you recommend some good varieties?"

Good climbing roses with pink flowers include: "Bantry Bay"; "Pink Perpétué"; "Albertine"; "Zephirine Drouhin"; "Compassion" and "New Dawn" (light pink).

Ground-cover rose ❧

"I want to plant some roses as ground cover. Do you think that the rose variety 'Bonica' would be suitable?"

Yes, "Bonica" is a good rose for ground cover and when fully developed will help to smother weeds. It has pale pink, double flowers, grows to about 3 ft (1m) tall and spreads to 4 ft (1.2m). If you want something less vigorous and more compact, consider "Kent" which has large trusses of white flowers and grows 18 in. (45 cm) tall, spreading to 2 ft (60 cm). The old polyantha rose "The Fairy" is also good for ground cover. It has soft pink, double flowers and grows about 2 ft (60cm) tall, spreading to about 3 ft (1 m) across.

A wall of roses ❧

"I'd like to grow a climbing or rambler rose against a 12 ft (3.6 m) high wall. What varieties would you recommend?"

It's not good to grow rambler roses, such as "Dorothy Perkins", on a wall as they are very prone to mildew in such situations. Choose instead a climbing rose such as "Aloha", pink; climbing "Etoile de Hollande", dark red; "Guinee", red; "Chaplin's Pink Climber", "New Dawn", light pink; climbing "Iceberg," white or "Compassion", pink.

Hanging around ❧

"I understand roses can be grown in hanging baskets. What varieties would you recommend?"

Growing roses in hanging baskets is a fairly new idea. The County Series of ground cover roses are ideal, including "Avon", blush pink; yellow "Gwent"; "Hertfordshire", carmine pink; and the deep pink "Wiltshire". Other suitable roses are: "Magic Carpet", lavender; pink "Nozomi"; "Peek a Boo", a patio rose with apricot flowers; and "Queen Mother", another patio rose with pink flowers.

Golden roses ❧

"I want to give my parents a gift on their golden wedding anniversary. Is there a rose called 'Golden Wedding'?"

Yes, there is a rose called "Golden Wedding". It is a cluster-flowered bush rose with yellow flowers. Bushes grow about 30 in. (76cm) tall and the double flowers have a light scent. There is also a Hybrid Tea rose called "Golden Years" which has large, double, golden-yellow flowers with a light scent. Both roses can be obtained at most rose nurseries.

Rose fillers ❧

"I have some shrub roses that flower only once and the border is rather dull afterwards. What could I plant with the roses to give a longer display?"

Low-growing perennials, such as *Geranium* "Johnson's Blue", catmint (nepeta), *Alchemilla mollis* and lavender, can be planted with the shrub roses to extend the season of interest. Lily bulbs could also be grown to flower after the roses have finished.

Name of the rose ❧

"I was given a bush of a shrub rose called 'Fantin-Latour' for Christmas. Can you tell me anything about it, please?"

"Fantin-Latour" is a very beautiful centifolia shrub rose. It was named after the French artist who specialized in painting roses and lived between 1805 and 1904. Little is known about the origins of the rose, but it appeared at the beginning of the century. Plants grow 7 ft (2.1 m) tall and as much across. The large, double flowers are pale pink in colour and are well perfumed. However, they appear only in summer and there is no repeat bloom.

A rose by any other name ❧

"What is rosewood? Does it come from a kind of rose? And what is satinwood?"

Rosewood is used in cabinet work for marquetry, inlaying and veneering. It has a bold, highlighted grain and an attractive colour.

It is called rosewood, not because it comes from a rose, but because of its rose-like scent. It is the wood of an Indonesian tree, *Dalbergia latifolia*, which is a member of the pea family. It is known as Indian rosewood, malabar rosewood, black rosewood, east India rosewood and blackwood. Other cabinet timbers such as kingwood and granadillo are also obtained from the genus *Dalbergia*.

The satinwood is the Indian *Chloroxylon swietenia*, a 50 ft (15 m) tree also known as the wood-oil plant. Its hard, durable timber takes a high polish and is used in veneering for its close grain and deep yellow colour.

Planting roses ❧

"Can you tell me the right time to plant roses? Is it best to buy container-grown plants?"

Plant roses between November and March. Container-grown roses can, however, be planted at most times of the year, provided they are looked after carefully and watering is not neglected.

Plant bare-root roses between November and March but only when the ground is not frozen or too wet. To ensure success, pour a good planting mixture or potting compost among the roots with some bonemeal before returning the rest of the soil to give the plants a good start. If you can plant in November and December the roses will have settled down and made new roots before the onset of winter. Make sure that the graft union is just below soil level.

Contained roses

"Can I grow patio roses in windowboxes and tubs?"

So-called patio roses are ideal for growing in all types of container, even in hanging baskets. Suitable varieties include: "Anna Ford", "Festival", "Robin Redbreast", "Shine On", "Sweet Dream" and "Top Marks". Suitable ground-cover roses for hanging baskets are: "Gwent", "Kent", "Magic Carpet", "Nozomi" and "Wiltshire".

Heeling-in roses

"I have purchased some rose bushes by mail order. They arrived the other day but the ground is not ready for them as it is very wet at the moment. How should I look after the roses until I can plant them?"

Remove the rose bushes from their packaging and plant them temporarily in a spare corner of the garden. Take out a trench with a spade and lay the roses in it at an angle, covering the roots with soil. This is known as "heeling-in". If the ground is too wet to do this, plant the roses temporarily in a large pot or tub, but transfer them to the garden as soon as conditions allow.

Moving roses

"When is the best time to move roses from one position to another?"

Move roses when they are dormant from November to early March when the soil is workable without being too wet. Cut back the shoots to within 18 in. (45 cm) of the ground and enrich the soil with bonemeal and decayed manure.

Mulching roses   🎕

"As my soil is light and sandy I have been putting manure on the soil around my roses. I have now been told that this can harbour pests and it is not a good thing to do. Can you tell me what to do?"

Ignore the advice you have been given. Mulching the ground around rose bushes does a great deal of good. It helps to keep the soil moist during the summer, smothers weeds and also improves the organic content of the soil.

A variety of materials can be used for mulching, including decayed manure, compost, bark fibre and spent hops. Some people lay cardboard over the bed and then cover it with a thick layer of compost. Black polythene laid over the surface of the soil also conserves soil moisture. You may be interested to know that the Royal National Rose Society is carrying out trials with several different mulching materials in its gardens at Chiswell Green, St Albans. The gardens open for the summer in June.

Deadheading roses   🎕

"Is it a good idea to remove the fading flowers from roses?"

It is well worthwhile removing the faded blooms. This stops seed forming and encourages new shoots to be made to produce more flowers. Cut back the stems with sharp secateurs above a bud and just below the old flower truss.

Feeding roses   🎕

"I find advice given on feeding roses is somewhat confusing. When is the best time to feed the bushes?"

To encourage roses to make good growth, feed them in early March with a proprietary rose fertilizer or Growmore fertilizer. Apply it in a ring around each bush. A further application can be given in May, followed by another in July. It is also important to mulch around the bushes in early spring with a layer of decayed manure or compost. This helps to keep the soil moist throughout the summer months.

Iron tonic for roses   🎕

"One of our roses has produced a shoot that has lost virtually all the green colour from the leaves. Can you help?"

The leaves are lacking in iron. As they are largely immobile in the plant the yellowing (chlorosis) starts with the youngest leaves and moves back down the stem. Iron is often in short supply in alkaline, chalky soils.

With such a severe case, it seems likely that the roots have got down to pure chalk in a patch in your garden. Correct by watering the soil around the plant, and the leaves themselves, with Sequestrene, treatment being given in March. This supplies the necessary iron in a form which cannot be locked up by the alkalinity of the soil.

Rose suckers

"I have some shoots on my roses with smaller leaflets than the rest of the bush and they are of a paler green. Are these suckers?"

Trace these shoots back to their point of origin and if they arise below the point of budding they are suckers. Scrape the soil away from their base and pull them off the bush with a sharp tug. This will also remove dormant sucker buds.

Above or below?

"Can you tell me the best way to feed roses? Should a dry rose fertilizer be used on the soil or a liquid fertilizer applied to the foliage?"

Although most people feed their roses with a dry fertilizer, applied at intervals through the spring and early summer, it is also beneficial to apply a foliar feed at certain times. The advantage of foliar feeding is that the nutrients are absorbed rapidly and give a quick response. This is useful where roses are growing in very alkaline and chalky soils and may be showing leaf yellowing as a result of mineral deficiencies.

Prune for success

"I have a rather splendid shrub rose 'Fruhlingsgold' which flowered well in early June. It is about eight years old and has reached 9 ft (2.6 m) in height with a spread of 7 ft (2 m). I would like to prune it but I am not sure how this should be carried out. Can you help?"

Your "Fruhlingsgold" shrub rose would seem to have reached its maximum dimensions and, as it is flowering well, prune it as little as possible. Cut out any dead and diseased stems after flowering and, if necessary, thin out overcrowded growths. Regular pruning, as with Hybrid Tea and floribunda roses, is not necessary for shrub roses.

Pruning new roses ❧

"I have bought some new rose bushes with bare roots. The stems look as if they have been cut back. Is any further pruning needed this year?"

The stems of your new roses will probably need to be cut back further. All newly planted roses should be pruned hard after planting. This is done to encourage strong growths from the base of each bush in the following spring. Always use sharp secateurs when pruning to ensure that clean cuts are made that heal over quickly. Cut just above an outward-facing bud with a slight slant away from the bud.

Prune back your roses annually or you will need a pair of binoculars to enjoy them.

Bend for flowers ❧

"I have an old climbing rose which I cut back severely last winter. Since then it has made several vigorous stems but no flowers have appeared. How can I make the plant flower again?"

The hard pruning has done your old climbing rose a lot of good. There is no reason why it should not flower again this summer. However, you must train the stems by arching them over and tying them to the trellis or supports. Bending over the stems will encourage side shoots to appear along their whole length, which should then produce flowers All side shoots should be cut back to within a few inches of their base. Do this without delay.

Silly roses

"Having moved house two years ago, the new garden had many overgrown roses. I cut them all back to just above ground level. The majority responded well but two bushes have gone silly. They are about 10 ft (3 m) tall and have not flowered."

You may have been over-enthusiastic when pruning. Cut back the stems of the bushes by about half their length to prevent strong winds rocking the bushes and damaging the roots. Growth will not be as strong this year but there is no reason why the bushes should not flower again. Feed in March with a high-potash fertilizer such as Phostrogen to encourage sturdy growth to produce plenty of flowers.

Pruning ramblers

"When is the correct time to prune rambler roses?"

Early September is a good time to prune rambler roses. Cut out some of the older stems that have flowered at ground level. Some of these older stems can be retained if there is space. Retain all the new, young growths made this season and tie them into place on their supports.

Pruning climbing roses

"I have planted a climbing rose in my garden. Should it be pruned in autumn or in the spring?"

It should not be necessary to prune your climbing rose as it has only just been planted. Train the main stems out and tie them to the supports. Any dead, diseased or weak growths may be cut out.

Overgrown rambler

"I have an 'American Pillar' rambler rose which has become very overgrown. When should I prune it?"

The ideal time to prune your rambler is in the autumn. Cut out some of the older stems at their base and shorten all the side shoots on the remaining main stems to within an inch of their base. Tie all the main stems into position on their support.

Rose cut-backs ❧

"Some of my bush roses have made very tall stems which sway in strong winds. Do you think it would be a good idea to shorten these tall stems to prevent the plants moving?"

It would be wise to prune your roses as you suggest, cutting the stems back by about half their length. This will prevent the plants moving and damaging the roots. Complete the pruning of the bushes early next year.

Neglected roses ❧

"We have recently moved house and in the new garden are several old rose bushes. They do not seem to have been pruned for some time as many of the stems are long and leggy, with all the leaves at the top. Can I prune the bushes now?"

Wait until next winter before pruning your neglected bushes. Mulch the soil with a thick layer of decayed compost, manure or bark fibre. This will prevent weed growth and keep the soil moist. It would also be wise to spray the bushes with either Rose-clear, Tumbleblite or Systhane fungicides against the common diseases such as black spot, mildew and rust.

Rose mildew ❧

"In June my rose bushes always start to be attacked by mildew which turns the leaves, and sometimes even the flower stalks, white. How can I stop this?"

Spray with Tumbleblite or Systhane and repeat a few times at two-week intervals. In dry weather (any water restrictions permitting), keep the soil well watered as mildew does seem worse in dry conditions. If you are planting up new bushes, try to plant those with less susceptibility to mildew, such as "Silver Jubilee", "Grandpa Dickson" or "Alec's Red".

Galled roses ❧

"I have found some odd pea-like swellings on a few of my species roses. Can you tell me what they are?"

The rounded growths are galls that are caused by a tiny wasp. Two related species of wasp cause similar swellings, but in one case the galls are quite round and smooth and are known as smooth pea-galls whilst in the other the galls are quite spiky and are known as spiked pea-galls.

No real damage is done by these insects or their galls. Gathering up the fallen leaves, or the galls which drop from them in autumn, would be an appropriate measure if one were really needed.

Black spot ❧

"I sprayed my roses with a winter wash and with a fungicide in March, but they are now losing leaves due to black spot. What can be done now please?"

The earlier sprays will have reduced the damage at the start of the season, but new infection will come in from outside sources. The best plan now would be to apply a good systemic fungicide such as Tumbleblite or Systhane. Repeat the treatment two or three times at two-week intervals.

Winter spot treatment ❧

"My roses suffered badly from black spot this summer. Is there anything I can do to avoid the same trouble next year?"

Many growers give their roses a winter drench of Armillatox or Jeyes Fluid to lessen the effects of disease in the following year. Before applying the drench rake up all fallen leaves and burn them to destroy disease spores. As soon as the foliage develops next April, spray the bushes with a fungicide such as Systhane.

Rust prevention ❧

"Is there a really effective way to prevent rust on our roses? Every year we seem to have an attack by midsummer."

Rust certainly is harder to eradicate than black spot. Gather up any fallen leaves that may remain under the bushes and then prune quite hard in early March.

As soon as any new shoots appear, spray with Bio Systhane or Tumbleblite. Repeat these sprays a few times at fortnightly intervals to protect the new growth.

The Royal National Rose Society has started a long-term trial examining roses for resistance to disease.

Disease-resistant roses ❧

"Roses in my area seem to get black-spot disease badly so I'd like to grow only roses that resist this disease. Can you give me some names of suitable varieties?"

Roses that are resistant to black-spot disease include: "Baby Love", "Magic Carpet", "Pink Favourite", "Allgold", "Flower Carpet", "Queen Elizabeth", "Escapade", "Alexander", "Arthur Bell", "Nozomi", "The Times", "Yesterday" and "Savoy Hotel".

Tunbridge ware toadstools ❧

"Whilst clearing up around an old rose bush we came across some tiny, greenish toadstools both on the dead bases of some of the rose stems and on a nearby fence post. Is this something we should be worried about?"

There is no cause for concern. The fungus you have found is known as the green wood cup, (*Clorociboria aeruginascens*), and grows on dead wood, especially oak. Infected wood becomes stained green and this was widely used in furniture known as Tunbridge ware, the stained wood being used for marquetry inlays. The fungus will not spread into any living tissue of your old rose bushes.

Life cycle ❧

"One of my rose bushes has a mixed greenfly population – some have wings and some do not. Can you tell me what determines whether wings will develop or not?"

Most greenfly species overwinter as eggs and the young that emerge are without wings. They feed and breed (without mating) on the winter host plant until population pressure, food quality or seasonal factors tell them that it is time to spread.

Winged forms then develop which fly off to find alternative host plants. Depending on the greenfly species involved, the alternative may be another plant of the same kind as before or a different type.

The winged forms then give rise to wingless offspring which breed on the host plant, and the cycle may be repeated a few times during the year. In autumn winged forms fly back to the winter host plant where they mate and then produce wingless forms that lay the winter eggs.

Gardeners' friend 🐝

"Can you identify a creature that I saw on my roses? It was grey to blue in colour with yellow patches and had six legs. There are quite a few of them on the rose leaves, but they don't seem to be doing any damage."

The creature you describe is the larval stage of the ladybird. They used to be called crocodiles by gardeners and children. The larvae feed on greenfly so they will be helping to keep your roses clean of these pests. Should it prove necessary to spray for a particularly bad greenfly attack, use Rapid insecticide which would not harm the ladybird larvae.

Hopping mad 🐝

"My lovely rose foliage is becoming covered with pale, bleached spots. Underneath the leaves are small yellow to white insects that take short, leaping flights when disturbed. I presume the two are linked; what can I do?"

Yes, the damage is being done by the pests you describe. For obvious reasons they are known as leaf-hoppers and usually you find the yellowish nymph stages with developing wings and whiter adults with folded wings. Control by spraying under the leaves with Tumblebug, Sybol or Safer's Rose & Flower Insecticide.

Rose greenfly 🐝

"Are there different sorts of greenfly that attack roses? We seem to have both red and green sorts and both large and smaller types."

There are at least five different aphid (greenfly) species that commonly attack roses, and several more that can be found from time to time. One species is actually called the rose aphid, but this can vary in colour from green, to pink, to reddish-brown! Fortunately they all respond to the same treatment.

Buzz words 🐝

"Last summer my rose leaves were severely damaged by what was identified as the leaf-cutter bee. Could you tell me the life cycle of this insect? I don't want to kill the bees, despite the damage they can do, but would like to know more about them."

The common leaf-cutter bee, *Megachile centuncularis*, attacks roses, amelanchier, lilac, privet, laburnum and a few other plants. It chews out semi-circular pieces of leaf and flies off to a suitable site which can be a rotting wooden post, a pot of compost or a piece of soft earth.

The leaf segments are then rolled into a tube and are fitted with a base. The cell thus formed is filled with pollen and nectar and a single egg laid before the top is sealed with a cap cut from a leaf. Several cells are inserted into the site, one on top of the other, and then filled in. Adults are active throughout June and July. The eggs hatch in late summer and the new adults emerge in the following June. It seems that the eggs may hatch, or the adults emerge, in reverse order to that in which the eggs were laid, as the upper ones come out first. The adult bees can be a nuisance to the keen rose grower, but they are also useful pollinators of garden flowers.

Rose help needed ❧

"Up until early July, the leaves of nearly all my large-flowered roses were constantly eaten away by yellowish-green shiny grubs. I don't know what they were, but can you tell me how to stop them attacking again please?"

The grubs would have been larvae of the rose-slug sawfly. Adults emerge from the soil in May and lay eggs on the foliage. The grubs feed through June and just into July, before dropping to the ground to get ready for winter, so there will be no more damage this year. During winter, cultivate gently around the bushes to expose or disturb the overwintering grubs in their silken cocoons. Next year in late May/early June, keep a look out for the first sign of damage. A spray with fatty acids or permethrin would clear up any attack.

Roses under attack ❧

"The leaves of several of our roses are being badly damaged by small caterpillars. They are eating off all the leaf surface, just leaving the network of veins intact."

The caterpillars are the larvae of the rose-slug sawfly and damage can be both rapid and severe. Hand pick or squash as many of the pests as you can find and then follow up with an insecticide spray to catch any missed. Tumblebug or Bug Gun would be suitable sprays to use.

Scaly roses ❧

"On some of my species roses I have found a scaly growth towards the base of the stems. Can you tell me what this is and how I should control it?"

The insect causing the problem you have found is the rose scale, also known as scurfy scale. Eggs are laid under the old scales in the summer and the new generation of nymphs settles in new feeding sites by autumn. Mating occurs in spring, thereby starting off the next generation. Control by pruning out infested shoots where possible or by spraying with a systemic insecticide such as Sybol or Tumblebug.

Rooting rose hedging

"I have been unsuccessful in taking cuttings from my rugosa rose hedge. If this can be done, can you tell me how and when to do it?"

Rugosa roses can be successfully propagated from hardwood cuttings taken in the autumn. Make the cuttings from firm shoots made in the current year. Cut them into 9–10 in. (23–5 cm) lengths, cutting just below a bud at the base and just above a bud at the top. Remove the lower leaves and thorns. In a shady spot, make a slit trench with a spade and pour some coarse sand in the base to assist rooting. Insert the cuttings to about 6 in. (15 cm), and firm the soil around them. In 12 months' time good roots should have formed and the plants may be lifted and planted in their permanent positions.

Rose cuttings

"I have two rambler roses in my garden, 'Albertine' and 'Veilchenblau'. Can I take cuttings from them and when is the best time to do it?"

Cuttings from your two rambler roses should root without difficulty. Take them in early autumn after pruning. Select firm straight stems of well-ripened wood. With sharp secateurs or a knife make the cuttings about 9–12 in. (23–30 cm) long. Trim each one below a bud at the base and above a bud at the top. Insert the cuttings in a slit made in the soil with a spade. Choose a position where the soil is well drained and put some coarse sand in the base of the planting holes to assist rooting. Leave the cuttings in place for a year, when they should have made a good root system. Lift them in autumn or winter and plant them in their permanent positions.

Rose cuttings

"I have a 'Chaplin's Pink' climbing rose. How can it be propagated? Does it have to be budded or can I take cuttings from it?"

The "Chaplin's Pink" climbing rose can be increased from cuttings and autumn is a good time to take them. Select young firm stems made this year, about the thickness of a pencil. With a sharp knife or secateurs make the cuttings about 9 in. (23 cm) long. Make sure you cut just below a bud at the base and above a bud at the top.

Insert the cuttings in a trench outside so that about 6 in. (15 cm) of stem is below ground level. Put some coarse sand in the base of the trench to assist rooting. Return the soil around the cuttings and make it firm. Good roots will have formed in 12 months' time, when the young plants can be put in their permanent positions.

Choosing your roses

For the latest information on availability of Britain's best-loved roses and where to source them refer to the excellent publication, Find That Rose *which is compiled and published annually by the British Rose Growers Association.*

Roses make great gifts for gardeners so why not celebrate their colour, fragrance and sheer quantity of bloom by choosing varieties perfectly matched for the gardener or flower arranger with a special occasion in mind?

Anniversaries

Diamond "Diamond Jubilee",

Golden "Golden Jubilee", "Golden Celebration", "Golden Days", "Golden Dawn", "Golden Moments", "Golden Wedding" and "Golden Years".

Ruby "Ruby Anniversary", "Ruby Celebration" and "Ruby Wedding".

Pearl "Pearl Anniversary", "Pearl Drift", "Pink Pearl" and "Sea Pearl".

Silver "Silver Jubilee", "Silver Anniversary", "Silver Lining," "Silver Wedding" and "Twenty-fifth".

General "Anniversary", "Happy Anniversary" and "Congratulations".

If it's a birthday to celebrate

Why not choose from this pick of seven bushes including: "Best Wishes", "Birthday Girl", "Celebration Day", "Congratulations", "Happy Birthday", "21 Again" and "Many Happy Returns".

Rose flushes for that special person

"Dearest", "Friend For Life", "Hero", "Little Flirt", "Lovely Lady", "My Choice", "My Love", "Pretty Lady", "Super Star" and "Valentine Heart".

Celebrate a wedding

"Bride", "Celebration Day", "Congratulations", "Glad Tidings", "Honeymoon", "Joyfulness", "Special Occasion" and "Warm Wishes".

And those new arrivals ✿
"Breath of Life", "Friday's Child", "Mother and Baby", "Mother's Love", "My Little Boy", "New Arrival" and "Peaudouce". And if it's twins . . . "Double Delight" and "Double Joy".

Celebrate retirement ✿
"Golden Handshake", "Good Luck", "Memory Lane", "Pensioner's Voice" and "Remember Me".

Rosy ideas for . . . ✿
Pots and hanging baskets
"Festival", "Kent" (and other members of the County Series), "Little Bo Peep", "Nozomi", "Peek A Boo", "Sunseeker", "Sweet Dream" and "Top Marks".
Arbours, pergolas, walls and fences
"Aloha", "Compassion", "Dublin Bay", Graham Thomas", "Leaping Salmon", "Penny Lane", "Summer Wines" and "White Cloud".
Covering soil and slope
"Avon", "Broadlands", "Flower Carpet" (white, pink and look out for new colours promised), "Pheasant", "Surrey" and "Swany".
Hedging and screens
"Alexander", "Ballerina", "Bonica", "Cornelia", "Mary Rose", "The Queen Elizabeth" and *Rosa rugosa*.

Mail-order rose nurseries ✿
Buying bare-root roses from specialist nurseries in the autumn is a particularly good way of buying a much larger range of rose varieties than would be found at a garden centre. Look out for their colourful catalogues for a wealth of ideas and varieties, including the latest introductions showcased at Chelsea and Hampton Court Flower Shows . . .

- C & K JONES Goldenfields Nursery, Barrow Lane, Tarvin, Cheshire CH3 8JF, tel. 01829 740663
- DAVID AUSTIN ROSES: Bowling Green Lane, Albrighton, Wolverhampton, Shropshire WV7 3HB, tel. 01902 373931
- FRYER'S ROSES: Manchester Road, Knutsford, Cheshire WA16 0SX, tel. 01565 755455
- GANDY'S ROSES LTD: North Kilworth, Lutterworth, Leicester LE17 8HZ, tel. 01858 880398
- JAMES COCKER & SONS: Whitemyres, Lang Stracht, Aberdeen, Grampian AB15 6XH, tel. 01224 313261

- MATTOCKS ROSES: Nuneham Courtenay, Oxford, Oxfordshire OX44 9PY, tel. 01865 343265
- PETER BEALES ROSES: London Road, Attleborough, Norfolk NR17 1AY, tel. 01953 454707
- R. HARKNESS & CO LTD: The Rose Gardens, Cambridge Road, Hitchin, Hertfordshire SG4 0JT, tel. 01462 420402

Soil and site

Loam defined   ❧

"What exactly is loam?"

Basically loam is a soil which contains equal amounts of clay, silt and sand enriched with humus – which is decayed organic matter. Loams that contain a larger proportion of sand are termed sandy loams and those with a larger amount of clay are clay loams.

Extra   ❧

"When wood chippings are used as a mulch do they take nitrogen from the soil? Presumably, extra nitrogen can be added. And should I rot the chippings down first?"

Wood chippings are invaluable for mulching and they do add to the soil's humus reserves. They also keep slugs away and suppress weeds. Unless they are rotted first, scatter 1 oz. per sq.yd. (28g/m²) of sulphate of ammonia over them to compensate for the nitrogen that is removed from the soil by bacteria when they rot them down. But ideally, they should be stacked and allowed to rot down before being added to the soil.

Top job?   ❧

"Is spent mushroom compost any good for top dressing?"

Spent mushroom compost has little nourishment value but it is useful to apply to the soil for its humus content.

However, lime content can be a problem. If your soil is fairly alkaline, it will be made more alkaline by adding the compost. Used as a top dressing, it will help to conserve soil moisture.

If you can obtain large quantities of mushroom compost, add it to the compost heap. Make sure you allow it to rot down with all the other vegetable matter.

Cover up ❧

"I have been advised to mulch the ground around my new shrub border with black polythene. This does not look very attractive. How can I disguise it?"

One way of disguising the black polythene mulch is to put another mulch on top of it, using bark fibre, cocoa shell or good garden compost.

Pesticide legislation ❧

"I am doing a project on pesticides towards my 'A' levels at school. Can you tell me the name of the legislation that controls pesticides in this country and any source of more information?"

The Food and Environment Protection Act of 1985 introduced strict controls over the supply, storage and use of pesticides and the Control of Pesticides Regulations of 1986 specifies these controls. A good source of further details would be the British Agrochemicals Association (which also looks after garden products). You can write to them at 4 Lincoln Court, Lincoln Road, Peterborough, PE1 2RP.

Adding lime ❧

"I have been given conflicting advice on when to lime the soil on my allotment. Should it be done each year, and if so, when?"

Soil should be limed only when it needs it. Ideally, soils for vegetables should be slightly acid with a pH of 6.5. If your soil is already alkaline with a pH of 7 or above, it does not need liming. However, if the soil has a pH lower than 6.5 it should be limed.

To find out whether a soil is acid or alkaline, purchase a small testing kit at a garden centre. The best time to apply lime is in the winter, but not when manure has been dug in recently.

Gathering seaweed ❧

"I understand that seaweed can be used as manure. Although I live near the sea, I am not sure of the legal position on collecting it from the beaches. Can you advise?"

Freshly gathered seaweed can be dug directly into the soil or it can be spread out and allowed to dry on the surface. Once dried, seaweed can be stacked until required. Wet material rots down quickly in a heap but gives off an offensive smell.

Gathering seaweed from beaches is an established practice. Contact your local council for permission.

Hoeing the soil

"Is it true that hoeing the soil between plants helps to retain moisture in the ground?"

Yes. It was a practice always followed by gardeners in the past. Hoeing the soil when it is fairly dry on the surface helps to create a surface mulch. Hoeing also kills off weed seedlings which would otherwise take a lot of moisture from the soil. If it is done in hot, dry weather the weed seedlings soon wither and die.

Hoeing can be avoided if the surface of the soil is mulched with rotted compost or black polythene. These mulches keep moisture in the soil and also prevent weeds developing.

Green manuring

"I have been told that I can improve the fertility of the soil on my allotment by growing a green manuring crop. What is the best type to grow and when should it be sown?"

The fertility of a soil can be greatly improved by growing a green manuring crop in it. The best time to sow is when the ground will be vacant of other crops for some time. For instance, if rye grass is sown in early autumn it will continue growing through the winter and can be dug into the ground in the spring. It is better still if the rye grass can be left to grow for a whole season. The crop helps to protect the soil from heavy rain in the winter and provides valuable organic matter when dug into the ground.

Crops such as mustard, can also be grown during the summer when a piece of ground becomes vacant for a short period; they can be dug in after a couple of months. Blue lupins may also be sown as a short crop during the spring and summer.

Making leafmould

"Can you tell me the quickest way to turn leaves into leafmould? I have four bags of dry beech and oak leaves. Do I put water on them?"

The best way to rot down the leaves is, first, to wet them. Then mix an activator, such as Garotta, with them. Press the leaves firmly into tough plastic bags. Tie them tightly at the top and make a few holes in the sides with a garden fork to allow air to enter. Keep the bags in a sheltered spot and cover them with sacking for insulation. Decomposition will be fast. Leafmould – crumbly and black – will be yours to remove after six months.

Composting sawdust

"Can I can add sawdust and wood shavings to my compost bin?"

It is important to have a good air supply through composting material and as sawdust is dense, especially when wet, it must be well mixed with other compost ingredients. Coarse wood shavings will take longer than soft materials to break down, but a small amount mixed in the heap should not pose any problems. Alternatively, stack the shavings separately in the open for at least six weeks and use them as a mulch as you would bark chippings.

Using bark chippings as a weed control

"Can you advise me on the use of bark chippings for weed control? Should they be used with a polythene sheet and what depth should they be laid?"

Use them to disguise a weed-control membrane or simply spread them 2 in. (5 cm) thick on to the soil. They should last for several years. Although large bark chippings last longer, they are not so effective at conserving soil moisture as small or medium chippings. Renew them only when they have integrated with the soil and are beginning to disappear.

Plant tonic

"Last year my windowbox plants started off well but they gradually deteriorated as the summer progressed. Should I have fed them do you think?"

The reason why your windowbox plants did not do well last year was probably because of a lack of plant food. This year, once the plants are well established, feed them with a liquid fertilizer such as Miracle-Gro or Phostrogen at weekly intervals.

The acid test

"I want to grow azaleas in my garden but I am told they need acid soil. What does this mean?"

An acid soil is one that is lacking in lime. Azaleas need an acid soil because the presence of chalk or lime renders iron unavailable to the plant, resulting in poor, yellowish foliage.

To tell whether your soil contains lime, small soil-testing kits can be purchased at garden centres. These indicate the pH level of the soil. Any pH figure below 7 means that the soil is acid, and figures above 7 mean, that the soil is alkaline and contains lime.

To make a soil more acid add peat and use fertilizers such as Miracid that are suitable for acid-loving plants such as azaleas, rhododendrons and camellias. Soils can also be made more acid by applying flowers of sulphur to them in the spring at 4 oz. per sq.yd. After a few months test the pH of the soil to see how much it has reduced the alkalinity.

Soil sickness ❧

"I have cleared an old rose bed as the bushes were spindly and weak. I intended to plant new roses in the same bed but I have been told that this is not wise and the roses will not do well. Is this true?"

The advice that you have been given is correct. As roses have been grown in the soil for many years it will now have become "rose sick". If you plant new roses in the same soil they will not thrive.

It would be best to grow something else in the bed and grow roses in a new position. If this is not possible take out large holes and remove the old soil from them. Fill the holes with fresh, fertile soil and plant the roses in it. Soil sickness is a difficult problem and affects all kind of plants. Apple trees should not be planted in ground where apples have been grown until two years have elapsed.

Shreds to dread? ❧

"I have recently bought a shredder to deal with the prunings from our garden. Can shredded conifer, holly and bay be used for mulching as I understand that some evergreens can poison the soil?"

Shredded material from evergreen plants such as conifers, holly and bay is perfectly suitable for using as a mulch around trees and shrubs, to help suppress weed growth and conserve soil moisture. However, fresh shreddings are best stacked in the open for a minimum of six weeks before use, so that bacteria can break down some of the compounds in the material.

How to manure ❧

"Can you tell me whether it is better to dig manure into the ground or put it on the surface and fork it in later?"

Most gardeners prefer to put manure in the bottom of the trenches as the ground is dug over. This saves another job of forking it in later. There is, however, no reason why you should not put manure around growing crops as a mulch. This helps to keep the soil moist and smothers weeds.

New Zealand flatworm ❧

"I have found what I believe may be one of the flatworms that eat earthworms. Is there any treatment that can be given? I am told that sightings should be reported; can you let me know where I should do this in Scotland?"

In the latest map charting the progress of the New Zealand flatworms through Scotland, there is a dot indicating a sighting close to Ullapool. Scottish sightings should be reported to Scotland Campaign, Cramond House, Kirk Cramond, Cramond Glebe Road, Edinburgh EH4 6NS.

Wood ash ❧

"Trying to be 'organic' I have burnt 'hard' garden rubbish in an incinerator. How do I use the ash?"

Wood ash can benefit soils as it contains variable amounts of potash. The potash content of the ash is highest when young, sappy twigs have been burnt. It is also very soluble so is best applied exactly when needed. Flowering and fruiting plants appreciate potash and the best time to apply it is in early summer. Avoid spreading it around acid-loving plants such as rhododendrons, camellias and heathers, as wood ash is alkaline.

Saving water ❧

"Is it safe to use water collected in a water butt from bath and shower waste for watering plants and hanging baskets?"

It is perfectly safe to use waste bath and shower water for watering plants and hanging baskets in the summer.

Potting compost

"Could you give me the formula for John Innes compost?"

John Innes Potting Compost No. 1 is made up by mixing seven parts sterilized loam, three parts peat, two parts coarse sand (all parts by volume). Add to each 10 litres, 28 g of John Innes base fertilizer and 6 g of chalk.

The John Innes base fertilizer is made up of two parts of hoof and horn meal, two parts calcium superphosphate and one part sulphate of potash (all parts are by weight). All ingredients must be well mixed together.

Maggots in manure

"I picked up some bags of farmyard manure whilst out recently in the car but on shaking them out found some areas of the manure to be infested with pale creamy maggots. Are these likely to attack any plants in my garden?"

The maggots would be larvae of one of the various flies that are attracted to manure. They perform a useful job in nature by helping with the breaking down of all kinds of raw organic matter from fresh manure through to dead animals. Although broadly related to cabbage root fly and carrot fly, these particular species will not attack your garden plants; they will simply pupate and turn into adult flies.

Soil matters

"I want to grow some geraniums in a windowbox. Can I fill it with soil from the garden?"

Ordinary garden soil will not give very good results in a windowbox as it is not of the right quality and texture. Choose instead a soilless compost or one containing loam such as John Innes Compost No. 3. Both types can be obtained in bags at a garden centre.

Compost mix

"I have an almost limitless supply of horse manure. Each year I collect a huge quantity of fallen leaves. Can I compost the two together?"

The leaves and horse manure should make good compost. Mix the leaves and manure together thoroughly or layer leaves and manure alternatively. The horse manure should help to speed up the rotting-down process.

Poor drainage 🦋

"Having recently moved to a new house I have discovered to my dismay that the soil varies in depth from 4–8 in. (10–20 cm), over what appears to be boulder clay. The water table is so high that water lies about in puddles after rain and dries to leave a hard crust. I am aware that lots of compost will help but it appears that if I grow roses, I need to choose varieties with small root systems. Can you recommend suitable kinds?"

No matter what size root system a rose has, it won't thrive in waterlogged soil. Before you put in roses or any other shrubs, it is vital that you improve the drainage. Do this by laying land drains in a herring-bone system of trenches, sloping to a soakaway or ditch. Alternatively you could use special water-ducting drainage strips that can be bought at garden centres.

Damp conditions can cause practical problems when it comes to planting time!

Read the label 🦋

"Some of the recommendations on insecticide bottles seem to have disappeared recently. Certain pests have gone from the labels and I am having to change from my usual tried and tested favourites."

The regulatory authorities are gradually working their way through all the different active ingredients and are imposing what many believe to be unrealistic requests on the suppliers.

Previously, if an insecticide controlled some types of caterpillar, then it was assumed, almost always correctly, that it would control virtually all other caterpillar species (subject to timing). Now each species to be included on the label has to be tested before it can be added to, or kept, on a label.

The cost of carrying out the necessary tests often greatly outweighs any revenue to be gained from perhaps a minor use, so the recommendations are being taken off labels. So always read the product label before use to ensure that your previous use is still a current recommendation.

Seaweed meal ❧

"I have some dried seaweed meal. How and when should I use it in my shrub and perennial flower garden?"

Seaweed meal contains more potash than nitrogen so will be ideal for your shrubs and perennials. It is best applied in late spring/early summer at a rate of 4 oz. per sq.yd. (100 g per m²) as a general tonic. It can also be used on lawns at the rate of 2 oz. per sq.yd. (50 g per m²).

Horse manure ❧

"Many riding schools locally have begun to bed horses using wood shavings instead of straw. Is horse manure with wood shavings as good as horse/straw manure?"

A mixture of horse manure and wood shavings that has been allowed to mature for a few months is excellent material for mulching or digging into the garden. It is a very friable material without the stringy bulk of straw, so in some ways it is easier to use.

Don't forget to feed ❧

"Last summer I used a soilless compost in my windowbox. The plants started off well but after a few weeks they made poor growth and looked miserable. Should I have fed them?"

Plants soon exhaust the nutrients in a soilless compost. Unless you feed, the plants will soon deteriorate. Once your plants are established this year, start feeding them with a liquid fertilizer at least once a week. This should keep them growing and flowering well all summer. Never allow the soil to dry out in the summer. In hot weather you may have to water at least twice a day.

Good compost ❧

"I bought a compost bin some years ago but have not been able to dry out the material to make good compost."

The best compost is produced when the heap is made up of several different constituents, kept in the right conditions: compost requires warmth, darkness, moisture and air.

Shredded compost materials that result in wet compost probably means that there is insufficient oxygen in the heap, so incorporate more bulky materials such as non-woody prunings, straw or farmyard manure to open up the heap.

N P K value ❧

"What, if any, is the N P K value of farmyard manure?"

The value of farmyard manure is that it adds organic matter to the soil. Nutrient levels are low, on average nitrogen 0.5–1%; phosphoric acid, 0.25–0.50%; potash 0.5–1%.

Grey leaves ❧

"I want to create a border devoted to white and grey plants. I plan to use white-flowered annuals such as petunias and tobacco plants but I am not familiar with grey-leaved shrubs which would be suitable for mixing with the white flowers. Can you recommend suitable shrubs?"

Shrubs with grey or silver foliage suitable for your border include: *Convolvulus cneorum*, *Olearia* x *scilloniensis*, helichrysums, *Lavandula* x *intermedia vera*, romneyas, *Potentilla fruticosa* "Vilmoriniana", perovskia, *Senecio greyi*, *Teucrium fruticans*, *Santolina chamaecyparissus*, *Salvia officinalis*, *Hebe pinguifolia* "Pagei", artemisias and *Cistus albidus*.

Bank on these ❧

"There is a wide ditch at the end of my garden where the soil is moist for most of the year. I would like to grow some ornamental plants on the banks. What would you recommend?"

There are a number of attractive plants that will thrive in the moist soil of your ditch. If there is plenty of space try the giant rhubarb, *Gunnera manicata*, and the skunk cabbage, *Lysichiton americanus*. Other suggestions are primulas, mimulus, astilbes, calthas, hostas, *Iris sibirica, I. ensata*, lysimachia, trollius and the white arum lily, *Zantedeschia aethiopica*.

Edge the beds ❧

"My rose beds tend to look dull and bare until the new leaves develop and flowering begins in June. What plants can I use to edge the beds to make them more attractive?"

There are a number of low-growing plants that are suitable for edging a rose bed. We suggest that you try some of the following: dianthus, violas, *Campanula carpatica, Lavandula* "Munstead", *Aurinia saxatilis*, helianthemums, spring bulbs such as *Tulipa kaufmanniana* and muscari, *Stachys lanata* and catmint (nepeta).

Plants for dry shade ❧

"There is a border in my garden which is in the shade of trees in the summer and the soil is very dry. I would like to grow a carpeting plant in the border. Is there anything that will grow in this situation?"

Yes, there are several plants that you could grow in the dry and shaded border. St John's wort, *Hypericum calycinum*, would be a good choice. It is almost evergreen and has bright yellow flowers in the summer. Once established it soon creeps over a wide area. Other plants that you could try are ivies, the variegated large-leaved periwinkle, *Pachysandra terminalis* and the deadnettles, *Lamium maculatum*.

North wall fruit ideas ❧

"I have an 8 ft (2.4 m) high, north-facing wall in my garden and I would like to train a fruit tree on it. What type of fruit would be suitable?"

Not many fruits will succeed on a north-facing wall. Morello cherries, however, are the exception and would be suitable for your wall. Plant a fan-trained tree this winter and attach the branches to horizontal wires fixed in the wall. The Morello cherry is self-fertile which means that a single tree may be grown. It is an acid variety and the fruit is used for making preserves but is too sour to eat raw. The white blossom in spring is highly ornamental.

Plants that resist rabbits ❦

"We have recently moved to the country and the garden is overrun with rabbits. I am able to put wire netting around some of the beds but others are impossible. Are there any plants that rabbits do not like? So far we have found that they do not touch geraniums and hostas."

The following plants appear to resist attacks from rabbits: agapanthus, alchemilla, aquilegia, astilbe, bergenia, colchicum, convallaria, cyclamen, dahlia, delphinium, eryngium, euphorbia, galanthus, hardy geraniums, helenium, hemerocallis, kniphofia, lamium, lupin, Michaelmas daisy, narcissus, nicotiana, poppies, primrose, pulmonaria, schizostylis, sedum, stachys, tagetes, trillium, verbena and viola.

Shrubs that are not usually harmed include: azalea, berberis, buddleja, ceanothus, choisya, clematis, *Daphne mezereum*, fuchsia, hydrangea, ilex, lonicera, tree peonies, philadelphus, rhododendrons, rosemary, sambucus, skimmia, spiraea, lilac and vinca.

Shrub selection ❦

"I have recently moved into a house with a little garden. Could you give me the names of some small shrubs that would be of interest for most of the year?"

Suitable shrubs include:
SPRING *Berberis buxifolia* "Nana", *Ceanothus thyrsiflorus* "Repens", *Cytisus* x *kewensis*, *Salix hastata* "Wehrhahnii", *Skimmia japonica* "Fragrans".
SUMMER *Caryopteris* x *clandonensis*, *Cistus crispus* "Sunset", *Fuchsia* "Tom Thumb", *Hebe* "Carl Teschner", *Potentilla fruticosa* "Red Ace".
AUTUMN *Abelia chinensis*, *Ceratostigma willmottianum*; *Cotoneaster conspicuus* "Decorus", *Hypericum* x *moserianum* "Tricolor".
WINTER *Euonymus fortunei* "Emerald Gaiety", *Mahonia aquifolium*, *Pachysandra terminalis*, *Sarcococca humilis*, *Ruscus aculeatus*.

Cover up ❦

"I have an ugly manhole in my lawn and I would like to screen it by planting a low-growing shrub near it. Can you suggest something suitable?"

Any shrub that you plant to screen the manhole must have flexible stems so that they can be pulled apart when it is necessary to open the manhole.

Cotoneaster horizontalis would be suitable, planted in a bed beside the manhole. It has prostrate stems which are covered in white flowers in the spring, followed by red berries in autumn and winter. The foliage also turns bright red in autumn. Another suitable shrub is *Juniperus sabina tamariscifolia*. This is a conifer with low-spreading branches.

Climbers on a west wall ❧

"Could you recommend some climbing plants that are suitable for a west-facing wall?"

Most climbing plants will grow happily against a west-facing wall. A few for your consideration are: wisteria, mauve or white flowers in spring; *Jasminum nudiflorum*, yellow, winter-flowering jasmine; climbing roses such as "Iceberg"; evergreen ceanothus, blue flowers in early summer; *Jasminum officinale*, white flowers in summer; *Solanum crispum*, lavender, potato-like flowers in summer; *Hydrangea petiolaris*, climbing hydrangea, white flowers in summer; *Chaenomeles speciosa*, better known as "japonica", early flowering.

Heights of perfection ❧

"Can you recommend a climbing plant to grow in a tub on a windy, west-facing wall which is in shade for most of the day?"

Climbers for your shaded wall include *Euonymus fortunei* varieties, such as "Coloratus" and "Silver Queen", both evergreen and initially needing support. You could also consider *Hedera colchica* "Sulphur Heart", large-leaved ivy with golden variegated leaves; *Hedera helix* "Goldheart", leaves splashed with gold; *Lonicera periclymenum* "Belgica", early Dutch honeysuckle and *Lonicera serotina*, late Dutch honeysuckle.

Grow the climbers in large tubs or better still, in a border beside the wall.

Plants for a damp site ❧

"I have a winter pond (60 ft wide and about 2 ft deep). It dries out between May and November. Some willows partially shade the site. What should I plant around the area?"

Apart from the willows that you have, there are several other good varieties. *Salix alba* "Chermesina" has orange-scarlet stems in winter. The young stems are the most colourful and all the growths should be cut back each spring to encourage lots of new stems to form. You could also plant the goat or pussy willow, *Salix caprea*.

Alders also do well in damp sites. Shrubs suitable for a damp site are *Cornus alba* and *C. stolonifera* for colourful stems, *Viburnum opulus*, *Spiraea* x *vanhouttei* and *Symphoricarpus*.

Provided the soil around the edges of the pond does not dry out completely in the summer you could prepare beds for perennial flowers such as astilbes, *Primula pulverulenta, Iris sibirica,* ligularia, lythrum, mimulus, rodgersias and houttuynia.

Wildlife garden ⅔

"A group of people I know are making a wildlife garden. A pool has been created to attract insects and animals but we need help and suggestions. Can you give us some further ideas?"

Now that you have installed a pool for amphibians, dragonflies and birds, you could grow teasels from seed to attract goldfinches which feed on the seeds. A bird box or two, a bat box and a "log house" for hedgehogs would also be good to have.

Why not have a wild-flower meadow to encourage insects and butterflies? If you plant buddleja bushes they will attract at least five different kinds of butterfly. Study *The Backgarden Wildlife Sanctuary Book* by Ron Wilson. This is a Penguin Handbook available from your local library. Another good book is *Creating a Wildlife Garden* by B. and L. Gibbons, price £10.95 (plus postage). It is available from RHS Enterprises, Wisley, Woking, Surrey GU23 6QB. You should also contact the Royal Society for the Protection of Birds, Sandy, Beds who have many leaflets on how to attract and feed birds in gardens.

Yellow foliage ⅔

"I am planning a border to be filled mainly with shrubs having yellow or golden foliage. Can you recommend any that I can grow?"

A few suggestions are: *Philadelphus coronarius* "Aureus"; *Viburnum opulus* "Aureum"; *Spiraea japonica* "Gold Flame"; *Berberis thunbergii* "Aurea"; *Lonicera nitida* "Baggesen's Gold" and *Ligustrum ovalifolium* "Aureum" (golden privet).

If your soil is acid you could grow some of the heathers and lings such as: *Erica carnea* "Aurea" and "Foxhollow", *E. cinerea* "Golden Drop" and *Calluna vulgaris* "Gold Haze".

Golden border ⅔

"I am thinking of planting a border filled mainly with plants having gold or yellow foliage. To form the foundation of the border, could you give me the names of a few trees and shrubs that I could grow?"

One of the best trees with golden foliage is *Robinia pseudoacacia* "Frisia". Another is *Catalpa bignonioides* "Aurea". The latter can be treated as a shrub to obtain the best coloured leaves. To do this, cut back all the stems hard in early spring. Strong new growth will result, covered in handsome leaves all summer. Other trees that you could consider are *Gleditsia triacanthos* "Sunburst" and the golden bay, *Laurus nobilis* "Aurea".

Shrubs that you could grow are: *Acer shirasawanum* "Aureum", *Berberis thunbergii* "Aurea", *Philadelphus coronarius* "Aureus" (golden mock orange), *Lonicera nitida* "Baggesen's Gold", *Ligustrum ovalifolium* "Aureum" (golden privet) and *Spiraea japonica* "Gold Flame".

Plants for clay soil ❧

"I have recently moved into a house on a new estate. The soil is clay and not very well drained. Can you give me a selection of plants that would grow in this type of soil? The garden faces south but is not very sheltered."

There are several plants that will tolerate areas of heavy clay soil that become wet in winter. If there are areas of constant standing water during the winter, the range of plants that you can grow will be much reduced. Before planting, it might be wise to put in a soakaway or land drains to help improve the soil drainage. Improve the structure of heavy clay by digging in plenty of organic matter and coarse grit.

A few suggestions of plants that are tolerant of wet soils include:
TREES – alder, *Alnus incana*; birch, *Betula pendula*; hawthorn, *Crataegus laevigata*; ash, *Fraxinus excelsior*; elder and sambucus.
SHRUBS – *Berberis stenophylla, Cornus alba, Hydrangea macrophylla, Hypericum beanii, Kerria japonica, Prunus spinosa, Salix humilis* and weigela.
HERBACEOUS PERENNIALS – astible, caltha, cimicifuga, gunnera, hosta, *Lysimachia nummularia*, monarda, trollius.

Seaside shrubs ❧

"As I live near the sea, can you give me the names of shrubs that will do well in the area?"

A good way of finding out what does best in your area is to take a look around local gardens and make your choice. In addition we can recommend the following: *Hebe* "Midsummer Beauty", lavender flowers; *Choisya ternata*, white, fragrant flowers; hardy fuchsias such as "Mrs Popple"; genistas; escallonias; tamarix; cytisus (brooms); *Senecio laxifolius*; yuccas; *Phlomis fruticosa*; santolina; and pittosporums.

Chalk these dozen up &#

"I want to plant some low-growing hardy perennials in chalky soil. What would you recommend?"

Low-growing perennials for a chalky soil include: *Ajuga reptans* (bugle), *Alyssum saxatile*, lamiums (deadnettles), helianthemums, *Polygonum vaccinifolium, Hypericum calycinum*, aubrieta, campanulas, arabis, geraniums, primulas, including primroses, and nepeta.

Thorny subjects &#

"What thorny shrubs can I plant around my house to deter burglars?"

The following are attractive ornamental shrubs. They are also well armed with thorns which should deter intruders: *Ulex minor* (dwarf gorse), berberis, chaenomeles (cydonia), *Genista hispanica* (Spanish gorse), rubus, *Poncirus trifoliata, Paliurus spina-christii* and roses.

Select climbers &#

"I have decided to divide my garden with a trellis fence and an arbour gateway. The trellis will be 7 ft (2.1 m) tall and about 24 ft (7.2 m) long. I would like to grow climbers on it that would flower at different times of the year. What would you recommend?"

In theory, it is possible to mark each month with a flowering climber but as flowering times overlap, you may well find that several are out together.

We suggest that you start in winter with yellow-flowered *Jasminum nudiflorum*. Progress into spring with *Lonicera belgica*. Brighten summer with a series of large-flowered clematis such as "Hagley Hybrid" and "Mrs Cholmondeley" and repeat-flowering climbing roses. For the autumn try *Vitis coignetiae*, famed for its leaves which assume brilliant sunset tints in October. A good book to advise you is *Best Climbers*, written by Stefan Buczacki (Hamlyn, £4.99).

Thorny subjects &#

"Can you give me the names of some thorny shrubs that I could grow to deter children from climbing into my garden?"

Try *Colletia paradoxa* which has large, sharp spines. Other shrubs worth growing are berberis, *Poncirus trifoliata, Genista hispanica* and ulex (gorse).

Growing to ground ❧

"To save weeding, I want to fill a border with ground-cover plants. Can you suggest what to grow?"

Suitable ground-cover plants for a border include; *Pachysandra terminalis, Hypericum calycinum*, heathers, ground-cover roses such as "Hampshire" and "Grouse", *Lonicera pileata*; bergenias; *Geranium endressii* and pulmonarias.

Boxed colour in winter ❧

"My windowboxes are full of colour in summer but dull in winter. Can you suggest plants for winter and early spring colour?"

The number of suitable plants for winter colour in windowboxes is limited but, even so, there is still a good choice. After the summer flowers have been cleared away plant winter-flowering heathers (*Erica carnea*), winter-flowering pansies, variegated-leaved trailing ivies, dwarf conifers, polyanthus and small plants of *Euonymus* "Emerald 'n' Gold". Small bulbs, such as snowdrops, crocus, dwarf irises, *Anemone blanda*, dwarf tulips and eranthis (winter aconites), will all provide winter and early spring colour.

Attracting butterflies ❧

"I want to grow plants that are attractive to butterflies. Could you give me the names of suitable kinds?"

Plants that attract butterflies include:
SHRUBS: buddlejas, lavenders, caryopteris, syringa and hebe.
PERENNIALS: scabious, coreopsis, nepeta, sedum, mentha, erigeron, centranthus, armeria, solidago.
ANNUALS: sweet alyssum, marigolds and candytuft.
   If you have a pond, water mint is most attractive to butterflies, as are dandelions and other similar-looking yellow flowers.

Plants beside the sea ❧

"I live near the sea and need advice on what to grow. Can you name some hardy perennial plants that like seaside conditions?"

Plants that normally do well near the sea include: fuchsias, hydrangeas, santolina, escallonia, lavenders, *Potentilla fruticosa, Artemisia* "Powis

Castle", nerines, penstemons, romneya, schizostylis, geraniums, kniphofia, alstroemeria, agapanthus and dianthus.

Shaded site ❦

"The site I have chosen for my herb garden is a little shaded, although the soil is reasonably moist and fertile. Which herbs would do best growing in such a situation?"

As the site is moist and not too shaded, any of the various mints (mentha) will flourish, while parsley and chervil will both grow better in partial shade in the summer.

Late summer scent ❦

"I have a sunny border and would like to grow shrubs in it. Can you suggest some that have scented flowers in late summer?"

There are a few fragrant late-summer flowering shrubs that you could plant in a sunny border. Some you might like to try include: *Elaeagnus pungens* "Maculata", *Itea illicifolia*, escallonia, *Romneya coulteri* (California tree poppy) and roses, in particular the highly perfumed old-fashioned types like the damask roses.

Dry plants ❦

"As my soil gets very dry in the summer and because of water restrictions I plan to grow only plants that will tolerate dry conditions. Can you make any suggestions?"

Shrubs and perennials that will tolerate dry soil conditions include: penstemons, cistus, phormiums, helianthemum, *Alchemilla mollis,* hypericums, alliums, hebes, perovskia, phlomis, sedums, bergenia, santolina, dianthus, eryngiums and irises.

Streamside plants ❦

"I have a small stream running through my garden and I would like to put some plants along its bank. Can you give me the names of some suitable kinds?"

Plants that like to be grown in damp ground beside a pool or stream include: *Acorus gramineus variegatus*, dwarf Japanese rush; *Houttuynia cordata, Iris sibirica, Primula japonica, Calla palustris, Caltha palustris*

"Plena", *Butomus umbellatus, Mimulus luteus, Scirpus zebrinus* and *Lobelia cardinalis.*

Plants for a ditch

"There is a ditch in my garden where the soil is always moist. Are there any plants that would like this moist soil? Last year I saw some plants that had bright yellow flowers similar to an arum lily growing at the edge of a pool. Could I grow these and what is their correct name?"

If you saw the yellow, arum-like flowers in early spring, they are most probably the skunk cabbage, *Lysichiton americanus.* They are very showy plants in the spring and make very large leaves in the summer. They flourish at the edge of pools and streams and should be ideal on the banks of your ditch.

Other plants that you could grow in the moist soil include astilbes, primulas, *Iris sibirica, I. kaempferi, Gunnera manicata* (giant rhubarb) if you have space, arum lilies (zantedeschia), rodgersias, mimulus and trollius.

Plants for a hot spot

"I have a bed in front of my house which faces south. It becomes hot in the summer and the soil soon dries out. What low-growing plants would you recommend for this position?"

The helianthemums or sun roses would be ideal for your sunny border. They are low growing and are available in many colours. Others that you could grow are: cerastium or snow in summer, iberis, hardy geraniums, *Anthemis nobilis,* chamomile, armeria, dianthus, *Chrysanthemum hosmariense, Genista sagittalis, Lychnis viscaria,* aethionema and dwarf achilleas.

Lime carpeters

"I want to grow some low-growing perennials for carpeting a border in my garden. The soil contains lime. What would you recommend?"

Suitable low-growing perennials you might like to try on your chalky soil include: varieties of bugle (*Ajuga reptans*), such as "Burgundy Glow", *Alyssum saxatile,* arabis, aubrieta, campanulas, such as *C. carpatica,* convallaria (lily-of-the-valley), lamiums (deadnettles), nepeta (catmint), *Hypericum calycinum,* geraniums, helianthemums and *Polygonum vacciniifolium.*

Seasonal shrubs ❧

"My garden is not very colourful at the moment and I would like to improve the situation by planting some winter-flowering shrubs."

There are many winter-flowering shrubs that you could grow. These include: *Viburnum tinus* "Eve Price", tough evergreen with pink flowers; *Viburnum x bodnantense* "Dawn", pink flowers on bare stems; *Sarcococca confusa*, evergreen with small, cream, scented flowers; *Lonicera* x *purpusii*, shrubby honeysuckle with scented flowers; *Hamamelis mollis*, yellow flowers; *Jasminum nudiflorum*, winter jasmine, yellow flowers; *Erica carnea* varieties, winter-flowering heathers; and *Abeliophylium distichum*, which has white flowers.

Low-level shrubs ❧

"I have a bed which has been cleared of weeds. Good quantities of home-made compost have been incorporated into the border. I want to plant low-growing shrubs in it this autumn. What would you recommend?"

The following shrubs will colour your border for most of the year: *Ceanothus* "Blue Mound", *Ceratostigma* "Forest Blue", *Cistus* "Sunset", *Cytisus ardoi-noi, Escallonia laevis* "Gold Brian", hardy fuchsias, *Genista pilosa* "Vancouver Gold", *Hydrangea* "Forever Pink", *Hebe* "Rosie", *Lavandula* "Blue Cushion", *Potentilla* "Goldstar", *Philadelphus* "Manteau d'Hermine", *Rosmarinus* "McConnell's Blue", *Syringa patula* "Miss Kim" and *Viburnum davidii*.

Let it grow! ❧

"I want to plant a border with low-growing plants to carpet the ground so that little maintenance is needed. Can you recommend suitable plants for the situation?"

Suitable low-growing plants for your border include: *Pachysandra termi-nalis* "Variegata" (*Hypericum calycinum, Erica carnea*), winter-flowering heathers, ajugas, *Cotoneaster dammeri, Lamium maculatum, Polygonum affine, Stachys olympica* "Silver Carpet", *Alchemilla mollis*, bergenias and *Juniperus horizontalis*.

Seaside screen ❧

"I have a flat with a terrace and stunning views over Hastings. The view is partly obscured by a block of flats. What can I grow to screen the flats?"

One way of screening the flats is to fix trellis to the parapet wall of your terrace and grow climbers on it. Or you could grow large shrubs in containers standing on the terrace. Suitable shrubs to try are: *Griselinia littoralis*, an attractive evergreen; *Olearia macrodonta*, evergreen with white daisy flowers; phormium, foliage shrubs; escallonias, evergreen, pink or red flowers; *Berberis darwinii*, evergreen, yellow flowers; *Ceanothus dentatus*, evergreen, blue flowers; and *Hydrangea* "Blue Wave".

Climbers for the trellis include *Campsis radicans*, vigorous, yellow flower in August; *Solanum crispum* "Glasnevin", blue flowers; *Lonicera japonica* "Halliana", yellow honeysuckle; *Passiflora caerulea*, blue passion-flower; and *Polygonum baldschuanicum*, "Russian vine", vigorous, masses of white dainty flowers.

Brew up ❧

"We have recently dug a very large boulder out of our garden and would like to have moss growing on it. Is there a preparation to encourage this? I believe we could put a mixture of milk and yoghurt over the surface."

To encourage a green covering to develop on your boulder, we suggest that you make up a strong brew of grass cuttings in water. Suspend a sack of fresh grass cuttings in a tank of water and leave it for a few days. Paint the green liquid produced over the surface of the boulder. Moss will eventually colonize the surface.

Fungi siege ❧

"We have discovered a weird white mould on some shepherd's purse weeds at the edge of our vegetable garden. The plants are distorted and thickly coated with a white deposit; it looks too thick for mildew. Will this spread to cabbages and other brassicas, or is it a good thing to encourage as a natural weed-control method?"

The strange coating on the plants is a complex of two different fungi, both plant diseases in their own right. Downy mildew (*Peronospora parasitica*) and white blister (*Albugo candida*) are the two fungi involved. It would be safer to weed out the shepherd's purse in this case.

Wicked weed ❧

"For several years, one of the beds in my garden has been infested with a fast-spreading weed. Weedkillers and digging are only short-term solutions. Would 2–3 in. (5–7 cm) of bark chips smother the weed?"

Your weed is ground elder, *Aegopodium podagraria*, which spreads by underground stems. One of the best ways of controlling it is to spray the foliage with glyphosate weedkiller between mid-June and mid-August. Glyphosate is the active ingredient in Tumbleweed, Roundup GC and Tough Weed. If the weed occurs among plants, try using Tumbleweed Gel, Tough Weed Gun or Roundup ready-to-use spray. It may be necessary to repeat the application of weedkiller if there is regrowth.

Unfortunately, a bark mulch will not stop ground elder, although it may make it easier to pull out if it roots into the loose surface layer.

Tropical effect ❧

"We have a glass, conservatory-type, swimming pool enclosure. I wish to fill it with tropical-looking plants. It is not heated but is ventilated. Can you suggest suitable plants?"

You will need to provide a minimum temperature of 10°C to be able to grow tropical plants. If you cannot do this, you could try hardy plants with a tropical appearance. Suggestions of plants to grow in a minimum temperature of 10°C are: citrus, *Cordyline australis*, strelitzia and *Yucca aloifolia*.

Hardier plants that will tolerate the winter cold include various bamboos, camellias, *Clivia miniata*, *Fatsia japonica* and *Crinum* x *powellii*.

Hypertufa blocks ❧

"Can you give me a recipe for making tufa cement blocks for a rock garden?"

The standard recipe for the hypertufa mix is as follows: 2 parts (by volume) moistened, sifted, sphagnum moss peat, 1 part coarse sand or fine flint grit, 1 part cement. Mix the ingredients thoroughly whilst dry and then add water, mixing all the time until the mixture is a consistency that can be cast into blocks.

This mixture can also be used for covering old, glazed, kitchen sinks to make an alpine or miniature garden. The sinks must be cleaned thoroughly and the glaze on the exterior chipped to aid adhesion. Just prior to applying the mixture, the chipped, glazed surfaces should be treated with Unibond which helps good adhesion.

Keeping roots at bay ❧

"I have a bay tree in my garden very close to two houses and a main drain. The tree is 20 ft (6 m) high. Could it damage the drain?"

It is never wise to grow large trees, particularly those with fibrous roots, such as willow and poplar, closer than 60 ft (18 m) from a house, otherwise roots may infiltrate and block drainage systems or damage foundations.

If this bay tree is growing very close to the house, it would be wise to remove it. If your soil is clay, consult a surveyor as the tree's removal may cause the ground to swell with moisture – a condition known as "heave" – which can damage house foundations.

A moving time for plants ❧

"Within the next few weeks we are moving house and I want to take some of the plants in the garden with me. What is the best way of transporting them to their new home?"

Elderly and well established trees and shrubs are not likely to move very well and you should leave them behind.

Most perennials should move satisfactorily: large clumps can be split into smaller portions. Plant them in boxes and pots filled with moist compost and, as soon as you can, replant them in the new garden and keep them well watered to get them well established.

Painting climbers ❧

"We have painted three walls of our cottage but the fourth is covered with climbers. How do we set about painting this wall? Do we have to cut the whole lot down?"

There is no need to cut back the plants. If you simply remove the ties, the shoots will fall away or can be prised away to allow you to work behind them. If the wall is damp apply a waterproof sealant before painting it.

First in, last out ❧

"I want to grow wallflowers and tulips together in a bed in my front garden. Which should be planted first, the wallflowers or the tulip bulbs?"

Plant your wallflowers first spacing them about 12 in. (30cm) apart. Afterwards place the tulip bulbs on the soil among the wallflowers so that they are evenly spaced out. Then plant immediately, using a trowel.

Good drainage is essential ❧

"I have bought an ornamental container in which I want to grow plants on my patio. There is no drainage hole in the base of it. Does this really matter?"

Yes, it does matter. Unless surplus water can drain away from the container the compost will become waterlogged and stagnant and the plants will fail. Could you drill holes in the base to allow water to escape? If you can do this, cover the holes with broken pots or rubble before adding a suitable compost in which to grow the plants.

That sinking feeling ❧

"We have bought a bungalow with a large garden for our retirement. At the moment it is all lawn but it is very wet. As you walk on it you sink down 3–4 in. (7–10 cm). Never having had a garden, we are starting from scratch. How can we get rid of all this water?"

The only way to get rid of the water is to lay drains. Dig a network of interlinking trenches 18 in. (45 cm) deep and 6 ft (1.8 m) apart. Lay tile drains, butting them together, along the base. Cover them with 6–9 in. (15–23 cm) of gravel. Direct the trenches, via a main trench, to a 6 ft (1.8 m) square and deep soakaway filled with bricks and rubble.

The long and the short of it ❧

"I have usually used a long stake when planting a new tree but I now see that short stakes are being used. Which is to be preferred?"

Traditionally, newly planted trees are given a long stake up to the crown of the tree. However, short stakes are often preferred these days as this allows some movement of the main stem without disturbing the root system. Both types of stake need to be put in position before planting, the stakes being inserted about 2 ft (60 cm) into the ground. Use rubber or buckle and spacer ties to support the main stem of the tree on the stake.

Holiday problem ❧

"I have a number of containers filled with plants on my patio. They need regular watering and I am wondering what is the best way to look after them whilst I am away on holiday in July. Have you any suggestions?"

Holiday watering is always a problem. The best solution is to ask a neighbour or friend to do the watering for you. Alternatively, invest in an automatic watering system so that small dripper tubes, connected to a main 12 mm tube, are led to individual containers. The drippers can be set to supply the right amount of water for each container.

An ill wind ❦

"We live on the coast, about half a mile inland and on a hill. Our property is surrounded by hedges and trees, planted mainly on a slope. Our concern is for an 18 ft (5.4 m) bay tree. One of its branches is bending in the wind and we are concerned that it will loosen the whole tree. Would a bay tree stand having the branches cut back by about one third and when would be the best time to prune?"

It would be a good idea to prune it as you suggest, removing about one third of its growth. Do this in May when the sap is rising and when the wounds heal quickly. New young shoots should appear soon. There is no need to paint the wounds as they heal much better if left exposed to the elements.

To fill or not to fill? ❦

"On a recent visit to Cambridge Botanic Gardens I saw a tree with a cavity in the trunk that had been very neatly bricked up. In a park not too far from my home there are several hollow trees but they are all left hollow. Would they be better if the hollows were bricked up?"

The modern method is to leave hollows empty. Any diseased wood is cut away to leave clean, healthy tissue, but the tree is then left to heal itself. Trials have shown that healing is generally better where no filling or wound painting is carried out, although if the hollow goes down inside the trunk a drainage hole may be drilled and perhaps a pipe fitted to drain the cavity.

Making a bog garden ❦

"I would like to make a small bog garden, about 6 ft (1.8 m) by 8 ft (2.4 m) but I am not sure how to set about it."

There is a very good description of making a bog garden in Dr Hessayon's *The Rock and Water Garden Expert*, available from most garden centres for about £5.

The important points are to use a butyl rubber liner set on top of 2 in. (5 cm) of sand and to make $\frac{1}{2}$ in. (5 cm) drainage holes in the liner, about 3 ft (90 cm) apart. Top the liner with a 2 in. (5 cm) layer of grit followed by a mix of 3 parts top soil, 3 parts peat and 1 part lime-free sharp sand. Ideally, make the hole about 18 in. (45 cm) deep.

Trees and shrubs

Small shrubs 🌿

"I have two small borders, one has a little early morning sun and the other is sunny for most of the day. Can you give me the names of small shrubs to plant in these borders?"

There are several small shrubs that you could plant in your two borders. If you choose a selection from each group they will provide you with colour at almost every season. All are suitable for both sun and shade except those marked, which only thrive in full sun. Our suggestions include:

SPRING: *Berberis buxifolia* "Nana", *Ceanothus thyrsiflorus* "Repens" (sun), *Cytisus x kewensis* (sun), *Skimmia japonica "Fragrans"*

SUMMER: *Caryopteris* x *clandonensis* (sun); *Cistus* x *crispus* "Sunset" (sun), *Fuchsia* "Tom Thumb", *Hebe* "Carl Teschner", *Potentilla fruticosa* "Red Ace"

AUTUMN: *Abelia chinensis*, *Ceratostigma willmottianum*, Cotoneaster conspicuus "Decorus", *Hypericum* x *moserianum "Tricolor"*, *Viburnum davidii*

WINTER: *Euonymus fortunei "Emerald Gaiety"*, *Mahonia aquifolium*; *Pachysandra terminalis*, *Sarcococca humilis* and *Ruscus aculeatus*.

Preserving leaves 🌿

"I would like to preserve some elaeagnus leaves in glycerine. Do I stand the stems in pure glycerine or should it be diluted in water?"

The glycerine should be diluted in water at the rate of one part glycerine to two parts water. Pour the glycerine into a bottle and add the water which should be warm. Shake it thoroughly and then pour it into a jar in which the stems will stand.

The bottom 2 in. (5 cm) of the stems should be placed in the mixture and left until traces of glycerine can be seen in the leaves.

Sturdy shrubs 🌿

"I have an east-facing wall immediately adjoining a public highway. What fast-growing and sturdy shrubs and roses would you recommend for this exposed position?"

Tough shrubs for the exposed border are *Mahonia japonica*, chaenomeles (flowering quince), *Euonymus fortunei, Viburnum opulus, Viburnum tinus, Berberis stenophylla, Berberis thunbergii* "Atropurpurea", *Mahonia japonica, Kerria japonica, Rosa rugosa* and pyracanthas. Pyracanthas are particularly good as they are evergreen, have white flowers in spring and masses of orange or red berries in autumn.

Climbers that you could train on the wall include: *Jasminum nudiflorum*, winter jasmine and variegated-leaved ivies such as "Goldheart" and "Sulphur Heart", also known as "Paddy's Pride".

Large hole for shrubs but small root ball!

Shrubs from seed ❧

"I would like to raise some shrubs from seed. Can you suggest plants that I can try?"

Shrubs that you could try raising from seed sown in spring include: acers, berberis, pyracantha, cotoneaster, potentilla, spartium, genista, hypericum, lavender, symphoricarpos, cistus and chaenomeles.

Shrub pruning ❧

"When and how much can we prune large hebe bushes and what can we do with an enormous tangle of Solanum jasminoides*?"*

Hebes can be cut back hard without doing harm. New growth will grow out from mature stems. The best time to prune is in spring. *Solanum jasminoides* can be treated in the same way, removing weak, congested stems and cutting back straggly growth in spring.

Seasonal berries ❧

"Can you give me the names of some shrubs that have colourful berries in the autumn?"

There are a great many shrubs with colourful berries. Some of the cotoneasters are outstanding. *C. horizontalis* is semi-evergreen and has flat branches covered in red berries. A good variety is "John Waterer" which makes a large shrub and also has red berries.

There are several pyracanthas or firethorns with red, orange or yellow berries; they are tough, evergreen shrubs.

Hollies are also outstanding evergreens. One of the best berrying kinds is "J. C. van Tol", self-fertile with bright red berries. *Ilex* "Bacciflava" has yellow berries.

One of the few shrubs with blue berries is *Viburnum davidii*. It is evergreen, but male and female plants must be grown together for berries to develop.

Moving times ahead ❧

"Please tell me if and when I can move, replant and trim back mock orange, forsythia and common holly."

The winter months, when everything is dormant, is the best time to replant your shrubs. If they are large specimens then, inevitably, there will be some root damage. If we get a cold winter you may find that they do not recover all that well in the following spring. Your philadelphus (mock orange) should be pruned after flowering.

Winter flowers ❧

"Could you give me the names of some shrubs that flower in the winter?"

Good winter-flowering shrubs include: mahonias, *Lonicera purpusii* (shrubby honeysuckle), *Erica carnea* varieties (winter-flowering heathers), *Hamamelis mollis* (witch hazel), *Garrya elliptica*, *Abeliophyllum distichum*, *Viburnum bonantense* and *Jasminum nudiflorum*.

Large shrubs for a bare plot

"I have recently moved house and the garden is almost bare with a wooden fence all round the perimeter. What large shrubs could I plant to provide some privacy?"

Large, evergreen shrubs for your garden could include: *Aucuba japonica*, *Berberis linearifolia* "Orange King"; *Camellia japonica* (but only on acid soils), *Choisya ternata*, *Cotoneaster lacteus*, *Elaeagnus* x *ebbingei*, *Eleaegnus pungens* "Maculata", escallonia, *Fatsia japonica*, *Garrya elliptica*, *Kalmia latifolia* (again only for acid soils), *Mahonia* "Charity", *Osmanthus delavayi*, *Photinia* x *fraseri* "Red Robin", *Pieris japonica* (acid soils again), *Pyracantha* "Mohave", *Viburnum tinus* and *V. burkwoodii*.

Tub shrubs

"I want to grow a few shrubs having attractive foliage in ornamental containers. Can you give me the names of suitable kinds which I can grow?"

Shrubs having ornamental foliage and suitable for growing in containers include: *Aucuba japonica* "Picturata", *Fatsia japonica*, *Buxus sempervirens* (box), *Juniperus chinensis* "Pyramidalis", *Laurus nobilis* (bay) and *Euonymus fortunei* "Silver Queen".

In addition, some shrubs have attractive flowers apart from their foliage and you could consider *Yucca filamentosa*, *Hydrangea paniculata* "Grandiflora" and *Forsythia* "Lynwood".

Particular care must be taken with plants in containers during the summer as the compost can dry out rapidly. Watering may be necessary two or three times a day in hot, sunny weather.

Wind-blown

"I want to plant some small trees and shrubs in my front garden which is exposed to cold winds. What would you recommend?"

Suggestions of suitable trees and shrubs for your exposed garden are as follows. Trees – laburnum, *Crataegus prunifolia* and *Sorbus aucuparia* (rowan). Shrubs – *Cotoneaster salicifolius* "Pendulus", holly, philadelphus (mock orange), *Rhododendron ponticum* (needs acid soil) and *Viburnum lantana*.

Air layering   ❧

"I have been told that it is possible to root branches of shrubs above ground level. Can you tell me how this is done?"

Yes, it is possible to layer a wide range of shrubs above ground level. It is usually called air layering. Make a slanting cut, about 1 in. (2.5 cm) long, in the stem of a shrub. Keep it open with a matchstick and surround it with moist sphagnum moss. Enclose the moss with a piece of clear polythene and tie it firmly at either end with string or tape.

Keep a close watch on the layer, as after some weeks roots will form and they can be seen easily through the clear polythene. Once a good root system has been made, cut off the new plant just below the new roots. Remove the polythene and pot the plant in a good potting compost. Once the pot is full of roots, plant it in its permanent position.

Scorched plants   ❧

"Practically all the plants in the seaside garden that I care for, except hebes, irises and escallonia, fail to flower for very long and quickly turn brown. The leaves also turn a crispy brown. I suspect that the trouble lies in the soil. It is extremely chalky and seems to lack substance. How do I reverse the problem?"

We suspect that your plants are being damaged by salt spray from the sea, particularly as you say that hebes, escallonia and irises are not harmed. These are known to be tolerant of seaside conditions.

You should concentrate on plants that are happy near the sea such as sea buckthorn, *Hippophae rhamnoides*, tamarix, olearias, *Senecio laxifolius*, griselinia, *Genista hispanica*, elaeagnus, *Cotoneaster horizontalis*, helianthemum. Most dwarf kinds of annuals should succeed, as well as gazanias. So much depends on how much protection you are able to provide against salty winds. To improve the poor soil, add organic matter to it in the form of compost or farmyard manure. Each spring apply a general fertilizer and mulch the surface of the soil with bark fibre or compost to conserve moisture.

Contain your festivities ❧

"This year I have bought a Christmas tree with roots and planted it in a large tub. I want to keep it for several years. After Christmas, can I keep the tree in the tub outside or must it be planted out?"

Your Christmas tree can be left in its container, but make sure there are drainage holes in the base. Stand it outside as soon as the festivities are over. Next summer, keep it well watered and do not allow the soil to dry out, or the tree will suffer.

Feed it with a liquid fertilizer during the summer to encourage it to make good growth. Stop feeding after August.

Ornamental trees ❧

"I want to plant an easy-to-manage tree of modest proportions in my garden this winter. What would you recommend? Are there any with colourful berries or fruits?"

The following are suggested trees for your garden. *Malus* "Neville Copeman", pale purple flowers in spring with red fruits in the autumn; *Crataegus prunifolia*, white flowers in spring and brightly coloured leaves in autumn; *Pyrus salicifolia*, the weeping pear with attractive silvery grey leaves; *Sorbus aria* "Lutescens", attractive whitish leaves in spring; *Salix caprea* "Pendula", Kilmarnock willow, weeping form of the pussy willow; *Robinia pseudoacacia* "Frisia", bright yellow leaves; *Prunus cerasifera* "Pissardii", pale pink flowers, purple foliage; *Prunus padus*, bird cherry, distinctive white flower spikes in spring; *Cotoneaster* x *watereri* "Pendulus", weeping habit, bright red berries in autumn.

Indian bean tree ❧

"Could you give me the name of my tree from the leaf I am sending? I grew it from a packet of mixed seed and it has now grown 6 ft (1.8 m) tall."

The leaf that you sent was the Indian bean tree, *Catalpa bignonioides*. It is a hardy tree growing to a height of 20 ft (6 m). There are some handsome specimens beneath Big Ben on the approach to Westminster Bridge in London and it is commonly seen in parks and large gardens in southern England. When mature the tree produces showy, white flowers in the summer which are followed by long bean-like pods. The golden-leaved form, *C. aurea*, is particularly attractive.

Ornamental trees

"I want a small tree for my garden which has attractive flowers in spring and colourful fruits or berries in the autumn. What would you recommend? I do not want a flowering cherry."

Why not try one of the ornamental apples? *Malus floribunda* is a Japanese crab making a small tree with arching branches which are thickly covered in pale pink blossoms in the spring. Small red and yellow fruits form in the autumn. Some varieties have fruits which can be used for preserves. "Dartmouth" is a popular variety with dark red fruits in the autumn.

Other good small trees to consider include *Cotoneaster* "Hybridus Pendulus", semi-evergreen with bright red berries in autumn, and *Crataegus prunifolia* which has highly coloured leaves in autumn and colourful berries which last well into winter.

Root of the problem

"Beyond the boundary of our house and 40–60 ft (12–18 m) from the property are three mature willows growing beside a stream. I estimate that they are now 50–60 ft tall and were pollarded about three years ago. I am concerned about the potential structural damage to my property. Can you advise me?"

You have every right to be concerned about the three large willows 40–60 ft (12–18 m) from your house. Their roots could pose a threat to the foundations, particularly if you are on a predominantly clay soil.

It is certainly not wise to have willows or poplars closer than 60 ft (18 m) from buildings. Have the trees examined by a qualified tree surgeon or surveyor to ascertain their potential danger.

Insurance companies are becoming more concerned about the proximity of trees to buildings and, in some cases, may demand higher premiums.

Fruit trees?

"On some Christmas trees we have looked at, there were some pineapple-like growths near the shoot tips. My husband and I would be very interested to know what could have caused these odd growths to appear."

The growths were caused by the feeding of an aphid-like creature known as the spruce gall adelgids. As the insects feed, the tree responds by producing the galls you have seen. The tree continues to grow normally and the gall dries up and turns brown and hard. Damage can be quite severe in some years and can reduce the value of the plants when being grown for sale as Christmas trees.

Cherry and amber gum ❧

"I have an oldish cherry tree that has started to produce quite a lot of amber gum from the trunk. Is this a sign of anything serious or just the result of the tree ageing?"

A cherry tree will produce this amber-coloured gum in response to an injury it has sustained. This "injury" could be natural cracking of the bark, a sign of bacterial canker attack or boring by caterpillars of either the goat or leopard moth.

Examine around the site of where the gum is being produced, looking for any largish holes in the bark. These would indicate the presence of boring caterpillars and it may be possible to kill these within the trunk by poking in a piece of strong, flexible wire.

Bacterial canker attacks the wood itself and eats away to girdle round the branch bases. In this instance, the gumming itself is not harmful to the tree so need not be removed or treated.

Weeping pear ❧

"I have an old tree of Pyrus salicifolia 'Pendula' in my garden. It is very handsome but the stems are very congested. Should I prune the tree?"

The growth often becomes congested on old trees of the weeping pear, *Pyrus salicifolia* "Pendula". It would be a good idea to thin out some of the older stems in winter. First remove any dead wood and then thin out some of the older wood. The effect of the pruning will be to encourage strong new growth.

Spotty sycamores ❧

"I have several large sycamore trees in my garden and last year the leaves showed a lot of unsightly black spotting. Is there anything I could do to prevent this happening again?"

The damage is due to attack by the tar spot fungus, *Rhytisma acerinum*. The fungus spends the winter on fallen leaves, and then in spring spores are forcibly discharged from the spotted areas to infect the new growth. There are no practical control measures for the infection on the trees, but gathering up the fallen leaves in autumn or winter should reduce attacks to some extent. Although unsightly, the spotting appears to do little actual harm in terms of general growth.

Mulberry cuttings ❧

"Can I take a cutting from a mulberry tree and when is the best time to do it?"

Mulberries can be increased by taking hardwood cuttings of firm young shoots in the autumn. Take them about 9 in. (22 cm) long and insert them outside so that the top 2–3 in. (5–7.5 cm) is above soil level. Put coarse sand in the base of the planting holes to promote rooting. The cuttings should have rooted in 12 months' time when they can be lifted and planted in their permanent positions.

Betula poser ❧

"My husband discovered some very odd-looking caterpillars on one of our young silver birch trees. They were feeding around the leaf edges, but were all in a 'S' shape with their tails in the air. Please could you identify and suggest a means of control."

The insects are larvae of a sawfly, and they do seem to prefer to feed in the odd fashion you describe. The damage to individual leaves can be considerable, but to the tree as a whole it is doubtful if they have any great effect.

If a lot of the leaves of your young trees are being attacked, then a spray with Phostrogen Safer's insecticide, Picket or Polysect should clear up the problem.

Skinned alive ❧

"Please can you tell me what is eating the leaves of several of my apple, whitebeam, and hawthorn trees? Can you suggest control measures?"

The pest responsible for the damage is the apple leaf skeletonizer. You may have found that the caterpillars eat the surface tissue of the foliage, leaving behind just the network of veins.

If the trees are not too large to spray, an application of the biological control bacteria sold as Dipel would be effective. The pest is just between generations now, so delay the application until new damage is seen in August, and repeat the treatment at the first sign of attack next year, usually in May.

Oak apples ❧

"This isn't truly a garden problem, but on an old oak tree just outside our garden there have been masses of these swellings. Some neighbours say they are oak apples, others say that oak apples are round and smooth. These were almost 1 in. (2.5 cm) across and irregular. What are they please, and can they attack any garden plants?"

The galls you have seen are the true oak apples and the round, smooth ones are more correctly called marble galls. Both result from feeding by gall wasps, and they have a very complex life cycle. They only attack oak trees.

Oak Apple Day, on 26 May, is at a time when new galls are at their best, and commemorates the return of King Charles II.

Change of habit ❧

"Six years ago we purchased a Betula pendula *'Tristis', expecting it to have pendulous branches with an upright leader. The tree has now grown to approximately 15 ft (5 m) but during the last 12 months the upright leader has drooped and become pendulous like the other branches. Is there any way in which we can correct this fault or do we, in fact, have a different variety?"*

Provided the tree is growing well and is in good health, it will soon produce a new upright stem or leader. This should break from the base of the old leader that has now become pendulous.

Take care with tree ties ❧

"A five-year-old alder tree in my new garden started to die off. An examination revealed that the main trunk had once been tied to a stake with polypropylene binder twine. This had resisted any rotting and had grown into the trunk, eventually cutting off the supply of water and nutrients to the top. What would you advise as the best material to use to tie up tree trunks?"

The best is undoubtedly the special tree ties, made from thick plastic or rubber. These are clearly visible, and include a method of increasing the size to allow for later trunk growth. Several types can be found in most garden centres.

Stumped for an answer

"I have an unsightly tree stump in the middle of my front garden. It has been cut a few inches above the ground and I would like to level it below the ground. How do I do this?"

Rather than use chemicals, such as ammonium sulphamate (Amcide) or saltpetre, to decompose the stump slowly, it would be better to use a professional stump grinder operator who will pulverize it, and the roots, with a machine in a short time. Your local hire shop will be able to help or you may find an arboricultural firm advertising in your local paper.

Timber!

"Whenever I cut a branch from a tree, the weight of the falling limb invariably tears away the bark lower down. How can I avoid this happening in the future?"

To overcome this pruning problem, always undercut the branch first. Make a cut with a sharp saw on the underside of the branch about 1 ft (30 cm) from the main trunk. Then, a little further out make a cut from above, right through the branch. This leaves a stub which can be cut off cleanly by first undercutting it and then sawing from above.

Without undercutting, the weight of the falling branch will tear the bark close to the main trunk.

Aspen invasion

"We returned from holiday to find our lawn plastered with sucker growths from our aspen tree. The furthest suckers were over 48 ft (16 m) away from the actual tree. Is there any way we can control these without damaging the tree or the lawn or, alternatively, can we spray the suckers and hope also to kill the tree?"

It is too late to apply any weedkiller to the suckers and digging or tearing them out is all that can be done now, although it is unlikely to be effective in the long run. When new sucker growth starts in spring spray with a brushwood or nettle killer as this will not damage the lawn.

Glyphosate may be effective in killing the main tree if there is enough leaf area relative to the tree size. Autumn would be the best time as the main sap movement would be downwards. This would also kill any grass hit by the spray, so protect it as far as possible. The weedkiller is deactivated by the soil, however, so any bare patches should be resown immediately.

Magnolia seed ❧

"We have a 25-year-old magnolia. Last autumn we noticed a cluster of pink lumps on one of the branches. Inside one we found some seeds."

Magnolias often produce seed pods, and it is worth sowing the seed if you want some more plants.

Wash off the sticky mass surrounding the seeds and sow them now in a small pot filled with seed compost. Stand the pot in a cold frame or greenhouse. The seeds may take 12–18 months to germinate, but when seedlings appear pot them individually in small pots. When they are large enough plant them outside.

Root pruning potted acer ❧

"I have an Acer palmatum *'Dissectum Atropurpureum' growing in a large pot but the roots are becoming too big for it. I would like to keep the acer in the same container, so can I prune the roots, and if so, when?"*

Do not prune the roots of your acer too severely as you may harm the plant. During the winter remove the acer from its pot and carefully tease out some of the old compost from among the roots. Retain all the fibrous roots and only shorten the thick, coarse ones. Return the plant to its pot, making sure that there is drainage material in the base. Add fresh potting compost, to replace the soil that was removed, and firm it well.

Acers can remain in the same pot for a number of years provided they are watered well in the summer and fed regularly in the spring and early summer.

Silver birch scourge ❧

"Why is it that so many silver birch trees seem to die and then snap off around 9 ft (2.7 m) or so from the ground? A lot of the trees around here seem to do this, and I am concerned that the same fate awaits my lovely Jacquemontii birch."

Birch trees "in the wild" are often attacked by the bracket fungus, *Piptoporus betulinus*, which causes a reddish rot of the wood, followed by the typical bracket-like fruiting bodies. Infected trees, as you have observed, do often snap off at a height of around 9 ft (2.7 m). It is unlikely that your tree would be attacked.

Witches' broom 🌞

"In our newly acquired garden there is a very old cherry tree. Up in the branches are some clusters of twigs which we thought were nests but now we find they are made of lots of little shoots all growing close together."

The shoots are making up what is generally referred to as a witch's broom. The growths generally arise following invasion by a fungus; one that is quite closely related to peach leaf curl.

No particular harm is done to the tree, but if they can be reached, the growths could be cut out. Do this in early summer to avoid any chance of silver leaf infection getting into the cuts.

Robinia in trouble 🌞

"The top of our young Robinia tree has died out and now there are small red lumps developing on the wood. Does this mean the whole tree will die, or is there some treatment we could give it?"

The red outgrowths are fruiting bodies of the coral spot fungus. This normally only attacks dead or dying tissue, so there would appear to be some underlying ill health associated with your robinia.

Cut out the dead wood and in spring apply a general, or a rose, fertilizer to the soil around the tree. With luck, the roots will still be healthy and new shoots will develop, one of which could be trained up to provide a replacement main trunk.

A few sprays of Supercarb may assist to ward off any latent coral spot infection.

Strange acorns 🌞

"Can you tell me why my acorn cups are so deformed? They don't seem to have proper acorns inside."

The distortion of the acorn cups is due to attack by a small gall wasp. This particular type of attack was first seen in south-west England in the early 1960s and it has spread quite widely.

The wasp lays her eggs in the flower buds in spring and the larval feeding causes the galling around the acorn. No control measures are possible, other than gathering up and destroying as many affected acorns as possible. Germination of infested acorns appears to be affected and there could be a serious threat to the British oak seed bank in future years. Squirrels, bank voles and badgers normally eat a lot of acorns as part of their autumn diet, so they could also be affected.

No berries ❧

"I have a 'Silver Milkboy' holly but it does not produce berries. Can you tell me why?"

The holly that was once known as "Silver Milkboy" is now known as "Silver Milkmaid" because it was found that it had female flowers.

If your plant flowers in the spring it is possible that it needs a male holly nearby for it to produce berries. If you have space, plant a male holly, such as "Silver Queen", "Golden Milkboy" or "Handsworthensis".

Lumpy lime leaves ❧

"I have recently come across a lime tree with odd-looking red 'spikes' growing out of the leaves. Can you tell me what causes these odd growths?"

The red growths are caused by feeding by the lime nail gall mite. The mites start feeding in May, and by June the odd-looking galls are developing, sometimes pale yellow, sometimes green and sometimes brown or red. The feeding appears not to interfere with growth of the lime tree.

Tree roots ❧

"I planted a eucalyptus tree in a piece of land 4 ft (1.25 m) from a path and a road. I am told that the roots will penetrate the road and cause it to crack. What should I do?"

Eucalyptus trees grow fast and develop an extensive root system which grows downwards and outwards. Inevitably, as the tree was planted just 4 ft (1.2 m) from a road, its roots will, in time, spread beneath it and may crack its surface. It is never wise to plant large trees close to a house, path or road, for almost certainly their roots will have a detrimental effect upon it.

Tree growths ❧

"On a recent Scottish holiday I came across a tree (which I couldn't identify) with lots and lots of odd growths on the trunks. Is it possible to tell what has caused them?"

Growths on tree trunks are variously referred to as galls, burrs or tumours. They can develop from a wide range of stimuli, including fungal or bacterial infection, insect or mite attack, or they can be composed of masses of vestigial roots or shoots. Generally trees are not particularly "put out" by these growths, and they can be very useful, for furniture-making or wood-turning, should the tree eventually be felled.

Wanted . . . small garden tree

"I want to plant a small tree in my garden. Can you tell me anything about Crataegus prunifolia? *How tall does it grow?"*

Crataegus prunifolia is an excellent small deciduous tree, particularly noted for its glorious autumn colours and colourful berries. It eventually grows 15–18 ft (4.5–5.4 m) tall. It will succeed in most soils provided they are well drained.

Black holly

"My variegated holly tree leaves have a black deposit on them. What is it?"

The deposit is of sooty moulds and these are living on sugary honeydew being produced by scale insects feeding under the leaves. If the tree is not too tall, spray with Sybol or Tumblebug to kill the scale insects and that will stop the honeydew production. The moulds will run out of their food supplies and after a month or two it should be possible to dislodge them with a forceful jet of water.

Strawberry tree

"I would like to grow a strawberry tree. Will it tolerate strong winds from the sea? Are the fruits edible?"

The strawberry tree, *Arbutus unedo*, is an evergreen that stands up well to coastal conditions. The fruits are edible but not very palatable.

Loquat leaf

"Could you identify the leaf I have sent? I think it is one of the evergreen magnolias. It is from a medium-size tree which produced goblet-shaped flowers last spring in a garden in Hampshire."

The leaf you sent is from a loquat tree, *Eriobotrya japonica*. It is a Mediterranean plant and flowers only after a very warm summer, usually from mid-autumn to early spring. Occasionally, it produces globular, pear-shaped fruits which are edible. The fruits of commerce are imported from warmer countries.

Corkscrew hazel ❧

"A friend has a nut bush in her garden. Some of the stems are twisted and distorted and others are straight and normal. Why are these stems twisted?"

Your friend has a bush of the corkscrew hazel, *Coryllus avellana* "Contorta", which is also known as Harry Lauder's walking stick because the stems are twisted and contorted. This is a curiosity and is usually grafted on common hazel which produces normal, straight growths. This is why you have both types of growth on one bush.

To retain the corkscrew growths pull out the straight, normal growths which arise from the base of the bush. Tear them from their point of origin to remove dormant buds. Do not cut them off with secateurs as this will encourage even more sucker growths.

Wanted . . . white silver birch ❧

"I would like to grow a small group of silver birches at the end of my garden. I want trees with really white stems and I understand that there are special varieties noted for their white bark."

There are several different forms of silver birch which have beautiful white stems. We can recommend: *Betula utilis jacqemontii*, "Jermyns" and "Silver Shadow"; *B. ermanii*, which has creamy white and pink bark; *B. papyrifera commutata* and *B. szechuanica* which has blue-green leaves.

Large magnolia ❧

"I planted a Magnolia 'Exmouth' about five years ago. It is now about 9 ft (2.75 m) high and has had several flowers. Having a very small garden I am concerned as to how tall the plant will grow."

Magnolia "Exmouth" can grow very large – up to 30 ft (9 m) or more in a favourable situation, so you will have to curb the enthusiasm of your plant by restricting root growth. Take out a deep trench around its root system and insert bricks or paving slabs to thwart further outward growth. With luck this should ensure more compact growth without affecting its flowering.

Hazel nut horror ❧

"We managed to beat the squirrels to our hazelnuts this autumn, hoping for a Christmas treat, but trying a few we found a number of the shells contained a little white, legless grub and not much nut! What was the pest and how did it get into the apparently sound nuts?"

The nuts have been attacked by the nut weevil. Eggs are laid on the young nuts in June, whilst the shells are still soft. The grubs feed on the developing kernel and normally then eat their way out through the shell to overwinter in the soil, pupating in spring. By harvesting your hazel nuts early, to beat the squirrels, the nuts still contained the weevil grubs.

Cultivating the soil around the bushes during winter will, with luck, disturb and kill any overwintering weevil grubs.

What a swell burr ❧

"Can you tell me what causes the swellings or burrs that appear on tree trunks from time to time? I use some of them in my wood turning and have never seen any explanation."

Tree swellings and other outgrowths are often caused by fungi or bacteria, and sometimes by insects, but the burr knots of apples and some other trees are groups of root initials and associated callus production. Other burrs are caused by groups of shoots all fused together, but what causes this to occur is still largely unexplained at present.

As a wood turner you will know that some burrs can be very useful in carpentry for turning and for veneer work.

Tree suckers ❧

"We have recently moved and have inherited a badly neglected garden. We have a particular problem with the roots of a tree which are producing suckers all over the lawn. How can we eradicate them?"

Several trees are rather prone to suckering, particularly after pruning or wind damage. It is not possible to apply chemicals to the suckers without harming the tree, so the suckers must be disconnected from the tree first. Sever the root between the tree and the sucker and then use a herbicide on the sucker.

Once a tree starts producing numerous suckers, it is virtually impossible to keep up with them all, and usually the only long-term solution is to remove the tree. Once it has been felled, the stump can be treated with a specially formulated herbicide to prevent further suckering. Individual suckers can be treated with Root Out, but be careful to follow the manufacturer's recommendations when applying it as the chemical is not selective and will kill grass and other plants that come into contact with it. Root Out is residual in the soil for around six months, after which replanting or reseeding can take place.

Azalea types ⠬

"There seems to be a confusing number of azalea types. Can you tell me the differences between Indian azaleas, Kurume azaleas and Knap Hill azaleas?"

Botanically, they are all rhododendrons. Indian azaleas are evergreen with small leaves and are usually grown as pot plants for indoor decoration. The Kurume azaleas came from Japan in the last century. They are evergreen and make low mounds of small leaves, covered in small, brightly coloured flowers in the spring. They can be seen at their best in massed plantings at the RHS's Garden, Wisley and in the Valley gardens at Windsor.

The Knap Hill azaleas are deciduous and have large, colourful flowers in spring. They were raised originally at the Knap Hill Nursery, Woking, Surrey.

Keeping problems at bay ⠬

"Last autumn, my 10 ft high bay tree, growing amongst rhododendrons and azaleas, started to develop a yellowing of the leaves. Starting with a paleness at the leaf edges, gradually the whole leaf turned yellow and then fell.

Looking in various books, it seems to match every nutrient deficiency condition known to man."

There may be a small amount of leaf spot fungus present, but the yellowing almost certainly started with dryness at the roots in the autumn. Softer-leaved plants are able to wilt under drought conditions, but hard-leaved subjects, such as bay, tend to suffer more severely.

Normal growth should resume as the warmer weather arrives and this can be helped along by an application of a general fertilizer, or of a rose food, followed by a few sprays over the leaves with Phostrogen.

Holey help ⠬

"My young aspen tree leaves are becoming full of holes and looking very tatty. What would be responsible for this, and can it be treated?"

Capsid bug is the responsible insect. Typically, these feed first on shrubs and trees, where they have possibly spent the winter in the egg stage, and then move on to herbaceous plants for the summer months.

Further damage can be prevented by spraying the leaves with Picket, Tumblebug or Long-Last.

No flowers ❧

"I have a five-year-old Azalea pontica growing in ericaceous compost in a very large tub. Normally, it flowers well but no flowers appeared this year. It is, however, making large quantities of leaves. Can you tell me why it does not flower?"

As your azalea is making so much growth you may be feeding it too much, making growth at the expense of the flowers. Try giving it some sulphate of potash to encourage more sturdy growth.

Monkey puzzler ❧

"I have collected seeds from a monkey puzzle tree. How and when do I plant them?"

Encourage your monkey puzzle (araucaria) seeds to germinate by placing them in a small pot filled with coarse sand. Stand it outside to allow the seed to become chilled, covering the pot with wire netting to deter mice eating the seed. In March or April sow the seed in warmth in a pot filled with a seed compost. The seeds will take several weeks to appear.

On the move ❧

"I have a large azalea which has been in the same place for a number of years but now has to be moved. When is the best time to move it and should I give it any special feed?"

Deciduous azaleas should be moved only when they are completely dormant between November and early March. Transplanting in November is often the most successful time because the warmth of the soil helps the roots to settle down before the advent of cold weather.

Evergreen azaleas are best moved in April–May or September–October.

Transplanting in the autumn is particularly recommended if your plant normally flowers profusely in the spring. In both cases, fork lime-free compost into the new site before planting. Alternatively, incorporate leafmould, coir, spent hops or bark fibre into the soil. Move the azalea with as large a root ball as possible. After transplanting, mulch the soil around the plant with a thick layer of compost or other form of organic matter to help conserve soil moisture.

Monkey puzzle

"We have just moved house and have a smallish garden in which there are several shrubs and a splendid monkey puzzle tree. Could you please tell me how quickly these trees grow? It is now about 15 ft (4.5 m) tall and, as far as we can ascertain, was planted sometime over the last 12 years. At the moment it looks attractive but I believe it can grow rather large."

Monkey puzzles, *Araucaria araucana*, are interesting trees introduced to this country from South America in 1795. The oldest trees in this country have attained a height of 80 ft (24 m) after nearly 100 years. The rate of growth does greatly depend on the local climate and growth is usually more rapid in mild, moist areas. However, you can expect your araucaria to put on about 9 in. (23 cm) of growth in a average season.

Although monkey puzzles are attractive in their early years they are not really suitable for small gardens.

Curious caterpillar

"I found an odd-looking caterpillar on my alder; with its big black eyes and hairy body my son said it looks like Dougal from the Magic Roundabout!*"*

This is the caterpillar of the lackey moth. The eyes are actually blue and the black spots are to frighten off predators. The moth lays its eggs in dense bands on a range of trees, including apples, and the caterpillars feed in large colonies under a protective tent of silken webbing.

Snowy Mespilus

"I was given a young snowy mespilus sapling in 1987. It is now a beautiful tree about 10 ft (3 m) tall. My worry is that the main trunk or stem is only 3–4 ft (0.9–1.2 m) from a bay window. Should I prune it? If so, when is the best time to do it?"

Although the snowy mespilus, *Amelanchier lamarckii* will stand pruning in the spring after flowering, we do not think that this would solve your problem. The tree can grow up to 20–25 ft (6–7.5 m) tall and you have planted it far too close to your house. If there are sucker growths coming from the base of the tree, we suggest that you remove rooted pieces in the winter and plant them in a more suitable position where they have space to expand. Afterwards dig out the old tree and plant something which will not grow so large in its place.

Choice tree

"Can you tell me whether I can grow Abutilon vitifolium *in my garden and how tall will it grow?"*

Plants of *Abutilon vitifolium* should grow happily outside in your part of the world and throughout the southern counties of England. It is a small tree making rapid growth to about 15 ft (4.5 m) tall. It produces masses of attractive violet or white flowers in the summer.

Maple seeds

"I am moving house later this year and with great regret will have to leave two fine trees of Acer *'Osakazuki' and* A. griseum. *I note that the trees are now displaying seeds. Is it worth collecting them to raise new plants?"*

Leave your acer seeds to ripen and collect them in the autumn. Encourage germination by stratifying the seeds over the winter. Mix them with sand in a pot and leave it outside for the winter, covered with wire netting to keep out mice.

Sow the seed thinly in the spring in a seed bed in a sunny, well-drained patch or if preferred, sow the seed in a pot of good seed compost. With luck, seedlings will appear within two months. You should have no trouble perpetuating *A. griseum* but as "Osakazuki" is a hybrid, seeds are liable to produce variable plants.

Shrub for chalk

"I would like to grow a shrub of Abelia grandiflora *because I admired a large bush covered in pink flowers last summer. Can you tell me whether it will grow well in my chalky soil? Does it need regular pruning?"*

Abelia grandiflora should grow well on a chalky soil provided it is improved with ample quantities of compost or manure. Also, mulch around the shrub each spring with the same materials or bark fibre.

Regular pruning is not required but cut out any dead and withered stems in early spring.

Shy azalea ❧

"I have had two azalea bushes for about seven years. Normally they are very beautiful but this year they have not flowered. They look healthy. Can you tell me why they have not flowered?"

Your non-flowering azaleas need a little potash to encourage them to bloom. Try top dressing them with 1 oz. per sq. yd (289 m²) of sulphate of potash now and again in February. Potash helps to balance the uptake of leaf-promoting nitrogen and induces flowers to form. Keep the ground around the bushes mulched with a thick layer of compost, manure or bark fibre.

Grow more ❧

"I have some azaleas in a border but they do not seem to make much new growth. Do they need any special treatment?"

Your azaleas may need feeding. Give them a seaweed-based fertilizer in the spring and summer. Also, put a thick mulch of decayed manure, leafmould or compost around the plants each spring. This helps to conserve soil moisture. In dry weather keep the plants well watered.

Soil for azalea ❧

"I have been given an evergreen azalea called 'Kirin'. Can you tell me what soil and situation it likes?"

Your azalea must have an acid, lime-free soil. It will not flourish if there is any lime or chalk in the soil and the leaves will turn yellow. First test your soil for lime. Small testing kits are available. If it is acid you can go ahead and plant the azalea after preparing the ground with acid peat, bark fibre and/or decayed leafmould.

If the soil is very alkaline it would be best to grow the azalea in a large tub of acid potting soil. Should it be slightly alkaline you could make it more acid with dressings of flowers of sulphur at 4 oz. per sq. yd (110 g/m²). It may be necessary to repeat the treatment until the soil is acid but test the soil for lime before applying more sulphur.

Layering azalea ❧

"I have an evergreen azalea growing outside. It is very healthy and there are several stems bent down close to the soil. If I peg these into the soil will they form new roots?"

You should have no difficulty in rooting the stems of your azalea that are close to the soil. July and August are good months to layer the stems. Prepare the soil by adding plenty of moist peat and coarse grit to it. Make a shallow cut on the underside of the stem with a sharp knife and bend it down into the prepared soil. Hold it in place with a wooden peg or stout piece of wire.

It will take at least a year for a good root system to develop. Sever the newly rooted stem from the parent and plant it in its new home.

Japanese maples 🌤

"I would very much like to grow a Japanese maple in a large pot or tub on my terrace. Can you tell me whether these maples can be grown in this way? What kind of soil do they like?"

Japanese maples are well suited to growing in large pots or tubs, as long as you ensure that there are drainage holes in the base of the containers. Use good potting soil – preferably one that is slightly acid.

The foliage is rather delicate and can be scorched in very hot sunshine. If possible, stand the plant where it can be lightly shaded during the hottest part of the day. Winds can also damage the leaves and a sheltered position should be chosen for your plant.

Extra special care must be taken in the summer – plants in tubs are often forgotten, particularly if they're out of the way – to ensure that the compost does not dry out and that watering is not neglected in hot weather.

Red maple 🌤

"For the second year running, the leaves of some of the maple trees in my long hedge have developed a bright red pimpling. I had hoped it would just go away! What causes the trouble and is there any control?"

The red pimpling is due to attack by maple bead-gall mites. Although some may consider the reddening of the leaves to be unwelcome, little actual damage is done as far as general growth is concerned, although the mites can spread to other species of acer.

On pale-leaved types, such as "Brilliantissimum", the attack is most unsightly. There is no effective chemical control, but as the mites spend the winter in sheltered spots on the shoots, severe autumn trimming or winter pruning should reduce population numbers and lessen attacks the following spring and summer.

Azalea cuttings ❦

"I have some bushes of evergreen azaleas and would like to take cuttings from them. When is the best time of year to do it?"

Cuttings of evergreen azaleas are not usually difficult to root. Take firm young shoots in July and early August. Make the cuttings 2–3 in. (5–9.5 cm) long and trim each one with a sharp knife just below a leaf joint. Insert them into small pots filled with a mixture of moist peat and coarse sand. Cover each pot with a polythene bag and keep the cuttings in a warm place with light shade from the sun.

Good roots may not have been made until the spring when the young plants should be potted separately in an acid, lime-free potting compost.

Snake bark ❦

"I want to plant a small tree which has attractive bark. Could you possibly suggest a few of the best types?"

You cannot do better than plant one of the maples with attractive bark. *Acer davidii* "George Forrest" has green and white vertical stripes on the bark and *A. grosseri hersii*, one of the snakebark maples, has attractive marbled bark and leaves that colour well in the autumn. *A. griseum* also has well-coloured foliage in the autumn and red peeling bark, which always attracts attention.

What a gall ❦

"I am bringing on a number of azaleas for Christmas, but sadly some are developing swollen leaves with a white appearance. How can I stop this from getting worse?"

The problem is a disease known as azalea gall. There was probably a very small amount of infection that went unnoticed last year but which is now developing severely. Pick off the swollen leaf clusters for burning and then spray a couple of times, a fortnight apart, with a copper fungicide. This will hopefully remove the infection and protect the new growth from attack.

Variegated maple ❦

"I have a bush of Acer negundo 'Flamingo'. It has very pretty variegated leaves. However, some shoots appear with plain green leaves which spoils the effect. Can anything be done to prevent these appearing?"

Acers with variegated leaves often revert to the plain green form. Nothing can be done to prevent it happening. Whenever stems appear with plain, green leaves they should be cut out at their base. If they are left they will grow more strongly than the variegated leaved stems and dominate the bush.

Butterfly tree

"I would like to know what to do with my buddleja or butterfly tree. It has flowered well for many years but this year, after coming into leaf, the shoots curled up and left bare branches. However, new growth is springing from the base. What should I do with it?"

As the main branches of your buddleja appear to be dead, cut them out at their base leaving the strong new basal growths. The shrub should soon recover.

Buddlejas respond to regular pruning. The branches can all be cut back close to their base in March each year. This will encourage strong new growths to develop which will flower in late summer.

Prune after flowering

"I am sending a shoot from a large bush in my garden. Can you possibly name it for me and tell me when it can be pruned? It has rounded, yellow flowers."

Your shrub is *Buddleja globosa* which normally flowers in early summer. It is well worthwhile having as it is easy to grow and normally flowers freely. Prune it directly after flowering, cutting out the stems that have carried flowers. The new growths made in the summer flower the following season.

Box cuttings

"I want to raise some box plants from cuttings. When is the best time to take the cuttings?"

The best time to take box cuttings is in the autumn. Select firm, young shoots and make the cuttings, with a "heel" of older wood attached, about 6 in. (15 cm) long. Insert them in small pots filled with a gritty compost. Stand the pots in a cold frame or greenhouse until new roots appear.

Buddleja under attack ❧

"I am enclosing leaves from my Buddleja globosa for examination; something seems to be eating them. Last summer the leaves developed holes and brown marks although I could not find any pests on them. The damage is starting again now."

The pest responsible for the damage is the figwort weevil. Like all weevils, the adults drop from the leaves and lie motionless when threatened, so they are not often seen at work. Both the larvae and the adults feed on the foliage of *B. globosa*, and also on *Phygelius* (also in the wild on figwort).

Control with a spray or two of Tumblebug or Sybol or Safer's Garden Insecticide.

Pruning buddleja ❧

"Can you tell me how to prune a bush of Buddleja globosa which has globular golden flowers? Is it treated like Buddleja davidii which I cut back in March?"

The two buddlejas you mention are pruned differently. The best way to prune *B. globosa* is to thin out weak growths in the spring and one or two of the older stems can be cut back to encourage new shoots to form.

If you treat it like *B. davidii*, cutting back all the growths severely, there will be no flowers in the following season.

Scented buddleja ❧

"Can you tell me anything about a shrub called Buddleja x weyeriana? How tall does it grow and when does it flower?"

Buddleia x *weyeriana* is a first-rate shrub growing up to 15 ft (4.5 m) tall. The rounded, yellow flowers are produced in late summer and have a very pleasant fragrance. The form most commonly seen is "Golden Glow". It is an interesting shrub as it is a hybrid between *B. davidii* and *B. globosa* and was raised in Dorset in 1914.

The shrub should be treated in the same way as *B. davidii*. Prune all the old stems hard each year in March. The flowers are carried on the new growth in late summer. You should find that the shrub will succeed in most well-drained soils and it is hardy.

Tree training 𝕖

"Last year I grew a plant of Betula platyphylla japonica (Japanese white birch) from seed. It is noted for its beautiful white bark. Does the tree need any special method of training to ensure that the bark is not blemished? Should the feathers be allowed to grow to thicken the main stem?"

Congratulations on raising your Japanese white birch. Train the tree in the normal way, allowing the main stem to grow until it reaches its desired height, before taking out the tip. Allow the feathers to grow, to thicken the stem, but keep them pinched. Eventually cut them off flush with the main stem. Any scars will soon heal over as the tree grows and bark forms.

Butterfly plants 𝕖

"I want to encourage more butterflies in my garden. Can you tell me the best plants to grow to attract them?"

Two of the most popular garden plants that attract butterflies are *Buddleja davidii*, a shrub flowering in late summer, and *Sedum spectabile*, a herbaceous perennial for the front of a border.

Other plants are: red valerian, sweet william, marjoram, scabious, lavender, candytuft, Michaelmas daisies, pot marigolds, forget-me-not, grape hyacinths and *Alyssum saxatile*.

Berberis freaks 𝕖

"Two of the shoots on a neighbour's berberis bush are wide and flattened and it looks as if several shoots have become joined together. Can you please explain what has happened, and is it catching?"

The flattening of shoots into wide, and often curled forms is known as "fasciation". The exact cause is not fully understood, and although it can be carried on by cuttings from the affected growths, this does not occur. It is not a condition that spreads from plant to plant. Among the suggested causes are pest, bacterial or frost damage, but the fasciation normally only affects a small number of shoots on a plant.

The affected shoots will generally revert to normal during the next growing season. The best treatment is to prune out the shoots, although leaving them does no harm.

Stopping reversion ❧

"I have a bush of Elaeagnus pungens *'Maculata'. Among the shoots with variegated leaves are some with plain green leaves. How can I stop these appearing?"*

It is not possible to stop the plain green-leaved shoots appearing on your shrub of evergreen *Elaeagnus pungens* "Maculata". All you can do is to cut them out whenever they appear. It is important to do this regularly as the plain green shoots grow more strongly than the ones with variegated foliage. If they are left the shoots with variegated leaves will gradually disappear and you will be left with a shrub with all plain green leaves.

Chilean glory flower ❧

"Last spring I sowed some seeds of the Chilean glory flower, Eccremocarpus scaber. *Planted out near a sunny wall the plants have been a mass of flowers. I was expecting orange flowers but they turned out to be red. Have I got a new type? Does the plant have to be raised from seed each year?"*

The flowers of *Eccremocarpus scaber* are normally orange but there is a form having red flowers which is the one that you have. There is also a strain known as Tresco Hybrids which has flowers in shades of yellow, red and orange.

The plants are perennial and will stand a certain amount of frost. However, it would be wise to protect the lower part of the plant against severe weather. You may well find that your plant has produced seeds. It would be worth collecting it. If the plant should be lost in the winter, sow the seed in early spring to raise some new plants which should flower during the summer. It does best in a warm and sunny spot.

Winter scent ❧

"Can you tell me anything about a shrub called mezereon which I am told flowers in winter and has scented flowers?"

The botanical name for the mezereon is *Daphne mezereum*. It is an excellent, small shrub with purple, scented flowers in February and March. It prefers a chalky soil. The flowers are followed by red berries which are poisonous and children should not be allowed to get at them.

Paper bush – a choice shrub for winter scent ❧

"Can you tell me anything about a shrub called edgeworthia which I believe has been used by the Japanese for making high-quality paper?"

Edgeworthia chrysantha, also known as *E. papyrifera*, is a choice Chinese shrub which has attractive, fragrant yellow flowers in late winter. As you said, it is used in Japan for making high-quality paper.

As the flowers are often damaged by inclement weather in late winter, it is sensible to grow the shrub in a container and keep it in a cold greenhouse for the winter. Stand it outside for the summer in a partially shaded position. In mild areas, such as in Devon and Cornwall, it can be grown outside.

Burning bush ❧

"I have had a burning bush plant, Dictamnus albus, for four years but it does not flower. Last year I moved it into a pot but it has still not flowered. Can you tell me what to do to make it bloom?"

It would be best planted in the garden rather than grown in a pot. Improve the soil, adding plenty of organic matter, and ideally adding a little lime if the soil is acidic, in the autumn. Choose a sheltered, sunny spot.

If it seems to be making soft, lush growth, feed it with sulphate of potash in the spring which should encourage more sturdy growth and improve flowering opportunities. Once established, avoid root disturbance. This is a very aromatic plant, the old flower heads are rich in oil, hence its common name.

Party trick ❧

"Can you tell me why dittany, Dictamnus albus, is known as the burning bush?"

Dictamnus albus is an attractive perennial, flowering in early summer. When the seed pods are ripening they give off a volatile oil. On a still warm day this can be ignited, without harming the plant, if a match is held near the seed stems, hence the common name – burning bush.

Red not purple ❧

"I have a large cut-leaved purple beech tree in my garden, but this year the new growth was spoiled by a coating of velvety red growths under the leaves. Can you tell me what this is and if there is any control on a large tree?"

The growths are caused by a type of mite known as the beech erineum gall mite. Feeding by the mites results in the formation of patches of dense hairs amongst which the mites live. The hairs soon turn red and then brown. No control measures exist other than trying to reduce mite populations by pruning out infested shoot tips from the lower branches.

Spring pruning

"I have some hardy fuchsias growing outside. At the moment the stems are like dead sticks. Should they be cut back to healthy wood?"

Although the stems of your fuchsias may seem dead, they could still sprout shoots in the spring. Wait until April before pruning. By then you will be able to see clearly which stems are alive and those that have been frosted.

Cut the dead ones back to their base. Stems with new shoots should be shortened back to where young shoots are appearing. Even if you have to cut back all the old stems close to their base, new shoots will soon appear from below ground level.

California glory

"Can you tell me anything about a shrub called Fremontodendron *'California Glory'? Is it hardy and what sort of soil and situation does it need?"*

Fremontodendron "California Glory" is a handsome large shrub, best grown against a warm wall. It is not hardy in all districts but it can be grown outside in most southern gardens. The plant is best grown in poor, well-drained soil to encourage tough sturdy growth. It does well on chalky soils.

The shrub resents root disturbance and pot-grown plants should be purchased. Little pruning is needed but any trimming to keep the plant shapely should be done in early April. The shoots are covered in brown hairs which are irritating and it is recommended that gloves and face mask are worn when handling the shrub.

Cut it out

"I have a large forsythia bush which has become very overgrown as I have never pruned it. When is the best time to do it and how do I go about it?"

The best time to prune a forsythia bush is after flowering in the spring. You will need sharp secateurs, long-handled pruners and possibly a small pruning saw for very thick branches.

First cut back the stems that have flowered to where a younger growth is appearing. This will grow in the summer and form a replacement shoot. As the bush is very overcrowded, you will also have to do some thinning. Aim to cut out some of the older darker stems, retaining the younger ones of lighter colour.

Neglected fig

"We have taken over an old garden and there is a big fig tree against a wall. It seems to be very overgrown. Can we cut back the branches?"

The old branches of your fig tree can be cut back in late March or early April. Do not prune all the branches at one time but spread the operation over two or three years. Try to retain as many of the young stems as possible and train these into position on the wall. The hard pruning should stimulate strong, new growth which should be tied into place in the form of a fan.

Soil for loquats

"I have germinated some loquat (Eriobotrya japonica) *seeds and at the moment the plants are about 8 in. (20 cm) tall. I intend planting them outside. What type of soil do they like?"*

The loquat is adaptable and thrives in most soils. Provided you enrich the planting holes with old manure or rotted garden compost, laced with bone meal, your plants should thrive. Plant them in a sunny, sheltered spot shielded from cold winds.

Flowers may appear in time but they are unlikely to produce fruit unless there is an exceptionally hot summer.

Burning leaves

"The beech leaves on our trees were attacked by insects this summer. Is it safe to compost them or should the leaves be burnt?"

The beech leaves should be composted as the insects will do little harm. It is a great mistake to burn leaves as, once composted, they add valuable organic matter to the soil.

Early forsythia

"I have a forsythia bush in a large pot. If I took it into my greenhouse, would it flower earlier than outside?"

Your forsythia will certainly flower early if it is taken into your greenhouse. Do this soon after Christmas. Do not give it too much heat, 7–10°C is about right. Stems may also be cut from bushes in the open after Christmas. Stood in water in a greenhouse the flowers will soon open.

Fremontodendrons for free ❧

"I have two fremontodendrons in my garden. One tree has seed pods. Can these be gathered and sown?"

Wait for the seed pods to ripen, then gather them and extract the seeds. Sow them immediately in small pots of gritty compost, covering the surface with $\frac{1}{2}$ in. (1.25 cm) of grit. Stand the pots in a cold frame. If the seed is viable, seedlings should appear next spring.

Irritating wall shrub ❧

"I have been given a fremontodendron. How do I care for it? Also, on the label there is a warning that it can irritate the skin."

Fremontodendron is a native of California and Arizona. It likes a south-facing wall and should be planted where it can grow unhampered to 15 ft (4.5 m) or more across. If it is confined and needs constant pruning, it may regress and become woody and ugly.

Its leaves are armed with tiny barbs which are easily detached when training in shoots and can irritate sensitive skin. Eyes are also vulnerable, so wear safety glasses, gloves and a long-sleeved shirt when cutting back errant shoots.

Good name! ❧

"I want to grow a forsythia bush. I came across one called 'Lynwood' in a local garden centre. Can you tell me anything about this variety and is it worth growing?"

Forsythia x *intermedia* "Lynwood" is one of the best forsythia varieties. The large, bright yellow flowers are borne in profusion. It has received a First Class Certificate and an Award of Garden Merit from the Royal Horticultural Society. Plants grow up to 7 ft (2.1 m) tall and as much across.

Maidenhair tree ❧

"I would like to grow a ginkgo or maidenhair tree in my garden but I am not sure how hardy it is. Do you think it would succeed here in Cheshire and does it need a special kind of soil?"

Ginkgo biloba is an attractive tree and is perfectly hardy. It will eventually grow at least 50 ft (15.2 m) tall. We can see no reason why it should not grow well in your district provided it is given a sunny situation and is planted in fertile, well-drained soil.

Gleditsia glitch ❧

"My mother's Gleditsia 'Sunburst' lost all its leaves this summer. It started to produce more, but these, too, were being eaten. Looking closely at them, a small caterpillar seemed to leap out and drop down on a strand like a spider would. Please help."

The rapid backwards movement of the caterpillar, together with the "hanging from a thread" act shows the caterpillar to be a member of the tortrix group. The same caterpillars would also have been responsible for the disappearance of the leaves.

   If the caterpillars are still present, stop further damage by spraying with Phostrogen Safer's Insecticide, Polysect or Picket. Look out for new damage next spring, as the overwintering caterpillars start their work, and repeat the spray if necessary.

Barren holly ❧

"I have a holly tree in my garden which flowers but sets no berries. Why?"

Hollies have male and female flowers and some varieties are male and others female. It is possible that you have a male holly which will never have berries, so it would be best to plant another holly which is self-fertile. "J. C. Van Tol" is a good variety which can be relied on to produce a good crop of red berries. It also has dark, shiny leaves with few spines.

It's a honey locust ❧

"Could you identify the plant from the piece I am sending? The foliage has a two-tone green colour and is now over 6 ft (1.8m) tall."

Your plant is probably the honey locust, *Gleditsia triacanthos* and possibly the variety "Sunburst". As you have found, its leaves, when they open, have a captivating two-toned hue. It is a very fine tree and commercially it is propagated from seeds or by grafting.

Splendid shrub ❦

"Can you give me the name of the piece of shrub that I am sending? What sort of soil does it like?"

Your shrub is *Genista lydia*. It is a first-rate plant forming a cascade of bright yellow flowers in late spring if it is allowed to grow over a rock or hang over a wall. It is not fussy about soil, provided it is well-drained. Plants can eventually grow 2 ft (60 cm) tall and spread out to 6 ft (1.8 m).

Cruel to be kind ❦

"The tips of the leaves on my young Gleditsia *'Sunburst' (honeylocust) tree have produced odd-looking swellings, rather like small peas. Can you tell me what this is and how to stop it happening again?"*

The swellings are the work of the honeylocust gall midge, an unwelcome arrival from North America that is now established in southern England.

In severe attacks the shoots can be distorted and the normally attractive tree made quite unsightly. As your tree is still young the best treatment would be to remove all the leaves showing signs of attack. There are several generations per year but the midge eventually overwinters in the soil. Next spring, around mid-May, apply an effective soil insecticide such as Sybol Dust to the soil and then continue to remove any galled leaves that are found.

Beauty bush ❦

"I bought a small shrub on a plant stall and I was told it was called beauty bush. I have been unable to trace the correct name for the plant and I do not know how to treat it. Can you help me?"

The shrub often called the beauty bush is *Kolkwitzia amabilis*. It is a very beautiful shrub when its pendulous branches are covered in masses of pink flowers during May and June. It is deciduous, fully hardy and makes an ideal small garden shrub growing 4–6 ft (1.2–1.8 m) tall. It performs best in well-drained soil in a sunny, open position.

Pruning tips for a Jew's mallow
"I have a large bush of Jew's mallow. When should it be pruned?"

Prune your Jew's mallow (*Kerria japonica*) bush by cutting back the stems that have flowered close to the older wood and where a young new shoot is appearing. Do this after the flowers have faded.

Kiwi Kowhai
"Whilst on holiday in New Zealand I saw many Kowhai bushes. Can they be grown in this country?"

The New Zealand Kowhai, *Sophora tetraptera*, is not fully hardy in this country but it is often seen outside in mild gardens in the south-west and the Isle of Wight. Elsewhere it is best grown in a large container which can be kept in the open in the summer but taken under cover for the winter.

In favourable situations grow the plant against a south-west facing wall.

New Zealand import
"Can you identify the piece of plant that I am sending? It is from a shrub growing in my daughter's new garden."

Your plant is a leptospermum, probably *L. scoparium*. The shrub comes from New Zealand and needs a warm, south-facing wall upon which to thrive. Winter can be difficult for it and a free-draining soil is essential.

There are some marvellous leptospermums, or tea trees as they are also known, in full bloom in the gardens of the National Trust property, Coleton Fishacre, where they thrive in the mild south Devon climate.

Colour change
"Can you explain why the flowers on my bush of Barnsley lavatera are changing to deep pink instead of remaining pale pink?"

It is not unusual for some clones of Lavatera "Barnsley" to revert to their parents' deep pink colour.

Guard against this colour change dominating your bush by cutting out all the stems that have reverted. With luck, your plant will then develop more stems with the white to pale pink flowers you want.

Himalaya honeysuckle ❧

"Could you name the plant from the cutting I am sending? It was growing in a garden hedge in Kent. Despite searching through my books, I cannot trace it. I know that part of its name is formosa and it may come from the Himalayas."

Your flower is the Himalaya honeysuckle, *Leycesteria formosa*. It is a hardy shrub, growing to at least 8 ft (2.4 m). The clusters of pendant flowers are white, surrounded by purple bracts and appear from June to September. Purplish red berries develop in the autumn which are said to be enjoyed by pheasants. The plant may be damaged in a hard winter, but fresh green shoots will appear again. To keep the shrub under control, prune it almost to ground level in the spring.

Tulip tree ❧

"I always thought that magnolias were tulip trees. I am now told that the tulip tree is something different. Which is correct?"

Although magnolias are often called tulip trees, the true tulip tree is *Liriodendron tulipifera*. The flowers are not very like tulips and they are greenish orange in colour.

Liriodendron is a very handsome tree growing to a great size and it is not suitable for a small garden. Young trees do not flower and it may be many years before blossoms appear.

Keep in trim ❧

"I have a bay tree trained as a ball. To maintain the shape when do I trim it?"

Begin trimming your bay tree in April and as new growths appear keep them trimmed at intervals throughout the spring.

Flower change ❧

"I have had a bush of Lavatera 'Barnsley' for several years. It flowers well for most of the summer but this year I noticed that some of the flowers were deep pink in colour and quite different from the normal soft pink colour. Can you explain what has happened?"

The deep pink flowers on your lavatera have reverted back to the original form. You may like to have the two-colour bush but it is possible that the stems with deep pink flowers will grow more strongly than the "Barnsley" form and could eventually suppress it. If this seems to be happening cut out all the stems with deep pink flowers at their base.

Laburnum seeds

"My neighbour has a fine laburnum tree which overhangs my garden. I have been told that it is poisonous. Is this true and what part of the tree is poisonous?"

All parts of the laburnum are poisonous. However, the green seed pods are the most likely parts to be eaten, particularly by children. They should be warned not to eat any plants or berries in the garden.

Some hybrid laburnums, such as the variety "Vossii", do not normally set seed. If your neighbour's tree is one of these, it should not be too much of a problem with children.

Multi-coloured laburnum

"In a garden close to where I live is a pink and yellow laburnum tree. At first I thought it had been grafted but on closer inspection found branches that had both yellow and pink flowers plus, in the centre of the tree, a lilac-coloured broom-like growth. Is this unusual?"

The tree that you have seen is unusual. It is called *Laburnocytisus adamii* and is a graft hybrid between *Laburnum anagyroides* and *Cytisus purpureus*. The inside core of the tree is laburnum and the outer covering is cytisus (broom). This gives rise to some branches with yellow laburnum flowers and others with clusters of purple broom flowers. In addition there are intermediate flowers of a coppery-pink colour. The tree originally came from a nursery near Paris owned by J. L. Adam in 1825.

Pruning lavatera

"My bush of Lavatera olbia rosea *made tremendous growth last summer. Can I cut it back in the spring?"*

Lavatera olbia rosea is a plant that can make rampant growth. By the end of the winter you are likely to find that some of the stems will have withered at the tips. We suggest that you cut these back in March and shorten any others that are encroaching too much on other plants. Any dead and thin, weak stems can be cut out at the same time.

Variegated tree mallow ❧

"Two years ago I was given a seedling of a plant the name of which the donor did not know. She understood it to be of the mallow or lavatera family. It has now grown 3 ft tall and has a long, leafy stem, resembling a stripped Brussels sprout plant. New leaves are cream coloured and mottled. So far the plant has not flowered. Could you possibly name it for me?"

Your plant is the variegated tree mallow, *Lavatera arborea* "Variegata". It is an attractive plant that can grow 4–6 ft (1.2–1.5 m) tall. The flowers resemble purple hollyhocks and they appear in the summer at the top of the stems. Plants are often found growing wild in sandy soil near the sea.

Lavateras can be short lived so it is worth taking cuttings which can be rooted from non-flowering stems taken at this time of the year. Prune back to 12 in. (30 cm) in the autumn to help reduce wind rock damage.

Cuckoo spit attack ❧

"About this time every year our lavender bushes and some herbaceous plants start to get attacked by cuckoo spit. Presumably the greenish creature inside the 'spit' is the cause. A simple cure, please?"

Cuckoo spit is the work of the creature hidden inside, as you suspect. It is known as a froghopper, as it hops and looks rather frog-like when adult. The spit is actually plant sap which the insect feeds on and then whips up into a froth. Although unsightly, and sometimes causing some distortion to new shoots, little damage is done, and insects can often be removed by a strong jet of water. In extreme cases use a general insecticide.

Dawn trim ❧

"I have a shrub of Viburnum bodnantense *'Dawn' which is getting quite tall. Can I prune it?"*

Prune *Viburnum bodnantense* "Dawn" after flowering, when its petals fade. New shoots will then grow strongly to flower the following year.

Bay watch ❧

"I have two different bay trees, bought as small plants and which I am training into shaped bushes. They have developed some encrustation under the leaves which none of my local nurseries can identify or suggest effective remedies for. (Rapid has not worked)."

The encrustations under the leaves are scale insects, which can be quite common on bay trees. The best control would be to spray with a systemic insecticide such as Tumblebug or Sybol. These get into the plant sap and so kill the pests as they feed on the sap.

The dead scale insects may not immediately drop off as their feeding tubes are deep within the leaf tissue, but they will eventually drop off, or could be picked off. If not controlled, the leaves will become blackened as sooty moulds grow on sugary honeydew exuded by the scale insects as they feed.

Tropical touch ❧

"I have grown a loquat plant from seed. What can I do with it now; can I plant it outside?"

The loquat (*Eriobotrya japonica*) is not fully hardy in this country but it should succeed outside in Dorset if you can plant it against a warm, south-facing wall.

Its main attraction is its large, leathery, evergreen leaves. Plants sometimes produce white, fragrant flowers after a hot summer. They appear in the autumn and are unlikely to set fruit.

Himalayan honeysuckle ❧

"Can you name the shrub shown in the photograph I am sending?"

Your shrub is *Leycesteria formosa*, commonly called Himalayan honeysuckle or pheasant berry. It has pendulous spikes of flowers which are surrounded with claret-coloured bracts.

Keep it young and attractive with appealing green stems by pruning it hard in the spring. Cut all old shoots to just above ground level. It will then produce strong new stems in the spring and summer.

Larch adelges ❧

"What causes the woolly growths on my larch tree? It looks like the woolly aphid that gets into apple trees, or is it a form of mealy bug? There is a pretty heavy attack."

The actual pest is known as the larch adelges. It is closely related to an aphid, but sufficiently different to have its own family. The "wool" serves as protection, exactly as with apple woolly aphid. The pests also produce copious sticky honeydew and a heavy infestation will result in needles browning and falling and in shoots failing to grow. The pest also causes gall formation on spruce trees.

Best control is by thorough sprays with a systemic insecticide such as Tumblebug or Long-Last.

Holly blotch ❧

"Every year the leaves on our otherwise splendid variegated holly develop brown blotches. Can you tell us what causes them and how we can cure the problem?"

The marks are the work of the holly leaf-miner. Adults are on the wing in May, laying eggs on the undersides of the leaves, generally beside the main veins. The developing larvae feed within the leaf tissue for some months, causing the unsightly blotch mines that you are finding.

It may be worth spraying the undersides of the leaves now with a general insecticide, but should any mines start to appear during the summer, remove them as they are found. Complete such leaf removal before the end of March next year to remove the pests before they emerge as adults to lay more eggs.

Sowing holly ❧

"I have been given some holly berries and would like to grow new trees from them."

Prepare the holly berries for sowing in the spring by mixing them with coarse sand in a flower pot and covering it with wire netting to exclude hungry mice. Place the pot in the coldest part of the garden to stratify (freeze and pulp) the berries.

In spring, remove the berries and sow them thinly outdoors, just covering them with soil. Seedlings soon appear.

You will have a mix of male and female plants but won't know which is which until they flower. So plant several in a group in the hope that some will be female and fruit.

Holly sex ❧

"I am confused about hollies. I want to grow a bush and I have been told I must plant both male and female varieties to have berries. I would have thought that 'Golden King' was male but it appears to have berries."

The names of hollies are confusing but you are correct in saying that, normally, both male and female varieties must be grown together to ensure a good crop of berries.

Despite its name "Golden King" is female. To make matters worse "Golden Queen" is male! They are both good varieties. "Camelliifolia" has handsome, spineless leaves and good crops of berries and "J. C. van Tol" is a useful variety as it is self-fertile and usually produces plenty of berries on its own. "Argentea Marginata" has white-margined leaves and plenty of berries, while a good yellow-berried variety is "Pyramidalis Fructu Luteo".

Vanishing berries ❧

"I have had a holly tree, 'J. C. van Tol', in my lawn for the past six years. It gets covered in small green berries but, apart from five or six, the rest disappear before maturing. This also applies to a 'Golden King' and a 'Silver Queen'. Cotoneasters and pyracanthas all flower and are covered in berries. How can I get my hollies to ripen their berries?"

There could be several reasons why the green holly berries are disappearing. Birds may be responsible or there may be a nutritional problem. Try feeding the soil with sulphate of potash now and see whether this has any effect. It is impossible for the *Ilex* "Silver Queen" to have berries as it is a male variety! Your holly must be wrongly named.

Flowering palm ❧

"Ten years ago we bought three Devon palms. Over the years we lost two of them but the third has flourished and is now about 8 ft (2.4 m) tall. A few weeks ago, what looked like a seed head appeared at the top of the palm. This has never happened before and we are worried that it has 'gone to seed' and will die. Can we do anything about it?"

Do not be alarmed. In recent years, Devon palms (*Dracaena australis*) have, because of hot summers, flowered freely. This has not affected their longevity and they have grown strongly the following year. There is nothing you have to do.

Dawn redwood ❧

"I saw an attractive coniferous tree growing in a container at a garden centre in April. The new young leaves looked like a larch. It was called dawn

redwood. However, the nurseryman could not tell me how big it would grow. Can you tell me how tall it will grow and is it suitable for a small garden?"

The correct name for the dawn redwood is *Metasequoia glyptostroboides*. It, like the larch, is a deciduous conifer and it is a very attractive tree. However, it is not suitable for a small garden as trees will grow more than 50 ft (15.2 m) – they will do this in 20 years!

The dawn redwood has an interesting history. Until 1941 it was known only from herbarium specimens. It was then discovered in China but it was not until 1947 that seed was sent to America and the rest of Europe a year or so later. It is now grown widely and is remarkable for its rapid growth.

Magnolia wonder ❧

"I have been reading about the wonders of the tree magnolia, Magnolia campbellii. *Can you tell me whether they grow anywhere in the London area where I could go and see one? I believe they flower very early in the year."*

A tall tree of *Magnolia campbellii*, or one of its many varieties, covered in large pink flowers in early spring, is a wonderful sight. The trees can grow to 60 ft (18.2 m) tall and some of the best specimens are grown in the Cornish gardens, particularly, Caerhays. However, there are good trees at Kew and at Windsor Great Park. They are also grown in the Sussex gardens at Borde Hill and Wakehurst Place. The flowering period is from February to late March. Unfortunately, the display is sometimes ruined if hard frosts occur.

Sacred bamboo ❧

"Can you tell me anything about a shrub called Nandinia domestica *'Firepower' which I admired recently in a garden centre? Would it be suitable for my district?"*

The shrub you have seen has decorative bamboo-like growth. It has small, white flowers in the summer and the foliage turns orange-red in the autumn. It should be hardy in your area.

Give it a sheltered position where it will receive plenty of sunshine. It will grow well in most fertile soils.

A change of colour ❧

"Can you tell me why I cannot get my hydrangeas to produce blue flowers? I have put rusty nails in the soil and used tea leaves but the flowers still remain pink. What else can I do?"

To have blue flowers, hydrangeas must be grown in acid, lime-free soil. As your hydrangeas are pink they must be growing in an alkaline soil. If the soil is very chalky you will not be able to have blue flowers. Rusty nails and tea leaves are not likely to help but alum (aluminium sulphate) may be tried. It is obtainable from a chemist.

Apply about $\frac{1}{4}$ lb. (110 g) per stem to the soil around the hydrangea in the autumn after leaf-fall and water it well into the ground. Repeat the treatment in early spring just before leaves appear. Again, water it well into the soil. The treatment may have to be repeated as the results depend on how alkaline the soil is.

Another way to obtain blue flowers is to grow the hydrangea in a large tub filled with an acid potting compost suitable for rhododendrons and heathers. Some varieties blue better than others. Among the best are: "Generale Vicomtesse de Vibraye", "Marechal Foch" and "Madame A. Riverain".

Climbing hydrangea ❧

"I want to cover a north-facing wall and I have been told to plant a climbing hydrangea. Is there such a plant? If so, would it be suitable?"

The climbing hydrangea, *Hydrangea petiolaris*, would be an excellent choice for your north wall. It may need support for a while but it will soon produce tendrils and be self-clinging. It produces big heads of white flowers in June and the leaves turn bright yellow in the autumn before they fall.

Firethorns (pyracanthas), are also good evergreen shrubs for training on a north-facing wall. They have white flowers in spring followed in autumn by red, yellow or orange berries. The colourful variegated-leaved ivies are also an excellent choice for a north wall.

Lace-cap hydrangeas ❧

"I want to grow a lace-cap hydrangea called 'Blue Wave'. Will it have blue flowers in an alkaline soil?"

Hydrangea "Blue Wave" will not have good blue flowers where there is chalk or lime in the soil. Plants must be grown in an acid soil to obtain the best coloured blue flowers. If your soil is not too alkaline you may be able to make it acid with alum powder applied in late autumn and again in the spring.

Step-by-step . . . rooting hydrangea cuttings ❧

"A friend has a large hydrangea bush and has offered me cuttings. When is the best time to take them?"

Hydrangeas can be propagated from cuttings taken now. Take the tips of firm shoots and make the cuttings about 3 in. (7.5 cm) in length. Stand them in a propagator and when good roots have been made pot the young plants up individually

Winter-flowering honeysuckle ❧

"I have been told that there is a honeysuckle that flowers in the winter. Is this true and is it easy to grow?"

Yes, there are winter-flowering honeysuckles. One of the best is *Lonicera x purpusii*. This makes a bush of medium size and has lots of small, cream-coloured flowers in winter. It is not difficult to grow and will succeed in ordinary, well-drained soil.

Other winter-flowering kinds are *L. fragrantissima* which has small cream, fragrant flowers followed by red berries in May and *L. standishii*, which is very similar to the others and is usually at its best in February.

Few flowers ❧

"I have several hydrangea bushes in my garden but they have not flowered for several years. They are planted in a bed under a large silver birch and with other shrubs and perennials around them."

The non-flowering of your hydrangeas is probably connected with their proximity to the large silver birch which is drawing on most of the water reserves in the soil.

Hydrangeas like a moist, retentive soil. Feed them in the spring and summer with a liquid fertilizer and mulch the ground around them with decayed manure or compost.

Hibiscus shrubs ❧

"I have two shrubs of Hibiscus syriacus – 'Woodbridge' and 'Blue Bird'. The flowers of the latter are falling fast. 'Woodbridge' is in full bloom but the leaves have turned a bright yellow. Both shrubs are several years old. I have been feeding them with a liquid fertilizer. What can I do about the problem?"

Hibiscus syriacus shrubs are not usually difficult to grow in ordinary good garden soil. However, they do like moist soil and a sunny position. The troubles you are having with your shrubs may be because of dryness at the roots. The soil should now be thoroughly moist but next summer leave a hose pipe trickling near each shrub when the soil shows signs of drying out.

Next spring put a thick mulch of compost, bark fibre or farmyard manure around each bush which will help to conserve soil moisture. Also feed each bush with Growmore fertilizer in March. These shrubs respond to hard pruning each year in March. The flowers are produced in late summer on the shoots made in the current season.

Hebe in difficulty

"We had several sorts of hebe, but many died out during the severe winter weather. Now, some of the leaves of the remaining ones are developing a dark spotting on the foliage. Can this be cured?"

The damage is due to attack by a leaf spot fungus, of which there are very many different species, living on a wide range of garden plants.

Cut back the infected shoots reasonably hard and then spray the regrowth with Dithane 945 or a copper fungicide to protect it from renewed attack.

Aromatic cuttings

"I have a curry plant in my garden which gives off a delicious smell in hot summer weather. When is the best time to take cuttings from it? Is this the plant used for making curry powder?"

The curry plant, *Helichrysum italicum*, is a small shrubby plant with silver foliage and heads of yellow flowers in the summer. It is not the plant used for making curry powder, although young shoots may be added to stews to give a mild curry flavour.

Cuttings of young side shoots, a few inches long, root easily in the summer. The shoots can be removed with a heel of older wood attached at their base. Insert the cuttings in small pots of gritty soil.

Whitebeam worry

"I have grown a whitebeam tree from seed and it is now about 6 ft (1.8 m) tall. It is planned to be the centrepiece of a new white border. I found the

leaves are now showing signs of some pest or disease with brown patches all over them."

The damage to your whitebeam is the work of slugworms. These are black, shiny caterpillars of sawflies and they graze off the leaf surface, rather than biting through the leaf. The damage is probably finished for this year and the pests will be pupating in the soil, to emerge next spring as adults.

Cultivate the soil lightly during the next few months, in the hope of exposing or damaging the pests. Next June or July, look out for a repeat of the damage and squash the pests by hand, or alternatively, spray with a Bug Gun or Bio Pest Pistol.

Blooming nice ❧

"Last September on holiday around Cape Cod in the United States, hibiscus plants were growing in many of the gardens. The beautiful satin flowers in various colours appeared on stout stems about 3 ft. (1 m) tall. I have not seen this particular hibiscus before. Could you tell me what it is and whether it can be grown in this country?"

The hibiscus that you saw in Cape Cod is most probably *H. moscheutos* or swamp rose-mallow. The flowers are certainly magnificent, often measuring 8 in. (20 cm) across. They can be grown in this country, particularly in mild areas, and are easily raised from seed in a warm greenhouse.

Several seed companies offer the F_1 hybrids "Disco Belle Mixed", also called "Les Belles".

Grow the young plants on under glass and plant in the open in a sunny position in early June. They also make good plants for containers on a sunny patio.

Unhealthy witch hazel ❧

"Last summer the leaves on my witch hazel bush turned an unhealthy, yellow-brown colour. The shrub normally flowers well but now seems to be unhappy. Have you any idea of what is going wrong?"

Your witch hazel (hamamelis) is suffering as a result of lime or chalk in the soil.

These shrubs must have an acid, lime-free soil. One way of overcoming the problem is to use a Sequestrene product or you can apply flowers of sulphur to the soil at 4 oz./sq.yd. (110 g/m²) in late winter. If the soil is very alkaline it will be very difficult to make it sufficiently acid for the hamamelis to thrive.

Each spring put thick mulches of peat or decayed compost around the shrub.

Blooming better ❧

"I have a large bush of Hydrangea arborescens *'Annabelle'. The flowers seem to be getting smaller each year. Can anything be done to improve their size? Incidentally, who is or was Annabelle?"*

If you want large flowers on your hydrangea bush you should prune it hard in March, cutting the old stems back close to their base. This will induce strong new growth in the spring which will flower later in the season.

"Annabelle" got its name after the town of Anna, Illinois, where it was first discovered.

Propagating hypericums ❧

"I have a bush of Hypericum *'Hidcote' and I would like to take some cuttings from it. When is the best time to do this?"*

Hypericum cuttings can be taken in July and August. Choose young shoots that have begun to harden at their base. Stand the cuttings in a shaded cold frame.

The leaves are likely to fall in the winter and should be cleared away. New growth should develop in the spring when the young plants can be potted individually.

Rusty rose of Sharon ❧

"I have a long stretch of rose of Sharon at the front of my cottage which was lovely until recently. Now the leaves are pale and unhealthy-looking and the whole effect has been spoiled. Can you advise me what I should do to correct the problem?"

The plants have been infected with hypericum rust fungus. At one time it was confined to the West Country but is now found more widely.

The best course of action is to cut the plants down to the ground and burn the cuttings. This may sound drastic, but new growth will develop next year. When new shoots do appear, spray a few times with a fungicide including rust on the label, such as Dithane 945.

Straight corkscrew hazel ❧

"I have a small bush of the corkscrew hazel. Whilst many of the stems are twisted, several coming from the base are straight and taller than the rest. Is this normal?"

It is common for plants of the corkscrew hazel, *Corylus avellana* "Contorta", to produce straight stems from the base. They are sucker growths arising from the common hazel on which the contorted form is grafted.

It is best to remove the sucker growths as soon as they are seen, otherwise they could take over the plant and eliminate the corkscrew growths. Do not cut them off with secateurs as this will only encourage more suckers to grow. Instead, pull them away from their point of origin with a sharp tug so that dormant buds are removed as well.

Holey trunk ❧

"We found some holes in the bark of an old hawthorn trunk, and cutting back into the wood exposed a number of bored channels. What insect would have done this?"

The channels were most probably eaten out by caterpillars of the goat moth. Both goat moth and leopard moth caterpillars bore into the wood and feed over a two- to four-year period, leopard moth caterpillars being yellowish and black-spotted, goat moth ones pink to yellow and red.

In the absence of the caterpillars, the way to identify the damage is to note that leopard moth caterpillars tend to feed singly and attack branches and trunks up to around 4 in. (10 cm) in diameter. The goat moth caterpillars tend to be present in some numbers, and feed mainly in the trunks, so the damage you describe was more likely due to the goat moth.

Layering a rhododendron ❧

"Could you tell me how to take cuttings from my rhododendron bush?"

Special equipment is needed to root rhododendron cuttings successfully. The easiest way for amateurs to propagate a plant is to layer a stem close to the ground in July or August. Bend it down to the soil and where it touches the ground make a slit in the stem. Dust the wound with hormone rooting powder. Prepare the soil by adding plenty of coarse grit and peat to it. Hold the layer in place with a wooden or metal peg.

It may take two years for the layer to make a good root system, when it can be severed from the parent in the autumn and replanted elsewhere.

Castor oil plant

"Can you solve a mystery for me? I thought that the castor oil plant was an evergreen shrub with shiny, green leaves. Last month I saw some big plants with reddish-purple leaves bedded out with summer annuals. These plants were labelled as 'Ricinus – Castor Oil plants'! Can you tell which is correct?"

The evergreen shrub, often used as a house plant and sometimes known as the castor oil plant, is correctly known as *Fatsia japonica*. The true castor oil plant is *Ricinus communis* and there are a number of different varieties, some with green leaves and others with bronzy-red leaves. The variety "Gibsonii" has handsome dark, red leaves and grows to about 5 ft (1.5 m) tall.

Ricinus plants are very poisonous and must be handled very carefully. Plants for summer bedding displays are raised from seed sown in the early part of the year in a heated greenhouse. The seedlings are grown on under glass and are planted in the open in early June.

Spotty rhodos

"I have seen a lot of rhododendrons this year with unsightly dark reddish spots on the leaves and have been wondering what the cause could be. Can you enlighten me?"

The cause could be attack by one of the many different species of rhododendron leaf spot fungus. Attack is encouraged by wet conditions in spring so the disease can be more severe in some years. Control measures are not really practical except on small garden bushes, when leaf picking and copper sprays may help to reduce attack.

Ornamental blackberry ❦

"Two years ago I purchased a plant from a market and was told it was an ornamental blackberry. I planted it out expecting it to climb. I now find that it is Rubus microphyllus *'Variegatus' which grows 2 ft (60 cm) high and spreads up to 6 ft (1.8 m) – no wonder it wouldn't climb! Can you give me any more information?"*

This relative of the blackberry has a small, mound-forming habit and purple-brown prickly stems. The leaves are marbled pink and off-white. It produces white, solitary flowers with a maroon calyx in spring followed by red berries in late summer.

Non-flowering rhododendron ❧

"My 'Elizabeth' rhododendron has small, pale leaves with some brown markings, and only produced one flower this spring. Does it need to be sprayed?"

There was evidence of a small amount of leafhopper feeding on the leaf sent to us, but the pale coloration and small size of the leaves, and the lack of flowering are the result of a lack of nutrients, and in particular a lack of iron.

Try a few waterings with Miracid soil acidifier and plant food over the leaves and the soil at roughly monthly intervals and this will supply all the necessary major and trace elements needed by acid-loving plants such as your rhododendron.

Blasted rhododendrons! ❧

"A number of the buds on our rhodos failed to open last spring and now we find they are covered with minute black pinheads. Can you identify and suggest a prevention?"

The buds are showing the effect of attack by rhododendron bud blast disease. Infection occurs in a rather unusual way: the spores of the fungus gain entry through tiny slits made in the leaves by the rhododendron leaf-hopper as it lays its eggs.

Remove infected buds now and next July spray with Picket, Tumblebug or use Safer's Garden Insecticide Concentrate against the leafhopper. Repeat the spray in mid-August.

Notched rhododendron leaves ❧

"Many of our rhododendron leaves have been nibbled around the edges. No pests have been seen."

The damage is being done by vine weevil adults, but as they feed mainly at night they are rarely caught in the act. Further damage can be prevented by spraying the foliage with Picket or Tumblebug a couple of times a fortnight apart, also spraying under the bushes where the pests hide by day. If damage is extensive, consider treating the soil with the biological agent nematode, which seeks out and destroys the larval stages of vine weevil.

Midget rhododendron ❧

"I have acquired a Rhododendron 'Goosander'. Could you please tell me how big it will grow and when it flowers? Will it grow in full sun?"

Your rhododendron is a dwarf, compact variety and will never grow very large. It produces mounds of flower trusses that are attractive pale yellow, flushed green, and have red spots. They open in late April and early May. It will probably succeed in full sun but most rhododendrons prefer dappled shade. "Goosander" is not fully hardy in all districts and may need some protection in the winter.

It must be grown in an acid soil that contains no lime. Mulch the soil around the plant each spring with a layer of decayed compost, rotted leaves or bark fibre.

Berry-less butcher's broom ❧

"I have a plant of butcher's broom but it does not produce berries. Can you tell me why not?"

To have berries on plants of butcher's broom, *Ruscus aculeatus*, you need both male and female plants as the flowers of the two sexes are produced on separate plants. Try planting more plants in the hope that you will have both male and female types.

Point taken ❧

"Can you name the shrub from the piece I am sending? It looks like a rose but the large thorns are not typical."

The piece of stem that you sent is from a rose called *Rosa sericea pteracantha*. It is a wild rose from the Himalayas and is usually grown for its large and attractive red thorns. The small, white flowers have four petals and are not particularly showy. Plants grow up to 8 ft (2.4 m) tall.

Tough rhododendron ❧

"Can you please give me some information on Rhododendron smirnowii*? I would like to have details of its height, colour, and whether it is peat-loving. Is it worth growing?"*

Although *Rhododendron smirnowii* is not often seen, it is well worth growing. Most rhododendrons must have an acid, peaty soil. They are very intolerant of lime or chalk. This species makes a compact bush. Growth is slow but can reach up to 10 ft (3 m). The bell-shaped, rosy-pink flowers appear in May and June. The undersides of the leaves are also attractively coated with a pale brown felt.

You can't overdo the peat when planting rhododendrons!

Feed and mulch your rhododendrons ❧

"Four or five years ago I planted a number of azalea and rhododendron bushes in my garden. Last year they did not make much new growth. Would you advise feeding them?"

It's well worthwhile feeding azaleas and rhododendrons in early spring. Apply Growmore fertilizer to the soil around the plants at 2 oz. per sq. yd (57 g/m²) or use a slow-release fertilizer such as Osmocote. Afterwards apply a thick mulch of bark fibre or rotted compost around the plants. This will help to conserve soil moisture. In dry spells keep the plants watered, using rainwater. A foliar feed at this time would also be beneficial, but do not feed after the end of July.

Dead-heading rhodos ❧

"I have been told that the green seed pods on rhododendrons should be removed after flowering. Is this a good thing to do?"

Yes, it is a good idea to remove all the green seed pods from rhododendron bushes. Instead of wasting energy on producing seed the plant puts all its strength into producing strong growth and new flower buds for next year. If you remove the old seed heads the plants should flower that much better next year.

Blotched rhododendrons ❧

"Some of our rhododendron leaves have small yellow spots on them and there appears to be a rusty deposit under the leaves. We have sometimes seen some unusual insects under the leaves but couldn't catch any to send. Please advise."

The yellowing on top with rusty marks underneath are typical signs of feeding by the rhododendron bug. The adult is $\frac{1}{4}$ in. long and has clearly netted wings, giving it the alternative name of lace bug. Although winged, the insect does not fly, so infestations tend to build up on individual plants. Damage can therefore be prevented by pruning out infested shoots in winter. Alternatively, spray the undersides of the leaves with Picket or Bio Long-Last in early and mid-summer.

Loosen those root balls ❧

"I have bought some rhododendrons in pots. The roots are in a tight ball. Do I leave them intact or loosen the root systems before planting the rhododendrons?"

Before planting your rhododendrons, loosen the root balls either with a fork or with the hands. When planting, fill the hole around the roots with a lime-free planting mixture or ericaceous compost to give the plants a good start.

Planting a rhododendron ❧

"I have bought a rhododendron in a plastic container. Should I plant it now or would it be better to wait until the spring?"

Your rhododendron would be better planted out in the ground rather than being kept in its pot until the spring. Plastic pots offer little protection to the roots and these could be killed off in severe weather. However, only plant when the ground is not frozen or too wet and prepare the ground well: add liberal amounts of decayed compost or an ericaceous planting mixture.

Cut for flowers ❧

"I have a large bush of flowering currant. Will it need pruning?"

Flowering currant bushes flower on the growths made in the previous season. Prune your bush after the flowers have faded. Cut back all the stems that have flowered close to their base.

Rooting hardwood cuttings ❧

"I have a flowering currant bush. Can I take cuttings from it and if so, when?"

One of the easiest ways of propagating a whole range of ornamental shrubs, including flowering currant (ribes), is by taking hardwood cuttings in the winter when the plants are dormant. Cuttings are made from firm stems made the previous season.

Insert the cuttings outside, preferably where the soil is light and sandy as rooting is more successful in this type of soil. Keep the top third of each cutting above soil level. Tread the soil firm around the cuttings and allow them to remain in the ground until the following autumn when they should have rooted.

Shrubs that can be increased now include: buddleja, forsythia, poplars, privet, weigela, symphoricarpos and willows, as well as blackcurrants and gooseberries.

Rowan problem ❧

"My self-sown, six-year-old rowan tree has developed a leaf problem which doesn't respond to my normal systemic fungicide spray."

The leaves have been attacked by the pear leaf blister mite, which also attacks pear leaves. The mites spend the winter inside the buds and then spread to developing new leaves in spring. The leaf spotting and pimpling is unsightly, but not really damaging.

There are no chemical controls and so the only action that can be taken, and then only with a small tree, is the removal of all the infected leaves. Do this each year as soon as the symptoms are seen.

No berries ❧

"I have two skimmia bushes but they never produce berries. Can you tell me why?"

Some skimmias have male and female flowers on separate plants and both must be grown together to ensure a crop of berries. It would seem that your plants are all of one sex, so try growing a plant of *Skimmia reevesiana* which has both male and female flowers on the same plant.
   This type does not like chalky soils.

Lilac suckers

"I have a beautiful old lilac bush in my lawn. I cut off all the suckers last year but, as a result, I now have 'millions' more. Is there anything I can do to stop them appearing?"

Cutting off the suckers has induced dormant buds to break into growth and, as a result, you now have a "forest" of suckers. The best thing to do is to trace each sucker back to a root. Then, with a sharp tug, tear the sucker from its point of origin. This should remove most of the dormant buds at the base of the sucker growth.

Yellowing leaves

"I have a pair of skimmia bushes which were planted together about six years ago. They have given us a lovely show of flowers and berries each year. Last year was an exception and I notice that the leaves are turning yellow. Can you tell me what is causing the trouble and how to overcome it?"

The yellowing of the skimmia leaves could be due to a lack of nutrients at the roots after several years of growth. Lack of either nitrogen or iron would result in yellowing foliage. It would be worth applying Sequestrene to the soil around the bushes early next spring, followed by rose fertilizer.

Lack of flowers

"Can you give me any reason why my bushes of Spiraea arguta *have not flowered this year? One is about 12 years old and the other is two years old, but it has never flowered. An eight-year-old* Viburnum carlesii *also does not flower. I mulch the soil annually with Forest Bark compost and add well-rotted manure plus Phostrogen throughout the season."*

You are overfeeding your shrubs so that the soil is excessively rich in nitrogen. This has resulted in the shrubs making leaf growth at the expense of flowers. Overcome this by top-dressing the root area with 1 oz. per sq. yd (110 g/m^2) of sulphate of potash. Apply it in August. Next year put it on in February and repeat in July. This will help both shrubs develop firmer shoots which should produce plenty of flowers.

Mountain ash

"Could you please tell me the lifespan of the rowan tree or mountain ash?"

Mountain ash trees should live, in spite of Essex being a relatively dry county, for anything up to 60 years. They grow very well at altitudes of up to 1000 ft (300 m) in Scotland, but the rainfall there is considerably greater than in southern England. Ensure they receive water in periods of drought.

Pruning lilac

"I have a large lilac bush. It has become very overcrowded. Can I prune it and when should it be done?"

The best time to prune your lilac bush is after flowering. Thin out some of the overcrowded growths and remove all dead and diseased wood. Old bushes can, if necessary, be cut back hard to induce strong new growth. After pruning, feed the lilac with a general fertilizer and mulch the soil with a thick layer of organic matter.

Dwarf lilac

"I have been given a small shrub called Syringa palabiniana. *Can you tell me how high it grows and when it flowers?"*

Your shrub is a dwarf lilac which grows to a height of about 4 ft (1.2 m). The pale pink flowers appear in May. It is an excellent shrub for a small garden and does well in most well-drained soils. It has been given an Award of Garden Merit by the Royal Horticultural Society. Botanists have decided that the correct name for the shrub is now *Syringa meyeri* "Palabin".

What's in a name?

"I went to buy some plants of Senecio laxifolius *at a garden centre but could not find any. Plants which looked similar were labelled* Brachyglottis *'Sunshine'. I was told these were one and the same plants. Is this so?"*

Yes, the plant names you have been given refer to the same plant. As you probably know, botanists are constantly changing plant names and it can be very confusing.

Senecio laxifolius is a first-rate, grey-leaved shrub which has yellow daisy flowers in the summer. It flowers best in a warm, sunny situation. It has also been known as *Senecio* "Sunshine" but botanists now decree that its correct botanical name is *Brachyglottis* "Sunshine". Not all nurserymen realize this and you will probably find all three names being used.

Pruning Goldflame

"I have a shrub of Spiraea *'Goldflame' which has become rather straggly. Can I prune it now? The young golden foliage is so attractive and I do not want to harm it."*

Do not prune your *Spiraea* "Goldflame" now that it is in full growth. The best time to do it is in March when the growths can be pruned back fairly hard. Afterwards feed the bush with a little bonemeal and it will soon be covered in strong, new shoots.

New willow

"I recently bought a shrub called Salix tricolour *from a garden centre. The foliage is most attractive but I cannot find out anything about it and I wonder whether you can help?"*

It is *Salix integra* "Hakuro Nishiki". It has also been known as *Salix integra* "Albomaculata". It was introduced from Japan by a Dutch botanist in 1979. It is grown for its attractive young, pink and white leaves and grows about 6 ft (1.8 m) tall. Plants will grow in ordinary garden soil and are happy where the ground is moist.

Pruning willow

"We have a beautiful 25-year-old weeping willow. Despite the removal of unwanted growth the tree now extends over a quarter of our garden. We have been advised to lop the tree. How severe should this be?"

The best time to prune your willow is when the leaves have fallen in late autumn. To remove large limbs requires skilled attention and we advise you to engage a professional tree surgeon – a list of approved arboriculturists can be obtained from the Arboricultural Association by phoning 01794 368717. Although lopping the tree will reduce its present size, growth will be vigorous after pruning and lopping will become a regular business.

This tree is, however, unsuitable for a small garden and in the long run it might be sensible to have it removed and replaced with something less vigorous.

Cut-leaved elder

"I have a green-laced elder, Sambucus racemosa 'Tenuifolia' growing in a container. Please tell me whether it will flower and fruit?"

Sambucus racemosa is commonly called the red-berried elder. "Tenuifolia" is as beautiful as a cut-leaved Japanese maple, and there is no reason why it should not flower and fruit.

Blighted lilac attack

"Our normally lovely lilac has been blighted by something, with most of the flower buds turning brown and shrivelling away. We haven't had any severe late frost, so what has caused the damage and what action should we now take?"

This blighting is actually due to a disease known as lilac blight. The disease is bacterial in nature but is often followed by the grey mould fungus.

Cut out all shoots showing signs of the damage and also any shoots showing any signs of cankers. Cut a few centimetres below the obvious sign of damage to be sure of eliminating all of the infection.

Next spring, in advance of any damage symptoms, it may help to apply a copper fungicide to the tree.

Gall damage

"On a large old willow tree at the bottom of our garden, some of the leaves have produced odd-looking swellings. Can you tell me what they are, please?"

The swellings on your willow tree leaves are the work of the willow bean-gall sawfly, *Pontania proxima*. Eggs are laid in the leaf buds during May and feeding by the larvae results in the willow producing the galls – those are the unsightly swellings you have found. Although the leaves look a mess, they cause little direct damage to the tree. When fully fed the larvae leave the galls by a tiny hole on the underside and pupate in the soil or on the bark of the tree. A second generation of adults emerges in July. No control is necessary, or indeed possible on a large, old tree.

Transplanting lilac ❧

"I have a three-year-old double white lilac. It flowered well this year but it is planted very close to a row of conifers used for screening. Will I be able to move the lilac?"

Your lilac tree, although it is only three years old, will have made a good root system. To move it satisfactorily, you will have to dig it up with the root ball virtually intact so that there is as little damage as possible to the roots. Early November is a good time to lift the plant as the soil will still have some warmth in it. Prepare the new position in advance with a good dressing of decayed manure or compost plus a dressing of bonemeal. Replant the shrub at the same depth it was originally. Return the soil around the roots and tread it firm. Mulch the surface of the soil around the lilac in the spring and make sure the soil does not dry out in the summer.

Green and gold ❧

"I have a bush of Spiraea *'Gold Flame'. Every now and then shoots with green leaves appear among the golden foliage. How can I stop this happening?"*

Nothing, unfortunately can be done to stop the green leaves appearing on your *Spiraea* "Gold Flame". It is simply reverting back to the original plain green-leaved form.

Whenever shoots with green leaves do appear, cut them out at their base. If left, there is a danger that they will eventually oust the stems with golden leaves because they grow more vigorously.

Lack-lustre lilac ❧

"I have a small lilac bush which this year has only produced a couple of flowers, and these were hidden in amongst the foliage. It is in full sun. Am I cutting back the foliage hard enough and when is the best time for it to be done?"

Your lilac is growing too exuberantly for quality flowers to form. Help balance the strong growth and leafy nature by top-dressing the root area with sulphate of potash. Repeat the dressing next February. Do not prune the shrub apart from cutting off the old flower heads as soon as they fade.

Christmas box ❧

"Can you give me the botanical name of Christmas box and tell me how to grow it?"

There are several different kinds but the most popular one is *Sarcococca hookeriana digyna*. It is a low-growing evergreen with small, white, deliciously fragrant flowers in winter. It grows well in shade and in most soils, including chalk.

Cotton lavender ❧

"My bush of cotton lavender has become very leggy. Can I cut it back? If I do, will the bush flower this year?"

Bushes of cotton lavender, *Santolina chamaecyparissus*, do become leggy after a year or so and need cutting back in early spring. Strong new growth will soon result. Flowers are unlikely to appear this year. Some gardeners grow the plant solely for its silver-grey foliage and prune it hard each spring.

Choosing a mahonia ❧

"A few weeks ago I saw a magnificent shrub with yellow flowers in a Devon garden called Mahonia lomariifolia. *Can you tell me whether it will succeed in my northern district?"*

Mahonia lomariifolia is a very handsome winter-flowering, evergreen shrub but it is not suitable for cold districts as frosts may damage it. Instead we suggest that you choose a hardier form such as "Lionel Fortescue", "Faith" or "Charity".

They must be given a carefully chosen position sheltered from cold winds, and soil well enriched with decayed compost and leafmould.

Powdery problem ❧

"Our mahonia bush has been plastered with what we assume is mildew since late summer. What would you recommend now to prevent attacks next year?"

Powdery mildew is indeed responsible for the white coating over the leaves of your mahonia.

Prune out the infected shoots now, removing the stems to a little below the last sign of mildew and then give a spray with Supercarb or Phostrogen Safer's Garden Fungicide. Next spring or summer, re-apply one of these fungicides at the first sign of attack. Keeping the bush well watered in dry spells will help to reduce the chances of attack.

Tender subject

"I am very fond of mimosa and I am told that it is possible to grow it outside in this country. Can you tell me whether this is true?"

Mimosa, *Acacia dealbata*, can be grown in the open in mild districts in this country, particularly along the south coast, but in very severe winters it may be cut back or even killed. Choose a sheltered position for it in the open, or train it against a south-facing wall which should give it protection. Plant in the spring so that tree is well established by the following winter.

Weird willow

"I came across a most attractive willow shoot recently where the tip had developed into a rose-like form. If I were to make a cutting of this shoot would the form be stable, and perhaps marketable?"

Sadly, no to both questions. The rosette growth, sometimes known as camellia gall, is actually caused by feeding of a larva of the willow rosette-gall midge. The adult midge lays her eggs singly in the buds in April to early May. Feeding by the pink to orange larvae results in the gall formation during summer. The galls turn brown in autumn and winter and fall from the tree as new growth starts up in the following year. The new adults emerge from the galls shortly afterwards.

Pruning mimosa

"I have a mimosa tree, which I think is really a form of an acacia, in my garden which is doing well and has fragrant yellow flowers in the early spring. Some of the branches have become straggly. Can I cut them back and when should it be done?"

Mimosa, *Acacia dealbata,* can be pruned after flowering in late spring. New growths should develop during the summer which will flower in the following spring. Use sharp secateurs to make clean cuts or a pruning saw if a large branch has to be shortened.

Magnolia seeds

"I have a five-year-old magnolia tree which has beautiful flowers each spring. Last year it produced red pips on three branches. I have removed the seed and kept some in a box. Four others have been sown in a pot. Am I doing the right thing?"

Ideally, magnolia seeds should be sown immediately they are fully ripe in late autumn. Use an ericaceous, lime-free seed compost and sow the seeds in pots or seed trays to a depth of about 1 in. (2.5 cm). Place the pots in a cold frame or in a sheltered part of the garden. Use rain water for watering as magnolias do not like lime. The seeds may germinate in the spring but it can take 12–18 months. Leave the seeds outdoors for another winter and do not throw them away as you may find they will germinate in the second spring.

Southern Rata ❧

"I have been sent some seed of Metrosideros umbellata. *Can you tell me anything about the plant?"*

Metrosideros umbellata is a New Zealand tree sometimes called the Southern Rata. It has attractive evergreen leaves and bright red, bottle brush flowers. It can be grown outside in this country only in very mild areas.

Sow your seed in a small pot of good seed compost stood in a heated propagator. Grow the plant in a large tub or pot and keep it in a frost-free greenhouse for the winter. Stand it outside for the summer in a sunny, sheltered spot.

To keep the plant to reasonable proportions, prune it after flowering.

Magnolia under attack ❧

"The leaves on my lovely magnolia are starting to be eaten. I cannot find any caterpillars or other pests, but quite large holes are appearing and a lot of notching is going on. Help please!"

Vine weevil will be responsible for the damage you describe. Adult female weevils emerge in May and June to feed on the foliage, feeding mainly at night.

Each weevil can lay around 100 eggs and the larvae from these, hatching from late July onwards, feed on plant roots. Prevent further leaf damage by spraying with BugGun! or Bugmaster and then in July apply beneficial nematodes to the soil, using Nature's Friends for Vine Weevil Control, BioSafe or Nemasys H.

Bare necessities ❧

"I have a large bush of Mahonia japonica. *It is healthy and flowers well. However, many of the stems have grown long and leggy. Can I cut them back and if so, when should this be done?"*

Mahonias tend to produce a few long and bare stems after several years. They can certainly be cut back, preferably to the junction of a young side shoot. Late April and early May is the best time to prune.

Propagating magnolias ❧

"I have a magnolia tree which I want to propagate. I have been told to air-layer a shoot. When should this be done?"

The best time to air layer your magnolia is in the spring. Select a stem about pencil thickness and make a slanting cut about 2 in. (5 cm) long and approximately 12 in. (30 cm) from the tip of the shoot. Dust the cut with hormone rooting powder and surround with damp sphagnum moss. Enclose the moss with clear plastic film tied at the top and bottom. Support the layer by tying it to a bamboo cane.

It will take several months for roots to form. When a good root system can be seen through the plastic, cut off the rooted layer just below the roots. Pot it in good potting compost and keep it in a shaded cold greenhouse until it has fully recovered.

Catch a crab ❧

"I want to grow a crab apple for its ornamental fruit. What are the best varieties to grow?"

Some of the best crab apples noted for their colourful fruits in the autumn are "John Downie", white flowers and orange-red fruits; "Eleyi", deep pink flowers and purplish red fruits; "Golden Hornet", white flowers and yellow fruit and "Red Sentinel", white flowers and deep red fruits.

Frost problem ❧

"We moved to Berwickshire recently. As it is subject to severe frosts can you tell me how I can protect some newly planted, small shrubs? They include Pernettya mucronata *which I think is sensitive to frost. I lost two of the shrubs last spring."*

As your garden is subject to severe frosts you must choose plants that are fully hardy. *Pernettya mucronata* comes from Chile and the southern tip of South America. It will stand up to frost but this depends on its severity. It is also a shrub that must have an acid, lime-free soil. To protect your shrubs, put a covering of bracken over them for the winter. Alternatively, you could put nylon fleece material over the plants for protection.

Mock orange cuttings ❧

"I have a bush of the mock orange called 'Sybille' which has a lovely scent. I would like to take some cuttings from it to give to friends. When is the best time to take the cuttings?"

July and early August is a good time to take cuttings from your mock orange (philadelphus).

Choose the tips of young shoots, made this year, that have begun to harden and turn brown at their base. Make the cuttings about 4 in. (10 cm) long and trim each one with a sharp knife below a leaf joint. Remove the lower leaves and insert the cuttings around the edge of a small pot filled with a mixture of equal parts moist peat and coarse sand or perlite. Put the cuttings in a heated propagator or cover them with a polythene bag until rooting occurs.

Cuttings can also be taken in the autumn. Choose young shoots and make the cuttings about 12 in. (30 cm) long. Insert them outside to about half their depth. Put some coarse sand in the bottom of each planting hole. This will assist rooting. These cuttings should have made good roots by the following autumn.

Striped kiwi ❧

"I have been given a plant of Phormium 'Yellow Wave'. It has most attractive yellow and green-striped leaves. However, I know little about its needs. Can you tell me what soil and position it likes?"

Your plant is a variety of New Zealand flax, *Phormium tenax*, which does well in coastal gardens. The plants are slightly tender and do not grow so well in cold areas. However, your plant should do well in your area [Bournemouth].

Grow it in a sunny spot and moist, but well-drained soil. "Yellow Wave" is an excellent foliage plant and looks superb when the sun lights up its colourful leaves.

Problem mock orange ❧

"I have a 'Belle Etoile' mock orange (philadelphus) but it won't flower. I pruned it fairly severely last year and it now has a 'forest' of straight stems. Will these ever produce flowers?"

It is possible that you have pruned your mock orange at the wrong time. It should be done after the bushes have flowered, cutting back the stems that have borne flowers. The growths made in the summer should flower in the following year. If you pruned in the winter you would have cut out most of the flowering stems.

It does seem to be growing very strongly and may be getting too much nitrogen. We suggest that you feed the shrub with sulphate of potash to encourage more sturdy growth.

Pernettya for ground cover

"Would pernettyas be suitable shrubs for ground cover? I have seen some plants with colourful white berries and would like to grow some for winter colour."

Yes, pernettyas are excellent shrubs for covering the ground and for their colourful berries in winter. They must have an acid, lime-free soil. To ensure a good set of berries it is wise to plant several varieties. One of the most reliable is "Bell's Seedling" which has dark red berries. Others are "Alba" and "Davis's hybrids" in a mixture of berry colours.

Tiny Tom

"On holiday in Cornwall recently, I saw a small rounded shrub with purple leaves similar to pittosporum. Can you tell me what the shrub is called, as I would like to have one in my garden."

The shrub that you saw on holiday is most probably *Pittosporum tenuifolium* "Tom Thumb". It is a first-rate dwarf shrub which thrives in the milder parts of the country.

It originated in New Zealand. The young leaves are green at first and then turn purple. In very cold winters it may suffer damage, but in most years it is happy outside in southern England. Grow it in a sunny position in well-drained fertile soil.

It has received an Award of Garden Merit from the Royal Horticultural Society.

Frost damage

"We have recently moved into a new house and garden and are finding some good shrubs in our new garden. One we have identified as a choisya (Mexican orange blossom), but the new shoots are all dead or dying. Please help."

A late frost would have been responsible for the damage. Cut out the browned shoots to below the point of damage and new growth will soon get under way.

Pieris cuttings

"I have a bush of Pieris forrestii and would like to take a cutting from it. Up to now I have failed. Can you tell me how to do it?"

The reason why you have not been successful with the pieris cuttings is probably because you have taken them at the wrong time. They should be taken in August and early September.

Choose young side shoots, a few inches long, that have begun to harden at their base. Make a clean cut with a sharp knife just below a leaf joint and remove the lower leaves. Insert the cuttings in small pots filled with gritty soil containing plenty of coarse sand or perlite. Cover the pots with plastic domes or polythene bags to keep the cuttings moist. Stand the pots in a cold frame or greenhouse or in the window of an unheated room. Roots should have developed by the following spring when the plants should be potted individually in a good potting compost.

Colourful kiwi

"On a visit to the Ventnor Botanic Garden on the Isle of Wight, I was very interested in their phormiums, which have yucca-like leaves in different colours. I was told they can only be grown in mild districts. Do you think they would do well in my garden in Dorset, which is not far from the sea?"

Phormiums are attractive evergreens which come from New Zealand. There are a number of new hybrids with leaves in reddish purple, cream and yellow. As you have been told, they are not fully hardy in all districts, but in your area they should do well. They are, in fact, good seaside plants. Grow the plants in well-drained soil and in a sunny situation.

Straggly perovskia

"I have a bush of perovskia 'Blue Spire'. It has spikes of pale blue flowers in late summer. It is now looking rather straggly. When can I prune it?"

As perovskia flowers on the shoots made in the current season, the best time to prune it is in early spring. The old stems can be cut back to within a few inches of their base. Strong new stems will appear to flower later in the summer.

Fireblight

"Is fireblight still a problem? I haven't heard much of it lately."

Fireblight certainly has seemed to be less of a problem in recent years. In the early days there was a lot of damage to hawthorns, pears and other trees. Once these had been removed, and measures put in place not to grow particularly susceptible varieties, such as Laxton's Pears or "Joseph Rock" sorbus, the problem became less acute. A major factor can be the weather at flowering time when, under suitable conditions, bees can spread the bacterial spores as they visit to pollinate.

Unhappy pieris ❦

"I have a pieris bush that does not look too well. It is in a pot outdoors and I am wondering whether it would be better planted in a border?"

Pieris are very beautiful spring-flowering, evergreen shrubs. They must have an acid, lime-free soil to succeed, so unless your garden soil is acid, it would not be a good idea to plant it out.

Your plant may improve if you feed it with a fertilizer such as Miracid. If it is in a small pot, move it on into a larger one using an ericaceous potting compost – as used for heathers and rhododendrons – or scrape away some of the surface compost and replace it with fresh compost.

Cherry blackfly ❦

"This spring our cherry tree had a very bad attack of blackfly, but it has almost disappeared now, without any spraying. Is it going to give a repeat performance, and how should we treat it?"

Cherry blackfly spends the winter in the egg stage on cherry trees and hatches out on the leaves during the spring. In May or June, winged forms develop and these fly off to summer host plants which include weeds speedwell and bedstraw. Some of the blackfly will stay on the cherry through to summer. The blackfly will return during autumn to lay winter eggs. The most effective control method is by spraying with a tar oil winter wash in December.

Pittosporum variations ❦

"Can you tell me the difference between Pittosporum tenuifolium *'Tom Thumb' and* P. t. *'Garnettii'?"*

Both these pittosporums are handsome ornamental shrubs with attractive foliage. "Tom Thumb" makes a dwarf shrub and has coppery coloured foliage which is green when young. "Garnettii" makes a large conical shrub with crinkly, creamy white foliage. In the winter the foliage is spotted with pink and red.

Power failure

"My flowering cherry was a picture in May, when in mid bloom, but by the end of the month most of the tips had shrivelled with just a few healthy shoots per branch. What caused it?"

The samples you sent would indicate a bad attack of blossom wilt, and there is also some bacterial canker present.

If the tree is not too large to get up into, the best advice would be to prune out all the spurs carrying wilted blossoms to prevent the infection getting back into the wood. This should be done as soon as possible – if left too late the larger cuts could be susceptible to infection by another disease, namely silver leaf.

Copper fungicide sprays in mid-August, September and October will help to control and prevent bacterial canker attack.

Spring-time autumn cherry

"In March my 'Autumnalis' cherry tree was covered in blossom. It is a 25-year-old tree and, until six years ago, flowered in the autumn. How can I make it flower at the proper time?"

Your cherry is *Prunus subhirtella* "Autumnalis". This usually flowers on and off from November to March, depending on weather conditions. In winter, the early blooms are often killed off by frost but more flowers appear as soon as there is another mild spell. Weather conditions are probably affecting the autumn flowering of your tree and nothing can be done about it.

No suckers

"Do any of the following shrubs produce suckers: Pyracantha *'Orange Charm',* Pyracantha *'Mohave',* Viburnum *'Dawn'?"*

None of the plants mentioned are inclined to sucker. If they do, it is usually because the root system has been damaged by digging. They are not grafted on to stock plants, so suckers do not normally appear.

Empress tree ❧

"I was recently in Washington, USA, and saw a large number of trees with blue, trumpet-shaped flowers. I was told they were Pawlonia tomentosa, *the Empress tree. I learnt that they originated in Japan where they are highly valued and the wood is used to make small boxes for brides. In the area around Washington DC the trees are fairly common, very invasive and considered to be rather a nuisance despite their attractive appearance. Can this tree be grown here and where can I get seeds?"*

Pawlonia tomentosa is a magnificent tree and can certainly be grown in this country, making specimens up to 80 ft (24 m) tall. The flower buds are formed in the autumn and are liable to be damaged by hard frosts in the winter.

Apart from the attractive flowers the large leaves are also very handsome. Plants are easily raised from seed from Chiltern Seeds, Bortree Stile, Ulverston, Cumbria LA12 7PB.

Tree peony ❧

"Some time ago I bought a cutting at a church bazaar. According to the label it is a tree peony lutea. Can you tell me anything about it?"

Your *Paeonia lutea* is a choice plant, producing yellow cup-shaped flowers in May and June. It also has handsome foliage.

Grow your peony plant in a sunny, sheltered situation and in good, well-drained soil, and feeding in the spring with a general fertilizer will help the plant to make good growth.

Cape fuchsia ❧

"I want to grow some phygelius or Cape fuchsias. When is the best time to plant them and what sort of soil do they need?"

Phygelius are slightly tender shrubby plants which should succeed in your area of Dorset. In cold areas cover the crowns of the plants with protective litter in the winter. Grow them in a sunny position in well-drained soil. Spring is the best time to plant them.

Several varieties are available including "Winchester Fanfare" and "Yellow Trumpet". The flowers appear in summer and into autumn.

Prune for better berries ❧

"I have planted a pyracantha which I want to train against a wall. To keep it neat and compact I understand that it needs regular pruning. When should this be done to best effect?"

To keep wall-trained pyracantha (firethorn) neat and compact, trim the growths back after flowering. Allow the leading stems to grow upward and outward without pruning. They will then produce larger clusters of berries.

Withering heights ❧

"Several of the shoots on my cherry tree withered just as the blossom was forming. What caused this and how should I treat it?"

Blossom wilt is the most likely cause of the problem. Infection causes the blossom and leaf clusters to shrivel but still remain on the shoots. The tips of the shoots may also die back a little way.

The only treatment now is to remove the shoot tips, cutting a little further back than any obvious sign of damage. There is no particular fungicidal recommendation, but it has been found that when a tar oil winter wash such as Mortegg has been applied for control of overwintering pest eggs, blossom wilt becomes less of a problem.

Soils for quince ❧

"I am very fond of quince jelly and I would like to plant a quince bush. Will it need any special type of soil?"

Quince bushes are not difficult to grow and they will succeed in any reasonable soil provided it drains well. Thin, shallow soils are to be avoided. Mulch around the bush each spring and scatter some general fertilizer in the root area.

Suitable varieties to grow are "Meech's Prolific" and "Vranja".

Blackthorn blossom ❧

"The blackthorn blossom was very beautiful this spring. Does this indicate bad weather to come?"

There are two species of prunus that flower early in the year. *Prunus cerasifera*, the cherry plum, flowers much earlier than *Prunus spinosa*, blackthorn.

The amount of blossom on both varies each year and is dependent upon the amount of new growth that the shrub produced in the previous season. This year both species did well for bloom but the fact that they flower when the weather is cold is not anyway out of the ordinary. The blossom of both species is not affected by cold weather and when their season approaches they will flower.

The only weather conditions that would prevent this happening is if temperatures dropped below zero by both day and night.

Mildew on quince

"The edges of my quince tree are rolling over upwards and appear to be more silvery-looking than normal. Is this some form of mildew and if so, how can I treat it?"

Earlier in the season, upwards-rolling of leaves is often the result of frost, but by June or later the cause would be powdery mildew, as you suspect.

A systemic fungicide would give control, but if there are any edible quinces on the tree such treatment would not have received the necessary official approval. Removal of the worst-affected shoots would be the only available treatment.

Scabby pyracantha

"My pyracantha bushes had masses of berries this year but nearly all of them developed brown to black cracked areas and the whole lot looked very unsightly. Can you tell me what the trouble was and how I can stop it another year?"

Pyracantha scab was responsible for the unsightly appearance of your berries. This is a fungal disorder which also attacks the leaves. It over-winters on the stems in little pustules and on the leaves still on the plant (but not on fallen leaves).

During winter, look for signs of the stem pustules and prune out any stems found bearing them. As new growth starts again next spring, spray with a carbendazim fungicide such as Supercarb or Spotless and repeat this a few times at two-week intervals.

If the disease shows signs of becoming a major problem, consider replacing the plants (in a new position) with varieties that show some resistance to infection, such as the red-fruited "Apache", the yellow-fruited "Golden Charmer" or the orange-fruited "Mohave".

Lime suckers

"I have a lime tree in my garden which produces masses of suckers around the base each year. It is a hard job cutting them out. Could you suggest another easier method of controlling them?"

It is natural for the common lime, *Tilia* x *europaea*, to produce thickets of shoots around the base of the trunk. There is no easy way of getting rid of the suckers, apart from cutting them out as close to their base as possible.

Chusan palm

"I understand that there is a palm tree that can be grown outside in this country. Can you give me its name?"

The palm you probably have in mind is the Chusan palm or Chinese windmill palm, *Trachycarpus fortunei*. Although it is certainly hardy in southern England it should be given a sheltered position as cold winds can damage the foliage. Young potted plants should be moved under cover if severe weather threatens.

Tamarix cut-back

"My tamarix is about 10 ft (3 m) high and the main trunk is leaning to one side. Can I cut the bush down to about 2 ft (60 cm) and start again? I don't want to kill it."

You can prune your tamarix to make it more bushy. It should not come to any harm and should soon make new growths. If your plant flowers in May it is *Tamarix tetrandra*. This can be pruned after the flowers fade in early June. If it flowers in August it is probably *T. pentandra*. This should be pruned between October and February.

Drastic yew turn

"I have some yew bushes which are spreading outwards. Can I cut back the stems drastically and when should it be done?"

Yews can be pruned back drastically if necessary. This should be done in early spring. The old stems may look very bare at first but fresh new growth should soon appear in the spring and summer. By the time autumn arrives there should be a good green covering of young foliage.

Waiting for yucca flowers ❧

"I have had a plant of Yucca filamentosa *in my garden for two years but it has not had any flowers. How much longer do I have to wait?"*

Yucca rosettes or crowns need to be about four years old before they flower. Your plant may well flower this year. Once a crown has flowered it will die but sucker growths take over. Once well established your yucca should produce flowers every year.

Yew seeds ❧

"I have collected some English yew seeds from beneath a tree reputed to be 1200 years old. How do I grow the seed?"

Yew is easily raised from seed and seedlings often appear naturally, particularly in gravel paths. Store the seed in damp sand for the winter and then sow it in small pots filled with a good seed compost in the spring.

Australian beauty ❧

"I have grown two seedlings of the Australian Waratah. They are now about 4 in. (10 cm) high. Can I plant them in the garden?"

The Australian Waratah (*Telopea speciossima*) is frost tender and will not stand the winter outside in this country. Why not grow your plants in pots and stand them outside in a sunny position for the summer? Move them to a frost-free conservatory or greenhouse in October for the winter.

Winter flowers ❧

"Could you name the shrub from the piece I am sending? The flowers first appeared in the autumn and it seems to be evergreen."

Your shrub is laurustinus, *Viburnum tinus*, a valuable evergreen producing whitish flowers all winter. It is a tough, easy-going shrub that is not fussy about soil and succeeds in a shaded situation. "Eve Price" is a very good form of it, having lovely pinkish flowers.

Rare beauty ❧

"Why is Viburnum x juddii *rarely mentioned in books and magazines? It is a most beautiful plant with an exotic perfume. Has it been renamed?"*

It is an excellent shrub and deserves to be known more.

It is a hybrid between *V. bitchiuense* and *V. carlesii*, producing its sweet-scented, pink flowers in April and May. It has a stronger constitution than *V. carlesii* and has been given an Award of Garden Merit by the Royal Horticultural Society.

The long and short of it ❧

"We have had a wisteria for seven years. It is healthy but it has never bloomed. Can you tell us why?"

Regular, twice-yearly pruning can encourage wisteria plants to bloom. In July, cut back the long, new growths to about 6 in. (15 cm). In winter after leaf-fall, shorten all the new side growths to two buds.

Feeding with a high potash fertilizer each spring can also lead to regular flowering. Sprinkle sulphate of potash at 2 oz. per sq.yd. (60 g/m^2) evenly over the root area when the soil is damp in February or March. Seed-raised plants may take up to 20 years to produce flowers. It is better to buy a grafted plant of a known variety. Overfeeding with a fertilizer high in nitrogen or manures may also delay flowering.

Pruning wisteria ❧

"When is the best time to prune an established wisteria?"

February is a good time to prune wisterias. Cut back all the side shoots on the main stems to within an inch of their base. In July summer-prune all the new lateral growths by shortening them to about 6 in. (15 cm) of their base.

Berry poisonous ❧

"The yew tree in my garden has lots of red berries which drop on the ground. Is it true that the seeds are poisonous?"

The red yew berries are highly poisonous and must not be eaten. Children must be made aware of the danger and toddlers kept from that part of the garden where the yew is growing.

Pruning weigela ❧

"We have a large bush of Weigela 'Bristol Ruby' in our garden that has not been touched for many years and is very overcrowded. When is the best time to prune it?"

Prune your weigela as soon as the flowers have faded. Aim to cut back the stems that have flowered, shortening them to a position where a new young shoot is appearing. This will grow during the summer and flower the following spring. Any dead, weak and withered stems can also be removed at the same time. To encourage the shrub to make plenty of new shoots, feed it with a general fertilizer which can be applied to the soil around the shrub at 2 oz. per sq.yd (60 g/m²)

No flowers or berries ❧

"My Viburnum opulus *is over three years old and looks healthy but it does not flower or have berries. Can you tell me the reason for this?"*

It is not unusual for relatively newly planted shrubs not to flower for a year or so after planting. The shrub has to make a good root system before it can become established and develop top growth. However, a lack of balanced nutrients, particularly potash, can encourage excessive leaf growth and inhibit flower formation.

Potash can be applied as sulphate of potash around shrubs at 2 oz. per sq.yd (60 g/m²) in early summer which should encourage the shoots to ripen and form flowers next year.

Berry blues ❧

"Two or three years ago I planted a bush of Viburnum davidii *specially for its blue berries. Although it flowers there have not been any berries. Can you tell me what is wrong?"*

You must plant more than one bush of *Viburnum davidii* as there are male and female plants. Berrying is a little uncertain with this shrub but if you get both male and female plants together you should have a good show of the beautiful blue berries. This low-growing shrub is excellent for ground cover in the front of a border.

Oversized ❧

"I have a myrtle bush which is growing too big. Can I cut it back without harming it and when is the best time to do this?"

Overgrown myrtle bushes can be cut back quite severely in March or early April. The bush may look rather bare for a few weeks but in May vigorous young growths will begin to appear and it will soon recover.

It is not likely that there will be many flowers in the summer after

534 °∞ Trees and shrubs

pruning. To help the plant make good growth, mulch the soil around it with decayed compost or manure after pruning. A dressing of bonemeal at 4 oz. per sq.yd (110 g/m²) will also help greatly.

Seaside gorse ⋟

"I have a bank which becomes very dry in the summer. I want to grow ground cover plants on it and I wonder whether Ulex gallii *would be suitable, particularly as I live near the sea?"*

The gorse, *Ulex gallii*, would be very suitable for covering a dry bank. It is a plant that will succeed in poor soil and a windswept position. It is relatively hardy at sea level, withstands salty winds and should be suitable for your garden. The spiny bushes become covered in yellow flowers in late summer and early autumn.

Male mistletoe ⋟

"Seven years ago I rubbed some mistletoe seeds into the bark of a 'Bramley's Seedling' apple tree. The seed developed and over the years the 'bunch' has grown but to my disappointment no berries have formed."

Your bunch of mistletoe, which has not borne berries, is a male. You will need to rub further berries into the bark to obtain more plants which may be male or female. With luck, there will be some females among them. There are no bisexual forms.

Blue berries ⋟

"I have two bushes of Viburnum davidii *which I planted for their beautiful blue berries. However, none have formed. Can you tell me how to get berries on my plants?"*

It is necessary to have both male and female plants of *Viburnum davidii* to get berries. It is probable that you have only plants of one sex. We suggest that you purchase a few more plants and hope that you have a mixture of both male and female plants.

No berries ⋟

"I planted several plants of Viburnum davidii *a number of years ago and was looking forward to seeing the blue berries. Unfortunately, none have appeared."*

Male and female flowers appear on separate plants of *Viburnum davidii* and as you have had no berries we can only assume that your plants are male. You will have to introduce some female plants and, to be sure they are female, wait until you can find some plants in berry at a garden centre.

Overhanging magnolia

"I have a magnolia tree which is beginning to spread out over a path. Can I prune the branches and if so, when should it be done?"

Magnolias do not usually need to be pruned but when branches get in the way some of them can be cut back using a sharp saw or secateurs. Do this after the tree has flowered.

Mistletoe to sow

"I have saved some mistletoe berries and I want to grow them on an old apple tree. How do I go about 'planting' them on the tree?"

Make a slit with a sharp knife in the bark of the tree and ease it back. Squeeze the seed into the slit. The fleshy berries should then stick firmly to the tree.

There are separate male and female mistletoe plants. Both must be grown together for berries to appear on the female plants.

Fake laburnum

"Three years ago I planted a laburnum tree named 'Battandieri' which flowered for the first time this year. Instead of hanging racemes of flowers my tree has produced bright yellow upright cones, rather like small sweet corns. Why has this happened and do I have an unusual tree?"

Your tree is not a laburnum, but a Moroccan broom (*Cytisus battandieri*). The flowers are typical of the Moroccan broom, and you will find that they have a rich pineapple fragrance which laburnum flowers do not possess.

Tender bloomer

"Last summer in Cornwall I saw some plants of a shrubby calceolaria which were covered in masses of small, yellow flowers. Can you tell me the full name of this plant, and is it likely to succeed in my garden?"

The calceolaria that you saw is most probably *C. integrifolia*. It is a first-rate plant and has been given an Award of Garden Merit by the Royal Horticultural Society.

It grows well outside in mild gardens in Cornwall but it is not fully hardy and needs winter protection. Plant it outside for the summer and take cuttings in August. When they have rooted, overwinter the plants in a frost-free greenhouse.

Mexican orange

"Can you tell me anything about a shrub called Choisya *'Aztec Pearl'. How does it differ from* Choisya ternata?*"*

Choisya "Aztec Pearl" is a first-rate, evergreen shrub. It was introduced by Hilliers nursery in 1989 and is a hybrid between *Choisya ternata* and *C. dumosa arizonica*. It has larger flowers than *C. ternata* and grows about 3–4 ft (1–1.2 m) tall. Fragrant flowers appear in the spring, pink at first, opening to white.

It is an excellent tub plant for growing on a terrace. It likes a sunny situation but needs shelter from wind.

Tree anemone

"I have been given a small shrub of the tree anemone. It seems to be evergreen. Can you tell me anything about it and what sort of situation it likes?"

The botanical name for the tree anemone is *Carpenteria californica*. It is a very beautiful evergreen shrub from California, producing single, white, scented flowers with golden stamens in the centre in early summer. It grows 6–10 ft (1.8–3 m) tall. To do well it needs a warm, sunny spot, preferably against a south-facing wall. It also needs well-drained soil. One of the best forms is "Ladham's Variety". Another is "Bodnant" which is said to be hardier.

Pruning time

"I have bought a bush of Caryopteris *'Worcester Gold'. Can you tell me what sort of situation it likes and when it should be pruned?"*

"Worcester Gold" is a golden-leaved form of *Caryopteris* x *clandonensis*, sometimes known as blue spiraea. It is an attractive shrub, producing blue flowers in late summer.

Grow it in a sunny situation in ordinary well-drained soil. Cut back all the shoots to within a few inches of the ground in March. This will stimulate strong growth which will flower in the summer.

Spring trim ❧

"I planted some bushes of Caryopteris *x* clandonensis *12 months ago. Do they need pruning now?"*

This caryopteris produces its blue flowers in late summer on shoots made in the current season. Pruning should be carried out in March, cutting back the old stems to within 4 in. (10 cm) of ground level.

Shrubby morning glory ❧

"Can you name the piece of plant that I am sending? It has attractive silvery foliage and flowers that look like a convolvulus."

Your shrub is *Convolvulus cneorum*. It is a most attractive, low-growing shrub, needing a sunny, sheltered position and well-drained soil. Unfortunately, it is not hardy in all districts and cannot stand hard frost in winter. It should, however, succeed in your Devon garden.

Bamboo flowers ❧

"I have a bamboo plant growing in my garden that was planted eight to nine years ago. It is a small-leaved variety with thin, yellow canes and is now about 10 ft (3 m) tall. This year it has produced no new green foliage. Instead, it has formed bunches of seed on each stem node. What are the prospects for the plant?"

As you probably know, bamboo clumps usually die when they start flowering. However, even when most of a clump dies a few offsets often remain and recommence growing. We suggest you leave your plant undisturbed and hope that a few new growths will emerge.

Pruning cornus ❧

"I have a large bush of Cornus stolonifera *'Flaviramea' which needs pruning as it is getting too big for where it is growing. When would be the best time to cut the stems back?"*

Cornus stolonifera "Flaviramea" is grown for its attractive yellow stems which look their best in the winter months.

The young, new stems are the most colourful and it pays to cut back the stems of the plant close to their base in March. This will encourage strong, new growths to develop which will brighten the garden the following winter.

White smoke bush ❧

"My smoke bush, which should have red leaves, has a lot of foliage covered with a white deposit. A friend says this must be the ash! Can you help, please?"

The white deposit on your smoke bush, cotinus, is powdery mildew. Infection is often more severe in dry summers and keeping the soil well watered in dry spells may help.

To control now, give a few sprays of Tumbleblite. After leaf-fall in autumn/winter, prune the shoots back to remove those that suffered from the mildew attack. Growth next year should then start off free from infection.

Tree anemone ❧

"I would like to grow a bush of the tree anemone, Carpenteria californica. *Do you think it will grow well in my garden in Sussex?"*

There is no reason why you should not be able to grow *Carpenteria californica* in your garden if you can give it a warm, sunny position.

It has beautiful white fragrant flowers in July. "Bodnant" is reputed to be one of the hardier forms.

Curbing rampant tendencies ❧

"I have a Clerodendrum thomsoniae *that I bought about 15 years ago but it has never flowered. It has made plenty of rampant growth. What am I doing wrong?"*

The fact that your clerodendrum has not flowered indicates that it is enjoying a high nitrogen diet. Curb the excessive vigour by feeding only with a high-potash tomato fertilizer which should encourage flowers to form. Feed and water only occasionally in winter when growth is much slower.

Tender palm ❧

"I have an australis sundance palm outside in a pot. The leaves are variegated green, red and yellow. It was purchased last year and is growing well and

seems healthy. When should it be repotted or can it be put direct in the ground? The plant is now about 4 ft (1.2 m) high."

Your plant is most probably *Cordyline australis* "Sundance", otherwise known as the cabbage tree of New Zealand. It is not fully hardy in all parts of the country, and even in Cornwall, plants were damaged in a severe winter a few years ago.

Keep your plant in a container so that it can stand in the warmest and most sheltered part of your garden. Damage occurs in the winter when water lodges and freezes in the base of the leaves. To prevent this happening, tie the leaves together for the winter and protect the main stem with sacking or other material. If your plant is already in a large container it will not need complete repotting. However, scrape away some of the surface soil and top-dress with fresh potting compost.

Nameless ❧

"We have a small tree in our garden which we have been unable to identify. Could you name it from the piece I am sending? The leaves turn red in the autumn and the berries are quite prolific."

The shrub is *Cotoneaster frigidus* "Cornubia". It is prized for its scarlet fruits and leaves which turn red before falling in the autumn. It ultimately grows to about 10 ft (3 m) tall. Birds enjoy the berries and it is a very desirable garden shrub. It has received an Award of Garden Merit from the Royal Horticultural Society.

Forever young ❧

"I have a bush of Cornus alba 'Sibirica' growing beside a stream, and the red stems have been very attractive through the winter. As the bush is getting large, can I cut it back? If so, when should this be done?"

If you want well coloured stems on your cornus each winter, you should prune it each March by cutting back the stems close to their base. This will encourage strong new stems to appear in the spring and summer. The young stems are at their best in the winter.

Winter sweet ❧

"I planted a winter sweet shrub early last year but it has done nothing. The leaves are feeble and the green ones soon wither. Can you advise me how to treat it?"

The winter sweet, chimonanthus, is a choice shrub producing highly fragrant yellow flowers in the winter. In this country it does need a warm and sunny position and in cold areas it is best planted against a sheltered, south-facing wall.

The trouble with your plant is that it is not happy where it is planted and you may have to move it to a more suitable position. It likes well-drained, fertile soil and is happy on chalk. This spring mulch the soil around the shrub with compost or manure and feed the plant in the spring and summer with a liquid fertilizer to encourage it to make strong new growth.

Propagating broom ❧

"Could you please tell me how to propagate a broom?"

There are several ways of propagating brooms. The easiest is to sow seeds in a pot indoors or in a greenhouse in early spring. Move the seedlings on into small pots before planting them in the open. If you have a named variety it will not come true from seed.

However, take cuttings from it in July or August. Choose firm young shoots about 4 in. (10 cm) long and insert them in small pots of gritty soil. Cover the pots with a polythene bag to conserve moisture and prevent the cuttings from wilting.

Another method is to layer a stem. Choose a stem close to the ground and peg it into the soil. Where it meets the ground make a slit in the stem about $\frac{1}{2}$ in. (1 cm) long and dust it with hormone rooting powder. Once the stem has rooted in about 12 months' time, it can be severed from the parent in the autumn and planted in a new position.

Broom blooms ❧

"I have a shrub of Cytisus battandieri *which flowered well in June. Does it need any regular pruning?"*

Cytisus battandieri (the Mount Atlas Broom) is a fine shrub with blooms that smell deliciously of pineapples.

The best time to prune it is after flowering when the shoots that have carried flowers should be shortened back to new, young growths. These will flower in the following year. At the same time some of the old stems may be cut out.

Pruning broom

"My broom bush flowers well but has grown straggly. Can I prune it and when should it be done?"

Broom bushes can be pruned and the time to do it is after flowering. However, care must be taken not to cut back the stems into old brown wood. The younger green shoots can be shortened by about two thirds of their length but if you cut back into older wood new growths will not form and the stems will remain bare.

When brooms become old and leggy it is probably best to scrap them and start again with a young plant. Cuttings of young side shoots can be taken in late July or August. Choose shoots that have begun to harden at their base and insert them in pots of gritty soil. Cover them with a polythene bag until they have rooted.

Training a broom

"I planted a Mount Etna broom some years ago and I want it to make a tree. When can I take the side branches off, and what should I do about the tuft of branches at the top of the plant?"

Now that your Mount Etna broom has a good head of shoots it does not need its side branches. Remove these during a mild spell next spring, ideally in mid-April. Encourage the top to spread and to assume more elegant proportions by thinning out any crowded stems.

Tie the remaining stems to a carefully constructed framework of canes with soft string. Within a year or so the branches will have set where you want them to and the framework can be removed.

Japonica jelly

"There are lots of large, yellow fruits on my 'japonica' bush. Are they edible?"

Yes, the fruits on your chaenomeles (japonica) bush are edible. One of the best ways of using them is to make jelly. A good recipe is: 3 lb. fruit, 1 lb. apples, water and sugar. Wash and cut the fruit into pieces. Just cover with water and boil slowly to a pulp. Strain through a jelly bag and add 1 lb. sugar to 1 pint of juice. Boil until the jelly sets and bottle.

Lantern Tree   ❧

"I have seen pictures of the Chilean lantern tree. Can you tell me whether it is easy to grow in this country?"

The Chilean lantern tree is *Crinodendron hookerianum*. It is an evergreen shrub with very beautiful lantern-like flowers in May.

It is not hardy in all but the mildest gardens, but it grows well in gardens such as Bodnant in North Wales and in western Scotland. It would be well worth trying in a mild area, like Surrey, but it does need an acid soil and a sheltered position.

Round the twist   ❧

"I was given a piece of twisted stem for a flower arrangement the other day and was told it was called Harry Lauder's walking stick. Can you tell me the name of the shrub from which it came?"

Your twisted stem came from a bush of *Corylus avellana* "Contorta", which is commonly called Harry Lauder's walking stick, or the corkscrew hazel.

It was discovered in a hedgerow in the middle of the last century and its twisted and curled stems are an attractive feature in the winter after the leaves have fallen.

In the summer, it is rather dull. However, the stems are useful in floral arrangements, particularly when covered in catkins. Shrubs can eventually grow to about 9 ft (2.7 m) tall.

Bottle brush seedlings   ❧

"Two years ago I sowed some callistemon seeds which came from Australia. They grew 7–8 in. (16–20 cm) tall but died in the winter. Last summer I repeated the process and also gave a neighbour some of the seed. They all failed. Why should ours die off in a greenhouse?"

Your callistemon seedlings died off in the winter because of cold, damp conditions. Once the plants have grown into a bush they are fairly hardy outside if they are given a warm and sheltered position in well-drained soil.

Sow the seed again in March in your greenhouse. Pot the seedlings individually as soon as they can be handled, using a potting compost containing plenty of coarse sand to ensure good drainage. Stand the plants outside for the summer in a warm and sunny position. When they fill their first pots with roots, move them on into slightly larger pots. Keeping them outside for the summer should help ripen the stems and stand up to colder conditions in the winter. Return your plants under cover in late September and, during the winter, give them very little water. Only water when the soil seems very dry.

Try to keep the greenhouse as dry as possible in the winter by ventilating it whenever possible. Your seedlings may have made soft, sappy growth which damped off in the winter in cold wet conditions. Try keeping the plants for the winter in a light place in an unheated room indoors.

No blooming good ❧

"I took a cutting from a bush of Cestrum elegans *over a year ago and it is now 5 ft (1.5 m) tall. However, it hasn't produced any flowers. Does it need grafting?"*

It is not necessary to graft plants of *Cestrum elegans* to ensure flowers, but encourage your plant to make flowering shoots by nipping out the tips of main stems in spring. They may need a year or so to mature before they will flower.

Buttercup bush ❧

"I bought a small plant in a sale. On the label it said 'Cassia yellow'. Can you tell me anything about the plant and whether it can be grown outside or needs a greenhouse?"

Your shrub is most probably *Cassia corymbosa*. Unfortunately, botanists have changed its name and it is now correctly called *Senna corymbosa*. Despite this, it is an attractive shrub producing masses of bright yellow flowers in late summer.

It is normally grown in frost-free greenhouses but in a mild district you may be able to grow it in the open against a warm, south-facing wall.

Walnuts under attack ❧

"We have a walnut tree in our garden which this year has produced leaves with raised lumps, under which are yellow hairy patches. Is this something to worry about and if so, how can it be controlled?"

The leaf affliction you describe is the result of attack by the walnut leaf gall mite. The symptoms look quite severe, and quite often virtually every leaf can be infested, but the effect on growth and cropping are minimal so no treatment is necessary.

In a nutshell ❧

"I have two nut trees. One is Corylus avellana *and the other is a red filbert. Both have been in the garden for about three years. Nuts formed this year but the shells were empty. Is this a common problem?"*

Nuts flower very early in the year and if the weather is unfavourable there will not be a good set. Frost will also kill off the flowers. The flowers on your nut bushes may not have been properly pollinated. Apart from this, nut plants raised from seed can give variable results and better crops are obtained if named varieties are grown, such as "Cosford" and "Kentish Cob". Grow two varieties together so that they will help pollinate each other.

Knobbly brooms ❧

"We are finding a number of knobbly swellings on our broom bushes. Do we have to dig the bushes out, and if so, is it safe to replant with other brooms?"

The swellings are galls due to feeding by a small mite, a distant relative of the blackcurrant big bud mite. There is no effective chemical treatment, but regular pruning out of attacked shoots whenever seen should stop the mite being a problem in your garden.

Choice tree ❧

"In a garden I visited last summer I saw a small tree with attractive variegated leaves. From a central stem the branches appeared in tiers or layers. The only name I could find was cornus. Do you think you could name the tree for me as I would like to grow one in my garden?"

The tree that you have seen is most probably *Cornus controversa variegata*. This is a very handsome and choice tree and the tiered effect of the branches is particularly appealing. This, combined with the whitish variegated leaves, has led some people to call it the wedding cake tree.

It was first introduced into this country at the end of the last century. It succeeds in most soils provided they are not too wet or arid. Eventually, after many years, trees can reach a height of at least 30 ft. (10 m) and spread to 40 ft. (13 m)

When to prune? ❧

"I have a lovely plant called Coronilla glauca *which has grown very spindly. It has not flowered this year. Can I prune it? I keep it in a cool greenhouse."*

Plants of *Coronilla valentina ssp. glauca* do tend to become straggly. To overcome this, prune back the shoots in March. When new growth appears, repot the plant in good potting compost. As it is almost hardy, we suggest that you stand it outside in a sunny spot in the summer. This should help the plant to flower better.

Trimming ceanothus ❧

"I have a bush of Ceanothus *'Gloire de Versailles'. It is covered in soft blue flowers at the moment. Does this shrub need pruning and when is the best time to do it?"*

Your ceanothus is one of the late flowering kinds and the best time to prune it is in early spring. Cut back the stems close to their base and the new shoots that form afterwards will flower in late summer.

Yellow bottlebrush ❧

"I have had a bush of the red bottlebrush shrub in my garden for some years. Last summer in a garden in Devon I saw what looked like a yellow bottlebrush. Is there such a thing?"

Yes, there are cream or yellow bottlebrush shrubs. One that is often seen in mild districts is *Callistemon pallidus*. This comes from Tasmania and has cream flowers. Another is *C. salignus* which has narrow leaves and pale yellow flowers. They need to be grown in a warm and sheltered position, and are not suitable for cold areas.

Summer snow ❧

"I have a sunny bank where the soil is poor and sandy. Would snow-in-summer be the best plant for ground cover in this situation?"

Snow-in-summer, *Cerastium tomentosum*, would be an ideal carpeting perennial for your sunny bank. The grey foliage is attractive all year and the plants are covered in masses of white flowers in June. It is invasive but can be trimmed back as required. It is certainly a tough, tolerant plant and a stock of new plants is easily raised from seed.

Lacking flowers   ❧

"I have a plant of Campsis radicans *trained against a wall in my garden but it produces few flowers. Is there anything I can do about it?"*

Sometimes called the trumpet vine, *Campsis radicans* is a vigorous climber which normally flowers in August and September. However, to flower well it needs a hot and sunny position. Flowers appear on the current season's shoots and so the side shoots can be cut back fairly hard in the spring.

To encourage more sturdy growth, which should improve flower quantity and quality, we suggest that you feed your plant with sulphate of potash. Apply 2 oz. per sq. yd (60 g/m^2) around the base of the plant. Give one dressing in February followed by another in July. Mulch the plant well with garden compost or peat to retain extra moisture. Once buds start to form, give the plant a weekly liquid feed to encourage more.

Deterring burglars   ❧

"Having been burgled recently, I want to have some really thorny plants beneath the windows of my house to serve as a deterrent. What would you suggest planting?"

One shrub that has large triangular spines and would deter any burglar is *Colletia paradoxa*, once known as *C. cruciata*. Other thorny subjects that you could plant include: berberis, blackthorn (*Prunus spinosa*), hollies, roses, such as *Rosa sericea pteracantha, Poncirus trifoliata* (bitter orange) and the double-flowered gorse, *Ulex europaeus "Plenus"*.

Colourful berries   ❧

"Can you help me with the name of a shrub that I saw in several places last autumn and winter? The branches grow flat against a wall and are covered in masses of bright red berries. Plants I have seen look so colourful that I would like to have a shrub of it in my garden."

We believe the shrub you have seen is *Cotoneaster horizontalis*. It is an easy-going shrub that is tough and hardy. The bright red berries in winter are certainly a colourful sight. Plants are semi-evergreen and are easily raised from seed. The flat branches look effective against a red brick wall but plants can also be used as ground cover and allowed to ramble over a bank.

Colour contrasts 𝕒

"I have planted a border with Choisya ternata *'Sundance' for its attractive yellow foliage. Can you suggest one or two purple-foliaged shrubs that I could grow with the choisya to provide a colour contrast?"*

Purple-foliaged shrubs that could be grown with the yellow-leaved choisya include *Cotinus* "Royal Purple", *Berberis thunbergii* "Atropurpurea" and *Pittosporum tenuifolium* "Tom Thumb".

Don't overdo the mulch!

March flowers 𝕒

"I have several winter-flowering shrubs and I would like to plant more. Can you tell me anything about Corylopsis pauciflora?"*

Corylopsis pauciflora is a very choice shrub, producing its primrose-yellow flowers in March and April. These have a faint cowslip scent. It likes to be grown in a partially shaded position and must have lime-free soil. Plants will eventually grow to about 6 ft (1.8 m) tall.

Improve the soil well with decayed manure or compost before planting and mulch the surface of the soil around the shrub each spring.

Camellias and lime ❧

"My camellia bush flowered well this spring but the leaves are now pale green in colour. I tested the soil and found that it was neutral. Is there a product that will improve the leaf colour?"

The product that you have in mind is most probably Sequestrene which helps to correct a deficiency of iron in alkaline soils. In very chalky soils iron is rendered unavailable to plants and as a result the foliage becomes very pale green or even yellow.

Sequestrene can be applied in the form of granules around plants that need an acid, lime-free soil. Another product that you can use to improve the health of your camellia is Miracid which is designed particularly for plants such as rhododendrons and heathers which must have an acid soil.

It will also help your camellia if you put a thick mulch of bark fibre or peat on the soil around the base of the plant. A single application of a slow release fertilizer, such as Osmocote, will also help to improve the colour of the leaves.

Not a bloomer ❧

"I received a camellia last year and it has made new growth, although it did not flower this year. Can you tell me when to feed it?"

As your camellia has made new growth we can see no reason why it should not flower next year. The rounded and fat flower buds should already have formed.

Only feed the plant in the spring and summer. Camellias do not like any form of lime and we suggest that you use a fertilizer such as Miracid which is designed for plants that need acid soil conditions such as camellias and rhododendrons. Give the first application in March.

Out of the bag ❧

"I have some camellia cuttings in a pot covered with a polythene bag. They look marvellous. When can I take the bag off?"

Remove the polythene bag, keeping your camellia cuttings warm and moist, when roots have been made and new shoots appear. If you find roots appearing from the bottom of the pot and new growth can be seen, it is time to remove the cover.

Pot the rooted cuttings individually and keep them in gentle heat until all danger from frost has passed. Plant them in the open in peaty soil or in a tub of lime-free potting compost.

Dusty camellias ❧

"My camellia leaves had spots on them and then the spots appeared to become open and dusty. Can you tell what the cause might be?"

The objects seen on your leaves are scale insects. They normally appear as brown, elongated creatures but eggs are laid under the scales amongst a mass of white, waxy threads. As the old scales die and fall off, the eggs and "wool" become visible. The young hatching from the eggs wander around for a while and then settle in a permanent feeding site.

Control by spraying with Tumblebug or Sybol.

Frosted camellias ❧

"Some of my camellia flowers get damaged by frost in the spring. Others in a shaded position are not affected. Can you explain why?"

The camellias that are being damaged are probably in an open position where early morning sun shines on the frosted blooms. In the shade the blooms thaw slowly and are not so badly damaged.

If possible, move the affected plants to a position where they avoid receiving early morning sunshine.

Browning leaves ❧

"The leaves on my camellia keep dropping off although they are green and shiny. Can you tell me why this is happening?"

The browning around the tips of the leaves indicates that the plant was short of water at some stage in the past months. Leaf and bud dropping in spring and early summer is generally related to a shortage of water in the previous autumn.

During dry spells, keep the plant well watered. Spraying overhead with clear water will also help it, plus regular feeds with Miracid or Phostrogen Acid Plant Food.

Camellia needs careful positioning &

"My camellia looks healthy but the buds always fall off before flowering."

There are two good reasons why camellia buds drop: inadequate water when the buds are forming in September, and exposure to early morning sunlight when the buds are frosted. It is vital, in autumn, especially on light soil, to soak the root area when embryo flower buds are developing.

In spring, when the buds are coloured and are about to open, rapid warming of frosted tissues can cause cells to rupture. Plants must be sited facing north, west or south but never east.

Camellia cuttings &

"I have a nice camellia bush and I would like to take a cutting from it. When is the best time to do it?"

The best time to take camellia cuttings is in late July or early August. Choose young shoots about 4 in. (10 cm) long that have begun to harden at their base. The cutting can be removed with a "heel" of older wood attached.

Insert the cutting in a small pot filled with a mixture of one part coarse, gritty sand and three parts moist peat. Dip the base of the cutting in a hormone rooting powder.

Camellia cuttings root most successfully in a mist propagation unit but if one is not available put the cutting in a warm, moist propagation case. If this is not possible, cover the pot with a polythene bag and stand it in a warm, light place indoors.

It may take three months for the cutting to root.

Spring potting &

"Will you please tell me when I can repot a camellia. Can I bring it into an unheated room for the winter?"

The best time to repot a camellia is in the spring when the roots are once again becoming active.

If the root ball is very tight with roots, tease out some of the older ones and trim them carefully. Keep the camellia outside for the winter or it can be kept in an unheated room. Keep it in a light place and prevent it from suffering from dry air by putting the pot inside a larger one with damp peat between the two. Alternatively, put the pot on a tray of gravel which should be kept damp.

Camellia drop

"I bought a camellia plant three months ago and potted it up in ericaceous compost. Since then the plant does not seem to have progressed at all, and some of the leaves and flower buds have dropped off."

The change in environment since you bought your camellia home from the shop may have caused the problem. But the plant should acclimatize soon and start new active growth.

For the next few months keep it out of direct sunshine and make sure the compost is always moist without being too wet. An occasional feed with Miracid should also help to bring it to life.

Sooty camellia

"The leaves of my camellia planted in the garden, not in a pot, are all black with what looks like soot, and before that they felt quite sticky. Can you explain please?"

The stickiness is due to honeydew falling on the leaves from a sap-sucking pest, such as greenfly and whitefly. On camellia, scale insects are the most likely culprit. Look for the small scab-like insects under the leaves, particularly along the main veins. Scale insects excrete honeydew as they feed, depositing a sugary substance which is rapidly colonized by sooty mould fungi. The mould does not attack the camellia, but looks unsightly and may reduce the efficiency of the leaves. Control by drench spraying Bio Long-Last under the leaves.

Ailing camellia

"All the leaves on my neighbour's camellia bush are curling and it seems to be dying. It was only repotted last year."

It is probable that this camellia has regressed because its potting compost has been allowed to dry out at some time. Camellias are avid moisture lovers and must be kept damp, particularly in hot summer weather. It is also vital to use lime-free (rainwater) water. Check that the drainage holes in the base of the pot are not blocked.

When repotting a camellia, always use a lime-free ericaceous compost and feed the plant in the spring and early summer with an acid fertilizer such as the liquid feed Miracid.

No flowers ❧

"I have had a camellia for ten years and it has never flowered. In an attempt to encourage flowering I have tried it in three different locations but without success. The foliage appears to be very healthy. The soil is sandy. How can I make it flower?"

It is odd for a healthy camellia not to flower. However, your soil may be too rich in nitrogen which has encouraged leaf growth at the expense of the flowers.

To rectify matters, feed your plant now, in the spring, with sulphate of potash applied at 2 oz. per sq.yd (57 g/m^2) around the base of the bush. Water this well into the soil. Hopefully, this will help to stimulate flower buds this summer which will open for you early next spring.

Spot the difference

"Can you tell me the difference between Camellia japonica *and* Camellia x williamsii?"*

Camellia japonica is a naturally occurring species and there are a great many varieties of it. The flowers are usually large and the leaves also large and glossy. Flowering is from February to May.

The williamsii camellias were raised by J.C. Williams at Caerhays Castle in Cornwall from a cross made between *Camellia japonica* and *C. saluenensis*. The flowers are often more graceful than the japonicas and the glossy leaves are usually smaller. These can be found in flower from November to May.

No camellia flowers ❧

"I have had a camellia in a large pot for five or six years, and it is now very reluctant to flower. What can I do?"

Plants in containers dry out very rapidly in hot weather in the summer and if your camellia became short of water at a critical period last summer this may have caused the lack of flowers this year.

Make sure the plant does not go short of water in the summer. Use rainwater whenever possible as tap water contains lime which camellias do not like.

Bud drop ❧

"I have a healthy-looking camellia loaded with flower buds. Last year many dropped off at this stage. How can I stop it happening this year?"

The usual reason for camellia buds dropping is because the plants have suffered a check in growth. If your camellia is growing in a container check that the root ball has not dried out. Severe winter frosts can also cause the buds to drop.

Camellia cuts ❧

"There are lots of straggly growths on my camellia. Can I can cut these out?"

It will improve your camellia bush if you cut back the straggly growths in May. This will encourage lots of new growths to form in the spring and summer. It will also help the plant if you feed it with a slow-acting fertilizer such as Osmocote.

Camellia seed ❧

"I have a large camellia bush which has a lot of seed pods like small crab apples. Can you tell me how I should plant them when they are ripe?"

When the camellia seed pods are ripe, remove the seeds and sow them straight away in small pots of seed compost. Stand the pot in a warm, moist propagating case until the seedlings appear. When large enough to handle, pot them singly in small pots.

Acid taste ❧

"I have three camellias in my garden which are not doing very well. I have decided to transplant them into large pots so that I can change their positions. Would a multi-purpose compost suit them or should I use soil from a growing bag? When should I move them and will they need pruning?"

Multi-purpose compost is likely to be too alkaline for lime-hating plants such as camellias. We suggest you use an ericaceous (lime-free) potting compost. Several brands are available at garden centres.

Autumn or early spring are the best times to move your plants. The only pruning that should be necessary is to shorten straggly growths.

Change of colour

"One of our large camellia bushes has developed a number of bright yellow leaves over the last year or so. Is this a mutation or something we should be treating?"

The yellowing may be the result of iron deficiency. There is probably enough iron in the soil locally and a suitable degree of acidity in the soil for camellias to grow well.

It is likely that as the camellia has been growing for many years, it could have used up the available supplies in the soil around the roots. Treat the soil and the leaves now with a chelated iron preparation such as Sequestrene.

Scaly camellia

"Can you please tell me what these objects are on the camellia leaves I am sending to you? They feel slightly woolly, but none of my friends have seen them on their plants, and my gardening books don't mention anything that sounds like them."

The objects are scale insects, or more precisely, the eggsacs of scale insects. The female scale insect remains over the eggsac after it is laid and the young hatch, by which time normally the female has died. To control these sapfeeding pests, spray with a systemic insecticide or with malathion.

Vegetables

Planting asparagus

"I want to make an asparagus bed. When is the best time to plant the crowns and how far apart should they be spaced? I have been told to apply salt to the bed. When should this be done?"

Plant asparagus crowns in late March and early April. Nowadays it is general practice to plant them in rows in a trench. Make this about 12 in. (30 cm) wide and 8 in. (20 cm) deep.

Build a mound in the bottom so that the asparagus roots can be spread over it. Cover them with about 4 in. (10 cm) of soil. Space the crowns in single rows, 15 in. (37 cm) apart. At one time it was thought that salt improved the growth of asparagus. It now appears that there is no foundation to this theory. Feeding with a balanced fertilizer in the spring will certainly help the plants to make good growth.

Asparagus attack

"Why is all the foliage on my asparagus bed disappearing? There appear to be some 'humpy-backed' grubs present and I wonder if these are responsible?"

The grubs you have seen are larvae of the asparagus beetle. Eggs are laid in June and July by the black and yellow, chequer-board-marked adult beetles and the grubs hatch out and feed for a couple of weeks before pupating in the soil. A new adult generation appears two to three weeks later and both adults and larvae feed on asparagus foliage.

Two or three generations appear each year and feeding can go on as late as October. To control, hand pick on a small scale or give a few sprays with a contact insecticide based on fatty acids, pyrethrins or permethrin.

Cut short

"I have had an asparagus bed for three years and started cutting the shoots this spring. How long can I go on cutting without harming the plants?"

As your asparagus bed is still young, you should cut the shoots for no longer than six weeks. Established beds can be cut for a maximum of eight weeks. All cutting should cease after the middle of June to allow the plants to produce foliage through the summer and build up the crowns for next year.

Asparagus and sprouts ❧

"I have twelve asparagus plants. They are four years old but do not produce many spears. Is it possible to grow other vegetables, such as sprouts, between them so that the space is filled in the autumn but without harming the asparagus?"

It would make matters worse if you grew other vegetables amongst your asparagus plants. If the asparagus is making plenty of foliage it would smother the other plants and they would not develop properly. Damage would also occur to the asparagus roots when planting the other vegetables. Concentrate on improving the growth of the asparagus plants.

Apply bonemeal around the plants in the autumn and feed with a general fertilizer in February and March.

Put a fairly deep mulch of decayed manure or compost around the plants in the autumn after cutting back the old foliage.

Asparagus damage ❧

"When the asparagus spears started appearing in spring, far too many came up 'lopsided' and were found to have damage to one side, just below soil level. Would slugs do this, and how can I stop whatever was responsible, next year?"

Yes, slugs would have damaged your asparagus stems, and the species involved would probably be the keeled slug that breeds below ground and rarely comes to the soil surface. Prevent attacks next year by watering the soil around the plants now, and again in early spring next year, with a biological slug and snail killer.

Planting globe artichokes ❧

"I would like to grow some globe artichokes in my garden this year. Is it better to start with plants or raise them from seed?"

Although globe artichokes can be grown from seed, the plants tend to be variable. It is better to plant rooted offsets of a named variety such as "Vert de Laon".

Plant the offsets in the open in late March or early April. Space them 3 ft (1 m) apart as they grow at least to this height. Plant each offset 2 in. (5 cm) deep. Choose a fertile piece of ground and a sheltered position.

If flowerheads appear in the first year, remove them to allow good plants to develop. Several heads can be cut from each plant in the second year. Cut them while the scales are plump and before they begin to open.

Globe artichokes ❧

"I have a clump of globe artichokes which I want to increase. How do I propagate the plant?"

Take suckers or offsets from it in March or early April. These form around the base of the plant.

Scrape away some of the soil and remove the offsets, preferably with roots attached, with a sharp knife. Replant without delay in their new positions about $2\frac{1}{2}$ ft (75 cm) apart.

Master chef ❧

"I planted some globe artichokes during the spring and a single head has formed on each plant. When is the best time to cut them? What is the best way to cook these artichokes?"

The artichokes are ready for harvesting when the heads are mature and just before they begin to open. The scales should be plump and soft. Cut the heads off the plant with a piece of stem attached. The best way to cook globe artichokes is to boil or steam them for about 45 minutes.

Before boiling them, cut the stalk off close to the base of the head. They may be eaten hot with melted butter or cold with a vinaigrette sauce. The base of the artichoke is the most succulent part.

Harvesting globe artichokes ❧

"I have grown some globe artichoke plants but I am not sure when to cut the heads for eating. Several opened into beautiful flowers before I could cut them."

Cut the globe artichoke heads when the scales are tight together but just beginning to open. Left too long, the flowers will appear, which means that you have left it too late. Cut off the heads with a short piece of stem attached. Removing the heads encourages new shoots to appear.

Global benefits

"A friend is digging up some clumps of globe artichokes and has offered me some. When is the best time for planting and what type of soil do they like?"

The best way to treat the artichoke clump is to take the rooted suckers or offsets off and replant these straight away. Late March and early April is a good time for planting. Choose a sheltered position and good, fertile soil. Apply a general fertilizer to the soil prior to planting.

After three years the clumps begin to lose vigour, and replanting should be carried out on a fresh site with young and vigorous offsets.

Artichokes under attack

"Our globe artichokes were badly infested with blackfly this summer, and in the end we cut them all down and burned them. If this should happen again, is there a safe spray we could use?"

Tumblebug carries an officially approved (under the Control of Pesticides Regulations, 1986) recommendation for use on any flower, fruit or vegetable. This could be applied to your artichokes with just a 24-hour wait before harvesting the heads. Check the labels of other insecticides if you wish to use an alternative product; permitted crops and spray-to-harvest intervals must be stated.

Sowing beetroot

"I have sown a row of beetroot but germination has not been very good. I intend making more sowings. What is the latest date for sowing to ensure a worthwhile crop?"

The poor germination of your beetroot seed could be because the soil was too cold. Now that it is getting warmer you should have better results. Beetroot can be sown at intervals until late June or early July. Some gardeners find that soaking the seed in tepid water for half an hour before sowing helps germination.

Harvesting beetroot

"I have grown some beetroot for the first time and seem to have a good crop. Can the roots stay in the ground for the winter or should they be lifted and stored?"

Except for very mild areas it is best to lift and store beetroot for the winter. This is best done in October. Lift the roots carefully with a fork and twist off the tops. Cutting the foliage with a knife can lead to "bleeding". Store the roots in boxes of dry sand or peat.

Monogerm beetroot

"Can you tell me what 'monogerm' beetroot means?"

Beetroot seed consists of a cluster of three seeds. If they all germinate the seedlings will have to be thinned to leave one at each position. "Monogerm" beetroot seed consists of one seed only. This means that thinning of the seedlings is minimized.

Beetroot modules

"I normally sow beetroot seed direct into the soil in early April. To save the job of thinning the seedlings, could I sow the seeds in modules and plant the seedlings out later at a suitable distance apart?"

Yes, beetroot seed can be sown in small pots or modules under cover for planting out later. This is a good system to get early supplies. For early crops, plant the seedlings out $3\frac{1}{2}$ in.(9 cm) apart, in rows 9 in. (23 cm) apart.

Less thinning is needed with monogerm varieties such as "Moneta". These produce one seedling from each seed cluster and the seeds can be spaced at the correct distance when they are sown.

Long or round?

"I have normally grown round beetroot. Is there any advantage in growing the long-rooted type?"

The round types of beetroot, such as the widely available "Boltardy" are usually grown for early supplies, and the long cylindrical kinds for storage. Varieties such as "Cylindra" are also useful for slicing, all of which are even in size.

Thinning beetroot

"I have sown some 'Boltardy' beetroot seeds and they have all germinated well. Do the seedlings need thinning out as they seem very crowded? Does watering help beetroot to make good growth?"

The beetroot seedlings will need thinning to ensure that you have roots of good size; carefully pull out surplus seedlings to leave them about 3 in.

(7.5 cm) apart. Watering is important and the soil must not be allowed to dry out. It is best to encourage good, steady growth ensuring the soil remains moist at all times. However, be careful not to overwater as this will encourage the leaves to grow at the expense of the roots.

Sowing broad beans ?❧

"I want to grow broad beans for an early crop. Is it worth sowing the seed in the autumn in my district?"

It would be well worth sowing broad beans in the autumn in your district [Gloucester], provided the situation is sheltered and the soil is well drained and not subject to waterlogging in the winter. Sowings can be made in late October and early November. If you have some cloches, put them over the young plants for protection and an earlier crop. A suitable variety for growing under cloches is "The Sutton" which is a dwarf variety. "Aquadulce Claudia", a taller variety, is also recommended for autumn sowing. Another way of protecting the plants is to cover them in the winter with nylon fleece.

Soil borne? ?❧

"The leaves of my broad beans are showing lots of brown spots and I am worried that this may be something that will get into the soil to infect plants next year. Can you please identify the problem?"

If the spots are quite small and powdery then bean rust would be present. On the other hand, if the spots are irregular in outline with no powdery feel then chocolate spot would be the disease responsible.

Neither will infect the soil, but will reduce further cropping of the beans. As cropping comes to an end, dig out the plants and bury them deeply inside your compost heap where they will rot away safely.

If there is an early attack next year, spray with a copper fungicide to prevent damage.

Early broad beans ?❧

"I want to grow some early broad beans under cloches. Is it best to sow the seed under glass in small pots or direct in the soil outside?"

Sow your broad bean seeds in modules under glass and, when the weather is favourable, plant them out under cloches in March. Put the cloches in position several weeks beforehand to warm up the soil.

Sowing broad beans 🌸

"I have tried sowing broad bean seed early but the results have not been satisfactory. Can you give me some tips on how to obtain better results?"

You may have sown your broad bean seed when the soil was still very cold. Covering the ground with cloches or floating film ahead of sowing should help to warm the soil and ensure better germination.

You could sow seed in modules under glass and plant out the seedlings when the weather becomes warmer and the soil has begun to dry out.

Singles or doubles? 🌸

"I have bought some 'Hylon' broad bean seeds. Should I sow them in a single or double row?"

Broad bean seed can be sown outside in February and March, provided the soil is not too wet. The choice is yours whether to sow a single or double row.

In a single row, space the seed 9 in. (23 cm) apart in the base of the drill which should be about 2 in. (5 cm) deep. Alternatively, if you sow the seed in a double, staggered row allow 9 in. (23 cm) between the seeds and leave a 2 ft (60 cm) pathway between the two rows.

Early beans 🌸

"I have some seed of 'The Sutton' broad bean. Can it be sown outside in the autumn to get an early crop?"

Broad bean seed can certainly be sown outside in November and early December to provide an early crop next spring. Success depends very much on the weather.

As "The Sutton" is a dwarf variety it is well worth covering the plants with cloches for protection or nylon floating film may be used. Another way of obtaining early beans is to sow the seed in modules in January under cover, putting the plants outside in early spring.

Black bean aphids 🌸

"Last summer my broad beans were badly affected with blackfly. What is the best way of dealing with it if the trouble appears again this year?"

A variety of sprays, such as derris and malathion, can be used against blackfly on broad beans. It is best to spray as soon as the pests are seen. If you prefer not to use sprays, pinch out the tips of the shoots after flowering. Ladybirds feed on the insects and it is a good idea to collect all the ladybirds that you can and put them on the plants.

Broad sowing 🛪

"Is there any advantage in sowing broad bean seed in the autumn compared with a sowing made in February?"

The main advantage of sowing broad bean seed in the autumn is that an earlier crop can be expected, although this does depend on the weather during the winter.

Sow the seed in late October and November in a sheltered position where the soil is well drained. "Aquadulce" is a good variety for autumn sowing. "The Sutton" is a compact variety useful for growing under cloches. If cloches are not available, it is well worth covering the plants with nylon fleece for protection.

Should the crop fail because of severe weather, sowings can be made in modules in a cold frame or greenhouse in January so that the plants can be put outside as soon as the weather is favourable.

Peas and beans fix lots of nitrogen for the atmosphere.

Pea and bean weevil, too ❧

"Each year in mid to late spring my overwintered broad beans have their leaves notched by what I have been told is a weevil. I don't know if this affects yields, but I would like to keep the plants free of damage if I could. What would you recommend?"

Your information is correct in that the damage is indeed caused by a weevil, namely the pea and bean weevil. The feeding on the leaves doesn't cause too much trouble, but the larvae of the weevils feed on the nitrogen-fixing nodules on the roots and this can reduce crops by almost a fifth.

If you dust the soil around the plants with Sybol Dust in early May the adult weevils should be controlled. As each female weevil can lay up to 1,400 eggs, reducing the number of adult weevils will be a great help in reducing damage to your crop of broad beans.

Missing beans ❧

"I sowed a couple of rows of broad beans a short while ago, but several failed to come up. Digging up the seeds, I found they had been eaten and black, many-legged creatures were inside some of them. I believe these are millipedes. I intend to gap up the spaces now, but can I protect the new seeds from attack?"

The creatures you have found are indeed millipedes and they are quite partial to a meal of broad bean seeds. Dust the planting holes with gamma-HCH or Sybol Dust to protect your new sowings. Once the seeds have germinated and produced shoots above ground they are much less likely to be attractive to the millipedes, so no action should be necessary for the rest of your earlier sowings.

Bean lucky ❧

"So far, my broad bean plants have been free from the dreaded blackfly. This is down to luck really, as no action has been taken. Is there anything I should do now to prevent a later attack?"

Remove the tips from the plants now, and the blackfly will be less likely to attack; they appear to recognize the bean plants by the colour of the new growth, as well as in other ways, such as smell or taste. Should an attack still take place, don't allow the pests time to breed. Spray at the first signs using Phostrogen Safer's Insecticide, Miracle Garden Care Rapid, or Murphy Tumblebug.

Saving a bean ❧

"I like to sow a couple of rows of broad beans in autumn, but used to lose a number to soil pests. I solved the problem with a seed dressing but find that it is no longer on the market. What would you recommend now?"

Dust the seed drills with Sybol Dust before sowing and work it lightly into the soil. This should control the millipedes and wireworms which are likely to be the main problems. It is also worth while sowing a few extra seeds at the end of the seed drill to fill up any gaps in spring.

Broad beans and blackfly ❧

"Is there any scientific basis for preventing blackfly attacks on broad beans by pinching out the tops of the plants in late spring? My father always used this method and it worked in most years, but I wondered why."

Colour of the host plant is believed to be one of the ways by which blackfly find their host plants. It is probably a difference of shade, rather than true colour, but the new growth of beans is paler than the old. It is thought that removing the young, paler growth at the tips of the bean plants encourages the pests to fly on, rather than land to feed.

Purple French bean ❧

"Can you tell me whether the purple-podded French beans are worth growing? Do the pods stay purple when cooked?"

Purple-podded French beans are well worth growing. The colouring of the pods is a novelty and most varieties have good flavour. The pods do not retain their colour after cooking and turn green. Did you know that there are also yellow-podded French beans which are also good to eat?

Colourful bean ❧

"Can you tell me anything about a bean called 'Rob Roy'? I am told it has colourful pods but none of my garden books mentions it. Can you tell me who can supply seed?"

"Rob Roy" is a climbing French bean. The cream pods are splashed with red. Apart from being very attractive the beans are tender and well flavoured. They are well worth a trial.

Seed can be obtained from W. Robinson & Sons Ltd, Sunnybank, Forton, Nr. Preston, Lancs, PR3 0BN.

Health warning

"In a herb book that I read recently it said that French beans were dangerous to eat raw. Is this true and why?"

Yes, French and other beans can be poisonous to eat in a raw state. They contain a protein called lectin which is harmful. However, this is destroyed when the beans are cooked, provided they are boiled for about 20 minutes or cooked in a pressure cooker. The lectin is not destroyed in a slow cooker because the temperature is not raised to a high enough level.

Early runner beans

"I want to grow some early runner beans this year. Can I sow the seed indoors and put the plants in the open at the right time? How soon can I sow the seed?"

Yes, you can make an early start by sowing runner bean seeds indoors or, preferably, in a greenhouse or cold frame in early May. Sow the seeds individually in pots or modules of good seed compost and stand them in a light, sunny window. If they do not get enough light the seedlings will grow thin and spindly.

Plant the seedlings outside in late May in prepared ground against a suitable support of poles or long canes.

Runner bean tubers

"Having stripped the runner bean vines from their supports, I lifted the plants and was amazed to find that they had swollen, tuberous roots. Are they affected with club root disease?"

Club root disease affects only members of the brassica family such as cabbages, sprouts and cauliflowers as well as wallflowers. It is natural for runner beans to produce tuberous roots. Normally they are killed off by frost but in mild areas, like Cornwall, plants can be left in the ground through the winter and will start into growth the following year without the bother of raising new plants.

Contain your beans

"I have only a small garden and there is no space for vegetables. I am very fond of runner beans. Could they be grown in large tubs on my patio?"

Runner beans can certainly be grown in large tubs on a sunny patio. Make sure first, however, that there are drainage holes in the base of the container. Plants can be purchased or raised at home. They should grow quite rapidly and must be kept well watered and fed each week with liquid fertilizer. When flowers appear spray the plants each day with water.

Holey beans ❧

"*Each year I save seed from my runner beans. Unfortunately, those that I saved from last year's crop have holes in them and insects inside the beans. What are these?*"

Your crop has been attacked by a species of bean seed beetle which lay eggs on the young pods in late May/early June. The larvae spend the summer inside the pods and emerge as adults the following spring.

As the larva eats a cavity the size of its own body, but does not always feed on the seed embryo, there is a chance your beans will still germinate. Start them off in pots to reduce the chance of rotting.

To prevent this happening again, only save seed from pods formed after June.

Poor crop ❧

"*I grew about 50 runner bean plants this summer but as in previous years, despite being pollinated by bees, the flowers did not set and I got few beans. My neighbours have experienced a similar problem. What can be done about it?*"

The real answer to dry set and lack of runner bean pods is not to grow runners, but to grow dwarf or climbing French beans instead. These don't require the intervention of insects for pollination. Being self-fertile, they set an enormous crop, regardless of the weather.

Running out of ideas ❧

"*I want to grow some early runner beans this year for a flower show. When can I sow the seed and what varieties would you recommend?*"

Runner beans are not hardy and need protection until all danger from frost has passed. For an early crop we suggest that you sow the seed towards the end of April in pots or modules in a cool greenhouse. Do not plant out in the open until late May or early June.

To get good crops, the ground needs to be fertile and liberal amounts of organic matter should be dug into the soil.

Good varieties to grow for showing are "Liberty" and "Enorma".

Has beans? 🐝

"Can you tell me why my runner beans failed to set last summer? There were plenty of flowers but not many beans. I was told to spray the flowers with water, but it did not make much difference."

This is a common problem. Red-flowered runner beans seem to be affected most and it might be worth trying pink or white-flowered varieties this year.

It is now felt that spraying the flowers with water does not solve the problem. However, poor setting is usually worse in hot, dry weather and a shortage of water at the roots could be a cause of the trouble.

Next summer, make sure that the soil does not dry out. As soon as the first green flowers appear, keep the soil soaked with water. Also, apply thick mulches of compost or other organic matter around the plants to help conserve soil moisture.

Dry set 🐝

"My white-flowered 'Mergoles' runner beans set well this year but when the beans were about an inch long many shrivelled and dropped off. Was this due to the hot weather?"

Your 'Mergoles' runner beans suffered from "dry set". This occurs when pollinating insects cannot enter heat-affected and partially deflated flowers and are therefore unable to pollinate them.

Next year mist the blooms regularly to try to keep them perky and wide open so that pollinating bees have no difficulty visiting them. It is also a good idea to run a perforated hose pipe along the centre of a double row and irrigate at night.

Sow soon for early cabbage 🐝

"How soon can I sow cabbage to get an early crop?"

If you sow seed under glass in March this should provide plants for maturing in early June. Grow the seedlings in small pots or modules and after hardening them off plant outside.

A sowing can also be made outside under cloches in late March and early April. "Hispi" and "Kingspi" are two of the earliest summer cabbages.

Spacing cabbages   ❧

"What is the correct distance for planting spring cabbage?"

Spring cabbages can be planted any time in late July/early August, 12 in. (30 cm) apart in each direction.

Sowing sprouts   ❧

"This year I want to grow my own Brussels sprouts. I want to have one variety for early sprouts and another for later supplies to last until late winter. What would you recommend?"

One of the best early sprouts is the F1 hybrid "Peer Gynt". This will give sprouts for the September–December period. "Oliver" is an even earlier variety. "Citadel" is another F1 hybrid for pickings from December to March. Sow the seed outside in shallow drills in late March or early April.

Sowing can be done earlier under cloches or seed can be sown in modules in a frame or greenhouse in early March. When large enough, plant out in the open in early April.

Spring "Pixie"   ❧

"I have been offered some plants of 'Pixie' spring cabbage. Is this a good variety to grow and when is the best time to plant?"

"Pixie" is an excellent spring cabbage. It has received an Award of Merit from the Royal Horticultural Society. It makes small plants with firm, compact hearts and is very suitable for small gardens.

Seed is sown in August, and the seedlings are ready for planting out from mid-September. Plant the seedlings 12 in. (30 cm) apart, each way. It is well worth covering them with cloches or fleece in early spring to obtain early supplies.

Cloche call   ❧

"I have been told that 'Hispi' cabbage can be grown under cloches or in frames for an early crop. When should the seed be sown?"

"Hispi" cabbage seed is normally sown outside in succession between March and July. For early cabbage, sow it in February under glass in modules for planting in the open in late April or early May.

Alternatively, make a sowing under glass in October. Plant the seedlings under frames or cloches in January. It is important to choose a warm, sheltered position for these early cabbages and the soil must be covered with cloches for several weeks in order to warm it up before planting out.

Sowing calabrese ❧

"I want to grow some calabrese plants this year but I am not sure which variety to grow. Can you recommend one or two? When should seed be sown and how soon can I expect to cut the heads?"

There are several good varieties of calabrese including the F1 hybrids "Corvet", "Caravel", "Green Comet" and "Express Corona". If your ground is infected with clubroot disease, grow "Trixie". This has tolerance against the disease.

Seed is available from Thompson & Morgan, Poplar Lane, Ipswich, Suffolk IP8 3BU. Sow the seed from early April until early July in shallow drills putting two or three seeds together, thinning them later to one at each position, 6 in. (15 cm) apart in rows 12 in. (30 cm) apart. The crop usually matures in 12–16 weeks from sowing.

Cabbages need a solid soil to grow well.

Cabbage is patchy ❧

"My spring cabbage plants do not look very good. Do you think it would be a good idea to feed them?"

It would be a good idea to feed spring cabbages in late February with a fertilizer rich in nitrogen such as nitro-chalk.

Purple cabbages ❧

"Some of my recently planted autumn and winter cabbages have developed a purpling of the leaves and do not seem to be growing at all. Feeding has not improved the colour or growth. Can you help?"

Attack by cabbage root fly is the cause of the purple discoloration and poor growth. If you carefully dig up the plants you will see that there is very little root present and you may also find the creamy coloured grubs of the pest. It is not really possible to control an existing attack although if you pull the soil up the stems as high as the first leaves and keep the plants well watered they may perhaps produce a new root system. Protect by a dusting with Sybol Dust.

Protect new plantings with squares of carpet underlay cut with a slit to fit closely to the stems or by covering the crop with Enviromesh.

Feathered foe ❧

"Wood pigeons have started to attack my various winter greens – cauliflowers, cabbage and broccoli. Is there any reliable control, other than netting, which I find a nuisance to remove each time I need to hoe?"

Netting is certainly the best answer, and several gardeners find they have to grow their greens in fruit cages to escape the ravages of local pigeon populations.

The late Fred Loads, a founder member of the *Gardener's Question Time* team, once said that pigeons need a straight flight path into the crop and placing a number of canes throughout the vegetable area would keep them away. It may be worth trying.

Blister attack ❧

"The leaves of quite a number of my brassicas, and especially my sprouts, have developed white, raised spots. Is this something that I should be seeking to control?"

The condition is due to a fungal disease known as white blister. It is specific to plants in the cabbage family and sprouts do seem to be particularly at risk. There will be a reduction in yield with infected plants and if the disease is not checked it can increase in severity from year to year. Remove and destroy the badly infected leaves, followed by a spray with a copper fungicide. Try to keep any new brassica sowings and plantings as far as possible from the old plants and at the end of cropping remove and carefully dispose of plant residues.

Club root 🌿

"I have purchased a piece of land at the end of my garden which was once used for allotments. To my dismay it seems that I have a serious club root problem. I plan to use May & Baker Liquid Club Root Control on it. I have also read that Dazomet can be used but I do not know where it can be purchased. I would be grateful for any help that you could give me."

Due to prolonged cropping with brassicas of different types on allotments, it is by no means unusual for club root to be present. The fungus is virtually specific to the cabbage family and it would be wise to avoid planting cabbages, sprouts, cauliflowers and turnips. If you do grow any from seed to transplant later, grow them in pots of sterile compost so that by the time that they are planted out there is a good root system. This may become infected later but the plants should be big enough to produce a crop.

The use of the May & Baker club root control that you have will delay infection of young seedlings sufficiently for a crop to develop. Dazomet can be used only by trained operators and cannot be bought legally for garden use. It does go a long way to eradicate infection. If there is a professionally trained and licensed operator in your district he/she may be able to treat your garden for you.

Whitefly problem 🌿

"After 45 years of successful gardening, I seem to have met my Waterloo! Millions of whitefly invaded my garden last year, decimating what should have been excellent crops of sprouts, spring greens and 'January King' cabbage. The tomatoes in my greenhouse had a black deposit on the skins. Is there anything that an amateur gardener can use to get rid of this pest?"

Two types of whitefly attacked your plants. One affects greenhouse crops and the other feeds on cabbages and their relatives. Sadly, both are difficult to eradicate.

Sprays which normally give some reduction in whitefly numbers include Long-Last, Sybol and Phostrogen Safer's Insecticide. Less easy to find but also effective is Savona. This and the Phostrogen product are based on soft soap and often work well when more potent chemicals appear to have lost their effect. Whichever product is used, it is essential to repeat the treatment every few days.

Outdoors, it also helps if new sowings and plantings are kept away from old crops. In greenhouses they can be controlled with the Encarsia wasp predator which feeds on the whitefly.

Useful wasps ❧

"I have found a number of objects on my cabbages and other plants, and I would like to know what they are. They don't move, but would seem to be some kind of insect."

The objects are greenfly that have been parasitized by a tiny wasp known as aphidius. Inside each of the attacked greenfly will be a wasp larva and when fully fed it pupates and in due course lays eggs in a further generation of greenfly.

Root of the problem ❧

"Some of my cabbage plants had swellings just below soil level which I feared were the dreaded club root. When I pulled them up, though, there was a little hole in each swelling and the insides were hollow, so I am having second thoughts. Any ideas, please?"

The swellings were the work of the turnip gall weevil. No serious harm is done except when attacks are on seedlings or very young plants. A seed dressing containing gamma-HCH would protect seedlings from attack.

Spotty broccoli ❧

"Some of my sprouting broccoli plants had a nasty spotting on the leaves this year. I have taken off all I could find, but what else should I do? Will it spread to my other cabbage and sprout crops?"

The spots are due to attack by brassica ring spot. The samples showed the typical dark, rounded spots about ½ in. (1.25 cm) across, followed by a yellowing of the leaves. The disease can attack all types of brassicas, particularly in wet winter weather. The infection normally passes from one crop to the next as new plants go in during spring alongside older, diseased ones.

If you can follow a three- or four-year crop rotation so the new brassicas are away from the previous year's crop, destroying all old crop remains as soon as picking is completed, the spotting should not return. A few sprays of Dithane 945 may help.

Liming the vegetable garden ❧

"Is it a good thing to apply lime to the soil in the vegetable garden each winter?"

It should not be necessary to apply lime to the soil used for growing vegetables every year. The only satisfactory way to find out whether lime is needed is to obtain a soil-testing kit and test your soil. Ideally, the soil should be slightly acid. Only if it is very acid is lime needed. You will probably find that it contains plenty of lime without more being added.

Cabbage protection ❧

"My spring cabbage plants get badly damaged by birds each year. I have tried bird-scarers without success. Can you suggest how I might deter the birds?"

The most effective way of deterring birds is to cover your spring cabbage plants with netting on a temporary framework. Some people have found "humming" tape placed around the plants is also effective in keeping the birds away.

Whitefly on sprouts ❧

"My husband has just found the first signs of whitefly on his sprout leaves. Is this the same sort as attacks greenhouse plants, and if not, is it any easier to control?"

No to both questions! The species of whitefly on brassicas is a much hardier one than that which lives under glass, surviving the hardest of winters, and it is just as difficult to control. Fortunately, it doesn't do as much damage as glasshouse whitefly, with its attendant honeydew and sooty mould problems.

It probably would be worth applying two or three sprays of fatty acids, permethrin or bifenthrin to try to nip the attack in the bud.

Flea beetles attack ❧

"In late summer my broccoli and cauliflower leaves were suddenly covered with dozens of little black beetles. They rapidly ate holes in the leaves. Could you tell me what they were and how I should have controlled them?"

The insects would have been a species of flea beetle. Attacks can be extremely severe on occasion, perhaps triggered off by particularly advantageous weather conditions a few weeks previously which allowed for rapid breeding.

Control would best be by a thorough spraying of both leaf surfaces with a fatty acids insecticide such as Phostrogen Safer's Insecticide for Fruit and Vegetables or a permethrin-containing one such as Tumblebug or Picket.

Ravaged cauliflower ❧

"Our cauliflower heads have been spoiled by vast numbers of tiny black insects. Some are dead and the others appear alive, but the cauliflowers are very unappetizing and have to be washed most carefully to get rid of all the unwanted livestock. What would they be, and how could we have prevented them?"

The insects are tiny predatory wasps, called diaeretiella, which lay eggs in aphids. All you could have done to prevent this was to spray early (controlling the first attacks of mealy cabbage aphids) so that the tiny wasps would not have been attracted to the crops. Some commercial growers introduce the wasps as a form of biological control to cut down on sprays.

Mealy cabbage aphids ❧

"My sprouts were spoiled during growth by a grey pest which caused the leaves to curl and become spotted and which also made them all sticky. Help please."

The pest was mealy cabbage aphid. As you found, this pest makes a real mess of the brassicas on which it feeds. Should attacks occur again, the best control would be to spray with the aphid-specific insecticide Rapid.

Alternatively, covering the crops with Enviromesh would stop the pests reaching the leaves.

Calamity cauliflowers ❧

"My husband's cauliflowers have been a disaster. Most of them were blind and the leaves didn't grow properly at all, just a main vein plus a frilly side bit. What went wrong?"

The condition you describe exactly fits a disorder known as whiptail which is due to a shortage of molybdenum. It is always worst in dry years and on acid soils.

Add lime in autumn or winter to next year's brassica plot and incorporate plenty of compost to hold water during dry spells.

Cabbage caterpillars ❧

"My husband's cabbages, and other greens, always suffer from various caterpillars during the year. Is there any really complete control?"

There are three main types of caterpillars which attack cabbages and related plants, namely the large and the small cabbage white butterflies and the cabbage moth. Holes are eaten in the leaves, and the caterpillars of the small butterfly and the moth also burrow down into the hearts.

A fair degree of control can be obtained by covering the crop with Enviromesh or similar covering to exclude the egg-laying adults. Where attacks have already started, you could spray the leaves with pyrethrum or permethrin or alternatively use the biological control agent *Bacillus thuringiensis*. Where the latter is applied, the caterpillars stop feeding almost at once and die shortly afterwards. It does need to be applied in good time, however, while the caterpillars are still feeding on the outer leaves.

Carrot fly crackdown ❧

"What are the best ways to stop carrot fly maggots ruining my crop every year? Nothing I have tried seems to give complete control."

Try a combination of methods this year. First, delay sowings until early June as this will then miss the damaging first generation of the pest. Then, if you haven't yet bought your seeds, try "Sytan" from Marshalls or "Ingot" from Unwins, both of which have shown some resistance to attack.

Dust the seed with Murphy Combined Seed Dressing before sowing, or treat the soil with Chlorophos, and then cover the plot with Enviromesh to exclude the adult flies.

Finally, lift the crop as soon as it is ready; damage is greatly increased if left after early October.

Carrot fly ❧

"I have not been successful with carrots in recent years because of damage from carrot fly grubs. I am not keen on using chemical sprays. Is it possible to trap the flies in any way?"

There are several things that you can do to lessen damage from carrot flies apart from using insecticides. Sow the seeds as thinly as possible to avoid thinning the seedlings. Disturbing the seedlings when thinning releases an aroma to which the flies are attracted. Another method is to sow late in mid-June to avoid the first batch of carrot flies. Covering the carrots with nylon fleece (Enviromesh) also forms a barrier and prevents the carrot flies getting at the crop.

Keep the hoe going through the growing season.

Save water ❧

"Should the ground between rows of carrots be mulched to keep down weeds? I have been told it is better to keep the ground well watered."

Yes, it is a good idea to mulch the ground between rows of carrots as it prevents weed growth and also conserves soil moisture.

In dry weather it may still be necessary to water the crop. Before mulching, pull out any weeds by hand. As the foliage develops it will form a canopy, suppressing weed growth.

Carrot trouble 🐾

"Several of our carrots appear to be stunted and the leaves are turning yellow and then red. Help please!"

Sadly, your carrots have become infected by virus, probably spread by the carrot willow aphid. Red leaf virus and motley dwarf virus combine to produce the symptoms you describe. There is no control, crops will not develop and digging up is the only treatment. Perhaps, in another year, growing the crop under a plastic cover would keep the aphids and viruses away.

Corkscrew carrot 🐾

"My son grew some carrots that were very forked and one did a complete corkscrew. What caused this, and would it be possible to get a corkscrew on demand with the right treatment?"

Forking of carrots can be caused by stony soil and also by applying fresh manure before sowing. Usually the roots divide up into two or more smaller ones, and it is much more unusual for a corkscrew effect to develop.

Possibly in heavy soil the divided roots would be forced to stay together and so become twisted, but it would be impossible to reproduce the exact conditions every time.

Violet carrots 🐾

"Some of the last carrots that we have dug up have a dark rot with a violet-purple coating. What is responsible for this condition?"

Violet root rot is the fungus responsible for the damage. It is a soil-borne disease which can attack many root crops. The best treatment is to dig out the soil where the infected carrots were growing, and to dispose of it safely.

Avoid growing root crops on the same site for four years or so, if possible. Brassicas are unaffected by the disease so could be grown on infected soil.

Planting celery ❧

"I have been given some self-blanching celery plants. When can they go out, and how far apart should they be?"

It's usually quite safe to plant self-blanching celery out in the open at the end of May/beginning of June, when frost is no longer a danger.

Celery needs a good, fertile soil, so a few days before planting, sprinkle a general fertilizer such as Growmore over where you intend to set your plants. To help blanch the stems, plant in blocks rather than separate rows, 6–9 in. (15–23 cm) apart. Water regularly, particularly in any dry weather, while a weekly liquid feed once the plants are established will help to encourage good growth.

Celery fly ❧

"My celery plants have developed a lot of blotchy marks on the leaves. What are they, and are they a health risk to the crop?"

The blotchy marks are caused by feeding by the maggots of celery fly. It is a type of leaf miner, but one that makes one large mine, rather than the more usual winding mines in the leaves.

Although unsightly it isn't really too serious, and generally can be controlled by squashing the caterpillars within the blotches, or removing the affected part of each leaf. Should there regularly be a severe attack, then it probably would be worth treating the celery with Crop Saver a few times.

Attacks normally start in May, and continue at intervals during summer and into autumn, and parsnips are also attacked. An alternative method of control is to cover the crop with Enviromesh to exclude the adult flies.

Self-blanching celery ❧

"Can you tell me whether self-blanching celery has to be grown in trenches in the same way as ordinary celery? Also, is it easy to grow?"

Self-blanching celery is easier to grow than ordinary celery and it does not need to be grown in trenches. It is not, however, as hardy. Sow the seed in a warm greenhouse in early March and grow the seedlings in modules or small pots.

Plant in the open in late May when danger of frost has passed. Really good fertile soil is needed and a general fertilizer should be applied before planting out. Plant the celery close together in blocks allowing about 9 in. (23 cm) between plants. Close planting keeps the stems partially shaded so that they are better blanched. Keep the crop well watered in dry weather. The celery should be ready for cutting from the end of July.

Sowing courgettes ❧

"I am very fond of courgettes and plan to grow some this year. Are there special varieties or can I grow ordinary marrows and cut them when small? Can I start the seeds off in my greenhouse to get an early picking?"

It is best to obtain special courgette marrows which have a soft skin. F1 "Green Bush", F1 "Defender" and "Burpee Golden Zucchini" are all good varieties.

The seed can certainly be started off in a warm greenhouse. Sow the seed in small pots or modules containing a good seed compost in early May. Plant outside in early June once all danger from frost has passed. Before planting make sure the seedlings have been hardened off and gradually accustom them to outside conditions. Stand them in a cold frame, covering them at night. By the end of May leave the frame fully open at night unless frost threatens. To give them a good start after planting out, cover the seedlings with cloches for a couple of weeks.

Courgette conundrum ❧

"One of my courgette plants has stopped cropping and has stunted growths. What would be the cause of this?"

Your courgette will have been infected with mosaic virus disease. This is spread by greenfly, and as they feed the virus passes into the sap. There is no control and as the plant is unlikely to resume cropping, and could act as a source of infection for your other plants, it would be best to remove it.

Starting marrows ❧

"I want to grow some marrows. Can I sow the seed now or must I buy some plants? What are the best kinds to grow?"

Marrow seed should be sown in late May. The soil should be warm enough to sow seed in the open where the plants are to grow. If you can cover them with cloches so much the better as they will give the young plants a good start. Sow two or three seeds at each position. If you do not have cloches, cover the seeds with jam jars. When the seedlings appear, thin them out to leave the best one at each position.

Seed can also be sown in small pots or modules under cover. When large enough plant them outside after all danger from frost has passed. Space bush marrows about 3 ft (1 m) apart and trailing kinds 4 ft (1.2 m) apart. In small gardens, bush marrows are more suitable. "Long Green Bush" and "Tiger Cross" are good varieties to grow.

A safe spray for courgettes? ❧

"My courgettes suffered a heavy mildew attack earlier this year. I am not keen to spray edible crops, but some drastic action was needed. What would you have advised?"

Products that have been approved for application to garden plants carry an official MAFF approval number so you can be assured that the necessary safety testing has been carried out. You should then check that the crop you wish to spray is listed on the label, or is covered by the words "for use on all flowers, fruit and vegetables".

The choice for powdery mildew on courgettes would be between the systemic fungicide carbendazim, and the organic fungicide sulphur. Either should be applied at the first sign of attack with one or two repeat sprays.

Dryness at the roots can be a contributory factor, so check this in the first few weeks after planting.

Fruit or veg ❧

"I know that fruit have pips or stones but vegetables do not. All the seed catalogues I receive list tomatoes and cucumbers under vegetables. Should they not reconsider this? I would also like to know what category is a marrow?"

Seed companies have always included tomatoes and marrows under vegetables and they always will. Although botanically classified as fruits, the following are normally regarded as vegetables: aubergines, beans, capsicums, chilli peppers, courgettes, cucumbers, marrows, okra, peas, pumpkins, sweet corn and tomatoes.

Bumper pumpkin ❧

"I have grown pumpkins for the first time this year. Would you please let me know the weight of the heaviest pumpkin ever grown?"

The current world record for a pumpkin is 836 lb. The variety "Atlantic Giant" was grown in America, but seeds are available in this country.

Novice pumpkin growers may well be pleased to produce fruits that weigh about 250 lb.

Allow your pumpkins to ripen and harden on the plants, but protect them from possible slug damage. Any large leaves that shield the fruits from autumnal sunshine may be taken off. Cut the pumpkins from their stems before frosts arrive and store them in a cool, dry room. Well-ripened fruits should remain in good condition until the following year.

Marrow mildew 🌾

"Is it possible to prevent mildew on marrows? Most years my plants get covered with it by midsummer, and I am sure cropping suffers."

Powdery mildew can be encouraged by dry soil conditions, so the addition of plenty of organic matter, before planting and as a mulch, plus adequate watering in dry spells should help. At the first sign of any attack, spray with a sulphur fungicide, or use Benlate or Supercarb.

Spray away 🌾

"The courgettes in the vegetable garden and the cucumbers in the greenhouse are all suffering from mildew attacks. How can I treat them; they are cropping now."

Keep the plants well watered in any dry weather and also spray a few times, at 14-day intervals, with Safer's Garden Fungicide (based on sulphur) or use Supercarb or Murphy Systemic Action Fungicide (based on carbendazim). No interval between spraying and picking is needed with these fungicides.

Next year, consider growing "Tyria" or "Marketmore" cucumbers which are claimed to be more resistant to mildew attack.

Harvesting courgettes 🌾

"I am growing some courgette plants for the first time this year. They seem to be healthy and are producing plenty of flowers. At what stage should I harvest the courgettes?"

Pick your courgettes when they are about 4 in. (10 cm) long. It is as well to check the plants each day as the courgettes swell rapidly and can soon become too big. Cutting them regularly also encourages more to form.

Rusty leeks ❧

"On our allotments most of the leeks seem to have leaves with rusty orange streaks and spots. We presume this is just fungus; is there any cure?"

Yes, the disease is leek rust, and there is no really effective cure. It can attack onions, garlic and shallots as well as leeks and can cause serious losses.

When harvesting the crops, destroy all unwanted residues and when sowing or planting new onions, leeks etc, keep them as far away as possible from any existing old plants. New crops can be protected from attack by a spraying with Dithane 945 or a copper fungicide, but it is necessary to spray in advance of any infection, and repeat every two weeks or so.

Leek moth menace on the allotment ❧

"I have been told that leek moth caterpillars are a problem where I have a new allotment. I didn't like to show my ignorance by asking what they looked like, so could you describe the pest, the damage and the control."

The leek moth is still relatively rare in this country, largely confined to the coastal areas of southern and eastern England. The small moths are rarely seen but they lay eggs at the bases of leeks in April and May and the small green caterpillars mine the young leaves. Later they penetrate to the growing points and eat holes in the young foliage as the leaves unfold.

The fully fed caterpillars pupate on old dead leaves and new adults emerge some two weeks later. There are two and sometimes three generations each year. Onions and shallots can be attacked as well as leeks.

Control starts by removing old leek plant residue as the crop is harvested to ensure no pupae are left around on the site. Frequent winter and spring cultivations will help to kill any pupae still present. Where damage has occurred a spray with a permethrin-based insecticide may help.

Transplanting leeks ❧

"I have grown some leeks from seed. When do I transplant them from their pots into the garden, and how far apart should they be?"

Transplant your leeks when they are about 8 in. (20 cm) high. Before you do so, give them a good watering, then in the prepared bed make 6 in.

(15 cm) holes with a dibber and drop one seedling into each. There is no need to fill the holes with soil as it will trickle back on its own when the plants are watered.

Space the leek seedlings 6 in. (15 cm) apart in rows 12 in. (30 cm) apart. If they are planted any closer the leeks will be smaller and slender.

Thunder flies ❧

"I am finding that the leaves of my leeks and onions have a silvery sheen to them, and there is a lot of fine spotting over the foliage. Is there something I can do about this?"

The silvery effect will be the result of feeding by thrips. Known also as thunder flies, the pests feed on the sap and cause the fine flecking, which gives a silvering effect when present in quantity. It may be too late, but sprays of a general insecticide after spells of thundery, close weather are usually effective.

Cos lettuce ❧

"I have never grown cos lettuce. Are they superior to ordinary lettuce? Should they be treated in the same way?"

Cos lettuce are generally regarded as having a better flavour than ordinary lettuce. They also have crisper leaves.

Sowings can be made throughout the spring and summer in the same way as ordinary lettuce. Cos grow best in cool, moist conditions. A good variety is "Lobjoits Green Cos" which can also be sown in the autumn. "Little Gem" is regarded as a semi-cos lettuce. It is small and compact with crisp hearts. It is only suitable for spring and early summer sowings.

Lettuce losses ❧

"I planted up my cold greenhouse with winter lettuce, but have already lost some through rotting off. How can I save the rest please?"

The rotting is due to the fungus *Botrytis* which is encouraged by moist, humid conditions. It often starts where the leaves touch the ground and then spreads. Water as little as possible, and ventilate as much as you can. When watering, keep the leaves and the necks of the lettuces dry. When doing any more planting, try building up little mounds of soil on which to plant.

In the bag ❧

"I would like to grow some early lettuce in my greenhouse. Could they be planted in growing bags? How soon can I sow the seed and what is a good variety to grow?"

Lettuce can certainly be grown in growing bags on greenhouse staging, close to the glass. For an early crop, sow the seed in early March. To avoid undue root disturbance, sow in modules and when the seedlings are large enough, plant them in the bags.

Suitable varieties are "Little Gem" and "Tom Thumb".

Friendly solution ❧

"How would you advise me to keep slugs under control on my lettuce crop? I have quite a lot just getting away, but in most years this is when the slugs start to attack."

The best control in this case would be to use a biological control agent Nemaslug or Nature's Friends for slug control.

These products contain the friendly nematode *Phasmarhabditis hermaphrodita*, which seeks out and penetrates the slug bodies. Once inside, a bacterium carried by the nematodes will overrun and kill the slug and then new nematodes are produced to seek out more prey.

Apply in water over a good area to ensure the best control and keep the soil moist in any dry weather. Obtain the Nemaslug via a local garden centre or send by post for Nemaslug to Defenders Ltd, PO Box 131, Wye, Ashford, Kent.

Coming a cropper ❧

"As we pull up our lettuce plants we are finding masses of white pests on the roots. Can you advise us please?"

The insects you are finding are lettuce root aphids. They spend the winter as eggs on Lombardy poplar trees, build up in spring inside small pouches on the leaf stalks and then fly off to attack lettuces.

Some return to the poplars in autumn, but where lettuces are grown round the year, they may stay with the new crops. Best control is to grow lettuce varieties such as "Avondefiance", "Debby" and "Lakeland" which are resistant to attack.

Lettuce downy mildew ❧

"My husband lost a lot of his greenhouse lettuces this year with a sort of mould. The leaves had pale and yellow areas which went mouldy and often the whole plant went soft and rotten after a few weeks. What would you advise, please?"

The damage sounds very much like downy mildew, to which lettuces under glass can be very prone. The best advice is for your husband to select varieties listed in seed catalogues as having resistance to downy mildew (although many different strains of the fungus do exist). "Action", "Beatrice", "Debby", "Dolly" and "Malika" should be satisfactory.

Lettuce virus ❧

"Some of our lettuces last year were rather distorted and seemed to have lumpy foliage and pale areas. My son thinks he read somewhere about a virus called big vein – is this correct? More importantly, can anything be done to prevent it?"

Yes, your son is correct, there is a big vein virus that attacks lettuces. Early attacks can have a stunting effect on the plants, and there is vein clearing and a bubble effect on the foliage. Interestingly, the virus is carried through the soil by a swimming spore of a fungus called *olpidium*.

There is no control other than removing affected crops. Grow lettuces in a new site each year, and raise them in pots of proprietary compost for planting out to avoid early damage.

Lettuce cutworms ❧

"A whole row of my lettuces was apparently eaten off at soil level overnight. I have plenty of slug pellets around and a humming line bird scarer. What do you think did the damage?"

The damage you describe is absolutely typical of cutworm attack. Cutworms are the caterpillars of various types of moths and they feed in the soil at or around ground level. Presumably the soil is looser along the row and therefore easier to move through. Prevent damage to further plants in the area by dusting the soil with Sybol Dust.

Take heart ❧

"Can you tell me if celtuce is a type of lettuce? When should the seed be sown?"

Celtuce is also known as stem lettuce and sometimes as Chinese and asparagus lettuce. It is not grown for its leaves, but for the heart of the stem which can be sliced and eaten raw in salads or cooked in a stir-fry.

Sow the seed as for lettuce in April, as soon as the soil has begun to warm up. Good, fertile soil is needed. Sow the seed thinly in shallow drills and thin the seedlings to leave the plants about 12 in. (30 cm) apart.

Novel salad leaves ❧
"I am told that there are several plants that can be used as substitutes for lettuce. Can you tell me what they are?"

A number of different leafy plants can be used as substitutes for lettuce, adding interest and colour to the salad bowl. They include: corn salad or lamb's lettuce, sow July–August; endive, sow May–August; radicchio, sow June–July; land cress, sow September; and claytonia, sow April–May.

Seed firms, such as Marshalls, Wisbech, Cambs PE13 2BR, phone 01945 466711 offer a collection of mixed salad leaves.

Onions from sets or seed? ❧
"Is it better to grow onions from seed or from sets?"

It is easier to grow onions from sets and because they start off as small bulbs they mature early. There is a danger that they will "bolt", however, and heat-treated sets should be grown to avoid this.

Tree onions ❧
"I would be grateful if you could advise me on tree onions. Should the onions that appear on the tops of the stems be used for cooking or ignored? There are also bulbs at the base of the stems. What is the best method of preparing and cooking these onions? I assume that there are no toxins associated with them?"

Tree onions are also known as Egyptian onions. The small bulbs that form at the tops of the stems, which need staking, are strongly flavoured. Use them in the same way as ordinary onions. They can be cooked or pickled. They do not contain any harmful chemicals. However, the small bulbs are fiddly to prepare and the plants are usually grown for their curiosity value.

Planting shallots

"I have been told that shallots should be planted on the shortest day. My books say plant in February. Can you tell me which is correct?"

Like garlic, shallots need a long growing season and they can certainly be planted on the shortest day if the soil is in a fit state. It would be well worth trying this early planting in your district [Exmouth] if you have a piece of well-drained soil.

Space the bulbs 6 in. (15 cm) apart in rows 8 in. (20 cm) apart. Plant with a trowel, leaving the top of the bulbs exposed. Where the soil is reasonably dry the bulbs can usually be pressed into the ground. The shallots should be ready for harvesting in July and August.

Sowing onions

"I want to grow some big onions for showing. What varieties should I grow?"

Good onion varieties for showing are: "Unwins Exhibition", "Marshall's Showmaster" and "Robinson's Mammoth Improved". Sow seed under glass as soon as possible.

Sowing show onions

"I have bought some 'Mammoth Improved' onion seed as I would like to produce big onions for our local show. When should the seed be sown?"

Onions for showing need a long growing season. Sow your seed as soon as possible in a warm greenhouse.

It is best to sow two or three seeds in modules or small pots filled with a good seed compost. This avoids pricking out the seedlings and disturbing the roots. When the seedlings appear, thin them to the strongest in each module. Plant the young onions outside in April in really good, fertile soil.

White rot warning

"In my new garden I have been warned by neighbours that onion white rot has been quite a problem. Is there anything I can do to reduce the risk of further attacks?"

Onion white rot can persist in the soil for eight years or so and there is no effective control available. Heavily manured plots do seem to suffer less and the onion variety "Norstar" shows some resistance to attack.

Should an attack occur, dig out the affected onions with a fair bit of the

surrounding soil and burn or otherwise dispose of them safely. Keep
onions, leeks and related crops off that area of soil for as many years as
possible.

Shredded onion leaves   ⅔

*"I wouldn't have thought that anything would eat onion leaves, but mine
have been almost shredded by a caterpillar of some sort. Can you identify
what is doing it?"*

The caterpillar is that of the leek moth which attacks onions, shallots and
garlic as well as leeks. There are three generations in most years, starting
in April to May, and the pests overwinter as pupae on plant debris. Leek
moths are mainly confined to the southern and eastern counties. To
control, destroy all debris as the crops are harvested, and cultivate well
and deeply in winter or between crops.

Onion neck rot   ⅔

*"Last year we lost quite a few onions during storage from a rotting at the top
of the bulbs. Is there anything we can do now to protect this year's crop?"*

Neck rot of stored onions often starts around harvest time, particularly if
wet weather coincides with damage to the onion stems. Bending over the
tops too soon can also result in injury and disease infection.

   Take care this year, if bending over the tops, to wait until they start to
die back naturally. After lifting, dry the onions off fully – a greenhouse
bench is ideal – to ensure there is no excess moisture around the necks.

Onion eelworm   ⅔

*"Last year, some of my onion seedlings failed to produce a proper root or bulb,
the leaves were twisted and bloated and then the plants died in early summer.
What would have caused this? I could not find any pests in the soil."*

The damage you describe is typical of that following eelworm attack. The
pests are microscopic in size so cannot be seen, but they can persist from
year to year. Weeds are often sources of reinfestation.

   This year, grow your onions on a different piece of ground and keep
weeds constantly under control. Follow a three- or four-year rotation of
crops as far as possible to reduce the chances of any build-up of persistent
pests. Onions could be followed by brassicas which are not affected by
eelworm, but avoid leeks or shallots.

Onions in trouble ❧

"My husband grew a good lot of onions this year, but just as they were getting to a decent size all the leaves started to die back and appeared tattered, as though eaten."

Onion moth caterpillars feed inside the developing leaves, eating them away from the inside. The caterpillars are a creamy green in colour and there can be as many as three and sometimes four generations in a year. With older onions the caterpillars penetrate to the bulb and result in a rotting.

New eggs are laid in April or May to start off the next year's attack. A spray or two then with a general insecticide would help to give control. For now, remove all onion plant residues.

Harvesting onions ❧

"I have two rows of onions that are growing well. When should I bend the tops over before lifting them?"

It is not a good idea to bend over onion tops to encourage them to ripen. Wait until they flop over naturally and turn yellow. Then the bulbs may be partly loosened in the soil by easing a fork around each one to partly sever the roots. Allow the foliage to turn brown before lifting the onions. Leave them on the surface of the soil to complete drying in the sun before storing them in a cool, airy place. Ripening can be completed by laying the bulbs on wire racks. This is useful if the ground is wet.

Roping onions ❧

"We used to have our onions 'strung up' by a friend who has died recently. Our own efforts do not look professional. Could you tell us how to do it correctly?"

Start by tying a length of fairly thick string or cord from an overhead beam. Tie a large knot at the base. Select your onions carefully, with the largest at the bottom. "Sit" the first bulb on the knot. Wind its stem around the string and set another bulb close to it, winding its stem tightly around the string. Continue in this manner with the bulbs nestling close to each other until you finish at the top. There is no need to tie each bulb to the string.

When a bulb is needed remove one from the top and work your way down. Remember, practice makes perfect!

Storing onions ❧

"I am having difficulty in drying off my onions outside, because of the wet weather, and I have put them in trays in a well-ventilated shed. What is the best way of storing the bulbs?"

Once onion bulbs have been thoroughly dried, the simplest way to store them is in net bags hung up in a dry and airy place.

The traditional way is to plait them in a rope so that they can be hung up. They can also be kept in shallow trays where air can circulate freely around the bulbs. Do not store them in polythene bags as dampness will collect inside.

Any onions with thick necks should not be stored as they will not keep. Use them up first.

Sowing parsnips ❧

"Last year I sowed some parsnip seed in March and very few came up. Can you tell me how I can get better results this year?"

Parsnip seed can be difficult to germinate if sown too early and when the soil is too cold. To overcome the problem, delay sowing until April when the soil should be warmer. Some gardeners overcome the problem by sowing the seed in soil blocks or modules in a greenhouse. The plants can then be set outside when conditions are favourable.

Another system that you could adopt is to "chit" or pregerminate the seed. Place a piece of moistened kitchen paper in the bottom of a plastic container. Sprinkle the seed over it and, after putting a lid over it, stand the container in a warm place.

Inspect the seeds each day and, as soon as there are signs of germination, carefully transfer them to individual pots of good potting soil. When large enough, plant the seedlings in the open garden. Always use fresh seed as old parsnip seed germinates poorly.

Parsnip seed ❧

"I have discovered a packet of 'Hollow Crown' parsnip seed which I have had for at least a year. Is the seed worth sowing now?"

Parsnip seed does not have a long life and if you sow the seed now germination is not likely to be good. It would be wise to purchase some fresh seed. Choose a variety that has resistance to the canker disease which can be a problem. Try "Avonresister" or F1 "Gladiator". Germination is not good if the soil is still cold. It pays to delay sowing until April or May.

Lifting parsnips 🌿

"I have grown some parsnips and I am not sure whether they need lifting and storing. Can you tell me if I can leave them in the ground until they are needed?"

Parsnips can be left in the ground all winter, the roots being lifted as required. However, as the foliage dies down it can be difficult to locate them and it is wise to mark their positions with canes. It also pays to cover the ground around them with straw or other material to make it easier to lift the roots if the ground becomes frozen.

Parsnip poser 🌿

"We grew some good parsnips, but quite a few have brown areas of damage down the roots. What would have caused these and how can we prevent this happening again?"

The damage would have been caused by slugs, probably the type known as keeled slugs. These feed almost exclusively underground so have been difficult to control in the past.

   Now control can be achieved by watering the soil with Defender's Nemaslug, or Miracle Garden Care's Nature's Friend for Slug Control. Delay application until March or April, when the soil temperature should have reached 5°C.

Roots in trouble 🌿

"We are just starting to lift our earliest parsnips and are finding rusty brown marks on the sides of the root. Is this parsnip canker or something else?"

The marks on your parsnips are the result of feeding by carrot fly. Parsnip canker attacks the crown and shoulders of the root whilst carrot fly feeds more on the side. Prevent damage next year by netting the crop to exclude the adult flies. Netting can be placed over the crop or place a simple barrier 2 ft (0.6 m) or so high around the crop as the flies move quite close to ground level.

Browned off ❧

"Last year my parsnips showed a lot of browning around the tops which a friend told me was due to canker attack. He said there were some resistant varieties available. Can you suggest one or two please?"

The original canker-resistant parsnip was "Avonresister", bred at Wellesbourne, a Ministry research station. More recent varieties are "Bayonet" and "Gladiator".

Parsnip canker is generally worse on soils that are short of lime and rich in nitrogen and in years when wet weather follows a dry early autumn. It is less of a problem with later sown crops and when the parsnips grow steadily throughout the year without fluctuations in water or nutrient supply.

Pea problems ❧

"My first sowings of peas failed to appear in any quantity, despite netting to keep out mice and birds. The peas I have been able to find have been eaten or have rotted away. Recommendations, please."

It is likely that there has been a combination of soil pests and diseases attacking your pea seeds. Before any further peas are sown, dust them with a combined seed dressing to protect against such damage.

Peas in a pod ❧

"I bought some sugar snap or mangetout pea seeds earlier this year but did not get round to sowing them. Is it too late to sow the seed in June? Are they grown in the same way as ordinary peas?"

Sugar or mangetout peas, which are eaten whole, can be grown in the same way as ordinary garden peas.

There is still time for you to sow the seed. Choose a piece of good, fertile soil and sow the seeds 2 in. (5 cm) apart in a 2 in. (5 cm) deep drill or take out a shallow trench, the width of a spade, and broadcast the seed in the bottom, covering them with about 2 in. (5 cm) of soil.

"Sugar Snap" is a good variety, growing to a height of 5–6 ft (1.5–1.8 m) and needs supporting with netting or pea sticks.

Pods in a curl ❧

"Many of my pea pods this year grew in a spiral fashion, or were somewhat bent. Why should this happen?"

Attack by pea aphid, when the pods were young, is the cause of them growing in a deformed manner. Prevent damage by spraying after the end of flowering with a general insecticide such as Phostrogen Safer's Organic Garden Insecticide, or with Tumblebug.

Shallow drills are best to sow peas and beans!

Pea marsh spot ❧

"Quite a number of our peas had small dark spots in the flesh. There was no outward indication, but they showed up on the peas that split during cooking. Advice please."

There is a classic disorder of peas known as marsh spot. It is due to a deficiency of manganese and is usually found on peas growing in marshy soil. The plants also may appear yellow and if the affected peas are sown the following year germination is very poor. Prevent or correct the problem by watering the crop and the soil, around flowering time – using manganese sulphate at 1½ oz. per 1 gal. of water (50 g/1 l).

Sowing peas

"I bought some seed of 'Kelvedon Wonder' peas earlier in the year but have not been able to sow them yet. How late can the seed be sown?"

"Kelvedon Wonder" is an excellent early pea, growing about 18 in. (45 cm) tall. Seed can be sown at intervals between April and July. It is resistant to mildew and it is a good variety for sowing in July for maturing in the autumn. If the weather is reasonable a worthwhile crop can be gathered from this late sowing.

Mangetout peas

"I would like to grow some mangetout peas next year. Are they easy to grow and what variety would you recommend?"

Mangetout peas are not difficult to grow and should be treated in the same way as ordinary peas. They are particularly noted for their sweet flavour. Good varieties are: "Oregon Sugar Pod", 3 ft (1 m) and "Sugarbon", 2 ft (0.6 m). Germination is poor if the seed is sown in cold soil. Warm the ground before sowing early crops with cloches.

Pinked peas

"My peas are growing very slowly and are only 1–2 in high. Every leaf has notching as though someone has been round with dressmaker's pinking shears."

The notching around the leaf edges is the work of the adult pea and bean weevil. The weevils are greyish brown so are not easily seen, and they drop off the plants and feign death at the first sign of danger. The larval stages feed underground, mainly on the nitrogen-fixing nodules on the roots, and this can depress growth.

The best control now would be to dust the plants and surrounding soil thoroughly with derris dust, or to spray under the leaves with Picket or Tumblebug. When sowing your next peas, dust the seed drill with Sybol Dust to prevent damage to the roots by the larvae of the weevil.

Pea moth prevention

"I hate finding caterpillars in my peas! Is there a reliable and fool-proof way to keep them out?"

Pea moths are on the wing from around mid-June to mid-August. If you keep your peas covered during that period with Enviromesh, then the moths will not be able to reach the plants for egg-laying.

The caterpillars hibernate in cocoons in the soil, so good cultivations will take care of most overwintering ones, but as the adults fly quite long distances to lay their eggs, netting provides the most reliable control.

Early peas ❧

"I want to sow some peas early this year. I plan to cover them with cloches for protection. What is the best variety to grow for an early sowing?"

The round-seeded peas are the hardiest and one of the best varieties to grow for an early sowing is "Feltham First". It is dwarf and is suitable for growing under cloches. Another hardy variety is "Meteor" and grows to about 18 in. (45 cm). Put your cloches in place several weeks before sowing to warm up the soil.

Why chit? ❧

"Why is it necessary to sprout potato tubers?"

Sprouting or chitting potato tubers starts them into growth and gives them a headstart when they are planted out in the spring.

Set the tubers upright in trays and keep them in a light place in a frost-free shed or greenhouse.

Blight advice ❧

"Is it good practice to plant potatoes in the same plot where potato blight has occurred in the previous year? I burnt all the old plants, but may have missed one or two potatoes and left them in the soil."

The potato blight fungus overwinters on potatoes in the soil and spores produced from these in the following year will infect the new crop. Even though blight spores are wind-borne – meaning that infection can also come from further afield – it would be better to move this year's potatoes to a new site.

Scabby potatoes ❧

"Is there any way to stop the small, round, scabby areas developing on our potatoes this year? I am told that liming encourages the trouble; is this correct, as our soil is pretty acid and needs liming?"

Your potatoes are infected with common scab. This trouble is encouraged by alkaline conditions and by a shortage of organic matter in the soil. Try to follow a three-year rotation with potatoes preceding the brassicas. You can then lime for your brassicas and it should be three years before the potatoes come back to that plot.

When planting, nestle each seed potato in a clump of grass mowings or fresh garden compost.

Varieties vary in their susceptibility to scab attack, and some resistance is shown by the varieties "Pentland Javelin", "Pentland Crown" and "Maris Peer". It also helps to water well in dry weather during the tuber initiation stage.

Potatoes growing more than sprouts ❧

"I have set up my seed potatoes in egg boxes in my usual way, but the young shoots are now feeding a mass of green aphids. What can I use to control them without affecting the subsequent potato crop?"

The insects would almost certainly be peach-potato aphids and these can be serious vectors of a number of potato viruses. Drench with a spray of Nature's Answer to Insect Pests to clear up the infestation.

The aphids could have hatched from a nearby peach tree, but are more likely to have been feeding on another plant close to where your seed potatoes are sprouting, and to have spread from there.

Sprouting potatoes ❧

"I have bought some 'Maris Bard' seed potatoes. I am told by friends that I should 'sprout' the potatoes by standing them in a tray before planting them outside. Is this really necessary and why is it done?"

"Maris Bard" is a good early potato and it is sound practice to "sprout" the tubers in trays before planting them outside.

The tubers should be stood on end close together with the ends containing the dormant buds uppermost. Kept in a cool but frost-free place, the dormant "eyes" will begin to grow and when planted out will be ahead of unsprouted tubers. This means that an earlier crop can be expected when the tubers are sprouted first.

Holey potatoes ❧

"Quite a few of my potatoes have small round holes eaten in them, as per sample. Could these be slugs or wireworms?"

The size of the holes, and the nature of the feeding inside the potatoes, shows that wireworms are responsible for the damage. Slug holes are quite a bit larger and the insides appear as if scooped out. Lift the remaining crop as soon as possible as damage increases quite a lot from now on. Next year, cultivate the soil well in advance of planting and if many wireworms are seen, incorporate Sybol Dust or Chlorophos into the soil at planting time.

Smash-less potatoes   ❧

"Last year we lost a lot of our potato crop due to feeding underground by slugs. Many of the potatoes were almost completely hollowed out. It may be a bit late, but is there still time to take any action this year?"

Yes, there is time for action to be taken to protect your potatoes from slug attack. Zeneca (formerly ICI) are selling a biological control for slugs, under the name of Nature's Friends for Slug Control. The pack is available from selected garden centres and contains a card to send off to that company for the actual product.

Alternatively, you can write direct to Defenders Ltd, Freepost, PO Box 131, Wye, Ashford, Kent TN25 5TQ. These friendly agents, "Nemaslugs" are nematodes that seek out and, with the aid of a bacterium, destroy the underground slugs. It is important to keep the soil moist after application.

Salad potatoes   ❧

"Are there special varieties of salad potatoes and do they need the same treatment as ordinary potatoes? Where can I obtain the tubers?"

Several different varieties of salad potato are available. They are all noted for their excellent flavour and can be eaten cold in salads or boiled in the usual way.

Cultivation is the same as for ordinary potatoes. Good varieties include: "Ratte", an old French variety; "Charlotte", firm, yellowish flesh; "Pink Fir Apple", long, thin tubers with pink skin and excellent flavour. Two new varieties are now on offer. "Linzer Delikatess" has excellent flavour-producing medium-sized tubers and "Belle de Fontenay" is an old French variety.

All these potatoes are available from S.E. Marshall & Co Ltd, Wisbech, Cambs PE13 2RF.

Potato puzzler   ❧

"Can you please tell me what is wrong with the enclosed potato? They all turned out like this and couldn't be eaten."

The little potato growths along the sides of the main tubers are a form of secondary growth known as gemmation. Secondary growth occurs when there is a period of wet after a long dry spell. During dry weather the potatoes virtually cease growing but the wet then induces a renewed burst of activity, resulting in new tubers starting to develop on older ones.

Apart from the difficulty in peeling, the tubers are quite all right to eat. Next year, keep the crop watered throughout any dry weather.

Drought victim?   ❧

"Can you tell me what causes the brown raised areas on my potato crop, and how it can be prevented?"

The corky patches are due to attack by common scab disease. The marks can be peeled off and the potatoes eaten normally, although when a serious attack develops the potatoes can look very unappetizing when lifted. This bacterial disease is usually encouraged by alkaline soils and is worse in dry summers.

Avoid liming the site for potatoes and add fresh grass mowings to the planting holes or drill at around a barrow load per 4 sq.yd. Water them well in dry weather. Varieties that are less prone to attack include "Pentland Javelin", "Pentland Crown", "Maris Peer" and "King Edward".

Spuds in trouble   ❧

"Some of the potatoes we are using in the kitchen have double rings of black spots just below the skin. What causes this, and is it harmful?"

The spots are the result of attack by leaf roll virus when the plant was growing. The damage passes down the vascular tissue of the stem and into the tubers.

The spots are not harmful, although they look unsightly, and are best "peeled out". Do not be tempted to save any of these potatoes for use as seed as all the crop would be infected.

Salad potato

"I plan to grow some 'Pink Fir Apple' potatoes this year. Are they grown in the same way as ordinary potatoes? Is it an early or late variety?"

"Pink Fir Apple" is a very old potato variety. Grow it in the same way as other varieties. It is a late variety and normally keeps well. Crops are not usually heavy but it makes up for this in flavour. The flesh is yellow and waxy, and the skin is pink.

Potato seeds

"I grew seven rows of 'Desiree' potatoes this year. Small green apple-like fruits appeared on all the plants. Can you tell me what they are and whether they are poisonous?"

The apple-like growths you have spotted on your "Desiree" potato stems are actually fruits containing seeds which, if ripened and sown, would produce new varieties. It is unlikely that they would be any better than the variety, but it is how new kinds are raised. The green fruits are poisonous and must not be eaten.

Hollow hearted

"Some of my 'Majestic' potatoes have brown, hollow centres but there are no signs of slugs and the outsides of the tubers have no bored holes. I know 'Majestic' is an old variety, but I have always had good results – until now!"

The condition you describe is known as hollow heart. This occurs when there is a wet spell late in the season and the tubers are pretty well mature. Growth starts up again, resulting in the hollow developing in the tubers. Large-tubered varieties, including "Majestic", often suffer most damage.

There is no real control, although regular watering during any late summer dry spells may help to keep damage at a lower level.

Blight fright

"When does potato blight normally occur? We lost a lot of our crop last year and would like to protect the leaves this year."

Potato blight is likely to attack in most years in the western extremities of Wales, and also in Cornwall.

The exact time depends on prevailing weather conditions, the blight being set off by a combination of warm weather and high relative humidity.

Spray as soon as possible, using a copper or a mancozeb-based fungicide. Repeat once or twice at 10–14 day intervals, or for longer in warm, humid conditions. Next year, consider growing a potato variety with some resistance to blight such as "Cara" or "Wilja".

Earthing up potatoes

"I am growing a few rows of early and late potatoes. I am told that I should have earthed them up. Is this necessary? When will the earlies be ready for lifting?"

Potatoes should be earthed up as you have been advised. This is done to cover tubers that form near the surface and prevent them becoming green. In this condition they should not be eaten as they are poisonous. It also helps to increase the crop.

Earth up the plants when they are about 9 in. (23 cm) tall. Hoe the soil thoroughly between the rows and draw it up into ridges around the stems. This should be done several times until the ridges are about 15 in. (38 cm) high. Early potatoes are ready for lifting when the flowers are fully open in June and July.

Potato blight fungus

"I lost most of my potato haulm last year to what I was told was potato blight. The leaves, and then the tops, turned black and died off early. Can this be prevented now?"

In your part of the country [Newcastle upon Tyne], the right time to spray against the potato blight fungus is July. Spores travel in the air and the infection develops when there is the correct temperature and humidity.

In north-east England, and in Scotland, mid-July is the normal time for attack to start. Spray thoroughly with a copper fungicide such as Bordeaux Mixture or Murphy Traditional Copper Fungicide. Repeat a few times at two-week intervals.

Potato problem

"I have just dug out some potatoes that I missed during harvest last autumn, and have found them to be full of holes. I have also found thin, wiry creatures present; are these wireworms, and if so, what would you suggest to stop them attacking my new crops?"

Yes, the creatures you found would be wireworms, the larval stage of the click beetle. Wireworms feed for four or five years before they are fully fed and ready to change into the adult form, so they could do considerable damage in your vegetable garden. Regular cultivations are probably the best control, exposing the larvae to the local robin population. Alternatively, dust Sybol Dust onto the soil before planting or sowing new crops and rake lightly into the surface.

Keeled slugs in potatoes ❧

"As we lift our main crop potatoes we are finding some with deep holes bored or eaten out. The entry hole, if that is what it is, is just under $\frac{1}{4}$ in. across. Help please."

The size of the hole indicates that the damage is being done by keeled slugs. They live underground and surface very rarely. Lift the rest of the crop as soon as you can; slug damage can increase ten-fold between the start and end of September. After lifting, water the plot with Fertosan Slug & Snail Killer.

Next year, water the potato site just before or just after planting the seed potatoes. Also, try growing "Pentland Dell" or "Pentland Ivory" which have some resistance to slug attack.

Potato blight ❧

"When is the correct time to apply a copper spray to stop potato blight disease? My husband lost a lot of his crop last year."

Timing varies throughout the country. In Fishguard blight is likely most years, and, if you want to be on the safe side, then the first fungicide should be given in late June. If the season is wet and warm, repeat the spray a few times at 14-day intervals.

It is possible to reduce the blight damage by careful choice of potato variety; posters at garden centres usually give details of resistance. "Cara" is one example of a good maincrop to try for its blight resistance, but it is always best to spray as well.

Skin deep ❧

"Could you recommend a potato variety that would be free from damage by scab marks? All the ones I have tried get small dark spots all over the skins."

Potato scab is most prevalent on light sandy soils lacking in organic matter, and in dry seasons. Liming also increases damage by common scab.

When preparing the plot, work in plenty of organic matter and when planting, sit each tuber on a bed of compost. If the compost is in short supply, add a barrow-load of mowings to every 3–4 sq.yd. of soil. Suitable varieties that are less prone to common scab include "Maris Peer", "Pentland Crown" and "King Edward".

Spuds it likes ❧
"Can I put potato peelings on my compost heap?"

You can, but make sure you mix them with some tougher woody waste such as hedge clippings and stems of herbaceous plants. You need to aim for a mix of about one-third tough waste to two-thirds soft (grass clippings and weeds, as well as potato peelings and other kitchen waste) as soft, sappy waste on its own tends to form a sodden mass which excludes the air necessary for successful composting. Do not, however, use the compost where you plan to grow potatoes or tomatoes, as the peelings may carry diseases.

In the dark ❧
"I am growing some 'Witloof' chicory for the first time. My plan was to force the roots in pots under the greenhouse staging, enclosed in black polythene to exclude light. I have been told that forcing can be done in an airing cupboard. Is this a good idea?"

Chicory roots can certainly be forced, as you have been told, in an airing cupboard. Ideally, the temperature for forcing should be between 10–18°C.

Blanched chicons will appear more quickly at the higher temperature and, as the temperature in your greenhouse is likely to be lower, we suggest that you will get better results with the airing cupboard method.

Also, try some in your greenhouse for later supplies. Put six good roots in a 9 in. (22 cm) pot of potting compost, and cover with a pot inverted over the lower one. Cover over the drainage hole to exclude light as forcing has to be done in total darkness.

Forcing rhubarb ❧

"I have several large clumps of rhubarb in my garden and I would like to force one or two to have some early sticks. Can the roots be forced in the open ground or must they be lifted and taken indoors?"

Rhubarb crowns can be forced in the open ground from December onwards. They must be covered to exclude light and, at one time, special clay rhubarb pots were used.

They can still be obtained but are rather expensive. Instead cover a root with a plastic bin, first putting straw or leaves over the crown to retain warmth. This will produce stems several weeks earlier than plants left in the open. If you want earlier supplies, lift the crowns in November and December after they have been frosted. Force them in black polythene sacks in a warm shed or greenhouse.

French leaves ❧

"Having enjoyed eating curled endive on holiday in France, I would like to grow some in my own garden. When is the best time to sow the seed and how is blanching carried out?"

Endive is more popular in France than over here. Plants are not difficult to grow and need very similar treatment to lettuce.

Sow the seed between May and August in shallow drills. Thin the seedlings to leave them 12 in. (30 cm) apart.

A new variety worth giving a trial is "Sally" (sold by Marshalls). The inner leaves can be blanched by tying the leaves together about two weeks before cutting. Blanching makes the leaves taste sweeter. Special blanching caps for covering the plants can also be purchased.

Forcing seakale ❧

"I would like to try growing seakale but as I have no greenhouse, can I blanch the plants outside and what is the best way of doing this?"

Yes, seakale crowns can be forced outside. The crowns are planted in March and allowed to grow through the summer. The old leaves are cleared away in the autumn and blanching can begin in January. Cover each crown with a 9 in. (22 cm) plastic pot to exclude the light. The drainage hole needs to be covered and the pots insulated. You should have blanched shoots ready for cutting in late March or early April.

Rhubarb, rhubarb   ❧

"I have previously found rhubarb to be very free of pest attack, but mine is now being devoured by slugs. Is this unusual? I had assumed that the oxalic acid content of the leaves would keep pests away."

Under warm, damp conditions slugs can be a problem. The leaf stalks may also be tunnelled by rosy rustic moth caterpillars, so the oxalic acid is no great protection. Try watering the rhubarb leaves and surrounding soil with Slugit liquid to stop further slug attack, leaving the necessary interval between treatment and picking.

New Zealand spinach   ❧

"I have planted some New Zealand spinach on my allotment. As this is the first time I have grown it, can you tell me when it will be ready for picking and eating?"

Pick your New Zealand spinach as soon as the leaves are large enough. It is best to pick the leaves and stems whilst they are still young as older leaves are inclined to be tough.

Attractive vegetable   ❧

"I have seen some spinach plants with bright red stems. Can you tell me anything about this vegetable? Can it be eaten or is it for ornament only?"

The seakale beet that you have seen is also known as Swiss or ruby chard. The bright red stems are certainly ornamental but the leaves may be eaten like ordinary spinach. The wide stalks and midribs can also be eaten in a similar way to asparagus.

Sow the seed outside in April, placing three seeds together 15 in. (38 cm) apart in rows 15 in. (38 cm) apart. When the seedlings appear, thin them out to one at each position. It usually takes about four months before the foliage is ready for cutting.

Spotty spinach   ❧

"I usually grow lovely spinach, but this year my crop is very poor. The leaves are covered with spots and a very poor colour. Can this be corrected, or must the crop be destroyed?"

The spotting is due to spinach leaf spot fungus. Normally damage is not too severe, but from time to time a severe attack does crop up. The best treatment would be to cut off all the foliage to remove the infection and then to spray a couple of times with a copper fungicide or with Dithane when regrowth starts. The new leaves should then be free from infection, but at the end of cropping, dig up and destroy all plant residues.

Continental flavour

"Dandelions grow freely in my small orchard. Is it true that the leaves can be used in salads?"

Yes, they are commonly used in this way on the continent.

Young fresh leaves may be picked from plants growing wild. However, the best leaves are blanched by covering the plants with upturned pots with the drainage holes blocked to exclude light. Do not use leaves from plants in lawns, as they may have been treated with chemicals.

Roots may also be lifted in the autumn and blanched in total darkness in a frost-free shed or greenhouse.

Mustard and cress

"I want to grow some mustard and cress for winter salads. As I have no greenhouse, can I grow it on a windowsill indoors?"

Mustard and cress is easy to grow indoors in a light window. Sow the seed in a shallow dish lined with damp kitchen paper. Keep it in a warm, dark place until the seeds germinate and then bring it into the light. Keep the paper moist at all times.

Mustard seeds normally germinate faster than cress. To be able to cut both at the same time, sow the cress first and follow with the mustard three days later. It normally takes about three weeks or so before the seedlings are ready for cutting.

Chinese cabbage

"I want to grow some Chinese cabbage but I do not know when to sow the seed. Can you tell me the best time to sow? Are the leaves cooked or eaten raw?"

Sown too early, Chinese cabbage is likely to run to seed. Ideally, sow the seed in July in good, fertile soil and you should have heads for eating in about ten weeks. Keep the plants well watered and never allow the soil to dry out.

The seeds should be sown in the open in rows 18 in. (45 cm) apart, thinning the seedlings to 12 in. (30 cm) apart.

Look out for reliable F1 varieties, such as "Kasumi" and "Harmony", which are less likely to run to seed and can be sown earlier in June. The leaves can be eaten raw in salads.

Sowing radicchio ?&

"Can you tell me anything about a vegetable called radicchio? When should it be sown?"

Radicchio is a red chicory and is grown for its red leaves. There are several modern varieties including "Red Devil". Sow the seed as for lettuce in June and July and the leaves will be ready in mid-September. They are used mainly in salads. Seed may also be sown in August to provide plants for growing under protection in the winter.

Chinese cabbage ?&

"I sowed some seed of Chinese cabbage in April but the plants went to seed. Why?"

Chinese cabbage is inclined to bolt if it is sown too early. Dry soil could also be the cause. The best time to sow is between June and August. Sowing in modules for planting out later avoids disturbing the roots and causing a check. Plants sown then should be given protection in late September.

Sowing celtuce ?&

"Can you tell me anything about a vegetable called celtuce. When should the seed be sown?"

Celtuce is the same as stem lettuce, grown for its thick main stem and not the leaves. The stem can be eaten raw or sliced and cooked.

To do well, grow it in good, fertile soil. Sow the seed in the spring in the same way as ordinary lettuce. Plants take about four months to reach maturity.

Winter salad ?&

"I am growing some 'Crystal Head' chicory. How soon can I cut the heads for eating?"

"Crystal Head" is a "Sugar Loaf" chicory and looks similar to Cos lettuce. It is grown as a winter salad or it can be boiled or braised. The inner leaves are folded together tightly and do not need blanching. The chicory can be harvested from October onwards. Cut the heads to leave a stump, from which new foliage will be produced for cutting later.

Salad days

"Can you tell me what is corn salad and how it can be eaten?"

Corn salad is also known as lamb's lettuce and is a useful substitute for lettuce. Sow the seed outside in July and August and thin the seedlings to leave the plants 4 in. (10 cm) apart. They will survive the winter well, as they are very hardy. Sowings can also be made in March and April for summer supplies.

A few leaves can be cut from the plants at a time, but whole plants may also be lifted.

Chinese leaves in difficulties

"We are growing Chinese leaves for the first time this year, and over the last week we have been finding small, bright yellow spots appearing on the leaves. We cannot see any pests apart from a small number of greyish aphids under the leaves. What is causing the spotting and how can we cure it?"

The spotting is a characteristic of the damage caused by cabbage aphid feeding. On cabbages the yellow spots tend to join up into irregular patches, but on Chinese leaves they seem to stay distinct. An under-leaf spray with Safer's Insecticide, Nature's Answer to Insect Pests or Tumble-bug would soon get rid of the aphids and prevent any further spotting.

Chinese caterpillars

"My Chinese leaves grew very well until the autumn, when they were suddenly attacked by a severe infestation of caterpillars. How late do caterpillars go on attacking crops?"

The attack would have been by caterpillars of the large white butterfly. Normally, caterpillars from the second generation pupate in August or early September, so unfortunately, you must have just caught a very late attack.

The pupae will overwinter and then emerge as the next generation of adults in April or May. Netting will keep the butterflies off the plants, and so prevent egg-laying.

Alternatively, the caterpillars could be picked off by hand, controlled biologically by spraying with *Bacillus thuringiensis* (as Zeneca Nature's Friends for Caterpillar Control or from WyeBugs) or chemically with Tumblebug, Polysect or Picket.

Sowing sweet corn 🌸

"Last year I sowed some sweet corn seed outside in late May. The plants did not do well and hardly any cobs ripened. Should I have sown the seed earlier?"

It would be well worthwhile sowing sweet corn seed under glass in April to produce plants ready for putting outside in early June. Choose an early maturing variety such as "Champ" or "Sunrise" and sow two seeds in each small pot or module. After germination select the strongest seedling and pull out the weaker one.

Before planting outside, gradually harden the plants off in a cold frame. After planting cover the plants with cloches if possible until they are well established. To assist pollination, plant in blocks rather than in long rows, spacing the plants 14 in. (36 cm) apart in each direction.

Baby corn 🌸

"Can you tell me how baby sweet corn is produced?"

To grow baby or mini sweet corn, choose an early variety or a special variety such as "Minor F1".

Sow the seeds in small pots or modules indoors in April for planting in the open at the end of May. Sow two seeds in each pot and pull out the weaker one after germination. Plant outside, spacing the plants closely together at about 6 in. (15 cm) apart. Harvest the cobs when they are 3–6 in. (7.5–15 cm) long. Each plant is likely to produce four to six small cobs.

Corn blocks 🌸

"I have raised some sweet corn plants in pots and have been told not to plant them out in rows. How should they be planted and when should it be done?"

Sweet corn flowers are wind-pollinated, so grow the plants in blocks to ensure effective pollination of the "silks" on the female flowers. Plant the sweet corn seedlings 14 in. (35 cm) apart in each direction in late May or early June.

It has been found that plants yield better if the ground is mulched. This can be done with black polythene laid on the ground before planting. Cut holes in the plastic to receive the plants. The polythene mulch helps to conserve soil moisture and also prevents weed growth.

Sweet corn problem ❧

"Many of my sweet corn cobs were full of earwigs when picked and a few were damaged where they had been eaten. Your advice please."

Earwigs need to feel pressure on both upper and lower surfaces when they tuck themselves away during the day, so it is not too unusual for them to be found in sweet corn cobs. It is unusual, however, for them to damage the kernels to any extent.

There would not be any easy control, but if you pack plant pots with straw or newspaper and put these on canes amongst the sweet corn you may find the earwigs would use those instead. It may also help to smear the stems of the sweet corn plants with Trappit glue which should deter any pests climbing up the stems.

Sweet corn aphids ❧

"Why should our sweet corn have suffered a terrible infestation of greenfly this year? What would they normally have attacked, and what control would you advise against any future attacks?"

The species of greenfly attacking your sweet corn would probably have been the potato aphid, *Macrosiphum euphorbiae*. This species attacks roses and related plants but then migrates to attack a wide range of other crops including sweet corn, beans, rape, lettuce and potatoes.

This species is usually quite widespread, but is only really numerous and damaging in certain years, probably related to weather conditions in spring. Control it by spraying with Tumblebug, which can be used on any crop, with just one day between spraying and picking edible crops.

Sweet corn smut ❧

"A few of my sweet corn cobs behaved really oddly this summer. They swelled up and almost exploded with masses of sooty black powder inside. What on earth went wrong?"

The sweet corn were attacked by maize smut. This fungal disease is pretty unusual, and looks quite alarming. It normally only occurs in very hot summers. There is no effective control in the garden but it is unlikely to occur again next year. Burn any plant residues remaining just as a precaution, and use a different piece of your garden for sweet corn next year.

Flea bitten 〰

"As my radish and turnip seedlings come up, the leaves become pitted with small holes. I believe this is due to flea beetle attack, although I have never been able to catch them at work. How should I stop further damage?"

Yes, flea beetles are responsible for the damage you describe. They only attack the first few leaves but attacks can be very severe. Prevent further damage by dusting along the seed drill as the new seedlings emerge, and along existing rows of small seedlings, using derris dust.

Repeat weekly, or after rain, until the plants are large enough to escape attack. The tiny yellow-striped, black insects jump off the leaves at the first hint of danger, so are not often seen at work.

Sowing celeriac 〰

"I am told that celeriac is a good substitute for celery. Is it easy to grow and when should the seed be sown?"

Celeriac is a good substitute for celery and is much easier to grow.

Sow the seed in modules or small pots under glass in March. Several can be sown together, thinning the seedlings to one per pot later. Plant in the open in May, spacing the plants 15 in. (38 cm) apart.

One for the pot 〰

"I have been given some black scorzonera roots. Are they eaten raw or should they be cooked? Are the plants raised from seed?"

Scorzonera roots are usually lightly boiled in salted water for about 15 minutes. They have a flavour similar to turnips. The roots can also be sliced, fried in butter and served garnished with parsley. The plant is perennial and is usually grown from seed which can be sown in April and May. Another sowing can be made in August to supply large roots for the following autumn.

Resistant swede 〰

"My husband and I are very fond of swedes, but each year our plants are very badly attacked by mildew. How would you suggest we prevent damage on the current year's crop?"

If you grow the variety of swede called "Marian" instead of your usual variety you shouldn't be troubled so much by powdery mildew.

"Marian" has been bred with resistance to both powdery mildew and club root fungi so is a very useful type. It will also help if the young plants are kept well watered in any dry weather.

Vegetable disasters ❧

"My swedes are all leaf and no roots and my sprouts blow open before they reach a decent size. What am I doing wrong?"

Your swedes are producing leaf and no root because they are growing in nitrogen-rich soil. This crop needs a good balance of phosphates to encourage roots to swell to a plump size.

This year rake into the surface soil sulphate of ammonia at $\frac{1}{2}$ oz. (14 g) and superphosphate at 2 oz. (57 g) each per sq. yd. (per m²).

The Brussels sprouts have "blown" because they have been planted in loose soil. Always set them, with a dibber, in ground that has been allowed to settle for several weeks. Do not fork it before planting.

Swiss chard ❧

"Can you tell me the difference between Swiss and ruby chard? Are they good vegetables to grow?"

Ruby chard has swollen red stems and Swiss chard has white stems. Both are excellent vegetables. Apart from the leaves the swollen stalks and mid-ribs can be eaten separately. Apart from their culinary use they are also highly ornamental and are worth growing in a flower border.

Swede storage ❧

"I have a good crop of swedes maturing and would like to know how best to store them. Can they be left in the ground until needed?"

Swedes are hardy and can be left in the ground until the end of the year, but they should then be lifted to prevent them becoming woody. If the weather becomes cold while they are in the ground, cover them with a thick layer of straw which should provide sufficient protection in all but the coldest areas. When lifted they can be stored in boxes in a cool, dry place, in a similar way to carrots.

Alternatively, you could build a swede clamp outdoors. Stack the swedes on a layer of straw in a sheltered, well-drained area and cover with another layer of straw. In very cold weather provide further protection by covering the straw with a layer of soil.

Sowing kohl rabi ❧

"I plan to grow some kohl rabi this year but I am told it is a brassica. Does this mean that it can be affected by the club root disease which is present in my soil and when should the seed be sown?"

Kohl rabi is a brassica and can be attacked by the club root disease. However, it does have resistance to the disease. If your soil is acid, apply lime to the ground this winter.

In good conditions kohl rabi can be harvested two months after sowing, and sowings can be made at intervals between April and September. It is a useful substitute for turnips.

Radishes in winter ❧

"I am growing some lettuce this winter in my frost-free greenhouse. The end of one border is vacant. Can I grow radishes in this space during the winter?"

Yes, it would be well worth trying some radish in your greenhouse this winter. It is important that you choose a suitable variety and one that produces less foliage than summer radishes. One that you could try is "Saxa".

Sow the seed as thinly as possible and thin the seedlings to leave them about 2 in. (5 cm) apart. Watering must be done very carefully and only when the soil shows signs of dryness.

Turnip trouble ❧

"Quite a number of my husband's turnip crop had split roots. He has not seen this type of damage before; any suggestions?"

The splitting of a number of root crops occurs when a dry spell is followed by heavy rain. During the dry period the skins of the roots become hardened and growth ceases. The rain activates new growth but as the hardened skin cannot expand the tissue splits.

Adding well-rotted organic matter to the soil before sowing, plus watering when necessary during dry weather will help to prevent similar trouble in another year.

Green manuring

"I want to sow a green manure crop on my allotment this autumn but I am not sure which one to use. Would fenugreek be suitable?"

Sowing a green crop for green manuring adds valuable organic matter to the soil. Fenugreek is best sown in spring and summer as a short-term green manure. It can be dug into the ground after 2–3 months. For sowing in the autumn we suggest you choose grazing rye or winter field beans. The latter can be dug in any time up to flowering. Grazing rye is valuable for improving soil structure. Cut back the top growth in the spring and allow it to wither before digging in the whole crop. Pick the blooms when they are fully open and before they begin to fade. Hang them up in bunches in a dry and airy place.

Know your mustard greens

"Can you tell me anything about mustard greens? I've seen them used in Chinese recipes."

Mustard greens are one of the Oriental greens that have become popular in recent times. Known botanically as *Brassica juncea*, mustard greens are coarse-leaved brassicas which have a spicy flavour. They are hardy plants and seed can be sown outside in July and August to provide greens through the winter.

To obtain good-quality leaves, which are usually cooked, lift some plants in September and grow them on under cover. Good varieties are: "Green in the Snow" and "Red Giant".

Know your Texel greens

"What are Texel greens and how are they grown?"

Texel greens are brassicas (*Brassica carinata*) and they are grown for their nutritious leaves. Seed is sown in spring and plants grow rapidly. The leaves can be cut as and when required for use in salads and they have a pleasant, spinachy flavour.

Fast mover

"Whilst digging over my vegetable garden recently I came across a number of semi-transparent caterpillars, whitish with brown heads. They moved quickly which should indicate that they are helpful creatures, but they look as if they could eat plant roots very easily! Can you identify them please?"

These caterpillars are the larvae of the swift moth. Both the garden swift and the ghost swift moths scatter their eggs over the soil and the caterpillars tend to feed on larger roots or in storage organs, such as tubers, so they are not that helpful. They feed for two or three years before becoming fully fed, prior to pupating.

The caterpillars will wriggle violently backwards when disturbed, but their normal forward motions are not as fast or purposeful as that of a predator such as the centipede.

Remove the caterpillars by hand when seen, hoe regularly to disturb and expose the pests, or apply a soil insecticide appropriate to the crops that are being grown.

Baiting wireworms 🎋

"Last year I converted a piece of worn-out lawn into a vegetable patch, but my potatoes and other root crops were very badly attacked by wireworms. What would you recommend I do to avoid this happening again this year?"

Wireworms can be a major problem in land recently converted from lawns, as populations under grass are normally quite high. Dig over the soil well before any planting or sowing and remove any wireworms found. A dusting with Sybol Dust should kill the remainder in the soil.

If you prefer not to use chemicals, then the best plan is to bait with half potatoes over the plot. Cut potatoes in half, spike them through with a skewer or thin cane and then bury them fairly densely 2 in. (5 cm) or so deep over the area to be cleared. Pull up the potatoes, using the skewer or cane, from time to time and remove any wireworms found.

Wireworms take up to five years to develop into the adult click beetle, so you will need to take precautions for the next few years. Good weed control will also help by removing possible alternative food sources for the wireworm population.

Slug eggs 🎋

"As I turn over the soil on my allotment, I am finding clusters of soft, shiny egg-like objects. Can you tell me what they are and whether I need to take any action?"

These are the eggs of slugs or snails. Normally they are laid in autumn or spring and hatch within a month or so, but those laid in late autumn often lie dormant until the spring.

Exposing them during digging may be sufficient to kill them but, if large numbers are found, water the soil with Nobble or Fertosan to ensure a clean start to the sowing season.

Potted veg ❧

"As an absolute beginner, I understand that vegetables can be grown in large pots outside. Can you tell me what vegetables to grow and when to sow them?"

It is possible to grow vegetables in large (12 in./30 cm) diameter pots or in growing bags. Suitable kinds are courgettes, marrows, lettuces, runner and French beans, potatoes, tomatoes, parsley and radishes.

If you use large pots, put a layer of crocks over the drainage holes and fill with John Innes No. 1 or 2. During the summer, feeding will be necessary with a high potash liquid fertilizer. Sowing dates vary, although seed of most kinds is sown in the spring.

Consult Joy Larcom's *The Vegetable Garden Displayed*, published by the Royal Horticultural Society, price £10.95. Most garden centres and book-shops should stock it.

Aphid attraction ❧

"Why is it that aubergines seem so attractive to aphids? Every year my seedlings, and later the growing plants, get plastered with these pests. What is the best control now?"

Aphids can be attracted both by leaf colour and by smell, so presumably the aubergine has the required qualities of both sorts of attractant. The best control is one which is applied early, before any damage has been done. This could be a drenching application of an insecticide containing fatty acids, pyrethrins, heptenophos or bifenthrin.

Alternatively, if a temperature of 18°C can be maintained, introduce a biological control such as *aphidius* from Defenders or *aphidoletes* from Zeneca Garden Care.

Aubergine minings ❧

"On one of my greenhouse-grown aubergine plants, several of the leaves now have these winding mines due, I assume, to a form of leaf-miner. Is there any recommended control?"

The best control is simply to squash any grubs that can be found in the mines – look for them at the wider end of each mine. Various species of leaf-miner exist, one or two being quite nasty, so it would be wise to get rid of all you can find.

Aubergines outdoors ❧

"Can aubergines can be grown outside during the summer?"

Aubergines can be grown outside in mild districts provided they are given a warm and sunny position.

Sow the seed in a temperature of 21–23°C in early April. When about 2 in. (5 cm) tall, pot each seedling in a 3 in. (7.5 cm) pot and keep them in a minimum temperature of 16°C. As they grow move them on into 6 in. pots. Nip out the tips of the plants when they are just over 1 ft (30 cm) tall to induce a bushy habit. Plants can also be planted in growing bags.

Sowing cucumbers ❧

"I plan to grow some cucumbers in my greenhouse this year. When should the seed be sown and what is the name of a good variety?"

Cucumbers need to be grown in high temperatures and a moist atmosphere. Sow the seed in a temperature of 21–23°C at the end of February for planting out in a greenhouse border at the end of March.

A good variety to grow is "Athene" which is an F1 all-female type.

If it is difficult for you to maintain a high temperature so early in the season, purchase chitted "Athene" seedlings. They are sent out in mid-April and are ready for potting and are available from: S.E. Marshall & Co Ltd, Wisbech, Cambs PE13 2RF. Phone 01945 583407.

Mildewy cucumbers ❧

"My daughter's greenhouse cucumber leaves were covered with a powdery white deposit and cropping finished far too soon. Is this preventable?"

Powdery mildew has attacked your daughter's cucumber plants. Prevent it next year by growing a resistant variety such as "Tyria" or "Carmen". These are all-female types so can produce a succession of cucumbers. Also keep the soil and the atmosphere humid for best results.

Cucumber care ❧

"I have some cucumbers growing in my greenhouse and the plants are now about 1 ft (30 cm) tall. When do I pinch out the tips? Do the plants need shade from the sun?"

Allow the main stems of your cucumbers to grow upwards, supporting them with canes or wires. Do not pinch out the tips of the main stems until the plants have reached the roof of the greenhouse. Side shoots that form should have their tips pinched out at two leaves.

Cucumbers like shade from the sun. Paint the outside of the greenhouse with a suitable shading distemper, maintain a temperature of 21–24°C and keep the atmosphere moist by damping down in hot weather.

Female cucumbers ❧

"Last year I grew some cucumbers but the fruit was bitter. Was this because the female flowers had been pollinated by male ones?"

Traditional cucumber varieties, such as "Telegraph Improved", produce male and female flowers. To prevent pollination and fertilization occurring, all male flowers should be nipped out. Alternatively, grow varieties that only produce female flowers, such as "Tyria", "Pepinex 69" or "Athene".

Problem cues ❧

"Some of our cucumbers seem to rot just behind the flower. Should we remove the faded flowers off the young fruits?"

There is no need to remove the flower remains, as they will fall off naturally, and are unlikely to be the cause of the rot. The damage would be due to the grey mould fungus, and this is encouraged by over-humid conditions. Cucumbers like humidity, but try to reduce it slightly to discourage the mould. A few fortnightly applications of Supercarb would also help to check the disease.

Cucumber whitefly ❧

"In recent years, my cucumber plants in the greenhouse have been consistently ruined by severe attacks of whitefly. Please help me to prevent similar loss again this year."

Start by washing the greenhouse structure thoroughly and then wash with Jeyes Fluid.

As soon as new plants are put into the house, hang up yellow sticky traps close to the tops of the plants. Should there be an attack of the whitefly, spray thoroughly with a fatty acid/soft soap product such as Phostrogen Safer's Insecticide or BioFriendly Pest Pistol.

By late June time, when temperatures have increased sufficiently, introduce the encarsia parasite, leaving the time recommended by the suppliers after the last soft soap spray. Make further introductions as necessary and the whitefly will be eradicated.

Taking a tumble   𝓔

"My husband's cucumbers in the greenhouse started off well and came into cropping but then the leaves became stippled with small pale spots, growth seemed to slow down and cropping virtually stopped. Help needed please."

The cause of the trouble is a severe attack by red spider mite (now more correctly called the two-spotted spider mite). Attacks are always more severe in hot dry seasons when the temperatures under glass reach very high levels and humidity often gets quite low. As the attack is now severe, best rapid control would be obtained by spraying with Polysect. Pay special attention to the youngest growth and undersides of the leaves. Next year, should the pest start to cause damage, introduce the predatory mite, phytoseiulus, to keep the attack under control.

Twin cucumber   𝓔

"One of my greenhouse-grown cucumber plants produced a twin fruit. What would have caused this and would there be any way to perpetuate this habit? I would think such a cucumber would sell quite well as a novelty."

Twin cucumbers are produced from time to time but there has never been any complete answer. It is usually just put down to a genetic fault. Virtually all greenhouse cucumber varieties are now all-female hybrids so no seeds are produced by which they could be propagated. Even if they did produce seeds, because of the hybrid nature of the varieties, the offspring would be very variable.

Okra details   𝓔

"I have seen some green pods called okra in a local supermarket. Can you tell me anything about them? Are they good to eat and can they be grown in this country?"

Okra, or Gombo, is a vegetable that is not often seen in this country, although seeds can be purchased from several seedsmen. It is a tropical plant and a relative of the hibiscus. "Long Green" and "Clemson Spineless" are two varieties available in this country.

Best results are obtained by growing the plants in a greenhouse, sowing the seeds in a temperature of 18°C in March. Once the seeds germinate, grow them in pots and put them finally in 6 in. (15 cm) pots. Pinch the tops of the stems when they are 12 in. (30 cm) tall to induce a bushy habit. Harvest the pods when they are young and about 3 in. (7.5 cm) long. They are used for adding flavour to soups and sauces.

Sweet peppers

"I have bought some sweet pepper plants and wonder whether they can be grown outside. I have a sunny, sheltered garden in Hampshire."

Sweet peppers or capsicums can be grown outside in the south and as your New Forest garden is sheltered you should be successful, particularly if you can cover the plants with cloches. Plant outside at the end of May when the first flowers appear, spacing the plants 15–18 in. (38–46 cm) apart in each direction. In other areas it is best to grow these peppers under cover.

Poorly pepper

"What has caused the pale and slightly sunken area on the side of some of my greenhouse-grown peppers? Most of the later ones are all right, but early ones showed a lot of damage."

The damage would be due to sun scorch. It is not too common a problem, as the leaves normally shield the developing pepper fruits, but perhaps earlier in the season the leaf cover was not large enough.

Prevent damage another year by applying Coolglass shading to the greenhouse glass.

Peppers in store

"I grew some chili peppers in my greenhouse last year. When I stored them in jars they all went mouldy. What is the best way of storing chili peppers?"

The best way to store sweet and chili peppers is to dry them in a warm spot indoors where air circulates freely. When crisp and there is no obvious trace of moisture, they can be packed into air-tight jars. Make sure the jars have been warmed in an oven first to ensure that they are not damp.

Pepper problem

"My greenhouse pepper plants are coming along well but have suddenly been attacked by greenfly which are making the leaves crinkle up. What

would be the best way to control them and then how should I prevent further attacks?"

To control the existing infestation, spray with Phostrogen Safer's Insecticide, Bio-Friendly Pest Pistol or Tumblebug.

To reduce the chances of renewed attacks, hang sticky yellow traps in the greenhouse, which should catch quite a few as they first fly in. Later in the season, consider introducing biological control agents. Both a parasite (*Aphidius*) and a predator (*Aphidoletes*) are available.

Yellow tomatoes ❧

"I usually grow ordinary red tomatoes but I see in a catalogue that there are also yellow tomatoes. Are they worth growing and should they be treated in the same way as the red varieties?"

Yellow tomatoes are noted for their delicious flavour and they are well worth growing. Some varieties may not yield as heavily as red tomatoes but they make up for this in their flavour.

Grow the yellow tomatoes in the same way as the red varieties. Seed can be sown in March in a warm greenhouse with a temperature of at least 15°C.

Productive windowsill ❧

"I want to grow some windowsill tomatoes, but not necessarily bush types. Can you give me the names of the best kinds to grow?"

The tomato plants best suited for windowboxes, hanging baskets and for small containers are the patio tomatoes. A good variety is "Tumbler". It produces superbly flavoured, small, bright red tomatoes which are borne in profusion on trailing foliage. It is excellent for growing in windowboxes and hanging baskets. Another fine variety is "Tiny Tim". It makes neat, compact plants for windowboxes and small pots on a patio. It produces an abundance of tiny, sweetly-flavoured, red fruits. Another good variety for growing in pots on a patio is "Minibel". The bushy plants become covered in small, red fruits of good flavour.

Seed can be obtained from Suttons Seeds Ltd. Hele Road, Torquay, Devon, TQ2 7QJ and Mr Fothergill's Seeds, Kentford, Newmarket, Suffolk CB8 7QB.

Off-colour toms

"Many of our tomatoes are ripening with distinct patches of yellow or orange instead of red. The flesh under the paler areas is also quite hard and appears unripe."

The tomatoes are suffering from a condition known as blotchy ripening. It is more troublesome in hot, sunny periods and is mainly related to high temperatures, high light levels and low levels of potash relative to nitrogen. Correct by ventilating as much as conditions allow, plus shading and damping down to reduce temperature levels, and feeding with a high-potash tomato fertilizer.

Cold tomatoes

"When can I plant tomatoes in my unheated greenhouse?"

Tomatoes can be planted in an unheated greenhouse from late May onwards. Single plants can be put in a large 10 in. (25 cm) pot or two can go in a growing bag. Try to maintain a temperature of 18°C by day and shut the greenhouse early to retain heat for the night.

Black mulch

"Can you tell me why some gardeners put black polythene around their outdoor tomatoes and other crops? I have seen this done in the Evesham district but I have not been able to find out why."

The use of black polythene around vegetable crops is widely practised nowadays. It is done to serve as a mulch which helps to keep the soil moist and also smothers weeds.

For outdoor tomatoes the sheeting can be laid out several weeks before planting to warm the soil ready for the plants. The edges need to be pressed into the soil to hold the sheeting down. Holes are made in the plastic through which the plants are inserted. Potatoes can also be grown through black plastic. The sheeting is laid over the ground after the tubers are planted. When the shoots appear, holes are cut in the plastic to allow the growths to come through. Apart from keeping weeds down and the soil moist, it saves earthing up the potatoes.

Feeding tomatoes ❧

"My tomatoes in growing bags started off well but are now not as good as they were. How often should I feed the plants?"

Tomatoes in growing bags soon exhaust the nutrients in them and regular feeding is necessary to sustain good growth. Feed once a week with a liquid fertilizer. There are several on the market to try.

Fern-like tomato leaves ❧

"The leaves of my greenhouse tomatoes are now growing all feathery and fern-like, with some curling of the stems. My friend says this is weedkiller damage. Is this right, and if so, is there any cure?"

The ferny outgrowths from the leaf edges and the twisting are typical signs of contamination by lawn weedkiller. It is rare for such plants to produce fruit, but when they do the tomatoes are usually oddly shaped with few seeds. The insides are often hollow and full of liquid not flesh, and these fruits are inedible.

   Contamination of this kind usually occurs by using a watering can for lawn weedkiller treatment and then for watering in the greenhouse. Even the most minute trace will cause the damage. Occasionally spray drift can occur when lawns are treated in windy conditions, and bottles of weed-killer stored in the greenhouse can also do the damage. Sadly there is little that can be done other than removing the plants.

Tomato leaf mould ❧

"Help please! My greenhouse tomato leaves have yellow patches on the tops with a brownish mould beneath. They look very poorly and I think cropping is suffering. Can this be controlled now, and stopped altogether in another year?"

There is an attack by tomato leaf mould on your plants. To control now, keep the greenhouse well ventilated and thin out the foliage if it is too dense. These measures will reduce humidity which encourages the mould. It would also be worth spraying a few times with Traditional Copper Fungicide to arrest the attack and protect the new growth.

   Next year, choose a tomato variety with resistance to this disease such as "Ida", "Shirley", "Piranto" or "Cyclon". The seed catalogues will advise you which varieties listed are resistant.

Blighted tomatoes ❧

"Towards the end of cropping, my outdoor tomatoes developed dark spots on the fruits. After picking, these areas appeared to sprout a small growth of mould and then tended to rot. Any advice to prevent such losses next year?"

It sounds as if your tomatoes had an attack of potato blight, no doubt coming in after the summer drought ended. Prevent attacks next year with sprays of Dithane or Copper, starting when growth is well advanced. Normally a couple of fortnightly sprays from late June, and then more if the weather is warm and wet (the same treatment as for potatoes) would keep the disease under control.

Blossom end rot ❧

"My husband started his greenhouse tomatoes off quite early this year, but each time he has done this in previous years the first fruits have developed a dark spot underneath. Can you explain what the problem is and how can he prevent it, please?"

The problem is called blossom end rot and it is caused by a number of cultural factors. Uneven watering can bring on an attack and often plants closest to doors or vents can suffer more than the others due to differences in water loss from the leaves. However, the main cause is related to a shortage of calcium in the fruit. There may be sufficient in the soil, but the various conditions interfere with uptake. The answer is to water the plants and the soil with a solution of calcium nitrate. This can be obtained by mail order from Garden Direct (the mail order side of Chempak) at Geddings Rd, Hoddesdon, Herts, EN11 oLR.

Ripening tomatoes ❧

"I have a good crop of tomatoes grown in the open but not many have ripened. If I cut off the fruit and take it indoors will it ripen under cover?"

Yes, it would be well worth your while picking your tomatoes and ripening them indoors from the end of September. If you wish, whole plants can be lifted and hung up in a well-ventilated greenhouse. Trusses of fruit can also be cut and hung up in a greenhouse or cool room to finish ripening. Individual fruits may be stood on a sunny windowsill or wrapped in paper and kept in a cupboard with a banana. These must be inspected frequently to see whether any have rotted.

Stem attack ❖

"My wife looks after all the greenhouse crops, usually very successfully, but this year a lot of the tomato stems rotted through and tomatoes above the rot failed to mature. Can you say what caused the rot and how I can stop it another year?"

Stem rot, caused by the grey mould fungus botrytis, would have been responsible. Attack usually starts at a point of damage, often where leaves have been removed, but then spreads to healthy tissue. High humidity and low temperatures encourage the disease. To prevent, cut off cleanly any leaves that need to be removed, keep excess humidity under control with good ventilation, but maintain a reasonably high temperature by not over-ventilating on cool days. A few sprays with Carbendazim will also help, timed to follow any major de-leafing operation.

Water gardening

Leaky pool ⚘

"There is a concrete pond in my garden but it will not hold water for long as there is a leak in one corner. What is the best way of repairing the leak?"

Rather than try to find and repair the leak which is causing the water level in your pond to drop, it would be more efficient to cover the concrete with a flexible liner of heavy-duty butyl rubber. Aquatic centres, usually attached to large garden centres, stock these.

Don't forget to "air" the butyl for a day or two before putting it in the pond to dispel noxious gases which might have built up within the layers of the material.

Fisherman cat ⚘

"I have an ornamental pool containing a number of ornamental fish. Unfortunately, my cat is also fond of fish and enjoys catching them. How can I stop her doing it?"

Try putting prickly leaved shoots of holly around the edge of the pool. The cat will not like walking on the prickles and, hopefully, it will keep her away from the edge of the pool and the fish.

Perhaps the most effective method is to stretch a net just above the surface of the water and make sure the edges are well anchored to prevent the cat getting underneath.

Feeding time ⚘

"When should I stop feeding my goldfish?"

You don't actually stop. On warmer winter days, if the fish are up and about you can give them a little food, but clear out any that's left uneaten after a couple of minutes.

When spring arrives and the fish start to come up to the surface, feed every couple of days to begin with. As their disease resistance will be at its lowest, give them a mix of standard floating food plus a few chopped worms and daphnia.

Lily leaves ❧

"I have been told that there is a waterlily with huge leaves that are capable of holding a child. Can it be grown in this country?"

The giant waterlily is known botanically as *Victoria amazonica*, and the leaves can be as much as 6 ft (1.8 m) in diameter.

It is grown in this country but as it comes from the Amazon it needs very high temperatures and a large, deep pool of water. It is only cultivated today in the large glasshouses at botanic gardens such as Kew. To grow these giant waterlilies successfully they need a water temperature of 30–32°C.

Preventing the big freeze ❧

"As I have fish in my pond, how can I prevent the entire surface from freezing over in the winter?"

The simplest way to keep a hole in the ice is to place a pan on the surface and pour hot water into it. Alternatively, pond heaters are readily available from water garden specialists and larger garden centres and these can be connected to the electricity supply used for the pump or fountain. On no account try to crack the ice by hitting it. The shock waves produced would harm any fish.

Clear water ❧

"To keep my pond clear I have used barley straw in it and after six weeks it is now clear. How long should I leave the straw in the water and when should it be changed?"

Barley straw can be used effectively in ponds to prevent algae problems from early spring to late autumn. The chemical released by the straw as it decomposes prevents the growth of new algae, so any existing dense areas of blanket weed should be removed before the straw is added.

The straw should be loosely broken up in net bags and supported by floats and replaced every two months.

Clearing duckweed ❧

"How do I get rid of duckweed from a garden pond?"

Each piece of duckweed is made up of a single, leaf-like structure from which is suspended a slender root. The plant overwinters at the bottom of the pool and rises to the surface again in the spring.

Short-term control can be effected by sweeping the pool surface with a net, however this is difficult where other free-floating, oxygenating plants are present.

There are no chemicals approved for amateur use for the control of water weeds in ponds and duckweed is difficult to eradicate. Only complete clearance, best carried out in April or May, including removal of the sediment, can hope to clear it. Even then, pond plants will need to be washed and kept in quarantine to ensure that no small pieces of duckweed have been left behind.

Fountains can add great movement to a pond.

Overwintering pond plants ❧
"How do I overwinter my pond plants?"

As the weather turns colder the underwater oxygenators should be cut back. Marginals should be cut back once leaves and stems have turned brown, but leave several inches of stem above water. Remove dead leaves and flowers from water lilies.

Floaters must be left to form their overwintering buds which will sink to the bottom, but you can keep some of these buds in a jar of water indoors. These will germinate early in the spring and if then returned to the pond will provide surface cover quicker than the buds left in the pond.

Non-hardy aquatics like water lettuce and water chestnut should be removed and overwintered indoors in water-filled containers.

Outdoor lily ❧
"I have been given an arum lily in a pot which stands in my frost-free greenhouse. I am told that it can be grown outside. Is this true?"

The arum lily, zantedeschia, can be grown outside in southern England, particularly if planted in boggy ground at the edge of a pool or stream. Strains such as "Crowborough" and "White Sails" have been grown outside for many years. There is no reason why your plant should not succeed outside in your district [Hampshire], provided it is given a sheltered position.

The blooms are likely to be spoilt in wet weather, so you may prefer to keep your plant in the greenhouse during the winter when it is likely to flower in April.

Plant it outside for the summer and repot in August. If it has grown large, it could be divided into smaller sections and some of these could be tried in the open garden.

Waterlilies ❧
"I understand that it is possible to grow waterlilies in a large tub. Is this correct and can you recommend suitable varieties to grow in this way?"

It is true that waterlilies can be grown in large tubs of water, but only if suitable miniature varieties are chosen that are happy in water 6–9 in. (15–23 cm) deep.

Good kinds to grow are *Nymphaea candida*, white, *N. tetragona*, white, *N.* x *helvola*, yellow, *N.* "Pygmaea Rubra", red, *N.* "Laydekeri Purpurata", red, and "Laydekeri Lilacea", rose. April and early May is the best time to plant them.

Water hyacinth info ❧

"I would like to grow a plant in my garden pool called the water hyacinth. When should it be planted?"

The water hyacinth, *Eichhomia crassipes*, is a floating aquatic. It has attractive green foliage and in hot summers spikes of lavender flowers appear. Late May and early June is the best time to introduce it to a pool.

The plant is not frost-hardy and must be lifted and kept moist and in frost-free conditions for the winter.

Weeds

Problem celandines   ❧

"Celandines grow thickly in three of my flower borders and I would welcome advice on how to get rid of them. I handweed as much as possible but there are so many little tubers on the roots that it is impossible to clear the ground properly."

Although celandines can be a nuisance, many gardeners find their golden, glistening flowers very attractive. There are several special forms, including one with white flowers, which are highly prized. Most of the foliage will now have died down and all that you can do is to fork out as many of the tubers as possible. Next spring, when the leaves appear, treat the foliage with a weedkiller containing glyphosate, such as Murphy Tumbleweed or Monsanto Roundup. This is a systemic weedkiller and may take several weeks to show any results. It will be necessary to repeat the treatment to get rid of the celandines altogether.

Wild onion   ❧

"Is there a weedkiller which will dispose of wild onion?"

It is possible to control bulbous weeds, such as wild onion, using weedkillers, if they are applied at the right time. After flowering is the best time, but before the foliage starts to die down. The weedkiller to use is glyphosate and allow three weeks for the chemical to work.

Apply it carefully and avoid contact with other plants. It is inactivated on contact with the soil so it poses no threat to other plants through the soil.

Curious pokeweed   ❧

"I would like to grow some pokeweed plants as the stems covered in dark berries are useful for flower arrangements. Can you tell me anything about the plant?"

The pokeweed, *Phytolacca americana*, is rather a weedy plant growing about 4 ft (1.3 m) tall. The flower spikes are white, followed in late summer by attractive, glossy, purple-black berries. However, the berries are poisonous and plants should not be grown where there are children around. The foliage also gives off an unpleasant odour. Plants are easily raised from seed.

Sticky weed ❧

"Could you tell me the name of the plant I am sending? I presume it is some kind of weed? It has a sticky nature."

The piece of plant that you sent is a weed commonly known as cleavers, goosegrass and, in some areas, Sticky Willy. The leaves and stems are covered in tiny recurved hooks, giving the plant a sticky feeling. The hooks enable the plant to scramble over nearby plants.

Cleavers are prolific seed producers, so plants should be pulled out as soon as possible and before they set seed. If there is a lot to remove, it would be best to have long sleeves and wear gardening gloves as the hooks can scratch tender skin. If the weed is growing away from cultivated plants it could be watered with Weedol to kill it. This, however, will not be possible if the weed is growing among ornamental plants.

Difficult weed ❧

"Could you identify the small bulbs that I am sending? I found them in a small, circular clump near the surface when I was weeding my herbaceous border."

The small tubers that you sent are from a plant called *Oxalis corymbosa* which is a pernicious weed. It is very difficult to eradicate.

If there are any more close by those you dug up, sift the soil carefully and try to remove all of them. Do not put them on your compost heap. Either burn them or dispose of them in a dustbin.

Persistent problem ❧

"Having recently moved to a new home, I have discovered that all the flower beds are smothered in muscari (grape hyacinths). I have spent hours trying to dig them out, but they seem very prolific. Is there any weedkiller that will get rid of them as I want to clear the beds for other plants?"

In situations to their liking, muscari can become invasive, although it is a lovely flower to have in the garden in the spring. To get rid of the plants try using glyphosate weedkiller on the foliage in early spring. This weedkiller has a systemic action and will affect all parts of the plant. It may be necessary to give more than one application and results may not be apparent for several weeks.

Problem knotweed ❧

"Can you please give me some advice on how to eradicate Japanese knotweed? I believe it was introduced to our garden some 40 years ago. Since then it has invaded 1½ acres of land. Last year we tried Roundup on a small patch but although it stunted the growth that year, it is coming up as normal again this year. We have tried sodium chlorate on another patch and it seems to be having the same results. Can you help?"

Japanese knotweed is one of our most troublesome weeds and is difficult to eradicate. In Victorian times it was a highly prized ornamental plant but they did not realize how invasive it would become.

Glyphosate (Roundup and Tumbleweed) is probably the best weedkiller to tackle it with. One application will not destroy it. When young foliage appears, you must re-apply it and continue for several years.

Borders full of ground elder ❧

"We recently took over an old, neglected garden and discovered the borders are full of ground elder. The roots are growing among peonies, forsythia, snowdrops and rose bushes. I have been told that the only way to get rid of the weed is to dig it out. Is this true?"

Ground elder is very difficult to eliminate when it is growing among cultivated plants. On unplanted soil it can be sprayed with Tumbleweed, Roundup or Tough Weed Killer. These, however, will kill any cultivated plant hit by the treatment. It may be possible to apply the weedkiller carefully around rose bushes and other shrubs avoiding contact with green stems.

Digging out the weed is the only other effective answer. Lift the cultivated plants in the autumn and plant them temporarily in weed-free ground. Afterwards, fork over the border, removing as much of the roots as possible. Any weed growth that reappears can be treated with weedkiller. It will take at least a year to eradicate the weed.

Ground elder menace? ❧

"I have seen plants of the variegated ground elder on sale. Surely no one wants this terrible weed in the garden?"

Fortunately, the variegated-leaved ground elder, *Aegopodium podagraria* "Variegatum", is not such an invasive menace as the type with plain green leaves. Many gardeners like it for its attractive cream and green foliage, particularly as it grows quite happily in shade and in any soil.

Tree stumped ❧

"We have just had to have a rather large tree cut down. How do we treat the stump to stop it regrowing as it is too big for us to dig out?"

Treat the stump with Root-Out, based on ammonium sulphamate which will eventually kill it. Bacteria and fungi will slowly attack the rotting stump and they can be helped by supplying regular doses of nitrogen in the form of sulphate of ammonia.

After several months you should find that pieces of the stump can be prised off and in time all the above ground evidence will have been removed.

Rooting out the problem ❧

"Can you please help me to get rid of a weed I have had for several years? It has a thick root which I have dug out in parts but it keeps growing back. I have tried several weedkillers without success."

The growths are from the roots of a Prunus species, most probably an old plum tree root stock. Digging out the worst roots would be the best solution, although difficult and involving some spoiling of parts of the garden.

A glyphosate weedkiller such as Tumbleweed, Miracle's Tough Weed Killer or Roundup should be effective, but for best results apply it in autumn as the sap tends to be moving downwards. Keep the spray off nearby cultivated plants.

Rust danger ever present ❧

"I have seen quite a lot of what appears to be rust fungus on groundsel weeds in my garden. Is this likely to be a danger to the cultivated plants in my garden?"

It is best to assume that any pest or disease found on weeds could spread to related cultivated plants. In the case of rust fungi they are, in the main, rather more specific than a number of other diseases, but even so it would be best to destroy the infected groundsel plants.

Killing ivy

"What is the best way to get rid of ivy which is growing in the bottom of an old hawthorn hedge?"

Brushwood killers, such as SBK, have been specifically formulated for problem weeds such as ivy and brambles. Ivy is best treated during the autumn and winter when you can spray a solution of SBK diluted with paraffin on the foliage and stems. Make sure that you cover as much foliage as possible and avoid the base of the hawthorn plants.

Difficult weeds

"I have some dandelions growing under my roses. I cannot dig them out without harming the roses, so how do I get rid of them?"

Spray Tough Weed Gun close to the leaves of the weed, keeping it off all green parts of the roses. If it comes in contact with brown woody stems, it will not do any harm.

Dig out dandelions before they set seed.

Resistant speedwell flourishing ❧

"Our lawn has a lot of speedwell in it and, despite trying many weedkillers, it is flourishing."

Speedwell is very difficult to eradicate as it is resistant to weedkillers. All you can do is encourage the grass to grow at the expense of the weed by feeding the lawn at intervals during the spring and early summer.

Rake out as much of the weed as possible and give repeated applications of a lawn weedkiller such as Bio Supertox in the spring.

Killing horsetail ❧

"Last year we moved to a neglected garden which is full of horsetail. We have tried digging it out but the weed has got among the roots of established plants. We've used glyphosate but this noxious weed soon reappears. Can you suggest other ways of killing it?"

As you have found, these primitive plants are extremely difficult to eradicate, particularly when they are growing among cultivated plants.

Before spraying with glyphosate in early summer, bruise the stems by walking on them. Painting each new shoot with Tumbleweed Gel is also worth doing, but it may take several years of treatment before you are rid of this weed.

Sowing shamrock ❧

"Could you let me know where I can get shamrock seed? I have been unable to find it in any catalogue."

Shamrock is not a distinct species of plant which explains why you have not found it listed. It is a variety of the white or Dutch clover, *Trifolium repens*. When a four-leaved form appears it can be propagated vegetatively and is often sold as Shamrock.

Seeds collected from the four-leaved form will not automatically produce seedlings with four leaves.

Clearing oxalis weed ❧

"My rose bed is full of oxalis weed and whatever I do it seems to get worse because of the small bulblets on the roots. Is there any way of getting rid of this weed?"

Oxalis is a very difficult weed to eradicate, particularly when it is growing among ornamental plants. Tackle the problem with glyphosate weedkiller.

Use a small dribble bar on a watering can to apply the weedkiller so that you can direct it accurately to the weed, avoiding the rose foliage. Where the weed is growing close to the rose stems, remove it carefully with a hand fork and endeavour to take away all the bulblets on the roots. It will be necessary to give more than one application of weedkiller.

These spiny seedheads are teasels

"I found some spiny seed heads outside my garden and I wonder what they are. I am sending one for you to see. Can you tell me what it is?"

Your seed head is a teasel, *Dipsacus fullonum*. It is a wild plant found growing in open spaces and near streams. It seeds freely and in a garden can become a nuisance. However, the flower heads are often dried for floral arrangements. One form of teasel was once used for combing woollen cloth.

Giant thistle

"Can you shed some light on a thistle-like plant that has appeared in our garden? In a matter of weeks it has grown over 9 ft (2.7 m) tall."

Your giant thistle with grey foliage is *Onopordum acanthium*, a biennial of great statuesque interest. It takes two years to mature, flower and die and, while doing this, adds great character to a sunny border. If you scatter the seeds in the open you will soon have dozens of youngsters to replace it.

Rusty thistles

"Whilst tidying up in the garden I have found a lot of old thistle plants with their leaves heavily infected with what appears to be a rust fungus. Is this a disease that could spread to, say, leeks or any other vegetable crop?"

Fortunately the species of rust on the thistles, known as *Puccinia suaveolens*, is specific to thistles, so it would not pose a threat to any garden vegetable crop.

Scalloped clover

"I have found some most unusual clover leaves in my lawn, with very wavy edges. It looks like they must have been nibbled by some creature; can you say what would have been responsible?"

The scalloped edges of these clover leaves are due to feeding by the pea and bean weevil. The adult weevils are partial to virtually any pea family leaf, so similarly notched foliage can be seen on quite a range of plants from clover, through peas and beans to wisteria.

A bind-of-a-weed ❧

"I have a shrub border which has become infested with convolvulus or bindweed, the type with large, white flowers. How can I get rid of it?"

The best weedkiller to use to kill the bindweed is glyphosate (Tumbleweed). It is absorbed into the whole of the plant and has a systemic action. It may take three weeks after application before results are seen. Because the weed has long white roots which penetrate large areas, new growth is likely to occur and it will be necessary to repeat the treatment. Great care must be taken to avoid getting the weedkiller on adjacent plants as these can also be harmed. Where the weed is growing amongst ornamental plants it is necessary to paint the weedkiller on the young growths of the weed. It is a laborious business but, if you are persistent, you will gradually eliminate the weed.

Growing nuisance ❧

"I have moved to a brand-new house and have dug the garden thoroughly. It is infested with mares tail weed which I am told can go 3–6 ft (1–2 m) deep. I am treating it with Roundup weedkiller. Am I doing right or is there anything else I can do?"

Common horsetail or mares tail (*Equisetum arvense*) spreads by spores or by rhizomes which produce green-branched stems, that look like miniature Christmas trees, in May. Away from shrubs and lawns, digging out the rhizomes can reduce the infestation if carried our regularly. For effective control it is necessary to use a glyphosate-based weedkiller such as Tumbleweed, Roundup GC or Toughweed. It is best applied between early June and August. Try to crush the weed before application. Protect nearby plants with plastic or some cardboard to avoid the spray damaging them. It may take several years of treatment before the weed is eradicated.

Chemical solutions: what to look for

Quite often gardening books and magazines will refer to a chemical's ingredient(s) rather than the trade name – this can be confusing to say the least. Listed over the next few pages, we have made the selection easier by giving the active ingredient together with the name you see on the garden centre shelf.

Note that chemicals are subject to the most rigorous testing and therefore can be removed from sale at any time. Likewise, new or reformulations may appear. The information is intended as a guide only and is subject to Government/manufacture change.

Chemicals must be treated with respect. Always follow the manufacturer's instructions carefully.

Garden chemical guide – Insecticides

ACTIVE INGREDIENT	PRODUCT NAME
Aluminium ammonium sulphate	Bio Catapult, Scoot, Stay-Off
Aluminium sulphate	6X Slug Killer, Fertosan Slug and Snail Powder, Growing Success Slug Killer
Benicarb	Doff Ant Killer, Doff Wasp Nest Killer,
Bifenthrin	Polysect Insecticide
Bioallethrin and permethrin	Bio Spraydex, Longer Lasting Bug Gun
Borax	Nippon Ant Killer Liquid
Butoxycarboxim	Plant Pin, Systemic Insecticide Pins
Dimethoate	Doff Systemic Insecticide
Dimethoate + Permethrin	Bio Long-Last
Fatty acids	Phostrogen Safer's Garden Insecticide, Safer's Insectidal Soap, Savona Rose Spray

Fenitrothion	Bio Fruit Spray
Heptenophos + Permethrin	Murphy Systemic Action Insecticide, Murphy Tumblebug
Lindane	Doff Ant Killer, Doff Gamma BHC Dust, Doff Weevil Killer, Murphy Gamma BHC Dust
Malathion	Malathion Greenfly Killer, Murphy Liquid Malathion, Murphy Malathion Dust
Metaldehyde (slug killer)	Murphy Slugit Liquid, Murphy Slugits, PBI Slug Mini Pellets, Slug Xtra
Methiocarb	Bio Slug Gard
Permethrin	Bio Flydown, Bio Sprayday, Fumite Whitefly Smoke Cone
Permethrin + Bioallethrin	Bio Spraydex, Longer Lasting Bug Gun
Permethrin + Dimethoate	Bio Long-Last
Permethrin + Heptenophos	Murphy Systemic Action Insecticide, Murphy Tumblebug
Pirimicarb	Rapid Aerosol, Rapid Greenfly Killer
Pirimiphos	Fumite General Purpose Insecticide Smoke Cone, Sybol, Sybol Dust
Pirimiphos-methyl + Pyrethrins	Kerispray
Pirimiphos-methyl + Resmethrin	Miracle-Gro Bug Spray, Sybol Aerosol
Pyrethrins	AgrEvo Garden/House Insect Killer, Bug Gun!, Py Spray Insect Killer
Pyrethrins + Fatty Acids	Phostrogen Safer's All Purpose Insecticide, Safer's Insecictidal Concentrate
Pyrethrins + Pirimiphos-methyl	Kerispray
Resmethrin + Pirimiphos-methyl + Tetramethrin	Miracle-Gro Bug Spray, Sybol Aerosol

Rotenone	Bio Friendly Insect Spray, Bio Liquid Derris Plus, BioSect, Derris Dust, Pbi Liquid Derris
Cresylic acid	Armillatox, Medo

Garden chemical guide — Fungicides

Bupirimate + Triforine	Nimrod-T
Copper	Bordeaux Mixture
Copper oxychloride	Murphy Traditional Copper Fungicide
Copper sulphate	Bio Cheshunt Compound
Myclobutanii	Bio Systane
Propiconazole	Murphy Tumbleblight II
Permethrin + Sulphur + Triflorine	Bio Multirose
Propiconazole	Tumbleblight
Sulphur	Sulphur Candles, Yellow Sulphur, Green Sulphur, Nature's Answer to Powdery Mildew and Scab, Phostrogen Safer's Garden Fungicide
Triforine + Bupirimate	Nimrod-T
Triforine + Permethrin + Sulphur	Bio Multirose

Garden chemical guide — Weedkillers

Amitrole + Diquat + Paraquat + Simazine	Pathclear
Amitrole + Simazine	Path & Drive Weedkiller
Ammonium sulphamate	Deep Root, Root-Out
Atrazine + Amitrole	Murphy Path Weedkiller
2,4-D + Dicamba	Bio Toplawn, Green Up Lawn Feed and Weed, Toplawn Feed with Weedkiller
2,4-D + Dicamba + Ferrous Sulphate	Triple Action Grasshopper
2,4-D + Dicamba + Mecoprop	SBK Brushwood Killer
2,4-D + Dichlorprop	Murphy Lawn Weedkiller
2,4-D + Dicamba + Ferrous Sulphate + Mecoprop	Gem Lawn Weed & Feed + Mosskiller, Green Up Feed and Weed Plus Mosskiller,

	Supergreen Feed, Weed & Mosskiller, Weed "N" Feed Extra
2,4-D + Mecoprop	Supertox, Toplawn Lawn Weedkiller, Verdone 2
2,4-D + Mecoprop-P	Gem Lawn Weed and Feed, Vitax "Green Up" Granular Lawn Feed and Weed
2,4-D + 2,3,6-TBA	Touchweeder
Dicamba + Benazolin + 2,4-D + Dichlorophen + Dichlorprop + Mecoprop Vitax	Green Up Lawn Feed "N" Weed Plus Mosskiller
Dicamba + 2,4-D	Lawn Builder Plus Weed Control, Pbi Toplawn
Dicamba + Dichlorprop + Mecoprop	New Supertox
Dicamba + MCPA	Green Up Liquid Lawn Feed "N" Weed
Dicamba + MCPA + Mecoprop	Bio Weed Pencil
Dichlobenii	Casaron G4
Dichlorophen	Bio Mosskiller, AgrEvo Moss Killer, Doff Moss Killer, Moss Gun
Dichlorprop + 2,4-D	AgrEvo Lawn Weed Killer, Doff Lawn Feed and Weed
Dikegulac	Cutlass
Diquat + Amitrole + Paraquat + Simazine	Pathclear
Diquat + Paraquat	Weedol, Weedol Gun
Diuron + Glufosinate ammonium	AgrEvo Path Weed Killer
Fatty acids	Bio SpeedWeed
Ferrous sulphate	Wide range of lawn products including – Gem Lawn Sand, Maxicrop Mosskiller and Lawn Tonic, Pbi Velvas, Phostrogen Soluble Mosskiller and Lawn Tonic, Vitax Lawn Sand
Ferrous sulphate + Dichlorprop + MCPA	J. Arthur Bower's Granular Feed, Weed and Mosskiller
Ferrous sulphate + Mecoprop + MCPA	Evergreen Extra

Glufosinate ammonium	AgrEvo Garden Weedkiller Concentrate, Murphy Nettlemaster, Tumbleweed General Purpose
Glyphosate	A wide range of weedkillers, including Murphy Tumbleweed, New Improved Leaf Action Roundup Brushkiller, Roundup GC, Tough Weed Killer, Weedclear, Tumbleweed
Glyphosate + Diuron	Weedatak Path & Drive
MCPA + Dicamba + Dichlorprop	Grasshopper Feed & Weed, Groundclear, Miracle-Gro Weed & Feed, Verdone Plus
Simazine + Amitrole	Path & Drive Weedkiller
Sodium Chlorate	Doff Path Weedkiller, Gem Sodium Chlorate Weedkiller

Useful addresses

How to get in touch with the organizations to give the gardener a helping hand . . .

ARBORICULTURAL ASSOCIATION, Ampfield House, Romsey, Hampshire S051 9PA, tel. 01794 368717

BRITISH AGROCHEMICAL ASSOCIATION, 4 Lincoln Court, Lincoln Road, Peterborough PE1 2RP, tel. 01733 349225

BRITISH BEDDING & POT PLANT ASSOCIATION, 164 Shaftesbury Avenue, London WC2H 8HL, tel. 0171 331 7281

BRITISH BEE-KEEPERS ASSOCIATION, National Agricultural Association, Stoneleigh, Warwickshire CV8 2LZ, tel. 01203 696679

BRITISH SOCIETY OF PLANT BREEDERS, Woolpack Chambers, Market Street, Ely, Cambridgeshire CB7 4ND, tel. 01353 664211

BUTTERFLY CONSERVATION, Box 222, Dedham, Colchester, Essex CO7 6EH, tel. 01206 322342

ENGLISH NATURE, Northminster House, Peterborough PE1 1UA, tel. 01733 455100

FLOWERS & PLANTS ASSOCIATION, Covent Garden, New Convent Garden Market, London SW8 5NX, tel. 0171 738 8044

THE GARDEN CENTRE ASSOCIATION, 38 Carey Street, Reading, Berkshire RG1 7JS, tel. 0118 393900

GARDEN WRITERS GUILD, 14–15 Belgrave Square, London SW1X 8PS, tel. 0171 245 6943

HEALTH & SAFETY EXECUTIVE (HSE), Information Centre, Broad Lane, Sheffield S3 7HQ, tel. 01541 545500

HORTICULTURAL DEVELOPMENT COUNCIL, Bradbourne House, Stable Block, East Malling, Kent ME19 6DZ, tel. 01732 848383

HORTICULTURAL TRADE ASSOCIATION, Horticultural House, 19 High Street, Theale, Reading, Berkshire RG7 5AH, tel. 0118 303132

INSTITUTE OF GROUNDSMANSHIP, 19–23 Church Street, The Agora, Wolverton, Milton Keynes MK12 5LG, tel. 01908 312511

THE INSTITUTE OF HORTICULTURE, 14–15 Belgrave Square, London SW1X 8PS, tel. 0171 245 6943

JOHN INNES MANUFACTURERS ASSOCIATION, Links View House, 8 Fulwith Avenue, Harrogate, North Yorkshire HG2 8HR, tel. 01423 879208

THE LANDSCAPE INSTITUTE, 6–7 Bernard Mews, London SW11 1QU, tel. 0171 738 9166

MINISTRY OF AGRICULTURE, FISHERIES AND FOOD, 3 Whitehall Place, London SW1A 2HH, tel. 0171 270 8080

PLANT BREEDING INTERNATIONAL, Maris Lane, Trumpington, Cambridge CB2 2LQ, tel. 01223 840411

PLANTLIFE, The Natural History Museum, Cromwell Road, London SW7 5BD, tel. 0171 938 9111

ROYAL SOCIETY FOR THE PROTECTION OF BIRDS, The Lodge, Sandy, Bedfordshire SG19 2DL, tel. 01767 680551

THE SOCIETY OF FLORISTRY, 59 Tree Tops, Portskewett, Gwent NP6 4RT, tel. 01291 424039

SOIL ASSOCIATION, 86–88 Colston Street, Bristol, Gloucestershire BS1 5BB, tel. 0117 929 0661

THE TREE COUNCIL, 51 Catherine Place, London SW1E 6DY, tel. 0171 828 9928

Garden societies

ALPINE GARDEN SOCIETY, AGS Centre, Avon Bank, Pershore, Hereford & Worcester WR10 JP, tel. 01386 554790

BRITISH & EUROPEAN GERANIUM SOCIETY, 4 Higher Meadow, Clayton-le-Woods, Chorley, Lancashire PR5 2RS, tel. 01772 4533983

BRITISH CACTUS & SUCCULENT SOCIETY, 15 Brentwood Crescent, York, North Yorkshire YO1 5HU, tel. 01904 410512

BRITISH CLEMATIS SOCIETY, 4 Springfield, Lightwater, Surrey GU18 5XP

BRITISH FUCHSIA SOCIETY, 15 Summerfield Lane, Summerfield, Kidderminster, Hereford & Worcester DY11 7SA

BRITISH GLADIOLUS SOCIETY, 24 The Terrace, Mayfield, Ashbourne, Derbyshire DE6 2JL, tel. 01335 345443

BRITISH HOSTA & HEMEROCALLIS SOCIETY, 36 Worgret Road, Wareham, Dorset, tel. 01929 552322

THE BRITISH IRIS SOCIETY, The Old Mill House, Shurton, Stogursey, Somerset TA5 1QG

BRITISH NATIONAL CARNATION SOCIETY, 23 Chiltern Road, St Albans, Hertfordshire AL4 9SR

BRITISH ORCHID COUNCIL, PO Box 1072, Frome, Somerset BA11 5NY, tel. 01373 301501

THE BRITISH PELARGONIUM & GERANIUM SOCIETY, 75 Pelham Road, Bexleyheath Kent DA7 4LY, tel. 01332 525947

BRITISH PTERIDOLOGICAL SOCIETY, 16 Kirby Corner Road, Canley, Coventry, West Midlands CV4 8GD, tel. 01203 715690

CARNIVOROUS PLANT SOCIETY, 1 Orchard Close, Ringwood, Hampshire BH24 1LP

COTTAGE GARDEN SOCIETY, Hurstfield House, 244 Edleston Road, Crewe, Cheshire CW2 7EJ

THE CYCLAMEN SOCIETY. Tile Barn House, Standen Street, Iden Green, Benenden, Kent TN17 4LB

DAFFODIL SOCIETY, The Meadows, Puxton, Weston-Super-Mare, Somerset BS24 6TF, tel. 01934 833641

THE DELPHINIUM SOCIETY, Takakkaw, Ice House Wood, Oxted, Surrey RH8 9DW

THE HARDY ORCHID SOCIETY, 1364 Evesham Road, Ashwood Bank, Redditch, Hereford & Worcester B96 6BD

EUROPEAN BROMELIAD SOCIETY, Grove Goch, Bodfari, Denbigh, Clywd LL16 4DE, tel. 01745 710423

THE HARDY PLANT SOCIETY, Little Orchard, Great Comberton, Pershore, Hereford & Worcester, tel. 01386 710317

THE HEATHER SOCIETY, Denbeigh, All Saints Road, Creeting St. Mary, Ipswich, Suffolk IP6 8PJ, tel. 01449 711220

THE HEBE SOCIETY, Rosemergy, Hain Walk, St Ives, Cornwall TR26 2AF, tel. 01736 795225

THE HENRY DOUBLEDAY RESEARCH ASSOCIATION, Ryton Organic Gardens, Ryton on Dunsmore, Coventry, West Midlands CV8 3LG, tel. 01203 303517

THE HERB SOCIETY, The National Herb Centre, Banbury Road, Warmington, Banbury, Oxfordshire OX17 1DF

HORTICULTURAL THERAPY, Goulds Ground, Vallis Way, Frome, Somerset BA11 3DW, tel. 01373 464782

JAPANESE GARDENS SOCIETY, Groves Mill, Shakers Lane, Long Itchington, Warwickshire CV23 8QB, tel. 01926 632746

THE NATIONAL ASSOCIATION OF FLOWER ARRANGE-MENT SOCIETIES, 21 Denbigh Street, London SW1V 2HF, tel. 0171 828 5145

NATIONAL AURICULA AND PRIMULA SOCIETY (MIDLANDS AND WEST), 6 Lawson Close, Saltford, Somerset BS18 3LB, tel. 01225 872893

NATIONAL AURICULA AND PRIMULA SOCIETY (SOUTHERN AREA), 67 Warnham Court Road, Carshalton Beeches, Surrey SM5 3ND

NATIONAL BEGONIA SOCIETY, 33 Findern Lane, Willington, Derbyshire DE65 6DW, tel. 01283 702681

NATIONAL CHRYSANTHEMUM SOCIETY, George Gray House, 8 Amber Business Village, Amber Close, Tamworth, Staffordshire B77 4rd, tel. 01827 310331

NATIONAL COUNCIL FOR THE CONSERVATION OF PLANTS AND GARDENS (NCCPG), The Pines, RHS Garden, Wisley, Woking, Surrey GU23 6QP, tel. 0483 211465

NATIONAL DAHLIA SOCIETY, 19 Sunnybank, Marlow, Buckinghamshire SL7 3BL, tel. 01628 473500

NATIONAL POT LEEK SOCIETY, 147 Sea Road, Fulwell, Sunderland SR6 9EB tel. 0191 549 4274

THE NATIONAL SWEET PEA SOCIETY, 3 Chalk Farm Road, Stokenchurch, High Wycombe, Buckingham HP14 3TB, tel. 01494 482153

NATIONAL TRUST, PO Box 39, Bromley, Kent BR1 3XL

NATIONAL VEGETABLE SOCIETY, 56 Waun-y-Groes Avenue, Rhiwbini, Cardiff, South Wales CF4 5SZ, tel. 01222 627994

NATIONAL VIOLA AND PANSY SOCIETY, Cleeway, Eardington, Bridgnorth, Shropshire WV16 5JT, tel. 01746 766909

NORTHERN HORTICULTURAL SOCIETY, Harlow Carr Gardens, Crag Lane, Harrogate, North Yorkshire HG3 1QB, tel. 01423 565418

ORCHID SOCIETY OF GREAT BRITAIN, Athelney, 145 Binscombe Village, Godalming, Surrey GU7 3QL, tel. 01483 421423

THE ROYAL HORTICULTURAL SOCIETY, PO Box 313, 80 Vincent Square, London SWIP 2PE, tel. 0171 834 4333

ROYAL HORTICULTURAL SOCIETY OF IRELAND, Swanbrook House, Bloomfield Avenue, Donnybrook, Dublin 4

ROYAL NATIONAL ROSE SOCIETY, Chiswell Green, St Albans, Hertfordshire AL2 3NR, tel. 01727 850461

THE SAINTPAULIA & HOUSEPLANT SOCIETY, 33 Church Road, Newbury Park, Ilford, Essex IG2 7ET, tel. 0181 590 3710

THE SEMPERVIVUM SOCIETY, 11 Wingle Tye Road, Burgess Hill, West Sussex RH15 9HR

THE TOMATO GROWERS' CLUB, 27 Meadowbrook, Old Oxted, Surrey RH8 9LT, tel. 01883 715242

VINTAGE HORTICULTURAL & GARDEN MACHINERY CLUB, 23 Willow Grove, Old Stratford, Milton Keynes MK19 6AY, tel. 01908 562660

WILD FLOWER SOCIETY, Woodpecker, Hoe Lane, Abinger Hammer, Dorking, Surrey

Seed Suppliers

B & T WORLD SEEDS, Whitnell House, Fiddington, Bridgwater, Somerset TA5 1JE, tel. 01278 733209

D. T. BROWN & CO LTD, Station Road, Pouton-le-Fylde, Lancashire FY6 7HX, tel. 01253 882371

JOHN CHAMBERS' WILD FLOWER SEEDS, 15 Westleigh Road, Barton Seagrave, Kettering, Northampton NN15 5AJ, tel. 01933 652562

CHILTERN SEEDS, Bortree Stile, Ulverston, Cumbria LA12 7PB, tel. 01229 51137

MR FOTHERGILL'S SEEDS, Gazeley Road, Kentford, Newmarket, Suffolk CB8 7QB, tel. 01638 751161

S. E. MARSHALLS & CO. LTD., Wisbech, Cambridgeshire PE13 2RF, tel. 01945 583407

W. ROBINSON & SONS LTD, Sunny Bank, Forton, Preston PR3 0BN, tel. 01524 791210

SEEDS-BY-SIZE, 45 Crouchfield, Boxmoor, Hemel Hempstead, Hertfordshire HP1 1PA, tel. 01442 251458

SIMPSON'S SEEDS, 27 Meadowbrook, Old Oxted, Surrey RH8 9LT, tel. 01883 715242

SUTTONS SEEDS, Hele Road, Torquay TQ2 7QJ, tel. 01803 614455

THOMPSON & MORGAN, Poplar Lane, Ipswich IP8 3BU, tel. 01473 688588

EDWIN TUCKER & SONS, Brewery Meadow, Stonepark, Ashburton, Devon TQ13 7DG, tel. 01364 652403

UNWIN SEEDS, Histon, Cambridge CB4 4LE tel. 01223 236236

Index